D1601173

ASSAULTING PARNASSUS

Theoretical Views of Creativity

Jock Abra
University of Calgary

UNIVERSITY
PRESS OF
AMERICA

Lanham • New York • London

British Cataloging in Publication Information Available

Library of Congress Cataloging-in-Publication Data

Abra, Jock, 1939–
Assaulting Parnassus.

Bibliography: p.
Includes indexes.
1. Creative ability. I. Title.
BF408.A23   1988   153.3'5   88–17148
ISBN 0–8191–7054–2 (alk. paper)
ISBN 0–8191–7055–0 (pbk. : alk. paper)

All University Press of America books are produced on acid-free
paper which exceeds the minimum standards set by the National
Historical Publications and Records Commission.

To my father and in memory of my mother

ACKNOWLEDGEMENTS

The title page of a book may bear only one name, but typically many people have contributed to its procreation. Certainly this is so in the present case. My interest in creativity--and my consequent musings about this most mysterious and seemingly irrational of human endeavors--was first piqued by the many artists, musicians, researchers, and above all dancers whom I observed, admired, and sometimes came to know. Several contributed helpful observations, but I particularly wish to acknowledge Winston Leathers for his unfailing interest, insight, and good fellowship.

However, a vast assemblage of notes, accompanied by sometimes indecipherable jottings of insights garnered whilst shaving, sleeping, or conversing, does not a book make. It was my students who impelled me to undertake the unromantic and often frustrating but necessary labor of organizing, expanding, and clarifying the jumble. They induced me to offer a course in the subject, and the lecture notes that I gradually developed have provided the nucleus for this book. Those students have served, and continue to serve, as remarkably patient, even sympathetic guinea pigs as I have tried things out, thought aloud, and, more often than I wish to remember, stumbled and fallen. Their questions, comments, and suggestions for further readings, even their baffled silences and slumberings, have all helped beyond measure. Anna, in The King and I, observes that if you become a teacher, by your pupils you'll be taught. Truer words were never sung. Obviously I cannot mention and thank every student by name, but Heather Carter, Susan Wood, Coby Britton, Fay Ferris, Maureen Pruegger, Jackie Bell, Barb Juschka, and Janice Ronaldson have contributed too much to remain anonymous. So have the members of the advanced seminar in creativity: Glenn Dawes, Karen Getty, Valerie Hazen, Sherry Kennedy, Philip Kuefler, Julien Lambert, Catharyn Miller, Denise Savage, Darlene Smart, Lori Walker, Adrian Shepherd, and Jennifer Watton.

The Psychology Department at the University of Calgary provided the space and time necessary for my sometimes leisurely labors. In particular, my several heads of department have been unfailingly understanding and supportive during several years of minimal productivity as I "went back to school" to acquaint myself with the literature. Clearly, the notorious "publish or perish" ethic is quashed when reasonable people occupy positions of responsibility. As well, my colleagues, despite their ofttimes widely divergent priorities and philosophical sympathies, have generally been conciliatory towards my rather unusual, even heretical interests. However, Ed McMullan deserves special mention. His neverending enthusiasm and encouragement have provided welcome antidotes for my periodic disillusionment with this project, and his insightful comments have invariably helped to improve it.

My late mother, Marion Abra, corrected many problems of language usage in the early chapters, and Miriam Greenblatt served as the capable copy editor. A grant from the University of Calgary Research Policy and Grants Committee assisted with the costs of typing and reproducing the manuscript. Alison Wiigs, Ann Camponi, and Fran Crucq, assisted by other members of the Psychology Department's secretarial pool, have skillfully re-typed my own portable's sometimes inaccurate excretions, and prepared the manuscript for printing. It goes without saying that none of these persons is responsible for any errors of fact, interpretation, or style that remain. For these, the writer alone must bear the brunt.

I wish also to thank the following individuals and publishers who gave permission for use of their materials: Sarnoff A. Mednick, J.P. Guilford, Albert Bandura; University of California Press, John Wiley & Sons, McGraw-Hill Publishing Co., Duke University Press, Alfred A. Knopf, Inc., Prentice-Hall, Inc., The American Psychological Association, Ablex Publishing Corp., Liveright Publishing Corp., Praeger Publishers, Abingdon Press, Macmillan Publishing Co. of New York, Michael B. Yeats and Macmillan London Ltd., New Directions Publishing Corp., David Higham Associates, Dent Publishers and Editions Gallimard.

Last, my sons Gord and Brian deserve special thanks. Perhaps the actual content carries little of their imprint. But they have helped me in more ways than they can possibly know.

TABLE OF CONTENTS

INTRODUCTION

Humankind has come a long way. At one time we existed in a largely hostile environment, which we neither understood, modified nor enriched to any marked degree. Balanced precariously in trees or huddled in caves, with survival our main concern, we languished at the mercy of seemingly whimsical, uncontrollable disasters.

Things have changed. We now understand many striking phenomena of our experience; the idiosyncrasies of heavenly bodies, climatic changes, and occasionally the behavior of our fellow creatures. We have sent our representatives to the moon and to the depths of the seas. More to the point, we have brought them safely back. We have learned much about how life begins and also how it ends. We have immeasurably increased our ability to avert disease, starvation, and natural cataclysm; for example, we have eliminated the once-dreaded scourge of smallpox. Of almost equal comfort, we can often predict and explain even those disasters that we cannot yet control.

The fruits of artistic genius, such as Shakespeare's plays, Beethoven's symphonies, Jane Austen's novels, and even Andy Warhol's Campbell's Soup cans entertain, stimulate, and enrich us. Thanks to our ubiquitous technology, our modern environment, with its fluorescent lamps, stereo components, reclining rockers, flush toilets, and electric toothbrushes, is almost entirely artificial rather than natural, peopled with products of our own devising.

Nevertheless, our ingenuity has been a decidedly mixed blessing, since it has also bestowed such less desirable progeny as nuclear weapons, as well as such minor irritations as junk foods and those penultimate inventions of the devil, transistor radios. Still, we seem to have made what resembles progress. Our lives seem richer, more satisfying, and certainly longer and safer than those of our distant predecessors.

It is our propensity for creative activity that has led to all these developments. Why are we driven to produce things that previously did not exist? What are creative people like? What is the creative process like? Such fascinating questions have often been asked, and some valuable answers have been provided, with which readers might wish to become familiar. Unfortunately, such interested persons face a formidable task. Apart from some brief summaries,[1,2] the various theoretical contributions are scattered throughout the literatures of philosophy, psychology, sociology, aesthetics, art criticism, and the history and philosophy of science. Several books of readings do provide excerpts from important sources[3,4,5] but these share some appreciable inadequacies. An author's actual intent may be severely compromised when a passage is isolated from its context. Also, technical jargon, without the benefit of introductory explanation, may challenge even a relatively sophisticated reader, and such sources supply almost nothing in the way of critical commentary.

The present work aims, therefore, to make the quest of those hypothetical interested laypersons somewhat less painful. It will first acquaint them with the major characteristics of the creative personality and the creative process. It will then critically discuss the theoretical ideas contributed by representatives of such traditions as psychoanalysis, existentialism, and scientific behaviorism. Thus it is intended, first, for the "enlightened" lay person, be he or she a practicing professional in the arts or sciences, an interested observer, or an undergraduate student seeking that elusive diploma. It is also hoped, however, that trained philosophers and/or psychologists will find it informative (although they should be forewarned that at times the discussion may seem elementary), since these theoretical writings have not, to our knowledge, been previously brought together in this manner. In short, we unabashedly seek to provide what might pass for a "textbook" on the topic.

Unfortunately, the requisite encyclopedic thoroughness is not easy to come by. There have been frequent discussions in the psychological literature about the characteristics of creative people, about the measurement and stimulation of creativity, and so on. But precious few bibliographies, journals, or textbooks enlighten would-be researchers about the mandatory theoretical literature they should consume. They must rely on word of mouth, suggestive hints dropped in works devoted to other topics, and above all on sheer luck. Reading by the shotgun method, wading randomly through mountains of irrelevant or dull verbiage hoping to hit periodic paydirt, may be a healthy antidote to narrow specialization, but it is a grossly inefficient practice that would drive a time-study engineer to drink. Furthermore, researchers will undoubtedly miss important contributions, particularly if they are buried in out-of-the-way sources. Nevertheless, at some arbitrary point they must shrug their shoulders, take the cover off the typewriter, and set to work, relying on others for advice about overlooked items. Only through such constructive teamwork will the necessary catalogue eventually develop.

Which raises another matter of concern. While reinterpreting and reworking various authors for general consumption, we have often wondered, "Am I getting it right?". And sometimes wonder has become unease, particularly when the ideas are difficult (e.g., Sartre) or poorly presented (e.g., Rank). Gradually, however, we have come to realize that a great work of ideas, like a great work of art, will provide many legitimate interpretations. Scholars have been arguing for centuries, for example, about what Aristotle "really said." Therefore, our reading of, say, Camus, may differ from someone else's in the ideas we deem noteworthy. However, one reason we have frequently included direct quotations from text is to show that our reading is at least defensible. (Another is to provide some feeling for the theorist's writing style.) Another purpose, then, is to stimulate discussion about the various theories, their meanings, implications, strengths, and weaknesses.

In view of our professed aim to be thorough, we might mention several topics that we have not included. First, the creative artist or scientist, the producer, is our main interest. Questions about the consumer or audience member, that is, about aesthetics and the psychology of art, will receive only an odd brief glance. Kreitler and Kreitler[6] and also Winner[7] both discuss the large amount of literature on these topics. Second, participation in music, painting, dance, and the like can reportedly help alleviate psychological disturbances, and enable patients to reveal the reasons for their problems. Still, this field of art therapy is again peripheral to our interests. The interested reader should consult Wadeson[8] or McNiff[9]. Last, the area of computer simulation and artificial intelligence has doubtless provided some worthwhile hypotheses, just as it has spawned so much computer-generated art and music. Again, we forego discussion. Our humanist biases have prevented our attaining either expertise or interest in this area. A thin excuse, but there it is.

A few words about the book's organization. Going Gaul one better, it comes in four parts. The first will focus on a smorgasbord of relevant topics, such as the definition of the term creativity, characteristics commonly found in creative personalities, and the various experiences they frequently report while going through the process. The remaining sections will spotlight theoretical accounts of creativity that attempt not only to describe it but also to grapple with the "how" and "why." We have grouped those accounts which seem to arise from a common tradition and which share some similar underlying assumptions about what human beings are like. Those included in part two assume us to be autonomous, that is, possessing free will. Those in part three see us as in some sense deterministic, because they attribute our creativity to causal factors beyond our own control. Part four includes those that straddle the fence, incorporating aspects of both premises.

The basic assumptions of each tradition will first be described in a general way, followed by its major representatives as variations on a theme. For each of these, we will first introduce some of its fundamental concepts and then try to show how these have been used to tackle the particular problem of creativity. In addition, whenever possible, we will examine a particular creative personality who seems to exemplify its ideas; for example, Leonardo da Vinci will represent Freud's views in action.[10] Last, in a section of critical commentary, we will discuss some of its major strengths and weaknesses.

A stylistic point also deserves mention. Concerning scholarly references in the text, we wish to avoid a monotonous parade of names and dates of interest only to the dyed-in-the-wool academic. Still, since the work of others should be properly recognized, superscript numbers will be used where reference seems appropriate, such as for direct quotations. An explanatory key for each chapter will be found in the Appendix, both to give credit where credit is due and to provide some direction for follow-up reading.

Now for a few words on terminology. The various accounts do not, as a rule, deserve to be called "theories," at least as that term is usually used. Not easily surrendering precise, testable predictions, they are more accurately labelled "frameworks," "perspectives," or "ways of thinking about creativity." Thus the various case histories, for example, will show that viewing productive people from a particular standpoint can shed additional light on their activities. The dangers of Procrustean methods--distorting complex characters out of all recognition to make them fit a particular ideology--are ever present (Freud's study of Leonardo provides the classic example of both the exercise and its weaknesses). Still, it is surprising how revealing this practice can be.

We must now make some confessions about the various approaches. They differ not only in their specifics but also in their fundamental beliefs about what human beings are like and therefore about how creativity can best be described. Yet, as will quickly become evident, they are without exception unsatisfactory. None remotely resembles a paradigm (in Kuhn's sense of the word[11]) and no such beast looms on the horizon. For example, they have for the most part attempted to explain only artistic creativity, while ignoring its other manifestations, such as science and business. We would hope, of course, that the hypotheses would have some general applicability, but the validity of that assumption will itself require our attention. In the same vein, it will be obvious that most perspectives ignore the known facts, such as the characteristics of creative people and their reliably reported experiences. In our view, any purportedly serious theory will sooner or later have to come to grips with these "data of creativity." So far, most have not.

By and large, judging by their minimal influence on one another, the theoretical and empirical contributions have developed independently. Theorists have apparently remained innocent of the facts, while empirical workers have eschewed theoretical reference as an effusion of the devil. Our remarks therefore will focus only on those facts about which the perspective clearly speaks, leaving readers to satisfy themselves about how well a particular perspective can handle the others.

With all their inadequacies, therefore, the accounts examined herein must be admitted in advance to be failures. Nevertheless, let us be perfectly clear about one point. We believe that they deserve attention. Failures they may be, but gallant, stimulating, and imaginative failures that have attempted to answer perhaps the most foreboding of all riddles. That our wideranging curiosity has, ironically, been unable thus far to explain itself is, perhaps, forgivable. But unless we begin with this admission, readers seeking final answers may feel frustrated by the end of the journey. Creativity may seem even more mysterious and awesome, a Gordian knot that defies our attempts to untangle it. Such periodic pessimism is shared, we suspect, by those who have spent their lives trying to understand it, but hopefully this early warning will somewhat soften the blow.

Psychology, particularly since it adopted the scientific method and the behavioristic dogma, has too often been content to wallow in trivia, emphasizing phenomena easily measured and hence open to reliable, conclusive investigation. Unfortunately, questions have often been asked which few people wanted answered in the first place. Here, on the other hand, is a topic whose importance few would challenge but whose difficulty is extraordinary. Therefore we must be charitable when explanatory attempts fall short.

I once asked a psychological colleague, who was committed to a scientific point of view, whether he preferred good (i.e., precise, unambiguous) answers to poor questions, or poor answers to great questions. He answered, as I suspected he would, "Good answers to poor questions." I'm afraid I disagree. Which is the main reason I have written this book.

Part I

PROBLEMS AND EVIDENCE

Here we will consider a heterogeneous array of matters, such as the problem of definition, along with some important attributes of the creative process and personality. No attempt will be made to treat these topics exhaustively. Since other sources have already performed this service, we shall confine our attention to matters bearing on the theoretical discussions to follow. Moreover, some possible topics--such as methods for stimulating and assessing creativity, or the education of gifted children--will be largely ignored. Important they certainly are; germane to our main purposes they are not.

Chapter 1

A PROBLEMATICAL POTPOURRI

In discussing creativity we face some sticky problems. Since our positions on these will pervade much that is to follow, and since the positions are debatable, it seems best to avow and also defend them right off the bat. Skeptical readers may remain unconvinced, but at least they will realize that the positions have been adopted only after consideration of other possibilities.

The Definition of Creativity

Few terms have their meanings so intensely debated. Definitions abound and all have major weaknesses.[1,2] However, our approach will emphasize the final product, such as a work of art or a scientific discovery. If the product displays the qualities that any creative product must possess, then it is by definition creative. Likewise, the individual who spawned it and the various behavioral and mental activities she or he underwent while doing so are ipso facto creative as well.

What distinguishes a product that we label "creative"? What crucial attributes must it possess? Majority opinion seems to agree on two. First of all, it must in some sense be original or unusual. The highly familiar and mundane do not, as a rule, qualify. This criterion should not elicit screams of protest, but the second perhaps will. A work, to be called creative, must also be judged to have value, merit, and/or quality. Originality, then, seems a necessary but hardly sufficient characteristic. As it is commonly used, the term "creative" is laudatory, expressing praise and admiration for someone or something; from this standpoint, therefore, all creative works will have novelty but not all novel works will be creative. A schizophrenic's frenetic painting or a deluded psychopath's theory of creation may be decidedly unusual, but few would deem them "creative." To avoid this problem, value judgments must be included as a criterion.

Therefore, Stein's[3] definition seems as acceptable as any. Creativity is the production of some novel or original work that is judged to possess merit by some knowledgeable group of people at some point in time. First, it is practical, since our day-to-day decisions about creativity's presence are usually based on some product we have experienced. Second, it solves the problem of the potentially talented but unproductive dilettante, who has long bedeviled creative endeavor, especially in the arts. These creatures will describe ad nauseum the brilliantly revolutionary novel or play that they have in mind, with which

3

one day they will astound the breathlessly waiting world. According to our definition, talking a good ball game is not enough. Nor is looking particularly "sensitive." Nor wearing the right clothes, attending the fashionable gathering places and snarling winningly at the bourgeoisie. Even having the de rigueur fixation on one's mother or father is not sufficient. In our view, people are not creative until they actually produce something worthwhile.

Furthermore, this definition should make creativity a somewhat more precise, unambiguous concept. Its presence is established by a tangible, material product that unlike a process, for example, is available, potentially at least, for others to experience and evaluate. Other criteria that have sometimes been used--such as personality characteristics, or psychological experiences, or the environment in which people work--may help us to understand and explain creativity. But they do not define it.

Our definition also states that the opinions of those who have had appreciable training in, and exposure to, a particular genre should carry special weight in assessing its works. History is, of course, rife with examples where such enlightened despots have been wrong, sometimes hilariously so. They may well disagree even among themselves. But these difficulties notwithstanding, surely we should still pay more heed to their opinions than to the untutored "man on the street" who knows nothing about art but knows what he likes. Democracy has no place in the evaluation of creative work, as Hamlet reminds us in his advice to the actors:

> This overdone, or come tardy off, though it make the unskillful laugh, cannot but make the judicious grieve; the censure of the which one must in your allowance o'erweigh a whole theatre of others (3.2).

Last, our definition recognizes that even these enlightened opinions can change. As any thoughtful critic will readily admit, they are written not in stone but in disappearing ink. The world's undoubted masterpieces will always speak eloquently, which is one reason why they are called masterpieces. But the judgment of history, the verdict that finally establishes their unquestioned greatness, is only handed down long after the event, after they have passed through many courts of appeal. Unfortunately, we who study creativity often cannot wait but must focus on current work. It is often difficult to discover the psychological characteristics or personal experiences of those who have long been dead. They tend to be rather reticent during interviews. Those still above ground can sometimes provide the only data.

We must also, in fairness, mention some less attractive features of our definition. First, it admits any product possessing the twin attributes of novelty and merit. Therefore, it includes those emanating from artificial sources, such as computers, or even from happy accidents. Statistical folklore has it that an infinite number of monkeys pecking away at an infinite number of typewriters would eventually produce all the great books. Is the monkey that happens to get lucky truly "creative"? To be consistent, we must ignore the agonized yelps of the humanist and answer in the affirmative. Fortunately, this difficulty in practice is negligible.

The importance we have attached to value judgments is more troublesome. They are notoriously biased and arbitrary; there are no inviolate, unquestioned rules available to conclusively establish quality. As we say, beauty is in the eye of the beholder. That is why disagreements, even among theoretically knowledgeable sophisticates, have been rife. How many immediate successes have eventually faded into oblivion as mere whims of fashion? On the other hand, how many masterpieces have at first met ridicule or apathy? According to the film Amadeus, Mozart was largely unappreciated during his own lifetime and died a pauper, while the now-obscure Salieri basked in popularity. J. S. Bach's sublime achievements were dismissed by his own sons as being hopelessly reactionary and not "with it." We hear of César Franck walking home alone through deserted streets after the premiere of his Symphonic Variations to tell his family that "it had sounded well, as he had known it would." Clearly, instant acclaim was not his to enjoy.

The year 1913 provided the most dramatic demonstration of how subjective value judgments can be. That year saw the world premiere of the Stravinsky/Nijinsky ballet The Rite of Spring by The Ballet Russe de Monte Carlo. The merit of the music, at least, is now widely admitted, and some audience members did applaud lustily. But a large segment expressed its displeasure with boos and hisses. A full scale riot broke out, the dancers had to be led from the theater under police escort, and at least one duel was fought.[4]

Supposedly the sciences are more impersonal and objective. Do they avoid these differences of opinion, and hence evaluation's arbitrary taint? Apparently not. Mendel's pioneering work in genetics was largely ignored during his lifetime. The seminal advances in physics during the early years of this century were rarely instantaneously appreciated. For example, even Max

Planck himself did not quickly understand the importance of his own work.[5]

In his widely read <u>Zen</u> <u>and</u> <u>the</u> <u>Art</u> <u>of</u> <u>Motorcycle</u> <u>Maintenance</u>,[6] Pirsig has argued that value judgments have historically been regarded with suspicion in Western thought precisely because they are so inherently subjective. Yet we cannot avoid evaluating everything we encounter--operas, quarterbacks, politicians, the weather, even hamburgers. In our eyes, some things are better than others, and every event possesses some amount of stimulus "quality." At heart we are all critics.

Why, then, if quality is such a fundamental aspect of our experience, has it received such scant attention? In Pirsig's opinion, it is because in ancient Greece an argument about the essential properties of truth was waged and won. Plato and Socrates held truth, or knowledge, to be objective, independent of any one mind or opinion. Therefore it could potentially be known by everyone. The opposition, the Sophists, saw truth as subjective, in the mind of the beholder. Supposedly there is no truth, but simply <u>someone's</u> truth.

The Platonic/Socratic tradition dismissed "quality" as an unimportant, even dangerous attribute, because if something so inherently subjective were given due recognition, then the entire view of truth would collapse like a house of cards. Since this tradition won the day, we in the West have had a knee-jerk bias to demand objective, publicly available, preferably measurable criteria to support ideas. Science, for example, probably our most influential method for gaining knowledge--has this bias. Hence it regards value judgments as inventions of the devil.

Similar suspicions are voiced in discussions of creativity. Some would argue that to establish its presence through something as arbitrary as value judgments will invite anarchy and eliminate the possibility of scholarly investigation. Let us train our lenses, say the doomsayers, on sheer <u>originality</u> or novelty, as Maltzman, for one, has done.[7] Now this tactic is defensible if originality is in the fact the matter of interest. But it cannot, we would argue, be used as a subtle ploy to learn anything about creativity. To reiterate, there is a world of difference between the merely unusual and the admirable (as Arieti[8] reminds us, it is particularly evident in dreams, whose contents are frequently most original but are much less often creative). Knowledge about the one may or may not tell us anything helpful about the other. This criticism can be leveled, Arieti has pointed out, at many of the studies searching for techniques to stimulate and encourage creativity. In fact, they have merely investigated originality. Conditions that help someone achieve new ideas will not necessarily lead to worthwhile ideas.

In short, the property of value or quality is inextricably entwined, in our view, with the concept of creativity. To ignore this attribute because it poses methodological/philosophical difficulties is unacceptable. It is, in Arnheim's phrase, "to be objective about nonobjective matters."[9] Our definition, despite its difficulties, seems the lesser of two evils.

In fact, we are personally more discomforted about including originality as a sine qua non of creativity. Prevailing opinion nowadays rarely questions this inclusion. But it is a rather recent one, probably stemming (as do so many of our beliefs about creators and creativity) from the attitudes of nineteenth century Romanticism. Admittedly, it does suit some types of creativity. Scientific work, for example, rarely wins renown unless it forges new directions. But many artistic masterpieces are "orginal" only in the trivial sense that absolutely any stimulus has something unique about it. Originality is hardly their primary, distinguishing attribute.

Consider the Greeks. In art, they eschewed novelty like the plague,[10] for their drama, sculpture, etc., was closely linked with religion and few activities are more conservative or resistant to innovation. Similarly, a Bach or a Mozart worked within the same forms and traditions as did many others, but simply took them to unequalled heights. Of Mozart, for example, one commentator has observed:

> There have been few great composers whose music was so intimately and organically tied to that of his predecessors as Mozart. Actually, one might call him a conservative, but a conservative who is fresh and unspoiled.[11]

Another expresses the matter even more directly:

> (Mozart) was, as we know, no revolutionary; he spoke the musical language of his time. He made liberal use of musical ideas of others, the urge for originality being as alien to him as to any composer of his time (italics mine).[12]

Similarly, Bach primarily represents the summit of a longstanding tradition, the Baroque. After his sublimities it languished, partly because its further development seemed inconceivable. Might we not therefore distinguish two types of creators: 1) the innovators such as Beethoven, Picasso and Martha Graham, whose "originality" is paramount, and 2) the perfectors such as Mozart, Bach and Sophocles whose immortality rests on other criteria? But if this distinction is allowed, then our definition faces almost incapacitating difficulties; in fact it veers uncomfortably close to untenability.

Be that as it may, we have reluctantly decided to retain originality as a defining attribute. A great deal of empirical work such as Guilford's[13] rests on it and in our day and age at least, it is widely accepted by both artists and critics as an important, even irreplaceable indicant of merit. As further solace, we agree with Gruber[14] that when we focus on the unquestioned "greats", the Shakespeares, Mozarts, Rembrandts, Einsteins, and Darwins whose qualifications for the label "creative" are beyond debate, the entire question of definition becomes somewhat superfluous. Whatever the standards and subtleties of wording, they deserve inclusion.

Democracy and Creativity

The general question of creativity's meaning poses a more specific problem. Does everyone possess the potential ability to be original? Or is it a rare gift, restricted to a special breed qualitatively distinct from the rest of humanity? These days the dominant prejudice appears to hold that "anyone can do it." Why is this so? First of all, to avow that "some people are more equal than others" would contradict certain fundamental, cherished American ideals. If all people are created equal, then all people should be able to create equally. In other words, the widespread reluctance to recognize genius as a special category is, as Arieti has put it, "based on pseudo-egalitarian premises."[15]

Second, in some respects everyone is creative. We all dream, every night, in remarkably consistent amounts[16] and with striking originality, the contents laden with symbols, hidden meanings, and so on, similar to those found in creative products. Thus it is accurately said "In dreams, everyone is an artist." Likewise, virtually all of us can acquire a language (in fact, this ability may be biologically innate[17]), and our use of it will be characteristically original. Even the driest civil servant will usually paraphrase ideas rather than recite them back by rote. Furthermore, we seem predisposed to receive original stimulation, for we routinely understand sentences that we have not heard before.

Indeed, according to Perkins[18] the psychological processes involved in creating are in no way unique or miraculous, but appear as well in other more mundane human activities. It relies largely on such ubiquities as reasoning, noticing, recognition and understanding rather than on, say, mysterious processes in some hypothesized unconscious mind. Can we say, then, that when Cézanne paints apples that resemble but do not

8

replicate the apples of experience, he simply "paraphrases" them, doing something that we all do? These are persuasive arguments. Yet in our view it is one thing to dream or speak with originality. To produce something tangible and permanent that others will admire is quite another, requiring special qualities.

Thus Rothenberg[19] convincingly argues that while dreams and creations certainly have some similarities, they also display important differences. Most notably, creating is a conscious, planned activity requiring high levels of personal control and manipulation of content, of motivation, effort and persistence, whereas dreaming is completely involuntary and automatic. Moreover, dreaming helps to keep us asleep and to dispel anxiety, while creativity as often induces high arousal and severe insomnia. Last, showing his psychoanalytic colors, Rothenberg asserts that a dream invokes censorship to disguise its actual meaning, while a creative work removes censorship. Thus in his estimation, "the creative process is the mirror image of the dream"[20] (italics mine).

Perkins too avoids a completely democratic position. Creativity's processes may be nothing special but its purposes are. It attempts to accomplish things which are extraordinarily different, due either to demands placed by others or by creators themselves. Necessity, for Perkins, is truly the mother of invention. Thus creativity is distinctive, if not, perhaps, in the processes involved, then in the people who do it. They willingly take up formidable tasks that ordinary folk, for one reason or another, prefer to shun. In brief, then, most of us seem to possess the foundations on which talent rests, but we lack some important superstructures.

Another factor promoting the democratic bias is the brand of psychology variously labeled "humanistic," "existential," or "third stream." In these circles, creativity has received such attention that it has attained almost buzzword status.* One assumption widely shared by Rogers, Maslow, Moustakas et al., is that everyone has the capacity to do it, if only they can achieve their potential as human beings, or self-actualize. Rogers seems the most fervent democrat in this group. He has provided a definition that openly avoids any distinction between

---

* The shelves of any reasonably "with-it" bookstore will be guaranteed to display titles such as "Ten Days to a More Creative Lifestyle," "How to Clean Your Own Oven the Creative Way," and "Creative Bestiality, Animal Husbandry, and You." Since publishers live and die by the law of supply and demand, we must assume that these emanations of pop psychology are being widely read, or at least widely purchased.

good and bad work.[21] Apparently anything new is automatically admirable. Hence, his astonishing statement that

> The action of a child inventing a new game
> with his playmates; Einstein formulating a theory
> of relativity; the housewife devising a new sauce
> for the meat; a young author writing his first
> novel--all of these are, in terms of our
> definition, creative, and there is no attempt
> to set them in some order of more or less
> creative (italics mine).[22]

To put it bluntly, this position seems at the least implausible, and some might prefer more derogatory modifiers. That the theory of relativity might arise from the same kind of person and through the same mechanisms as a new meat sauce simply defies credulity.

Fortunately, Maslow has restored some semblance of sanity by carefully distinguishing between two meanings of the word "creative."[23] It can, he notes, refer to genius, exemplified by such as Shakespeare, Mozart, and Einstein. But it can also designate a day-to-day lifestyle that is individualistic, uninhibited, and spontaneous. The first type of creativity is rare, shown only by a special few. The second type (with which Maslow was mainly concerned) everyone, supposedly, has the potential to achieve. Most notably, he was emphatic that it probably had little relationship to, and would shed little light on, the workings of genius.

But, as so often happens, a leader's message has been ignored by most of his followers. They have spread the gospel that a "creative lifestyle" will conjure up masterpieces that will make continents quake. Unhappily, this suburban misconception has usually yielded work of questionable merit, work that only close relatives and employees of the "creator" would wish to pay money to witness. We have no quarrel with people practising creative activities in order to enrich their lives, actualize their potentials, or come to terms with, say, their latent heterosexuality. But more than enough tomes have already pursued these awesome purposes. We do not wish to do so here.

By creativity we mean something rare and special. The true genius is, in our view, qualitatively different from the rest of us, and so must be the processes by which he or she produces. We do not believe that everyone has the mysterious disease called talent, nor do we believe that inventing a new meat sauce is sufficient evidence for its presence. Helpful environmental conditions are necessary for this talent to develop; hostile circumstances can certainly suppress it. But no amount

10

of effort or encouragement will bring it forth from a source where that potential does not exist.

Since this stance is likely to be provocative, let us defend it in a different context. Most of us can accept, without undue discomfort, the concept of the "natural athlete." Some people readily accomplish physical activities without much thought or effort; others, equally motivated, trip over their own shadows. And the rest of us, even with a lifetime of concerted practice and the best of coaching, could not come close to emulating the particularly gifted. Bobby Orr, Martina Navratilova, Guy Lafleur, Pelé, O. J. Simpson, Nadia Comenici, Willie Mays, Babe Didrickson, Julius Erving--they are a breed apart. Certainly they had to work hard. But how many others have worked even harder under equally beneficial circumstances of training and failed miserably? If the concept of natural talent seems reasonable for athletes, why is it so unthinkable that artists and scientists might possess something similar? The belief that "everyone can do it" may appeal to our sense of democracy and fair play. Unfortunately, it is probably inaccurate, a foundation of sand upon which it would be foolhardy to build a theoretical house.

The "Data" of Creativity

In discussing the various perspectives, we will use a method for evaluating ideas that science has found very effective. The sciences all study some type of empirical phenomena (or facts or data, as they are also called), that is, events that are observable, measurable, and conveyed to us through our senses. These events are also said to be "publicly available" and "objective" since, potentially at least, one person's observations of them can be checked and verified by other witnesses. After all, people do make mistakes and even have hallucinations. But when several agree, their observations can be said to be reliable or repeatable, and our confidence that those observations are reasonably accurate can thereby increase.

Scientific hypotheses, or theories, try to encompass and explain these phenomena, to state how and why they occur. Therefore, theories may develop via the method of induction, in which the various facts are collected first and then the theory "grows out of them." It is now widely questioned whether true induction is, in practice, either possible or desirable.[24] But however theories come about, they are certainly, in science, answerable to the facts and must account for them adequately. Otherwise, no matter how impressive a theory's logic and beauty, it will be rejected. Similarly, scientific theories must be unambiguous, making precise, testable predictions about phenomena as yet unobserved, so that if these predictions do not materialize,

11

the theories must be either modified or scrapped entirely. In other words, scientific theories can be proven wrong; they are distinguished by their falsifiabilty, and science progresses, according to some opinions, by the criticism and disproof of unworkable ideas.[25]

It is this insistence on empirical support for its ideas that provides science with its special advantages over other methods of inquiry.* The proof is in the pudding: by adopting this bias we seem to have gained more understanding of the world's mysteries. Therefore, this same approach would seem desirable for evaluating the various theoretical attacks on creativity. Unfortunately, the "data" at our disposal lack, at first blush, certain properties that data usually possess, notably measurability and objectivity. We must therefore try to show that they nevertheless can provide acceptable criteria.

The so-called "data of creativity" fall into two categories. The first, personality characteristics found in creative people, seem scientifically respectable. While these characteristics have been assessed using different techniques that vary widely in precision, in theory they can be objectively and reliably measured because they are observable. Moreover, several characteristics have been consistently found, so that we will be able to generalize concerning "the creative personality."

It is the second type of data that poses problems. Creative workers have provided many anecdotes and informal observations describing their experiences.[26,27] These, then, exemplify the method of introspection, in which one examines one's inner mental life, or conscious experience, and attempts to report the results of this self-analysis to someone else. Introspection was frequently used by psychologists during the late 19th and early 20th centuries when Wundt/Titchener "structuralism" was in vogue. Subjects were exposed to various stimulus situations, such as lights flashing and bells ringing, and were asked to describe their experiences.

---

* A theological approach, for example, promotes ideas extraordinarily immune to disproof. Here, when facts and theory collide, the facts are often dismissed as incorrect. The theory, a dogma or unquestioned truth, is inviolate. Galileo's problems originated when he used a scientific approach to test Copernicus' notion that the earth was not the center of the universe. The Inquisition, more theologically inclined, didn't much care what his data said. The prevailing dogma said that the earth was the center, and that ended the discussion.

The results were decidedly mixed; the method's deficiencies were glaringly revealed. A person's consciousness is private and subjective rather than publicly available and objective. Only that person can directly observe it. Others can share it only when the person describes it to them. Anyone who has tried to communicate a particularly intense emotion or experience will realize that words often cannot do the job. We fall back on pitiful ejaculations such as "well, you know...like, you know...like WOW!," which are not particularly informative. An expression to which we often resort at such times precisely captures the difficulty. "Words fail me!"

Introspection is also troubled because, in the same situation, several people often describe their experiences using different, yet strikingly similar words. One might report "a blazing bright light," another "an intense fiery glow." Since each person's consciousness is private, we cannot tell whether they actually had different experiences or were simply describing the same one in different words. Is one person's experience of "orange" the same as another's? No one knows. Thus it is very difficult for us to do reliability checks on someone else's observations.

Two final problems should also be noted. The so-called Heisenberg Uncertainty Principle currently bedevils all the sciences. When any phenomenon is observed or measured, its properties change. Now this seems particularly true of consciousness. If I try to examine and describe mine, it will probably part company with the ordinary consciousness I have when I'm not looking at it, so to speak. Therefore my descriptions will not reflect my usual experiences in the same situation. As well, according to the psychoanalysts, we have an unconscious mind that is not observable but that nevertheless crucially affects our actions. If this is so, then people probably do not observe even their own mental qualities accurately. (This is only one of the many persuasive arguments Nisbett and Wilson[28] raise against the introspective method.)

In light of these difficulties, how can we accept introspective reports as firm "data" for evaluating our theoretical perspectives, assigning the same importance to them as to a precise measurement from a recording device? In defense, we will not try to show that these reports are any less subjective than they seem, but rather that more legitimate data face precisely the same problems. Nowadays, we realize that most facts are not nearly as "hard" as more innocent times supposed. Dickens' Mr. Gradgrind,[29] a stereotypic nineteenth century arch-empiricist, believed that "the facts" would lead inevitably to theoretical truth and the best of all possible worlds. He has gone the way of the horse and buggy (as Dickens clearly knew he would).

13

As the first witness for the defense, Polanyi has pointed out[30] that truly objective, impersonal data are probably impossible to attain. Personal, _tacit_ interpretation can never be avoided. The "data" are always observed through someone's sensory receptors, and that person's biased, arbitrary opinions will affect decisions about meaning and the response warranted. Even if we could confine ourselves to completely objective events, we probably would not want to, since the resulting knowledge would be trivial. Likewise, Kuhn has reminded us that the experiences from the same, supposedly objective events can be variable.[31] Each "fact" resembles an ambiguous figure, such as a Rorschach ink-blot, which can be interpreted in many ways depending on the biases of the observer. When these biases change, Kuhn asserts, in a real sense the empirical world will also change, at least as we perceive it.

Second, our sensory receptors continually receive vast arrays of stimulation, most of which we ignore. Still, a myriad of potential data exist "out there" in that "blooming, buzzing, confusion" (to borrow William James' apt phrase), and someone must decide which deserve emphasis in evaluating a theory. These decisions are equally biased and arbitrary; there are no firm, inviolate canons to help them. Which facts are important? It's a matter of opinion.

What, then, are the genuinely distinctive, crucial attributes of "data"? Surely, it is their reliability. If several observers agree about a phenomenon, then it should be given some weight. Its characteristics, its importance, and its meaning will still be debatable, but at least it will have been experienced by several persons. A special virtue of science is, then, its insistence on verifying its ideas with public observation.

As we will shortly discover, creative people often report[32] what sound like similar experiences. For example, in one study over 50 percent of those interviewed reported that after finishing their labor they felt detached from the final product; as if it were someone else's work rather than their own. Surely it would be pedantic and even silly to ignore such appreciably reliable reports on purely methodological grounds.

Furthermore, other problems with introspection should become, in practise, less troublesome. The Wundt/Titchener approach foundered mainly on the reef of inadequate communication, on the inability of introspectors to convert a private, personal experience into some form of viable revealing expression. However, this approach used trained but hardly talented introspectors. Creative people, on the other hand, should well fit the latter role since introspection, the effective communication of personal experience in some form, is the very stuff of their business.

14

To repeat, the creative experience is inherently subjective and private. Should we, as some might prefer, therefore ignore it as a hopelessly unscientific quagmire? Or should we take the bull by the horns and rely on verbal self-reports? We prefer the latter option since, with all their problems, self-reports can supply some intriguing possibilities.

We must, however, reject yet another possible tactic with which we already have some experience. An attempt could be made to provide an objective, operationally defined, and thus scientifically legitimate measure of the creative experience. Experimental aesthetics attempts to use scientific data as an indication of aesthetic matters (see Kreitler & Kreitler[33] for an extensive review of this literature). It uses measurements such as EEG readings, pupilary dilations, heart rates, and the like as an attempt to scientifically establish beauty. Which of several pieces of art is better? Which particular sound pattern is generally preferred? A reading on some instrument will supply the criterion. However, the results of these studies have been, in my view, laudably scientific, overwhelmingly empirical, and laughably trivial. They cry out for satire. Why have they advanced knowledge but little?* Because an aesthetic experience is by its very nature subjective, private, and arbitrary. That a particular measurable response should accompany it helps us not one iota in understanding it. To insist on objective criteria to verify it is (to use Arnheim's phrase again) "to be objective about nonobjective matters." Methods are a means to an end; we should choose those that will best answer the questions we ask. To make measurement the sine qua non of intellectual inquiry is to attach more importance to the method of study than to the topic of study. Which is a classic case of the tail wagging the dog.

The best scientists, on the other hand, cheerfully admit that their method is limited and cannot do everything. We might listen to Einstein on this point:

---

* Arguably, science is no better than any other method of investigation so long as it simply verifies the obvious, that is, ideas also held by "common sense" or prevailing belief. It attains preeminence only when it verifies the not obvious, when its findings surprise us and tell us things about the world that we would not otherwise have suspected. Thus, most scientific theories that attract great interest (again, Einstein's is an obvious example) do so, at least in part, because they make counterintuitive predictions, which subsequent testing nevertheless shows to be accurate. By this criterion also, experimental aesthetics has been a dismal failure. The examples we have encountered have been quite bereft of surprises.

15

> I asked Einstein one day, "Do you believe that
> absolutely everything can be expressed
> scientifically?" "Yes," he replied, "it would
> be possible, but it would make no sense. It
> would be a description without meaning--as if
> you described a Beethoven symphony as a variation
> of wave pressure."[34]

Any experimental aestheticians who have not already slammed this
book shut in disgust might take heed!

The Stages of the Creative Process

Having discussed the problems of studying the creative process,
let us next examine some fundamental aspects of it. A more
detailed description will be provided later on, but hopefully
this sketch will help the reader understand some of the personality
characteristics of those who must endure this process, along
with its typical experiences. Also, our later deliberations
will specify several stages of the process and separately examine
each. This approach is debatable. Therefore, after noting some
influential examples, we shall attempt to defend it.

The different stages suggested by various authorities seem,
once differences in terminology are surmounted, quite similar.
Table 1.1 presents several typical analyses. We will now discuss
their main components.

Table 1.1

Some Proposals of the Successive Stages in the Creative Process

Author	Stages (Time/Progress ⟶)			
Wallas[35]	preparation	incubation	illumination	verification
Stein[36]	preparatory/ education	hypothesis formation	hypothesis testing	communication of results
Hutchinson[37]	preparation	frustration	achievement	verification

1. Preparation. It is generally agreed that a potential
creator must first learn the background material and techniques
of a field before contributing to it in any original way.
Stein[38] provides the only dissent here. While accepting the
importance of this phase, he questions its inclusion in the

16

creative process proper since it is not unique to that process. This phase can also prepare someone for many different sorts of activities.

2. Incubation/frustration. It is also commonly assumed that bright ideas will follow the preparatory phase neither immediately nor automatically. For some time, little of worth will be harvested. The role of conscious effort provides the main controversy about this phase. In the well-known view of Wallas,[39] various bits of knowledge supplied by preparation "incubate" in the unconscious mind, simmering and interacting with one another like the ingredients in a stew. Thus various possibilities are considered below the level of conscious awareness. A classic paper by philosopher/mathematician Poincaré has endorsed this view:

> Most striking at first is this appearance of sudden illumination, a manifest sign of long, unconscious prior work. The role of this unconscious work in mathematical invention appears to me incontestable, and traces of it would be found in other cases where it is less evident.... These sudden inspirations...never happen except after some days of voluntary effort which has appeared absolutely fruitless and whence nothing good seems to have come.... These efforts then have not been as sterile as one thinks; they have set agoing the unconscious machine and without them it would not have moved and would have produced nothing.[40]

Poincaré goes on to say that the bright ideas that do rise to the mental surface will invariably be worthwhile. Moreover, even in such supposedly hard-nosed disciplines as science and mathematics, they must also satisfy aesthetic criteria and be not only logical but also "harmonious" and "beautiful." According to this view, the unconscious filters out the unproductive possibilities, the blind alleys, and the dead ends. Or, in Poincaré's words:

> All goes on as if the inventor were an examiner for the second degree who would only have to question the candidates who had passed a previous examination.[41]

It is immediately obvious that the process as here depicted closely resembles the gestation of a child in the womb. In both cases, the progenitor is consciously uninvolved with and has little control over the growth and maturation of the eventual result. For Hutchinson, however, this stage features much more

conscious bumbling and thrashing around.[42]   The worker wanders
down blind alleys, apparently getting nowhere fast.   Typically,
he or she will feel stupid, incompetent, and frustrated.   The
problem may become so hateful that the inventor will resort to
any evasive activity--sharpening pencils, brewing countless cups
of coffee, or even deigning to visit the dentist.   He or she
may contemplate throwing it over completely and joining the
army.   But the problem will not leave the inventor alone, dominating
both dreams and consciousness.   Furthermore, feelings of guilt
may intensify the agony if, like most creatives, she or he is
conscientious and views idleness as the devil's playground.   In
short, racked on a classic approach-avoidance conflict, the inventor
is   driven   both   towards   and   away   from   the   work.   Stein's
corresponding stage, that of hypothesis formation, includes both
the conscious and unconscious components as well as aspects of
the inspiration stage to follow.[43]

     3.   Inspiration.   Supposedly this dramatic, storied moment
supplies the seed from which all else follows; both theorists
and laypersons assume its importance.   The individual obtains a
"bright idea."   The figurative light bulb clicks on and the
individual gasps "Aha" or "Eureka" (as Archimedes supposedly
did as he watched the water rise in his bath).   Inspiration
may strike at any time and its whimsical unpredictability provides
many colorful anecdotes.   We have all heard that a falling
apple helped Newton conceive the idea of gravity.   Poincaré
discovered a mathematical solution as he boarded a bus (an
ill-timed inspiration, this case suggests, could be dangerous
to life and limb).

     For some reason, insights often arrive when the recipient
is either lying in bed at night or shaving.   Perhaps the answer
lies with Rollo May's notion that ideas come in the transition
between work and relaxation.[44]   Inner censors are relaxed and
thought can free wheel.   But not always.   Consider a particularly
famous insight as described by the fortunate beneficiary, physicist
Enrico Fermi:

          We were working very hard on the neutron-induced
          radioactivity, and the results we were obtaining
          made no sense.   One day, as I came to the
          laboratory, it occurred to me that I should
          examine the effect of placing a piece of lead
          before the incident neutrons....I was clearly
          dissatisfied with something: I tried every
          "excuse" to postpone putting the piece of lead
          in its place.   When finally, with some reluctance,
          I was going to put it in its place, I said to
          myself, "No, I don't want this piece of lead

18

here; what I want is a piece of paraffin." It was just like that; with no advance warning.[45]

Perhaps no example more clearly reveals the mysterious, arbitrary, and almost God-given nature of inspiration. Why paraffin, of all things? Why not tin? Or wallboard? Or a peanut butter sandwich? Yet Fermi's seminal experiment won him the Nobel Prize.

Dreams can also be fruitful although, judging by reports, not as often as we might suspect. The main difficulty, probably, is not that dreams are barren but that they are rather poorly retained. Many slumbering creators keep notebook and pencil handy on their nightables, hoping that any important "Ahas" will awaken them. Still, Kekulé reportedly dreamt of a snake biting its own tail, which to him suggested the rather unapparent association that the benzene molecule must have a closed-ring structure. As well, Singer dreamt of the idea for his sewing machine. The problem was to find a way to copy the action of hand sewing; a needle pierces the cloth, and then a hand pulls the needle through on the other side. Singer dreamt that a rider on a horse was rushing at him. The rider carried a spear with a hole in its point through which was threaded a yellow ribbon.[46]

4. Verification/hypothesis testing. In this stage, the person attempts to convert a profound insight into a finished product that can be communicated to others. The artist must refine and polish; the scientist, already convinced himself of a new theory's validity, must verify it, either empirically, logically, or mathematically, to win over more skeptical colleagues. In this phase, the creator must shift to a more critical, objective perspective, and view his or her work through the eyes of others. This is no easier to do than for parents to evaluate their own children with detachment (and certainly many creative products have had visages that only a parent could love).

Once more, frustration and even trauma are endemic. As the creator labors to "get it right", she or he may agonize for weeks over one word in a poem, or one gesture in a dance that, to the audience, will be gone in an instant. To be an artist or scientist might seem to the uninitiated like a glamorous career. The verification stage firmly corrects this delusion. Yet, to anticipate a later point, it is skill in this stage that separates the successes from the failures.

5. Communication of results. This phase has often been overlooked, but a few investigators have paid it the attention it deserves.[47,48] The evaluations of other people, we have

19

learned, will decide whether a product stands or falls. Other
factors that follow its completion can also affect those
evaluations, such as marketing and public relations skills, the
opinions of critics and other influential tastemakers, even the
political, economic, and meteorological climates. A complete
account of the process cannot afford to neglect these important
matters.

Why Stages?

We must now defend our breakdown of the creative process
into component stages, because this practice has some questionable
aspects. Contrary to the impression that many psychology textbooks
convey (when they condescend to discuss creativity at all),
these hypothesized stages do not _explain_ the process. They
merely _describe_ it, and they are themselves phenomena that require
explanation. Furthermore, any such analysis wildly oversimplifies
the process and so may actually hinder rather than help
understanding. All analyses imply that the various stages occur
in a discrete, linear sequence, succeeding one another with the
automatic inevitability of stations on a railway line. It is
more likely that they overlap and interact with one another in
a much more fluid, flexible manner.

Conceptually, of course, preparation must preceed inspiration,
since someone is unlikely to obtain insights about a field of
which one is ignorant. Still, in practice, a creator frequently
will understand and appreciate the work of his or her predecessors
only _after_ having tried to improve upon their work. By the
same token, as the saying "out of the mouths of babes" brings
home, too much knowledge about other contributions can indoctrinate
a creator with the dominant perspectives and inhibit the ability
to conceive alternatives. _Citizen Kane_, widely recognized as a
landmark of the film genre, was the first film its director,
star, and co-author, Orson Welles, ever made. By his own admission
he knew almost nothing about the medium, but, in his opinion,
this ignorance was bliss. _Citizen Kane's_ revolutionary techniques,
still eye- and ear-catching after some forty years, were discovered,
according to Welles, "because we didn't know any better."[49]

Likewise, the stage of verification, which supposedly follows
inspiration, can sometimes actually _provide_ it. During revisionary
work, new insights often appear. A choreographer may notice
natural forms and shapes that ordinarily might escape the eye.
A playwright's germinal conception will grow and change, gathering
ideas for specific lines of dialogue, character development,
and pieces of stage business as he rewrites. How many show-stopping
moments in the Broadway musical theatre have originated during
the ulcer-ridden "out-of-town tryout"? "Harry", the producers
wail, "Act Two is dying half way through. Can't you give us

20

something to wake everybody up?" Poor beleaguered Harry, who laboured under the misconception that his work was done, burns the midnight oil, singlehandedly keeping up the tobacco and coffee industries' profit pictures. But the result is sometimes a "10:30 miracle" like "Sit Down You're Rocking the Boat" from Guys and Dolls, or "Brush up Your Shakespeare" from Kiss Me Kate.

In short, the verification stage, by awakening dormant sensibilities and new perspectives, will often yield dividends. Two respected creators, regarding this stage:

> (People) have asked me how I ever found time
> to know anything that was going on in the world
> about me when my life was so completely absorbed
> by this world of writing. Well, it may seem
> to be an extraordinary fact, but the truth is
> that never in my whole life have I lived so
> fully, have I shared so richly in the common
> life of man as I did during these three years
> when I was struggling with the giant problem
> of my own work.
>   For one thing, my whole sensory and creative
> equipment, my powers of feeling and
> reflection--even the sense of hearing, above
> all my powers of memory, had reached the greatest
> degree of sharpness that they had ever
> known....For three years I prowled the streets,
> explored the swarming web of the million-footed
> city and came to know it as I had never done
> before (italics mine).[50]

> When my creative energy flowed most freely, my
> muscular activity was always greatest. The body
> is inspired....I might often have been seen
> dancing; I used to walk through the hills for
> seven or eight hours on end without hint of
> fatigue. I slept well, laughed a good deal--I
> was perfectly vigorous and patient.[51]

An artist acquaintance has perhaps more accurately described the real course of events.[52] Creators conduct a continuous dialogue with the medium, often attempting many possibilities with the medium responding either positively or negatively. Thus a series of small "inspirations" occur continuously, both before, during, and after revision. Stein, for one, seems to agree with this notion when he asserts that hypothesis formation and hypothesis testing alternate.[53]

Still and all, however, in principle we must accept the idea of stages. It is the smooth, linear progression from one stage to another that we question. The various stage-like components fit most introspective reports and they are defensible for descriptive purposes. Moreover, if nothing else, they bring home the point that the creative process is not a unitary, homogenous entity but involves several different types of thought, so conceptually it is likely that all stages must occur at some point in the process. Stein also adds that "staging" can help us understand those unfortunate malignancies called "creative blocks," wherein the worker's creativity "dries" and productivity plummets. An extensive discussion of these matters would be peripheral here, so the interested reader is referred to Stein's work. Essentially, he demonstrates that, depending on the stage in which the block occurs, both the cause and the remedy will differ.

Chapter 2

THE DATA OF CREATIVITY I: SOME CHARACTERTISTICS

OF CREATIVE PERSONS

What are creative people like? Are they really as mad as hatters? Longer of hair and dirtier of fingernail? Impractical, pie-in-the-sky daydreamers? Lazy, parasitic layabouts, sponging off the largesse of the hardpressed taxpayer? Invariably homosexual?

In this chapter we shall discover the accuracy of some common preconceptions. Several sources provide extensive discussions, but we shall limit ourselves to those having relevance for the theoretical accounts. We shall also try to avoid ideas that have inadequate empirical backing and stand on little more than blind intuition or common sense. Lombroso, for example, in a historically interesting but dubious study,[1] asserted that creative people tend towards stammering, "vagabondage," rickets, and sterility. In defense of these conclusions, he listed well-known individuals who displayed each attribute. Lombroso did not establish that these attributes occur more frequently among creators than in the general population. But if his assertions are accurate, then stimulating creativity will be an easy matter. Simply geld everyone and outlaw Vitamin D.

At first glance, assessing personality characteristics might not seem especially difficult. After all, these characteristics are revealed by a person's behavior, which can can be publicly observed and potentially measured. In practice, however, personality assessment faces all manner of pitfalls. Some of these we shall, in due course, confront. However, we do not wish at this time to belabor questions of methodology, but simply to acquaint the reader with some of the frequently used techniques.

Methods of Study

Psychology's various measuring instruments probably provide the most indicative data. Tests such as the MMPI pose specific questions about personal matters, and answers can be scored in an objective, impersonal manner. This type of approach has even been used retrospectively by Cattell and his colleagues.[2,3] They do not administer the test directly to a subject. Instead, from biographical data such as information about habitual lifestyle and behavior patterns, they decide what an eminent person's answers might have been and assign a "score" on a variety of characteristics. A personality profile is then constructed, showing the individual's position along each of sixteen dimensions

23

of personality. For example, one such hypothesized dimension has extremes of <u>cyclothymia</u> and <u>schizothymia</u> (jargonistic monstrosities which resemble extraversion and introversion respectively). Scientists, as a group, usually fall towards the latter end of this continuum since they are typically withdrawn and internally preoccupied loners. Obviously, interpretive bias is more likely here, especially in deciding what the often vague material in a biography "means" and translating it into a quantified characteristic. But certainly objectivity is still the aim of those using the MMPI.

Another form of assessment, more subjective, uses tests such as Rorschach and other projective techniques, and indepth personal interviews. In these, an interviewer talks at length with the subject in order to draw conclusions about the latter's thoughts, feelings, and opinions about a variety of matters. Clearly, given amorphous, open-ended nature of this situation, the biases of the interviewer can greatly influence both the responses and the interpretations obtained. Different assessors will often draw different conclusions from the same interaction so that reliability suffers. Yet the flexibility of these procedures may encourage revelations that more precise techniques do not allow.

The <u>living in</u> method, developed by Barron, MacKinnon and their co-workers,[4],[5] is a particularly attractive approach. Certainly it has supplied some valuable data. A group of creatives, representing a particular discipline such as writing or architecture, is gathered together, observed, and evaluated intensively over a period of several days. All manner of techniques are used, ranging from the most objective instruments to the most amorphous of group discussions. Because it covers the entire spectrum, this many-faceted approach is perhaps the most sensible.

Personality Characteristics

For our purposes, the debate about preferable methods is slightly academic, since most of the creative characteristics we will discuss have appeared under a variety of assessment techniques. Occasionally we shall follow Lombroso and mention case histories that exemplify a particular characteristic, but in most cases other, more objective evidence exists to verify it. We shall also go beyond merely reciting the qualities found, and attempt to show how each might help creative work, and also, given that work's peculiar requirements, why it might induce that characteristic in its practitioners. These explanations, however, should be taken as the hypotheses that they are.

24

1. <u>Flexibility</u> <u>of</u> thinking. Creativity, by definition, requires originality, so an innovative person must be able to produce alternatives to commonplace ideas. Rigid thinking, exemplified by the "can't teach an old dog new tricks" mentality, clings to the obvious even when it is inappropriate or incorrect. Rigidity, which, incidentally, increases with such factors as age and damage to the frontal lobes of the brain,[6] will obviously hinder creative thought.

Flexibility may seem so obviusly necessary as to need no mention. Is it not almost tantamount to saying that we must think creatively in order to be creative? Certainly it is the attribute emphasized by most of the psychological tests that attempt to predict and/or assess someone's potential for creative work. Thus Guilford's Unusual Uses Test measures the ability to conjure up strange, bizarre uses for common objects (such as hammers). Likewise, his Divergent Thinking tests examine the fluency of ideas by asking the person to name all the things that are, for example, white and edible (flour, sugar, salt, snow, and shaving cream come quickly to mind).[7] In like fashion, Mednick's Remote Associations Test,[8] presents triplets of words, such as hammer, uppercut, and musical and the testee must discover another word that is a reasonable, but not obvious or dominant associate of all three. (As flexible minds will have surmised, one correct answer to the preceeding triad is "hit.")

Yet there seems to have been an unfortunate tendency, at least in testing/assessment circles, to treat flexibility as the <u>sine</u> <u>qua</u> <u>non</u> of creative work, when its antithesis, a relentless, dogmatic stubborness in the face of all opposition, may sometimes be equally important. At the least, other important qualities, without which flexibility is nothing, should also be assessed.

2. <u>Confidence</u>. Under this heading we will discuss a cluster of related attributes. Creative people are, as a rule, self-assertive, dominant, and self-sufficient. They are more independent and less catering to authority. They have great "ego strength" and are not given to self-criticism. This does not mean that they are swaggering, boastful braggarts (although some are), but they do believe, privately at least, that their talent is genuine and their products worthwhile. Such brimming self-confidence can be ill-founded and when it is, we call it delusions of grandeur. In the genuine article, however, it is reinforced by creative deeds.

Many creatives <u>have</u> been notoriously arrogant. Koestler mentions, among others, Darwin, Newton, and Pasteur.[9] Also, the philosopher Hegel reportedly began his lectures by saying,

25

"I may say with Christ that not only do I teach Truth, but that I myself am Truth." [10] Even the young Einstein was not popular with acquaintances because of what they perceived as an exaggerated opinion of his own worth. [11] His familiar image as the humble, fatherly bumbler, the archetypal absent-minded professor, came later in life. Playwright George Bernard Shaw also possessed a particularly formidable ego. One anecdote concerns his play Saint Joan, which presents Roman Catholicism in a sympathetic light. Contrary to the prevalent belief, Shaw was convinced that, given the attitudes of her day, Joan of Arc received a fair trial. The theologians, he felt, bent over backwards to be just and impartial, giving her every opportunity to defend herself. Shaw was therefore asked whether he would convert to Catholicism. He replied in the negative, on the grounds that the Catholic Church could not have two popes. [12]

As Rollo May has emphasized, [13] confidence is crucial. It is perhaps the major difference between talented persons who fulfill their potential and others of promise who do not. Why is it so important? Several reasons can be suggested. First, creative work often starts with a vague, nebulous hunch, with what poet Stephen Spender called "a dim cloud of an idea." [14] Confident persons, having the courage of their convictions, will pursue this beginning and develop its potential where others, less sure of themselves and their talent, may dismiss it. When the same idea later on brings fame and fortune to someone else, they are left with the poor consolation that they thought of it first.

Secondly, confidence is necessary to cope with public opinion. General consensus tends to be conservative and more comfortable with the familiar than with innovations that upset the status quo. In all likelihood, true innovations will at first be rejected and condemned with their progenitors to scorn, ridicule, or, worst of all, indifference. It is crucial, in the face of these reactions, that the creators reaffirm their products' merit and their own talent. Thus Llewelyn Powys asserts that when writing, once the pen is in hand, one must ignore others' possible opinions, and work away with careless, proud indifference. [15]

Creative work also involves great psychological risk. In a very real sense, its practitioners strip off their psychological clothes in public; exposing themselves, their abilities, and their limitations. In the words of critic Stanley Kaufmann, "A work of art of any kind is a tremendous investment of ego, of self, of nakedness." [16] For Stephen Spender, the purpose of poetry is to "achieve nakedness." [17] So exposed, creators invite arbitrary judgment. If it be harsh, their ability to work effectively can be devastated.

26

History tells of many, however, who have persevered over early adversity, powered mainly by their substantial egos. For years the great modern dancer/choreographer Martha Graham performed whenever sufficient funds could be scraped together, often before loyal but minuscule audiences. Her violent, earthy movements, at odds with the graceful, ethereal style of classical ballet, were a ready target for satire. (That traditional film staple of the Yuletide season, White Christmas, features one example. The production number called "Choreography," obviously has Graham as the target of its barbs.) Fortunately, Graham's faith in herself and her work rarely flagged.[18] In psychology, Sigmund Freud's preoccupation with human sexuality deeply offended the Victorian morality of his day. Polite society rarely discussed sex and presumably performed it (reluctantly?) under the covers with the lights out. It found Freud's theory of infantile sexuality (according to which children can experience sexual desire long before puberty) a repugnant product of a depraved mind. Yet Freud, whose ego has rarely been surpassed, could dismiss the outraged clamor as simply the ravings of misguided ignoramuses.

This ubiquitous self-confidence has some corollaries. First, typical creatives are not particularly liberal or democratic in temperament; not given to seeing "the other fellow's point of view." More often they are dogmatic about the inherent superiority of their own ideas. For example, in the psychoanalytic movement's early years, a circle of followers gathered around Freud, agreeing with much of what he had to say. However, men as brilliant as Jung, Adler, and Rank inevitably began to produce independent ideas of their own. To Freud, such dissent was both a professional and a personal affront. The heretics were almost literally stripped of their credentials and drummed out of the lodge. Similarly, Martha Graham was adamantly possessive of the great roles she had created for herself. The members of her company, whom she expected to be her obedient, unquestioning, and expressive tools, could not possibly tackle them. With her dauntless single-mindedness, Graham continued to perform long after she should have retired, until eventually she had to admit that her powers had slipped. However, she would not help others learn her roles, or cooperate in having them recorded for posterity. No one else, she felt, could possibly do them justice.[19] Fortunately, the dances were salvaged and they are still performed successfully today.

Second, for Willy Loman, in Death of a Salesman, the supreme accomplishment was "to be well liked." Willy must have firmly muzzled his innovative tendencies, for, while creatives may be respected they are not usually popular. Some of this they bring on themselves since they do not value, and are not particularly adept at, social relations. But their foreboding self-confidence

27

can also discourage intimacy. As every politician knows, the high road to popularity and election is paved with feigned humility, but pride goeth before a fall. Louis Pasteur was apparently almost barred from the French Academy of Sciences, despite his obvious credentials, because his unseemly arrogance had irritated so many members.[20] Martha Graham is another example: revered, even immortal in her later years she had unfortunate bouts with alcohol, which may be explained by her lack of close friends.[21] In the presence of such a legend, everyone would be respectful and polite, bowing and scraping with a "Miss Graham" this and a "Miss Graham" that, but few would call her "Martha" or telephone to ask her out for coffee.

Still, periodic failures are not an impossibility, for even the greatest have had their disasters: Shakespeare, for example, gave us not only <u>Hamlet</u> but also the dubious pleasures of <u>Titus Andronicus</u> and <u>King John</u>. Balanchine and Ashton have choreographed dances that were performed once, hastily withdrawn from the repertoire, and seen no more. How does someone respond when he has removed his clothes only to be told that, on this occasion at least, he appears ugly and deformed? Such failures can be traumatic, as the novelist Henry Miller reminds us:

> Finally, I came to a dead end, to a despair
> and desperation which few men have known, because
> there was no divorce between myself as a writer
> and myself as a man...to fail as a writer meant
> to fail as a man.[22]

How does a creator prevent public failure from incapacitating further effective work? Making excuses is probably the most common recipe. (Psychologists label this device <u>rationalization</u>.) The hostile reception can be blamed on the ignorance or stupidity of the public and critics; it is over their heads, or too good for them, or ahead of its time. Such assertions can comfort the bruised ego simply because they do often contain a germ of truth. Shaw provides a rarer antidote (effective for the most dauntless of egos), which is self-ridicule. At one point he penned a one-act comedy called <u>Overruled</u>, which played in a triple bill along with two other short pieces by Pinero and James Barrie. <u>Overruled</u> was a dismal flop, yet the morning after its premiere, when any feelings of depression and inadequacy would be at their height, Shaw could view events in the following way:

> Pinero's playlet fell flat, mine fell flatter,
> and by contrast, Barrie's charming piece----worked
> as it never had before or since. The relief
> to the audience after the Pinero-Shaw
> mystifications was stupendous. They simply howled

28

for Barrie, whose pleasant little comedy made them realize how much they hated us. Next morning (the producer) rang me to suggest a few cuts. I replied that there were only two possible cuts--Pinero's piece and my own. I advised him to advertise a WARNING in capital letters, with the following simple statement beneath: "Mr. Barrie's piece commences at 10, before which the theatre bars are open."[23]

Last, when one must admit personal failure, having reliable, loyal supporters to lean on can be most comforting. Their undiminished faith in one's talent can help restore flagging confidence. Musician/composer/accompanist/lover/father-figure Louis Horst played this role for the young Graham, observing, "Every plant needs a wall to grow against. I am Martha's wall."[24] Two other noted female choreographers, Isadora Duncan[25] and Agnes de Mille[26], have acknowledged the necessity of the TLC and financial support that their mothers provided during long spells of public apathy. The importance of loyal followers to the success of any creator receives too little recognition.

3. Tolerance for ambiguity. Creative people are generally less conventional than are the unkempt masses. They are more comfortable with uncertainty; they find puzzles that lack clear, final answers to be intriguing and stimulating rather than threatening. Like mountain climbers, they perceive obstacles not as threats, but as challenges to be overcome "because they are there." An inventor expressed precisely this intolerance for any obstacle

which stood in the way of whatever I wished to accomplish. Were such an obstacle thought beyond one's power to remove it, the fact constituted a challenge.[27]

Likewise, composer Lukas Foss has suggested that successful creators are by nature gamblers, comfortable with risks and prepared to take them.[28] In his opinion, works most often fail because they are "too safe." In support, a study of junior high school students showed that the most creative 10 percent were much more prepared to take chances, for example, to guess wildly while grappling with a difficult problem solving task, than were the least creative.[29]

We summarize this conglomeration of attributes with the term tolerance for ambiguity.[30] Barron showed doctoral candidates a set of drawings, some of which were precise geometric shapes such as circles and triangles, while others were vague forms open to many possible interpretations. The more creative subjects

29

preferred the ambiguous drawings. According to Barron, the trait revealed is fundamental, because creators must be ready to abandon known systems of classification in favor of alternatives. They will prefer stimuli that suggest new possibilities. Why do they develop these preferences? Perhaps, Barron suggests, their families and friends have provided interpersonal situations that were vague and unpredictable. They learned that, with perseverence, they could solve them and gain more personal satisfaction while doing so.

A study of three hundred eminent personalities suggests that this notion may have merit.[31] Their backgrounds may have shown a great deal of diversity, but one factor was strikingly reliable. Many had fathers who were "idea men," dreamers who were prone to gamble everything on some questionable venture; more often than not, losing everything. Thus the eminent person had frequently experienced the unfortunate consequences of risk taking and had learned that failure is not the end of the world. Erich Fromm[32] asserts that during the Middle Ages various supreme and inviolate authorities provided final, unambiguous answers to humankind's eternal questions; the unquestioned dogma of the Catholic Church explained the meaning and purpose of life and death, and rigid feudal systems irreversibly established one's place in the social order at the time of birth. In this way citizens were without the freedoms that we take for granted, but they did have the security that certainty provides.

More recently, however, events such as the Reformation and the French Revolution have changed this comfortable state of affairs. We are now immeasurably more free to make of life what we wish, but we have paid the price of a concomitant increase in anxiety, doubt, and insecurity. Many people, Fromm argues, find these experiences repugnant, and longing for security will align themselves with any totalitarian system that offers it. Hence the attraction of Fascist and Nazi regimes. (Their rigidly authoritarian practices also provide another comfort, that is, adherents can avoid responsibility for their own actions. How often, at the Nuremberg trials and later, was the defence heard that "It wasn't my fault; I was simply doing what I was told!") We would expect that this description would not apply to those of a creative outlook. They desire <u>anything</u> <u>but</u> security, which they find more boring than comforting.

4. <u>Internal</u> <u>locus</u> <u>of</u> <u>control</u>. This characteristic obviously would fall within the rubric of the previous section, except that it seems not to have been verified empirically. Therefore it should be regarded more as a hypothesis to be tested. Rotter has distinguished between people possessing <u>internal</u> as opposed to <u>external</u> <u>locus</u> <u>of</u> <u>control</u>,[33] and developed a psychological test to determine the category in which someone

belongs. The first type, rugged individuals, assume responsibility for the results of their actions, whether successful or not. (The type has been immortalized ad nauseum by novelist/philosopher Ayn Rand[34] and is also to be seen in countless westerns.) Those with an external locus of control, on the other hand, believe events to be beyond control and attribute individual triumphs or failures to external factors such as society, other people, fate, the stock market, the phases of the moon, and so on. If they are to work productively, creatives must believe in their ability to manipulate the world around them. Without an internal locus of control creatives would not be able to do what it is they do: create.

5. Insecurity. We must now contradict some earlier observations. Judging by many introspective reports at least, creative people are often riddled with doubt about the quality of their products and the authenticity of their talent. Thus we have van Gogh slashing his paintings to ribbons in fits of hatred, Franz Kafka ordering that his unpublished manuscripts be destroyed at his death,[35] and Tolstoy, shortly after completing Anna Karenina, writing to a friend:

> My Anna, when I reread it, seemed to me such execrable stuff that I find it difficult to recover from my feeling of shame and I don't think I shall ever write anything more.[36]

The creative psyche seems ingenious, not only at conceiving new works, but also at discovering ways to make itself miserable. It probably is partly itself to blame. Characteristically, creators have high standards for achievement and so set difficult, even impossible goals for themselves. Witness Goethe's call to arms, "The first and last task required of genius is love of truth."[37] Eternally dissatisfied with their works, viewing them as dismal failures even when others have found them meritorious, they tend to be perfectionists.

Mass communication has probably helped promote creative unease, especially in the young. Beginners who are constantly bombarded with the polished, sophisticated contributions of mature professionals can be devastated, since their own efforts, in comparison, may seem hopelessly inept. Not realizing that those same professionals also had to persist through trial-and-error apprenticeship, beginners may give up entirely or, more insidiously, try to copy the professionals. Given the recent advances in the mass production of art, this factor is undoubtedly more threatening than ever. Shakespeare is on film and TV, Bach and Mozart on radio, and Balanchine on videotape. Beginners can no longer try their wings in innocent isolation. As someone said, the advent of musical recordings is the main reason why so many contemporary composers and performers sound alike.

But undoubtedly the greatest reason for creative insecurity is the fear of "losing it" or "going dry." The very nature of the creative process encourages this unhappy state. It is generally believed (perhaps unjustifiably) that everything depends on the moment of inspiration. Unfortunately, inspiration is characteristically whimsical; it cannot be programmed or timetabled. Heavy reliance on such a capricious event can lead to insecurity for the creator. The errors, dead ends, and blind alleys so characteristic of the incubation/frustration stage would be joined by feelings of stupidity and inadequacy. Playwright Neil Simon's sentiments are typical:

> You know, it frightens me too. The whole aspect of "Where does the creative urge and the instinct all come from?" Because when you don't know where it comes from, it's a mystery, and it frightens you. Say it could turn off at any moment. (italics mine).[38]

Nor are these fears of "losing it" merely another symptom of the unsteady temperament of creatives: it happens frequently. How many young novelists, playwrights, or scientists have made a promising start, caused a brief furor, and are never heard from again? Even the mature and established can experience lengthy dry spells.

Also contributing to these emotions is the undeniable fact that many achievements owe as much to luck, accident, or serendipity as to anything else. The discoveries of penicillin and the X-ray are two well-known examples.[39] Millikan's famous "oil drop" experiments, which established conclusively that electrons were actually unitary particles, depended on a series of fortunate flukes.[40] (This may be the reason why undergraduate students, in their laboratory assignments, have a notoriously difficult time replicating his results.) Archaeologist F. G. Rainey has provided a particularly amusing example of serendipity at work:

> I was digging in the West Indies.... I knew that the only sites in the West Indies were shell heaps. That's where you found everything. Great piles of seashells.... When we got down to the bottom of the shells, we stopped, because that was the bottom of the site. We knew that. One day, I'd had a very big luncheon and I went to sleep after lunch, it was siesta and a very hot day. The foreman thought, "Oh well, it's a hot day, let the boss sleep." I slept.

Some of our workmen finished...the bottom of the shell and, nobody was there to tell them to stop.... When they got beyond the sterile stuff, they began to turn up the kind of painted pottery that nobody had ever seen before in the West Indies. At that point they woke me up, and I made my first discovery....I'm absolutely certain it was because I ate too many beans for lunch.[41]

Yet while luck may have played a part, he must still have had the insight to profit from its gifts. Many investigators before Roentgen had noticed the X-ray phenomenon, but they invariably dismissed it as an unimportant "mistake." In Louis Pasteur's famous dictum, "Fortune favors the prepared mind."[42]

6. Paradoxical personalities. On occasion, we have blatantly contradicted ourselves about creators' typical characteristics, finding them to be, for example, both self-confident and riddled with doubt, both capable of flexible thought and dogmatically narrow-minded. To further complicate matters, there are still more inconsistencies. They can be both selfish and unselfish, detached from their work and emotionally involved in it, accurate of memory and deplorably absent minded. Once more, Einstein supplies a ready example:[43] humble and arrogant; the wisest of patriarchs and the most childlike of innocents; possessing a legendary ability to focus for long periods on one problem, coupled with an openness to virtually every person, cause, or appeal that landed on his doorstep.

Readers who prefer neatness will undoubtedly be as perplexed as Maslow[44] and McMullan[45], who also have puzzled over this propensity for displaying seemingly contradictory, mutually exclusive properties. How can this be? To begin, several writers have noted that such paradoxes are almost essential to the creative act itself. Thus Rollo May, discussing what he calls the paradox of courage,[46] asserts that creative persons must labor in both certainty and uncertainty; they must be fully committed and confident in the "rightness" of their ideas, but also realize and even enjoy the fact that they could be wrong. In May's words, "Commitment is healthiest when it is not without doubt but (when it occurs) in spite of doubt."[47] In the same vein, Holton adds:

To be able to see and use...polar opposites lies close to the very meaning of genius. The seemingly ambivalent style of thinking, acting and living is therefore not merely "good copy" but needs to be considered as one aspect of (an) unusual ability to deal with the ambiguities

33

inherent in the chief unresolved problems of science.[48]

McMullan has provided an intriguing explanation for this phenomenon.[49] However, it is first necessary to digress to supply some background. It has persistently been asserted that we can think about the world in two fundamentally different ways. Ornstein, in his influential book The Psychology of Consciousness,[50] has distinguished between linear and nonlinear thought. The former is characteristically verbal, analytic, and logical. One idea preceeds another in time, as do words in a sentence or steps in a mathematical proof.

Nonlinear thought is qualitatively different--a "new ball game," so to speak. It is intuitive and visual rather than logical and verbal, featuring vague "gut reactions," or what Polanyi has called tacit understanding,[51] as when we know something but we cannot express it in words. The various component ideas seem to occur simultaneously, so the sense of time passing and of one idea preceeding another is absent, hence, "nonlinear". This form of thought comes to the fore particularly during the various altered states of consciousness. Regardless of the method used to obtain these--whether dreams, meditation or artificial chemicals--the reported mental experiences tend to be strikingly similar,[52] suggesting that all may tap the same psychic fountainhead.

Ornstein has shown that different parts of the brain may control these two types of thought; specifically, the left and right hemispheres seem specialized for linear and nonlinear thought, respectively. But for our purposes the important point is that creative thought of any kind seems to alternate between the two modes. Even such definitively linear activities as science, mathematics, and philosophy require healthy injections of inspirational, intuitive thought to succeed, as both Poincaré[53] and Einstein[54] have avowed. On the other hand, artistic pursuits also need critical, analytic detachment, notably during the stage of verification.

This view of the creative process has many advocates. For Nietzsche,[55] the two opposing forces of Dionysus (representing surging vitality, intuition, and emotion) and Apollo (representing form, order, and reason) were both involved in art, and battled one another for supremacy. Romantic that he was, Nietzsche held that in the best art, notably that of archaic Greece, the Dionysian principle gained the upper hand. When in classical times Apollonian tendencies prevailed, Greek art, in his opinion, went into decline. And for Rothenberg[56] creativity exemplifies so-called Janusian thinking (after the Roman god Janus, who had two countenances that faced opposite directions). The essential

34

point, however, is that if these views are accurate, then any creator must be almost, in a sense, "schizoid", a Jekyll and Hyde functioning in two distinctive, almost contradictory modes.

How has McMullan thereby explained creators' paradoxical characteristics? He suggests that as they oscillate between the two modes, their personal qualities may likewise change. Nonlinear functioning would encourage selfishness, humility, emotional involvement, and the like, while linear functioning would bring forth the opposite qualities, such as altruism and detachment.

7. Androgyny. As we now know, the typical creative personality is not exactly a model of consistency, but one paradoxical quality at least seems understandable. Creative men are often found to prefer activities and express values that are typical of women. Similarly, creative women in some ways lean towards more masculine interests and attitudes. (On this latter point the literature is admittedly contradictory[57]. Some authorities, notably Roe[58], state this to be the case, but Helson's extensive studies on creative women suggest that they are in some ways less masculine.[59]) This does not mean, we hasten to add, that most creatives are homosexual; some are, but then so are some bankers and used car salesmen. We refer here to a cerebral rather than to a physical orientation.

The paradox before us, then, involves a mental outlook that half the time is at odds with the body in which it is placed. With surprising reliability, introspection finds the right side of the body to be more "masculine" and the left more "feminine." This would suggest that the two sides of the brain might show a similar sexual specialization, with the left side having the more masculine tone (the body's right side is controlled by the left side of the brain, and vice versa, since the anatomical connections cross the midline). We have previously learned that both modes of thought, and hence both hemispheres, contribute to creative work. Rephrasing this statement in terms of the present argument, both masculine and feminine thinking are necessary. Thus the frequent assertion that creative thought is "androgynous." The sexual paradox, therefore, seems reasonable. Creative persons must be in contact with both genders of their psyche, so their sexual orientation might well migrate towards neutrality.

But are creatives more likely to be overtly homosexual? Although conclusive statistics are not available, most authorities seem to reject this supposition.[60] However Gedo[61] expresses the minority opinion, for the arts at least, citing its frequency both among contributors (e.g., Michelangelo, Sappho, Tchaikovsky, Proust, Gide and Tennessee Williams) and also consumers. He

35

also provides some explanations for this supposed state of affairs. For one thing, of course, homosexuals are freed from domesticity's demands on time and energy, demands that, for example, may have sidetracked many talented women during their potentially most productive years.

But mainly Gedo argues, from a more psychoanalytic perspective, that the drive to create arises from the same source as does the orientation. More specifically, male homosexuality at least may be adopted as a defence, to escape from an excessively intimate, stifling relationship with a woman, usually the mother. This intense drive to maintain one's sense of separation in turn fuels an overriding need to be different in every way, to detach oneself from the surrounding cultural milieu. Thus is bred the drive for distinctive originality which is supposedly creativity's hallmark.

8. Sex. We here refer to gender rather than activities. The preceeding section notwithstanding, it is undeniable that more eminent productivity has come from men. Women have more than held their own in literature (Jane Austen, the Brontes, George Eliot, Virginia Woolf, et al.), choreography (Isadora Duncan, Martha Graham, Doris Humphrey, Agnes de Mille, Twyla Tharp, et al.), especially in their contributions to children's literature[62] and to the interpretive/performing arts such as singing, dancing, and acting. But they are rare among mathematicians, scientists, and musical composers.

Why this sex difference? Perhaps simply because we cannot always assess productivity accurately. Historically, women have undoubtedly received less exposure. For example, Germaine Greer points out[63] that a woman's painting was often credited to a man to increase its value. Thus Frans Hals' famous The Jolly Companions was actually painted by Judith Leyster. In the same vein, a strong prejudice held that women were incapable of anything worthwhile; witness Dr. Johnson's statement: "Sir, a woman's preaching is like a dog walking on his hind legs. It is not done well; but you are surprised to find it done at all."[64] A vicious circle resulted. Women's work was either dismissed or consigned to dusty attics, damp cellars, or furnaces, thereby strengthening the belief that women produced but little.

Most critics being male, their masculine priorities and attitudes also worked against any distinctively feminine style receiving a fair hearing. Among other things, such critics have decided that arts like oil painting, where women have been in short supply, are "major," while such predominantly feminine forms as handicrafts are "minor." And of course, women have reigned supreme in the domestic arts. Could not a case

36

be made that the siring and rearing of children are accomplishments second to none?

Still, when all is said and done, the sex difference seems something more than a measurement artifact. Even Greer, whose feminist credentials are impeccable, accepts this conclusion. So we must pursue its explanation, and many of our perspectives do offer suggestions. Now environmental/cultural factors are often assumed to cause the sex difference. They may well do so, as we shall see, but the uncritical acceptance or the dismissal of this explanation is merely unverified propoganda parading in the guise of established truth. As we shall soon learn, the question is very difficult to answer conclusively because of methodological problems, so we shall consider as well other explanations which may seem less compelling, notably Freud's. In an early review of the sex differences literature, Wooley wrote:

> There is perhaps no field aspiring to be scientific where flagrant personal bias, logic martyred in the cause of supporting a prejudice, unfounded assertions, and even sentimental rot and drivel, have run riot to such an extent as here.[65]

Plus ça change, plus c'est la même chose!

9. <u>Naivete</u>. Here is yet another paradox of sorts. We might be tempted to associate creativity with sophistication, enlightenment, and worldly wisdom. Be that as it may, its practitioners are also found, as a rule, to be rather naive and innocent about the world. They tend to be impulsive, uninhibited, and given to open emotional display, so they are frequently labelled "temperamental." They have great vitality and are enthusiastic about their activities and about life in general. They tend to be slightly impractical, at least by prevailing standards, because they regard economic matters as unimportant and, as a result, usually have poor heads for business. All these attributes suggest the rubric "childlike" (not, we hasten to add, "<u>childish</u>," a term with very different connotations) and again, many eminent individuals, notably Einstein and Franz Schubert, have been so described.

While qualities such as innocence and honesty may seem rather peripheral, in fact they may be the very stuff of creative talent. The painter Matisse stated, "Study as hard as you like, but guard your naivete....It will be all you've got some day."[66] Goethe thought naivete to be the most important of all qualities,[67] and Picasso maintained that "It is enthusiasm of which we have the most need, we and the young."[68]

37

Why are these qualities so important? Consider Hans C. Andersen's story The Emperor's New Clothes. Everyone had been told that if they could not see the emperor's marvelous new suit of clothes, then they were fools. Naturally, everyone was awestruck by it, except one little boy, who had not been told what he should see. So, not knowing what was "correct," he alone saw the truth. The suit of clothes was imaginary and the emperor was actually naked. Alexander Graham Bell's editor says somewhere that the inventor's childlike naivete provided both his weaknesses, such as extravagant enthusiasms and fits of impatience, and also his strengths, such as freshness of vision, scrupulous concern for truth, thirst for knowledge, and a neverending tendency to wonder. Now we can appreciate Einstein's purported statement that he invented a new theory of the universe because he couldn't understand the old ones.

10. Alienation. The archetypal creative is rather introverted, placing minimal value on social matters and interpersonal relations. Many first-rate scientists, for example, are socially inept. We hear that Cavendish, when told to attend a dinner to meet some foreign dignitaries, "broke away and ran down the corridor, squeaking like a bat."[69] As a result, creatives often feel "different," somewhat removed from general society. Playwright Neil Simon has verbalized these feelings:

> I always picture myself as that person at a cocktail party standing in the corner and watching. And I've always felt, and I think this is very true of most writers that I know, we are observers rather than participants..... I'm always sort of on the outside, watching it all, noting it...because I find it harder to relate to life personally--much easier to go upstairs, put a piece of paper in, and live my life there.[70]

The term alienated seems to capture this collection of attributes and feelings. Once more, we can suggest a variety of contributing factors. First, although a few creative activities, notably film-making and choreography, allow one to work "in a crowd," more typically they require large doses of solitary confinement. The worker need not find this sentence enjoyable. Many writers, for example, detest the awful moment when they must close the study door and leave the rest of the world behind. Playwright Moss Hart, noting that he frequently worked with others, especially George S. Kaufman, guessed that he preferred collaboration simply because it provided company during work.[71] But the worker must find it bearable. Possibly, therefore, someone inherently more antisocial would be more likely to try creating. Putting it differently, the social butterfly who

38

constantly needs other people around would probably not attempt, say, poetry or ceramics.

The converse is also possible. Some aspects of creative activity might also encourage alienation. We shall develop this point more fully later on, but general society, as a rule, views creatives with a complicated mixture of ambivalent emotions not guaranteed to increase their sense of belonging.[72] On the one hand recognizing that progress depends on their contributions, society grudgingly grants them respect. But it also tends to resent them and has often imposed social and even legal sanctions against them (Galileo's problems with the Inquisition being a particularly dramatic example). Creatives are considered egocentric know-it-alls, openly parading their superiority; dangerous malcontents, blatantly rejecting basic values; and above all, genuine threats to the most esteemed status quo and social order. No, the typical creative is not widely sought, either as a dinner companion or as an ideal match for one's child.

Creatives, for their part, know only too well that they are held in disrepute and even ridicule, and that their line of work is not widely understood. To compound their frustration, they must nevertheless maintain some sort of dialogue with this wider, suspicious, and unsympathetic public, because they need it as judges and audience for their work. Now consider a talented chef who concocts a feast to titillate the palates of the most discriminating gourmand. Suppose his actual consumers are those for whom "Turf n' Surf" is the ultimately sophisticated sustenance. They berate the harried waiter to "take away this gluey glop and bring me a T-bone," or smear the entire dinner with ketchup. The unfortunate chef, between bouts of tearing out his hair, will undoubtedly conclude that he is simply on a different wave length from the rest of humanity.

Communication is a two-way street; both donor and recipient must be competent to hold up their ends. Unhappily, consumers of creative work are too often woefully ignorant, so that products may fail through no fault of their own. Creatives often must feel like refugees from a far-off land, trying to make themselves understood to those who share neither their language, their traditions, nor their priorities.

But the prime precursor of their alienation is unquestionably their perceived unimportance to society. It is hardly news that creatives are underpaid, but this is merely one symptom of a more basic disease, i.e., widespread public apathy and indifference. Even ridicule is easier to bear than neglect. Anaïs Nin, in her diary, repeatedly asks herself why she struggles to write when no one cares,[73] and Virginia Woolf observed:

(The world)...does not ask people to write poems
and novels and histories; it does not need them.
It does not care whether Flaubert finds the
right word or whether Carlyle scrupulously
verifies this or that fact. Naturally, it will
not pay for what it does not want. [74]

In light of the hostility and lack of understanding on
both sides, creatives may well be tempted to drop out of society
entirely. Why continue such a hopeless dialogue? This sentiment
has been nicely expressed in Howard Fast's story The First
Men. [75] A group of high I.Q. children is given the best of
education and upbringing under highly controlled, isolated
circumstances, to help them maximize their potential. What miracles
of ingenuity, it is wondered, what astonishing social improvements,
will this special group provide? Clearly, the children care
little for these popular priorities, for they immediately direct
their huge reservoirs of talent and energy towards one goal,
the complete separation of their subculture from general society.
They alter the time sequence of the commune in which they
live, so that they lag behind the rest of the world by one
ten-thousandth of a second, producing a barrier impenetrable
from either side.

But such a solution is not practical. The mutually
antagonistic partners, like it or not, need each other, although
the antipathy will probably not disappear. It seems advisable,
then, that creatives should not waste their energies wishing
that things were otherwise, but accept these realities and get
on with their work. 'Twas ever thus.

11. Self-discipline. If our hypothetical "man on the street"
holds one stereotype about creative work, it is that it is
easy, and an excuse to sponge off welfare. Creatives, he believes,
spend their days lounging about in cafes, dashing off occasional
masterpieces, and imbibing in all sorts of illegal and legal
substances. Many dilettantes who practice such a lifestyle,
have unfortunately reinforced this inaccurate scenario. What
is forgotten is that these highly visible frauds usually do
little creative work. True creatives are much less conspicious,
holed up as they are in studios and laboratories.

Rosner and Abt have published some revealing interviews
with genuine creative figures, [76] suggesting that the realities
are rather different. Their work is hard and frustrating; both
demanding of time and energy. It requires enormous self-discipline
because, in the words of one artist, "There is no one making
you go into the studio." Typically, they are organized and
systematic, working to deadlines imposed either by others

40

(publishers, granting agencies, and the like) or by themselves. They routinely set daily quotas of either a certain number of hours or a certain amount of produce. Their productive times may differ, some being "morning" and others "night" people, but that time will be inviolate. Relentlessly compulsive, they allow neither domestic, social, or economic demands, nor vacations, nor rain nor snow nor gloom of night to interfere.

As the saying goes, "Creativity is one percent inspiration and 99 percent perspiration." Persistence and (for one noted cartoonist) "stamina"[77] are as important as sheer talent. In fact, in one survey some inventors voted "perseverance" as the most important ingredient for success; "imagination," perhaps a more obvious candidate, was a distant second.[78] Sometimes the naturally talented fail to fulfill their potential because, when everything comes too easily, they do not develop these important commodities. In Martha Graham's words, "Everyone is born a genius, but in most people it only lasts a few minutes." [79]

There are, of course, some exceptions to these rules. Several composers, for example, had such incredible natural facility that they seemed able to conjure up masterpieces almost before breakfast. Mozart produced his last three symphonies in six weeks. Schubert, in one month shortly before his death, produced his last three piano sonatas, a string quartet, and the song cycle Schwanengesang.[80] Nor did quality suffer, for every work is a rare achievement. But these are exceptions. Beethoven is more typical. His manuscripts, pockmarked with violent crossings out and changes, clearly show his agony as he sought a satisfactory statement.[81]

Why is stick-to-it-iveness so important? Two stages of the process, preparation and verification, particularly require hard work. Acquiring the requisite techniques and background knowledge involves much drudgery, routine practice, and even rote memorization. Dancers, for example, must spend years hanging onto the barre, training their bodies to be flexible instruments of expression and undergoing what Martha Graham fittingly called "the discipline to achieve freedom." [82] There are no short cuts. There is no easy way. If there were, it would have been discovered long before now.

So, too, for the verification stage. Converting a vague image in the "mind's eye" into a product that accurately captures it "out there" is, for most creators, a desperate struggle. Even countless revisions never quite seem to get it right. Drama critic Walter Kerr has accurately described the situation:

> The play that comes to be is born of a battle. The battle goes on inside the playwright as he

41

measures what he can have against what he must have. It goes on within, and with, his many colleagues as a group mind comes into being to make public what has hitherto been private. It goes on within, and with, the audience as the experience is tested to see whether a thousand minds will hold it true...We don't have to praise this condition of life, this possibly unacceptable profession. We do have to recognize it for the unavoidable contest it is, and cry accordingly.[83]

And yet the successful are distinguished as much as anything by their ability and willingness to revise. Their first rough drafts may not differ noticeably from those of amateurs, but their final versions will because they are fighters who refuse to compromise.

Even the dramatic moment of inspiration, which seems so easy and effortless, usually comes after much preliminary work. It is a mark of naive amateurs to wait for inspiration before setting to their task. Productive professionals know that they must get to work first. Likewise, professionals will not allow fluctuating moods to affect their work[84], whereas amateurs work only when they "feel like it." Inspiration may not come during actual work, but one must be struggling with a problem before it will appear at all. Professionals also realize that constant creative activity, however unproductive, sharpens the perceptions and conscious awareness. Chances are thus increased that some event will cause (in the words of Henry James) "the imagination (to wince) as at the prick of some sharp point."[85] Creatives may be productive because they are sensitive, but it is equally plausible that they may be sensitive because they are constantly producing.

They may be successful for the same reason. As Simonton has recently shown,[86] the greatest creators are usually distinguished not only by the quality of their finest achievements but by the sheer quantity of their total output. They produce more than do others as well as better. Thus Joseph Haydn's vast array of symphonies, quartets, masses, and so on, and Picasso's more than 20,000 works represent the rule rather than the exception. Could this greater volume perhaps explain their eminence? For by sheer probability, would it not increase the chances of quality periodically appearing? W. H. Auden put the matter precisely: "The chances are that, in the course of his lifetime, the major poet will write more bad poems than the minor."[87]

42

Simonton therefore proposes a constant probability of success model, which holds that the chances of any one product being successful are constant across all creators. If this is the case, then those who do produce more should achieve more success. In support, Simonton shows that the greatest creators are indeed usually precocious, (i.e., in the manner of Mozart, they start younger) are more productive each year, and frequently live longer* than do their less eminent colleagues. All these attributes would augment one's lifetime productivity. In short, Simonton clearly agrees with Gruber[88] that distinguished lives are characterized by continuous effort. The crucial importance of their persistence is thus once more indicated.

12. Selfishness. The Muses are jealous mistresses, making demands of time and energy on those laboring in their service. Therefore, a creator's obligations to family and friends must take second place. To be a loving helpmate may seem glamorous in theory, but the realities may feature economic privation and countless lonely evenings spent watching television. Furthermore, creatives may exploit others in pursuit of their goals. For example, Joyce Cary's novel The Horse's Mouth portrays one Gulley Jimson, a painter of doubtful talent but unmistakable commitment.[89] He uses the money for his family's food and clothing to purchase paint and brushes. Although he is "hooked" on art instead of heroin, he otherwise resembles a drug addict who sacrifices everything to support the habit.

Apart from Ayn Rand's propogandist writings, selfishness is usually seen as a disreputable quality. To find it in those who are often perceived as the crowning glory of humanity has sometimes evoked surprise. Maslow, for example, was forced to admit that his self-actualized people were not in every way particulary admirable.[90] But desirable or not, selfishness is crucial. An altruistic willingness to sacrifice one's work in order to live for others has destroyed more than one promising career. Graham Greene's novel The End of the Affair[91] shows how an unhappy but engrossing relationship undermines a writer's commitment, dedication, and hence productivity. And Oscar Wilde through one of his characters, has said:

> You know I am not a champion of marriage. The real drawback to marriage is that it makes one unselfish. And unselfish people are colorless. They lack individuality.[92]

---

* Actually, the relationship between longevity and eminence is curvilinear. Simonton shows that the eminent tend either to die young, as did Mozart and Schubert, or to live to a ripe old age.

43

13. "Creeping like a snail, unwillingly to school." Perhaps melancholy Jacques, in As You Like It had creators in mind, for certainly they persistently express a hatred of school. Isadora Duncan called it a prison.[93] Clark attributes Einstein's strong bias against all things German to his bitter experiences in the rigid, authoritarian gymnasium where he was first educated.[94] As always, there are notable exceptions. James Joyce, for one, excelled in and by all reports enjoyed school.[95] But distaste seems to be the more typical reaction.

Once more, several explanations can be summoned for these feelings. Creatives--ever independent, strong-minded and even contrary--do not easily accept the regimentation and dictatorial authority found in most schools. Unquestioning obedience is not their most obvious trait. Also, even as children they usually have strong opinions about their main interests and may regard unrelated training as simply a waste of time. And their opinions may be somewhat justified, since school grades (as several studies have shown) predict creative achievement with no accuracy whatsoever.

As well, as Torrance's pioneering work has clearly shown, creative children often have a difficult time in school.[96] They are not usually popular with either teachers or classmates and, sad to say, they sometimes bring their problems on themselves. Their different interests and attitudes, their sexual androgeny and social introversions are unlikely to induce popularity equal to, say, the star of the football team. Often bossy, self-centered, rebellious, and generally hard to handle, they openly express their distaste for the entire educational system. Given the mutual antipathy, both parties undoubtedly sigh with relief when the ordeal has ended. Clearly this strained relationship anticipates that which will develop later between creatives and society in general.

Before we abandon pedagogy, however, we might tentatively consider a hypothesis. Might not this hostile attitude be less pervasive among prospective scientists than artists? Science seems to require more familiarity with the previous work of others and with what is called "the literature," since it is on these foundations that new work will be built. It was Newton who said, "If I have been able to see farther than others, it was because I have stood on the shoulders of giants."[97] (This view is nowadays less firmly held. As we shall in due course discover, Kuhn's pioneering analysis of the history of science[98] argues that it does not always progress in this linear, cumulative manner. In fact, the greatest workers--the Einsteins, Newtons, et al.--do not build upon but revolt against previous work. Be that as it may, they must at least become familiar with that work.) However, in the arts, where the sense of

44

teamwork seems less pervasive, many competent practitioners are noticeably ignorant of and uninterested in anyone else's work. When they attend to it at all, it is more as something to react against rather than to build upon.

Given these differences, might a child of, say, chemical leanings perhaps view education with less distaste than would another more given to flights of poesy? Unfortunately, this seemingly compelling hypothesis also appears wanting, since college grades do not predict creative success in the sciences any more accurately than in the humanities.[99] Contradictory also is Simonton's evidence concerning the relationship between amount of formal education and creative success.[100] In general, this relationship conformed to an inverted U, with the most eminent usually having a moderate amount of schooling, rather than either too little or too much. Of special note here, however, are the only moderate differences in education between eminent scientists and artists. The latter typically possessed some college experience (albeit not enough for a degree), while the productive scientists most frequently had some graduate education, but less than that needed for an advanced degree.

14. "Age cannot wither her, nor custom stale her infinite variety." Cleopatra, given this accolade, probably lacked creativity, since people's best work most often appears during their younger years (but then we do not usually count the arts of the boudoir among the standard media of expression). This aging effect was most strongly substantiated by Lehman's classic study.[101] An eminent person's best achievements usually appeared in the early or mid-thirties, followed by a rather rapid rate of decline thereafter. Admittedly, the specifics differed somewhat across fields of endeavor. The natural sciences, particularly chemistry, physics, and mathematics showed the youngest peaks, (thus verifying the widespread belief that the lastnamed at least is a "young man's game"[102]) whereas philosophy, prose literature and the social sciences ripened somewhat later.* To complicate matters further, various forms within a field seemed differentially susceptible to the aging effect; in music, for example, chamber music and symphonic productivity peaked earlier than did light opera or musical comedy. But within these limits, the pernicious effects of age were invariable.

Not all would accept Lehman's generalizations wholeheartedly. For one thing, like virtually every statement about creative

---

*   The eminent psychoanalysts may represent another exception to the "early ripe, early rot" phenomenon. With the exception of Freud himself, most of them produced their major work in their fifties or even later.(103)

people, they have their notable exceptions. Many artists--Haydn, Tolstoy, Verdi, Titian, Martha Graham, and Picasso, to name a few--were still producing effectively well into their twilight years. Gauguin barely began to paint until mid-life, foregoing a banking career to embark on this perilous venture. (Readers wishing elaboration about such examples of longevity are referred to Butler.[104])

Dennis, furthermore, argues that one's quantity of production declines much less precipitously with age[105,106] and also notes several methodological problems with Lehman's work, such as historians' reluctance to cite an older person's work in their textbooks. After correcting for these, Dennis concludes that the productive peaks actually appear much later in life--in the forties, for most disciplines--and that the age decline, more severe in the arts than in the sciences, does not set in until the sixties.

Simonton, too, questions the decline.[107] His constant probability of success model, when modified to the problem, now asserts that over one person's lifetime, the chances of a particular work achieving success remain constant. But does not the more rapid decline with age of quality than of quantity immediatley disparage this assertion? Should not their rates coincide? As Simonton rightly points out, the comparison is complicated by a variety of factors. Most notably, creators die at different ages, so that when we compare young and old we compare different individuals. Perhaps the less capable contribute a disproportionate number of observations to the advanced ages, thus keeping quantity high but devastating quality. When Simonton corrects for these problems, by devices beyond the scope of this book, he finds strong support for his model.

Nevertheless, for various reasons we remain skeptical of both Dennis' and Simonton's findings and conclusions, suspecting that Lehman's are accurate, at least in broad outline. Moreover, this opinion seems to be widely shared (see, for example, Krebs[108]). Our opinion rests partly on the appreciable empirical and anecdotal evidence, but also on more theoretical grounds. Briefly, virtually every creative attribute that we have discussed changes over the life cycle, so we have an almost embarrassing number of possible reasons for an age decline. Indeed, Lehman lists no less than sixteen possible causes for his findings, some of which we will include here as we proceed.

First, the elderly are not known for their flexible thinking; in fact, it is well documented that rigidity increases with age. It may be that "we get too soon old and too late smart," but knowledge that comes with age is usually well worn and works against perceiving fresh alternatives.

Self-confidence may also decline. Young people seem remarkably sure of themselves and unintimidated by the prospect of failure. Albert Camus, for example, said that he wrote his play <u>Caligula</u> when he was 25, "the age when one doubts everything except oneself."[109] Karen Horney holds that young persons often exaggerate their potential abilities and prospects, invariably expecting to take the world by storm.[110] These grandiose expectations later life, in most cases, could not possibly fulfil; even appreciable achievements may then seem unsatisfactory. Such persons may come to perceive themselves as failures and their self-confidence suffers.

But surely confidence will <u>increase</u> with age if people gain success and renown? Perhaps not. They will have learned, for one thing, how capricious and unreliable inspiration can be. They will also be in the uncomfortable position of having to compete with themselves, since everyone will be expecting even greater feats. If an unknown neophyte authors a fiasco, nothing has changed. But an established reputation loses the freedom to fail. Choreographer Antony Tudor, for example, after producing a steady stream of masterpieces during the 1930's and 1940's, suffered a lengthy dry spell. Why? Dancer Sallie Wilson, a renowned interpreter of Tudor's works, theorizes that he felt he could not top himself.[111] Beginning a new work is intimidating enough without the additional burden of knowing that one is expected to succeed. (Tudor himself, however, attributes his reluctance to his declining physical powers, as he can no longer devise and demonstrate the steps effectively.[112])

Other qualities also change with age. Childlike, enthusiastic innocence <u>is</u> more typical of the young, and may be replaced later by the jaded boredom of the world-weary sophisticate. Resources of energy, stamina, and strength are also depleted, which would affect productivity in most fields, but especially in physically demanding ones such as dance. As Lehman points out, the mature may be hampered by unhappiness in their personal lives or disillusioned by lack of early success. Paradoxically, success and fame too easily won may also wreak havoc by breeding complacency and a resting on one's laurels. The dash of insecurity arising from the need to prove oneself may well be fundamental.

Consider also the memory, which at first blush might seem irrelevant or even harmful to creativity. Would it not supply only familiar and venerable ideas at the expense of those more novel? The Greeks, however, clearly felt otherwise. According to their legends, the Muses' parents were Zeus and Mnemosyne, the goddess of Memory. As Stephen Spender tells us:

> Memory exercised in a particular way is the natural gift of poetic genius....Imagination

47

itself is an exercise of memory. There is nothing
we imagine that we do not already know.[113]

Remembered sensations, images, and experiences are the poet's
raw material, but virtually every creative field uses mnemonic
elements in some way. Given that memory is so basic, its
well-documented decline with age[114] may be another precipitating
factor.

Lastly, the notorious Peter Principle provides another enemy
for the elderly.[115] With tongue planted firmly in cheek, Peter
proposed that, in hierarchical organizations such as business
or the military, as long as individuals do their jobs well,
they will demand, and obtain, promotions to higher positions in
the hierarchy. Sometimes these entail quite different duties,
but only when people begin to function inefficiently will these
promotions cease. Thus, the Peter Principle: within a hierarchy
a person inevitably rises to his or her own level of incompetence.
Scientists, for example, who have garnered early acclaim will
thereby advance within the scientific and academic communities.
They will find themselves editors of journals, advisors to
governments, members of innumerable paper-pushing committees,
and the like. Hence, they will have less time and energy for
their research, and their productivity will decline. It is
perhaps for this reason that the output of American winners of
the Nobel Prize declined by 30 percent during the five years
following the award.[116] Likewise, one study found that laboratory
scientists who were paid more (presumably because they had
accomplished more) were expected to perform a greater number of
different activities.[117] The very best workers were involved
in too many activities and consequently were spread too thin.

In conclusion, we might also mention another possibility
occasionally voiced, that creativity does not so much decline
as change with age. Simonton[118] analyzed the content of various
plays and found that aged playwrights will more probably deal
with religious and spiritual experience and challenge the importance
of material well-being than will their younger colleagues.
Similarly, Edel[119] implies that the motives for working may
well also change, which could affect one's type of work. Thus
the later Yeats fought his despair and anger at death's increasing
imminence, by expressing these emotions in his poems.

Chapter 3

THE DATA OF CREATIVITY II: COMPLICATIONS

We must now consider some matters that muddle our neat portrait of the typical creative personality. Some of these are psychological, others methodological. We shall deal with each in turn.

Fictional Characteristics

The hypothetical "man on the street," holds some rather powerful stereotypes about creative people. We will discuss two of these that are particularly inaccurate.

1. "Great wits are sure to madness near allied/ And thin partitions do their bounds divide." John Dryden's aphorism[1] has come down to us in many guises, but the essential idea remains that creatives are "a bit dotty" or even "nutty as fruitcakes." It is a longstanding belief, since none other than Plato may provide its sire. In a seminal statement, he wrote that a poet, when "inspired," is "possessed...beside himself, and reason is no longer in him."[2] (A careful reading of this passage suggests that Plato had in mind, not the "possession" of the mad man, but a very different, more divine frenzy bestowed by the godly Muses.)

The Romantic era, that particularly influential source of contemporary stereotypes, particularly emphasized this belief. Supposedly, every artist was consumptive, overly sensitive, doomed to an early demise, and, above all, neurotic; prone to sudden changes of mood, acute depression, and explosive temper. Thus the great criminologist Kretschmer could write:

> Mental disease...leads in the overwhelming majority of cases merely to the diminuation of mental power, and ineffectiveness...but in a few exceptional cases of men...of great talent, it leads to the activity of genius....Were we to remove the psychopathic inheritance, the demonic unrest from the man of genius., nothing but an ordinary talented person would remain (italics mine).[3]

Similarly, for Lombroso, genius was simply one type of insanity reflecting like all others biological deterioration of the brain brought on by hereditary factors.[4] More recently, Freud has propounded the belief that both neurosis and creativity arise from the same fountainhead, i.e., from factors buried in the unconscious mind. It would follow, then, that treatment of

49

these factors could be a mixed blessing, for it might "cure" both a person's psychological problem and talent. Bertrand Russell, in his Satan of the Suburbs, depicts a psychoanalyzed Hamlet who has become wonderfully "normal" but is now deadly dull company.[5] For this reason, many troubled creators have avoided psychological therapy, assuming that their hangups were the price they had to pay for obtaining those inexplicable inspirations.

Several contemporary authors have also shown why the two afflictions might be expected to coincide, at least on occasion. Hutchinson notes that the frequent frustrations and failures of creative work might well encourage personal problems.[6] Moreover, Pickering has shown how serious disturbances actually helped six individuals attain their successes.[7] For example, Darwin seemed remarkably healthy during the voyage to the Galapagos, but after his return home he became a lifelong invalid, although no organic causes were ever found for his affliction. Pickering attributes it to psychological factors (we would nowadays label it a conversion reaction). He points out that by retiring to his bed, Darwin avoided all manner of interruptions, such as administrative and social duties, thereby obtaining the solitude he needed to contemplate and arrange his vast accumulation of observational evidence. Only in this way could he sway the doubters. In short, his illness did not help him gain his insights, which had been simmering long before, but it did facilitate their refinement and verification.

Pickering also describes several cases (ironically, Freud himself is one) in which the person's psychoneurotic problems evidently did supply insight. Consider, for example, novelist Marcel Proust's Remembrance of Things Past. He clearly worked out his overly intimate relationship with his mother, and his guilt about the responsibility he felt for her premature death, by reliving the happier times of childhood when she was still alive. Such personal "confession" is, for Freud, the major impetus for creation. Storr, too, has described some cases that fit the Freudian bed.[8] Novelist Ian Fleming's James Bond, urbane and woman-conquering, apparently served as a wish fulfillment for the author; being everything he was not.

Storr also argues that some typical creative behaviors closely resemble various types of pathology. The "schizoid" character is unable to accept uncertainty or ambiguity. More importantly, he or she tends to be emotionally isolated from other people, a recluse who feels both superior as well as weak and vulnerable. Satisfaction is sought from things or events because it cannot be obtained from human relationships. Creative activity often attracts such people. Besides being solitary, it can result in fame and notoriety, and thus reinforce feelings of superiority and power. Storr unconvincingly advances Albert Einstein and

50

more successfully suggests Isaac Newton as exemplary schizoids. Newton in particular was the definitive social misfit; hostile towards others and suspicious that they would steal his discoveries.

Storr also cites the similarities between some creatives, notably Henrik Ibsen and Igor Stravinsky, and the obsessive-compulsive. This type dislikes disorder, squalor, and ambivalence, which she or he will struggle unceasingly to eliminate. At least a touch of this affliction, it would seem, must be present in _every_ creator to supply the necessary persistence and perfectionism. Michelangelo provides perhaps the preeminent example. At the risk of his life, he dissected human cadavers to learn principles of anatomy necessary to his art.*

One factor seems particularly responsible for the belief that neurosis and creativity go together. Some eminent creators have had severe, and highly publicized, psychological problems. We remember the painter van Gogh, composer Robert Schumann, philosopher Nietzsche, dancer/choreographer Vaslav Nijinsky, and the writers Dostoevsky and Strindberg, whose illnesses have all made good copy. Despite this persuasive evidence and opinion arrayed before us, we must nevertheless reject the notion that the two "diseases" must accompany one another. Moreover, Hutchinson, Pickering, and Storr--their preceeding arguments notwithstanding--would all seem to agree. Pickering is adamant that his cases are exceptions to the rule. Storr sees the creative as not "normal" (i.e., average) but as a different kind of deviant from the neurotic. Both have unusual access to their inner psychological world, but the creator can control this gift while the neurotic cannot. Storr cites Charles Lamb's observation, that "the true poet...is not possessed by his subject, but has dominion over it."[10]

Let us, therefore, summon our rebuttals. We will first challenge the idea that neurosis is a necessary causal condition, i.e., that a person cannot create unless he or she is already "unstable." If this were so, then, as we noted earlier, treatment of illness should also damage productivity. According to Stein,

---

* Sandblom(9) has shown that physical as well as psychological illness can facilitate creative work, by driving the afflicted either to express and work through, or compensate for it. Vivaldi's asthma, for example, forced him to turn from the priesthood to music and Toulouse-Lautrec's dwarfed, ugly appearance, which made him persona non grata in polite society, may have stimulated him to paint. In addition, Chekhov's lengthy battle with tuberculosis, Sandblom speculates, may have contributed to the resigned, passive attitude which we know from his plays as definitively "Chekhovian."

this prediction has rarely been evaluated,[11] but those studies that are available indicate that therapy is usually beneficial. Fried found that psychoanalysis helped a group of artists control some anxieties and depressions that had interfered with their ability to work systematically.[12]

We must also raise a methodological objection. Even if the two conditions do accompany one another, it is not necessarily true that neurosis causes creativity. It is equally plausible that creativity might produce neurosis, as Jung has argued while rejecting Freud's position.[13] For Jung, artists inevitably face conflict because two forces are at war within them, i.e., the ordinary human desires for such routine pleasures as happiness and security, set against the ruthless passion for creating that overrides personal desire. Thus the artist is called to a greater task than are ordinary mortals. "(He or she) must pay dearly for the divine gift of creative fire."[14] Neurosis could indeed develop.

Given that the causal relationship is doubtful, we will now question that neurosis need even accompany creativity. First, while remembering the troubled van Goghs and Nijinskys, we tend to forget the many creators who were disgustingly "normal." Joseph Haydn was the most even tempered and generous of men. J. S. Bach, to all appearances, functioned like a successful businessman, doing his job and doing it well. Stubborn, intractible, and somewhat humorless he may have been. But neurotic? Not unless the fathering of twenty children indicates instability. It was Oscar Wilde who rebuffed the Romantic tradition most effectively:

> The only artists I have ever known, who are personally delightful, are bad artists. Good artists exist simply in what they make, and consequently are perfectly uninteresting in what they are. A great poet, a really great poet, is the most unpoetical of all creatures. But inferior poets are absolutely fascinating. The worse their rhymes are, the more picturesque they look.[15]

Even those creators who have problems will probably achieve their best work during their lucid moments. Schumann's recurrent bouts of depression, for example, were accompanied by lower rather than greater productivity.[16] As both Hutchinson and Virginia Woolf[17] have stated, creativity protects the health of the genius since problems develop more often when one is prevented from working. The point is really this: People with problems will be found in any large group. Does the population of creatives have more than others? Several studies have answered this question

52

in the negative. Havelock Ellis found that of 1030 individuals listed in the Dictionary of National Biography, only 44 (4.2 percent) were clearly insane.[18] If anything, this proportion is <u>lower</u> than what we would normally find. Likewise, Juda found that a group of 294 artists and scientists contained no more psychotics (other than a marked excess of psychopaths) than did the general population.[19]

Terman, in a classic study, delineated a large group of <u>gifted</u> children (as revealed by their high scores on the Stanford-Binet intelligence test).[20] Their intellectual achievements were then assessed periodically during their later lives to determine whether they fulfilled their potential. Clearly, by a variety of criteria, they did, but more germane to our present discussion, they also showed a <u>lower</u> incidence of such psychological problems as "nervous breakdown," drug and alcohol abuse, and suicide than would a random sample. Now, as we shall shortly discover, intelligence and creativity are no longer thought to be synonymous. Still, this select group undoubtedly contained more creatives than does the general population. In addition, the criteria used to indicate later success--such as articles and books published, patents and copyrights taken out, and the like--certainly suggest unusual creative ability amongst members of the sample. There is every reason to suspect that these results would hold for a set of creatives as well.

Admittedly, creatives do show evidence of psychopathology on psychological tests. Barron's group of writers fell in the upper 15 percent on most of the MMPI's measures of disturbance.[21] However, they also showed a combination of characteristics not found among the genuinely disturbed, such as excessive ego strength, self-confidence, personal effectiveness, and independence. The reasonable conclusion--which most authorities would nowadays accept--is that creative people differ both from average humanity and from your friendly neighbourhood neurotics. It is a disease of a special kind, a deviation in a different direction.

We conclude with another objection that is more of a warning. If we assume that neurosis and creativity are handmaidens, we may dismiss a great work as "nothing but" a psychological symptom, akin to phobias, hallucinations, or bad dreams. This may compromise our ability to appreciate it. Freud could study artists' problems while still admiring their products, but others, it would appear, have trouble doing so. Vernon W. Grant's position is worth investigating.[22] His examinations of some individuals who exhibited acute psychological distress (notably van Gogh, Edgar Allan Poe, and Strindberg) are generally worthwhile, but with novelist Franz Kafka he has accumulated a healthy coating of egg on his face.

53

Kafka's stories reek of loneliness and isolation, of guilt and vague, undefined danger. The Trial is typical. The protagonist, Joseph K., is accused; he has no idea who his accusers are or, indeed, what his crime is. Nevertheless, he automatically assumes his guilt (to be human, it is implied, is to be guilty), but tries busily to defend "his case." Inevitably, he is tried, convicted, and executed "like a dog." This certainly sounds like rampaging paranoia, although, as playwright Harold Pinter points out,[23] this kind of thing happened all the time in Europe during the 1930's and 1940's and in some places still does; a knock on the door in the middle of the night and someone "takes you away."

Likewise, Kafka himself unquestionably was a troubled person who led an unhappy, even tragic life (although he never came under psychiatric treatment). His Letter to His Father reveals his strained relationship with and fear of his father (which probably explains his perennial obsession in his writing with arbitrary, tyrannical authority). His diary expresses tortured doubts of his own worth and indulges in orgies of self-chastisement for deluding himself that he can write (a clear exception to the creative's usual self-confidence/arrogance). It also reveals his sexual problems; he several times withdrew from marital engagements, partly out of loathing for this expected activity.

Apparently, Kafka never intended many of these stories to be read, since he instructed that they should be destroyed.[24] Therefore he seems to have written for the classic Freudian reasons, to work through and to "confess" his problems. With these facts in mind, Grant then asks by what criteria we can distinguish work that is "normal" from that which is not. Neither pathology of personality or in product, he asserts, is sufficient by itself. But if these are combined with work that is obscure and fails to communicate precisely, then the work is disturbed. Now Kafka's writings are certainly at times ambiguous; authorities have argued endlessly about their interpretation and, as Camus aptly observed, "the whole art of Kafka consists in forcing the reader to reread."[25] Hence, Grant concludes, Kafka fulfills the three criteria, allowing us to dismiss his work as "only" pathological. Furthermore, anyone who admires it must likewise be suspect:

> Kafka will have an appreciative and understanding public among those who to some degree share his emotional afflictions...the lonely and seclusive, the guilt-ridden and the religiously preoccupied...it is doubtful whether many mentally healthy persons will find (his writings) memorable.[26]

We have two answers to this argument. First, that worthwhile products will always be clear and obvious is a debatable criterion. The reductio ad absurdum would label comic books, Harlequin Romances, and advertising jingles as the pinnacles of Western culture, and reject Hamlet because no one has been able to make head or tail of the protagonist. Actually, a multileveledness, an ambivalent complexity that allows us to return to a work continually for fresh insights, is often pinpointed as a defining attribute of great art.[27]

Second, and more important, why must we distinguish normal from pathological art? If a work fulfills that ultimate criterion, if it produces that vague sense of excitement in the pit of the stomach, the "gut reaction" that is the sine qua non telling us we are in the presence of quality, then "that is all ye know on earth, and all ye need to know." Even if that work and its author are both stark staring bonkers, and even if it takes us much leisurely contemplation before we can decode the work's many messages, does this really matter?

Surely what is important is not that Kafka was disturbed (he probably was) but that his work is effective (it certainly is). Those who have dealt with government bureaucracies, military authorities, or hospital administrations will find that his scenarios are not delusional but frighteningly accurate. In fact, we often label bizarre but only too real occurrences as "Kafkaesque." If our admiration for him ipso facto verifies our own sickness, then we will happily abandon sanity.

2. Intelligence. Until recently, terms such as "gifted" and "talented" have been used indiscriminately for persons of both high intelligence (as assessed by IQ tests) and creative ability. Cox' famous study of retrospective IQ is exemplary.[28] People's IQs are often computed by comparing the age at which they accomplish a particular skill with the average age of accomplishment. Thus, precocious achievement will yield a high IQ score. Using biographical data, Cox determined the age at which various persons had attained certain abilities and then computed their "intelligence." Where the average IQ is theoretically 100, by her reckoning J. S. Mill had an IQ of 190, Goethe 180, and Mozart (who probably dashed off a string quartet while coming out of the womb) 155. Some of Cox' criteria, such as age of learning to read and to use algebra, do suggest intellectual attainment, but others, such as writing poetry and composing symphonies, resemble creative abilities. Yet she draws no distinction between the two types. Likewise, Terman's longitudinal study lumps intellectual and creative achievements together in determining whether a child has fulfilled her or his early potential.

Guilford was among the first to argue that the two are not synonymous.[29] IQ tests emphasize verbal, logical, linear thought, which Guilford labels convergent thinking, while creativity also requires a hefty nonlinear component, or divergent thinking. If this distinction is valid, then IQ scores should not predict creative potential accurately. Judging by the bulk of the evidence, they do not.[30] Guilford felt that special tests of creative ability were needed, and we have since seen many of these marketed.

Today, the popular bias is that scores on a good creativity test should relate only moderately to IQ scores. If the correspondence is excessive, then the test must be measuring intelligence rather than creativity. In practice, the two scores typically correlate quite closely at the lower end of the IQ distribution, but beyond a certain level (about IQ 120, according to several authorities), they part company.[31] In other words, a slightly above average intelligence seems necessary for creativity (and certainly we would not expect a retardate to be innovative), but additional gains will be of little further help.*

Do these results prove that the two attributes are actually different? Not at all, since creativity tests have been carefully designed so as to be independent of IQ. That they do not measure intelligence does not automatically prove that they do measure creativity. They simply may not be measuring much of anything. This troublesome possibility gains credence when we note that many of them predict subsequent creative productivity with only moderate success.[35]

Nevertheless, in our opinion there are both empirical and theoretical reasons for thinking the intelligence-creativity distinction genuine and not simply an artifact of the way tests have been constructed. First, the difference between linear and nonlinear thought is now widely accepted. It seems reasonable, then, to regard "intelligence" as a trait reflecting the first type, and "creativity" as involving both. Thus, for example, IQ will measure those abilities useful academically (and probability of school success does increase with IQ score). However, the

---

*   Simonton(32) provides a variation on this theme. He suggests that some fields of endeavor, such as the physical sciences, may require more intelligence than do others, such as the social sciences, for creativity to appear. Thus an Einstein who revolutionizes the former may exceed a Freud in intelligence. However from the standpoint of Gardner(33) and Guilford(34) different fields require different kinds of intelligence. If this is the case, then such comparisons across fields become meaningless.

highly creative may well have trouble in school and will probably hate it. In short, creative thinking does seem to be a different category. In poetry, for example, all things are possible, according to Allen Tate:

> if you are man enough...the sea boils and pigs have wings....In poetry, the disparate elements are not combined in logic, which can join things only under certain categories and under the law of contradiction.[36]

Secondly, it has been shown that a group of high IQ subjects can be reliably separated into high and low creatives[37] and that these two groups display different personality characteristics. The high creatives show a greater sense of humor and playfulness; more unconventional career aspirations (wishing to be writers or inventors, rather than lawyers, doctors or professors); greater independence, introversion, and impulsiveness; and more willingness to take chances than do the high IQ-low creatives. When given a picture, such as a man sitting in an airplane returning from a professional/business trip, and asked to imagine "what is happening here," they construct strikingly different scenarios:[38]

A _high IQ subject_. Mr. Smith is on his way home from a successful business trip. He is very happy and he is thinking about his wonderful family and how glad he will be to see them again. He can picture it, about an hour from now, his plane landing at the airport and Mrs. Smith and their three children all there welcoming him home again.

A _high creative subject_. This man is flying back from Reno where he has just won a divorce from his wife. He couldn't stand to live with her anymore, he told the judge, because she wore so much cold cream on her face at night that her head would skid across the pillow and hit him in the head. He is now contemplating a new skid-proof face cream.

The variation in imagination is immediately apparent. Now if creativity and intelligence were not independently varying entities, it would not be possible to form these two groups reliably, let alone show such persistent personality differences between them.

We suspect that a high IQ-low creative person might migrate either to scholarly, academic work (cf. Ibsen's Professor Tesman, in _Hedda Gabler_, who is particularly good at sorting out and arranging someone else's inspirations) or to criticism. For it was the late Kenneth Tynan, himself a first-rate assessor of

57

things dramatic, who defined the critic as "someone who knows the way but can't drive the car."[39]

Conceptual Problems

We must now confront underlying difficulties with the content of Chapter 2 that may have troubled the reader. Some of these we can surmount but, regretfully, others will be intransigent because they stem from the very nature of creativity.

1. The generality of creative characteristics. There are many manifestations of creativity and many different fields within which it is expressed. We think, for example, of innovative actors, musicians, poets, painters, choreographers, biochemists, geologists, economists, business executives, advertising designers, hair stylists, auto mechanics, plumbers, and so on ad infinitum. At first glance these various fields would seem to demand quite different abilities and personalities. We might ask, do an inventive flower arranger and football coach have anything in common? Are there any qualities that appear in every line of work? Our previous discussion assumed just such sweeping generalizations.

Investigations of intelligence have faced similar questions. Is it a nonspecific mental ability, equally useful in any and all situations, or are there different types of intelligence, having more limited applicability? Most pioneering IQ testers assumed that "intelligence is intelligence is intelligence." However, Spearman, for one, saw the need for not only a "g" factor but also various "s" factors.[40] A person having more "g" would be more effective in general, since it was relevant to any intellectual functioning; the "s" factors came into play only in certain specific situations. Thus Spearman formally expressed a popular belief viz., that a brilliant professor who can solve a foreboding equation between gulps of coffee may be hopelessly inept at coping with a primitive environment.

Likewise, students of creativity have thus far emphasized a "g" factor while virtually ignoring the more specific requirements of various fields. Someone with "talent," they have apparently believed, should succeed anywhere. Guilford raised a voice of dissent against the prevailing dogma. His structure of intellect model[41] hypothesizes many mental operations, which presumably have varying importance in different endeavors.

Still, the prevailing tendency to run roughshod over what is an obvious difficulty may be defensible. First, many individuals have shown ability in more than one field. The classic example is the Renaissance man, such as Leonardo da Vinci, who besides being a masterful painter was a scientific thinker of great imagination, anticipating by several centuries inventions such as the submarine and the airplane. As Dr. Samuel Johnson put it:

> True genius...is a mind of large general powers, accidentally determined to some particular direction, ready for all things, but chosen by circumstance for one.[42]

The biologist/biographer Dubos agrees:

> It is often by a trivial, even an accidental decision, that we direct our activities into a certain channel....Every decision is like a murder, and our march forward is over the stillborn bodies of all our possible selves that will never be.[43]

Hutchinson, discussing this point, has also expressed poignant agreement:

> The arts and sciences, I believe, roughly classify themselves from the creative aspect, not on the basis of content and method, as so many aestheticians have vainly tried to show, but rather according to the demands they make upon the intuitive faculty...Each discipline contains a range of all these elements...The identity of great disciplines of thought has its roots ultimately in the intuitive faculty, no matter how many poles they are apart in superficial content. In the heated imagination of genius philosophy is translated into poetry, and science reaches the heights that music yearns for. A great scientific discovery or experiment, a great piece of music, or of art or of poetry, forged at an intense level of mental operation...all have this in common: they open windows whose casements frame a new view of reality, which, as we strive to comprehend and to appreciate, gives us some slight conception not only of what has already been fashioned, but also of the grandeur and magnificence of the unknown, the yet-to-be-discovered. And with wonder comes humility.[44]

Several empirical studies have supported these assertions. White re-examined the 300 geniuses who had been studied retrospectively by Cox and found that most of them had been active in _five_ _to_ _ten_ _fields_, with the _versatility_ _index_ being

59

highest for nonfiction writers, statesmen, and philosophers (averaging 7.5 fields) and lowest for mathematicians (2.7).[45] Furthermore, creative architects,[46] writers and mathematicians,[47] scientists,[48] and even Air Force captains[49] all show some comparable psychological characteristics, even though their interests are widely diverse. Likewise, Cattell and Butcher (in the study described previously) found similar personality profiles among creative artists, scientists, and writers of imaginative literature.[50] In their words:

> We had actually expected some major differences between those talented in science and in the arts (but)...the really remarkable feature of these findings...is the high degree of similarity and consistency of the personality picture across all areas.[51]

And, as a final point, we shall shortly find the creative process, introspectively, to be quite similar in different sorts of activities.

All in all, some sweeping generalizations about "the creative personality" do, therefore, seem justified. But if this is so, we must then ask why someone might choose one field over another. If their personalities are so comparable, why does one prefer biochemistry and another poetry? This problem has, as we shall later see, been completely ignored by most theories, although Hutchinson tentatively suggests that the chosen field will be that in which inspiration comes most easily. This is really no answer at all, since it solves one riddle by posing another: Why does inspiration come more easily in that field? But at least he has asked the question.

2. This changing world. The next problem relates to the previous one. To repeat an earlier observation, our current stereotypes about creative people and the work they do owe a great deal to the Romantic period. At other times, these have been viewed quite differently. For example, in medieval times, artists--more craftspeople or artisans--performed an honorable function but one not thought to be particularly mysterious or wonderful. Typically, they produced work systematically and to order, because it was their job. Moreover, as the great Romanesque and Gothic cathedrals demonstrate, they often produced it anonymously. Our modern assumption, that individual artists should express their own particular vision and should therefore take the audacious step of signing their work, we owe to the Renaissance.

Likewise, we usually assume these days that creative work requires healthy doses of something called imagination. Yet, as Engell has clearly shown,[52] this presumed psychological property was virtually unknown until it was hypothesized during the Enlightenment in the writings of Hobbes, Locke, Leibnitz, et al. They saw it as a quality that supplemented reason and was necessary to explain our more intuitive, "emotional" mental processes.

The concept of the imagination reached its full flowering, however, during the Romantic period, in the hands of, among others, Wordsworth, Keats, and particulary Coleridge. Our abilities to sympathize with other people, to relate intimately to nature, and to experience passion and feeling were all laid at its door, because all these require that we step outside ourselves and identify or empathize either with external events or other persons. As well, the imagination allowed us to interpret, rather than merely receive, the information from our senses. In short, for the Romantics, it was the source of the human psyche's most valued abilities and even of truth itself.

Artists, particularly poets (and most particularly Shakespeare) were thought to possess the greatest amounts of imagination. The poet was therefore a sanctified being and poetry was the road to truth. (We must suspect the objectivity of this belief, given that its fervent advocates were, almost without exception, poets.) Thus Wordsworth:

> Imagination, which, in truth,
> Is but another name for absolute power
> And clearest insight, amplitude of mind,
> And Reason in her most exalted mood.[53]

For our purposes, the important point is that prior to the Romantic era, this henceforth crucial attribute went unnoticed; therefore, in a real sense, creativity did not require it. When inspiration was mentioned at all, it was not attributed to the person's own ability but to some external, usually omnipotent agent, i.e., God or the gods.

Other notable recent changes in the nature of creative work include a steep decline in the role of religious expression, and an equally dramatic rise in the importance attached to originality. Indeed, the sometimes almost neurotic seeking after novelty may be the most characteristic quality of modern art. Perhaps, therefore, whereas creators could once deepen and ripen their particular styles of working over their lifetimes, they must nowadays virtually compete with themselves. They must constantly strike off in new directions or risk that ultimate chastisement: they merely repeat themselves. One immediate result has been to enhance the aging effect. Lehman found that in almost every field, creators' best achievements appear

61

earlier in life than was the case several hundred years ago, and that the decline in productivity with age is now much more pronounced.[54] Moreover, the magnitude of this effect is probably underestimated, given our much greater longevity.

Lehman attributed this finding to our greater haste to put our work before the public; formerly, lengthy delays such as Darwin's seem to have been more the rule than the exception. This may be part of the story, but we also advance another possibility. Might not originality be an attribute more accessible to the young? When it becomes creativity's primary mark, might their elders not be penalized and withdraw from the race? The triumvirate of great Greek playwrights, Aeschylus, Sophocles, and Euripides, exemplifies this point. Each produced his greatest work at what seems to us an incredibly venerable age.[55] It was also the Greeks who bowed to none in their distaste for originality in art.[56]

The twentieth century has seen other changes also in the conception and nature of creative work. For example many art forms now require appreciable technological expertise; we think of ironwork sculpture, computer art, and electronic, synthesized music. These days, detached, impersonal scientists can be found laboring not only in laboratories but also in studios and lofts. Artists of an earlier day would not have soiled their hands with such unseemly, pedestrian travail.

Which brings us to our point. Given these fundamental changes in the very nature of creative activity, might not a very different type of person, of quite different personality, be attracted to it? Might we not suspect that the contemporary artist, with his or her distinctive interests and abilities, is quite different from, say, the "back to nature" buff of Wordsworth's day, and that both part company with the artisan of the twelfth century who labored anonymously to serve God and the nobility? If those earlier practitioners were given an MMPI would they not, in all probability, lack many of the qualities we have noted, while displaying others? To cite only one example, it would be most surprising if our artisan were not obedient, conforming, and highly religious.

According to Hess at least,[57] feminine creativity has particularly suffered from these changes. In ancient time, he argues, gifted women actually faced fewer institutional and social constraints and were freer to practice and take art seriously. In support, think of classical poets such as Sappho, to say nothing of the Bayeux embroidery, a masterpiece of the Middle Ages that was probably both designed and executed by nuns. Paradoxically the Renaissance, that dramatic awakening to the virtues of individuality and personal expression, had precisely the opposite effect for women. The point we must bear in mind, then, is that the generalizations in Chapter 2, perhaps legitimate for modern workers, may be far off base for others.

3. Whom to study? In alluding to creatives' various characteristics, we have assumed that creatives can be precisely and reliably identified. Unhappily, this is not always so. Nevertheless, the decision must be made, and at least two types of approaches have been used to make it. Predictably, each has its weaknesses.

One possibility is to use predictive criteria, such as psychological tests. Here, as the label suggests, we try to pinpoint in advance those who will likely become creative, and then assess their characteristics. Thus Guilford's various tests have greatly influenced our impressions of creative people simply because they have so often been used to decide who those people are. Such tests have real advantages because they provide an objective, reliable criterion--a test score--for making that difficult decision, and they insure that the subjects will be available for later testing and observation. Unfortunately, since these tests do not on the whole predict creative success accurately, those labeled as "creative" may not in fact be so. As a result, the conclusions drawn from such samples should be taken with a grain of salt.

The second general method, more retrospective in nature, focuses on those who have already been stamped as creative by their contributions. Since we observe them "after the facts are in," can we not be more confident that we are dealing with the genuine article? In fact, this is by no means certain. Designating someone or something as "creative" always involves an arbitrary, value-laden judgment and such decisions are not easily settled.

We must therefore examine the various criteria used to choose these individuals. The judgment of experts? Probably less fallible than lay opinions, but even they can err about the candidates they nominate and, if they differ among themselves, matters become complicated. The number of products produced? An unambiguous, precise criterion, but notwithstanding their modest relation,[58] quantity by no means guarantees quality, as the "publish or perish" ethic esteemed by North American universities has firmly substantiated. Someone producing the most will not invariably produce the best. Nominations by colleagues and fellow workers? Presumably, knowing the field particularly well, they should be more capable of choosing its illustrious members. But their judgments can be influenced by personal animosities brought on by grant proposals rejected, products harshly criticized, or quarrels over theoretical matters.

The preferable retrospective criterion is probably generally acknowledged eminence, choosing those for study whose greatness no one in their right mind would question, such as Shakespeare, Mozart, Madam Curie, Rembrandt, Newton, et al. The problem is that such universal agreement rarely develops during a person's lifetime. History does not hand down its judgments hastily, so the nominees will have long departed. Modern psychology, with all its triumphs, and the claims of parapsychology notwithstanding, cannot yet interview and test the deceased.

We must also note some difficulties that any retrospective study, of either the living or the dead, will face. Biographical information may be unavailable or of questionable accuracy. Stories, legends, and so forth can become so exaggerated with retelling as to border on rumor. Even carefully researched studies must be suspect. That mysterious, mercurial quality, "personality," can be perceived in a variety of ways. Biographers, consciously or otherwise, may emphasize the qualities pertinent to their point of view. Thus Freud's study of Leonardo, it has been suggested, is more informative about Freud than about Leonardo.

Autobiographies, interviews, objective testing, and the like eliminate these biographical middlemen and assess persons directly. Yet they may be surprisingly unrevealing about themselves. If studied long after their productive years, they will likely have changed appreciably. Their previous characteristics and experiences will have to be summoned from memory, either their own or that of others "who knew them when." Need we mention that memory can suffer lapses?

As well, persons may, for a variety of reasons, play an artificial role to present themselves in a certain light. Artists, for example, may unconsciously adopt the trappings of neurotic behavior simply because they too accept the popular stereotype that if one is an artist, one must be neurotic. In turn, this can engender a self-fulfilling prophecy; the characteristic will be found because practitioners expect it to be found. Or the subject may wish to achieve notoriety. In her autobiography, My Life, Isadora Duncan adopts a decidedly theatrical, even flaky, demeanor. According to at least one intimate source,[59] her publisher encouraged this stance from her because the "Isadora legend" would hype sales. Or the person may simply be a liar. Dylan Thomas' interviews are a mass of contradictions, defying attempts to sift out truth. Which is hardly surprising, since he was also, reportedly, not above plagiarising from others far less talented.[60]

Of course less selfish motives can also sometimes produce fabrications. Legend has it that baseball immortal Dizzy Dean gave every interviewer different information, even about such supposedly unambiguous events as the date and place of his birth. Reportedly, Dean was only trying to help each of them obtain a fresh, original story.

4. Subject variables. This last problem requires that we digress briefly to explain something about scientific methodology. To determine whether one thing has caused another to happen we must conduct a controlled experiment. We develop two situations that differ in only one way, the difference being called the independent variable. We then compare the events that occur in the two situations; if these also differ, we can confidently conclude that the independent variable has caused these changes. It is, after all, the only difference between the situations, and it seems reasonable to assume that if those situations had been identical, then the events occurring in them would also have been identical.

But if we allow more than one independent variable to vary between the situations, an occurrence called an experimental confound, we can no longer know which variation has caused events to change. Either or both could be responsible. Thus, if we observe that ice cream melts more rapidly in a hot than a cold room, but we also placed different brands of ice cream in the two rooms, our experiment is confounded. Either the difference in room temperature or in brand could be liable.

These matters particularly vex psychological experiments, where we wish to observe how the behaviors of subjects change in different situations. For example, wondering whether overcrowding might cause violence, we might vary the population densities in different cages of animals and determine whether the number of aggressive acts also varies. But to avoid confoundings, we obviously must compare subjects who are in every other way identical, so we can assume that if they had been treated alike they would have behaved alike.

Given that any two subjects, human or animal, will differ notably one from the other, is such a seemingly foolish assumption ever possible? It is, if we do two things. First, we must place a large number of subjects in each group and compare the average behavior exhibited by the two groups. Then we assume, instead, that the average behavior of the groups would be comparable if they were treated identically, which is more realistic. The second (and for our purposes, crucial) consideration is that we must assign our subjects randomly to their groups. Each one must be placed in a particular group--in our previous study, in either the high or low density conditions. If each is assigned by random methods, such as by the flip of a coin, so that any subject has an equal chance of being placed in either

65

group, then we will obtain two groups that are, on the average, highly similar. Thus random assignment is essential if causal relationships are to be discovered.

Now consider the somewhat different <u>subject</u> <u>variable</u> <u>experiment</u>. Here, subjects are not randomly assigned. Instead, some characteristic that they possess (which is, in most cases, also the independent variable to be studied) predetermines the group in which they will be placed. Comparing men and women, or high and low IQ subjects, or young and old subjects, or wealthy and poor subjects--all of these are subject-variable experiments, because the subjects do not have an equal chance of being placed in either group. In turn, since the groups will differ in the type of subjects that they contain, these experiments are inevitably and hopelessly confounded. The differences between men and women, for example, are countless--their biological characteristics, the environments established by their parents and peers, even the length of their hair (usually). Any or all of these factors could cause behavioral differences between them.

Are not such experiments, then, a waste of time? Fortunately, not entirely. They will reveal that the two factors vary together--or, <u>correlate</u>. But factors can certainly be correlated without being causally related or, to put it another way, all cause-effect relationships will also be correlational, but not all correlations reflect a cause-effect relationship. People who drive more expensive cars will also, as a rule, take more trips to Hawaii, but clearly the size of one's car payments does not cause one's vacation plans.

Hopefully the reader will by now have anticipated the problem we must raise. Comparing creative with uncreative people is a subject variable experiment. That the former tend to be more selfish or egocentric or younger does not prove that their creativity produced these qualities or, for that matter, that these qualities are responsible for their creativity.* The correlations we noted in Chapter 2 do provide helpful information about "what happens." Creative people have more self confidence.

---

* This was the gist of our disagreement with assertions that neurosis causes creativity. Even if the two "diseases" do accompany one another (which is itself doubtful), this only establishes a correlation. Likewise, to uncritically blame environmental factors for the sex difference in creativity is premature, since it too reflects a hopelessly confounded, subject variable comparison. However, if female productivity increases in the future, as these factors change, then this explanation will gain some credence.

Fact. Those correlations can also be useful for prediction. Children with higher ego strength are more likely to become creative. Fact. But these relationships cannot tell us <u>why</u> things happen the way they do. When we attempt to <u>explain</u> someone's creativity by referring to his or her correlated attributes, we must tread warily, which is why we labeled our attempts as <u>hypotheses.</u> We were dealing in the realm of conjecture, and our explanations must be taken on that level.

Chapter 4

THE CREATIVE PROCESS I: PREPARATION AND INCUBATION

What is the creative process like? The various experiences that practitioners report will provide more data with which our theoretical perspectives must come to grips. In our deliberations, we shall focus more elaborately on the individual stages introduced earlier.

Preparation

In any field of endeavor, it seems necessary first to learn something of one's craft. In the words of composer Igor Stravinsky:

> No matter what the subject may be, there is only one course for the beginner; he must at first accept a discipline imposed from without, but only as a means of obtaining freedom for, and strengthening himself in, his own method of expression (italics mine).[1]

Someone who has never studied the rudiments of music is unlikely to compose masterpieces, just as someone ignorant of biochemistry and physiology is probably disqualified from the race to discover cancer's cure. This point needs emphasis because it is fervently believed, in some circles, that any "discipline imposed from without" will stifle talent. In fact, too little can be every bit as harmful as too much. An "education for creativity" will aim to instill, not slavish conformity to existing forms, but the necessary technical and psychological tools.

Several authorities have studied the environments in which creatives are trained and have advanced some useful suggestions about how these might be improved.[2] We shall attempt to summarize the major conclusions. As we might have expected, the primary agents of socialization are not overly helpful. Their main purpose being to foster society's values, they are more apt to encourage popular rather than unprecedented paths. This will help to breed reliable, conscientious pillars of the community, but not necessarily creators.

1. **Domestic environment**. We might expect this to influence creativity if anything does, but according to Mansfield and Busse's extensive review[3], such variables as birth order, forms of parent-child interaction, family size, and religious commitment have effects that are always complex and sometimes outright contradictory. However birth order at least may play a significant role, since according to the majority of studies, the eldest

sibling is the most likely to attain eminence.[4] Unfortunately the explanation of this correlation, even if it is genuine, is obscured by the plethora of confounding variables.

The parents' roles would seem likely to be especially critical and here, happily, some general statements can tentatively be made. The parents of MacKinnon's creative architects, for example, seemed to run to a type. They showed great confidence and trust in the child, and gave him or her freedom to explore the world and make independent decisions.[5] They established clear standards of right and wrong, but downplayed dogmatic religious beliefs while encouraging the child to explore alternatives. Thus morality was depicted as a personal opinion rather than as a preordained truth. In general, they encouraged independence, especially by maintaining rather remote emotional ties. Albert, too, finds that for the mathematically and scientifically eminent, the relationship with parents was usually rather distant (although not hostile).[6] Perhaps Eisenstadt provides culminating support for the facilitating effects of parental remoteness. He found that the frequency of orphanhood among geniuses far exceeded that for the general population.[7]

Inhibitory parents, on the other hand, discourage "book learning" and seemingly impractical academic and/or artistic pursuits, particularly if their own priorities lean more towards profits and country club memberships. The child who rejects these values (and most creatives do) will face powerful inducements to change; thus, students in an art school often found that their parents withdrew emotional and/or financial support when they chose this questionable form of education.[8] Likewise, the child who does not worry about being sociable or well-liked (and most creatives do not) but who prefers solitary activities along with frequent bouts of daydreaming, may be quickly bundled off to the nearest psychiatrist. Clearly, parents of talented children must be informed about the behaviors they typically exhibit, so these can be at least reluctantly accepted.

2. <u>Schools</u>. Torrance's studies have dramatically shown how destructive the typical school can be.[9] In a democracy, those funded by the public are arms of socialization, aiming to inculcate values and attain a virtuous mean. In the words of one educator, "When I am finished with my class, the slow children are a little faster and the fast children have slowed down a little."[10] Stereotypic teachers will reward courteous, obedient behavior while disciplining those who refuse to accept their say-so on faith, who ask embarrassing questions and demand evidence to support opinions. Thus the children learn not only to respect an enlightened but fallible human being, but also to revere an all-seeing, all-knowing guru.

70

In the same vein, school curricula emphasize situations having a "right" answer, i.e., the one that the teacher prefers. Other solutions will be chided as not only "different" but "wrong," and genuinely "off the wall" contributions will be curtly dismissed as "silly." Internalizing this kind of blind obeisance can destroy any latent originality, which almost always requires rebellion against authority figures. Prospective innovators must learn to stick to their guns.

But what of those schools specialized for training selected youngsters in specific pursuits--art colleges, music conservatories, ballet academies, and the like? Would they not provide more sympathetic environments and more relevant curricula? Several extensive investigations of such institutions have been conducted[11] and, surprisingly the Getzels and Csikszentmihalyi study at least suggests that even performance therein may not be overly indicative.[12] Students obtaining the best grades in studio courses and the highest originality ratings by their teachers were generally more successful in their subsequent careers, but those achieving the best academic grades were more likely to fail as artists; these grades were reliably negative predictors. As well, students whose work was rated highly by the staff but poorly by laymen, generally did not succeed and eventually gave up art. Those who "made it" were rated highly by both types of judges. It would seem, then, that the stamp of approval from an instructor is a necessary but not sufficient criterion for success.

As well, Getzels and Csikszentmihalyi point out, these institutions also represent a voice for tradition and the status quo within the profession. They decide what kind of work and what kind of person will be admitted to artistic status. They introduce students to the realities of a professional career, such as intense competition, excessive work demands, starvation incomes, and impoverished living conditions. These may rudely awaken those with dreamy misconceptions about the glamorous life of an artist, and who may therefore renounce the activity. But let us not bewail this weeding out process; best that those unsuited to the career's demands be discouraged early on. Any good training school in part performs this censorial/editorial function. As well, nothing prevents students who are denied the union card/diploma/ piece of paper from practising their art if they so wish.

3. A disclaimer. We have paid our homage to the currently popular attitude that schools are beneath contempt and teachers are without exception Hitlerian autocrats posing undeservedly as little tin gods. Now let us sound some discordant notes. First, schools and teachers represent majority society, which financially supports them. As such, they are expected, first

71

and foremost, to pass on its prevalent values. Majority society, as a rule, will distrust the voice of nonconformity and will revere genuine innovators only after they have had the good grace to die. It is hardly surprising, therefore, that educational institutions are not overly conducive to originality; instead, we should perhaps be thankful for anything they achieve in this line. Criticizing them for not serving purposes that the majority does not wish them to serve is unfair. Schools will not change until the public's attitudes do.

In addition, while creative children do have difficulties in school and usually hate it, the fault does not lie entirely with the institution. Stubborn, contrary, independent, and selfish as they typically are, they can be a handful in the classroom. A pedagogue is charged (oh dubious privilege!) with shepherding a roomful of youngsters, kicking and screaming, to drink from the fount of knowledge. A short fuse with a rebellious individual is understandable.

It is also fashionable, among those seeking an "education for creativity," to bemoan any sort of scholarly regimentation or authoritarian control. Stifling originality! Inhibiting inquiring young minds! So run the slogans of the doomsayers. Admittedly, gifted children probably will benefit from sympathetic, stimulating environments. Teachers charged with their nurture probably do need special training to learn how to channel those independent tendencies. But when complete freedom and spontaneity are advocated as _ipso_ _facto_ desirables, when "doing your own thing" and "doing whatever you feel" are elevated to the status of self-evident truth, when any sort of discipline or training becomes anathema, then it is time to evacuate the bus. For the _reductio_ _ad_ _absurdum_ of individual freedom is _sloth_, and nothing valuable has ever come from it.

There is nothing wrong with learning to respect authority any more than there is anything wrong with learning to respect the basic rights of any other person. That respect is only dangerous when it becomes slavish reverence. Persistent belligerence may indicate not talent but only thoughtlessness and insensitivity. Moreover, children who are sure that no one can teach them anything probably condemn themselves to an ignorance of the basics. To produce effectively, they must acquire technique, persistence, and self discipline. Even the greatest pianists must spend years practicing their scales. Even an Ulanova or a Baryshnikov must sweat it out every day at the barre under the watchful eye of the ballet master. Willingness to work hard under highly regimented conditions while others less committed were out "doing their own thing" is a major reason for their success.[13]

72

D. H. Lawrence learned to work in water colors by copying, in painful, arduous detail, the works of mature masters.[14] This required him to develop the necessary techniques of the medium and also, he suggests, helped rather than hindered his developing his own style. This intriguing approach could have other applications, e.g., in teaching youngsters how to write correctly and with "style." While unquestionably a boring, unimaginative, plodding way to work, it may also be more effective.

In short, we must remember that there is no easy way. If there were, it would have been discovered long before now. Nor, as Maddi has so persuasively argued,[15] are these puritan virtues applicable only to the preparation stage. Every aspect of creative work requires persistence. Bright ideas do not come easily. Frustration, as we shall shortly see, is an unavoidable experience as we try both to obtain the ideas and to refine and polish them afterwards. In addition, the world has never been sympathetic and never will be; its apathy is as certain as death and taxes. Therefore, those who embark on a creative career must learn to be tough and to persevere.

It could be argued, then, that for this reason, if no other, a healthy dose of routine education is beneficial for creatives. The sooner they learn that they are "different" and that their values and attitudes are likely to be unpopular, the sooner they will develop the necessary defenses to "cope." If they are exposed as children to only the most encouraging of atmospheres they are likely, when they eventually come face to face with the real state of affairs, to suffer a debilitating shock.

To help the pendulum swing back towards moderation, therefore, let us briefly play devil's advocate and defend what we might call an excellence in adversity syndrome. No conclusive statistics have come to our attention, but a surprising number of talented creators seem to have arisen from environments that were anything but ideal. How many writers have come from rural or even backwoods locales? Michelangelo's father persistently discouraged the child's compulsive need to practice his art, as did Handel's. Chaim Potok has movingly portrayed a young artist, Asher Lev, who, because of the indefatigable demands of "his gift," contravenes the tenets and attitudes of his fundamentalist Jewish upbringing.[16] He experiences intense domestic opposition, but he perseveres because he must. Nietzsche mentions that the circumstances under which he conceived Thus Spake Zarathustra were anything but favorable.[17] He was in poor health, the weather was cold and rainy, the sea was noisy, and so on. And yet the ideas came forth, proving, to his satisfaction at least, that "everything decisive arises as the result of opposition."[18]

73

Along the same lines, recall Eisenstadt's demonstration[19] that eminent persons had more frequently experienced premature loss of one or more parents. Such bereavement can, he guesses, sometimes increase the child's likelihood of creating by demanding greater responsibility, independence, and adaptability to a suddenly changed environment. Furthermore, feelings of insecurity and especially of guilt, so common in bereaved children, can provide stimuli to and reservoirs of energy for productive effort. Similarly Barron[20] suggests that the ubiquity of grief and ordeal in the typical creator's life could encourage a necessary tolerance of, even preference for, ambiguity. He or she will learn that with hard work, perseverance, and perceptual sensitivity, some sense can be made of the inexplicable. As Barron puts it:

> In (creative individuals) I would posit a stronger initial impulse to render experience intelligible, combined with an unusual ability to pay attention and to organize percepts effectively for prediction, both of these factors being present in a situation which is exceptionally depriving in terms of intelligibility or susceptibility to classification.[21]

Even anthropological evidence seems to verify our position. Cross-cultural studies of creativity have been rare but Margaret Mead[22] has contrasted two vastly different milieu. In Samoa, even the most rudimentary departure from routine artistic forms, say, in a tribal dance, is excessively admired; nothing is ever criticized. The result is a culture steeped in happiness and mental health but with little originality. In Mead's words:

> If each individual were permitted to feel that the slightest change was in fact creative, something could happen to the impulse to make major changes... they have been stimulated to desire no beauty, to search for no new knowledge which their culture does not immediately and fully provide.[23]

How different is the island of Bali! Here has arisen an artistic culture of extraordinary richness and variety, where virtually everyone is deeply involved in music, dance, and visual art. And child-rearing practices break every "always encourage" rule. When Balians display their artistic wares publicly, the best they can hope is that the audience will observe in silence, rather than hoot, jeer, or even walk out in disgust. This society, therefore, may court neurosis, fear, and even boredom. Still, Mead implies, its inhabitants retain their health because their creative drives release their suppressed personal and social feelings.

74

At the risk of overkill, the same message is communicated by the "writers' colony" that novelist James Jones established with his royalties from From Here to Eternity, and other novels. In this seemingly idyllic environment, would-be novelists could work free from anxiety, financial worry, and interruption. By his own admission, it failed dismally.[24] Nothing worthwhile was produced, because people in heaven do not struggle. They vegetate. Still on the same note, Arieti has described the constituents of what he calls a creativogenic culture, a culture that encourages and stimulates creativity.[25] These beneficial factors--such as freedom of thought, widespread access to education, economic support, and so forth--are, Arieti admits, particularly prevalent in North America. Yet, sadly, this same culture has produced, per capita, relatively few eminent creators, while Germany, with its notoriously heavy-handed and authoritarian educational practices has produced many.

How can this be? Arieti argues that such environmental factors do not by themselves guarantee anything. Personal, psychological considerations are equally important, and American culture promotes some potentially inhibitory values. Children are encouraged to be outgoing and socially adept, because it is important to be popular and well-liked. Daydreaming, perhaps indicative of a rich inner life, is taken to signify laziness or "lack of drive," and is discouraged. Material acquisition and economic security are emphasized, so children must be "practical" in setting their goals. Not surprisingly, such priorities tend to nip potential talent in the bud. But above all, it seems to us that supremely happy, well adjusted, environmentally advantaged children might not be particularly driven to create. To succeed in this arena, as in sports, you have to be hungry!

Incubation/Frustration

Supposedly, their entrance to this second stage distinguishes creative people from others similarly prepared. A "germ" of an idea, which suggests something to be puzzled about, seems to initiate the transition. Henle, following in William James' footsteps, has discussed a gap or discontinuity in knowledge and understanding that demands attention and solution.[26] A gap is not a passive vacuum but is intensely active, beckoning with almost hypnotic power. It can easily become an obsession, producing torture and sleepless nights until it is solved. Gaps arise from knowledge, because one cannot be perplexed about matters of which one is ignorant, so the preparation stage supplies the ingredients not only for finding answers but, even more important, for asking questions.

Anecdotal reports verify the plausibility of this analysis, Stephen Spender called the gap "a dim cloud of an idea."[27] Sculptor Henry Moore reported that at the seashore "out of millions of pebbles passed...I choose to see with excitement only (a few)" (italics mine).[28] And for writer Henry James:

> Most of the stories...have sprung from a single seed...the wandering word, the vague echo, at touch of which the novelist's imagination winces as at the prick of some sharp point.[29]

It is also widely agreed that commencing work is fruitless until one has discovered this nut that needs to be cracked. Robert Burns stated:

> I have two or three times in my life composed from the wish rather than the impulse, but I never succeeded to any purpose.[30]

Bertrand Russell asserts:

> What has come first is a problem involving discomfort. Then comes voluntary application involving great effort. After this, a period without conscious thought, and finally a solution, bringing with it a complete plan of a book.[31]

And Goethe advises:

> My counsel is to force nothing and rather to trifle or sleep away all unproductive days and hours, than on such days to compose something that will afterwards give no pleasure.[32]

The picture before us, then, is that this preliminary "Inspiration One" begins the process by supplying a focus for contemplation, while the better known "Inspiration Two" provides its solution. To solve a newspaper's crossword puzzle, it is necessary not only to discover the answers to the various questions, but also to pick up the newspaper. This seems so obvious that its importance can be missed. But Getzels and his colleagues[33] have avowed that creatives are distinguished not so much by their abilities for problem solving as for problem finding. They must have, apparently, a healthy masochistic streak, searching diligently for something to frustrate them. An observation of Einstein's is indicative:

> The formulation of a problem is often more essential than its solution, which may be merely a matter of mathematical or experimental skill.

To raise new questions, new problems requires creative imagination and marks real advance in science.[34]

There have been precious few empirical investigations of the creative process that are genuinely impressive, but Getzels and Csikszentmihalyi[35] have conducted one. They presented some art students with a series of objects that the latter were asked to represent in any way they wished. Students were free to handle, arrange, and examine the objects before they set to work. Getzels et al. could therefore determine a <u>problem finding score</u> by measuring the number of objects manipulated, the amount of exploratory behavior shown while selecting and arranging the objects, and the uniqueness of the objects finally chosen to draw.

Thus the situation forced the students to practice overtly, where it could be observed and measured, a "trial and error" process that normally would occur privately. The problem-finding scores (particularly the number of objects manipulated and the amount of object exploration) correlated highly with the originality and aesthetic value of the students' still life drawings (as evaluated by several professional judges) and, even more important, with their later success in the profession.

Still, the beginning supplied by Inspiration One <u>is</u> only a beginning. Before Inspiration Two makes its leisurely appearance, mistakes, blind alleys, and changes of direction are almost routine as one agonizingly awaits it. It is because of these ordeals by trial that "frustrating" seems to aptly describe this stage and vindicate Hutchinson's account of it over Wallas/Poincaré. The latter make it seem all too easy when, more typically, agony precedes ecstacy. Paper is hurled into the wastebasket after only a few tentative words are written. Some random chords are pecked out on the piano, to be followed by an angry fist crashing down on the keys and a grimaced expletive. Sleep gives way to tossing and turning. At such times, one can sympathize with Yeats:

> Better go down upon your marrow-bones
> And scrub a kitchen pavement, or break stones
> Like an old pauper, in all kinds of weather
> For to articulate sweet sounds together
> Is to work harder than all these.[36]

To compound the torture, most <u>creative blocks</u>, or dry spells appear during this stage. When inspiration simply will not come, when every attempt resembles beef stew, then the person will definitely be "frustrated." It seems defensible at this point, therefore, to examine some of the reasons for these

77

afflictions along with some of the remedies that have been suggested. Our discussion will be somewhat cursory, since these matters are peripheral to our main purposes. The reader seeking elaboration should consult Stein.[37]

1. Interference. Many behaviors are incompatible; even the most adept would be hard pressed to mow the lawn while washing the dishes. Therefore a dominant response tendency can block or even obliterate a less obvious possibility that nevertheless may be more desirable. Thought processes are equally susceptible to such interference. It is a major cause of forgetting[38] and, in problem-solving of both the parlor game and real-life variety, how often do we miss the solution because "we were looking at it the wrong way?"

Interference can also produce creative blocking. Koestler points out that often a problem will be "in the air," puzzling many individuals.[39] But through intellectual snowblindness, most will miss the forest because of the trees. When Darwin solved the mystery of evolution by suggesting the mechanism of natural selection, more than one scientist experienced the distasteful emotion, "It's so obvious; why didn't I think of it?" The competing alternatives were, after the fact, recognized for the errors that they were.

A variety of techniques are available to help a creator overcome these blocks. Role playing, in which one pretends to be different people, can force one to view the world from other perspectives. Brainstorming[40] encourages groups of people to throw out any possible solution to a problem, no matter how ridiculous it might seem. The atmosphere purports to be nonevaluative, one in which "anything goes" (whether it is possible, in practice, to establish such an atmosphere is debatable). Only later are the ideas reviewed more critically, to separate wheat from chaff. The underlying belief is that many fruitful ideas are suppressed because of fear of ridicule.

Similarly, in a series of studies, Maltzman and his colleagues[41] have trained subjects to produce unusual responses to stimuli in a free association situation. More specifically, the same stimulus, such as "table", is presented repeatedly, but the subject must change the response to it each time. Original responding is thereby increased over the course of a session, but whether this tendency bears any long-term dividends in real life situations is a moot point.[42]

Two seemingly opposite techniques can, strangely enough, both be beneficial. Sometimes, extensive contemplation of a problem will only increase dominant fixations and further suppress other alternatives. So withdrawing from it--taking a vacation,

78

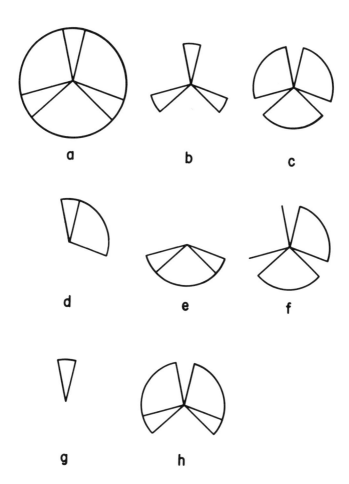

FIGURE 4.1   Alternate configurations of a figure-ground relationship
(after R. Arnheim. _Toward a Psychology of Art_. Berkeley: U. of
California Press, 1966, p. 294.   Used with permission of the publisher.)

listening to music, immersing oneself in unrelated activities,
or simply wasting time--can, according to many creatives, sometimes
work wonders.[43] Yet Sakurabayashi had some observors study
reversible figures, in which two equally dominant figure-ground
relationships usually alternate, and found that with prolonged
inspection they became aware of further, less obvious configurations
(see Figure 4.1).[44] Furthermore, Eskimo artists reportedly will

contemplate a soapstone for some time, until the figure which "resides within it" becomes apparent to them. Only then will they set to work.

When is it better to persist and when to lay off? There is no easy answer, since each of these incompatible practices may yield dividends, but some evidence hints that the former may more often be helpful. Gall and Mendelsohn[45] administered Mednick's Remote Associations Test and then, after an interlude, readministered the items the subject had initially missed. Some subjects spent the intervening time working on those missed items, others free associated to them a la Maltzman, while still others "incubated", i.e., practised an unrelated, diversionary task. Subsequently, the prolonged inspection approach produced more solutions on the missed items, while the virtuous idleness condition produced the fewest.

Still, individuals themselves must undoubtedly learn through experience which option works best for them, and under what circumstances. Many report that they can almost sense whether a day will be productive.[46] Given positive feelings, then, persistence is recommended, but unmistakably "bad vibes" indicate that it is probably time to adjourn to a movie.

Various drugs have also been periodically advocated as liberators from interference. Thus, some creators have worked effectively under the influence of opium (S. T. Coleridge, Elizabeth Barrett Browning), alcohol (Edgar Allan Poe, Baudelaire), and mescalin (Aldous Huxley). However most authorities would agree with Arieti[47] that, while these artifical aids may provide novel ideas, they probably hinder the more critical, detached thought that is necessary to select ideas of merit. Therefore, they are at best a mixed blessing for productivity, to say nothing of their effects on health.

Discussing a problem with others can also be helpful, since they may supply fresh alternatives. Moreover, as we try to put our problem into words, we often find ourselves saying things that we did not realize we knew. It was one of Freud's great insights that, amidst mountains of worthless verbiage, a few gold nuggets of inspiration may suddenly flow forth to indicate the solution to a difficulty. Therefore, Freud's system of therapy, called psychoanalysis, emphasizes free association. By such circumlocution, we may also discover a new way of conceiving even a highly familiar topic. Writing can provide similar dividends. As we slave over a typewriter, or battle writer's cramp, we may find unforeseen words appearing on the page.

2. Moods. Most creatives report that fluctuating moods do not affect their productivity.[48] The lab or studio is, in a real sense, a separate world, so moods are left outside with the overshoes. One mark of the amateur dilettante is that he works only when "he feels like it"; professionals are more relentless. Within the working space, however, moods can be critical, and the compulsive rituals professionals sometimes practice are means to achieving productive ones. Thus Stephen Spender smoked and drank coffee incessantly, neither of which he otherwise did. Jean-Paul Sartre wrote in a coffee house, surrounded by noise and bustle. Zola pulled the shades to keep out the sunlight. Perhaps most bizarre of all, Schiller kept rotten apples in his desk and wrote with his feet in a bucket of cold water.[49] But if the strategy works, who can say it nay?

Creative activity seldom requires one to associate with other people, but where this is the case, the quality of those interactions can also be important. Thus, film directors Sidney Lumet and Franco Zeffirelli both need cooperative atmospheres. When Lumet encounters tension, he stops work to "have it out,"[50] while Zeffirelli has walked away from several projects simply because an atmosphere of love with his colleagues did not develop.[51] On the other hand, choreographers Jerome Robbins[52] and Antony Tudor[53] thrived on confrontation and crisis; they seemed to go out of their way to antagonize others. But again, it is the results that matter.

Apathy, the feeling that one's work doesn't matter is, by general consensus, particularly insidious. Norman Mailer believes that a great writer must assume above all that it is important to be a great writer.[54] Picasso said, "The essential...is to create enthusiasm....It is enthusiasm of which we have the most need, we and the young."[55] Even the greatest can fall victim to bouts of indifference and unproductive "dry spells" will invariably follow. Bertrand Russell's letters clearly reveal that the 1914-1918 war brought on a lengthy one:

> All that one has cared for is dead, at least
> for the present; and it is hard to believe
> that it will ever revive. No one thinks about
> learning or feels it of any importance. And
> from the outer deadness my thoughts travel to
> the deadness in myself--I look around my shelves
> at the books of mathematics and philosophy that
> have sunk again into the state of lethargy that
> I have had at intervals since the war began....I
> want someone to take me in hand and order me
> about, telling me where to live and what to do
> and leaving me no self-direction at all....It

81

leaves me with no interest in anything, and not enough energy to get into a better frame of mind by my own efforts....My impulse is just to sit still and brood.[56]

As this example suggests, apathy can spring from a variety of sources. Persistent neglect, which produces the feeling of being ignored, undervalued, and underpaid. Isolation from others who share similar attitudes, interests, and enthusiasms. The completion of a large project, such as a novel may produce "post-criterion drop", demonstrating that the sense of excited involvement cannot easily be shifted from the completed project to another. This may explain why Nobel Prize winners afterwards show marked drops in productivity.[57]* Lastly, too much praise and recognition can lead to apathy. Germaine Greer asserts that poisonous praise--encouragement too easily won often bestowed by paternalistic males--is one reason why few women have succeeded as artists.[59] It stifles any motive for them to take their work seriously and strive to improve.

How can apathy be controlled? Any human activity can seem silly when examined with detachment, so in order to avoid cynicism, a creator must lose perspective and become involved. Other people's enthusiasm can also provide defense. As well, apathy resembles a physical condition in which one's body chemistry seems to change, so exercise, proper diet, and other such health aids may help to control it. Mozart, we note, reportedly composed after physical exercise.[60] On the other hand some other popular treatments seem not only ineffective but harmful. Vacations of excessive duration tend to increase apathy, perhaps by promoting emotional detachment. Too much rest or sleep will stimulate but one desire, for yet more rest and sleep.

Since self-confidence is so crucial, cowardice, self-doubt, and fear can also be destructive moods. Contrary to popular opinion, anxiety such as "stage fright" does not afflict only young pianists before a recital. Successful and mature artists are also susceptible, even to the extent that a tragic fini can be written to careers.[61] The slightest failure by a performer because of, say, a temporary desertion of technique can initiate

---

* Many behaviors display just such a goal gradient effect.(58) In their initial phases they are practised with leisurely inefficiency but, as the finish line looms ahead and anticipated reward becomes more imminent, they become more intense. Thus, a rat will run faster as it proceeds down an alleyway and approaches food, and students will procrastinate over assigned essays and at the last moment stay up all night to finish them.

anxiety about a repeat and, in turn, a self-fulfilling prophecy. Sir Laurence Olivier reports that at his career's height he battled an almost incapacitating stage fright, induced by anxiety that he might forget his lines.[62] According to Gedo,[63] responsibilities can also diminish confidence. So too can the destruction of a grandiose self-concept when one must at last admit that one's accomplishments hardly rival those of the most eminent.

Why is anxiety so pernicious? Most creative blocks stem from interfering, competing responses. Many studies have demonstrated that as anxiety increases, so does the dominance of the most common response tendency.[64] In other words, the harder we try, the more we will perform obvious behaviors and miss alternative possibilities. If this dominant tendency is desirable, then all is well. But all too often, especially in problem solving and creative situations, it is only an interfering nuisance. This is probably the reason why the more intensely we search for a solution, the more it will evade us, only to make an effortless, fickle appearance during mundane activities. For such activities are, above all, times of low emotional arousal.

We have, then, yet another contradiction before us. Both apathy and anxiety, underarousal and overarousal, reduce efficiency. However the so-called Yerkes-Dodson function[65] shows that in many difficult situations, precisely this relationship appears; performance is best at a moderate level of arousal/anxiety. We hasten to add that this relationship does not explain the observations about creatives, since the Yerkes-Dodson function itself needs to be explained. But we can be comforted that one creative paradox, at least, appears elsewhere as well.

Can anxiety be successfully treated? A variety of techniques are available for dealing with the clinical variety (see Costello[66]) and some might be applicable to the creative kind as well. Let us mention one, which had at least one successful employment. Apparently Serge Rachmaninoff became depressed because of the failure of his Piano Concerto No. 1, and a creative block resulted. He sought out Dr. Nikolai Dahl, a hypnotist, whose administrations helped to the extent that Rachmaninoff could complete his concerto No. 2, which is dedicated to Dr. Dahl.[67] Musical compositions have been dedicated to many people, but this may be the only case where a physician has been singled out for such an honor.

In conclusion, we offer a few personal suggestions for battling the frustration stage. The first step is to realize its inevitability. Often, while struggling with an ongoing problem, we fondly remember completed projects because their finished versions now seem so polished and serene. We ask ourselves:

why is the current project so agonizing? Actually, the others provided anxious moments as well; we have simply forgotten. Therefore, a daily diary can be helpful in order to record our moods while working and to remind us later on how we actually felt. In addition, since those previous difficulties did eventually lead to a satisfactory resolution, our confidence can be restored that the process will be repeated.

Simultaneously working on several projects which require different approaches can also help rescue a day from being a total waste. A change can be as stimulating as a rest. And lastly, people must discover for themselves their most amenable working conditions. There is no "right way" to work. Hammerclavier Hammerschmidt, the poetic virtuoso of the tuba, may practise in the outhouse at midnight with a canary perched on the shoulder, but that does not mean that others should. The method that produces results is the preferable one.

Once these necessary conditions are discovered, one must be brutal in insisting on them. When one's name is on the program, so to speak, one's psychological life is on the line. No one else will share the burden of failure. The greatest frustration of all is to fail because external factors prevented one from doing one's best work. Creatives should not be reasonable in enduring situations they find discomforting; they should make waves. On this point there can be no compromise.

Chapter 5

THE CREATIVE PROCESS II: INSPIRATION AND BEYOND

According to popular belief, successful creation must include a dramatic moment of "aha," when the solution to a riddle suddenly appears. Likewise, it is assumed that the process will soon take a much easier course. In this chapter, we shall consider the various events that typically occur during and after an insight.

Inspiration

The supreme moment does not lend itself easily to verbal discussion. Both self-evident and supremely nonlinear, it might seem to be the altered state of consciousness par excellence. Still, at least two matters deserve our attention, one probably more foreseeable than the other. First, we shall ask what the experience of inspiration is like psychologically. Second, we shall pose a more heretical question: is inspiration really necessary?

1. Do the colored lights turn on? It is rather difficult to determine characteristic qualities of an inspiration because many creatives are loath to discuss the process at all. They often fear that, like the watched pot that never boils, a psyche too closely observed may no longer yield insights. For Henry Moore, "It is a mistake for a sculptor or painter to speak or write very often about his job."[1] Playwright Edward Albee has observed:

> If you intellectualize and examine the creative
> process too carefully it can evaporate and vanish.
> It's not only terribly difficult to talk about,
> it's also dangerous. You know the old
> story----about the centipede. (He was asked)
> 'It's amazing and marvelous how you walk with
> all those hundreds and hundreds of legs. How
> do you do it?'.... The centipede stopped and
> thought...and thought about it for awhile, and
> he couldn't walk.[2]

Nevertheless, many introspective reports are available and, considering how subjective this moment is, they show surprising agreement. Hamlet provides a famous example. Following his encounter with the ghost, he is at first uncertain how to proceed. Suddenly the appearance of his actor friends triggers an idea:

85

I have heard,
That guilty creatures sitting at a play
Have by the very cunning of the scene
Been struck so to the soul that presently
They have proclaim'd their malefactions;
For murder, though it have no tongue, will speak
With most miraculous organ. I'll have these players
Play something like the murder of my father
Before mine uncle. I'll observe his looks;
I'll tent him to the quick. If he but blench
I know my course.....The play's the thing,
Wherein I'll catch the conscience of the king.
(2.2)

Hamlet's actions, then and later, are typical of those
receiving inspiration's largesse. First the idea will seem certain
and beyond question. Recipients' first reaction will be "of
course," and amazed at the idea's simplicity, they feel stupid
that it was not discovered earlier. They may then fear that
someone else may have beaten them to the solution (which can
happen, since "being scooped" is an occupational hazard,
particularly in science).

Usually the inspiration will be brief, summarized by a
single sentence, phrase, or equation. Entire novels have flowed
from such a nucleus, as if one is "unravelling a ball of twine
from out of the unknown."[3] However, it will also suggest many
corollaries and implications, which will tumble out in such
abundance that the recipient's pen or typewriter will literally
be unable to keep up. Tchaikovsky has described this white
heat:

I forget everything and behave like a mad man.
Everything within me starts pulsing and quivering;
hardly have I begun the sketch, than one thought
follows another. In the midst of the magic
process it frequently happens that some external
interruption wakes me from my state....Dreadful
indeed are such interruptions. Sometimes they
break the thread of inspiration for a long time.[4]

Coleridge's infamous "Man from Porlock" demonstrates how calamitous
interruptions can be. The poet had just conceived Kubla Khan
and virtually had it written out in his head, when the interloper
distracted him for a crucial hour, effacing much of the material.
The poem resembles an archaeologist's piecing together of a few
disjointed fragments from a vanished civilization.

During inspiration, as well, detachment and separation from
the work will be lost. One's sense of individuality and of

86

self will disappear, as will the dichotomy between subject and object. Creator and created become unified in what Rollo May has called the encounter.[5] Time seems to stand still, suspending one in an ever-present "now." This psychological departure from the ordinary, mundane world can breed absent-mindedness. The scientist Ampère, reportedly, was particularly prone to this affliction.[6] While riding in the country, he became so absorbed in a problem that he dismounted and walked slowly along, leading his horse. When he arrived at his destination, he was missing his horse, which he had left somewhere behind. On another occasion, he wrote a formula on the back of a dusty cab. When it suddenly drove away, he had to dash madly in pursuit to prevent the precious inspiration from being obliterated in a car wash.

There will be feelings of great excitement, rapture, and elation. Motivation and commitment, lagging during earlier phases, will be renewed. And lastly, like zealots who obtain enlightenment, the creator will want to share the discovery with others. In the words of one, "I usually have to resist the impulse to rush up to strangers and tell them about it."[7] Previously, the creator preferred seclusion to avoid the painful question, "How's it going?". Now the door will be open and visitors welcome; in fact, they may have difficulty escaping.

It is notable that Tart's altered states of consciousness--brought on by dreams, hypnosis, and various drugs such as mescalin and marijuana--produce experiences strikingly similar to those just mentioned.[8] Perhaps their psychological mechanisms overlap.

2. Is inspiration necessary? That a "eureka" is a sine qua non for creative success is a view by no means unanimously held. Actually, throughout history the pendulum has oscillated regularly, with inspiration now being emphasized, now minimized. Its current popularity again demonstrates how greatly Romantic biases have influenced our attitudes.

In medieval and baroque periods, as we have seen, the artisan was expected to produce work systematically "to order." A Bach or a Haydn, for example, dependent on ecclesiastical and/or noble patronage for a livelihood, routinely composed a new cantata for next Sunday's service or an intriguing string quartet to entertain the guests at a forthcoming ball. They could not afford to wait for an unpredictable bolt from the blue. Were Bach interviewed on a contemporary talk show and asked "Why do you compose?", he probably would reply, "Because it's my job; it pays the bills." And to the query "How do you do it? What's the secret to your success?" he would likely retort, "There is no secret except hard work." The sense of mystery would be negligible.

During the Romantic era the pendulum swung the other way. Still, Edgar Allan Poe, among the most romantic of writers judging by his dates and life style has, ironically, denied relying on anything besides planned, conscious labor.[9] In addition, the older views may be making a comeback. Several influential moderns, notably Stravinsky,[10] have openly debunked inspiration's importance. Choreographer George Balanchine was often heard to say that "Inspiration does not come on suddenly, like a stomach ache."[11] Rather, since his dancers were available for only a few precious rehearsal hours, "My Muse must come to me on union time."

Furthermore, Gruber has convincingly argued that it wildly oversimplifies the usual state of affairs to attribute everything to one dramatic "inspiration."[12] He perused Darwin's personal notebooks and journals to determine how the latter's thinking actually developed. Darwin was supposedly the definitive inductionist, systematically gathering his observations during the Beagle voyage without any theoretical preconceptions. Then his inspiration came in the fall of 1838, as he read Malthus' work on population, that natural selection could provide the explanation. Gruber in fact shows that most of Darwin's theoretical ideas appear in his notes years beforehand, albeit in germinal form. Apparently he posed as the arch-inductionist because he fully anticipated that his ideas would set off a storm of controversy. He pretended that he had been reluctantly been driven to his unorthodox views by sheer weight of the evidence. As we know, his attempt to head off controversy did not entirely succeed.

Gruber maintains, then, that inspiration is not a dramatic "moment of truth" but a more gradual growth process, with an idea growing and disappearing in the person's thought. In the same vein, Hutchinson[13] has hypothesized a continuum of creative thought. Conscious, rational effort occupies one extreme, intuitive insight the other, and all sorts of intermediary possibilities lie in between. Different occasions, he proposed, may involve different concentrations of inspiration, since his subjects reported that, while it sometimes affected their work, at other times it was notably absent (although most felt that inspiration accompanied their best efforts). They also intimated that as they grew older, they worked more methodically, relying craftsmanship and experience rather than inspired frenzy. As a result, they also became less subject to frustrating trial and error.

In summary, we do not wish to deny inspiration's importance, since so many workers have emphasized it, but simply to point out that its role is probably more spasmodic and more complex than is often supposed.

Verification/Hypothesis Testing

If and when inspiration finally arrives, creators still face frustrating and even cruel labor. For they must now find the means to share that insight with others. This requires that they view their attempts as if through the eyes of others; with critical detachment. It isn't easy. In the words of Anatole France:

> The scissors work in the cold light of the dissecting room. They cut out all that is adventitious and preserve only the healthy flesh.[14]

As we contemplate the finished product, it may make proficiency seem easy. A glance into what Ghiselin has called "the sweat and litter of the workroom",[15] however, will give the lie to this comfortable misconception. A chef who concocts a gourmet extravaganza may confidently parade, before the eyes of guests, a steady stream of succulent dishes, but behind the scenes is a culinary mess. For Vera Volkova, the late and beloved teacher of ballet, the dancer's classroom is "our kitchen." There, mistakes can be made and difficult feats attempted without risking public failure. There, dance's physical and mental demands need not be hidden. But in the dining room of the performing stage, before the paying customers, everything must seem effortless.

During verification, creators may be hard put to maintain motivation, especially if inspiration seems self-evident and they think their work finished. How many scientists collect their data and jot down preliminary hypotheses on scraps of paper, but somehow never quite get around to the drudgery of writing these up for publication? Like someone skimming through a familiar murder mystery, the excitement diminishes once they know what happens, so they may prefer moving on to something else.

But the other extreme can also pose problems. Some workers, like Penelope awaiting the tardy Odysseus, never finish their revising. Like possessive mothers, they keep their progeny tied to their psychic apron strings. Thomas Wolfe, by his own admission, relied on his editor to tell him when his work was done.[16] We picture the editor tearing the manuscript away from Wolfe's grasping hands, as he pleads on bended knee to make "just a few more changes." According to Storr, such compulsion reflects

89

not only perfectionism gone amuck, but also fear of the intimidating prospect of public exposure and possibly negative judgment.[17]

In the face of such obstacles, accomplished professionals are distinguished from the mediocre and inexperienced not only by the quality of their inspiration but also by the command of their craft. Their early drafts may be similar to a novice's, but each draft improves upon the last, so that the final result will be worlds apart. The novice may correct flaws in each revision, but also may introduce others, so progress suffers.

Thus, persistence to revise in order to communicate effectively is also crucial for success. Why do some practise it almost to excess, while others of equal potential hardly do so at all? Our perspectives provide few helpful answers, but Arieti proposes a mysterious agent called the endocept.[18] This vague, ideal image hovers in the mind's eye of the creator, who tries desperately to represent it "out there" in the external medium. It is a Holy Grail floating just out of reach, a siren to the creator's tortured Odysseus. Under its beckoning magnetism, every creator resembles the pathetic/ heroic Don Quixote pursuing his unreachable ideal of perfect love and chivalry. Accordingly, the creative process seems not only to be "pushed" by such desires as self-expression but also "pulled" by the need to give form to this amorphous goal, and it is this need that supplies persistence. Thus Langer's assertion[19] that the expression of one's vague feelings, to clarify them for oneself, is artistic creativity's primary purpose. Communication to others is merely a peripheral by-product.

Many introspective reports have verified the endocept's plausibility. Oscar Wilde writes:

> Dorian, from the moment I met you, your personality had the most extraordinary influence over me. I was dominated, soul, brain and power by you. You became to me the visible incarnation of that unseen ideal whose memory haunts us artists like an exquisite dream (italics mine).[20]

And Isadora Duncan observes:

> Already famous, sought after in every country, I had only to pursue a triumphal career. But, alas! I was possessed by the idea of a school--a vast ensemble-- dancing the Ninth Symphony of Beethoven. At night, I had only to shut my eyes and these figures danced through my brain in mighty array, calling on me to bring them to life. 'We are here. You are the one at

whose touch we might live!'...I was possessed
by the dream of Promethean creation that, at
my call, might spring from the Earth, descend
from the Heavens, such dancing figures as the
world had never seen. Ah, proud, enticing dream
that has led my life from one catastrophe to
another! Why did you possess me?...Small
fluttering light, just ahead of my stumbling
footsteps, I still believe, I still follow you.[21]

But does tough-minded science depend on such vagaries?
According to textbook accounts, its theories come about through
induction, arising from the empirical facts available by an
almost relentless, largely unimaginative process. This scenario
is largely dismissed nowadays,[22] and Polanyi[23] provides another
which seems more plausible. He begins with a paradox first
pointed out by Plato. A problem whose solution we already
know is no problem. But if that solution is unknown, we could
have no idea where to look for it. How then could we ever
discover it?

Polanyi answers that **feelings** of deepening coherence
characterize scientists' searchings. Initially the vision of
that solution is foggy, but it has sufficient coherence to
guide intuition, and hence their imaginations, along the right
track. It facilitates "enlightened guessing" so they invariably
make the right choice for the myriad decisions they face.
Thus it gradually emerges by degrees from the mist. Einstein,
discussing relativity's discovery, has reportedly verified this
account:

> There was a feeling of direction, of going straight
> toward something definite...(which was) clearly
> to be distinguished from later thoughts about
> the rational form of the solution.[24]

According to Polanyi, scientists' endocepts come from
actual reality "out there" which those scientists are
attempting to unravel. In this they differ from the
artistic brand, which presumably reside entirely in artists'
imaginations. However others such as Popper[25] would hold
that a scientific idea is equally an act of imagination.

That great actor and fine visual artist, Dirk Bogarde,
summarizes the notion of the endocept:

> How do you paint the intangible, how do you
> paint all the love which I have had and which
> this sodding train is taking me away from?[26]

Is this not the problem faced by every artist and scientist, viz., how to make the intangible concrete? It is also another source of frustration, for if there is one thing on which most agree, it is that the final product never satisfactorily captures the endocept's essence. Henry Miller's experience is typical:

> The artist expresses himself by and through imperfection.... One gets nearer to the heart of truth (in the sense that) he ceases to struggle....I accept a priori my inability to realize the perfect ideal. It does not bother me in the least.[27]

Still, hope springs eternal that the vision will at last be captured in form, allowing others to share its magical power. That is why, Arieti suggests, many creators return to the same themes--van Gogh to his self-portraits, Mendelssohn to his "Songs Without Words," and Skinner to reinforcement contingencies as determinants of behavior.

The endocept is a reasonable hypothesis also because it is difficult to see how work could proceed without it. As creators try, err, and revise, they <u>work</u> <u>towards</u> <u>something</u>. They know only vaguely where they want to go but more precisely where they do <u>not</u>. A poet tries a certain word. "No, that's not right." Another. "That's a bit more like it." Still another. "<u>That's</u> what I want!" The decisions made may seem arbitrary, but they are made with confidence. They indicate that creators do not thrash blindly around in a vacuum, like rats in a maze, but rather, seem to be guided and led.

The Creator as Medium

We usually assume that a creative product originates from <u>someone</u>, e.g., an artist or scientist, and that it is his or her responsibility. Theirs the laurel wreaths and also the overripe fruit. Actually, introspective reports suggest, at some point the work often seems to "take over" so that the helpless creator follows rather than leads. Creators may feel at such times that they have little control over the process and that the result is <u>not</u> of their doing. That result has come about, not through their voluntary decisions but through automatic, reflexive processes, in the manner of a waste product or (to borrow A.E. Housman's apt label) "a secretion."[28] Perhaps, like spiritualism's storied "mediums," a creator simply provides the body for otherworldly spirits to communicate with earth-bound souls. Nietzsche has written:

> It was on these two roads that all <u>Zarathustra</u> came to me...perhaps I should rather say, <u>invaded</u>

me....One can hardly reject completely the idea
that one is the mere incarnation, or mouthpiece,
or medium of some almighty power.[29]

That most astute philosopher/poet, Winnie the Pooh, provides
further verification of this point.[30] He composed a bit of
verse to honor that hyperactive interloper in the Hundred Acre
Wood, Tigger, and therein referred to Tigger's weight as measured
in pounds, shillings, and ounces. Piglet objects: shillings
obviously relate not to pounds (weight) but to pounds (currency).
Pooh agrees that this may well be the case ordinarily, but in
writing poetry, one has to let things come however they will.
The shillings also wanted to be included, so he had done so.

An extreme version of this situation was recently reported
in the popular press (and thus should be taken with a grain of
salt). One Rosemary Brown, an "average London housewife," literally
functioned as a medium for great composers of bygone days.
Bach, Schubert, Chopin, Gershwin--she purports, arrive and dictate
compositions to her; pieces that they "didn't have time to
write while they were alive." She is an untutored pianist,
often cannot play the works they "give" her, and yet several
musical authorities have vouched for the compositions' stylistic
accuracy. Here are Mrs. Brown's impressions of some of her
visitors:

> Schubert is very modest and he always apologizes
> for disturbing me. Bach is very strict. He
> never talks. He just dictates his music and
> then goes. Beethoven is kind and I am pleased
> to be able to tell you, he is no longer deaf.
> Actually my favourite musician is Mozart but
> he has only come to see me once or twice....The
> naughtiest one is Chopin. He visits me in my
> bedroom and when I am undressing to have a
> bath.[31]

Only in Chelsea! In the same vein, the creator may be
quite taken aback by the finished work, which often will differ
from the initial vision. Playwright Harold Pinter is adamant
when he says he has no more idea what will happen in his plays
than anyone else; even he is often surprised.[32] His fellow
dramatist, Arthur Miller, sees this as a healthy sign:

> If I can't get ahead of a character, and yet
> he keeps talking, I know I've got something.
> If I can get ahead of him, controlling him, he
> hasn't acquired a life of his own. The play
> is a dead duck.[33]

Gertrude Stein agrees:

> So how can you know what it will be? What
> will be best in it is what you really do not
> know now. If _you_ _knew_ _it_ _all_ _it_ _would_ _not_ _be_
> _creation_ _but_ _dictation_ (italics mine).[34]

Another common occurrence further verifies the medium concept. Only those of suicidal inclination should ask a creator to explain the meaning of his/her work, for the invariable response will be acute irritation, coupled with a growled retort that "The work says it all!" Puzzled consumers, for whom it does nothing of the kind, may take this as yet another indication of creators' unsteady, contrary temperaments. For surely those who produce a work should understand it if anyone does? In reality, they very often do not, which is probably the real reason for their response. It is enlightened critics' main task to provide the possible interpretations.

As final support, we refer to creators' frequent feelings, once the work is complete and some time has elapsed, that it is not theirs. No less than 50 percent of Hutchinson's interviewees reported this sense of detachment, with statements such as "When I have finished a particular piece of work, I feel as though it had nothing more to do with me" and "Reading over my efforts later, it does not seem that they are familiar to me."[35] Given that during the process itself one's feelings of control and responsibility may also fluctuate, these surprising yet quite reliable observations become more understandable.

Problem Solving and Creativity

It is tempting to regard these two activities as interchangeable, for they do have striking similarities. The most obvious is the moment of inspiration that provides the solution to a baffling puzzle. As well, both are subject to frustrating blockages and unproductive trial and error before this enlightenment appears. It is likely, then, that we can increase our understanding of the one by studying the other. But only to a point, because running roughshod over their differences will lead to dangerous oversimplification of the creative process.

Problem solving usually refers to situations such as anagrams, Maier's two strings, Luchins water jars, etc. that possess a correct answer (see Bourne, Ekstrand and Dominowski[36] for an extensive discussion). Experimenters, their subjects, and anyone else will agree on what it is and when it has been found. On the other hand, creative situations, such as composing symphonies and writing novels have more arbitrary criteria. The validity or "rightness" of a solution depends on a value judgment. Thus, to a problem-solving inspiration we exclaim "That's right!"; to a creative one, "That's good!" As a result, a completed problem, such as a crossword puzzle, seems perfect within itself. It defies improvement, so it also seems a trifle dull (for what is less interesting than a problem whose solution we know?). But creative works, because they are never perfect, are never finished.

Some important implications follow from this distinction. The component processes and typical experiences of the two activities, we suspect, are comparable prior to solution but afterwards part company. For example, in problem solving the stage of verification is virtually nonexistent, because once inspiration arrives, to all intents and purposes the work is over. But in creation, finding an effective way to communicate the insight to others is crucial.

Judging by reports, postinsight experiences may also differ. The solution to a problem, for example, seems quite focused, answering only that particular problem. A creative insight, however, as we have learned, provides a host of related ideas. Moreover, anxiety and insecurity are indigenous to creative work, making self-confidence an important attribute. Why? Because success and the agreement of others is never certain. Creators know too well that others have suffered from delusions of grandeur. Will their efforts also be weighed in the balance and found wanting? That is why painters hide their canvasses and playwrights spend opening night in the washroom relinquishing their dinner. Problem solvers face no such traumas; they know when they are right.

If these differences are as important as we suspect, then the relation between problem solving and creative ability may be substantially lower than is sometimes supposed. Are eminent contributors to the arts and sciences also accomplished at tasks such as crossword puzzles and Rubik's cubes? It would not surprise us if they were not. If the answer was indeed negative, then it would explain why some tests of "creativity," which in reality more closely resemble problem tasks (such as the Remote Associations Test[37]), have little predictive accuracy.

Training for Verification

As mentioned previously, this distinction has some implications worth pursuing. The first, which can be dealt with quite briefly, concerns a gap in our knowledge about how

95

to facilitate creativity. We have seen that success depends as much as anything on the ability to revise successfully, and to achieve a polished, evocative product. How can we help the novice to improve at sensing weaknesses in his or her work and eliminating them? It is one thing to have them pointed out by someone else and quite another to correct them oneself. This hurdle too many students never clear, which must severely hamper their chances for professional success.

Unfortunately, precious few techniques exist to help this stage. Stein, for example, is vague on this topic, which reflects more on the field at large than on him. While it deserves far more attention than it has thus far received, we should warn that answers will not be easy to come by, given the very nature of the verification stage. If the attributes of a worthwhile product are arbitrary and uncertain, how do we teach someone how to achieve them? It is difficult to provide directions to a city when neither its name nor its appearance are known.

Consider writing. Students can and do learn to write correctly (at least in theory) because the rules of grammar and spelling, defined and agreed upon, resemble a problem's solution. But that is not the same thing as learning to write well. Teachers may know an effective style when they see it but, because it is an individual matter, be unable to provide much helpful advice. If they highhandedly dictate their own particular preferences, then the student's work will remain only a pale reflection of another's. It is hardly surprising that so few students ever acquire a personal, effective style.

Art and Science

The second implication of the creativity-problem solving distinction will need more leisurely perusal. We have previously asked whether there is a nonspecific creativity, a "g" factor that influences every field. Art and science provide a particularly obvious version of this question. Are they, in the last analysis, comparable activities requiring highly similar abilities, or would they attract rather different sorts of creators?

The remote past seems to have downplayed their differences. For the ancient Greeks, music, closely akin to mathematics, rested on systematic, logical principles of acoustics.[38] The anonymous artisan who carved Notre Dame's gargoyles, so far as we can ascertain, had much in common with the engineer who constructed its flying buttresses. And the Renaissance seemed little surprised by Leonardo's success at both endeavors. Once more, Romanticism seems responsible for modern attitudes. In reacting against the Enlightenment's rational, scientific approaches to knowledge, it believed that subjective, "artistic" pursuits, such as poetry, were quite different and ultimately more valid paths to truth.

However, as we shall see, their similarities are once more being emphasized. Our comparison of art with science will journey along many highways and byways. To help the reader stay on course, let us first sketch our intended route. Initially, we shall examine some differences that have been proposed. Some of these are little more than figments of popular imagination, and we shall point out their inadequacies as we proceed. Others will merit more serious consideration. As we finally try to decide how similar they actually are, we will lean heavily on the distinction between creativity and problem solving.

1. Possible differences. One obvious proposal concerns their topics of study. Supposedly, science deals with the external world of objective reality, gathering empirical data through observation and proposing theories that develop from and attempt to explain those observations. Art, on the other hand, expresses more subjective, individual matters. Kohut's view is typical; scientists are more "detached," trying to understand and express phenomena remote from themselves, while artists are more self-expressive.[39]

This position poses several difficulties. Many artists such as landscape painters, playwrights, and nature poets, take a great deal from the empirical world, while some branches of science, mathematics and theoretical physics, take almost nothing. Admittedly, an artist uses "interpretation," representing the world not "as it is" but as she or he experiences it. But we now realize, as we saw in Chapter 1, that scientists do likewise. Observers having different theoretical or personal biases will give quite different meaning to the same empirical observation and will also disagree about which data deserve attention.

And do scientific explanations grow inevitably from accumulations of data, via the method of induction? The philosopher Hume showed long ago that pure induction is impossible, because all possible observations can never be conducted.[40] Popper has argued, then, that any theory, such as Newton's, requires an interpretive "leap" beyond the data and is as much a subjective interpretation of nature as is a painting or a poem.[41] It originates, not in nature, but in Newton.

As a second possible difference, perhaps art--a right hemisphere, nonlinear activity using imagination and intuition--deals with our emotional, affective experiences, while science is more logical and linear? This is a frequently heard distinction. Langer defined art as "the creation of forms symbolic of human feelings",[42] (which by implication science is not).

97

Kant held that the progressive steps of scientific thinking can be clearly stated in language, because science has certain logical, agreed upon rules of procedure and method, but artistic genius makes its own rules which cannot be reduced to a formula or even stated precisely.[43] As well, successful art possesses an intangible "spirit" (we might nowadays call it "pizazz"), while scientific work is judged by more logical, objective criteria.

Still on the same lines, Bruner says that art increases our understanding by "connecting" seemingly unrelated events, particularly by using metaphors, to reveal unexpected but still valid similarities.[44] Thus, an artistic idea has "generality," implying a range of possibilities beyond its immediate, superficial content. Now science also employs metaphors (e.g., computer simulation of mental processes) and lawful generalizations (such as the Boyle-Charles law of gas volumes), but its combinations can be logically and elegantly defended, often by using mathematics. Artistic combinations, however, are logically inexplicable, verified at a deeper, more emotional "gut reaction" level.

Given such beliefs, science may come to be demeaned as a more plodding, unimaginative pursuit; thus Maslow admits: "If I wanted to be mischievous about it, I could go so far as to define science as a technique whereby noncreative people can create."[45] These attitudes miss the mark, for in practice science also employs aesthetic, intuitive processes. Perhaps its ideas can be verified by the classic criteria, but many introspective reports suggest that aesthetic values are equally important. Einstein's best ideas often arrived first as images or fantasies, set apart by their beauty and emotional appeal.[46] Poincaré's mathematical ideas, he asserted, forced their way into consciousness mainly because of their elegance.[47] In his opinion, a mysterious censor in the unconscious eliminated excessively unattractive ideas during incubation. Intuitions also seem important. Often the solution to a puzzle will be evident before the means of logically or empirically verifying it. Gauss reported that "I have had my solutions for a long time, but I do not yet know how I am to arrive at them."[48] Polya said, "When you have satisfied yourself that the theorem is true, you start proving it."[49]

On the same theme, most scientific experiments and theories sink quickly into merciful oblivion. But a few become "classics," discussed in innumerable undergraduate classrooms and received with interest and even amazement. Do these classics practice science more logically? Is their methodology more invincible or their data more numerical? Actually many of them are rather deficient in these linear qualities. They succeed, like poems or paintings, by producing an intangible aesthetic exhilaration. The work of the Swiss psychologist Jean Piaget provides a ready example. His "experiments" are methodologically lax, easily torn to shreds by any reasonably competent undergraduate. But the ideas behind them are so appealing that they have now become, after some early resistance, widely admired and even venerated.

A third possible difference. Perhaps science progresses while art does not. Science accumulates observations. Older theories are discredited by new facts, so the new theories advanced to handle those facts must be "better." Thus the cliches that today's average schoolboy knows more about the world than Newton or Galileo, and that science builds upon its ancestors, as witnesses Newton's statement, "If I have been able to see farther than others, it was because I stood on the shoulders of giants."[50] Thus Mr. Gradgrind, Dicken's caricature of a committed scientist/empiricist, who fervently believed that we would eventually understand everything that matters if we relied on "fact" and only on "fact."[51] However, art can hardly be said to progress in this sense. The work of Shakespeare, Rembrandt, Mozart, et al. remains unrivalled, and a case could be made that the ancient Greeks reached the highest pinnacles of all. Thus, every art has its enduring "classics," ultimate standards against which new work is compared (and usually found wanting). But sciences use the word "classic" very differently. We almost never compare a new theory with Newton or Pythagorus, because it is <u>assumed</u> to be better.

By way of rejoinder, this portrayal of art history seems accurate enough but that of science is called into question by Kuhn's widely read <u>The</u> <u>Structure</u> <u>of</u> <u>Scientific</u> <u>Revolutions</u>.[52] He argues that, if science progresses at all, it is not by a smooth, inexorable march towards some final light at the end of the tunnel. Instead, long periods of comparative stasis, in which gains are consolidated, are periodically interrupted by sudden, dramatic leaps. More specifically, a prevailing <u>paradigm</u> dominates a science (a mature, highly developed one, such as physics, at least) at one point in time. The paradigm, a set of biases and assumptions shared by all workers, determines the investigations and ideas deemed worthwhile. Newton's views of the universe, which for several centuries bestrode physics and astronomy like colossi, provide a ready example. Paradigms provide a certain security, pointing out problems needing attention. Those working within the paradigm, practicing <u>normal</u> <u>science</u>, devote their lives to solving them. There will always be some <u>anomalies</u>--phenomena that conflict with the prevailing paradigm--but these will be regarded suspiciously and probably ignored entirely, because they unsettle this comfortable state of affairs. Thus science, like the human <u>psyche</u> from which it grew, can apparently repress discomforting events.

Eventually, however, enough anomalies accumulate that the paradigm seems increasingly inadequate and even stifling. A sense of progress is gradually replaced by one of stagnation. Now the discipline is ripe for a revolution, i.e., the replacement of one paradigm by another, although the old paradigm is not evicted until such a relief candidate is available. When a revolution occurs (such as Einstein's views supplanting Newton's), those ignoble anomalies suddenly become interesting and even crucial, for in a real sense they provide the new paradigm's raison d'être. Furthermore, even previously important data will be reinterpreted from the new standpoint and acquire quite different meaning. In short, Kuhn asserts, when a paradigm changes, the empirical world also changes. For example, those believing that the earth is flat and those avowing its rotundity will interpret the same phenomena, e.g., the sun's setting in the west, very differently.

But how does this affect our picture of scientific progress? In Kuhn's opinion, a revolution accelerates it, but one could argue that the discipline is thereby set back to square one, where it must start over. Admittedly, science often leads to technology, which undoubtedly progresses. We have more inventions, treatments for disease, domestic aids, and so on than in former times. But let us not confuse these with science. We may have more paraphernalia than the Greeks, but do we really understand the empirical world any better? It is a moot point. Sometimes, it seems, the more we learn the more puzzled we become. In brief, it is doubtful that art progresses; and perhaps the same may be said of science.

As yet another possibility, perhaps art is more competitive and science more cooperative? The supply of artists far exceeds demand, so economics may be partly to blame. Moreover, they usually work alone; committees do not produce masterpieces. (Although John Kenneth Galbraith is said to have muttered, "These days there are no great men, only great committees.") But above all, if each artist presents a personal vision, then in a real sense he or she competes with every other for the sympathies of the audience. Scientists, however (according to this scenario), build on one another's work and often work in teams. Ideally, then, it should be immaterial who discovers something, so long as someone does. Perhaps, therefore, scientists might be less selfish, egocentric, and obsessed with personal reputation?

This distinction will not bear scrutiny. For every titanic artistic ego, like Richard Wagner's, there has been an Isaac Newton to match. Some artists have indulged in devious back stabbing, but Haydn and Schumann, for example, acted most generously towards Mozart and Brahms, respectively, openly admiring and promoting their work.[33] And certainly science can feature

100

competitions for reputation not always fought by Queensbury's rules, as James Watson's The Double Helix so clearly reveals.[54] Watson, the co-discoverer (with Francis Crick) of DNA's molecular structure, reveals science, not as a plodding pursuit conducted by robots in white lab coats, but as an extremely human, frustrating, devious, and ultimately exhilarating process. His book was written about their race to discover DNA. He admits that "reputation, reputation Iago" drove them on against others, notably Linus Pauling, because he and Crick knew full well that a Nobel Prize awaited the victors. There was glee when the opposition barked up a theoretical blind alley. There were dirty tricks aplenty. Watson gained access to Rosalind Franklin's X-ray photos of DNA without her knowledge, and these helped greatly in solving the structural riddle. Since Franklin herself might have reached the answer had she had a fair opportunity to interpret her own data, there have been thinly veiled accusations that Watson and Crick "stole" the prize from her.[55]

Holographer Dennis Gabor, for one, agrees with Watson's picture, maintaining that he knew only two scientists, Einstein and Max Born, who were genuinely interested in the secrets of nature only and were not competitive.[56] For Gabor, everyone else wants to show how clever they are. Watson himself has persistently argued, in light of his own experience, that science is as effectively motivated by competition as are other activities.[57] Putting several scientists to work on a problem independently, not sharing their knowledge but working against one another, may be more expensive and ulcer-inducing, but it may also be more productive. In support, Torrance found in a controlled study that children in a competitive situation produced better solutions to a problem than did control subjects.[58]

Several less seminal differences might also be noted. Scientists perhaps must be more familiar with the work of others, if only to check that their planned investigations have not been "scooped." Which is a real possibility, as Wallace and Leibnitz learned to their sorrow. Darwin beat Wallace to the punch on evolution, while Newton anticipated Leibnitz' invention of the calculus. However, many artists seem surprisingly uninterested in other work, past or present, perceiving it as something to react against rather than build upon. As well, it is highly unlikely that two artists might produce, say, the identical painting. Yet, when all is said, this rule has too many exceptions on either side to carry much weight. Many scientists read little, skimming the latest Table of Contents only to be sure that their current projects remain undone, while more than a few artists stay abreast of new developments, talking and writing about them with interest and enthusiasm.

Lastly, the word "science" implies, to some minds, the handmaidens of measurement/quantification (making some form of mathematics indispensible) and technology (computers, test tubes, etc.). For artists such matters are irrelevant and perhaps even intimidating. But again, a seemingly seaworthy craft springs leaks, for some scientific work requires only the technological skill to wield pencil over paper, while artistic enterprises such as sculpture and electronic musical composition require intimacy with complicated materiel.

   2. Evaluating ideas. We turn now to some apparently more genuine distinctions. First, and probably foremost, are the criteria used to evaluate ideas. In science, they may be judged aesthetically in the early going, but beauty is only necessary, not sufficient. Ideas still must, at some point, be logically, mathematically, and/or empirically verified. Above all, if they don't "fit the facts," they must be modified or thrown out entirely, regardless of their intuitive appeal. As a result, scientific theories must be precise to the extent that they can be proven wrong. Which, for Popper, distinguishes them from other types of ideas.[59] And in all likelihood they soon will be proven wrong. Almost perversely, then, a theory that quickly becomes obsolete is better than one that hangs around; the latter was probably too vague for precise testing. Popper holds, in fact, that science progresses by criticizing and disproving incorrect ideas. It grows, not towards truth, but away from error, becoming less wrong.

   Reality, as we might have guessed, is more complicated. Textbooks may trumpet the platitude that a few contradictory observations will shoot a dominant belief down in flames. This rarely happens since science explains away or perhaps ignores embarrassing findings. As well, a scientist with time, energy, and ego invested in a pet theory will understandably be loath to forego it. Playing by the rules, when faced with contrary facts, she or he should surrender like a good sport and admit, "Yes, I'm wrong. Darn it anyway. And I had my Nobel Prize speech all prepared and my tuxedo rented."

   Actually, this scientist will probably choose more devious tactics, perhaps revising a theory to "explain" the anomalies or finding a way to discredit them. In so doing, he or she may reduce the theory's precision, clarity and, in the long term, its influence, as Hull's theories of learning demonstrate. The early version[60] was laudably falsifiable, stimulating a host of empirical tests. These revealed many flaws. His subsequent versions, which tried to "predict" these heresies[61] were so vague that they gradually faded from view.

102

Einstein reportedly played the game in a similar manner.[62] Since his theory "felt right," any contradictory observations must be wrong and their errors would eventually be found. They usually were. Thus, even in science, more theological attitudes sometimes prevail. Be that as it may, its ideas are still answerable to the facts.

As for artistic ideas, at one time they also had to agree with generally accepted canons of design and content. Since the Renaissance, however, the criteria have become arbitrary. Nowadays, people will disagree not only about whether a certain work possesses the crucial properties but also about what those properties are. Timelessness seems to be as acceptable as any. A masterpiece will not lose favor with the changing winds of fashion but will have staying power, partly because of its multileveledness (to borrow the Kreitlers' phrase[63]). Like the sphinx, almost hypnotically ambiguous, it yields a plethora of fresh insights on different occasions.

The two pursuits, then, decide merit by almost contradictory criteria. Science prefers precision, clarity, and quick obsolescence, while art advocates ambiguity, infinite variety, and longevity. Which probably explains, among other things, Freud's mixed fate. His influence in science has been limited because, in the opinion of many, his vague postulates defy disproof. But his provocative insights into the mysteries of the human psyche have, according to artistic criteria, rarely been bettered. Hence his huge effect on the arts; modern drama and literature, for example, would have taken quite different directions had he never surfaced.

3. Public access. As Kuhn has pointed out[64], public access provides a second difference. Whereas science/philosophy was once widely read, nowadays it is elitist and almost secretive. Conducted in jargon and symbols, it requires specialized training. The average person readily admits an inability to understand, comment on, or evaluate it.* Art, on the other hand, once the exclusive domain of nobles and ecclesiastics, has become increasingly populist, especially with recordings, prints, paperbacks, and other inexpensive paraphernalia being mass marketed. Today's Everyperson, confident that their opinion is

---

* Some scientists see this as unfortunate and even dangerous. Since people pay for and are greatly affected by scientific research, they should not remain ignorant of its harvests. Thus, Canadian biologist David Suzuki uses his very popular, informative radio and TV programs to acquaint the public with the latest scientific developments.

as good as anyone else's, freely judges any art with which they come in contact.

Although this distinction may seem trivial, it could affect the type of person choosing each career. A prospective artist, while personally a recluse, might need to show off, to seek (in Freud's famous phrase) "Honour, power, wealth, fame and the love of women."[65] A budding scientist, while equally reclusive, might prefer to withdraw completely into science, seeking respect from only a small group of peers. In other words, both artist and scientist desire recognition, but from different segments of humanity.

Which returns us at last to the main point. We tried to distinguish art from science to decide whether they might require different abilities and hence attract different sorts of people. We found an ample supply of information but it neither helped nor defended our assertion that the artist and scientist are actually different breeds. Fortunately, Kuhn has provided a theory that will perhaps help us defend this suspicion.

4. <u>Two types of scientist</u>. Kuhn has distinguished between two brands of scientist, the <u>normal</u> and the <u>revolutionary</u>.[66] The first, by far more common, work within a prevailing paradigm, providing answers to the questions it poses. They are, to use Kuhn's own label, "problem solvers," because the paradigm will conclusively decide whether their contributions are worthwhile. Revolutionary scientists, on the other hand, advance new paradigms. They are a more "creative," almost an artistic breed since, according to Kuhn, a paradigm's superiority is decided by value judgments. (Others, pre- and post-Kuhn, have suggested similar distinctions. Thus, Cannon contrasted <u>guessers</u> (revealers of new directions) and <u>accumulators</u> (collectors of facts)[67], while Kaplan pitted <u>routine</u>, productive science, leading to technological innovation, against <u>oddball</u> science.[68]) The new recruit seems neater, simpler, even more beautiful.

In Kuhn's words:

> Since no paradigm ever solves all the problems it defines and since no two paradigms leave all the same problems unsolved, paradigm debates always involve the question, Which problems is it more significant to have solved? Like the issue of competing standards, that question of values can be answered only in terms of criteria that lie outside of normal science altogether, and it is recourse to <u>external criteria</u> that most obviously makes paradigm debates revolutionary (italics mine).[69]

104

Admittedly, the new paradigm may also seem empirically better, since it will encompass those very anomalies that destroyed its predecessor. What is often forgotten in the headlong stampede onto the new bandwagon is that there were undoubtedly other phenomena that this outmoded alternative handled more capably. But these will typically be swept under the rug or modified so they fit the new religion. Now normal science closely resembles the textbook version. Since a paradigm decrees how data are to be interpreted and which data are important, so long as it remains in vogue such data can provide the necessary objective standard for theoretical decision making. Furthermore, there will certainly be an impression of progress when so many heretofore embarrassing puzzles are conquered.

Kuhn in fact argues that textbooks misrepresent science by portraying only the normal brand. If that is so, then should not those choosing science as a career be those who find normal science appealing? Normal science differs markedly from art; ergo, most scientists should differ from artists. But why, then, did most of our apparently clear-cut differences collapse? Probably because in portraying science and scientists, we included the revolutionaries, the misfits who, from Kuhn's perspective, are almost artists in disguise (and remember Einstein's attachment to the violin!). Their personalities and working practices only muddied our lens, rendering science more "artistic" than it usually is.

If we confined our attention to the normal, problem-solving scientists, how might they differ from artists? Kuhn has pictured them (perhaps somewhat unfairly) as rather plodding and unimaginative, neither seeking novel ideas nor valuing them until they have been objectively, publicly substantiated. These normal scientists prefer precise, unambiguous concepts to the "multileveled" and perceive worldly phenomena as coherent, logical, and measurable. Therefore, they might be somewhat intolerant of ambiguity, finding it not intimidating, but irritating. But the revolutionary brethren of these scientific foot soldiers might, like artists, be more willing to venture out on imaginative limbs and gamble on subjective, unverified hunches.

In this regard, Knapp[70] guesses that science (by which he seems to mean normal science) prevails between periods of religious orthodoxy and more casual, secular heterodoxy. It is less stoic and doctrinaire than stiff-upper-lip religion, but more so than the other extreme of an implied continuum.* We might guess

---

* Knapp's connecting the psychologies of science and religion raises some intriguing, if slightly peripheral possibilities. Given that science arose when religious orthodoxy was on the

(although Knapp does not) that artists and revolutionary
scientists--less compulsive, more emotional and
self-expressive--should occupy that other extreme.

Anne Roe's studies of scientists provide some empirical
support for hypothesizing differences.[71] Admittedly, she rarely
compared scientists to artists, and did report many qualities
that can be found in both groups. But when subsequently she
compared her study of scientists to an earlier one of painters,[72]
she did find some differences between the two. The artists
moved earlier to specialized training and had less formal education,
so they might have shown lower IQ scores, a point not verified.
(Knapp, too, found that scientists on the whole choose their
careers later in life than do artists.[73]) In addition, Roe's
scientists tended to have fathers in the professions, while the
artists' family backgrounds were more variable. (Here Knapp
parts company; his scientists came usually from the lower
socioeconomic strata, the artists from either the highest or
lowest.) In Rorschach and interview testing, the scientists
showed healthy, if rather remote, parental relationships, while
the artists had unresolved oedipal problems. Still, the ubiquitous
chicken and egg must be resurrected. Frequently, parents disapprove
of artistic interests and career choices. This could produce
the troubled relationships, rather than the latter determining
the career decision.

Emotionality also differed. Delight, dismay, anger, euphoria,
and the like occur during both activities. Artists, however,
often can express these in their work, subtly or openly, while
scientists, whose products are impersonal and detached, cannot.

-----

wane, and that it reigns supreme in our secular age, perhaps
its underlying faith in reason, order, and logic, together with
its unambiguous criteria for making decisions, provide the same
comforts and defense mechanisms that religion once did. Note
the similarities. Science substitutes the inviolate dogma of
"the fact" for that of Holy Writ. Its Nobel Prize winners and
the like become canonized saints who deserve our unthinking
reverence. It uses foreign tongues (mathematics and computerese)
as the Church once used Latin, to discourage lay persons'
understanding, thus denying them admittance to the inner sanctum
because they were insufficiently knowledgeble. They must take
the enlightened minority's decrees "on faith," without question.
The Church sold indulgences to smooth the path to eternal bliss.
So too do telethons and door-to-door blitzes convince the public
that their largesse to science will keep those modern
devils--cancer, heart disease and even herpes--from their doors.
Our cure for all ills and our comfort for all distress, is
science, perchance, the new opium of the people?

Furthermore, both groups showed the typical sexual androgyny, but the artists were more open about sexual matters and more passive and submissive in their general demeanor, while the scientists clung more stubbornly to their opinions. Lastly, Roe suggests some differences between the two acts themselves. The initial discovery may in both cases be self-expressive, but painters expose themselves more in their finished work, while a scientific report's author is stylistically hidden. As well, scientific work, unlike the artistic, has focus and direction. Therefore, like Kuhn, she sees it to be a problematic rather than creative activity.

Liam Hudson's[74] distinction between two types of thinkers, based on their performance on various psychological tests, also echoes the present distinction. Convergers are more comfortable with problem-solving situations such as conventional IQ tests than with the more open-ended, "creative" variety, whereas divergers show the reverse preference. And the former make up the bulk of the scientific population, while the latter are usually found in the arts.

Furthermore, Hudson reports marked personality differences between these two types. Convergers display more conventional attitudes, more respect for and deference to authority, are less prone to both humor and violence, more likely to marry, less likely to divorce, and even show different patterns of sleeping and dreaming. Still, their suppressed violent/aggressive tendencies, when released, seem unusually intense. Elaborating on this last point McClelland[75] speculates that scientists may harbor deep aggressive feelings which they only control with difficulty. For this reason, they attempt to subjugate the external world to impersonal laws. He suggests too that they work almost obsessively and dislike deep personal contact or open emotion. They therefore prefer more "impersonal" arts, such as music or photography, over painting or poetry which are more personally revealing.

5. Some questions about the arts. Before ending this section, we might apply Kuhn's notions to several artistic matters. First, various schools or "isms", such as classicism, impressionism, romanticism, and so on, have for a time dictated styles of work. Are these akin to scientific paradigms? Was Beethoven, who almost single-handedly overthrew one dominant tradition and founded another, a revolutionary like Einstein? Certainly an artistic revolution will dramatically change the type of new contribution as well as the interpretations given to previous ones (as witness the bombastic renderings of Mozart and Bach by nineteenth-century conductors[76]).

However, Kuhn classifies disciplines as pre-paradigmatic when their state of development is such that one paradigm does not exclusively hold sway but several compete. The social sciences warrant this classification and so too, it would seem, do the arts. In the romantic era, for example, one school, headed by Brahms, preached a return to the classicism of Beethoven and Mozart, while the Liszt- Wagner crowd propagandized a "music of the future." Similarly, the twentieth century has produced "serialists" (Schoenberg/Webern/Berg), "neoclassicists" (Stravinsky), and "nationalists" (Bartók), all of whom part company with one another.[77] Clearly, no single outlook is close to being universally accepted.

Also, artistic and scientific revolutions differ. Both are precipitated by dissatisfaction and a sense of stasis, but in art these feelings stem, not from empirical anomalies, but from a sense that everything which can be said in the dominant form has been said. As well, the major adherents of an overthrown scientific paradigm will become passe, of only historical interest. Whereas artists from earlier epochs may fall temporarily from fashion (as did Bach during the classical era and as have romantics like Liszt in our day), but will usually be resurrected to win their permanent place. In other words, artistic fashions will return, but those of science, once they wane, wax no more.

Lastly, is there an artistic species analagous to the normal scientist? Interpretive, performing artists, we suggest, might fit this description. They too begin with a set of preconceptions handed down by someone else, such as a script, score, or piece of choreography. They have leeway to find their own particular solution to these puzzling stimuli, but there are limits. They still must work within a preconceived framework rather than providing their own. Do performing artists display personality profiles similar to normal scientists? It seems a question worth pursuit.

Communication of Results

We move now to the last stage of the process. Man does not live by bread alone, and a product's success does not depend solely on its merit. Many other factors of a management/business variety come into play after it is finished. Creative work of any kind is a highly competitive business, so political, marketing, and public relations savvy are important considerations, whether we like it or not. In the long run, it is unlikely that such skills can compensate for an inferior product, but a good one can founder without them.

108

While popular stereotype may portray the creator as an airy, impractical daydreamer incapable of writing a press release or balancing a budget, it is not always accurate. Many fine workers, e.g., Shaw and choreographer Merce Cunningham, can hold their own in any business conference, and by all indications both Bach and Will Shakespeare knew on which side their bread was buttered.

Yet once this is said, it must be admitted that many creatives are unquestionably incompetent at and thoroughly dislike these matters. Why so? First of all, creators must now be gregarious, practical, and economically realistic--skills, as Stein points out, not needed earlier in the process and not usually stored in their psychological armory.[78] Also, training institutions have, until recently, done little to teach such skills, so graduates have had to learn them in the marketplace.

Lastly, the work into which creators have poured so much time and energy has, up to now, been exclusively theirs. Although some sense of detachment will have begun to set in, the feeling will be compounded when they must share that work with others. In fact, during this phase they sometimes resemble parents at their offsprings' nuptials, pushed hither and yon by photographers and florists and having little influence over the course of events. Now that their work is done, they may feel rather left out. Notice the artist wandering aimlessly around a gallery at his or her opening, as a fashionable audience munches its wine and sips its cheese. Between devastating remarks about the economy, so-and-so's hat, and the terrible catering arrangements, these consumers may deign to cast a casual glance at a painting over which our artist has sweated buckets of blood. One patronizing remark from them can make it all seem pointless.

Because creators so often find this stage difficult and painful, they often defer to what Stein[78] has called intermediaries, i.e., individuals who, one way or another, intervene between creators and their general public, influencing the success of their interaction. Their role is important, yet it has received relatively little attention in discussions of the creative process. We shall therefore examine two examples, one of which will receive additional scrutiny later on.

Entrepreneurs: Serge Diaghilev

Unmistakably, managers, agents, public relations experts and the like crucially influence creative success. A symphony orchestra or ballet company desperately needs good management or promotion, but the requisite combination of artistic sensibility and business acumen is quite rare and extremely valuable. Too often, the occupants of these positions are either frustrated artists who think balancing a budget is beneath contempt, or hard-nosed business people determined to run the organization with the crude efficiency of a fast food dealership, not realizing that in this context a heftier profit margin (or, more accurately, a smaller deficit) is not the main index of achievement.

Impressario Serge Diaghilev, the founder/driving force behind the Ballet Russe de Monte Carlo, best demonstrates the talented entrepreneur's value.[79] By general agreement, the Ballet Russe was among the most important of all artistic organizations; dictating standards and influencing every sphere of society in the years just before and after the 1914-1918 war. The list of those who at one time or another contributed to its destinies reads like a who's who of twentieth century art. Composers Stravinsky, Ravel, Debussy, Prokofiev, and Satie; designers Bakst, Benois, and Picasso; choreographers Fokine, Massine, Balanchine, and Nijinsky; dancers Karsavina, Pavlova, Nijinsky, Lifar, Massine, Dolin, and Markova. But the Ballet Russe was much more than a helter-skelter conglomeration of talented individuals. It was an integrated whole, a Gestalt. Surprisingly, it attained success, not by pandering to conservative tastes and offering the familiar, but by emphasizing novelty. Its radical productions (The Rite of Spring being the most notorious) stimulated constant controversy.

Diaghilev was the Ballet Russe's heart and soul, the irreplacable component. Without him it would not have come into being, and after his death it quickly languished. Yet Diaghilev's special talents were not so much those of the creative artist as of the "intermediary" extraordinaire. He was unsurpassed at recognizing genius in others, especially the young or unknown, at bringing these prodigies together, and at supplying the necessary resources so that they could collaborate in comparative harmony. A master psychologist, he was a supreme promoter, fund raiser, and diplomat who could twist even the most foreboding of temperaments to his purposes and wheedle funds from even the most reluctant purse. For him the end justified any means.

Ironically, this nonartist fitted the stereotypic creative personality as have few others. He was fiendishly devious and manipulative, vain, neurotically hypochondriac, wildly temperamental, and openly deviant sexually. The ultimate taker of risks, ever willing to gamble on new productions and untried talent, he annually accumulated monumental deficits. In true creative fashion, these economic matters did not concern him. He had a legendary tenacity and persistence in pursuit of his goals[80] and was almost neurotically possessive of those who worked for him. When Stravinsky accepted a commission to develop his Histoire d'un Soldat elsewhere, Diaghilev took it as almost a breach of trust and showed no interest in the work whatsoever.[81]

110

He reveled in the scandals, not least because of their publicity value. Unfortunately, his neverending search for novelty was, in some opinions,[82] his eventual undoing. It led to a decline in standards; absolutely anything that was different came to be desirable. Still, Diaghilev was undoubtedly a creative genius. His product was nothing less than the Ballet Russe, and few have achieved more.

Critics

While these aisle sitters obviously affect creative success, they have received suprisingly little attention. In correcting this oversight, we shall first discuss the nature of their work which is frequently misunderstood. As well, criticism seems a strange career to choose, inviting notoriety and antipathy rather than popularity, so we shall suggest some possible personality traits of those who do so choose. And later we shall ask our theoretical perspectives to comment on their work. In all this, we shall on occasion resort to introspection, since we have practiced criticism ourselves. (In penance for this sin, we have also received our share of critical slings and arrows as a producer.)

1. The need for criticism. Are critics necessary? Despite their periodic gaffes, we must answer affirmatively. Were we to indiscriminately accept everything, the steady deluge of pap would quickly bury quality work. Moreover the best critics also play a more positive role, interpreting difficult works (which may be their most important task) and publicizing worthwhile novelties to encourage the attention of an ordinarily conservative public (e.g., The New York Times' John Martin almost singlehandedly promoted America's fledgling modern dance movement[83]) and informing not only the present but also the future of "what it was like to be there on that night."[84]

In science, according to Popper,[85] criticism is equally crucial, since human progress depends on the disproof of erroneous ideas. In his view, it allows open societies to discover and eliminate errors while totalitarian ones, by discouraging questioning, are doomed to woeful obsolescence. Scientists, then, should welcome adverse opinion, for it will uncover their work's worthwhile aspects.

Similarly, Dr. Johnson believed that the targets of his critical wrath should thank him, as he did the assailants of his Lives of the Poets, for:

> I would rather be attacked than unnoticed. For
> the worst thing you can do to an author is to
> be silent as to his works. An assault upon a

111

town is a bad thing; but starving it is still worse.[86]

Many professional critics are likewise nonplussed when negative reviews anger creatives. The critic wants only to help, to collaborate rather than confront. Don't creators understand? This attitude seems decidedly unrealistic, as Stanley Kauffmann has recognized:

> A work of art of any kind is a tremendous investment of ego, of self, of nakedness....If someone tells you you're deformed after you've exposed yourself, the more truthful he is, the more you hate him....If (someone) hates me for negative things I've written about him, I never resent it in the slightest. Why shouldn't he?....I don't expect them to be reasonable.[87]

Finally, we humans cannot experience anything--be it movies, paintings, or hockey games--without automatically judging its merit. We grade exam papers, cheer quarterbacks, and boo referees. We praise those who risk and succeed, but are merciless to those who fail. Even in the sexual arena, where animals breed indiscriminately, we choose our partners raptly. For Pirsig, therefore,[88] science's emphasis on value-free perception is unrealistic; we simply cannot do it. Similarly, Bertrand Russell states, "I do not admit that a person without bias exists."[89] That being so, surely the presumably more enlightened voice of the critic should not only be heard but carry special weight as that censure which must o'erweigh a whole theatre of others. Why we have this judgemental tendency is a fascinating question which our theories should face (Pirsig does not), but if we are all critics at heart, to summarily lynch those that practise the profession (more than one artist's fantasy) seems pointless. Criticism will not go away.

As well, let us remember, a critic's power varies greatly across media. In science, full-time critics virtually do not exist. Journal editors, while choosing the research to publish, rarely comment publicly on it, the readership being sufficiently knowledgeable to decide for itself. In addition, their skill as active researchers, rather than as evaluators, has usually gained them their position, so they may later be judged by those they now judge. The consequences are mixed. On the one hand, journal editors are probably more sympathetic and constructive. They understand how painful is even kind negative opinion, let alone needless sarcasm (many artistic critics, judging by their remarks, do not). This artistic variety need fear only angry letters (which they can ignore or even welcome as proof that they are widely read), or glasses of punch flung in

112

their face (thus did dancer Sallie Wilson, to wide applause, chastise Clive Barnes).

On the other hand, science's judges, actively involved as they are, may be less sympathetic to radical ideas that challenge their own. If they allocate funds for granting agencies, they may actually invoke censorship by preventing an unknown neophyte with a seemingly hair-brained idea from pursuing it; without funding, much research is impossible. In the arts, few critics possess such ultimate power, since a writer, for example, needs only paper, typewriter, and wastebasket. At any rate, the general public, certainly affected by science, has little say in its machinations. A small group of "backroom boys," clad in labcoats and huddled in presumably smoke-filled laboratories, decide yay or nay.

In this, the arts differ. In the more commercial, pop-mass fields, public opinion is all-powerful and critical influence nil; no one cares what Pauline Kael thinks about Return of the Jedi, or William Littler about the Sex Pistols. However, critics can affect more serious, adventurous work, bringing obscure novelties to their potential audience's attention. Undoubtedly, one favorable paragraph in The New York Times can repay twenty years'[90] pianistic practice. Likewise, as William Goldman's The Season reveals, critics fundamentally influence the commercial Broadway theatre. There, the "hit or flop" philosophy decrees that a show either "gets the reviews" and prospers, or faces instant demise. Thus, a few rumpled Osirises (the number varies with newspaper bankruptcies) pronounce life and death. Their flattering remarks (often lifted hilariously out of context, since even a devastating notice will contain the odd unpejorative phrase) adorn every marquee and ad. PROVOCATIVE DRAMA (Kerr, Times) or SLAMBANG MUSICAL SMASH (Featherbed, Akron Garmentworkers Monthly)-the practice continues, although customers may pay no heed whatever.* But suppose they do. Why? Certainly the upward spirals in ticket prices and Manhattan muggings discourages their venturing[90] Times Squareward without reassurance. But also, Bookspan suggests,[91], they may simply be too lazy to form their own opinions. For the critic's power the public should blame itself,

---

* Producer David Merrick, "the abominable showman," located seven gentlemen, each having the same name as one grouch on the aisle. He wined and dined them before taking them to his late, unlamented musical, Subways are for Sleeping. Their quotes then allowed his ads to trumpet, in all legality, "Wonderful Show" (Howard Taubman), "Great evening in the theatre" (Walter Kerr), and so on. Merrick failed to mention that these particular gentlemen did not write reviews.

and it may also console itself that the said power is nowhere what it once was. Diana Rigg reports:

> By 1572, a player staging a casual performance risked brutal consequences: 'to be grievously whipped and burnt through the gristle of the right ear with a hot iron of the compass of an inch about, manifesting his or her roguish kind of life.' Second offences were judged to be felonies and third offenses entailed death 'without benefit of sanctuary or clergy.'[92]

2. Criticism <u>and</u> creativity. Is criticism (we must next ask) a creative act? Let us first distinguish <u>critics</u> from <u>reviewers</u>, those ignorant hacks appointed through being insufficiently literate to write readable obituaries. Isadora Duncan mentions one scribe who continually chided her lack of musicality, a talent in which she took justifiable pride. He was, she later found, quite deaf, unable to hear a note![93] But true critics <u>are</u> artists, similarly seeking not only to think through but also to express personal impressions of an experience that lacks right answers. Critics announce their presence, not by their opinions, but by their reasons for holding them and by the style with which they defend them. In fact, critics will usually dismiss evaluation as an uninteresting, necessary evil demanded by editors and public. Thus, we may well disagree with critics while still enjoying their musings, whereas upon concurring with the typical reviewer, we wonder where we went wrong. Too, critics must possess rare perceptive and interpretive powers, to recognize quality and to discover what a work actually says, since its producer will typically only vaguely understand. Indeed, many critics see this interpretation as the most interesting and important part of their job. Hence the critical art, like everything great, will stand the test of time and speak with clarity to the future. Likewise, a critic's ability, Kauffmann for one suspects,[94] can be sharpened by instruction, but only where some natural talent exists.

Still, direct life experiences supply the artist's material, while critics need both life and art for their work. Should we then call them parasites? Kauffmann, while rejecting this deprecation, sees criticism as a lesser art. As does Simon,[95] although critical and artistic processes seem to him very similar. Yet for Oscar Wilde, reportedly,[96] criticism <u>surpassed</u> art, precisely because it encompassed two very different phenomena.

To lay rest another misconception, critics are <u>not</u> invariably failed artists who have been driven by their inadequacies reluctantly to another career, so their every perception is colored with envy. In fact, while some great critics (such as

114

Shaw, Schumann, Berlioz, and Johnson) have had impeccable artistic
credentials, and while famous critics have sometimes turned to
creation (Walter Kerr has written and directed for Broadway,
and Kenneth Tynan has penned Oh, Calcutta! which box-office
criteria at least decreed a masterpiece), a superior artist,
egocentrically self-centered, may well make a disastrous critic.
Dylan Thomas' editors, for example, had to water down his venomous
judgments of others' work before printing them.[97] Indeed, untalented
artists, athletes, and scholars frequently make the best teachers
and commentators, for when something is difficult, we must think
more deeply about it. Very few current NHL coaches were themselves
star players, whereas Bobby Orr was an abominable coach, having
little understanding of others' limitations or of the skills he
found so natural.

Nevertheless, dance critic Anna Kisselgoff[98] feels that,
while critics needn't be good at the field on which they comment,
they should have extensive training and experience in it. She
studied both ballet and modern dance because "you just don't
look at something for the first time and write about it."[99]
For Bookspan too[100] a critic of performance should have had
some performing experience, to understand the hazards and efforts
involved. In addition, it goes without saying, any critic will
have experienced many works in the genre to provide needful
standards of comparison; a naive critic is a contradiction in
terms. Genuine critics, then, prefer to do what they do, to
sit in the audience and consume. Rosner and Abt's informative
interviews[101] reveal that most chose their careers because they
wanted, not to dance, or paint, or compose, but to write.
They are not failed artists but successful journalists. As a
result, Kerr[102] denies their power hunger, asserting that not
one would resign if that power was obliterated. Inveterate
gossips, they so love the theatre that they can't shut up
about it. Boundless enthusiasm for quality, not jaded cynicism
for garbage, sets them apart. Witness Kerr's remarks about My
Fair Lady (which admittedly deserved superlatives):

> A show so dazzlingly melodic and visually rich
> in its first act that it scarcely needed a
> second--and so emotionally binding in its second
> that you wondered why you were merely dazzled
> by the first....(it) invites any and all
> performers to simply lift the lid from its treasure
> chest and avail themselves of its glistening
> baubles.[103]

Let the caricature of the cantankerous critic be consigned to
mothballs.

At any rate, contrary to another common objection, critics have every right to comment about fields in which they may be unskilled. Theirs is an art form related to, yet diverging from, others; it's a different job. Here is Dr. Johnson again:

> You may abuse a tragedy though you cannot write one. You may scold a carpenter who has made you a bad table, even though you cannot make a table. It is not your trade to make tables.[104]

But if Concerned Reader avows anything, it is that critics should be "objective," somehow avoiding personal bias to evaluate each work on its own merits.[105] Curiously, some critics agree that they should merely describe rather than judge, so readers can decide for themselves. Others, while seeing a need for evaluation, agree that it should keep a work's particular aims in mind. Thus, film critic Judith Crist: "I don't judge a Disney film on the same terms on which I judge a Bergman film."[106] Up to a point, these attitudes seem defensible. If a work seeks only to be an amusing diversion and succeeds, should it be lambasted for not being something else? As well, a critic's narrow, inflexible biases will prevent insightful comments on the genuinely innovative. To do so, critics must constantly rethink their attitudes about "what is good." And certainly those who mount vituperative vendettas simply out of personal or political animosity should be condemned to covering weddings and fashion shows.

Still, these demands are at bottom debatable. Is absolutely any underlying artistic purpose equally acceptable? Does, therefore, a well-produced, profound statement of Nazi philosophy warrant raves? Clearly this will not do. At some point we must judge a work's aims, as well as its success in meeting them. Moreover, asking critics to be "objective" is asking the impossible, given that we all evaluate. And anyway, by suppressing their opinions they would become mere reporters, their writing vapid and sterile. As Bertrand Russell put it, "A book, like any other work, should be held together by its point of view."[107]

Thus, Tynan openly plumped for virtually every working-class, kitchen drama, such as John Osborne's Look Back in Anger, that saw the British fog.[108] For him, every good play had a political attitude, preferably well left of center. Hence his fondness for Brecht and his impatience with Terence Rattigan (he of Separate Tables), who aimed to "entertain" and not offend the bourgeois audience personified by Aunt Edna. To Tynan, a playwright not offending Aunt Edna isn't doing his job.

Those were Tynan's biases, openly admitted, so we were hardly done a disservice. In other words, a review is only

116

one person's opinion, a truism that honest critics will avow more fervently than anyone. If readers nonetheless attach cosmic importance to their every utterance, they are hardly to blame. Actually, "average theatregoer" should probably consult anyone except a critic while contemplating ticket purchase. Introspectively, the prospect of later writing a notice greatly affects perception, e.g., we will attend with unusual intensity, thus gaining very different impressions from someone seeking only casual diversion, apres dinner and drinks, and pres dancing and debauche.

But Concerned Reader is not finished yet. He will doubtless still assert that critics' comments should be "constructive", meaning that they should act in part like teachers. A student, to improve, must be informed about errors and about possible remedial action, and certainly creators learn little from remarks like "Mr. X's latest epic is the largest pile of rubbish since Sodom and Gomorrah." Interestingly, many critics do see themselves clad partly in this pedagogic guise,[109] but readers rather than creators seem their main targets. And others clearly disagree entirely. Otherwise, how could they feel free to say virtually anything that is not outright libel about the latter? Or perhaps, in instructing them, they believe that sparing the rod spoils the child? George Jean Nathan has attempted to defend their frequent cruelty.

> Any sound dramatic critic must periodically be guilty of vulgarity and bad manners. If a plawright--insults invited critical attention by hitting it in the face with a contemptible and overly odiferous cheese pie, it is pretty hard to figure out why he should not be hit in the face, in turn, with an even larger and juicier critical equivalent. The critic who meets excessively bad manners in such artistic directions with good manners may be a gentleman, but he is a damned weak, ineffective and unread critic. Good manners are for press agents.[110]

To put it bluntly, this is hogwash. It assumes that an artist intentionally, out of pure spite, has produced "odiferous" work. None to our knowledge have ever done so. In our view, the creative person is a rare, valuable commodity. When he or she fails, we should not lie. But "nays" can be rendered in different ways, and cruelty is never justified. There is too much of it in the world as it is, and surely the arts, those supposed "civilizers," should work to eliminate it rather than add to it. As well it may convince that creator never to risk again. Fortunately, some critics[111] do accept responsibility towards creators. Walter Kerr says somewhere that critics must encourage writers, even after failure, to keep trying, because "what we need more than anything are next plays." That's the teacher for our school.

All of which makes us ask, why do critics react venemously to incompetence, as if they had been insulted? Disappointment we understand, but anger? Goldman[112] says simply that criticism is a lousy job, demanding much consuming of mindboggling ineptitudes, so only a perversely bitter unemployable will long remain (and apparently serious critics do frequently burn out[113]). As well, many critics want renown. Being controversial is one way to obtain it as is, Kauffmann points out, playing to the would-be sophisticates who prefer to dislike everything and for whom "enthusiasm" is a four-letter word. Furthermore, America has long valued the irritable curmudgeon like H. L. Mencken or George S. Kaufman. Is there anyone who does not secretly treasure the latter's scathing indictment of one play: that he saw it under unfair circumstance, when the curtain was up?[114] And lastly, critics who have not themselves created may not appreciate the torment induced by a sarcastic notice--hence Bookspan's injunction that they should all try that other side of the fence. Still, other artists, from whom we might expect more understanding, oftentimes display unrivalled cruelty towards failure. Here is Shaw:

> The artist...who accounts for my disparagement
> by alleging personal animosity on my part is
> quite right. When people do less than their
> best, I hate them, loathe them, detest them,
> long to tear them limb from limb and strew
> them in goblets about the stage or platform....The
> true critic is the man who becomes your personal
> enemy on the sole provocation of a bad performance,
> and will only be appeased by good performances.[115]

Thus we propose another explanation. We begin with a vivid memory. Ken Dryden, goaltender supreme, (always excepting, unhappily for Canadians, that Horatio of the freeze, the Soviet Union's Vladislav Tretiak), led the Montreal Canadiens to an unprecedented four consecutive Stanley Cups during the late 1970's. His temporary "retirement" over a salary dispute showed his importance; the team, otherwise intact, plummeted to mediocrity. We take you now to the 1979 playoffs. Dryden, standing in his accustomed place but suddenly merely mortal, encounters a streak of inadequacy. The Montreal fans, demanding perfection, are restless. At first only a few boos assault our ears but, as Dryden's difficulties and the opposition's score both continue to mount, the Bronx cheers become a torrent. At the buzzer, the dauntless Dryden, once master of all he surveyed, exits with head bowed. Next game the raspberries reappear undiminished and Dryden, now completely shaken, fans on the first two shots. Heretofore, he is more irreplaceable than Atlas, but suddenly one Bunny Larocque, holder of the Guinness record for most splinters accumulated in backside, now tends the twine.

Like carnivorous wolves, we too seem angered by weakness, especially in those who risk rare achievement and come up short. So too the critic? John Simon, himself an infamous assassin, says that, contrary to rumor, he does not enjoy writing a scathing notice, but it cathartically releases and cleanses his anger at ineptitude so he can approach subsequent work fresh.[116] We surmise from this that critics' seemingly insensitive cruelty, like their tendency to judge, simply manifests a pervasive human tendency. So before censuring them, let us look to ourselves. We do not begin to understand why we possess this sadistic tendency that, in the extreme, can cause us even to jeer the physically and psychologically handicapped. It seems completely maladaptive and destructive. Yet we cannot dismiss it as confined to a small, diseased minority. It is far too widespread. So here is another question for our theoretical perspectives.

3. Who becomes a critic? What type of person chooses a critical career? Is William Archer correct when he asserts that the first necessity for a dramatic critic is the ability to sleep while sitting bolt upright?[117] Informative personality data from tests are not yet available,[118] so we shall substitute some informal prediction/guesswork. First, critics will doubtless encounter hostility from both creators and public, as witness Sir Thomas Beecham's reply when he was asked to endow a university chair of criticism. "Gladly, so long as it's an electric chair!" (Sir Thomas, presumably, would serve as the electrical conductor.) Prospective critics must at least endure, and even enjoy, such hatred. Frequently labeled sadistic, they may in fact lean more towards masochism, and in this way at least perhaps resemble judges in other fields. Do we not also marvel at the strange souls who volunteer to referee soccer and expose themselves to the certain wrath of 100,000 fanatics? At the least, they must certainly have wondrously thick skins!

In many respects critics' profiles may resemble the typical creator's. They too seem introverted, shy, and aloof. As a result, they display a similar Jekyll-and-Hyde paradox, albeit not within their personalities. Oftentimes the most brutal literature flows from a veritable Caspar Milquetoast, in comparison to whom even Walter Mitty would seem like Attila the Hun. As well, critics, like most artists, waste little time wondering why they do it. Several, when this question was asked of them, were openly nonplussed because they had never thought about it. Clearly, their career's peculiarities had not struck them. Then too they, like creators, must possess healthy egos

119

(as several readily admit[119]); otherwise they would not inflict their opinions on others. In addition, they must obviously possess the same need not only to understand an experience but also to share it through communication. Lastly, they also will frequently display a naive streak, at least as regards the antipathy their negative pronouncements evoke. Wide-eyed innocents, they wonder why others are so upset.

But differences arise. Criticism requires at least equal linear intellectuality but perhaps less right hemisphere imagination than does creation. Kenneth Tynan's succinct description bears repeating: "A critic knows the way but can't drive the car."[120] If so, then most of them should fit the high IQ, low-creative category several times delineated,[121] and described by Schiller:

> The reason for your (inability to create) lies, it seems to me, in the constraint which your intellect imposes upon your imagination.
> .....Apparently it is not good, and indeed it hinders the creative work of the mind--if the intellect examines too closely the ideas already pouring in, as it were, at the gates...In the case of a creative mind, it seems to me, the intellect has withdrawn its watchers from the gates, and the ideas rush in pell-mell, and only then does it review and inspect the multitude. You worthy critics, or whatever you may call yourselves, are ashamed or afraid of the momentary and passing madness which is found in all creators....You reject too soon and discriminate too severely.[122]

Should this hypothesis be valid, then, the aforementioned personality differences (see Chapter 3) between this category and high IQ, high creatives should also distinguish creators from critics. Hence, the former should, for example, fear risks and mistakes (although critics who choose their calling because it's "safer" are in for a surprise), possess a less robust sense of humor, and have enjoyed and done well in school.

Relevant here is Bruner's distinction[123] between children who want to learn about the world for themselves, and those who prefer to get ideas from others (as, in a real sense, critics do). Predictably, the former prefer problem solving; the latter, rote learning and regurgitation. Disturbingly, analytic ability, so important for effective criticism, seems poor in that second group. If therein lie most of the critics, we can understand why good ones are so rare. At any rate, we suspect that critics may resemble teachers and missionaries as much as creators. They too wish to inform, educate, and convert others (and several, notably Kerr and Simon, did begin as teachers).

With that, we leave empirical matters and turn to theory. At the outset, we mention two restrictions. First, for each perspective, we will initially present some basic premises, but the uninformed reader should realize that our versions of, say, Sartre or Freud are hardly exhaustive. They dwell only on those ideas relevant to the discussions of creativity. Those readers seeking completeness might consult Hall and Lindzey,[124] Maddi[125] or Sahakian.[126] Second, we reiterate that most accounts have quite ignored the foregoing facts of creativity. It seems pointless to recite, in each critical commentary, the same gloomy catalogue of evaded data so we will consider only those most relevant to the perspective in question.

Part II

THEORIES OF PERSONAL AUTONOMY

The perspectives in this section assume that human beings possess free will. They are capable of making decisions that are not influenced by antecedent factors beyond their control. Therefore they must bear the responsibility for their choices. These perspectives also avow that creativity occurs because of the very nature of the human species and/or of existence. Therefore, it is a universal tendency that is automatic and even inevitable, in many ways the most fundamental of all activities. To be human is to be creative. In a real sense, it is not the presence of creativity so much as its frequent absence that requires explanation. Why are so many people not creative?

Chapter 6

EXISTENTIAL APPROACHES I: BASIC PREMISES AND ALBERT CAMUS

Most of existentialism's major themes have been voiced
repeatedly over the centuries but, by general agreement, this
philosophical position was formally baptized when the nineteenth
century's angry man, Kierkegaard, took pen in hand to demolish
the writings of Hegel. It has particularly come into its own
since World War II, it being de rigueur for all would-be
intellectuals of the 1950's to brazenly display in back pocket
or brief case their copies of Sartre's Being and Nothingness.
They may even have read it. Modern psychology has been as
much influenced by this movement as has any field, as we shall
learn in the chapters to follow.

Existentialism

To discuss existentialism as a general philosophy is not
only fiendishly difficult, it is almost a contradiction in terms.
For, to anticipate a later point, it is above all a philosophy
of the individual. Truth, for example, is a subjective and
idiosyncratic, rather than a universal and objective, concept.
There is no "truth," but only someone's truth. What is valid
for one person may or may not be so for another. Thus, one
slogan emblazoned on existential banners reads, "Thou shalt not
generalize." As a result, existentialism actually refers, not
to one integrated philosophical system, but to many emanations
from some disparate and often contrary personalities.

It is equally difficult to decide who should be included
in this category. Many who would seem to qualify, such as
Karl Jaspers, have themselves rejected the existentialist label
because it suggests that their ideas might have some general
applicability (which is unthinkable). Other likely candidates,
such as Albert Camus, have had the label rejected for them,[1]
since they do not accept some characteristic beliefs.

What are the beliefs shared by all members of this club
that does not know who its members are and denies, as a matter
of principle, that shared beliefs are either desirable or possible?
It would seem futile to try to answer this question. Nevertheless,
rushing in where wise men have feared to tread, we shall do
so.

1. Dreadful freedom. One belief common to them all, at
least according to Jean-Paul Sartre, is that "existence preceeds
essence." The term essence refers to a human nature or a set
of general properties that are true of, and found in, every
human being. If we possessed such an essence, then "each existing

125

'man' would only be a particular example of a universal conception, the conception of 'man'."[2]

From an existential perspective, we are thrown into the world, possessing only this <u>existence</u>. We are totally free to decide how we will respond to it and what we will make of it. It is these free choices, and the acts that follow from them, that create or construct our individual properties, or essence. Thus, what we do determines what we are (not the other way around, as science would have it). In other words, existence preceeds essence.

This position implies, in turn, that people's nature is continually evolving and fluctuating. With a few exceptions to be noted later, they cannot be pinned down to a set of permanent, irreversible properties. Any subsequent act can negate or at least revise a previous essence. The statements "Harry is a barber" or "Harry is depressed" might be true <u>now</u>, but they could be contradicted by something Harry does in the future. Thus, people, like kaleidoscopes, never remain fixed or predictable; they are forever "becoming."

It is for this reason that the characters in plays or novels written from an existential perspective often cannot be easily pinpointed as being this or that. For example, in Harold Pinter's play <u>The Homecoming</u>, Ruth is, at various points, a wife, a mother, a sister-in-law, a daughter-in-law, and finally a prostitute. Moreover, this last role is particularly fitting, for as critic Walter Kerr has observed, the prostitute is a definitive existential character:

> The whore, by definition, lacks definition. The whore performs no single social role, she is what each new man wishes to make of her. She is available to experience, and she is an available experience. She is eternally "between trains," and she is known in passing and as something passing. In fact, she is simply unknown. Existentially speaking, we are all life's whores to the degree that we are in motion and have not arbitrarily codified and thereby stilled ourselves.[3]

The prostitute's skillful role-playing makes her interactions with her customers resemble a highly formalized ritual. In fact, Jean Genet has intimated, in his plays such as <u>The Balcony</u> (which is set in a brothel) and <u>The Maids</u>, that such highly ceremonious, stylistic playing of a variety of roles is typical of human existence.

Since each person is free to make of existence whatever he or she can, it follows that people in general cannot have much in common with one another. Each is unique, and his or her properties will tell us little about anyone else. Heidegger, for example, has viewed the person as inescapably a being-in-the-world,[4] whose existence, rooted in a particular time and place, has a down-to-earth, everyday, banal quality. It features concrete, specific events, such as a cigarette being smoked here and now, or a landlord demanding the rent this minute. (Ironically, Heidegger himself apparently hoped to induce, from the unique character of an individual existence, some general abstract statements about Being as a universal category. This seems, at least from an existential perspective, an attempt to reconcile opposites, so it is hardly surprising that Heidegger never did publish it.[5] At any rate, since his final aim was to understand Being in general, Heidegger denied that he was an existentialist.[6])

This revolutionary view of human existence led Kierkegaard to his revolt against the prevalent philosophical systems of his day, which professed grandiose statements about existence in general. Since such systems completely ignored the realities of everyday life, they had little value for the individual who simply wanted to gain some understanding of her or his particular existence. Philosophy had, according to Kierkegaard, become a pie-in-the-sky, academic game. But if it concerned itself, as it should, with these genuine problems it would become the most practical pursuit of all. Ever since, existentialism has above all aimed for relevance.

Since there are no general truths about existence, writers can discuss only their own existence, since that is all they have to go by. Hence existentialism actually refers to a set of philosophies (theoretically, at least, a set of infinite size), each describing a particular situation. Which partly explains its great appeal in our day. The unquestioned truths of the past--the various religious, political, and psychological systems that have purported to provide final answers--all of these have been found wanting. Above all, our two devastating world wars--along with our innumerable "conflicts," "crises," "skirmishes," and so on--have shown all too clearly where these various "isms" can lead. Widespread disillusionment has followed, for which an attitude that "Truth is in the eye of the beholder" has seemed an attractive remedy.

2. Corollaries. Let us now examine some related matters. First, it is striking that many "existentialists"--even those, like Sartre and Camus, more philosophically inclined--have presented their views in literary forms such as novels, plays, and films. Why should this be? Because works of literature,

127

first and foremost, portray an individual character rooted in a particular existence. Thus they avoid abstract, sweeping statements that are so tempting when philosophy is presented philosophically.

Second, existentialists routinely express almost vitriolic hatred of both academics and scientists. Reportedly, Sartre was grievously insulted when told he resembled an engineer.[7] Harold Pinter's portrait in The Homecoming of Teddy, the "Doctor of Philosophy," is devastating. Teddy is so detached from everything that he can stand thoughtfully by and watch while other members of his family seduce his wife. And it is glaringly obvious that few existentialists have occupied academic posts. Why is this? Both scientists and academics, almost without exception, assume the world to be reasonable and coherent. Scientists accept the concept of determinism (that events happen for reasons). They propound laws, which are simply categorical statements, or generalizations that summarize a variety of individual phenomena and state what they all have in common. Thus the behavioral scientist, for example, will ask in what ways the action of various people resemble each other.

Existentialists, denying that such generalizations are possible, find these activities ridiculous. Also (and here we move to a third, particularly important corollary), they deny the coherence or logic of the world. They believe that both existence and the universe are absurd, whimsical, chaotic, and anything but deterministic. Human beings, having free will, can interpret existence however they like and become whatever they wish. So existentialists reject a fundamental scientific tenet as an outrageous lie. This theme of absurdity colors much existential writing, so let us pursue it. We feel (we are told) anxiety (or angst), dread, and anguish, not because we are neurotic but simply because we are alive. To be human is to be anxious; it is inherent to our condition. Thus Sartre, for example, responds to his existence with nausea. In short, in these circles paranoia runs rampant.

Why do they insist on being so unrelievedly bleak? Because, above all, they have felt anxiety, dread, and the like and, as a group, they have tended to trust feelings and emotions rather than reason and logic. The latter can become sidetracked and confused by objective, general concepts, but feelings and moods are more personal and hence more trustworthy. To gain valid understanding of our particular existence, we should pay them heed. They are the starting point, the preeminent "data of existence," as it were. Philosophical analyses of our condition follow after, as attempts to understand them.

128

And those emotions find our condition to be decidedly dismal. Why do we feel this way? First, because there is no order, no coherent answers to tell us "what it's all about." Our existence, therefore, seems meaningless, stupid, and even pathetically funny and, as Fromm has reminded us,[8] most of us tolerate ambiguity rather poorly, feeling uncomfortable when we lack certainty. Secondly, because in one crucial respect, we are not free. We cannot become that which we most want to be, which is immortal. Inevitably, sooner or later, we will die and our existence will end. For Camus, death is "God's great insult."[9] As a possibility, it permeates our existence for, as has often been observed, as soon as we are born, we are old enough to die.

Our trauma is increased because we are aware of this situation. We don't know when we will die, but we know that we will. In this context, human activity can seem trivial and even silly. It places exaggerated importance on worldly events such as political developments, budget speeches, profit margins, and Stanley Cup Playoffs that, ultimately, cannot change anything that really matters. In actual fact, despite our self-important posturing, we resemble pawns in a cosmic game of chess. We don't know the players, but we understand (if we honestly confront our situation) that at any moment, arbitrarily and whimsically, they can knock us off the board and continue the game without us. As Gloucester observed, "Like flies to wanton boys, are we to th' gods; They kill us for their sport" (King Lear, 4.1).

Which returns us to a point made earlier, viz., that existential themes frequently surfaced long before Kierkegaard. For example, Shakespeare's credentials seem quite in order; at least many of his characters mouth typical sentiments. Here is only one example of many, a famous soliloquy from Macbeth:

To-morrow, and to-morrow, and to-morrow,
Creeps in this petty pace from day to day,
To the last syllable of recorded time;
And all our yesterdays have lighted fools
The way to dusty death. Out, out brief candle!
Life's but a walking shadow, a poor player
That struts and frets his hour upon the stage
And then is heard no more: It is a tale
Told by an idiot, full of sound and fury,
Signifying nothing. (5.2)

For Sartre, at any rate, our anxiety and nausea also spring from a third source, which is the terrible responsibility that our freedom places on us. In his words, "Man is condemned forever to be free."[10] If I can make of my life whatever I wish, without any antecedent causes or unquestioned truths to guide me, then that life becomes entirely my own doing. I

129

must evolve my own particular meaning alone and isolated. I have no comforting answers or easy excuses to lean on. Thus my freedom is not, as I might at first have thought, a liberating breath of fresh air, but rather a dreadful burden that I cannot put down. Furthermore, my responsibility is even more onerous because it is not only to myself but to humankind in general. In freely choosing myself, I provide my personal, editorial statement of my ideal, of existence as I think it should be. As each of us goes about our life, then, we bear--like Atlas--the burden of humanity on our backs.

Sartre agrees that to avoid this responsibility, many people will pretend that some ultimate meaning is to be found in existence. But those who refuse to live authentically, who take refuge in such comforting but cowardly lies, are, to Sartre, guilty of **bad faith**; they are **salauds** (translated, roughly, as "filthy stinkers" no less).

3. **Creativity**. We will, before long, examine some analyses of creativity advanced by particular writers, but at this time we wish to read between the lines of the preceeding generalizations. For they suggest a view that has not, to our knowledge, been expressed in so many words. From an existential perspective, a creator's labor seems nothing less than a microcosm of all human existence. Like every person, she or he struggles neverendingly with a formless, unstructured situation. The blank paper stares back at the would-be author. The canvas, tightly stretched and cured, awaits the first tentative strokes of the painter's brush. The dancer slouches casually, hand on hip and boredom on face, challenging the choreographer's inspiration and secretly hoping that it won't come before the next cigarette break.

What should a creator do with these universes? He or she is free to devise any solutions, none of which are, objectively speaking, particularly correct. There are no inviolate canons, no givens, to provide comforting answers, any more than there are in life. Why use yellow rather than red paint for that spot in the upper left hand corner? Or a dominant seventh rather than a diminished fourth? Or an arabesque rather than a pirouette? Personal preference provides the only guide. The dilemmas of the creator, like those of existence, were once solved by unquestioned "isms," but artists, like people, have come to reject them, thus gaining the decidedly mixed blessing of freedom. Nowadays, rules are made to be broken.

That creator, like Everyperson, labors in anguished doubt because of the terrible responsibility he or she feels for the results. Is it good enough? What will others think of it? The enterprise can seem silly, because ultimately it cannot change the things that really matter. Whether one finishes this murderer of sleep or whether one quits in disgust, life will go on and the silent cosmos will unfold as it should.

Nor can compulsive effort prevent the inevitable. Sooner or later, it must be finished, even though one can always envisage yet a few more touches. The writer, confronted by a publisher's inviolate deadline, pleads for more time, like Desdemona facing the homicidal Othello and crying, "Kill me tomorrow; let me live tonight. But half an hour! But while I say one prayer" (5.2). To no purpose. Why not persist longer or, for that matter, finish sooner? No reason at all.

And yet, according to this proposal, the process offers its compensations. It implies that we create in order to learn about and even to define ourselves. If we envolve our essence from our freely chosen acts--"I do therefore I am," to paraphase Descartes' famous dictum--then the arbitrary, subjective decisions that we make while we evolve a product will show us our own personal preferences. These will become objectified in that product where we can contemplate them and, in turn, ourselves. The "that sort of bear" phenomenon, first described by that noted existentialist poet and philosopher, Winnie the Pooh, exemplifies this motive. If Pooh did something (such as discover the North Pole) that revealed something about himself that he had not previously realized, he invariably muttered "that sort of bear."[11]

Somewhat similarly, Kreitler and Kreitler[12] and also Getzels and Csikszentmihalyi[13] have suggested that the creative act seeks not so much tension <u>reduction</u> as tension <u>definition</u>. Vague, free-floating anxieties about such onerous and ultimately insurmountable matters as the meaning of life and the inevitability of death are difficult to control. Confronting them is like belaboring a room full of floating feathers. But if we redirect and focus our metaphysical anxiety into something specific, concrete, and above all potentially solvable, such as a creative task, something about which we can worry instead, we may attain some comfort. In this view, then, the creative person truly, in Camus' words, "lives doubly."[14] Working, he or she confronts the same challenges and anxieties as in living. Through arbitrary, personal choices she or he evolves a product. Precisely as one evolves one's life.

4. <u>Harold Pinter</u>. A seminal artistic development of the twentieth century, the so-called <u>Theatre of the Absurd</u>,[15] is represented in virtually every Western country. It includes, besides those existential philosophers such as Sartre and Camus who have periodically turned to drama, such notables as Samuel Beckett, Eugene Ionesco, Jean Genet, Tom Stoppard, and

N. F. Simpson. They have all, in various ways, leaned heavily on existential tenets, portraying an existence that is absurd, illogical, and incomprehensible. Some of these works are gloomily depressing, others hilariously funny, and still others (including probably the greatest of the genre, Beckett's Waiting for Godot) manage to be both.

From this august company we have selected Harold Pinter to personify the existential approach to creativity. These days, his plays are probably the most frequently performed but, more relevantly, he is, according to critic Walter Kerr at least, "the only man working in the theatre today who writes existential plays existentially."[16] A Beckett or a Sartre produces a philosophical treatise as much as a dramatic work, showing through logical, systematic revelation that the world is absurd. He presents both his characters and their dilemmas as examples of universal phenomena. Indeed, the former typically have a decidedly Everyman quality, which implies that their travails reveal what life in general is like. Obviously, such work is inherently contradictory, because it uses the very properties that existence supposedly lacks to defend the author's views. In Kerr's words:

> We are first offered a concept, a statement of essence....(Mr. Beckett) forms an abstract concept of man's nature and role and presents it to us in its original conceptual form, individualizing it only slightly....even when we wish to make an anticonceptual statement, even when we wish to say that man has not been and cannot be defined, we do it by conceptualization, by starting from a definition.[17]

But, Kerr persuasively argues, Pinter alone avoids this pitfall, because he does not defend the premise of absurdity but simply presents it:

> "I don't conceptualize in any way," Pinter has said....Watching a Beckett play, we immediately engage in a little game of "concept, concept, who's got the concept."...Watching a Pinter play, we give over the scramble to stick pins in ideas and fix them forever to a drawing board. We feel that the drawing board isn't there and that our eager thumbs would only go through it.[18]

Why does Pinter have this unique effect? First, he purports not to understand his characters himself, and so provides almost no background information about their personalities or motivations.

132

As a result, we cannot impart easy, precise explanations for their actions. In the film The Servant, for example, a butler (brilliantly portrayed by that much underrated actor Dirk Bogarde), employed by a young, rather decadent lord, gradually takes over the latter's life, becoming the dominant rather than subservient factor and eventually destroying him. We have no idea why the butler does these thing. Easy sociological, political, or economic reasons, for example, simply will not suffice. He just "does them."

The notoriously inconsistent behavior of Pinter's characters also illustrates the unpredictable kaleidoscope of human "becoming." For example, in The Homecoming again, Lennie, an uneducated, small-time hood and pimp can suddenly fling this question at the philosopher Teddy:

> Do you detect a certain logical incoherence in the central affirmations of Christian theism?....How can the unknown merit reverence? In other words, how can you revere that of which you're ignorant? At the same time, it would be ridiculous to propose that what we know merits reverence.[19]

We laugh at something so flagrantly "out of character." But our laughter has an uneasy edge. Is there nothing on which we can rely?

This obscurity is typical of Pinter. As he has said:

> The explicit form which is so often taken in twentieth century drama is...cheating. The playwright assumes that we have a great deal of information about all his characters, who explain themselves to the audience. In fact, what they are doing most of the time is conforming to the author's own ideology....When the curtain goes up on one of my plays, you are faced with a situation...two people sitting in a room which hasn't happened before...and we know no more about them than I know about you, sitting at this table. The world is full of surprises. A door can open at any moment, and someone will come in. We'd love to know who it is, we'd love to know exactly what he has on his mind, but how often do we (italics mine)?[20]

Thus, Pinter rejects other playwrights' confident assurance that they can speak for their characters, creeping inside and manipulating them like literary puppeteers working their marionettes. In a famous episode, he dramatically expressed

133

these sentiments:

> He received a letter which read "Dear sir, I
> would be obliged if you would kindly explain
> to me the meaning of your play The Birthday
> Party. These are the points which I do not
> understand: 1. Who are the two men? 2. Where
> did Stanley come from? 3. Were they all supposed
> to be normal? You will appreciate that without
> the answers to my questions I cannot fully
> understand your play." Pinter is said to have
> replied as follows: "Dear Madam, I would be
> obliged if you would kindly explain to me the
> meaning of your letter. These are the points
> which I do not understand: 1. Who are you?
> 2. Where do you come from? 3. Are you supposed
> to be normal? You will appreciate that without
> the answers to your questions I cannot fully
> understand your letter."[21]

Thus, Pinter's characters are truly "existential," lacking any
predictable consistency or essence.

A second reason for his plays' distinctively existential
ambience is that events are often unexpected and incomprehensible
(and again, he asserts that he himself rarely knows what will
happen next). Which again places before us a world where anxiety
is pervasive. In The Birthday Party, for example, two hoods
arrive to "take Stanley away" because he has defied "the
organization." We never learn who these hoods are, what Stanley
has done, or what this mysterious "organization" is. No one
in the play seems to know either, but they quite accept this
puzzling state of affairs as entirely in the natural order of
things. In The Homecoming, the wife Ruth, after allowing herself
to be seduced by her in-laws before the benign gaze of her
husband, agrees to stay with them as a live-in prostitute,
while he heads back to America to look after the children. It
all seems completely commonplace. No one is surprised or exclaims,
"Hey, wait a minute!". In this world of complete freedom and
anarchy, anything goes.

The unmistakable sense of the here and now also contribute
to the plays' existential atmosphere. Other contributions to
the genre seem decidedly abstract; their settings are anywhere
and anytime. But Pinter's overflow with an almost overpowering,
even oppressive down-to-earth quality. This particular room,
these specific people seem almost hypnotically concrete. As a
result, even the most everyday actions such as lighting a cigarette
or lifing a teacup seem ominously significant.

134

We might also briefly mention other devices that, according to Esslin, help Pinter achieve his effects.[22] His brilliant dialogue so accurately mimics the essential qualities of everyday speech that we suspect he must have a tape recorder in his head. His characters chatter on at length about irrelevant trivia, rarely saying what seems appropriate in the situation. They pause and stumble and (most characteristically) repeat themselves ad nauseum. Witness this exchange in The Caretaker:

Davies: Who was that feller?
Aston : He's my brother.
Davies: Is he? He's a bit of a joker, en'he?
Aston : Uh.
Davies: Yes...he's a real joker.
Aston : He's got a sense of humor.
Davies: Yes, I noticed.
        Pause
        He's a real joker, that lad, you can see that.
        Pause
Aston : Yes, he tends...he tends to see the funny side
        of things.
Davies: Well, he's got a sense of humor, en'he?
Aston : Yes.
Davies: Yes, you could tell that.[23]

Again, something besides Pinter's accurate ear is thereby established. Clear communication and interpersonal understanding are forlorn possibilities, so in our lonely isolation, not expecting to be understood, we try desperately to bang our message across in sledge-hammer fashion. As well, in a chaotic world we must hang on for dear life to anything unequivocal. The brother has a sense of humor. That much we know. It isn't much, but it's a comfort of sorts.

To many observers, Pinter's plays seem discomforting and even weird. Why? Probably because we are much more familiar with the very different "well made play." There, everything is crystal clear. Events are explained, the characters make sense and speak coherently, so that we understand everyone and everything. Every line of dialogue communicates some information. The plot unravels with calendar-like inevitably, displaying an obvious beginning and end. But as Pinter himself has repeatedly pointed out, life itself is rarely like that. In a real sense, then, his plays are much more realistic. It is their almost unbearable accuracy, perhaps, that makes us squirm; it is all too close to home.

In conclusion, Pinter deserves our attention not only because he has presented existential themes but also because (if we accept his statements at face value) in creating he has practiced

135

what he preaches. He writes, it seems, to see what will happen and to attain in the product "out there" his own personal, subjective understanding. Not knowing what to believe, he works it through and discovers it in his work.

5. <u>Commentary</u>. As it stands, we have here not so much a fully developed, integrated theory as a "model," "metaphor" or "way of thinking about" creativity; this must be admitted at once. Many issues are not so much brushed over lightly as left entirely untouched. We are told nothing, for example, about why someone might choose a certain style of expression or a particular creative field. Nothing about why creators might possess the personality characteristics or undergo the reliable experiences that they do. Above all, little about what qualities might distinguish them from those less adventurous souls who choose not to confront their situation "doubly." Undoubtedly, the existentialist would dismiss such charges. Their answer would require those ultimate inaccuracies, i.e., sweeping generalizations. He may have a point. Gruber, for example, has argued that since the product that results is unique, so too must be each creative act. To completely understand such an act, we must study it, seeking a theory of the individual.[24] From his standpoint too, generalizations about creativity would be largely uninformative.

Be that as it may, the existential perspective, despite its narrow scope, does provide extraordinarily appealing answers to a few questions, including perhaps the most fundamental of all, that of motivation. A host of creators have described their labors as being just such voyages to define and discover themselves.[25] Storr has pursued this notion that creativity may be a <u>quest for identity</u>.[26] In doing so, he has attempted to answer at least one problem apparently ignored by the foregoing existential account, viz., the difference between those who are driven to create and those who are not. Noting the notoriously paradoxical personalities displayed by creatives, Storr suggests that they might find the basic question "Who am I?" particularly perplexing and turn to creating to find out, while less complicated souls, more "sure of themselves" (in the existential sense), would not. Accordingly, a creator's inconsistent qualities, such as sexual androgyny, become not merely interesting yet essentially peripheral phenomena but the very stuff of productivity. This notion, obviously, poses another problem, i.e., why <u>do</u> creators have paradoxical personalities? Still, it deserves further study.

In addition, this notion can shed light on the critic's choice of a masochistic career. According to Simon, when Pauline Kael was asked her opinion of a particular movie, she replied, "I don't know, I haven't written my review yet."[27] For many critics, in fact, the main attraction of writing a notice is not the saying of "yea or nay" but the chance to work out for themselves a satisfying, intelligible impression of an ambiguous event.

Does this also explain, perchance, our anger when a critic's opinion, or indeed any work of art, does not meet with our approval? Since it is an interpretive statement of opinion, it reveals that not everyone responds to the world as we do and that, in the last analysis, there are no final certainties in life, but only opinions. We are insecure enough in our choices without constantly being reminded of how arbitrary they are.

An explanation of the sex difference can likewise be proffered; I am indebted to Fay Ferris for this interpretation. If we are driven to create in order to achieve satisfying interpretations of ambiguity, perhaps women, encouraged from infancy to seek wifehood and motherhood, have faced fewer doubts than men about the ultimate purpose or meaning of their lives or about their expected role.* Hence, they have not needed to create. Nowadays, however, many women are torn between their historically conditioned, traditional roles and those preached by feminism, feeling guilty or even traitorous if they simply stay home and raise children. Which may explain the evident rise in distaff creativity, much of it clearly investigating what it means to be a woman.

However, we must needs offer some negative observations. We have here an intriguing analysis of what we might call the creator's "push," i.e., the force that impels one onward from behind. The amorphous, ambiguous medium challenges an inherent need for personally satisfying answers. But creators also seem to be "pulled" towards that vague, amorphous image in the mind's eye that Arieti has called the endocept.[28] They labor in existential doubt and infinite choice only so long as they lack inspiration. Once it arrives, they move with the certainty of a laser, desperately trying to express something. As the words tumble out faster than the typewriter keys will fly, the process now seems anything but arbitrary.

---

* Shaw's play Man and Superman vividly contrasts male and female certainty. The male protagonist, ignorant of first priorities, devotes himself to various trivial pursuits. The heroine, knowing that getting married and having children, fulfilling the "life force," is all that really matters, waits with growing impatience for him to come to his senses and propose. But as his dithering persists, she eventually takes the unheard-of step (to the Victorians) of proposing to him. At some point, we must get on with it.

137

As Poincaré has observed, the mind does not face an infinite array of alternatives, a supermarket of ideas as it were.[29] Those that are sterile, it never contemplates, because a mysterious editorial filter, which seemingly operates at Checkpoint Charlie between the unconscious and conscious minds, stamps only the passports of worthwhile ideas. The existential account tells us nothing about this guiding vision of what must be, which directs every arbitrary choice. Nor does it explain our need to communicate. If we seek, alone and in isolation, only personally satisfying interpretations of reality, why endure the frustrations of verification so others can share them? Likewise, why take the risks of show and tell? Perhaps (the existentialist might reply) because verification seeks not communication but greater clarity. As we know, the product will change from the initial conception, taking on a life of its own. Therefore, we often realize "what we really think" only when the finished version lies before us.

Another weakness, which flows from a basic problem with existential tenets, will lead us to propose a modification to perhaps make it more palatable. Even those otherwise sympathetic have doubted that we have complete freedom to become absolutely anything. Clearly, this premise is far too extreme, so that Maslow, for example, finds it "just plain silly."[30] No amount of willing will allow us to fly unaided or to run the 100 meter dash in two microseconds. Whether we like it or not, those two great determinants of behavior, heredity and environmental experience, do limit our options.

Much the same can be said of creative work. No medium can become absolutely anything. Literary forms are restricted by the expressive potential of words, dance by the movement capabilities of the human body, and science by the limitations on observation and measurement. To succeed, therefore, at both existing and creating, we must accept, work within, and even enjoy these boundaries, while yet pushing them as far as they will go. Which can actually work to our advantage (at least in creating) because truly infinite choice could well be so intimidating as to be incapacitating. Thus, poet John Dryden has observed that rhyme surpasses blank verse in that it:

> bounds and circumscribes the fancy. For imagination in a poet is a faculty so wild and lawless that, like an high-ranging spaniel, it must have clogs tied to it, lest it outrun the judgment.[31]

Since the various media present different possibilities, an important key to a creator's success is discovering the one most suitable for expressing a particular vision. Is he or

138

she trying to say something verbally that sounds or movement or paint might capture more effectively? According to choreographer Doris Humphrey, such inappropriate aims, e.g., attempting to convey a very involved or subtle scenario, are the most frequent reason why dances fail.[32] Those fortunate enough to discover their comfortable niches early in life, become child prodigies of the Mozart/Mendelssohn ilk.

Albert Camus

We turn now to this writer who has above all emphasized the inherent absurdity of human existence. He has also attached particular symbolic importance to the creative act, which he sees as nothing less than a microcosm of that existence. We will examine two of his major philosophical statements separately, for they not only part company rather frequently but are at times almost directly contradictory (in existential circles, of course, consistency is not necessarily a virtue). For each, we shall also elucidate the view of creativity that it professes.

The Myth of Sisyphus

This legend, for Camus, allegorically represents the nature of human existence. Sisyphus was condemned by the gods to roll a stone up to the top of a mountain, but each time he succeeded it trundled back down, forcing him to begin again. And again. For the rest of eternity. The gods, presumably, thought that "there is no more dreadful punishment than futile and hopeless labor."[33]

How does this sordid tale represent our condition? In Camus' opinion, we humans have a persistent desire, or nostalgia, for explanation and understanding. We are inherently curious. Unfortunately, we are placed in a situation that has no answers to offer. Existence is a mammoth Rorschach test that we can structure however we wish, with no answer being any better than another. The absurd, then, arises from our basic need to wrestle some kind of meaning from an existence that has none:

> But what is absurd is the confrontation of this
> irrational and the wild longing for clarity whose
> call echoes in the human heart....The absurd
> is born of this confrontation between the human
> need (for reasons) and the unreasonable silence
> of the world.[34]

Thus, our nostalgic quest is futile. Our eternal metaphysical questions about the meaning of life are answered only by a cosmic silence.

From this beginning, Camus faces the quandry often posed to particularly morbid existentialists: If life is so miserable, why shouldn't we kill ourselves and end the agony? How can we, while admitting that our lives are absurd, still value them sufficiently as to choose to prolong them? Or as Camus puts it:

> There is but one serious philosophical problem, and that is suicide. Judging whether life is or is not worth living amounts to answering the fundamental question of philosophy. All the rest--whether or not the world has three dimensions, whether the mind has nine or twelve categories...comes afterwards....Does the absurd dictate death?[35]

In other words, to be or not to be, that is the question!

We can try to avoid our absurdity, of course, by becoming involved in our daily routine. But eventually, at some point it will hit us between the eyes. Yet even then we can still escape, by taking a logical leap and affirming, through blind faith, a conclusion that flies in the face of the evidence. (Psychologists would call these leaps defense mechanisms.) Camus' great predecessor, Kierkegaard, for example, took the religious leap when he accepted our absurdity and, illogically, took it as further proof for the necessity of God.

Camus will not leap. Unlike Sartre, he doesn't stick nasty labels on those who choose such artificial comforts, but he cannot bring himself to follow them. A leap, by relinquishing our demand for explanation, is a surrender. It admits that there are some things beyond our understanding, that "There are more things in heaven and earth than are dreamt of in our philosophy." In his eyes, therefore, a leap is a philosophical suicide, because it allows the absurd to defeat us. The absurd is the most reliable fact of our existence, the one thing of which we can be sure. To deny it seems to him incomprehensible, tantamount to Descartes avowing that "I think, therefore I am" and then deciding "but I don't think that I think."

For Camus, we must continually stare the absurd in the face and keep it consciously in mind; we must struggle with and revolt against it. Yet we must never hope that this battle can be won, for that is impossible. When we acknowledge our absurd status in this way, and remain determined not to leap but to confront it, we achieve lucidity. The absurd can never be eliminated. We know this. We are defeated before we start. So if we choose to live authentically and confront the absurd, we really have only two reasonable choices: suicide or recovery.

140

Camus rejects suicide because it constitutes another unsatisfactory leap; it accepts the victory of the absurd. True absurd persons, on the other hand, will not admit defeat. They consistently demand that which they know they can never have, i.e., understanding, so they forego any hope. But they retain their scorn for this indomitable adversary. That is their only sin. And it is also their recovery. They choose to live on, not denying life's essential absurdity but resisting it. This hopeless, doomed revolt provides the only value and majesty to human life. Therefore, "the important thing is not to be cured, but to live with one's ailments."[36]

The definitive absurd person, then, is that antithesis of the suicide, i.e., the condemned criminal. The former, afflicted with life, chooses death. The latter, forcibly conducted to death, insistently reaffirms, to the last moment, the value of life. No one lives more intensely, every crucial second. Camus' magnificent novel, The Stranger, presents such a hero, Mersault. He is at first caught up in a mundane, humdrum existence. However he is condemned to death, and as his execution day approaches, his life becomes increasingly intense; he cherishes every precious moment to the full. Similarly, in The Plague, Dr. Rieux knows that he cannot stem the tide of a bubonic plague that is sweeping the city of Oran. Whether his patients live or die is entirely beyond his control. Yet he continues to struggle against hopeless odds to help them.

Thus, to Camus, the gods were wrong. By condemning Sisyphus to futile, hopeless labor, they did not punish him, but allowed him an existence of unsurpassed authenticity:

> The struggle towards the heights...in which the whole being is exerted towards accomplishing nothing...is enough to fill a man's heart...One must imagine Sisyphus happy (italics mine).[37]

We must also direct our attention to one further idea, which we might call the doctrine of quantity. The Achilles heel of every existential system is ethics. If there are no ultimate, inviolate truths, then morality must also be arbitrary. No particular act is automatically preferable to or better than another, and virtue is only a matter of opinion. Thus, Camus maintains, Ivan Karamazov uttered his famous cry that "everything is permitted," not in joyful affirmation of the universe's bounty, but in bitter resignation at its moral neutrality. But given this state of affairs, what then constitutes a good life? Camus answers that it is not the quality of our acts that matters (there are no standards of quality) but the quantity. Not the best living, but the most living; the more we do, the better we have lived. Therefore, with Nietzsche, he holds that "what counts is not eternal life, but eternal vivacity."[38]

1. Sisyphus and creativity. Absurd creators are the most dramatic examplars of human lucidity. In their work, they do not try to explain their situation, because they know that to express an idea or communicate any message about the human condition is to assume that such explanations are possible. Such romantic practices break the fundamental commandment, "Thou shalt not hope." Moreover, they do not seek to obtain a personal understanding in their work (as in the version of existential creation discussed above) or try to slip in, unnoticed, some subtle thematic message. Both of these leaps temporarily lose sight of the absurd, resulting in what Camus derisively dismisses as "thesis art."

Absurd creators are therefore denied innovators' usual aims and comforts. They practice their art, presumably, while clad in hair shirts and flagellating themselves. Still, as we say, "hope springs eternal," so such artists must be eternally vigilant against surreptitious wishes to express and/or communicate something. They must continually remind themselves that their only authentic purpose is to describe their situation artificially in another form, to show the "what" but never the "why." Thus, absurd creation is "the great mime," using symbols and images to represent something incomprehensible. Hence, for Camus, "If the world were clear, art would not exist."[39]

Is it possible, in practice, to carry off this harrowing approach to creative work? Can we eschew the persistent hope that we can not only describe the world but make sense of it, at least for ourselves? Can thesis art be avoided? Perhaps if we choose to work in visual art or music, which are inherently abstract and representational. But literature, and especially fiction, provides an almost insurmountable challenge. Which is precisely the reason why absurd artists, given their love of the perversely contrary, would probably choose to write. Has anyone pulled off a lucidly absurdist approach in this genre? Camus is decidedly unsure, realizing that here even the most committed tend to founder. As we shall shortly learn, Kafka seems to have come remarkably close, and Dostoevsky's early novel, The Possessed, in its portrayal of the would-be suicide Kirilov, seems to have succeeded admirably at failing. Unfortunately, the later works, Crime and Punishment and Brothers Karamazov, were both spoiled by unseemly notes of hopeful optimism.

The doctrine of quantity also comes into play. The universe, constantly bombarding us with stimulation, provides an inexhaustible number of possible subjects. Absurd creators will try to "say everything," to represent every sensation, even

142

though they know this to be hopeless. Eventually their work will end, not because they will run out of topics but because they die. Like the tortured van Gogh, in his last year phrenetically splashing great gobs of paint on canvas to "get it all down," they race against time.

Naturally, they lose, so it goes without saying that their work will be a catalogue of failures. Like all existing persons, they are defeated before the opening kick-off. Undoubtedly, they will also be dissatisfied with their efforts, oftentimes to the extent of repudiating them.* They will be contradictory and obscure, because those properties are intrinsic to the universe they represent. They cannot change anything. Why bother? Because we are human beings and we exist to bother. Creators must continue their revolt because, as sculptor Robert Engman put it, through creating man "dignifies himself,"[41] just as Sisyphus does by compulsively pushing his rock up the mountain. Creating, like existing, is an absurd, futile, exhausting, frustrating, ridiculous way to spend our time. But what else can we do?

We can now understand why, for Camus, such artists are the definitive absurd human beings. They doubly confront the absurd dilemma in both life and work, realizing all the while that both activities are hopeless and have no future. But by abandoning hope and accepting the doctrine of quantity they will, like Sisyphus, become perversely free. They will realize that, in artistic expression, the sky can be the limit and absolutely anything be acceptable.

    2. <u>Franz Kafka</u>. Although we have dealt with this writer earlier (see Chapter 3), we will now do so again within the present context, since Camus himself saw Kafka as a particularly apt personification of absurdist practices.[42] Camus does not dwell on either Kafka's personality or its effect on his work. There is no reference, for example, to his notoriously involved relationships with either his father or with the opposite sex, matters that would provide rich fodder for a theorist of psychoanalytic persuasions. Ignoring them is, of course, quite

---

* In this context, Koestler(40) relates a revealing story about Picasso. An art collector spent a considerable sum of money for one of his paintings. He showed it to the master, who glanced at it briefly and snarled, "It's a fake." Somewhat nonplussed, the collector later purchased yet another work "by Picasso." Again the painter dismissed it as "a fake." When the same events occurred yet a third time, the exasperated collector asked, "How can it be that there are so many paintings around, bearing your signature, that are fakes?" Replied Picasso, "I often paint fakes."

in keeping with Camus' own absurdist principles; presumably the nonfiction writer is equally bound not to seek explanation but only to represent. Hence, this study provides, perhaps, the only example extant of an authentically absurdist biography. Several of Kafka's seminal works are simply described, to show that they are (or, in some cases, are not) consistent with this doctrine.

The unique situation we call "Kafkaesque" presents strange, almost dream-like events in a highly realistic, matter-of-fact way. The opening sentence of The Metamorphosis is typical:

> When Gregor Samsa awoke one morning from uneasy dreams he found himself transformed in his bed into a gigantic insect.[43]

As so often happens in Kafka, his characters completely accept such a decidedly bizarre occurrence. Astonishment is not in their repertoires. We, the readers, are thereby also hoodwinked and only several paragraphs later do we stop and exclaim, "Hey, wait a minute!". Their everyday, down-to-earth qualities likewise increase our gullibility. Samsa, for example, is that most mundane of drudges, a commercial traveler, and his greatest worry about his strange affliction is that his boss might be angry.

It is this oscillation between the natural and the extraordinary that gives Kafka's work its unique quality and makes it an exemplary portrait of absurdist principles. The world is assumed to be unpredictable and human understanding to be impossible; absolutely anything can and probably will happen. So Kafka, displaying in spades the absurd artist's cardinal virtue, does not try to interpret this world but simply to put it on display with its make-up removed. As well, he clearly practices the ethic of quantity, because the same distinctive atmosphere and the same kinds of events appear in all his works. This repetition, which for Grant was compulsively neurotic,[44] is for Camus supremely admirable. As has often been noted, it is differences of opinion that are responsible for the success of horse racing.

And yet, since truly absurd creation is a hard master, not even Kafka can sustain it. He too, like Dostoevsky, eventually leaps into metaphysical hope and comfort. The Trial, we are told, expresses the requisite authenticity. The protagonist, Joseph K., is accused of unspecified crimes by unknown authorities, is tried, condemned, and eventually executed without ever understanding what he has done, who his accusers are, or why they judge him. He accepts without question that his ignorance is in the natural order of things. That's the way the world

144

is. Yet he persists to the very end in trying to defend himself, to get some evidence in support of "his case," and, above all, to understand. But, we suspect, he fully realizes in advance that all his frenetic activity is in vain and that the fate against which he struggles is inevitable.

So far, so hopeless. But in The Castle, a later novel, unseemly romanticism intrudes. A certain village is totally controlled by and directed from a mysterious castle, the officials of which are held in the utmost veneration, although no one in the village has communicated with them, or indeed has ever been inside the castle. K., a land surveyor, is hired by the castle, but is given neither job description nor meaningful work to do. He tries various ploys, both devious and otherwise, to clarify his situation. To no avail. He is thwarted at every turn.

The difference between this K. and the Joseph K. of The Trial is that the former clutches a nagging, persistent faith that ultimately he can get some information. It is even implied that he might succeed, and so scornful human pride and the never ending, doomed struggle are here replaced by hope of eventual victory. Therefore, in Camus' opinion, this K. allows the absurd to defeat him, while Joseph K. never does, even at the moment of his death. For he dies "like a dog,"[45] as he always knew he would, but his nostalgia remains intact. The Castle, then, is a "cradle of illusions."[46]

3. Commentary. The absurd approach, obviously, describes art and artist, not as they usually are, but as they could and should ideally be (at least in Camus' opinion). Ironically, he betrays his own slightly romantic tinge when he cheerfully admits that it has rarely, if ever, been consistently achieved. Furthermore, this approach emphasizes the artist's metaphysical attitude while working more than the product that results from that work. Hence, it would be quite futile to seek the approach's attitudes towards many of creativity's phenomena.

Once more, then, some might challenge its place amongst salient proposals. Despite its limited scope, we have few doubts on this score (an opinion with which Maddi, for one, seems to agree[47]). Its accuracy about certain aspects of creative work is compelling and indeed unsurpassed. It emphasizes creators' agonized toil. Their sweat and frustration. Their private awareness that ultimately their efforts must be futile. In their solitary struggle to force that unyielding, indomitable adversary called "the medium" to relinquish its secrets, failure must be the final reward. Yet these creators, cursed by their authenticity, cannot bring themselves to retreat into some more comfortable, less risky occupation. Like Don Quixote, they must

145

needs tilt at their windmills, persistently trying to "reach that unreachable star."[48] As scenic designer Robert Edmond Jones reportedly said to a class of eager (and obviously naive) students, "I can see that some of you are doomed...doomed to become artists."[49]

Still, from this very defeat absurd creators can wring a grim, perverse satisfaction that prevents their labor from becoming merely masochistic. Like any Camusian hero, they may be pawns hopelessly overwhelmed by cosmic adversaries. But they are the pawns who fight the good fight. In this sense, they are not depressing but exhilarating. We must imagine Sisyphus happy!

However, even leaving aside some metaphysical difficulties, we must still recognize that this portrait, which in some ways has such psychological validity, in others simply does not coincide with most introspections. For example, creators rarely report keeping the absurd in mind while they work, so apparently this attitude operates unconsciously if it does so at all. Which means that creators are hardly models of lucidity. Likewise, contrary to absurdist commandments, does not every creator experience, at least periodically, moments of satisfaction and even euphoria, and allow dreams of success to intrude upon his or her struggle? Yes, these delusional fantasies may be fleeting and inaccurate, but for the recipient they are nonetheless genuine.

In fact, if these emotions did not sometimes appear, we doubt that creators would continue to work. Being as subject to the laws of reinforcement (existential dogma notwithstanding) as the rest of us, they will eventually cease an activity not producing some kind of payoff. We suspect that Camus must himself have encountered some such satisfactions frequently; otherwise his literary output would have suffered.

In the same vein, consider his assertion that authentic creative work must not try to convey any hidden messages but must only represent, mainly by way of symbols. Now it is widely agreed that we do use symbols to express the inexpressible,[50] but most artistic work pursues other goals as well. In fact, we might argue that many masterpieces attain their greatness in part through their grappling with the fundamental, recurring themes of human experience. Similarly, on the other side of the proscenium, audience members receiving these communications will, almost instinctively, expend much time and energy trying to understand them.

Furthermore, it is not only literary works that sometimes aim for thematic statements and for communication. So too do supposedly more abstract media. In painting, what of all those religious canvases in the Raphael/Leonardo lineage? And no message

146

could be more powerful and unmistakable than that of Picasso's Guernica. In music, we have the programmatic tone poems of Richard Strauss, the nationalist compositions of Lizst, Wagner, and Bartók, and the impressionistic representations of Debussy and Ravel, to say nothing of innumerable opera, ballet, and musical theatre scores. The list is endless. Complex and obscure the message may be; the attempt at communication may even fail completely, leaving its puzzled audience quite in the dark. But obviously the attempt is made and made often.

In sum, The Myth of Sisyphus flies in the face of the data, promoting an approach that neither creators nor audience members have frequently practiced. We must wonder, then, whether it can greatly help the psychologist, that crass utilitarian, who wishes to understand creativity not as it might be but as it is. Now this objection might ordinarily be somewhat beside the point, except that it reveals Camus' blatant contradiction of one of existential philosophy's most enduring edicts, one with which he himself has sympathized.[51] A moral system must begin with the real facts of human behavior, with our unthinking, intuitive, and therefore most genuine responses. A plague on pie-in-the-sky, academic ideas that lack relevance! And yet Camus can deny that we should hope for success while creating, or try to send and to receive thematic messages (all of which we do routinely and reflexively), while advocating other reactions that seem beyond our capabilities.

Admittedly, from an existential angle, inconsistency is hardly a capital offence. Still, we might be tempted to earmark Camus, as Olivier did Hamlet in his well-known film, as a man who could not make up his mind. Actually, a further irony here raises its metallurgical head. Camus' own literary works (his plays, at least) are themselves singularly guilty of trying excessively to communicate ideas. Caligula, for example, wears its philosophy on its sleeve, and this didacticism badly weakens its dramatic impact. Which led the late Kenneth Tynan to classify it as that rarest of all theatrical animals, the "bad great play."[52]

A related difficulty with this approach lies in its emphasizing the artist's underlying attitude rather than the quality of work. The resulting standards of judgment would be, to put it bluntly, unacceptable. Is second-rate work that grows from the correct metaphysical posture preferable to vintage work that is produced for such purposes as personal expression or to put bread and butter on the table? Such standards would, perforce, demean many achievements that most of us have agreed to call "great." Of course Camus may not equate authenticity with greatness at all, and he may have been quite unconcerned with the attributes necessary for the latter. If that is so, then we must question the applicability of his ideas to understanding creative work.

The doctrine of quantity poses similar problems. If every act is equivalent and sheer frequency is the only guide, then the one who creates most must also create best. Surely this will not do either. What of those "writers" who churn out formula fiction, such as Harlequin romances, in a matter of days, and have literally hundreds of "novels" to their credit? Admittedly, such mind-boggling productivity requires skill of a sort, but should it relegate Tolstoy and Austen to second place? And what of those "composers" who can knock off several advertising jingles before breakfast? Should we doff our hats to them rather than to the rather unproductive Beethoven and Brahms, who sweated blood over every note? It could be argued, in rejoinder, that hacks lack definitive absurdity because the requisite attitudes of authenticity and lucidity are missing. Actually, the ultimate cynics, they often realize full well how patently ridiculous are their exploits. But exploits pay the bills.

Furthermore, this doctrine again contradicts the facts of behavior. As we have seen, every human being almost instinctively expresses value judgments and preferences. Thus, for typical creators, not all depictions of the universe are equivalent; some seem, for whatever reasons, superior and these they will choose. But if Camus has made the creator's task difficult, he has made the critic's not only irrelevant, but virtually immoral. A critic would evaluate creative products? Verboten; every one is equivalent. A critic would seek their thematic meanings? A pox on him or her; art should merely describe. Let the critic, decree Camusian canons, forthwith be eliminated.

The Rebel

As mentioned previously, existential approaches have problems handling morality. The doctrine of quantity, for example, is clearly an unsatisfactory base on which to build an ethical system, as Camus himself eventually admitted. If every human act is equally acceptable, then, in his words, "We are free to stoke the crematory fires or to devote ourselves to the care of lepers."[53]

It is this weakness that his later work, The Rebel, seeks to rectify. The Myth of Sisyphus asked whether the absurd demanded suicide and found the answer to be negative. The Rebel asks whether it demands, or at any rate allows, murder. The answer (again negative) follows from our typical response to that absurdity. As we contemplate our unjust, incomprehensible condition, we demand explanation and understanding, so that this

148

ridiculous outrage can be ended and "that which has been built upon sand should henceforth be founded on rock."[54] This metaphysical rebellion is also directed against the waste and stupidity of our inevitable deaths. So Camus' counsel is that of Dylan Thomas:

> Do not go gentle into that good night,
> Rage, rage against the dying of the light.[55]

Now any rebellion is directed against something, in this case against no less than God himself. So when we rebel metaphysically, we do not deny Him, but we certainly do denounce Him as the author of evil, the absurd, and death. Hence, metaphysical rebellion is inherently blasphemous; it expresses human pride and our refusal to let God push us around any longer. Unfortunately, with this stance we place ourselves in a cosmic Catch-22. God's Almightly Decree does provide standards of right and wrong, such as the Ten Commandments, that are inviolate and beyond dispute. Our rebellion, by rejecting God, must also reject His ethical systems, and therefore opens the door to morality becoming arbitrary.

Precisely this paradox tortures Ivan Karamazov. He rejects God because He is murderous and allows the suffering of children. But Ivan must therefore also reject God's values, such as "Thou shalt not kill." He has thereby legitimized the very act that stimulated his rebellion in the first place, i.e., the murder of children. The aim of Camus is to break this paradox by seeking a genuinely human set of values that we can then substitute for those that God so high-handedly dictated. How can we discover such values? By those choices we make passionately and instinctively rather than intellectually and logically--"in the heat of battle," as it were.[56] In rebelling, for example, we establish those beliefs for which we are willing to risk punishment, death, and even eternal damnation and it is these, according to Camus, that should provide the basic standards for exemplary human conduct.

Metaphysical rebellion establishes that our first, most fundamental value is human solidarity. Clearly, we rebel in the name of all humanity, because we demonstrate our willingness to sacrifice ourselves even for eternity. Therefore it would be illogical to rebel only for ourselves. Thus, our rebellion "transcends the individual"[57] and involves us with others, revealing that we are all in this struggle together against the Almighty. And so the first human value becomes, to paraphrase Descartes' famous dictum, "I rebel, therefore we exist."[58] If any of us denies this "we are" and lives instead in solitary isolation, then that person becomes a "stranger." (This is precisely

149

Mersault's condition in the novel bearing that title. No one else, not even his mother or his lover, is important to him.)

This position has two implications. First, murder becomes unacceptable, not because it is "evil" but because for us to kill someone makes no sense when we have just, through our rebellion, defended that person's right to live. The Myth informed us that to keep the absurd ever before us is the cardinal virtue. We have now shown that we accept this not only for ourselves but for everyone. Yet if we kill someone, he or she can no longer confront the absurd. We cannot deny a person this basic right any more than we can deny it to ourselves by committing suicide. Thus, rebellion always affirms life and creation rather than death and destruction. A second implication is that free, unambiguous human communication becomes crucial; only through it can our solidarity survive. Every misunderstanding leads to isolation and thence to a kind of death.* In Camus' words, "Clear language and simple words are the only salvation."[60] Arise, ye prisoners of jargon!

1. Creativity as rebellion. The Rebel's portrayal of creative work is summarized by the phrase, "Art is the activity that exalts and denies simultaneously."[61] Van Gogh is said to have observed that "God must not be judged on this earth. It is one of His sketches that turned out badly."[62] Every artist is, in a sense, trying to improve upon the mess He made of things in His shaky first draft, when He invented a world lacking coherence and shot through with absurdity. Thus, artists portray the world not as it is but as it could be--as Nietzsche put it, "No artist tolerates reality,"[63]--and in this sense an artist is the definitive rebel.

---

* Two of Camus' plays each depicts one of these corollaries.(59) Caligula is the definitive rebel who wants the impossible, i.e., whatever he cannot have. He wants his extensive power to be truly infinite, but in his rebellion to reach this goal he erroneously neglects the ties that bind him to his fellows, acting with unrelieved cruelty towards them. Eventually, he accepts death because he learns that we cannot be free at others' expense.

In The Misunderstanding, a long-lost son returns home, but he chooses (for quite obscure reasons) not to reveal his identity to his family. He takes a room in their hotel where, it develops, they make a business of killing and robbing their guests, a fate he duly suffers. Moral: communicate openly. Both plays are "actor proof," combining contrived plots with dialogue that no performer could bring to life. But philosophically they make their points.

150

In one significant departure from The Myth, Camus attacks the problem of style and suggests two possibilities. Each of these emanates from one answer to the problem of "what to do about reality." At one extreme is a type of art, obviously not rebellious, that totally accepts things as they are. Such art we might call religious because it implicitly reaffirms God's work. One example, ironically enough, would be that which emanates from totalitarian, fascist, and/or Stalinist regimes (art that is often labeled "super realism"). For its simplistic, propagandist, "ours is the best of all possible worlds" tone again swears by "what is." (In such societies, the artist who does not take such a positive stance is, of course, in deep trouble). This realistic art, which does not interpret but simply displays, resembles the type promoted in The Myth. This approach is quite impossible to carry off completely because it requires "indefinite enumeration"[64] and even in a lifetime not every sensation can be represented.

The other type of style features total denial. It rejects this God-given world, retreating into an artificial "sealed world"[65] devised in the artist's own fantasy. There he or she can reign supreme, understanding why things happen the way they do and introducing the clarity and logic that the real world lacks. A novel's plot can unfold precisely, its characters can make sense, and, above all, it can have a comprehensible beginning, middle, and end. In the extreme, such romantic escapism totally banishes reality, resulting in work that is completely abstract and formal. However this approach, too, cannot be completely realized, because even the most abstract painting will borrow something from the real world. Every color, shape, and so on exists somewhere, given that the world presents infinite possibilities. Some duplication is unavoidable.

Genuinely rebellious art, however, is to be found somewhere between these fictional extremes. As we noted earlier, it both denies and exalts reality. The artist "borrows" some of the world's properties that are worth retaining, thus reaffirming the essential beauty of that world and of its creatures. But the plagiarism is not total. The artist also modifies and paraphrases, competing with creation by introducing improvements missing in God's work and giving it coherence. Above all, such an artist tries to correct His greatest blunder of all, inevitable death, by giving earthly creatures immortality. Captured in the work and so protected in a sort of artistic Lenin's Tomb, they can avoid their stupid, absurd death and oblivion.

Rollo May has observed, in this regard, that creativity requires an intensity of emotion, a vitality, that is rage.[66] It may ostensibly be directed against social or political injustice (as witness such angry writers as Dickens, Sinclair Lewis, and Britain's "angry young men" of the 1950's), but ultimately this rage rails against the greatest insult of all: death.

Therefore rebellious art is the ultimate act of blasphemy. It is a Tower of Babel that exalts humankind and puts it in sinful competition with God, attempting to usurp and improve upon His definitive function. It does not deny that His work has some merit, but it is rebellion nevertheless against its less desirable aspects. We can now understand why Camus holds sculpture to be "the greatest and most ambitious of the arts."[67] It tries to retain the essence of God's finest creation, the human being, while improving upon it by making it immortal. Sculpture seeks:

> the gesture, the expression, or the empty stare which will sum up all the gestures and all the stares in the world. Its purpose is not to imitate but to stylize.[68]

While we will not extensively examine a personality fitting The Rebel's views, we might dally briefly, as does Camus, over Marcel Proust's epic Remembrance of Things Past. In this "fictional autobiography," Proust tried to recreate the events and characters of his early life in almost exhaustive detail. Nevertheless, the result was much more than a mere tape recording, because he evidently took a good deal of authorial license. Furthermore, in good rebellious fashion, he refused to admit "what is"--in this case, that the past was gone forever--because he clearly wished to relive and resurrect that past. In this attempt, therefore, he showed how the art of the novel can redesign creation itself.

Camus does not tell us in The Rebel how the doctrine of human solidarity enters this picture, but he does so elsewhere.[69] Artists may believe themselves to be alone in their work and, as a rule, they are (at least in a physical sense). Still and all, through their work they speak for everyone, since they express and communicate matters of common concern:

> (The artist's) vocation, in the face of oppression, is to open the prisons and to give a voice to the sorrows and joys of all.[70]

This hypothesis sheds some light on a crucial creative quality: the need not only to get bright ideas but also to communicate them. Perhaps it is artists' intuitive sense of human solidarity that drives them to share their insights about how God's work can be bettered. Thus, like all rebels, they act not only for themselves, but in the name of everyone.

152

2. Commentary. The Rebel's account of creativity seems much more realistic than The Myth's and avoids many of the latter's weaknesses. Camus clearly implies that creators can hope for some measure of success as they formulate alternatives to God's abomination. Likewise, the doctrine of quantity is openly rejected, since "indefinite enumeration" of the world's properties becomes not an ideal but an impractical, even rather pathetic pursuit of the impossible. Thus, Camus shows the way for the development of some rebellious standards of aesthetic judgment. Presumably, superior works express the shared themes of human existence powerfully and give substance to human solidarity. Such criteria have much to recommend them.

In addition, we are told, rebellious artists do not completely confront reality but, at least in part, leap away from it into an artificial world of their own devising. While retaining something of the world, they change a great deal, not only representing but also interpreting. This prospectus corresponds much more closely to usual practice--not least because creative work certainly does function at times as a kind of escape. One of its major attractions is that in the studio, study, or laboratory we can control and manipulate events as is seldom the case in reality. Time can stand still. The world, with its insurmountable difficulties and above all with its mortality, can, temporarily at least, be held in abeyance.

As well, the critic's labors, at least by implication, are now viewed more sympathetically. Indeed, every creator's act now amounts to constructive criticism, trying to improve upon and eliminate the flaws in Someone Else's Work (i.e., God's) and showing how He should have done it instead. And surely if creators are justified in expressing rage against Divine Creation's shortcomings, then critics may also scream when mortal produce insults their sensibilities.

The Rebel also, we might note, seems much more optimistic in tone. Besides suggesting that creators can now hope for some measure of success, it admits that God's contribution has meritorious aspects worth keeping. As well, while it still assumes our absurdity to be inescapable, it does hold out the very real possibility of human togetherness, understanding, and communication. Our painful metaphysical situation thereby becomes somewhat more tolerable than in The Myth where, it is implied, we must each confront our absurdity in isolation. Nowhere is the "we're all in this together" theme in evidence. No one helps Sisyphus push his rock, or comforts him when, yet again, it rolls back down the hill. Actually, from the standpoint of The Myth, Camus seems in this later work to have fallen into the same soft bed as did Kafka, Dostoevsky, et al. He too has seemed to weary of fighting unwinnable battles and has allowed

153

hope to raise its beautiful/ugly head. Thus, The Rebel's decidedly more positive, even romantic veneer seems a good deal more accurate than the harsh, uncompromising Myth. But perhaps it sacrifices a bit of grandeur?

Still, (to adopt a more derogatory stance) The Rebel's description of creativity does not jibe excessively with the actual state of affairs either. Artists rarely, if ever, report that they consciously confront their typewriters or easels to blaspheme God or to defeat death. (We shall later discuss possible connections between creativity and death.) If these rebellious motives do operate, they are apparently a well-kept secret within the artistic fraternity. In fact, they seem far too metaphysical for workaday practice. To repeat, vicious rumors have it that some first-rate creators labor (oh cowardly leap!) simply in order to make money.

As well, other varieties of metaphysical rebellion may or may not supply the cosmic glue to unify the human race, but this clearly does not fit the typical creatives' experience. As we have learned, they usually feel not solidarity with but isolation and even alienation from their fellows. Admittedly, they may still represent metaphysical rebellion in the name of togetherness and so furnish a convenient symbol for the absurdist philosopher, but their experience is very different.

Let us finish with several positive comments of a more general nature. First of all, Camus is undeniably a superlative writer. Even in translation he manages to be both dignified and impassioned, both intellectually stimulating and emotionally appealing. Thankfully, his prose avoids that detached, dégagé quality so pervasive in philosophic writing. When we combine these qualities with his talents for the memorable turn of phrase and the wryly sardonic metaphor, we have a writer who will elicit tears of admiration/jealousy from anyone who has, on occasion, struggled to produce a few readable sentences on paper. In discussing him, the temptation is irresistable to simply quote at length, for it is impossible to state his views any better than he has himself.

He does require careful rereading. He can be difficult because he sometimes uses familiar words in unusual ways. Fortunately, he has a way of approaching an idea from several directions, so that a difficult passage will, as a rule, be clarified later. But above all, he must be read slowly because his ideas deserve careful contemplation. Admittedly, stylistic competence would hardly by itself gain Camus inclusion here. But it is a hefty bonus that places him in graceful counterpoint to others with whom we will later have cause to do battle.

Lastly, in either of its variations, Camusian existentialism seems, despite all its harping on absurdity and hopelessness, anything but depressing. By confronting the fundamental, enduring issues that concern us all and by emphasizing authenticity, integrity, and honesty, it puts to shame those academic philosophies which eternally belabor questions that no one in their right mind would want deciphered.

155

Chapter 7

EXISTENTIAL APPROACHES II: JEAN-PAUL SARTRE

We turn now to this most vociferous and visible existentialist, novelist, playwright, philosopher, political activist, and refuser of the Nobel Prize. (Predictably, his motives for the last named were complex--see Stern[1] for a further exposition--but essentially he wanted to protect his much cherished freedom and independence.) We will not attempt anything like a comprehensive review of his thought, since there is much that is tangential to our interests. Rather, we will direct our gazes towards a few concepts, presented most fully in his seminal philosophical work Being and Nothingness[2], which have some fascinating possibilities for understanding the creative act. In this endeavor we shall do some simplifying, because Sartre under full literary sail can be a formidable adversary. There are passages in Being and Nothingness that we can peruse twenty times and still, in dismay, ask, "What?". In particular, we shall avoid his terminological monstrosities such as being-for-itself, being-for-others, and so forth and, at the risk of oversimplification, substitute our own. While admittedly his hyphenates possess great subtlety of meaning, they lead into complications interesting only to the professional philosopher, while providing a semantic quagmire into which even the most sympathetic reader can easily sink.

The Fundamental Project and The Gaze

Existentialists from Kierkegaard onward have distinguished between two possible states of being for the human species. The first, the subjective self, refers to my particular being as an individual. It is unique; it cannot be categorized or described by generalizations glommed from other people's properties. It is condemned to be free, so it is always under construction as I freely choose my arbitrary acts. As a result, it continually changes, like a kaleidoscope, and cannot be predicted, because its momentary status may well be negated by some future act I commit. Obviously, for existentialists the continuous evolution of its properties is what human existence is all about.

The second type of being, the objective self, refers to being in general, an impersonal, independent commodity that is external to any particular individual. It is a static, unchanging, predictable human nature that we supposedly all will possess both now and in the future. The Hegelian generalizations that scientists, philosophers and, yes, psychologists scatter around as they fit people into neatly labeled categories represent attempts to describe it.

157

Sartre maintains that individuals, in reality, do not possess such objectivity at all. It is a fictional ideal. We are condemned to subjectivity and freedom, separated from this kind of static, defined essence although we wish passionately to have it. Thus, existence is a lack, for which our feelings of desire provide the introspective evidence. Hence, a human "is a being which is not what it is, and which is what it is not."[3] While the objective self may describe what we are ideally, it has little connection with what we are as we exist in reality.

We long for it to be otherwise. We want that permanent essence, and our incompleteness is yet another source of human unhappiness and suffering. Thus, the objective self represents a potential or possibility towards which we continually strive and which we spend our lifetimes trying to achieve. Our subjective selves grow and are created, not in arbitrary anarchy, but towards this final goal. Our freely chosen acts not only define those subjective selves momentarily; they are also further attempts to become (subjectively) what we are (objectively). Our primary aim, then, our fundamental project, is to unify the two selves and to "coincide with ourselves."

Need we say that this can never be? What we most want, we cannot have. Existentialism being what it is, this project is an exercise in futility, an impossible dream reminiscent of Sisyphus. The subjective can never become objective, the free can never become the deterministic, because then it would no longer be human. God is the only being that can attain the impossible union and be what He is. Moreover, this objective self is not an already existing potential, similar to one of Plato's Ideals. Not only is it unknown to us, it does not even as yet exist. It is only defined after the fact, in the past, once our choices have been made and our cards have been played. We have been that (since the past cannot be changed) but we are already something else, and beforehand we can be, and will become, virtually anything. In other words, in this lifelong search we have no idea where we are trying to go until we don't get there.

An apt metaphor for this quandary is the ass attached to a cart.[4] Before it dangles a carrot that is tied to the end of a stick. The stick, in turn, is fixed to the shafts. Every effort exerted by the ass to reach the carrot pulls the cart forward but gets it no nearer the carrot, which is forever hanging hypnotically, frustratingly, just out of reach. So too is objective being. Thus, the two types of being are inherently distinct and independent, and yet logically each depends on the other and neither has any meaning without the other.

There are at least two occasions, however, when I can approach objectivity. One is at the moment of death. Then, for the first time, I have no further possibilities and my essence remains fixed. Then my past will suddenly coincide with my future and I will be what I have been because, like a time lapse photograph freezing me in the midst of some ongoing act, death "petrifies" me.* Admittedly, this frozen essence itself may change over time, if those who survive me change their opinions of me and assign different characteristics to me (e.g., when one generation regarded J. S. Bach as a mediocre has-been, and the next saw him to be a sublime master). The difference is that, while alive, we are responsible for these changes in our essence. Once dead, we are not, because they are out of our hands, administered by others. Thus, "To be dead is to be a prey for the living."[6]

Another such occasion arises when I interact with another person. When the Other contemplates me, and I come under his gaze or look, I may experience a kind of death by becoming, in his eyes, a type or an example, an object rather than a free, unpredictable subjectivity. Under his gaze, he can "possess" that subjectivity and I will experience shame, which is simply the feeling of being an object for the Other. I may cease being a perceiver, i.e., the center of my own perceptual universe, in which all things revolve around me. Instead, I may realize that, in his eyes, I am just another object of perception, another peripheral event in a field of which he is the center.[7] And so his gaze makes me conscious, in a kind of visual rape, of being a petrified "object that is looked at," lacking freedom and subjectivity.

Let us borrow Sartre's dramatic example of this change in perspective.[8] Suppose I am peeking through a keyhole and observing some situation. Suddenly I hear footsteps; someone is watching me. No longer the perceiver, I am now the perceived. I am seen. Before the Other appeared, my act was one of free

---

* Particularly in his plays and novels, Sartre has emphasized that death ends our options to become something other than what we so far have been. In the words of Stern,(5) "Dead...my present has slipped away, my future possibilities have disappeared, and I have become entirely my past....As long as we are alive, we are 'on reprieve.' The man who was a coward in his past, and is still alive, has kept his freedom to 'naught' this past, to project himself toward a heroic future....In this sense we say that death petrifies us forever as we are at the moment it strikes us" (italics mine). Thus the characters in Sartre's literary works are often concerned about dying "at the right time," when their good sides are showing, so to speak.

subjectivity. Now it is on display for that Other, and I will experience it very differently.

Why does the Other's gaze threaten and perhaps destroy my freedom? Because I realize that by his contemplation he is reducing me to an object and categorizing me, since I do the same thing whenever I contemplate others. I instinctively label them as "handsome" or "well dressed." I make sweeping statements such as "Harry is moody," which reduce Harry to a predictable, unchanging essence. I imply that Harry will be like that both now and in the future. In Maslow's terms, my portraits <u>rubricize</u> him.[9]

Unfortunately, the Other's gaze informs me that he too possesses free subjectivity and his own perceptual universe of which <u>he</u> is the center. At first, he seemed like any other object "out there," but it is soon obvious that he differs dramatically from the rest. The world that I perceive, he also perceives, but differently and in a way that I can never know or share. "Thus suddenly an object has appeared which has stolen the world from me."[10] If I, as subject, reduce others to objects, then they, known now to have subjectivity also, must objectify <u>me</u>. Under their gazes I get a taste of my own medicine.

Supposedly, then, a struggle for perceptual and psychological supremacy must ensue whenever two freedoms interact. They cannot both remain the centers of their perceptual universes, any more than the earth and the sun can both be the centers of the solar system. Something has to give. When faced with such a confrontation, therefore, we can react in either of two ways. Remember the game played by children, in which each participant tries to outstare the other, with the one who first looks away being declared the loser? Likewise, as the first possibility, each of us can try to "outgaze" the other and retain our subjectivity while reducing our adversary to an object. But this contest is no longer only a game, because the stakes are higher. Here (to switch the metaphor), two solitary Gary Coopers face one another using not revolvers for weapons but retinas. The town isn't big enough for both of us. Neither of us will physically die, but psychologically one of us certainly will.

However, a second option presents itself. I may voluntarily give over the struggle and surrender my freedom, so that the Other can keep his. I may choose to reduce myself to a pure object, who exists only in his gaze as a kind of psychological parasite. Why would I decide to do this? Because the Other possesses that objective self of mine that I have spent my life pursuing. Through his gaze, he has come to see and know me precisely in the way that I want to and don't. Therefore, he provides a rare opportunity. If I can see myself through his eyes, as the Other sees me, then I may locate the missing piece in my psychic jigsaw puzzle.

The sadist and the masochist provide classic versions of these two reactions. Sadists try to debase their adversaries/lovers into helpless, totally dependent "things" over whom they can exercise complete, arbitrary power. Masochists choose to debase themselves, to be manipulated, humiliated, and reduced to pure objectivity, because potentially they can regain their freedom by voluntarily giving it up. Both of these enterprises are, as Sartre shows at some length, ultimately doomed. They founder on inescapable paradox, the seeds of which are contained in the old joke that "a sadist is someone who makes a masochist happy."

Let us consider only the masochist's failure (for it will be relevant to Sartre's study of Jean Genet). If I am of this persuasion, I will debase myself before the Other and try to become a particularly important object in his gaze. Thus, contradictorily, by losing myself (the subjective version) I can find myself (the objective version). I must then cherish the Other's freedom above all else, because if he loses his status as a pure subject, he will also lose his ability to possess me as a pure object. In turn, I will lose my chance to regain it parasitically through him.

And yet I still desire above all that he love me and attach importance to me, for only then will I become a pure object, complete in his gaze. Unfortunately for my ontological sanity, as soon as he does this he loses his subjective freedom. By becoming attached to me and needing me, he ceases to be the pure, unencumbered subject I need him to be. His love endows me with subjectivity (which I do not want) and degrades him into his own objectivity. The twists of Sartre's unerring logic begin to be apparent.

The essence of the gaze is captured quite successfully by the legend of Perseus and the Medusa. Any objects coming under the Medusa's gaze were turned to stone and literally petrified. However, Perseus held up his shield before her, in which her own image was reflected. In one version of the myth she was herself petrified, when her gaze was "turned back on herself" and she saw herself as others saw her.

This fascinating (and by psychologists too much ignored) concept of human interaction has some implications that deserve mention. First, for Sartre, all such interactions, particularly those involving love and/or sexuality, inevitably feature such power struggles. Reciprocity or equality are romantic fictions.

161

A relationship can be no more symmetrical than can the sexual act itself; there must always be an active/dominant donor and a passive/submissive recipient. Each partner needs the other, but in a very different way because each plays a different role. One participant is always the lover, who worships and gazes at the adversary/accomplice; the latter is the beloved, who is worshipped and gazed at. In short, the coupling of the sadist and masochist provides both the reductio ad absurdum and also the microcosm of all relationships.

As well, Sartre's long-time companion, Simone de Beauvoir, has applied the concept to the psychology of women.[11] They have long been treated as sexual objects, evaluated mainly by their physical attractiveness. Conscious of being gazed at, therefore, they have, by and large, accepted object status and relinquished their subjective freedoms, becoming unassertive, dependent, and obsessed with their appearance to others. For the typical woman, the important question has not been "Who am I?" but "What do they think of me?".

Lastly, R. D. Laing has interpreted the schizophrenic personality along these lines.[12] Under the gaze of others we all feel selfconscious, but potential schizophrenics (for obscure reasons) feel it particularly intensely. Constantly aware of being stared at, they may find it traumatic simply to walk down a street or past a line of people. Therefore, to protect their sensitive subjectivity from petrification by all these gazes, they hide it from view. They fabricate and display a highly artificial public self that features bizarre, psychotic behavior. In this tragic role, they are actually "split" (the literal meaning of the term "schizophrenia") between their artificial and their genuine selves.

Creativity

These Sartrian notions suggest two approaches to creativity. In both, it is seen as yet another attempt on our part to attain power and dominance, this time over the external world and its objects. In fact, these approaches may well represent two different ways of saying the same thing; readers may judge for themselves. An experience of the writer's will serve to introduce them both.

In Victoria, B.C. languishes the storied Empress Hotel. Here, expatriate matrons of empire still pridefully out-English the English. Here, "r's" are softer, upper lips stiffer, and neck lines more rigid. Here, where "high tea" is still served promptly at 4 PM, "The Good Queen" refers not to Elizabeth II but to the city's namesake. For these displaced patricians, Kipling still seeks India's eternal secrets and Gordon, at this

162

very moment, awaits his relief at Khartoum. Next to the Empress snuggles a tiny, tranquil park, delightfully isolated from the urban hurly-burly. In it, one may leisurely contemplate the meaning of existence, the inevitability of death, and Team Canada's latest belaboring by the Russian hockeyists.

In this park someone, in a moment of rare insight, has placed some magnificent totem poles. They demand the contemplation of my gaze, for they pose a formidable riddle. "Why," I must ask, "would anyone undertake the taxing labor of carving an image on a tree?". Admittedly, historical cum religious motives were largely responsible. But do these totems not also reflect the same human need that has given us graffiti scratched on lavatory walls, lovers' initials painted high up on unscalable cliffs, and twigs whittled into miniature steamships? By all appearances, we simply cannot leave our environment alone.

Why not? Why do we expend so much time, energy, and tears on such seemingly useless pastimes as art, science, sports, and games? Sartre answers that these are all different manifestations of our fundamental project, our neverending, hopeless quest to unify our evolving subjectivity with permanent objectivity.[13] Our subjective selves lack that final potential precisely because they are always changing. But the attributes of an environmental object remain fixed. My "moodiness" may be here today and gone tomorrow, but a tree's "woodenness" is now and always will be. Perhaps, then, if I can appropriate or take over that object and make it a part of me, I can therby acquire its attributes, and above all that permanence I presently lack.

This is what all the aforementioned gratuitous activities are, in different ways, trying to do. A work of art, for example, which I have created, is a synthesis of myself (since I "did it") with an external, objective event (the medium) that is separate from me. And it certainly possesses that static finality that I so desire. As such it becomes a way for me to stop time and my relentless flight towards death, to freeze myself in my tracks. Oscar Wilde's story The Picture of Dorian Gray presents a fascinating variation on this theme. Dorian, a handsome youth, lives to be young and attractive. The idea that he must eventually age and lose these qualities is thus, for him, particularly horrifying. However an artist paints his portrait. It is so lifelike that it literally "becomes" Dorian; the portrait's face gradually ages, while the living Dorian remains eternally youthful, i.e., unchanging. Which, then, is the "real" Dorian Gray?

As we might have guessed, however, a work of art must likewise fail as a technique for unifying the subjective and

163

objective. I can no more completely incorporate a work external
to myself than a sadist can completely gratify all his or her
desires at the expense of a masochist. My product can never
attain that elusive dual oneness because, while it may capture
objectively what I am at the instant of its completion, I, the
artist, will continue to change while it will remain fixed, so
I will soon transcend it.

    Hence artists' eternal dissatisfaction with their work and
hence their continual desire to change it. They are trying to
bring that work "up to date," but of course they can never do
so. Presumably, an artist would only be eternally satisfied
with a work produced at the moment of death, because that self
would thereafter be his or her petrified being. As Sartre has
said, regarding the sculptor Giacometti:

> Almost as soon as (his statues) are produced
> he goes on to dream of women that are thinner,
> taller, lighter, and it is through his work
> that he envisions the ideal by virtue of which
> he judges it imperfect. He will never finish
> because a man always transcends what he does.[14]

    Still, we can now understand why we take these seemingly
trivial activities so seriously: they express our fundamental
Diogenesian search. Moreover, they can give us a sense of our
importance and necessity in this otherwise fluctuating,
incomprehensible world. Yet, Sartre emphatically informs us,
when athletes or artists swell their chests with prideful arrogance
because of their apparent successes, they are lying to themselves,
and so become salauds. They refuse to recognize that actually
they matter not a whit and that life will continue on its
merry way perfectly well without them.

    The concept of the gaze provides Sartre's second approach
to creativity. When we interact with Others, we can seek the
sadist's dominance, but we can also voluntarily submit as does
the masochist, taking our being from them and evaluating our
actions through their eyes. Many creative people, Sartre suggests,
practice this second reaction. According to his fascinating
autobiography, The Words,[15] he himself did so. The child Sartre
played a series of roles to impress the watching adults, first
by persistently reading books and later writing countless stories,
pretending all the while to be unaware of their prying presence.
But once he had allowed those Others to label him as "the
reader" or "the child prodigy," he then must fulfill those
labels or suffer guilt, that powerful motivator which ever since
has driven him to write compulsively. Sartre's evocative prose
describes the mechanism:

My truth, my character and my name were in the
hands of the adults. I had learned to see
myself through their eyes. I was a child, that
monster that they fabricated....(I was) condemned
to please....I sometimes wonder whether I have
not consumed so many days and nights, covered
so many pages with ink, thrown on the market
so many books that nobody wanted, solely in
the mad hope of pleasing my grandfather....My
commandments were sewn into my skin; if I go a
day without writing, the scar burns me...and
since all writers have to sweat,..we're all
galley-slaves, we're all tattooed.[16]

But eventually he becomes a genuine writer when he realizes
that he has the same power over his characters as the adults
have over him. He can control those characters' destinies,
even kill them off with a stroke of his pen. In the world of
his imagination, the masochist becomes the sadist. But is he
now free of the gaze? Not at all, since now he writes for the
effect on posterity. To be read, and therefore in a sense
seen, by generations yet unborn is to symbolically defeat death
and attain immortality:

The Giver can be transformed into his own Gift,
that is, into a pure object (the book)....I
would hand myself over to the consumers.[17]

Varying this notion of the gaze somewhat, we can also
understand other aspects of creativity. We exist amongst many
external objects, both human and inanimate. This "environment"
can, as the more dogmatic versions of behaviorism assert,[18]
control us and determine our characteristics (as witness the
truism that "human behavior depends on environmental factors").
Yet we can also gain preeminence over it. After all, our
modern environment is, to repeat an earlier point, almost entirely
of our own making, peopled with products that we have devised.
It may create us, but we can also, and have, created it.

Do we not have here (with a little shuffling) the necessary
ingredients for a Sartrian gazal struggle, pitting the individual
not against someone else but against her or his surroundings,
with each having the potential to master and control the other?
Admittedly, Sartre's scenario only unfolds when two subjective
freedoms interact. But if we equate freedom with creative ability,
as seems at least plausible, then the analysis should still
apply. If this much is allowed, then one way for individuals
to bring their environmental adversary to heel is to modify it
through their own freely chosen, creative activities. When I

165

slap graffiti on a blank wall, then that wall no longer gazes impersonally back at me. I have imposed my selfhood on it.

From this standpoint, then, creativity arises from the same unavoidable struggle for dominance that, for Sartre, permeates every human interaction. Is this, perchance, an overly melodramatic portrayal? We think not. In trying to force one's medium to yield up its possibilities and express one's vision, a creator does wage a battle, an exhausting struggle between (to quote Walter Kerr again) "what he can have and what he must have." Will that environmental phenomenon remain stubbornly intransigent and emerge victorious, or can it be wrestled to the ground?

What is Literature?

But what of the interaction between a creator and the audience? Might the gaze have something useful to say about this? Sartre has pursued this point in What Is Literature?,[19] and come to a rather surprising conclusion, at least as concerns the dyad of author and reader. To anticipate, he apparently views it as an exception to the usual power struggle, since it is possible (and indeed crucial) for both participants to retain their freedoms. This is because they do not confront one another directly but through a mediator, the book. Like a Henry Kissinger practicing shuttle diplomacy, it carries messages between two potentially antagonistic parties, while keeping them separated from each other's throats.

Sartre begins by denying that the various arts have anything in common, or are "parallel." Each employs different elements, so that they can tell us little about one another. (In our terms, then, he denies a creative "g" factor.) Even poetry and prose, which both use words, do so quite differently. The poet uses them "for themselves," the way artists and musicians employ color and sound. But the prose writer, alone among artists, exploits elements as signs; words stand not only for themselves but for other things. With this debatable assertion, Sartre confines his analysis to the writer-reader relationship.

Writing, for Sartre, is a notable example of human freedom and subjectivity. Since we are, by nature, not free not to choose, writers, like all authentic persons, must make decisions and take sides on the issues about which they write. They cannot and should not be impartial, seeking only to represent the world; they should try to change it, to serve some kind of evolutionary/revolutionary purpose (although not necessarily in the narrow political sense of these words). Engaged, committed writers' words are "actions" or (more melodramatically) "loaded pistols." In fact, Sartre cheerfully evaluates other writers, past and present, mainly by asking whether they were an "irritant for their age."

However, writers do not labor for themselves but for others. They can never experience their work as do readers, who come to it only after it is finished. For writers, their work is too much a part of themselves, always in a suspended state of construction, never complete, because they could always change something. In addition, as they write they are more aware of the activity itself than of the concepts coming to life under their pen. The future is a series of blank pages that they must fill, while from the readers' standpoint the pages have already been filled. Even afterwards, as they re-read, writers cannot attain the readers' perspective. The latter forsee, predict, and guess what might be on those pages yet to come. Writers already know.

In other words, writers always meet themselves as they read, and touch their own subjectivity. They want their work to become an impersonal object, but they cannot achieve this themselves. Only the eyes of others can do it, so they need readers to finish the task they have begun. But readers can only fulfill their complementary role if they too remain a "pure freedom," retaining their subjectivity and acting, not as passive sponges or objects of perception, but as active, dynamic perceivers--gazers rather than gazees. After all, readers cannot experience the book as an object unless they approach it as a subject. Therefore, "all literary work is an appeal...to the reader's freedom to collaborate in the production of his work."[20]

For this egalitarian partnership to succeed, then, readers' activity must also be creative. Like literary princes arousing dormant sleeping beauties they "stroke" and "awaken" the words the writers have previously laid to rest on the page. And writers (for their own selfish purposes) must help readers function in this active way. If the latter simply internalize certain specific effects passively, if they are inattentive or incapable, then the writers' efforts will have been wasted. But if readers are functioning at their best, they will:

> Project beyond the words a synthetic form, each phrase of which will be no more than a partial function of the "theme," the "subject," or the "meaning."[21]

Thus for fully participating readers, holding up their end, the words provide only an intitial stimulus for their own conscious activity. They not only read but "muse" about what they read. This activity writers may certainly guide and suggest by the words they produce, but they cannot and should not try to

167

control it. They must never try to affect readers or "overwhelm" them by dictating particular emotions, thoughts, or experiences (otherwise readers will lose their precious subjectivity). The distinguishing characteristic of bad writing, such as cheap pulp fiction or propaganda, is that it does precisely this. No, writers must simply present, and let readers make of it what they wish. Thus, reading is:

> an exercise of generosity, and what the writer requires of the reader is not the application of an abstract freedom, but the gift of his whole person...Thus, the author writes in order to address himself to the freedom of readers, and he requires it in order to make his work exist (italics mine).[22]

Or, to put it succinctly, "reading is directed creation."[23]

Now Sartre recognizes that writers may themselves be impassioned about themes they wish to express, especially if they are "committed." But the decision to write presupposes that one "withdraws" somewhat from these strong feelings and does not try to force them onto one's anticipated colleague. In other words, readers must be able to assume that writers are in an attitude of generosity. However, readers, too, must be in this attitude, valuing and preserving the freedom of the writers to produce the books that they wish. Each partner recognizes the subjectivity of the other and works to maintain it, so that the partnership can become authentic. Let us allow Sartre to summarize this position:

> Precisely because the universe is supported by the joint effort of our two freedoms...however bad and hopeless the humanity which it paints may be, the work must have an air of generosity....The one who writes recognizes, by the very fact that he takes the trouble to write, the freedom of his readers, and...the one who reads, by the mere fact of his opening the book, recognizes the freedom of the writer. The work of art, from whichever side you approach it, is an act of confidence in the freedom of men...the result of which is that there is no gloomy literature (italics mine).[24]

168

According to this penetrating analysis,* then, we have here a notable exception to the power struggles that supposedly characterize all human interactions. Here we find not confrontation but generosity, not a perceptual battle for supremacy but a sharing of freedoms. Furthermore, Sartre's disclaimers notwithstanding, we see no reason why this analysis could not be applied fruitfully to other media as well (and Sartre himself uses analogies from other arts, especially painting, to buttress his arguments). Apparently, therefore, works of art can provide a kind of shield or wall through which two psyches can collaborate without either coming out the loser. In this, they resemble those glass windows sometimes placed in the aquaria of Siamese fighting fish, which allow these voracious combatants to confront and glare at one another without doing any damage.

Jean Genet

Sartre has provided several biographical studies of creative personalities, notably the poet Beaudelaire and the painter Tintoretto, in which the concept of the gaze figures prominently. However, it particularly influences his fascinating study of Saint Genet: Actor and Martyr,[26] so we shall follow him along this path. Jean Genet, whose plays (such as The Maids and The Balcony) and novels (such as Our Lady of the Flowers), mixing perverse, fantastic sexuality and obscure allusion, have outraged, stimulated, amazed, and sometimes bored his audiences. Jean Genet, who has been openly admired by some of Europe's most renowned intellectual figures (including Sartre), while spending much of his adult life behind bars. Jean Genet. Brilliant artist and despicable criminal. Playwright and thief. Poet and homosexual. Jean Genet. Object of "the gaze."

It is difficult to summarize briefly the complicated highways and byways of Sartre's exposition. Never given to using one word where twenty would do, Saint Genet even by his standards is excessively verbose. This is not to say that it does not contain some marvelous passages, for few philosophers (or novelists for that matter) have equaled Sartre's ability to use metaphor and imagery to bring an otherwise obscure argument to life. As with Camus, the temptation is irresistible to simply quote him at length.

---

* Stern asserts that it did not originate with Sartre but with Croce.(25) Sartre has several times been accused of being slipshod in acknowledging his obvious intellectual predecessors, notably Nietzsche and Adler. Perhaps this simply indicates his dislike of scholarly, academic practices.

He begins with a bygone instant when Genet, under the gaze of the Other, died of shame and lost control of his own selfhood. This seminal event provided the psychological quandary that he has spent his life trying to resolve. An orphan from early childhood, he acquires life's necessities not, like most children, by natural right but through the kindness and largesse of others who have no inherent obligation to him. Therefore, "this child has more than enough of gifts";[27] he must be continually grateful to others. It is quite fitting, then, that he should choose to receive his selfhood from them, just as he receives everything else. Under their gaze, he will relinquish his free subjectivity and become an object in their eyes.

One day he is caught stealing. A voice declares, "You are a thief." It may not have happened this way, but Genet believes that it did. In an instant, gazed at and named a "thing," he learns what his essence is to be. A thief. Still free to be guilty, he can no longer be innocent. He is "pinned by a look, a butterfly fixed to a cork."[28] In this way he is cut off from the normal, law-abiding citizens whom Sartre calls the Just. They need an outcast, a scapegoat to personify all the despicable vices they themselves possess but cannot admit, because of their moral beliefs. (Psychoanalysts use the term projection when we assign our own undesirable qualities to someone else.) Genet thus becomes a useful Other for good men, their image in the mirror. They will not let him out:

> By the gaze that surprised him....the collectivity
> doomed him to Evil. They were waiting for him.
> There was going to be a vacancy; some old convict
> lay dying on Devil's Island.[29]

Furthermore, the Just have inculcated their values inside him; he believes as fully as they that stealing and murder are wrong. Hating what he is and what he must be, he is thereby also denied self acceptance. For this reason too he will assign priority to his objective self, which he is to the Others, over his free subjectivity. On the side of the objects named rather than those which do the naming, his appearance to them will become his prime reality, and he will play whatever role they give him (hence the actor of the title). To "get in touch with himself" he must try to see himself in a detached, impersonal manner, as others see him.* This will be his quest.

---

* Many of Genet's plays display a highly stylized, ritualistic role playing. In The Maids, for example, two female servants pretend to be "madame." They put on clothes, and adopt her

170

The only free choice left to him is to decide, of his own accord, to be what he already is. Only by becoming an even more despicable arch-criminal than they want can he take the initiative, retrieving both his dignity and his life. Hence, "I was a thief, I will be the thief."[30] Thus, "He remains in his place conspicuously when nobody has requested him to leave it."[31] By such seemingly submissive, acquiescent acts does he gain the same perverse dominance over his oppressors that a masochist has over sadists. They need him. Therefore, in a sentence that aptly summarizes Sartre's analysis, "This is a game in which the loser wins."[32]

All these undercurrents are expressed in Genet's role of the passive homosexual "queen." His brute pimps and criminals possess, via their gazes, his (Genet's) objective being. When he submits to them, and they penetrate him sexually, they place their beings inside him, where he can hopefully steal them and, in turn, obtain his own. The more stupid and vapid those pimps appear, the less intrinsic being they seem to have, the more Genet desires them. Perhaps this psychological parasite can "take it over" from them and so view himself through their eyes. Once more, Sartre supplies a helpful metaphor:

> That head is unoccupied, he is going to be able to install himself in it, like a hermit crab in an empty shell.[33]

The only quality these lovers must possess is indifference to him. The Other, whom they represent, is by definition uncaring, so if they return Genet's affection, they lose prestige. No, they must take him by force, for only by being made to submit can he truly internalize the Other. Again, loser wins.

We must now leave these pornographic matters, for homosexuality and criminality fail to fulfill Genet's quest. Therefore, he tries a second gambit, that of the Aesthete, the decadent seeker after beauty, pretense, and artificiality. Again (not surprisingly) failure. So, at last, the Writer becomes his third and final persona or metamorphosis (although his purpose remains to regain his lost being through the gaze of the Other). This vilified outcast knows that the Just will hate what he

---

social roles and even her personality quirks. In addition, they take turns playing each other playing madame. As if this were not enough, Genet has directed that the two maids should be acted by adolescent boys. Thus, young boys play older women who play each other each playing madame. It is a "whirligig" in which we are never quite sure who is who.

writes, but their scorn and ridicule fulfill his masochistic need for humiliation. Once more, loser wins.

He first tries poetry. Do his perverse motives demand that he write badly? Not at all, for he soon realizes that the Others prefer inferior poems, so writing beautiful ones is the quickest road to failure and "martyrdom." For Sartre, however, Genet's early poems, such as Funeral Rites, are not successful because they demand to be paraphrased and interpreted in linear terms, whereas the best poetry is untranslatable. Which indicates that here is a natural prose writer still seeking a medium. In his first great novel, Our Lady of The Flowers, he at last comes to terms with himself. Henceforth,

> He must walk in the broad daylight of prose....(Poetry) has been only a transition.[34]

Our Lady was written entirely in the solitude of his prison cell. At first blush it reveals no attempt whatever to communicate. Seeking excitement and relief from boredom, Genet simply writes down his fantasies. He uses a decidedly unusual criterion for making artistic decisions, i.e., sexual arousal. His creations--Divine, Our Lady, Gabriel, et al.--must provoke erection and orgasm of "the capricious and blasé little fellow he carries between his thighs"[35] or he rejects them. Thus Our Lady is an "epic of masturbation."[36] At this early stage, he does not think of creation as a career. Each work is an isolated "offence," done only for excitement. When it begins to bore him, he finishes it hurriedly or even leaves it incomplete. Each book, he says, will be his last. Like a literary Sarah Bernhardt, forever doing farewell appearances, he may not write for months. Then his favourite themes will once more arouse him and he will take pen in hand (the phallic symbolism is obvious).

But gradually the writing rises above this monistic, onanistic level and becomes, clearly, Genet's latest attempt to reach his psychological goals. In it, he still seeks himself, that elusive objectivity. While writing, he thinks only of his characters. But as soon as the ink is dry he stands outside himself, reading his own thoughts, like someone gazing at himself in a mirror. Like every creator, he vacillates between two roles, now standing inside the work and now outside, as witness his frequent authorial instrusions, such as "I am growing bored with Divine," in the midst of an exposition. Involved, he is the masturbator seeking excitement; detached, he is the writer/creator. His dealings with Divine, the passive drag queen, particularly betray this schizophrenia. Genet clearly identifies with her, so at one point she is Genet and at another a character whom he contemplates and writes about.

172

But now (as we might have guessed) he encounters an insurmountable obstacle. He tries to read his writings and see himself but (for reasons we have discovered in What is Literature?) he cannot. This definitive pariah, the Just's rejected Other, created a new universe on paper where he thought he could attain complete power. Unfortunately, he meets only himself in his writing, rather than Another who is himself. He must admit that he needs the collaboration of readers, representatives of the Other, to finish the job. As a result, like a graffiti poet seeking immortality on the side of a subway car, he now writes in order to be read, to affect the Just. We readers may sense that we intrude into his private fantasies, but we also realize that he expects our gaze. As we run over the words he has written, we "caress Genet physically."[37]

If we, the Just, hate his book or even censor it, that is fine, for this shows that he has gained our attention. If we imprison him for it, so much the better. Before he wrote, he was nothing to us. Horrified by thieves in general, we simply ignore a particular thief, such as Genet, and delegate his punishment to our hirelings, the police and magistrates. Like the baseball personality (was it Branch Rickey?) who told reporters that he didn't care what they wrote about him, as long as they wrote something, Genet wants to bring our "dead gaze," which as a child had petrified him, back to life and make it again "sparkle."

But what if we ignore him? That alone could deny him his goal. But if he writes about crime beautifully he need have no fear. The aesthetic depth of his style, images, and inventions will force us to read him and, in turn, gaze at him. At last he approaches his goal, to become the definitive object for the Other. Moreover, he has gained the upper hand and will turn the tables on us. We made him a thief to serve as an object of hatred. Now, as a poet of theft, he will make us see him as he wants to be seen. Our police and magistrates can protect us against his crimes, but not against his poetic depiction of crime.

It is with words that Genet will lay his traps....The trap is a book...black strokes on paper sewn together.[38]

Genet has still more devious purposes in mind. The Just had established their values within him, so that he hated himself for what he was. For this too he will have his revenge, by instilling his values within us and forcing us to recognize that, unconsciously, we share them. In Sartre's opinion, many of Genet's stylistic idiosyncrasies, such as continuously using the present tense and the first person pronoun "I," help to involve us in the portrayed events, so that we identify with the feelings and desires of the characters. In short, we experience empathy. But of course these experiences, supposedly our own, are actually Genet's and, unfortunately for us, the world which he depicts is a world of crime. We address him freely, in our generosity, but we are trapped. While accepting and admiring his formal skill, we also accept a content of distasteful criminal and sexual acts that ordinarily would horrify us. We are forced to admit, for example, that a graphic depiction of homosexual intercourse has moved and even aroused us. So for Genet:

> poetry is the art of using shit and making (the reader) eat it.[39]

By these means do Genet's values take us over, and voluntarily.* Let us allow Sartre's evocative prose to summarize this intriguing argument:

> The decent man very gingerly sticks his toe into this still water, then makes up his mind and dives in....(He discovers) I am bad, a homosexual, a monster....His (Genet's) procedure has not varied since the time when he was a young hoodlum who let himself be taken by the Pimps in order to steal their ego. He let himself be taken by readers; there he is on the shelf of a bookcase, someone takes him down, carries him away, opens him. "I'm going to see", says the right thinking man, "what this chap is all about." But the one who thought he was taking is suddenly taken.[41]

In a real sense, then, Genet puts himself into his books; in fact, he "dissolves himself" in and lives on in them. He is his work. He may not be able to see himself there, but he will "put himself into circulation" so Others will. In this:

> The scapegoat is taking his revenge. He has

---

* Festinger's studies of cognitive dissonance(40) verify Sartre's analysis. Persons holding a particular political or moral opinion will sometimes change it if they can be coerced into playacting the role of someone holding the opposite opinion. But this will only work if they believe they were led to state this opposing position voluntarily. If they conclude that they were somehow forced to act in this inconsistent way, then they can justify their compliance, and their opinion will remain unchanged.

174

been the object of their gazes and now they
are the object of his.[42]

Thus, his ten years of literature resemble a psychoanalytic
"confession" of what he actually is. But just when he might
seem to have conquered his demons, the existential world's inherent
contrariness makes his victory short-lived. Unhappily, readers
do not honour Genet for his writing about crime, but in spite
of it. They admire his talent but condemn his subject. He is
still not taken by them for what he is. In addition, this
masochist wants the Just to hate him. When they become
understanding and even sympathetic to his plight, when liberal
bleeding hearts bewail the unfortunate early experiences that
forever perverted him, they cease to be the Just. He can no
longer even commit a crime, because some sophisticate will have
it hushed up, and if by chance he is convicted, writers will
testify for him in court and prison authorities will treat him
kindly because he is, after all, a famous writer.

So, paradoxically, his hard-won freedom and influence is
"dreary." Like an old soldier who fought for peace but now
misses the excitement of war, or an athlete whose multi-year
contract guarantees lifelong security, success and recognition
bring only boredom. He no longer knows quite why he writes.
So now his own tables are turned. Before this loser won.
Now, the winner at last, he loses. Or, in Sartre's words:

> In winning the title of writer Genet loses the
> need, desire and occasion to write.[43]

Sartre wrote this pessimistic prognosis, implying that Genet
was "finished," before Genet produced his greatest plays such
as The Balcony and The Blacks. Nevertheless, it may be indicative
that with success Genet has turned to yet another artistic
medium. Perhaps this latest metamorphosis, the Playwright, shows
less need to display and reveal himself?

Dancers

The concept of the gaze has such untapped potential that
we will provide two biographical examples of it. Some activities,
by their very nature, might reduce their practitioners to "gazed
at" objects of perception, impersonal commodities filling whatever
image the viewer/customer desires. Dancers, a group with whom
the writer has been closely associated, might be expected, we
will suggest, to internalize such a dehumanized status.

Sweeping generalizations about any heterogeneous population
naturally court disaster, so we must immediately limit our scope,
using Siegel's distinction between academic and expressive dance.[44]

The first, exemplified by classical ballet, resembles a museum. Predictable and conservative in form, it preserves a particular style and code of manners. The more personal expressive dance, on the other hand, emphasizes self expression and originality. Seeking new forms or the transformation of old ones, it is inherently experimental and often revolutionary. An obvious example is American modern dance (and Siegel believes that American dance generally has internalized expressive values much more than has Europe).

Judging by their highly individual dance approaches, Isadora Duncan, Martha Graham, Merce Cunningham, et al. would, in personality, probably fit Sartre's free, subjective perceiver. Consequently, we confine ourselves to academic dancers in such large institutions as The New York City Ballet, The National Ballet of Canada, and England's Royal Ballet. These employ large, anonymous corps de ballets, since their repertoires lean heavily towards classics such as Swan Lake/Sleeping Beauty, or works recognizably in that tradition, such as the "neo-classics" of George Balanchine.

Ethereal, unworldly glamor and romance is the classical female dancer's public image, which is why so many star-struck pre-pubescents dream of occupying her place. The ballerina, barely in contact with the earth and thus with all things crassly physical, skims lightly across the stage on her toes and leaps effortlessly into the air or is borne aloft by her doting cavalier prince. Glorious sounds from uncounted and unseen musicians impel her every movement. The world, like those musicians, is at her feet.

A more brutal contrast between appearance and reality is difficult to imagine. Several sources graphically portray it. Agnes de Mille, both an inventive choreographer and perhaps the most compelling of all dance writers, has poignantly described in her witty, insightful works such as Dance to the Piper[45] and Speak to Me, Dance With Me,[46] her long, painful labors in obscurity before she became an overnight success. Mazo's wonderfully evocative Dance Is a Contact Sport[47] chronicles the grueling day-to-day backstage life, the rehearsals, performances, and tours, of a typical New York City Ballet season. A series of interviews in Gruen's The Private World of Ballet[48] shows what many renowned figures think about their lives and work. And of course the film The Turning Point brought home to a much wider audience some realities of the dance profession.

What are those realities? First, poor pay. Although dancers can now actually live on their wages, they still earn less than plumbers or mechanics. Only international stars can afford such luxuries as a home and car. Constant pain. Ballet technique--with its five positions of the arms and feet, its turn out from the hips, its pointed feet, stretched legs, erect back, and lifted torso--is a Procrustean bed for which the human body was never designed. The eternal struggle to make it fit will always produce pain, but so long as its anatomical location keeps changing, the orthopede need not be visited. But knees and ankles do give way and careers do end, as when some thoughtless choreographer demands a dangerous movement. The men risk chronic back problems by hoisting up those ballerinas (who seem somewhat less ethereal from underneath). And if you would retain your illusions of her glamor, do not peruse her feet. The wages of dancing _en_ _pointe_ are bunions and blisters by the score. Fatigue. The dancer's day begins with a technique class whose physical and mental demands make the average hockey practice seem like bird watching. No matter how the previous night has been spent--performing, carousing, or even sleeping--morning will find dancers everywhere hanging grimly onto the _barre_, lowering their bodies in yet another _plie_. Then will follow a day of taxing rehearsals, perhaps another class or two, and sometimes an evening performance for the _coup_ _de_ _grace_.

Yet these physical demands pale beside the psychological ones. Mobile Sisyphi, every dancer pursues impossible perfection. If, momentarily, they forget this truism, a mirror will remind them. Like the Wicked Queen's in Snow White, it does not lie; every minuscule flaw is mercilessly revealed. A hefty ballerina being a contradiction in terms, every dancer fights a neverending Battle of the Bulge; beside their diets, an anorexic's will seem gluttonous. The supply of dancers far exceeding demand, there will be continuous competition, competition for places in the best schools and companies, and for the juiciest roles. Extensive touring provides another terpsichorean trauma. But hold! Is not here at least glamor and romance? Journeys to far-off lands? Titled admirers jostling at the stage door? A TV interviewer even more moronic than most asked about the "fun" of touring. A dancer replied, "Oh, it's terrific fun--if your idea of fun is Hibbing, Minn. on Saturday night!." Touring is living out of a suitcase. It is antiseptic hotel rooms, dirty, drafty backstage areas, and all-night short-order restaurants of doubtful hygiene. It is sitting all day on a bus, then trying desperately to force your protesting body to perform rare physical feats that night. Touring makes long-term relationships with someone outside the company very difficult, and raising a family virtually impossible. Dancers have been known to suffer nervous breakdowns on tour.

Worst of all, the arbitrary judgments of directors and choreographers control the dancer's fate. Mazo shows how New York City Ballet members lived and died by Balanchine's every glance; it could mean a solo part or a terminated contract. Ballet originated in the courtly life of Versailles, and companies retain its rigidly hierarchical social system. They are not democracies but throwbacks to feudal fiefdoms, and the dancers are the serfs, doing what they are told without complaining (at least not within earshot of the lord of the manor) or the company will find someone else less vocal. The company organizes virtually every aspect of their lives, so rarely must they exercise personal responsibility or independence. As Mazo puts it:

> In the company, as in the army, you don't have to think. People tell you what to wear, and where to go and what time to show up. Balanchine offers advice on diet (protein), pets (cats) and hobbies (plants and cooking). He gives the girls perfume for Christmas, so that they don't have to worry about that choice....So all a dancer really has to do is dance, try for roles and aim at advancement inside the company.[49]

The company may even rule (usually negatively) on such personal matters as love, marriage, and pregnancy. Director Lincoln Kirstein openly views every reproductive act by his distaff employees as heretical. Anyone can have babies. Like nuns, these women have chosen a higher calling. Ballerina Allegra Kent, by audaciously mothering three children, became a virtual outcast; Balanchine no longer wished to devise new roles for her.

And always, the greatest enemy of all, time, looms in the wings. It is fitting that a dying swan should be the most familiar image for this most ephemeral of the arts. Like the last rose of summer, dance's tragic beauty rests partly on its transientness. In the words of Walter Sorrell:

> As time is the most fragile fabric of which our life is made, so is the moment it takes the dancer to move. This moment is an ecstatic state of being; it is telescoped timelessness. Because of it, the urgency, the power of immediacy is stronger in the dance than in any other art form.[50]

By inviolate decree, ballet is for the young. Soon the dancer will labor not to improve but simply to delay decline. Soon the automatic will become the difficult and then the impossible. Then the dancer must pick up the pieces of his or her life and find a new career. Retirement can be as shattering for the dancer as for the athlete.

We have supplied this background to show that by all logic there should be no dancers (and virtually every one has wondered, while enduring yet another interminable rehearsal, or gazing blankly out a Greyhound window at yet another wheat field, "What am I doing here?"). And so we must ask: who would choose a career offering such intangible rewards and such constant castigation? Dancers' personality characteristics have not been studied empirically, so our answers, relying on informal observation, should be treated as hypotheses to be tested rather than as firm data.

First, classical dancers learn from childhood to accept externally imposed authority and discipline without question. A class from a first-rate dance academy, such as the National Ballet School of Canada, will display poised youngsters with precise, assured techniques, who dress alike, look alike, and suppress any individuality or youthful rebelliousness. They are being trained for the corps de ballet, and the third swan from the left must resemble the other swans. It is both exhilarating and depressing to watch children who look like nothing so much as a superbly talented group of trained seals.

Second, dancers must be intelligent. They must learn quickly because rehearsal time is valuable and no one will wait. That Hollywood cliché, the understudy who fills in for the star, happens all the time in ballet companies, and the "quick study" is the one who will get to do Giselle on two days notice. They need infallible memories. If a male dancer forgets to catch his ballerina, she will land flat on her backside, and ballerinas in full tantrum can be awesome to behold. Therefore, dancers like Michael Somes[51] who remember every step in every ballet they ever learned will never lack for work. Thus, we give the lie to the saying that "a dancer's brains are in her feet." They must combine intellectual feats that would challenge many a Ph.D. with an intuitive empathy for both music and drama.

Still, far too often dancers are incredibly naive and innocent. Unlike expressive dancers, many of whom are college graduates, few ballet dancers have persevered beyond high school. They wish only to "make the company" and if it is to happen at all, it should be by the late teens. Once in, they live like cloistered monks, rarely meeting outsiders, lacking the time, energy, and money to read anything besides potboilers, let alone attend many plays or concerts. As a result, for every worldly, enlightened Erik Bruhn, Violette Verdy, or Edward Villella, we can find ten who are appallingly ignorant not only about world affairs, economic realities, and "great literature and philosophy" but even about their sister arts. For example, dancers obviously must be musical, but few have much knowledge about the technical or historical side of music. Even more astonishing, most know

179

almost nothing and care less about the history of or latest developments in their own art. Teaching music appreciation or dance history to a roomful of dancers must be among life's more ungrateful activities. They wish only to dance themselves, and nothing else matters. Marcia Siegel expresses a similar suspicion:

> In some way that isn't entirely perverse, dancers appreciate their own elusiveness in the culture. Their attitude toward filming their work is one of mistrust, and beneath their toleration for critics lies an unarticulated hostility. I often feel dancers would rather not have us see deeply into their work or meditate on its implications. They prefer to remain inaccessible to scholarly analysis, to exclude themselves from the normal processes of historical evaluation. They do what they do for their time.[52]

To the continuous frustration of those concerned about their welfare, they also, too often, refuse to contemplate their futures. Most will express some vague notion about teaching after they retire, although they will admit, when pressed, that convincing uninterested, untalented youngsters to point their feet and hold their backs straight possesses little allure. Likewise, while most expressive dancers eventually attempt choreography and often will start their own companies, relatively few ballet dancers[53] show much interest in such pursuits. (According to Klosty,[53] more than 74 percent of Merce Cunningham's former dancers have themselves gone on to produce creative work in some field. No ballet company, we suspect, could come close to matching this astounding figure.) Instead of simply interpreting someone else's ideas and be created on, wouldn't they like to create something themselves? Not terribly often. All in all, the ballet dancer is the definitive here and now, existential being.

We have left until last the most indicative characteristic of all. This set of quotes from Gruen's interviews will provide some hints.

> The fact of the matter is that ballet dancing is the most unnatural thing in the world. You're constantly in agony, but you've got to come out onstage and make it seem as though it were the most natural way of moving.[54]

> (Question) What are the tortures of being a ballet dancer?
> (Answer) It's like going to the dentist every day.[55]

180

To begin with, you can't go on in this business unless you're prepared to always be in pain somewhere. You've just got to accept it. If it were up to me, I would put a large sign over the door of our school....'All Ye That Enter Here, Be Prepared for Ninety-Nine-per-Cent Failure Every Day!'[56]

I will tell you something--I believe that basically every dancer hates it. It's just that nobody wants to admit it. I hate it also. But I go to the barre every morning anyway. I force my body until it hurts.[57]

Finally, ballerina Merle Park dares speak the name of the attribute which the others have clearly implied:

"Of course, we are all masochists."[58]

They are. They must be. And so, after this lengthy sojourn, we are at last ready to attempt our Sartrian explanation of the dancer's psyche. We would expect to find every one of the aforementioned personality characteristics in those who, under the gaze, have chosen to relinquish their subjectivity and gain their selfhood, not freely, but parasitically through the eyes of others. We will argue that academic dancers are, and indeed must be, those who have accepted the status of objects of perception. Otherwise they would not choose to endure this demanding profession.

Sartre, in discussing our relationships to the Other, notes that our own bodies are unique objects in our perceptual worlds.[59] At times, I can experience my body as part of me, as when it performs some act and I feel that "I did that." It can also be an object external to myself, as when I contemplate a wound on my leg, and gaze at it through the eyes of Another, such as a doctor. At such times, my body becomes an "it." Now the dancer's instrument of expression is not an external medium such as canvas, paper or test tube. It is the dancer's own body. We will argue, in a nutshell, that dancers react to that body primarily in the second manner, as an object of perception, which in turn must make them Sartrian masochists.

First of all, the dancer's body does, in a real sense, provide an object on which someone else expresses creative impulses. The dancer is to the choreographer as canvas is to the painter and marble to the sculptor. Now admittedly the choreographic process usually is not totally a one-way street, a "Simon says" in which the choreographer says "jump" and the dancer asks only "how high?" In practice, the latter may actively contribute

181

by offering suggestions and by choosing, among several possible variations of a movement sequence, the one that feels better.* Thus, in dance, the dialogue or conversation between the creator and the medium is literally realized. Someone wishing to compose on a completely passive, dehumanized object would not opt for choreography. (Although some choreographers, especially Alwin Nikolais, are sometimes accused of dehumanizing their dancers and treating them as simply elements in a larger mosaic of design. It may be symbolic that Nikolais once ran a marionette theatre.[60]) But that having been said, this relatively democratic scenario usually holds only when small dances--solos, duets, and the like--are being created. For reasons of simple efficiency, the larger the group the more dictatorial the process. And certainly the dance's final form will still, in the last analysis, be the choreographer's decision, with the dancer providing the body on which those decisions are carried out.

Furthermore, during the stage of verification, every artist must try to critically evaluate the product "through the eyes of others." This is difficult enough to do at the best of times, but for the dancer it is impossible. We can never see ourselves as others see us (as witness Genet's doomed quest). Therefore, dancers must rely on opinions from teachers, directors, audience members, and (the most critical viewers of all) other dancers to discover their appearance.

And above all, they must rely on their image in a mirror. These mysterious apparati provide the distinctive feature that quickly identifies a large room as a "dance studio." Whichever way dancers turn, they confront a reflection of themselves. Now a mirror image of myself is a strange perception. It is me. Yet it is not. It is detached. Yet it is affiliated. In the film Duck Soup, Groucho Marx, clad in nightgown and

---

* Many noted choreographers have a favorite dancer with whom they continuously work, e.g., Ashton with Fonteyn, Kenneth MacMillan with Lynn Seymour, and so on. The reason, undoubtedly, is that with that dancer there is a mysterious, often intuitive, and not verbalized "meeting of minds" that stimulates the choreographer. The relationship of George Balanchine to his various pet ballerinas perhaps best exemplified this point. Balanchine was famous/notorious for preferring to compose for women, and for young women at that. Invariably, at any point in time, he had one individual (at different times Vera Zorina, Maria Tallchief, Tanaquil LeClercq, and Suzanne Farrell) who was the focus of his talent, and also (almost inevitably) of his affections; all (with the exception of Ms. Farrell) became his wives. When they no longer inspired him, he moved on to someone else, both professionally and personally.

slippers, faces another character on the other side of a mirror, who is identically dressed. The Other copies Groucho's every move precisely. Groucho waves? The "image" waves back. Groucho spins daintily and careens off mirror right? So too does the image. Yet Groucho suspects what ve know, i.e., that the mirror's occupant is not his image at all but someone else. And therein hangs a tale. Spending so much time, as do dancers, gazing at yourself in mirrors must do something to your head.

But (it may be objected) cannot artificial aids, such as films and videotapes, show dancers their own image accurately? Unfortunately, these too can be grossly misinforming, as readers will realize who have suffered through watching themselves on TV. The image thereon rarely coincides with the one we have of ourselves. In addition, others will assuredly assure us that "It doesn't look at all like you!" But do they lie? We can never know.

Lastly, every aspect of dancers' careers depends on how others perceive and evaluate their body, and how it functions. Dancers are continually "gazed at," perhaps not as blatant sex objects (although no honest balletomane would deny that sexuality is part of the "dance experience") but certainly as sense objects. Because, in dance, we directly and sensuously apprehend human bodies in sublime activity, it communicates an electric immediacy equalled by no other art form.

For all these reasons, we suggest, dancers will inevitably become both narcissists and Sartrian masochists, obsessed with the appearance of their own body and especially its appearance to others. They will come to regard it as an "it," separate from themselves. They must learn to correct "it" through muscle memory and kinesthetic feedback, and to accept "its" pain and fatigue as the necessary price of their profession. It will become an object in their own eyes, just as it is in everyone else's.

It is quite unsurprising, then, that the typical dancer will also display the personality characteristics of the masochist. But does dance attract those who are already (for other, unknown reasons) masochistic? Or, alternatively, does it induce masochism in otherwise free individuals who choose to dance? To this chicken-and-egg question we provide no answer. We suggest only that dance and masochism (the type portrayed by Sartre, we must emphasize) are and must be correlated.

We wish to close this discussion on a more optimistic note. It might seem, from the preceeding, that dance lacks any positive rewards and that therefore those who practice it so fervently must be a neurotic breed. Let us now correct

183

this impression. The experience of moving freely through space is a "high," a Maslowian peak experience[61] like no other. It taps our every resource to the limit, combining the physical release of the most demanding sports with the emotional and intellectual fulfillment of an art. It suspends us beyond our humanity in time and space. Snoopy, that wonderful dog in Peanuts, understands. Periodically, he can be seen careening around like some demented dervish mounted on a drunken pogo stick. Then, in the last panel, he confides, "To those of us who know, dancing is the only thing." It is. It certainly is. Which is why dancers more or less willingly endure all the garbage that the career demands.

What is this mysterious experience like? Here is Jorge Dunn:

> When I dance, I do not feel that I am dancing. It is not I who dances. It is a force that propels me. It is a force that one does not understand....Sometimes there are vibrations. Often they come from the people you love, or from the public.[62]

Perhaps our analysis can also shed some light on this experience. What is this self that is lost? Could it be that objective, "gazed at" self, that the dancer has heretofore constantly received from The Others? Now the master, he throws it back in their faces. Look at me. Like Genet, the masochist gaining dominance, he can force them to pay attention and see him as he wishes to be seen. The powerless, temporarily, becomes a figure of supreme power.

According to this notion, then, dancing resembles an addiction. Any addicting event, such as tobacco or heroin, will both satisfy a need and also reinstate that need, trapping people in an inescapable cycle. The more dancers need to show themselves to others, the more they will need to see themselves as others do. And vice versa. As dancers will readily admit, then, they are addicted. (Fortunately, dancing is one of the few activities not yet indicted as a cause of lung cancer!) But above all, we insist, this kind of commitment is not neurotic. Masochism can be exhilarating!

Commentary

On the face of it, Sartre's perspective seems to say little about many of creativity's phenomena but, as we have doubtless implied, we see great potential for development along these lines. Let us first indicate the possibilities regarding the fundamental project. Perhaps most basic of all, we can thereby

184

understand why we expend such effort on, and attach such importance to, seemingly useless activities like sports and artistic pursuits, why we reduce ourselves to the brink of neurosis to improve our poems or lower our golf scores. After all, these do represent, in different guises, nothing less than our enduring quest for psychic unity.

As well, we remember the mysterious endocept in the mind's eye, which a creator neverendingly, and imperfectly, tries to express. Does this not resemble, and perhaps stem from, the vague vision of an objective self, which also hovers tantalizingly, like the yoked donkey's carrot, just out of reach? Or consider creators' classic twin reactions to their work, i.e., dissatisfaction and "I didn't do that!" At the moment of its completion, when they have attained an external, enduring statement of what they are, they may momentarily coincide with themselves. Hence they experience a sense of ecstatic unity with it. Unfortunately, their beings continue to fluctuate while their work remains unchanged, so the latter soon expresses what they were rather than what they now are. Creators' growing dissatisfaction with their work accordingly becomes understandable. In a sense, they are quite right that they didn't do it--at least in their current personae.

Having expressed our admiration of this aspect of Sartre's work, we must nevertheless raise some objections. First of all, as we also said of Camus, creators simply do not report such abstract, ontological motives for their work, and by existentialism's own standards, failures to portray existence as it is genuinely experienced every day are serious failures indeed. At best, therefore, this approach seems applicable to only a small minority of creators. Now ordinarily this would not concern existentialists, with their bias against generalizations. Yet Sartre presents his tenets, in Being and Nothingness at least, as highly abstract, theoretical statements that he clearly believes have wide, if not universal applicability.*

We can raise a similar objection to Sartre's study of Genet. While it is undoubtedly a stimulating, imaginative account

---

* As more than one critic has noted, that philosophers so committed to individuality and uniqueness should indulge in abstract theorizing is at the least incongruous. Yet when Sartre states that we are all afflicted with freedom and therefore can possess no general, essential properties, he thereby identifies some general properties that we all possess. Strictly speaking, existentialists' observations should apply to no one except themselves. Even writing a book to attempt to convince others is almost a contradiction in terms.

185

of a provocative and important creative figure, are its concepts at all applicable to other such individuals? Even within the heterogeneous, diversified creative population, Genet seems atypical as regards life experiences, personal qualities, and the type of work produced. How valuable, then, in a general sense, can be the resulting interpretations? The existentialist would again retort (this time with more justification) that Sartre wished only to understand <u>Genet</u>; his legitimacy to be a creative Everyman is entirely beside the point. Nevertheless, those accustomed to generalizations will remain dubious.

We must now come to grips with a problem that is both basic and serious. Human beings, we are adamantly informed, have complete freedom to become anything. Their past actions, i.e., what they have been, provide their only unchanging essence, but that past essence exerts no influence over, and does not predict, their future choices (if it did, then their freedoms would be severely compromised). Now this position does provide one acceptable tenet: people are to be judged simply by their actions, by <u>what</u> <u>they</u> <u>have</u> <u>done</u>.[63] Therefore, someone's genius, for example, is only established after the fact, by the free choices he or she has made. All of which accords with our bias that products, rather than personality characteristics or psychological experiences, must be the primary indicant of creative ability.

But in another respect this position becomes troublesome. It clearly denies that genius, or indeed <u>any</u> personality trait, can become persistent and reliable (at least prior to death). Although someone's previous acts may have earned the label "genius" <u>thus</u> <u>far</u>, that person's <u>future</u> acts may or may not continue to do so. We will simply have to wait to find out. Everyone becomes an equal candidate for future immortality, regardless of their previous track records. Although a Beethoven may already have produced a series of supreme symphonies, including the revolutionary Eroica, he is no more likely to compose the equally revolutionary Ninth than is some obscure haberdasher.

Now admittedly the past doesn't guarantee anything. Some individuals, such as the composer Rossini, have been initially productive and then lapsed into quiescence. Others, like the painter Gauguin, have come out of the woodwork after few early indications of ability. But such cases are rare. The most accurate indicator, surely, of future success, is <u>past</u> success. If we had to choose between Beethoven and the clothier as the more likely candidate to compose the Ninth, and wager our life's earnings on our choice, there is little doubt where most of us (including, we suspect, Sartre himself) would lay our money!

Let us turn now to the notion of the gaze. Unlike the fundamental project, it does seem to jibe with the facts of introspection. We have all, surely, experienced both the desire to dominate and the desire to submit to others. As Adler has emphasized (see Chapter 11), the power motive fuels many human endeavors, possibly including creativity, and Sartre's account of this motive has rarely been bettered. Let us, therefore, pursue its possibilities. It can nicely explain the sex difference in creativity. According to Simone de Beauvoir,[64] women have historically been the Other, taught to think of themselves as objects of perception. They have therefore received their selfhood from others, who have imposed labels such as "passive," "dependent," "untalented." Such self concepts could devastate any potential women might have had. Moreover, the gaze implies a solution of sorts to that most perplexing of riddles, shaving's facilitation of inspiration. Perhaps not the shaving per se but the gazing at oneself in a mirror is responsible. Temporarily seeing ourselves approximately as others do, we confront our objectivity. Which, we are told, is precisely why we create.

Or consider the notoriously paradoxical qualities of the creative personality, and in particular the oscillation between self confidence and insecurity. As we have seen, in any Sartrian interaction, it is a moot point whether the gazer or the gazee, the sadist or the masochist, has more power. Thus, the combatants' sense of power should also wax and wane, and so should creators' sense of assurance and control, of power and domination, over both medium and audience. Likewise, we have seen that creators invariably perceive themselves as alienated from and struggling with general society, since they have very different priorities and attitudes. This too suggests an antagonistic rather than cooperative relationship with their consumers. Lastly, our needs for power may explain our ubiquitous tendency to evaluate virtually every event we experience. If we accept "whatever is" from the world like passive sponges, then we allow it to rule, reducing us to the ranks of the gazees. But when we accept or reject that world, nodding our heads in approval or else screaming "No! It should be thus rather than thus," we thereby assert our active freedom to choose. Then the world lies at our feet.

Hoffer has also recognized the importance of power motives in creative work.[65] His true believers are fanatics who willingly relinquish selfhood to immerse themselves in some political or religious cause, wanting only to be small cogs in a large mass. The most extreme of these, Hoffer asserts, are failed authors, artists, and scientists who, frustrated because they cannot produce as they would like, often become ardent patriots and singleminded zealots. Moreover, he notes, so-called men of words--poets, philosophers, and artists of questionable talent--have been in the vanguard of virtually every mass revolutionary movement of recent times, as witness, among others, Marat, Robespierre, Lenin, and Mussolini, as well as virtually every member of the Nazi inner circle. Above all, of course, Hitler himself was a frustrated artist. According to those who knew him during his early days as a bohemian painter in Vienna, he showed neither unusual lust for power nor virulent anti-semitism.[66] These came later. Thus, it seems, the potential "man of words" has a particular need for dominance. He will try first to satisfy it through creative work, but when he realizes that he will never produce masterpieces, he may turn to other, more insidious outlets.

In view of the gaze's appreciable explanatory power, then, it is ironic that one of Sartre's most extensive discussions of creative activity, What Is Literature, should pull the rug out from underneath it. We wish, therefore (defending Sartre against himself), to take issue with this stand and argue that the usual power struggles do ensue between creators and audience. We quite agree that they must work not only for themselves but also for others. Clearly, they must not only be able to get bright ideas but also need to communicate them. Otherwise, they would certainly forego the toil and frustration necessary to make the product intelligible, let alone take the psychological risks of putting that product on public display. But when Sartre holds that the creator/audience dyad is, and should be, symmetrical, we part company. When others attend to a creator's work, they admit his or her importance (as Sartre himself has asserted in Saint Genet). If it should influence them to think or feel differently, then the creator has gained power over them. Then too, consider once more those receptions following a ballet, play, or opera. The artist, usually economically deprived and politically impotent, temporarily can dominate the political and social elite, who pay him homage. Knowing who he is, they whisper admiringly to one another as he sweeps by while he, although ignorant of their separate identities, bestows upon them, like any regal personage, a condescending smile. This heady moment can, for the artist, repay much day-to-day privation.

Yet this interaction is as multi-faceted as is any gaze. Who needs who? The audience may scream "Bravo!" and "Author! Author!," but they thereby provide the one thing their partner/adversary needs. An actress takes her bows after another triumph. With each raising of the curtain, a humble smile of gratitude warms her countenance. But a scornful grimace of hatred replaces it as the curtain descends. She realizes that without their receptive passivity, she has nothing.

Sartre himself vacillates on this point and, in doing so, places impossible demands on writers. On the one hand, they must be committed revolutionaries, seeking to change and irritate their age. Which certainly suggests that they should try to sway their readers to their own point of view. How can writers do this while still remaining in the requisite attitude of generosity, respecting readers' freedoms and not trying to influence them unduly? Writing is an occupation difficult enough without its being required to serve two contradictory psychological masters.

This debate between cooperative and competitive motives bears on the creator/critic relationship. The latter, with few exceptions, will see it as a collaboration between two equal partners working for the same ends. Hence, as we have seen, they are often surprised and even hurt when their negative comments are angrily received. They were only trying to help. Similarly, they will invariably deny that they possses that much power (no one doubts the reviews' ability to "make or break" more than does the reviewer who writes them) or that it attracts them in the least. These attitudes seem to us deluded, even fogbound. Goldman[67] vividly describes the power possessed by the New York Times' theatrical critic (at the time, Clive Barnes). A certain producer, well aware of the importance of Barnes' pronouncement for his latest enterprise, reported that, on the opening night,

> In the darkness, along the sides of the house, the publicity staff and various managers and producers crept in silence, peering towards Barnes to see if he was enjoying himself. It was, as one of the producers told me afterward, "a ...ing outrage--grown men with field glasses trying to see if one guy is laughing or not.[68]

Contrary to rumor, most critics are human. Could any of us remain immune to such heady wine as this? To seeing our name emblazoned three stories tall in Times Square, inducing the multitudes to sample delights of that new musical laff riot, Crime and Punishment? To knowing that myriads of talented persons languish at our mercy and hang on our every utterance? To realizing that one devastating paragraph from us can destroy a lifetime of dedicated sacrifice?

Creators, however, recognize the relationship realistically for what it is, a battle of wills between two indomitable adversaries, like the dominance struggle of the gaze. For critics routinely shatter What Is Literature's most fundamental commandment, i.e., thou shalt not infringe on the freedom of thy partner. When they pass judgment, or even advance constructive criticisms, they imply, "You should have done it otherwise."

189

Clearly creators are not given the latitude to work however they wish, without risking condemnation.

In sum, we find it more sensible to view the creator/ audience interaction as a power struggle, with the former needing to dominate external objects, whether human or inanimate. Before leaving Sartre, we might also glance briefly at several problems with the gaze that are admittedly tangential to our topic. First, two widely read books, Fromm's The Art of Loving[66] and May's Love and Will[67] have each disputed his description of that most dramatic of interpersonal relationships, the one we call love. They quite agree that it can involve a Sartrian contest of wills; they disagree that it must. For them, not only is cooperative, symmetrical love between two people possible, it actually constitutes love in its highest form. The gazal variety is only one possibility among many, and a rather immature possibility at that.

We must also, on introspective grounds, question some matters of detail. Clearly, for Sartre, the gaze encompasses the entire moment when we are recognized by the Other and enter his or her consciousness. Eye contact is only a part, but an integral part nevertheless, of that moment. In my experience, it can be equally dehumanizing when the Other does not look my way if, say, we pass one another on the street. Blank, glazed visage fixed firmly ahead, staring either past me or even right through me as if I were invisible, the Other seems to deny my importance and indeed my very existence. Is not this also supremely petrifying?

Part III

THEORIES OF ANTECEDENT CAUSATION

The perspectives in this section all assume that creativity is due to some factor or factors beyond creators' control, so that they are the servants rather than the masters of the process, and the product that results is, in a real sense, not their responsibility. These perspectives differ, often drastically, about what those antecedent factors might be. But they are united on the more basic matter that some such factors are necessary for creativity to occur at all. Thus, in contrast to the views espoused in Part II, it is the presence rather than the absence of creativity that needs to be explained.

Chapter 8

SUPERNATURAL/THEOLOGICAL APPROACHES

This framework attributes creativity to events that are mystical, spiritual, and therefore, almost by definition, unknowable. Supposedly creators are occupied, temporarily or permanently, by divine forces that control their labor and speak through them; in short, creativity is a gift of the gods. For several reasons, our discussion can be relatively brief. If something by its very nature defies human understanding, then little more can be said about it. Furthermore, such explanations have not been popular in our secular age, which, perhaps naively, prefers to see its worldly phenomena as natural and potentially comprehensible, open to scientific investigation and control.

Still, theological views deserve their moment in the sun. They have some intriguing implications, and in earlier times various versions were often accepted without question. For the ancient Greeks, for example, the nine known branches of art and science were each supposedly supervised by a mysterious goddess called a Muse; thus, Terpsichore and Polyhymnia controlled the dance and sacred song, respectively. These muses were believed to bestow or withold inspiration upon a creator as they saw fit, so he/she languished at their mercy.

In the Platonic dialogue The Ion, Socrates provides several reasons why inspiration should be laid at the door of such divine sources.[1] First, if creators themselves controlled it, then they would be able to deal effectively with all the arts. But since their talents are restricted to a particular field, presumably the locus of this talent must depend on the Muse with whom they are on intimate terms (apparently, the scourge of specialization was as rampant in Plato's day as in our own). Secondly, poets must be little more than soothsayers or interpreters for the gods, a medium through whom they speak, because otherwise they would be able to create continually, without interruption. Whereas in actuality, dry spells are common, and poets may well conjure up one or two great products and then lapse into silence.

The Book of Genesis provides a particularly fascinating description of creativity as a divine, omnipotent act. During that hectic six days, we are told, God/Yahweh produced a supreme achievement, beside which even the greatest fruits of human enterprise pale into insignificance. (Although some cultures see creation as a bad mistake, the unfortunate harvest from one of God's weaker moments.[2] Had He been more mindful, He would not have produced such misery.) Nothing of comparable originality has been produced either before or since (the claims

193

of the antimatterists, the black holists, and the like notwithstanding). No other invention provides so many possible interpretations and has stimulated more contemplation and commentary than the universe and human existence (how many undergraduate philosophers, pink of cheek and fuzzy of chin, have reflectively intoned, "What does it all mean? Why are we here?".) No other product has shown such staying power, or ability to communicate effectively in so many times and places. Even the most insensitive person has been by turns bemused, depressed, intrigued, and exhilarated by God's invention.

More recently, Tolstoy[3] has provided a noteworthy example of this approach. He begins by asserting, with Camus, that human solidarity and communication are preeminent values, which art must, first and foremost, try to encourage. In fact, art occurs because we can experience another's joy, sorrow, despair, and so on. Artists should express their various emotional feelings. If the audience can gain infection (we might call it empathy) by sharing them, then the work is good, because it has substituted a sense of oneness for that of separation. Supposedly: infection depends on three factors: (a) the individuality with which the artist conveys feelings, (b) the clarity with which he or she expresses them, and (c) the sincerity of the expression. This lastnamed, assigned special importance, refers to the intensity with which the artist feels the emotions expressed. Thus, Tolstoy maintains, primitive or peasant art is invariably more powerful than that from the upper classes because it is more sincere.

But which feelings provide better subject matter? Superior work will express, not pleasure, sexual satisfaction, or some such, but the religious perception of its age, current feelings about such questions as the meaning of life and the highest good. In our day, when Christian values (according to Tolstoy) should hold sway, the best art will express humility, purity, compassion, love, and above all brotherhood. It will unite us all by transmitting the simple joys of everyday life that we all, regardless of race, religion or geographical location, can understand. Elitist art, which speaks only to a privileged, educated minority, Tolstoy rejects out of hand. Which leads him to some astonishing preferences. He dismisses, among others, Beethoven's Ninth Symphony, along with his own War and Peace and Anna Karenina. Like Ko-Ko, the Lord High Executioner in Gilbert and Sullivan's The Mikado, he's "got a little list" of pet peeves deserving decapitation. It warrants repeating in toto:

> Bad art, deserving not to be encouraged but to
> be driven out, denied, and despised (is) art
> which does not unite, but divides, people. Such,
> in literary art, are all novels and poems which

194

transmit Church or patriotic feelings, and also exclusive feelings pertaining only to the class of the idle rich such as aristocratic honor, satiety, spleen, pessimism and refined and vicious feelings flowing from sex - love - quite incomprehensible to the great majority of mankind. In painting we must similarly place in the class of bad art all the Church, patriotic, and exclusive pictures; all the pictures representing the amusements and allurements of a rich and idle life; all the so-called symbolic pictures, in which the very meaning of the symbol is comprehensible only to the people of a certain circle; and above all, pictures with voluptuous subjects--all that odious female nudity which fills all the exhibitions and galleries. And to this class belongs almost all the chamber and opera music of our times, beginning especially from Beethoven (Schumann, Berlioz, Liszt, Wagner), by its subject matter devoted to the expression of feelings accessible only to people who have developed in themselves an unhealthy, nervous irritation evoked by this exclusive, artificial and complex music.[4]

Inclusion in such an august list of rejects is almost a compliment. On the other hand, are not greeting card verses--which speak gushingly and simplistically about peace, love, and above all motherhood--to be viewed as the very summit of perfection? Clearly, these Tolstoyan criteria simply will not do.

Ambivalence

If creativity is the definitive act of the gods/God, then what does it mean if human beings create? When they do so, they temporarily at least take on immortal demeanor and become "like gods," which thereby stimulates several conflicting emotions, with the overall feeling being decidedly ambivalent. On the one hand, when we create we strive towards omnipotent perfection, dramatically verifying, from a Judeo-Christian standpoint, that we were born in God's image and can simulate His work. (And many creators do report feeling, at times, an almost godlike sense of power over their media and therefore over all earthly, material phenomena.) Romantics such as Blake and Shelley vocally avowed such a notion.[5] Supposedly, a universal mind or power was resident within all things and the creative arts, particularly poetry, simply tried to express this divine omnipotence and so regain humanity's unity and oneness with God. From this angle, then, human creativity becomes perhaps the most reverent of all acts.

195

But by the same token, it could also indicate a deplorable lack of humility, the ultimate heresy deserving swift and awful retribution. We have earlier seen Camus portray it this way. So too does the legend of the Tower of Babel (Genesis II:3-9), wherein humankind sought to construct a tower whose "top would reach unto the heavens," bringing them up to God's level and thus threatening His superiority. But our distant ancestors faced a formidable adversary. He introduced different languages onto the earth, making communication and the sharing of knowledge much more difficult, and so easily frustrated their puny attempts to emulate Him.

This is one reason why many religious institutions, particularly those of a fundamentalist persuasion, show suspicious attitudes towards any sort of innovation. It was the Puritans under Cromwell who closed England's theatres and invoked a tradition of severe censorship from which the institution is only now freeing itself. Such reactionary attitudes cry out for satire, and Flanders and Swann, among others, have happily obliged with the pungent observation that "If God had meant us to fly, he would never have given us the railway."[6]

Many of our enduring myths and legends also express this attitude that the inquiring or innovative mind is getting too big for its boots and is risking divine retaliation.[7] Prometheus, who stole fire from the gods and gave it to humankind was, for this act of blasphemy, bound to a mountain, where a vulture ate out his liver for the rest of eternity (the gods, evidently, can devise particularly gruesome tortures when they are contravened!). Oedipus, driven to seek enlightenment and understand himself, whatever the cost, discovered to his horror that he had, unknowingly, killed his father and married his mother. His relentless curiosity had caused him to see too clearly; in recompense, he blinded himself. Faust acquired great knowledge only by selling his soul to the Devil. Icarus flew too close to the sun, so that his wings melted and he fell into the sea. That an equally dastardly fate might await anyone else who exceeds his station led G. B. Shaw, with tongue planted firmly in cheek, to write to violinist Jascha Heifetz:

> My wife and I were overwhelmed by your concert. If you continue to play with such beauty, you will certainly die young. No one can play with such perfection without provoking the jealousy of the gods. I earnestly implore you to play something badly every night before going to bed.[8]

And of course our own traditions tell of Adam and Eve's temptation by their slithering, unappendaged compatriot. By dining on history's most infamous piece of fruit, they abandoned

Eden's state of blissful innocence, gaining not only enlightenment but also sin and suffering. This mixed blessing posed for the first time our most enduring quandary, i.e., is ignorance bliss?

To repeat, then, human creativity stimulates, from a theological point of view, ambivalent emotions. This volatile mixture of admiration and suspicion is in part responsible for the checkered relationship between creators and the societies that have housed them. On the one hand, societies have had to admit that creators are valuable; they contribute to the quality of life and the great god of progress. In Arieti's poignant phrase, "A new painting, poem or scientific achievement...increases the number of islands of the visible in the ocean of the unknown."[9] In agreement, any number of desperate politicians have avowed that "talented children are our most precious resource."

Other, more negative attitudes are equally in evidence however. Creative work almost inevitably promotes change and threatens the status quo, and creators will often transgress the norms, mores, and even formal laws of a society (once more, Galileo's clash with the Inquisition is instructive). As a result, it is usually futile to convince those same politicians, once elected, to put their money where their mouths are. Will they commit even minuscule funds for the support of artistic and scientific work or for the training and stimulation of our talented youngsters? Not if it means even minuscule cutbacks in their privileges. For privately politicians, like the voters who elect them, regard innovators as necessary but troublesome malcontents.

To complicate matters further, a theological perspective suggests still other interpretations of human creativity. It could be viewed as an attempt not to become but to follow God, to try to uncover the marvelous workings of His "invention" and to understand what He hath wrought. Einstein repeatedly avowed such a motive:

> 'What we strive for,' he cried, 'is just to draw His lines after Him...I'm not a family man. I want my peace. I want to know how God created this world. I am not interested in this or that phenomenon, in the spectrum of this or that element. I want to know His thoughts, the rest are details.'[10]

Einstein was not religious in the formal sense of avowing a particular faith, but he was imbued, apparently, with a deep "religiosity," i.e., he believed unequivocally in the universe's basic harmony, order, and lawfulness, and in a divine omnipotence. In his words again:

197

'I believe in Spinoza's God who reveals himself
in the orderly harmony of what exists...not in
a god who concerns himself with fates and actions
of human beings.'[11]

This unshakable faith in the Creator's guiding hand undoubtedly
determined Einstein's stance towards one of twentieth century
physics' most famous controversies. Do the laws of strict
determinism, as he believed, still hold for particles making up
the atom (electrons, protons, and so on)? If this is so, then
we can hope eventually to describe and predict their behaviors
with absolute certainty. Or rather, as Bohr and others maintained,
do their behaviors fluctuate randomly, so that those behaviors
can never be described exactly but only by a statistical
distribution showing a range of possibilities? Einstein rejected
this second possibility with perhaps his most famous aphorism,
"God does not throw dice with the universe."

Lastly, human creativity can theologically be viewed as an
attempt to communicate with or to glorify the Almighty. Many
creators have labored selflessly to serve God, seeking neither
personal statement in their work nor fortune or fame. Examples
abound. Much pre-Renaissance art, such as the Romanesque and
Gothic cathedrals and the wonderful medieval tapestries and
paintings, came from unsigned "Anonymous," who presumably worked
for these reasons. And perhaps things have not changed so
much as we might think. Even today's supposedly more secular,
Bohemian artists report, when questioned, a surprising frequency
of religious belief; 43 percent of one group of art students
stated that they regularly attended worship services.[12].

In the same vein, the theatre from the time of the ancient
Greeks has frequently functioned as a religious institution to
glorify the gods/God and exalt the spirit of mankind. Its
tendency for profane irreverence and skepticism is a relatively
recent development. So too is music's secular employment in
concerts, radio broadcasts, rock festivals, and the like. For
centuries, serious compositions were intended almost exclusively
for services of religious worship, as witness the sublime masses,
cantatas, and oratorios of Palestrina, Bach, Handel, et al.

Indeed, according to Coulson,[13] the divergence of artistic
creativity from religion has harmed both, but particularly the
latter. He asserts, following Cardinal Newman, that since the
objects of religious faith cannot be proven empirically, their
acceptance requires an act of that same imagination which influences
the arts, particularly poetry. This imagination, then, enlarges
our sense of reality beyond the material, so that atheism may
merely indicate an inadequate imagination. Breaking the vital
link with artistic sensibility renders religion a dry and dusty

thing, "the prisoner of practical men and their needs."[14] James
Joyce also saw religion and poetry as seeking similar ends:

> There is a certain resemblance between the mystery
> of the mass and what I am trying to do....I am
> trying in my poems to give people some kind of
> intellectual pleasure or spiritual enjoyment by
> converting the bread of everyday life into
> something that has a permanent artistic life
> of its own.[15]

In the Beginning: Omnipotent Creativity

As we have already suggested, many creators, especially
those of bygone days, have personified the theological approach.
Yet a particularly apt example has, to our mind, never received
the attention it deserves. We refer to no less than God Himself,
the ultimate Creator as He is depicted in the Old Testament,
particularly in Genesis. Given that He accomplished a creative
feat of unrivaled magnificence, why should we not contemplate
Him, not merely as a remote figure of reverential awe, but
also as a particularly talented Creator, displaying attributes,
experiences, and emotions (albeit on a cosmic scale) similar to
any other? Why should we not approach Genesis as, at least in
part, a sort of personality/biographical study of the Almighty?

When this is done, as we will now try to show, many seemingly
prosaic Biblical passages take on new light. Likewise, many of
His inexplicable or even horrifying actions become comprehensible,
precisely because they are so typical of creative personalities.
In the exercise to follow, we will not indicate every conceivable
similarity between divine and mortal creators; this task we
leave to scholars of greater theological expertise. Rather, we
wish to demonstrate its intriguing possibilities, so a relatively
brief exposition should suffice.

An initial disclaimer seems called for. We will be practising
a sort of reverse anthropomorphism, assigning some extremely
human characteristics to the Almighty. Some might see this
practice as the height of sacrilegious blasphemy, particularly
when those characteristics are not flattering. Others, more
irreverent, might raise precisely the opposite objection, viz.,
that such an earthy portrait teeters on the brink of the quaint,
a mirror image of Thornton W. Burgess at his most unbearably
coy.

We assure both assailants that our purpose is both serious
and pious. Has not the unrelieved awe in which God has historically
been held actually done Him a disservice? Is not the benevolent,
flawless, grandfather-in-flowing-white robe bequeathed to us by

formal religion and Hollywood spectacular much more blasphemous? Such a dull, insipid doughnut would not have produced a boiled egg, let alone something as mind-boggling as the universe. God must have been (and is) much more fascinating, complicated, and intimidating. Which, as we will try to demonstrate, is precisely how the Old Testament depicts Him. Thus, we seek to reclaim Him from the Old Folk's Home for Indigent Artists and from the boring perfection to which he has been consigned, to make Him once more truly the Living God. The defense rests.

Let us begin with the first verses of Genesis: "And the earth was without form, and void; and darkness was upon the face of the deep" (Genesis I:2). Like every creator, God evidently began with the existential dilemma, the undefined, ambiguous medium having many interpretative possibilities. For musician Lukas Foss, it is "the dizzying emptiness of the blank page."[16] For D. H. Lawrence, holding a brush fu of color in front of an untouched canvas is like "diving into a pond."[17] In this sublime moment, when overt actions have not yet begun to restrict one's options, everything is still possible.

Moreover, God's formless void presented truly infinite alternatives; to paraphrase Cole Porter again, "Anything Went." Evidently, the cosmos had remained static throughout eternity, so that God's first inspiration was to realize that change was possible. Not only did He create, but he "created creativity." Since there were no historical precedents or unquestioned canons to help Him, His first attempts must have been little more than trial-and-error dabblings. More than any subsequent creator, He had only His arbitrary, subjective preferences to guide Him. This is clearly suggested by the revealing comment, "And God saw the light, that it was good" (Genesis I:4). Apparently, He relied on the same criteria for making His decisions as have creators ever since; He kept something because He liked it, because it seemed to "work." We imagine Him, then, lips pursed, piercing eyes asquint, powerful hand resting thoughtfully on formidable chin, muttering, "Let there be light" (Genesis I:3), not as a thundering authoritative edict, but rather as a highly tentative, groping, "Let's see how that looks!". Unfortunately, Genesis is silent about His other trial balloons, less pleasing, that were assigned to the celestial wastebasket. We suspect that there were many.

After the sixth day, when His first draft was finished, He apparently pioneered another common experience. Many creators report that they find a work especially satisfying at the moment of its completion (presumably, the doubts return later). Stephen Spender, for example, reports that at this moment he invariably thinks the poem to be the best he has done.[18] So too for God. We are informed that, "And God saw everything that He had made, and behold it was very good" (Genesis I:31, italics mine). That "very," absent from the descriptions of the previous five working days, betrays his profound, and understandable, feelings of self-satisfaction.

Following this intensive, fruitful effort, and then the well-earned rest on the seventh day, other typical events occurred. We now know how frequently the work will take over, go its own way, and become something quite different from what its author envisaged. Never has this happened more dramatically than here! God's greatest invention of all, human life, had such an independent tendency "built in." On the face of it, what an inspiration! Endow His progeny with the ability to make decisions and thus to practise the same sublime process that He had just invented. Let humankind, created, also be able to create. No other artistic product has had the same potential for going its own way. Poems, for example, once written, do not as a rule write other poems.

Adam and Eve's first decision was whether to use this incredible ability. Should they remain "innocent," eternally resident in Eden and therefore subservient to God, or eat of the forbidden fruit and gain knowledge? Now God commanded that they not eat of the fruit, but obviously, given His omnipotent power, He could have prevented this had He so wished. Why place it in Eden at all, except as a test, as an opportunity for them to make this crucial decision on their own? To enforce a completely master-puppet relationship, to counteract their endowed independence by pulling every string, would have compromised His greatest inspiration. Actually, might He not secretly hope that they would choose to nibble?

But what has this episode of humankind's gaining knowledge to do with their ability to create? Actually, it is clear that the word "knowledge," in its Biblical usage, refers at least partly to creativity (and not only in the narrow biological sense of species reproduction). The serpent promises that if they eat of the fruit, "Your eyes shall be opened and ye shall be as gods" (Genesis III:5, italics mine), i.e., they will take on the definitive divine attribute, which is creativity. They shall know "good and evil," to make possible the arbitrary, subjective value judgments without which creative work is impossible. Most indicatively, several Biblical passages (e.g., Genesis VI:5 and Genesis VIII:21) almost casually interchange the words "knowledge" and "imagination," and the latter certainly implies creative ability.

Unhappily, by inventing a product that could itself create, God placed Himself in an eternal quandary that has bedeviled His stage of verification ever since. On the one hand, every

201

new invention conceived by His mortal progeny would further substantiate their creative independence and thus accredit His invention. But what to do if (as could well happen) they evolved a world of which He did not approve? Again, He could certainly intervene and crush it, but that would ruin everything.

We must imagine, therefore, a God trapped on the horns of His own dilemma, vacillating continuously between "hands off" and "hands on," now wishing to control earthly developments, now to leave them alone. Some of His subsequent acts became rather more comprehensible when seen in this light. At several points, He obviously concluded that enough was enough. One such instance led to the destruction of Sodom and Gomorrah, the cities of the plain, "because their sin is very grievous" (Genesis XVIII:20). Now "sin" is specified by God's arbitrary value judgment; a sin is an activity of which He does not approve, and never mind what anyone else thinks. The residents of the doomed cities weren't acting as He would wish, their independence threatened the entrenched hierarchy. So, like a celestial Brezhnev taming Czechoslovakia, He sent in the tanks.

Similarly, He bestowed the Ten Commandments when it seemed time to show who was boss and to unequivocally state the rules. Again, these suggest His preoccupation with reasserting His power. First of all, it is notable that, with one exception, every commandment is proscriptive, stating something that we should not do. This betrays His concern with limiting freedom and independence, and setting boundaries to our innovative tendencies. This far and no further. In addition, while some commandments make good psychological and/or sociological sense, others seem arrogant in the extreme. They resemble the rantings of a sullen King Lear, stung because His progeny have shown insufficient respect. "Thou shalt have no other gods before me." "Thou shalt not make unto thee any graven image, or any likeness of anything that is in heaven above, or in earth beneath" (Exodus XX:3-4). Why not, for heaven's sake? Why would our attempts to give Him form, in wood or stone, so offend His tender sensibilities? Perhaps because, if we were to conceive Him in our image, giving Him human attributes, the dominance relationship would be reversed and the tables turned, as if a statue were to suddenly grasp the sculptor's chisel and modify his or her features. Whereas previously He had been the Creator and we the created, now the vice would be versa, an unacceptable possibility when His powers seemed to be slipping.

Let us now briefly elucidate other similarities between mortal and divine creation. First, we have learned how a creator will frequently, with hindsight, come to hate his or her works. Seemingly hopeless flops, they deserve only to be hidden from sight or, preferably, destroyed altogether. Now note this Biblical observation, "And it repented the Lord that He had made man on the earth, and it grieved Him at His heart" (Genesis VI:6). God's reaction to His disenchantment was typical. He brought on the flood (Genesis VI-VIII) to allow Himself to make sweeping revisions. Still, not everything was dross; a few bits seemed worth keeping. Therefore, "And of every living thing of all flesh, two of every sort shalt thou bring into the ark, to keep them alive with thee" (Genesis VI:19). But after this fit of artistic pique, God seemed contrite. "And the Lord said in His heart, I will not again curse the ground any more for man's sake; for the imagination of man's heart is evil from his youth" (Genesis VIII:21). Clearly, He has become resigned to His creation's innovative abilities and the threat that they represent.

Consider now that ultimate tragedy which has befallen so many mortal creators, notably Shakespeare, Shaw, Ibsen, Browning, Mozart, Michelangelo, and the like. Eventually, they become revered and venerated. Their works are dissected to the marrow bone by earnest scholars seeking academic advancement. In school classrooms, unwilling young horses are dragged, kicking and screaming, to these waters and made to drink. Reluctant musical acolytes dutifully belabor their Mozart, Beethoven, and Schubert, reiterating Für Elise or the Minuet in G over and over until both they and their progenitors are ready to commit hara-kiri. Then, released from pianistic bondage, where do they turn for pleasure and sustenance? To the tender mercies of the Top Forty.

We learn early on that we go to the theatre, concert hall, or art gallery, not joyfully for entertainment, but reverently for education and spiritual uplift. We must dress properly, mind our manners, and not slouch in our seats. Polite applause is de rigueur, but extremes of emotional display (either favorable or otherwise) are unacceptable. In short, we must behave precisely as if we were in church. This, in a nutshell, is the tragedy. When we deify creators, we effectively destroy their immediacy and blunt their impact. To put it succinctly, we castrate them.

Has God not suffered a similar unhappy fate? These days, has not this perfect, infallible, omnipotent Almighty, whom we must worshipfully revere and whose name and pronoun we must perforce capitalize, has not He become a bit of a bore? Yet when we read the Old Testament from the present perspective, we are immediately struck by His joyful, exhilarating vitality, His propensity for the same foibles, weaknesses, and miraculous inspirations as the greatest of humanity. Now He becomes a truly fascinating figure deserving of our genuine respect and admiration. We suspect that God is no more thrilled by His omnipotent status than Shakespeare would be with his. We suspect that the living God would have no more use for the average bishop than the living Shakespeare would have for the average teacher of literature. We suspect that He would dismiss the average Church service, that soporific supreme, as the least suitable of all ways for us to express our admiration for His genius. In other words, the interaction between God and humankind seemed much more informal and "down to earth" in Old Testament days, when He was forever sticking His sacrosanct nose into everyone's business. But as we have come to revere Him we have also (aside from those highly formalized rituals one morning per week) come to ignore Him.

Thus He has undoubtedly discovered, as have countless mortal creators, that the public's memory is short unless you keep producing new masterpieces. As the saying goes, you're only as good as your last play. Unfortunately, creating the universe is a hard act to follow. What do you do for an encore? Perhaps, like an aging, passe movie star who no longer is offered parts, He would much prefer to regain the limelight and reassert His influence and control over worldly affairs. Perhaps one day He will return to do so. Perhaps He already has.

Given that so many of God's experiences typified those of creatives, would His personality profile be similarly similar if we could, perchance, administer a cosmic MMPI? About His most productive age and His attitude towards the schoolroom we are left in the dark, but certainly he possessed self confidence, even arrogance, in spades. Witness the tribulations he arbitrarily imposed on the loyal Job. Or that most unseemly episode involving Abraham and his son Isaac (Genesis XXII:1-14). Abraham's wife, Sarah, had finally, in his extreme old age, borne him a son, whom he dearly loved. God commanded Abraham to take Isaac up on a mountain and sacrifice him for a burnt offering, simply to prove his (Abraham's) loyalty. That at the crucial moment God stayed Abraham's hand does not, for us, forgive this incredible display of self-centered arrogance.

God's covenant with the Israelites also founded that popular creative practice of acquiring supportive disciples as walls to lean against. As has often been the case since, those disciples found their special status to be a mixed blessing. Like most creatives, He turned out to be a jealous, domineering partner. He decreed that they were to have no other gods before them. They were to remain loyal and steadfast no matter how overbearing He might be. As more than one Jew has lamented, being the chosen people has seemed to mean being singled out for special suffering. In addition, has any mortal rivaled God's unpredictable, paradoxical personality, with His capacity for generosity, love,

204

and devotion coupled with sudden, inexplicable bouts of jealousy, highhandedness, and cruelty? God's gender is nowhere clearly indicated, so He/She/It seems to have been the androgynous creator par excellence.

Commentary

As we have tried to show, various religious accounts, particularly in the Old Testament, provide an unusual and intriguing "way of thinking about creativity," an analogy in the manner of cybernetics or computer simulation. Yet a chicken-and-egg question must immediately be raised. Should we take Biblical creation as a description that can increase our understanding of the human version? Or (as more pious souls might prefer) should we see human creativity, rather, as providing a path to help us grasp the mysterious workings of the Almighty? Does the computer simulate human thought, or vice versa? We have clearly preferred the first option here, but the choice seems largely a matter of taste.

We should first mention some phenomena, in particular several reliable creative experiences, that fit the theological perspective. First, consider the ubiquitous medium experience. When the creator, an inspired secretary, feels that an unknown source dictates his or her produce, which then takes on its own life and pulls the creator along in pursuit, the intervention of some divine agent certainly seems plausible. Thus for some Romantics, notably Shelley, poetry should forego conscious choice and rely instead on intuition and passionate feeling. Only then can it avoid merely personal expression by contacting and revealing the Godhead.

Second, the moment of inspiration itself, so mysterious, unpredictable, and awe-inspiring, certainly suggests omnipotent involvement. In fact, the word "inspire" literally means "to breathe in," referring to the breath of life that God reportedly forced into Adam's nostrils (Genesis II:7). This implies that when we become inspired, we again take in something from God that allows us temporary access to one of His most characteristic abilities. Hence, composer Joseph Haydn reportedly avowed that his composition The Creation, among others, came from divine grace; similarly, he declared that "When my work does not advance, I retire into the oratory with my rosary, say an ave...immediately ideas come."[19]

The striking similarities between creative and religious inspirations, which have been extensively discussed by Hutchinson[20] particularly suggest their similar origins. (And both resemble the properties of the altered states of consciousness which have been summarized by Tart.[21]) Consider a typical religious

205

insight, such as Saul's encounter with the vision and voice of God on the road to Damascus (Acts IX), in which he was overwhelmed and instantly converted to Christianity. There is the same absolute certainty about its validity (which usually cannot be verified objectively) as in the definitive creative inspiration. The same loss of self-consciousness, the same oneness with external phenomena (in the same manner of May's <u>encounter</u>), the same loss of time and place awareness, and the same missionary zeal to share the insight with others. "Go ye therefore and preach the gospel" is a command upon which any number of creatives have acted.

Similarly, both religious and creative zealots will vacillate between euphoria and despair, at one time convinced that their beliefs are right, at another that they are unworthy. Like many creators who have been dissatisfied with their work, religious figures such as St. Paul, St. Francis of Assisi, John Wesley, and Martin Luther have felt persistently inadequate.[22] Both groups seek an unattainable perfection and, as they contemplate their lives and works, notice only the gap between "what is and what ought to be."

Certain Biblical passages also interpret other phenomena. Consider, for example, the sex difference in creativity. Almost immediately, we are informed:

> And God said, Let us make man in our image, after our likeness: and let them have dominion over the fish of the sea, and over the fowl of the air, and over the cattle, and over all the earth, and over every creeping thing that creepeth upon the earth
> So God created man in his own image, in the image of God created he him; male and female created he them (Genesis I:26 & 27).

Somewhat later we learn that:

> And the Lord God caused a deep sleep to fall upon Adam, and he slept: and he took one of his ribs, and closed up the flesh thereof;
> And the rib, which the Lord God had taken from man, made he a woman, and brought her unto the man.
> And Adam said, This is now bone of my bones, and flesh of my flesh; she shall be called Woman, because she was taken out of Man (Genesis II:21-23).

In other words, man was made "in God's image," and presumably was thereby more directly endowed with His various characteristics, including creative ability. On the other hand, elsewhere we are given a different picture:

> But of the fruit of the tree which is in the midst of the garden, God hath said, Ye shall not eat of it, neither shall ye touch it, lest ye die.
> And the serpent said unto the woman, Ye shall not surely die: For God doth know that in the day ye eat thereof, then your eyes shall be opened and ye shall be as gods, knowing good and evil.
> And when the woman saw that the tree was good for food, and that it was pleasant to the eyes, and a tree to be desired to make one wise, she took of the fruit thereof, and did eat, and gave also unto her husband with her; and he did eat (Genesis III:3-6).

Here, woman initiates the attainment of knowledge, setting us on to the path of independence from God, so that we will "be as gods" and "know good from evil." In this, she seems mainly responsible for our becoming creative in our own right.

Certainly these passages will, in our day and age, garner little sympathy, implying as they do that women are not only inherently second-class citizens but also rather unreliable and scatter-brained. But let us not underestimate how much these same passages have, over the ages, influenced public opinion and been used to rationalize women's shoddy treatment.

The Bible paints a similarly ambivalent portrait of critics. One of the notable acquisitions from original sin and the fall from grace was the ability to evaluate, to "know good from evil." On the whole, the Old Testament seems rather sympathetic to this pursuit. For example, an entire book is devoted to Judges, who generally seem to be held in high regard, as a primary source of wisdom and virtue:

> Nevertheless the Lord raised up judges, which delivered them (the Israelites) out of the hand of those that spoiled them (Judges II:16).

And again:

> Speak, ye that ride on white asses, ye that sit in judgment, and walk by the way (Judges V:10).

We have no idea if the white asses came from too many hours
spent sitting on dusty aisle sets, but certainly it is herein
implied that evaluators know what is best for their underlings;
even when chastising the latter, it is more in sorrow than in
anger.

Yet the New Testament seems to provide several stern
injunctions to the critic:

> Judge not, that ye be not judged.
> For with what judgment ye judge, ye shall be
> judged: and with what measure ye mete, it shall
> be measured to you again (Matthew VII:1-2).

Or: "Let he who is without sin cast the first stone" (John,
VIII:7).

Nevertheless, creators are enjoined by Jesus not to be
angered by critical antipathy but to be grateful:

> Blessed are ye, when men shall hate you, and
> when they shall separate you from their company,
> and shall reproach you, and cast out your name
> as evil....Rejoice ye in that day, and leap
> for joy; for behold, your reward is great in
> heaven....
> But I say unto you which hear, Love your enemies,
> do good to them which hate you,
> Bless them that curse you, and pray for them
> that spitefully use you.
> And unto him that smiteth thee on the one cheek
> offer also the other (Luke VI:22-23, 27-29).

But on balance, we assume, celestial circles must view the
critical dodge sympathetically. After all, God Himself has retired
from creative work, we are told, to sit in judgment over us
all as to our suitability for admission to the Kingdom of
Heaven. Does He enjoy turning thumbs up or down or does He,
like most critics, see it as merely a boring, necessary evil?
Perhaps it is indicative that we will get our final reviews
not from God but via St. Peter. At any rate, no mortal critics
can, to our knowledge, condemn the incompetent to eternal fire
and brimstone (however much they might wish to on occasion).

But is not the theological account embarrassed by scientific
creativity? For does not science, with its preference for
naturalistic, materialistic explanations, demand at least an
agnostic, if not an outright atheistic, stance? In fact, popular
misconception notwithstanding, science rests on several fundamental
beliefs that cannot be empirically verified and that fit a

religious view quite comfortably. Consider its article of faith called determinism, which assumes that the universe is not (as existentialism, for example, would have us believe) chaotic, whimsical, and absurd but is ordered and lawful. Surely it is but a small step from here to accepting the idea of some Master Planner who devised this amazing riddle, of which scientists spend their lives trying to untangle a minuscule part. Once more, Einstein in particular has voiced this attitude:

> Everything is determined, the beginning as well as the end, by forces over which we have no control. It is determined for the insect as well as for the star. Human beings, vegetables, or cosmic dust, we all dance to a mysterious tune, intoned in the distance by an invisible piper.[23]

From such a standpoint, it becomes equally believable that insights might come about because that "invisible piper" provides hints towards the eventual solution.

However, we must now face some special difficulties with this perspective (leaving aside its silence about much of creativity's data). Biblical simulation can be a very entertaining parlor game and it is notable, as we have tried to show, how numerous are the analogies between human and divine creators. Yet it is questionable that this exercise adds much to our understanding of creativity. It is distressingly barren in suggesting further directions for investigation or in opening new vistas. To repeat, if we hold that our creativity has omnipotent origins, then we must largely restrain our curiosity. There is little more to be said because our most sublime ability becomes, in the last analysis, incomprehensible and uncontrollable. If we choose to believe that we create simply because we are created in God's image, then we provide ourselves with yet another fait accompli.

In fact, this exercise in simulation closely resembles the practices of religious fundamentalists. They too search diligently for Biblical passages that seem to support their favorite dogma or grind their favorite axe. Should dogs be forced to clothe themselves? Should garbage be collected only on Tuesdays? Should pistachio nuts be banned from ice cream? Simply cite chapter and verse. Since the Bible is so wonderfully vague (and in comparison, even the Delphic oracle's pronouncements are marvels of precise lucidity), such passages can invariably be found. We are quite confident that others, also using the Old Testament, could paint a very different portrait of the Divine Creator than we did here.

Chapter 9

PSYCHOANALYTIC APPROACHES I: SIGMUND FREUD

Within this tradition, we will discuss several perspectives whose differences, at first glance, seem more noticeable than their similarities. At the outset, therefore, let us ask what beliefs they share. The first is a thoroughgoing determinism, the assertion that the universe is lawful, coherent, and orderly. A phenomenon never happens without reason but is always caused or determined by other events that potentially can be specified. Once this has been accomplished, we can say that we understand and have explained that phenomenon. A deterministic view of human beings, then (in marked contrast to existentialism, for example), assumes that all our actions and experiences are comprehensible.

This belief is also firmly held by other perspectives otherwise quite disparate from psychoanalysis. It is the type of causal events emphasized that particularly distinguishes the latter. It assumes that our mental life includes an unconscious component. Although we ourselves are unaware of its constituents, still they can crucially affect our thoughts and actions. Thus, our creativity, for example, is determined by factors not easily accessible to our own understanding. They lie dormant, lurking unseen beneath the surface like a Loch Ness monster. With these general points in mind, we will now discuss some influential donors to this tradition, pointing out their similarities and differences where it seems appropriate to do so.

Freud, the Viennese physician who founded the psychoanalytic movement and first proposed many of its essential ideas,[1] has profoundly influenced our modern view of ourselves. For this reason alone he belongs in the select pantheon reserved for the likes of Marx, Darwin, and Einstein, and no purportedly enlightened person should remain ignorant of his contributions.* Therefore, it seems advisable to review some of them, although they have been widely disseminated and several excellent introductions are available.[3,4]

---

* It is necessary to say this because it is still fashionable in some quarters to dismiss Freud as an overrated charlatan whose superstitions do not deserve serious attention.(2) In our opinion, one need not accept every Freudian hypothesis (we ourselves shall have cause to criticize many of them in due course), but one should be familiar with them because of their great influence.

Basic Hypotheses

A quick summary is difficult, because Freud's writings were copious. They were also sometimes blatantly contradictory, so our version may part company with others. A major assumption is that we wish to avoid severe emotional shock, anxiety, or trauma, such as that experienced when our self-image is threatened. To do so, we often employ defense mechanisms, various protective devices that we use unconsciously. Freud and others have described a host of these, but we will mention only a few to convey their flavor.

Rationalization employs an incorrect explanation for personal failure. To admit our inadequacies could be traumatic, so we make excuses. A classic example is the tennis player who stares accusingly at the racquet after blowing a shot. Compensation makes up for failure in one endeavor by an intensified drive for success in another, e.g., the frail, shy nonathlete who tries to succeed at scholarship. As we shall see, compensation was emphasized by Freud's disciples/adversaries, Adler and Jung.

A particularly important defense mechanism is repression, which is essentially a technique to induce forgetting. Any distasteful or socially undesirable experiences and desires we "push down" from consciousness into the unconscious, so that we are no longer aware of them. Still, like other unconscious events, they can exert an influence, particularly by causing disturbed, neurotic behavior. Freud was first and foremost a practising physician wishing to help his patients, and he felt that if these repressed traumas could be brought back to consciousness, they could be recognized and "worked through." Hence, his system of therapy, called psychoanalysis, is basically a set of techniques for improving memory.

In the primary method, free association, patients lie on the proverbial couch (the butt of countless satirical cartoons) and talk ad infinitum about whatever comes into their mind. One thought leads to another, which leads to another, until eventually (in theory) they will be reminded of the repressed problems. But for our purposes, dream interpretation is a more relevant technique.[5] Freud hypothesized a vague psychic force or energy called libido, which was a manifestation of sexual energy. There is only a finite amount of it, but some must be expended in keeping those unconscious skeletons locked in their closets.[6] Like vicious dogs kept chained up out of sight, they struggle ceaselessly to be released into the light of day for an airing. Dreams provide an opportunity to let off steam, because during sleep the custodian/censor guarding the kennel is less vigilant. Still, if these shocking matters were openly expressed--in screaming headlines, as it were--they would scandalize the patient's moral sensibilities and she or he would quickly awaken. Consequently, they are disguised, like wolves in sheep's clothing; thus, dreams say one thing and mean another. Their superficial or __manifest content__ represents, in coded form, their actual, hidden meaning, the __latent content__. They are full of symbols, which always represent something else (for example, any long, narrow object, a __phallic symbol__, invariably signifies the male organ). Nevertheless, the interpretation and decoding of these nocturnal, esoteric screenplays gives a therapist another key for unlocking the secrets of the unconscious.

As the preceding example suggests, Freud concluded that the unconscious' constituents almost invariably had a sexual meaning. While this stance is decidedly arbitrary, based mainly on his own interpretations of his patients' revelations, it is not quite so ludicrous as his critics have proclaimed. He surmised, correctly, that sex is a basic, biological, and very powerful motive which, more than any other, encounters restriction and suppression. This is so in our day (our much trumpeted liberality notwithstanding) and was even more so in Freud's, when Victorian mores still held sway. That having been said, there is still little question that Freud became obsessed with matters sexual to the exclusion of other possibilities.

Consider, for example, the famous __Oedipus complex__,[7] named after the king immortalized by Sophocles who, unknowingly, killed his father and married his mother. This sordid scenario, Freud asserted, is inevitably reenacted around the age of four in the fantasy of every male infant's unconscious __psyche__. He desires sexual relations with his mother and so hates his father, whom he fears will emasculate him (the so-called __castration complex__) because he is a rival for her affections. Such obviously unacceptable feelings the child represses, but his subsequent personality development will crucially depend on how he resolves them. Homosexuality, for example, could result from an unsatisfactory working through of Oedipal tendencies.

Nor are females immune from such bizarre experiences; supposedly, they undergo the mirror image, desiring their fathers and hating their mothers. However, noticing that they lack the masculine genital equipment and concluding that they have __already been__ castrated, they feel __penis envy__.[8] Their perceived anatomical depletion causes them to feel psychologically inferior as well. (A female friend of the writer provided the most succinct rebuttal to this notion: "The only time I feel penis envy is when I have to urinate while on a camping trip.")

We must also introduce Freud's famous personality structure, its supposed components being the id, ego, and superego.[9] The first named, present from birth, forms the most primitive, archaic

213

part of the mind and gives rise to our most animalistic, uncivilized tendencies, often of a sexual kind. Completely unconscious and thus communicating but little with the real world, it obeys the pleasure principle, seeking immediate gratification of its wishes and desires without recognizing the demands of that world or the need for any compromise or denial. In other words, it "wants what it wants when it wants it."[10] Id function, then, closely relates to primary process, which is concerned with satisfying these basic needs and instincts. This process dominates newborn and infant behavior but becomes submerged in later development, although it still surface periodically in dreams and in various pathological conditions (Suler[11] has surveyed the theoretical and empirical investigations of this topic).

The ego, in contrast to the id, is present in the conscious mind. Thereby in touch with and aware of the real world's characteristics, it can obey the reality principle. Realizing that the id's demands are unrealistic, it tries to modify and channel them so that they can, if at all possible, be satisfied without upsetting society. So the ego acts as a kind of mediator between the id and its eternal adversary, civilization. Ego function closely relates to secondary process, which gives rise to this realistic outlook and--like linear, left hemisphere thought--is logical, detached, and critical. It develops somewhat later than primary process during childhood, but in later life becomes dominant.

Last is the superego, resembling the familiar notion of the conscience. It arises from the resolution of the Oedipus complex, as the child internalizes society's attitudes about right and wrong. Therefore it attempts to deny those asocial id impulses, producing tension and guilt.

Why is Freud important?

Although it is a slightly peripheral matter, we might pause briefly to ask this question, since it is so fashionable these days to belittle Freud. He can be, and has been, called to task on several grounds, but we shall mention only two. First, some of his especially colorful ideas--the castration complexes, penis envy, and so on--do strain credulity.[12] A newcomer's invariable response to Freud is "Oh, come on!" Now ordinarily this would hardly trouble us since, as the history of ideas time and time again reveals, common sense is extremely fallible. Still, about matters psychological, it should, in our opinion, be given some weight. People themselves are the topic of study, so they should be able, introspectively, to evaluate the merit of an idea. If it does not, at a "gut reaction" level, seem to jibe with their experience as human beings, then this must, at the least, give us pause.

214

Secondly, Freud's theory clearly violates the canons of good scientific theorizing.[13] His hypotheses and concepts are vague, by their very nature defying measurement and observation (for example, an unconscious process is almost by definition unobservable). As a result, the theory lacks the falsifiability that Popper and many others see as the hallmark of good theorizing. It cannot be pinned down to precise, unambiguous predictions or proven wrong. Rather, after the facts are already known, it can explain almost anything that happens and therefore, perhaps, it explains nothing, because such post hoc explanation resembles betting on a completed horse race. Freud always considered psychoanalysis to be a science,[14] but many would dispute his evaluation.

These valid criticisms explain why large parts of modern psychology, so committed at all costs to being scientific, have been relatively unsympathetic to Freud. His greatest influence seems to have been in more artistic fields. Twentieth century drama, literature, and art, for example, would have taken quite different paths had he never written, and works of almost every vintage have by now received their Freudian interpretations. Tomes perusing Hamlet's Oedipus complex, for example, would fill a library.

What, then, are his seminal ideas, those which lead us, in the face of all these embarrassments, to nevertheless pay him heed? The first is unconscious motivation, the hypothesis that we do things for reasons that we ourselves do not understand. Contrary to wide belief, Freud did not invent this notion; it had been espoused in various guises ever since Plato.[15] However, he was the first to popularize it, to extensively describe its possible effects, and to suggest precise methods for exploring it. The prevalent nineteenth century view that humans are rational and enlightened beings, who make decisions after logically weighing the alternatives, was thus dramatically contravened. For Freud, we choose blindly and irrationally, influenced by determinants unknown to us.

It was his second contribution, his insistence on the primary importance of the sexual drive, that most assured his notoriety. Freud is as responsible as anyone for the remarkable speed with which puritanical Victorian morality has been supplanted by openness and even candor. Whether this be progress is debatable. Rollo May, for one, has argued that we have gone from one extreme to the other; where formerly we denied sex, now we have become obsessed with it.[16] The anxieties and neuroses spawned by our repressions (assuming Freud is correct in this) have been replaced by a host of new ones quite unknown to the Victorians. In some circles, the preoccupation with "making it" regularly has become almost obsessive, and the strange delusion has developed that discovering yet another position for intercourse will somehow solve the enduring problems of human existence.

Thirdly, Freud was hardly the first to avow that "the child is father to the man," but he certainly helped foster modern psychology's article of faith that the first six years or so of life crucially affect subsequent personality development. Partly from him, then, have come our modern concerns for child-rearing practices, parent-child interactions, and the like.

His last notable bequest is the decidedly unflattering, even ugly picture he painted of human nature. The unconscious, that decisive determinant of our destiny, was for Freud little more than a garbage dump, a compost heap of base, primitive impulses only tenuously held in check by society's moral restrictions. Our civilized veneer is dangerously thin; beneath it boils the anarchic passion of the jungle beast. Freud realized[17] that this devastating portrait delivered yet another blow to human pride, already staggered first by Copernicus' heliocentric theory (which removed the earth, and therefore human affairs, from the center of the universe and cast it out to the periphery), and secondly by Darwin's theory of evolution (which categorized humans as mere animals, akin to the chimpanzee and aardvark, rather than as unique, qualitatively different lords of the universe).

As is well known, neither Freud's nor Darwin's views were received at first with open arms. Perhaps the incredible bloodbath of World War I, as much as anything, helped to convert the masses of humanity. The political and military stalemate of trench warfare seemed unbreakable. Essentially, two huge armies slaughtered each other by the millions, with little discernible change in either territory or attitudes. At its height, the war seemed destined to last forever. Graves[18] and Remarque,[19] among many others, have poignantly described how the early, naive enthusiasm for the war was gradually replaced by disillusionment and cynicism. Because, worst of all torments, people no longer understood what they were fighting about.

In the face of this overwhelming evidence of human stupidity, both Freud and Darwin began to make sense. Our inherent goodness no longer seemed quite so tenable. One of Freud's most powerful monographs, produced in 1915, mused on the bloodshed.[20] People are surprised by it, he argued, because they viewed human nature incorrectly to begin with. Freud and his colleagues were saddened and appalled by war, but not surprised:

> We may already derive this consolation--that
> our mortification and our grievous disillusionment
> regarding the uncivilized behavior of our

world-compatriots in this war are shown to be unjustified. They were based on an illusion to which we had abandoned ourselves. In reality our fellow citizens have not sunk so low as we feared, because they had never risen so high as we believed.[21]

And those still skeptical about his views must have been given pause by the rise of Fascism and National Socialism. Those same beastly, subhuman tendencies were now not only recognized but stressed and honored. Certainly, some of Freud's ideas may cause our common sense to shudder, but the course of human events suggests that his best have rarely been equaled.

Creativity

Freud's interest in art and literature was lifelong, and his expertise appreciable. He was fascinated by creative people, especially artists, musing in print about Dostoevsky, Ibsen, Michelangelo, and Leonardo da Vinci, among others. His thinking owes much to his theory of dreams, emphasizing yet another, less neurotic defense mechanism called <u>sublimation</u>[22]. Here, those socially unacceptable tendencies languishing in the unconscious are redirected or rechanneled into more acceptable expressions, such as works of art. So these, like dreams, speak subtly in symbolic code and can similarly be interpreted to reveal their unconscious referents.* This exercise Freud himself practised, most notably in his study of Leonardo (to be discussed shortly), and others have done so many times since. Let us consider only one example of it, which to our knowledge has not been previously attempted. This analysis was suggested by a student, Fay Ferris.

The paintings of the noted Canadian artist Emily Carr display many apparent phallic symbols, such as trees and totem poles. Now as far as we know, Ms. Carr never had, during her entire lifetime, a satisfactory sexual relationship. By her own admission, when her father attempted to describe the facts of life to her, she was horrified by the brutality of it.[24] She instantly rejected both her father (to whom she had previously been close) and all things sexual (whether this reflected his overly graphic portrayal or simply her own reticence is unclear). But might we not suspect that her suppressed sexuality could have given

---

* Freud did not always approach art in this analytic spirit. His discussion of Michelangelo's <u>Moses</u>, (23) for example, simply tried to understand its superficial, manifest meaning, i.e., "what is happening," but did not pursue the underlying personality which gave rise to it.

rise, through sublimation, to the evident symbolic content in her work?

But we do Freud a disservice if we imply that, for him, sex provides the whole story. Elsewhere,[25] he asserts that artistic works, like dreams, seek to fulfill several kinds of wishes, of which erotic desires are only one. Equally important are those of personal ambition. In probably his most famous statement about creativity, he argued that the artist wishes to win "honor, power, wealth, fame, and the love of women, but he lacks the means of achieving these satisfactions."[26] Therefore, that artist retreats from the frustrating world of reality into a world of his own construction, where in fantasy, at least, he can achieve this personal aggrandizement.

In amplifying this theme,[27] Freud first notes that children's games, like art, display imagination at work. Also like artists, children attach great importance to their playful activities. "The opposite of play is not serious occupation but--reality."[28] On the face of it, adults no longer play because it is not acceptable. Actually, Freud suggests, they simply substitute the more private pursuit of daydreaming. Artists, too, resembling both children and the gatherers of wool, indulge in play, but for them it also serves to advance their work. This notion an unusually humble Isaac Newton, for one, seemed to find acceptable:

> I do not know what I may appear to the world;
> but to myself I seem to have been only like a
> boy playing on the sea-shore, and diverting myself
> in now and then finding a smoother pebble or
> prettier shell than ordinary, while the great
> ocean lay all undiscovered before me.[29]

In all these activities, then, unsatisfied wishes motivate fantasies; in turn, the fantasies fulfill those wishes. "We begin by saying that happy people never make fantasies, only unsatisfied ones."[30] (Even children's play, seemingly so innocent, earns this blanket condemnation.) In particular, artists, in their inspired gaming, can sometimes satisfy their ambitions. Most novels, for example (in Freud's opinion, at least) feature a hero who triumphs over all and wins the woman's admiration. By identifying with this protagonist, the writer enhances his own sense of superiority, so his work is, literally, "egocentric."

Given that other desires besides the specifically sexual can be sublimated, why are some people particularly adept at using this mechanism? What sets artists apart from other run-of-the-mill daydreamers? Supposedly, artists have a "laxity" or "flexibility" of repression,[31] which allows them to lift the lid off the seething cauldron of the unconscious, peek in, and

then use the constituents constructively. And why do they have
this ability? The answer, for Freud, probably lies in genetic
endowment. Or, in his words:

> It is the innate constitution of each individual
> which decides...how large a part of his sexual
> instinct it will be possible to sublimate (italics
> mine).[32]

Furthermore, in this passage (and others), it becomes eminently
clear that Freud is no democrat when it comes to talent.
Artists are a specially endowed, privileged minority. Not everyone
can do it.

But how do artists thrill and involve us when they
share their fantasies, whereas others only succeed in boring us
when, say, they describe their dreams? This is the fundamental
secret of their talent. Partly, artists can alter their bizarre,
ordinarily unacceptable characters and themes, softening and
concealing what is offensive, so that we, the consumers, are
taken in.[32] We can therefore experience them at an unconscious
level, without realizing it, in a surreptitious, titillating
"foreplay." Just as dream content is disguised so as to slip
out of our psyches without upsetting the moral watchdog, so
artistic content is disguised to slip in. Thus, we can live
dangerously without the threat of guilt. And so, in freeing
themselves from their own frustrated desires and wishes, artists
offer a similar liberation to the audience. In brief, then, a
work of art, like a dream, may seem innocuous but it invariably
disguises immoral content.

Artists can also deflect our awareness by giving us purely
formal pleasure.[34] As we admire their skillful manipulation of
a medium--their effective turns of phrase, flow of melody, or
sequences of movement--we will overlook the underlying pornography.
Freud concludes, therefore, that we honor and revere artists
because they put us, unbeknownst to ourselves, in touch with
these ordinarily inaccessible pleasures. As a result, an artist
"thus achieves through his fantasy what originally he had achieved
only in his fantasy--honor, power, and the love of women."[35]
His/her work solves the problem that motivated it in the first
place.

While this set of aesthetic principles seems at least worth
pondering, Freud elsewhere ventures an unusual opinion. One
criterion of quality, which is perhaps accepted above all others,
is longevity or staying power. Something is great that many
cultures and eras have chosen to call great. Freud disagrees;
something that does not or even cannot last can still be beautiful:

219

A flower that blossoms only for a single night
does not seem to us on that account less lovely.
Nor can I understand any better why the beauty
of perfection of a work of art...should lose
its   worth   because   of   its   temporal
limitation....Since the value of all this beauty
and perfection is determined only by its
significance for our own emotional lives, it
has no need to survive us and is therefore
independent of absolute duration (italics mine).[36]

It is a provocative and, as presented, eminently reasonable
argument.

We might conclude this section by asking about Freud's
ambivalent feelings toward artists and their work, for, as Spector
has noted,[37] his writings betray both his admiration and
disapproval. Admiration is understandable enough, since many
will share this response to great work. But disapproval? Freud's
own narrow, restrictive attitude to things sexual seems partly
responsible for this reaction. In his opinion, works of art
not only subliminally express such matters but also use rather
devious, sneaky tricks to fool our moral sensibilities. In
other words, the very pinnacles of human civilization, ironically,
originate in our most base, primitive tendencies and so seem
slightly unkempt.

A second reason, probably, is that prevalent emotion called
jealousy. In part, Freud envied artists' lax repression, which
allowed them to parade their deepest desires relatively openly,
something that the rest of us (including Freud) are too rigid
and uptight to do. As well, Spector points out, Freud several
times mentioned their special talents for winning the affections
of the fairer sex. During his long and difficult courtship of
his own wife, Freud showed a rare gift for torturing himself
with fits of jealousy.[38] He continually doubted his ability to
gain her undying affections and worried that he might be supplanted
by another. It is understandable, then, that he might resent
those who, in his opinion at least, could storm the bastions
of the female heart with such ease.

We now turn to a case history cast in a Freudian mold.

Leonardo da Vinci[39]

About this renowned artist/scientist, by Freud's own
admission, we know little. However, he has taken the few fragments
that are (according to him) reasonably well established and
fashioned a fascinating portrait. First, Leonardo was noted
for his methodical, sometimes lackadaisical work habits. In

220

addition, he seems to have been rather quiet and withdrawn, not given to competition or temperamental display. Sexually, he seems to have been barren. There is no evidence (we are told) that he ever embraced a woman in love. Since he surrounded himself with beautiful (and largely untalented) male "pupils," he was widely thought to be, and was formally accused of being, homosexual. In Freud's opinion, however, these liaisons probably were unconsummated as well.

Lastly, of course, Leonardo, the definitive Renaissance Man with interest and expertise in many fields, was insatiably curious. This desire to understand everything, which gave him the label of the Italian Faust, supposedly was so overpowering that it eventually led him to study every aspect of nature. Hence, in later life he turned to science, to the detriment of his art. Freud quotes him as stating:

> One has no right to love or hate anything if
> one has not acquired a thorough knowledge of
> its nature....If you little know it, you will
> be able to love it...not at all.[40]

To Freud, these clues all suggest a temperament whose emotional and sexual feelings had been redirected into intellectual inquisitiveness. But why did Leonard remain aloof from the ordinary human passions? Psychoanalysis, naturally, can supply some answers.

Freud begins with a childhood memory (let us hope, only a fantasy) that Leonardo reported. A vulture opened his mouth with its tail and struck many times with its tail against his lips. Freud then shows, through some involved but ingenious reasoning, that this must be interpreted as follows: "Through the erotic relations to my mother I became a homosexual."[41] How so? The tail's phallic connotations are obvious, so the scenario does suggest the passive homosexual act of fellatio. However, since the vulture also, in many cultures, symbolizes motherhood, it suggests, as well, memory of nursing at the mother's breast. In sum, the fable unites masculine and feminine themes.

Now we do know that Leonardo, born illegitimate, was somewhat later (the date is a mystery) adopted by his father. The vulture fantasy leads Freud to conclude, therefore, that Leonardo was for some time raised by his natural mother, because it implies a memory of being violently, even erotically, suckled. It meant "my mother has pressed on my mouth innumerable passionate kisses."[42] She must, then, have taken her little son as a sexual substitute for her missing male. Henceforth, for Leonardo,

221

women would be both mothers and seducers, and his feelings towards them would forever be ambivalent.

Around the age of three, infants supposedly pass through a period of intense curiosity about everything (as any parent will agree who has been bombarded by their endless questions). For Freud, of course, this curiosity originates from sex. The one question they really want answered is, "Where do children come from?" If this curiosity is discouraged, it will be repressed, perhaps to be sublimated into a general inquisitiveness about everything except sex. This is precisely what happened with Leonardo; due to his confusion about his mother, he suppressed his desire to "ever again (experience) such tenderness from women's lips."[43] The women in his paintings, supposedly, betray this ambivalence. Consider the famous Mona Lisa smile. It is both seductive and maternal, warm and passionate like an archetypal earth mother, but also cold, aloof, and even cynical.

Freud also provides a plausible explanation for another development. One radical new practice of the Renaissance was to substitute natural for theological explanation, and reliance on one's own observations rather than on preordained dogma. Now such dogma emanated from sources that clearly resembled father figures, i.e., the ancient philosophers (notably Aristotle) and the authorities of the church. How was Leonardo, among others, able to reject them? Presumably, he had already rejected his own father, partly because of the latter's initial desertion but also because his (Leonardo's) overtly erotic relationship with his mother would intensify the normal Oedipal rivalry. Freud cites several bits of seemingly innocuous evidence, such as the note Leonardo wrote in his diary when his father died, to show that he harbored a repressed death wish for his father. Ever the arch-determinist for whom everything had an explanation, Freud somewhat wryly observed:

> It is only a triviality to which anyone but a psychoanalyst would pay no attention....To him nothing is too trifling as a manifestation of hidden psychic processes; he has long learned that such forgetting or repetition is full of meaning.[44]

Let us now adopt a more critical stance towards some aspects of this interpretation (other difficulties we shall leave until later, since they pervade all of Freud's work). For one thing, it is not at all clear why Leonardo did not redirect his mother hatred/ambivalence into overt homosexual activity. The vulture fable, by Freud's own admission, suggests such tendencies, and overly intimate maternal attachment is a common whipping boy, in psychoanalytic circles, for explaining homosexuality.[45]

Why was _any_ kind of sexual focus, male or female, suppressed and redirected?

He does admit two major flaws. The "choice of the defense mechanism," why a particular individual uses one rather than another, has been a persistent thorn in the side of psychoanalysis. Rarely is there a satisfactory answer, and certainly there is nothing here to tell us why Leonardo selected sublimation to deal with his awakened and then repressed sexual childhood fantasies. Even more troublesome, why was he so good at it? From whence came his rare talent? In keeping with the bias expressed earlier, Freud suggests that biology of the "organic bases of character"[46] will probably provide the answer.

Yet despite all these difficulties, Freud's _Leonardo_ remains compelling. In our opinion, it should be taken as a work of art rather than of science and approached in that light. Like any worthwhile artistic product, it is arbitrary and personal, not necessarily _accurate_ but certainly _fascinating_. It resembles, more than anything, a finely crafted detective novel. A few subtle, easily neglected clues are used to piece together, after the fact, a plausible hypothesis of "who dunnit," the guilty party being not the butler, but the mother. An Ellery Queen or Hercule Poirot will, like Freud, ignore contradictory evidence and indulge in delightful leaps of logic. Such flaws do not lessen our addiction to their deeds (especially during the summer months), because part of our enjoyment comes from discovering those flaws. A whodunnit that neatly accounted for every bit of evidence would be boring indeed. Similar sentiments apply here.

Commentary

Although glaring weaknesses in Freud's thought will doubtless have occurred to the reader, let us begin with its attractive aspects. First, that creativity might substitute for sexuality is rather more credible than it might seem. For one thing, the two activities show remarkable similarities, particularly in their various stages. An initial preparation (foreplay? flirtation?) slowly builds up tension that is released in a climactic moment of either inspiration or orgasm. Feelings of emptiness, aptly labelled "post-coital depression," may follow either act. And, above all, both can give rise to the birth of a new phenomenon, which, in either case, will be unpredictable and possessed of unanticipated attributes. Having a mind of its own, it will go its own way to become what it will become, notwithstanding the wishes of its sires.

Consumers of creative products also show some almost sexual responses. Consider those viewing an attractive painting. Are they content to admire it from afar? They are not. They must "own" it or "possess" it, so as to avoid long separations and the sharing of its charms with strangers. Lovers will sacrifice pride, youth, and bank balances to capture a heart with which they are obsessed; so too will members of the audience.

In the same vein, note the similarities between the creative process and other ways through which the unconscious supposedly reveals itself.[47] In free association, like creativity, extensive mental blocking, along with apparently aimless associative meandering, suddenly ends. Perhaps impelled by a casual word or a trivial incident, insight arrives, popping up like a cork from a wine bottle, to solve (temporarily, at least) a chronic problem. Dreams, too, have provided both therapeutic and creative insights. If we concede that the unconscious does speak through these media, then we must at least suspect that creative revelations arise from the same source.

Freud manages to turn to his advantage another point which might seem to present difficulties. In his view, should not someone who is sexually active also be uncreative? In this sense, the abstinent Leonardo was an ideal specimen for Freud's microscope. Yet many creators--Wagner, Liszt, Raphael, and Bertrand Russell, to name a few--were remarkable sexual athletes. Still others, such as J. S. Bach, Rubens, and Bernini, were happy, model husbands.[48] And Edvard Grieg composed his piano concerto in A minor while in the midst of the (presumably fulfilling) labors of his honeymoon! From whence came enough libido, to say nothing of adrenalin, to carry on both of these exhausting pursuits?

Few have surpassed Freud's talent for explaining seemingly embarrassing facts, and he puts it to good use here. Briefly, completely satisfactory sex will become dull and routine (advocates of the swinging life, take note!):

> The value the mind sets on erotic needs instantly sinks as soon as satisfaction becomes readily obtainable. Some obstacle is necessary to swell the tide of the libido to its height.[49]

Thus, someone with the sex life of a rabbit will still seek other, exciting worlds to conquer (such as creative work?) that provide barriers to achievement. Which suggests that the sexual drive is doomed to frustration; either too little or too much will be unsatisfying. This argument's main virtue, naturally, is to render Freud's explanation untestable, another exercise at which he was a past master. People can be creative because their sex life is rich or because it is barren. The gelding thus becomes virtually the only unlikely candidate. (But then we think of the renowned _castrati_ vocalists of Handel's day, to say nothing of Lombroso's sterile geniuses.)[50]

We wish next, putting words in his mouth, to suggest how Freud might handle some creative phenomena that, to our knowledge, he confronted either only incidentally or not at all. First, why the reliable medium experience, that "someone else did it"? In his analysis of Jensen's _Gradiva_,[51] Freud briefly implies that during creation, we tap different, usually unavailable parts of our minds, i.e., the unconscious. At this time, then, we are genuinely in a different "head space," so that when we return to the earth of ordinary consciousness, we may well feel that the result is not our doing. In a sense, it isn't.

Similarly, we can now understand creatives' _inability_ to explain their work. Thus Dylan Thomas cared greatly that the words in his poems should sound suitable but was cheerfully unconcerned about a poem's underlying meaning. His attitude was, "Your meaning is as good as mine."[52] Even such a staunch egoist as G. B. Shaw could voice similar sentiments.[53] And certainly from a psychoanalytic standpoint, creators should no more be expected to understand their own produce than patients should understand the meaning of their own dreams. Both will need a trained interpreter to help them, and both may well reject the translations, saying, "That's not what I meant at all." Nonetheless, in Freud's opinion, those translations are more likely to be accurate. The analyst knows best.

1. _The_ artist and communication. But why do artists, unlike others with repressed problems, need to tell tales on themselves in public? _Why_ their _need_ to communicate? Here, several possibilities suggest themselves. First, artists, like sexual exhibitionists, might need (for whatever reason) to parade themselves and their sexual attributes publicly. This desire, like any other, could be sublimated into an artistic display before an audience. A later psychoanalytic spokesperson, Weismann, has asserted this view:

> Not only the actor but all creative artists have some need for as well as an ability to exhibit. These qualities are to be found in writers, composers and painters who are certainly not considered to be performing artists....Acting will attract those who have excessive inner needs for, and urgent insatiable gratification from, exhibiting themselves. Psychoanalytic investigation reveals that these are individuals who have failed to develop a normal sense of identity and body image during the early maturational phases of infancy.[54]

225

James Jones pithily acknowledges the same need:

> I do think that the quality which makes a man
> want to write and be read is essentially a
> desire for self-exposure and is masochistic.
> Like one of those guys who has a compulsion to
> take his thing out and show it on the street.[55]

All of which adds a slightly altered, more literal meaning to
Stephen Spender's observation that a poet tries to "achieve
nakedness."[56] A Portrait of the Artist as a Young Flasher!

A second possible answer rests on yet another defense
mechanism, projection, in which we bestow our own undesirable
qualities onto other objects or people,[57] (the pot calling the
kettle black, as it were). By putting these qualities "out
there," we can protect ourselves by denying that we have them;
also, they become easier to work though.* Clearly, projecting
them into a work of art could accomplish similar purposes.
Moreover, at one point Freud at least implies his agreement,
stating that "a dream...is a projection."[59] This being so, the
same could be true of a work of art, given their similarities.
From this standpoint, then, artists produce not so much to
communicate their suppressed tendencies as to purge themselves
of these tendencies in a kind of exorcistic rite.

We may also, with a little shuffling, explain critical
pursuits. Presumably with the superego's development comes our
insistent tendency to judge every event experienced. This
puritanical watchdog, on guard against any hint of immorality,
will not allow any of us to remain neutral, but perhaps it is
overly dominant, even nagging, in those who become professional
evaluators. Like stern parents, they restrain the artist, that
overgrown child who subtly expresses id impulses. Spender, for
one,[60] sees the creator-critic relationship as resembling that
between parent and offspring. All writers, he suspects, secretly
wish to impress someone, often a parent or teacher who did not
believe in them, and in their minds the critic may symbolize
that significant figure.

Freud's thoughts on psychological development also hint at
the critic's personality. Supposedly, everyone passes though
various phases (successively, oral, anal, latency, and phallic)

---

* This second view of the process seems generally preferred.
Bruner, for example, holds that we externalize our qualities
outside ourselves so that we can contemplate them with
detachment.(58) We proposed a similar possibility while discussing
existential approaches (see Chapter 6).

during which different anatomical locations provide primary pleasure. A fixation at a particular stage (either through its excessive pleasure, or frustration) will later produce a distinctive character. "Anal" types--compulsive, inhibited, remote, and aggressive--fit our hypothetical critic to a T, that shy bird who cannot unleash his or her imagination and who fears taking risks but pummels those who do. Are critics, perchance, slightly "tight-assed?"

Freud's developmental notions have also been used by Hudson[61] to explain convergent and divergent thinkers. According to his (Hudson's) fixation hypothesis the former, found primarily among scientists, must fixate during the latency period. For this eventuality supposedly breeds persons who think in an orderly, analytic manner, and prefer to be rule bound, to deal with the external world and to treat the personal in an impersonal way. In contrast the divergers, usually artists, must fixate somewhat later, during adolescence, since this would instill objective, rational abilities but with a preference for imposing them on a subjective, personal world.

2. Creativity, women, and age. A Freudian explanation for the sex difference seems even more overt (if also more debatable) in his writings. His frequent, often rather derogatory musings on the female psyche are largely superfluous here (and probably anywhere) but, for better or worse, we offer a few tidbits. Supposedly a young girl experiences penis envy when she notices her lack of that curious male appendage. Typically perceiving herself, thereby, as mutilated and incomplete, she internalizes the same contempt for her sex that men feel[62] and hence a walloping inferiority complex. Apparently, then, few women possess either the self-confidence or the willingness to risk which, unfortunately, creative work requires (although Freud only states directly that "women (have) less capacity for sublimating their instincts.")[63] Alternatively, Freud several times asserts that women (for complicated reasons) never resolve the Oedipus complex properly,[64] so their superegos are undernourished. Consequently, they are less able to judge objectively, with detached scrutiny. Since creativity requires these abilities, it would thereby suffer. But why, then, are there so many first-rate female critics?[65]

Still, women who do create apparently represent, for Freud, a second solution to penis envy. Sometimes, he asserts, a woman will convince herself that she does have a penis (a process called disavowal[66]), will therefore "harden herself" (apparently Freud himself was not immune to Freudian slips!), and will try to act like a man. He used this mechanism mainly to explain female homosexuality, mentioning only incidentally that it might also be sublimated into an "intellectual profession."

227

But the infrequency with which creative women have sired children, along with their sometimes more masculine interests and attitudes, makes his extension of it to the creative realm seem likely. Indeed, Watson, in The Double Helix,[67] portrays one such individual in Rosalind Franklin, that very capable scientist whose X-ray photos of DNA Watson and Crick "borrowed" (rather questionably) for their own use. However Watson favors an environmental rather than Freudian explanation for her intimidating character. In a most sympathetic epilogue, he argues that in the largely masculine scientific subculture, an intelligent woman must either "out-macho the machos" or be ignored or, worse, patronized. In addition, he praises Franklin's great courage in continuing to work effectively until shortly before her death, although she knew she was mortally ill.

Freud did touch briefly on one field in which women have worked successfully. We include this passage mainly to show how bizarre he can sometimes be:

> It seems that women have made few contributions to the discoveries and inventions in the history of civilization; there is, however, one technique which they may have invented--that of plaiting and weaving....Nature herself would seem to have given the model which the achievement imitates by causing the growth at maturity of the pubic hair that conceals the genitals. The step that remained to be taken lay in making the threads adhere to one another, while on the body they stick into the skin and are only matted together.[68]

Recognizing that such incredible ideas on feminine mental life might provoke the odd ripple of dissent, he then adds,

> If you reject this idea as fantastic, and regard my belief in the influence of lack of a penis on the configuration of femininity as an idee fixe, I am of course defenceless.[69]

So you are, Dr. Freud, so you are!

Finally, on more reasonable ground, we can ask why creation is more typical of the young. Remember Hamlet's insensitive berating of his mother, for becoming involved with the hated Claudius:

> You canot call it love; for at your age
> The heyday in the blood is tame, it's humble
> And waits upon the judgment; (3.4).

Since, as this passage declares, the sexual drive does decline with age (although not nearly as precipitously as youth's more manic apologists would have us believe), so too, then, should the urge to create.

3. <u>Difficulties with Freud's theory</u>. But we must now play a more pessimistic tune and turn to some trouble spots. Here, we are frequently indebted to Spector, whose thoughtful and extensive critique of Freud's views on art is recommended reading.[70] Initially, we should note a gaping omission. Freud frequently discusses artists but has almost nothing to say about scientific creativity. Perhaps it defies his treatment, since it lacks the same sense of personal expression and rarely uses symbols. Alternatively, since Freud firmly regarded himself as a scientist, perhaps he felt that he could not analyze this species objectively.

Undoubtedly, some psychoanalytic interpretations, whether provided by Freud himself or by his more enthusiastic followers, will cause our common sense to blink in amazement. In the extreme they demand satire, and Crews, for one, has happily obliged with a hilarious pseudo-psychoanalytic interpretation of Winnie-the-Pooh.[71] Admittedly, interpreting symbols must be among life's more ungrateful activities, because those interpretations must always be arbitrary; we simply lack the means, as yet, to validate them conclusively. Even if the content of a dream or work of art does symbolize something else (which is itself debatable), to specify that "something else" is only to state an <u>opinion</u>. Leonardo's vulture may mean precisely what Freud maintains, or something quite different, just as a telephone pole may represent the phallus, or an oil rig, or the moons of Jupiter, or (oh heresy!) simply a telephone pole.

What is irritating about Freud and his brethren is their insistence that these interpretations are not stimulating possibilities (which they are) but gospel truth (which they are not). Fortunately, some of his successors have been less dogmatic. For Jung, the same dream can have many meanings, and it is the interpreter's task not to impose one but to suggest alternatives.[72] Presumably the dreamer can recognize intuitively which possibility is valid. In other words, a Freudian will assert, "This is what your dream means." A Jungian will ask, "Could it mean this?". As things stand, the second approach seems eminently more defensible.

Which brings up a related problem. Any interpretation, being arbitrary, will reflect the interpreter's own biases and beliefs. As evidence for this assertion, some influential theories of personality largely formalize their own authors' personalities

229

and backgrounds, i.e., Jung himself aptly personifies his own theory.[73] This is hardly surprising. Such a theorist will develop his views in part by contemplating his own experience as a human being and then generalizing his observations to the rest of humanity.

Freud was as susceptible as anyone to this practice so that, as Spector has convincingly shown, the Leonardo monograph is more descriptive of Freud than of Leonardo. Following his own precepts, he seems to have been working through some problems rather close to home. For example, the domestic situation he concocted, with its overly intimate, even incestuous mother and its detached father, precisely fitted his own. Moreover, as Spector shows, he brazenly ignored some known facts about Leonardo that did not fit that situation. His study of Dostoevsky displays similar editorial license.[74] If the resulting portraits were accurate, all this would matter not a whit. But is projection the road to validity? At any rate, the Leonardo begins to resemble infinitely receding images in a set of contraposing mirrors. We, the audience, observe Freud as he studies Leonardo. Who contemplates his Mona Lisa. Who, in turn, thoughtfully observes us.

We must next ask, are creative works "self expressions" of an artist's own personal psyche, or does she or he simply give form to more universal themes and values? Freud clearly favors the first alternative, and he is certainly not alone. Romantics, existentialists, and humanists have all agreed on this much at least. Introspective reports also provide frequent support. Here is Dylan Thomas:

> I hold a beast, an angel and a madman in me...and my problem is their subjugation and victory, downthrow and upheaval, and my effort is their self expression.[75]

Other perspectives, such as the theological, have leaned towards the second alternative. As well, Freud's great adversary, Jung, as we shall shortly learn, gave it particularly profound expression.[76] Jung agrees that art can function as a kind of therapy to work through personal problems, but this yields only minimally interesting neurotic art. Great art, quite a different matter, rises above an individual life to communicate universal matters, speaking "from the mind and heart of the poet to the mind and hearts of mankind."[77]

In like manner, playwright Arthur Miller asserts that a dramatist partitions himself out among his various characters.[78] Each is partly expressive of him and is partly an independent creation in its own right. Contrast this with Freud's assertion

230

that a writer identifies almost entirely with one character, the protagonist/hero.[79] Miller agrees with Jung that "confession may be the beginning of art, but never its end."[80] As well, both would deny that we can gain insight into an artist's personal psyche by interpreting his or her work. Obviously the jury is still out on this issue and no tallies are available to reveal the majority's sentiments. But we should at least realize that Freud's assumptions about art, in this regard, are by no means universally accepted.

We return, next, to a familiar problem. For Freud, creative behavior occurs for the same reasons and stems from the same sources as does neurotic behavior, i.e., the repressed garbage dump of the unconscious. He is adamant on the point. Here is only one passage of many: "The motive force (for art) is the same conflicts which drive other people into neurosis."[81] A work of art is symptomatic of underlying problems and is an attempt to confess or resolve them. We examined the avowed neurosis/creativity partnership at some length before (see Chapter 3), so we need not reiterate our arguments here but simply observe that the bulk of the evidence calls Freud into question. Even when someone does create in order to confess a problem, the process may be much more conscious and even cynical than Freud would have us believe. Storr, in commenting on the famous statement that artists seek "honor, fame, and the love of women," points out, correctly, that many have knowingly pursued, and used their work to obtain, these benefits. After all, it is common knowledge that art can produce them. Many artists, like athletes, labor in part because they admittedly enjoy the limelight. And what does that cliche-ridden line of seduction, "Come up and see my etchings," tell us? That being perceived as an "artistic person" has long been one gambit for enticing someone else to adjourn to the bedroom or the jacuzzi.

We turn now to one overriding omission in Freud's perspective that, on reflection, produces several weaknesses. As aestheticians have long noted, a work of art has two basic components, viz. content--which is its meaning, message, or theme ("what it says")--and form--the style, techniques, and medium that it uses to express that content ("how it says it"). Thus, Shakespeare, in A Midsummer Night's Dream:

> And as imagination bodies forth
> The forms of things unknown, the poet's pen
> Turns them to shapes, and gives to airy nothing
> A local habitation and a name. (5.1)

Various aspects of the form-content relationship have long been debated. Which is more important? Are they necessarily distinct, or can they overlap? Must a work have both? (A

231

work lacking any form whatsoever is inconceivable, but one without content is at least theoretically possible.) We do not wish to immerse ourselves in these sloughs of despond. Tiptoeing quietly past, let us simply state that, in practice, most if not all works will possess both qualities.

For our purposes, the important point is that Freud's is exclusively a theory of content; it informs us why an artist expresses the themes she or he does. Apart from the decidedly atypical ruminations on Michelangelo's Moses,[82] Freud completely ignores formal matters. Not only that, he showed remarkably little interest, either in his writing or as an artistic consumer, in work of mainly formal appeal, such as abstract art.[83] As well, he expressly ignored pornography, which presents sexual matters not surreptitiously but blatantly. Neither type of art fitted his theory, so they became persona non grata.

On the other hand, Freud himself[84] and many of his followers have openly admitted a curious preference. They will focus on second-rate work that contains obviously bizarre, subliminal content ripe for interpretative plucking--fairy stories, myths, gothic romances, and the like--while ignoring superior contributions that happen to be less suitable for depth analysis. Here, for example, is Bergler's all too typical opinion:

> (It is) immaterial for psychological evaluation, whether (the artist) is a good or bad writer.[85]

At best, then, the theory can say little that is helpful about many types of art, including some of the greatest. And surely any approach more interested in the mediocre than in the sublime, which regards questions of value as simply irrelevant, stands indicted almost by definition. Among other things, it will, perhaps, answer questions that concern most of us only incidentally, i.e., how and why does a hack produce hogwash, while remaining stoically mute about a much more fascinating riddle: from whence cometh the masterpiece?

Several other Freudian failings, it would seem, are due to this neglect of formal matters. First (in common, admittedly, with other perspectives), Freud says nothing, either overtly or implicitly, about why someone might choose a particular medium (painting, sculpture, or biochemistry) or style (Gothic, Bauhaus, or neo-Neanderthal) for expression. Both of these decisions, we would suggest, are made largely from formal considerations. Given that a person has something to say, how can he or she say it most comfortably and naturally? In which style and medium will she or he feel "at home?" After all, a particular theme can be expressed in many ways, as the Oedipus legend itself so clearly demonstrates. It has been portrayed dramatically by Sophocles, choreographically by Martha Graham (in Night Journey), novelistically by Dostoevsky (in Brothers Karamazov), and psychiatrically by Freud himself.

But, most damning, Freud provides little enlightenment about perhaps the most important question of all. What factors set the rare genius apart from the rest of neurotic humanity? What is the source of his or her talent? If two neurotics simply express the same underlying conflicts, why does one earn a Nobel Prize while the other merely receives a hefty bill from the analyst? To cite specifics, why did Leonardo show such supreme talents, unlike the thousands of others who have also had overly intimate mothers?

Other than some vague references to genetics/anatomy (which, given the present state of knowledge, are little more than stabs in the dark), Freud has little to say here. His disinterest in formal matters once more seems to be culprit. It seems likely that the presence of greatness is announced, first and foremost, by the power, style, and imagination with which its themes are represented. Or to put it differently, a masterpiece possessing admirable form but paucity of content (although not trivial content) is quite conceivable, as witness abstract art, but one having great content poorly expressed is not. Some of the worst abominations imaginable have attempted to grapple with cosmic themes and have fallen flat on their overly pretentious faces. The Oedipal theme has been expressed both grippingly and also soporifically. Succinctly, greatness is distinguished not so much by what it says as by how it says it. In the words of Alexander Pope:

> True wit is Nature to advantage dress'd;
> What oft' was thought, but ne'er so well express'd;
> Something, whose truth convinc'd at sight we find,
> That gives us back the image of our mind.[86]

Freud admitted this weakness in his approach on several occasions. In his discussion of Dostoevsky, he observed that when faced with the creative artist, analysis was forced to lay down its arms.[87] And in the Leonardo:

> As artistic talent and productive ability are intimately connected with sublimation, we have to admit also that the nature of artistic attainment is psychoanalytically inaccessible.[88]

233

Chapter 10

PSYCHOANALYTIC APPROACHES II: JUNG AND RANK

Any discussion of the psychoanalytic movement must begin
with Freud, but he was far from alone in providing seminal
contributions either to our general view of ourselves or to
our understanding of creativity. In this chapter we shall consider
two others who at first closely followed the founding father
but who later diverged to provide provocative proposals of their
own. Both of these disciples shared many of Freud's biases,
so these need not be repeated. Instead, we shall focus on
their points of departure.

Carl Jung

Initially, Jung was in the forefront of the Freudian entourage,
adopted by the master as the fair-haired heir apparent.[1]
Consequently, the rupture between them, brought about by Jung's
later theoretical heresies, was both professional and personal,
leaving deep wounds on both sides. While accepting in principle
the dictum that sex was an important motive whose denial could
produce neurosis, Jung adamantly denied that this one mechanism
might explain virtually every idiosyncrasy of human behavior.
In general, he viewed the unconscious much more positively. It
was not merely a compost heap of primitive tendencies. It
also encompassed the person's best possibilities, and so could
drive one towards positive, affirmative acts that would actualize
this dormant potential. As well, it contained not only memories
of past experiences (real or imaginary) but also an almost
mystical sense of the future.[2] Its coded messages communicated
not just what had been but what was to be; in Dickens' terms,
it contained both the Ghost of Christmas Past and the Ghost of
Christmas Yet to Come.

However, his most suggestive proposal was probably that of
the collective unconscious,[3] another region of the psyche besides
the more generally accepted personal unconscious. Supposedly,
it stores a kind of wisdom of the ages that has been passed
down from our ancient predecessors. As we share certain inherited
biological, anatomical structures, so too do we all possess
some common behavioral tendencies, experiences, wishes, and
memories. Unlike the personal unconscious, which seems to lie
closer to the surface of mental life, analytic techniques cannot
bring the collective component back to conscious awareness, because
its contents were not repressed but have been buried since our
conception.[4]

The famous archetypes are its most important inhabitants.
These mysterious, primordial archaic images seem to possess special

235

significance for all people everywhere. For example, forms such as the cross and the mandala are invariably assigned religious or mystical importance because of their fascinating, almost hypnotic power.[5] Yet we miss the essence of this notion if we simply equate archetypes with specific forms. They are, rather, <u>tendencies</u> or <u>potentials</u> for certain forms, which organize the images that we actually do produce. They can be represented in many variations and still retain their essential meaning. Therefore, the archetypes, only indirectly expressed, are seen dimly, as "through a glass darkly."

The arguments that Jung summons to support these difficult ideas are compelling. First, a devoted student of anthropology and archaeology, he was struck by the frequent recurrence of certain symbols, legends, and myths in various societies, both ancient and contemporary, that had had no contact whatsoever with one another. For example, von Franz has described how different cultures have portrayed the miracle of creation itself, along with typical creative experiences;[6] the thematic similarities are unmistakable. So too do certain religious rituals and practices crop up with almost monotonous regularity. Jung concluded, reasonably, that these similarities are not accidental but reflect our shared predispositions to react predictably to events of great significance, such as birth and death.

Secondly, like Freud, he was led to his beliefs by his clinical experiences. His patients sometimes reported textbook Freudian dreams that expressed personal fantasies. But other dreams had an impersonal, universal quality seemingly quite divorced from the dreamer. Sometimes the events and ideas therein were completely unfamiliar, yet invariably the dreamer would attach special importance to these dreams, and their themes would tend to recur. Such novel, inexplicable content suggested that the unconscious itself is creative (in dreams, every person is an artist) and that the collective unconscious was now speaking.

Jung's third defense is more logical than empirical. The archetypes, like any unconscious mechanism, must remain shadowy and arbitrary to the skeptic, because they cannot be directly observed. But Jung correctly points out that the human body is a "museum of organs." Its structures are the product of long evolutionary development, so it represents a kind of race memory for our ancestors' biological characteristics. Likewise, we all possess certain inherited behavioral "instincts," such as eating, sleeping, and reproducing. (Jung warns, however, that <u>instincts</u> and <u>archetypes</u> must not be confused. The first term he reserves for purely biological inherited tendencies, the second for more psychological, mystical ones.) He quite justifiably asks, then, why it is unthinkable that we might also succeed to some ancestral psychic attributes.

236

Which brings us once more to the interpretation of symbols, an exercise to which Jung has made classic contributions.[7] In his opinion the human mind produces symbolic events spontaneously. As evidence, we dream automatically during sleep, and in remarkably reliable, predictable amounts. (Kleitman[8] has summarized some experimental work, showing that about 20 percent of sleeping time will be spent dreaming.) Thus Hamlet's "perchance to dream" is unduly irresolute. Dreams are the third certainty. Furthermore, to Jung they obviously possess far more than superficial meaning; so too do myths, fairy stories, romances, and the like.

In discussing this latent content, he insisted on a distinction between signs and symbols. A sign will have a specific, precise meaning or referent, but a symbol will be inherently ambivalent, possessing various and often inexpressible connotations. Whenever we face events either too vague or too awesome for our rational understanding, we resort to symbols to try, however unsatisfactorily, to give them form.

In Jung's opinion, Freud had confused the two representations and so had treated symbols as if they were signs, giving them, in dreams and elsewhere, fixed interpretations and stating, "This is what they mean." Jung, on the other hand, like most philosophers before him, held that the same symbol might have quite different meanings for different people, or even for the same person on different occasions. Furthermore--since sex was not, for him, the be-all and end-all--the message need not necessarily be pornographic. Even an obvious phallic symbol could represent fertility, healing, or the life force rather than the male organ itself. Therefore, as we mentioned previously, Jung preferred to suggest various interpretations, believing that the recipient was best able to recognize the valid alternative. In addition, if the first decoding was off base, subsequent dreams would attempt to correct it by communicating the same message in a different form.

The Psychology of Types[9]

Finally, we must grapple with Jung's famous delineation of various personality types. Introverts and extroverts are the two most fundamental. Introverts set the self and subjective psychological processes above external events. They are motivated by inner needs and mental life, and tend to be reflective, detached from others, and loners. In the extreme, they may retreat completely into a narrowly egocentric, internal fantasy life having no connection to reality.

Extroverts, on the other hand, are conditioned by objects and external events, which work like magnets to determine decisions and reactions. They are the definitive "hail fellows well met," boisterous, back-slapping "joiners" who place great store on their interactions with and effect on other people. In the extreme, they may be so caught up in "objects" that they lose themselves entirely.

What determines a particular person's preference? Here Jung admits defeat, but suggests that the answer will probably be found in physiological differences (like Freud, when faced with an unsolved puzzle he leaned toward biological, reductive hypotheses).

Predictably, the picture becomes more complicated, because Jung was not so naive as to think that everyone would fit neatly into one of these pigeon holes. First of all, only rarely will a person be exclusively one or the other; one tendency will dominate consciousness, but for most of us, some aspects of both will periodically appear. As well, for Jung the unconscious tends toward the opposite of conscious life, to compensate for the latter's omissions. As a result, a conscious extrovert would have the subjective, personal factor reigning supreme in his or her unconscious, as its manifestations, such as dreams, would show. According to this theory of opposites, then, we all, like actors, wear psychological masks in public, hiding important aspects of our personalities behind a disguise or facade called the persona (a term that originally denoted the masks worn by the actors in classical Greek theatre). Again this notion severely blurs the demarcation between the two categories.

As a further complication, realizing that even within these two groups individuals can differ markedly from one another, Jung distinguished four types of psychological functioning. Supposedly, people may prefer to respond to the world primarily by thinking, feeling, sensation, or intuition. Let us now briefly describe the eight resulting categories (two psychological types, each containing four possible response modes). The thinking type emphasizes intellectual processes. If one is an extrovert, these are based on objective, external "facts," or data, while an introvert's would express subjective ideas. The feeling type relies on emotions and desires to make decisions. Now an introverted form of this function seems clear enough, since feelings are decidedly subjective. But a feeling extrovert seems almost a contradiction in terms. Yet Jung argues that someone may experience beauty, value, or love for an object or other person because she or he has internalized the opinions and responses of others. Thus, this arch-bandwagon jumper's emotions do in fact depend on external events; for this slave of the fluctuating world of fashion, even emotions lose their personal character.

238

At any rate, thinking and feeling, both <u>rational</u> <u>functions</u> (since both base their judgments on reason), are opposite and therefore compete with one another. When one is dominant, the other will be suppressed into the unconscious, so that the thinking type will be deficient in feeling, and vice versa. The two <u>irrational</u> <u>functions</u>, which depend more on the intensity of perception than on reason, are similarly competitive. The sensation type is influenced by sensory experiences, those stemming from external objects if one is an extrovert (an enthusiastic consumer of sunsets, mountains, and various flora and fauna) and by more internal stimulation if an introvert. The intuitive type depends more on internal, involuntary events, such as hunches, to make decisions. The distinction between the introverted intuitive and sensation types is only vaguely delineated, but the extroverted version seems more comprehensible. Characteristically preoccupied with future possibilities and above all with novelty, he or she becomes bored when things become well defined, predictable, and familiar. Such a person tends, therefore, to be fickle, initiating movements and then leaving others to clean up the pieces while he or she moves on to something else (Mr. Toad, in Grahame's <u>The</u> <u>Wind</u> <u>in</u> <u>the</u> <u>Willows</u>, seems a classic example).[10] Let us allow Jung to clarify the four functions:

> <u>Sensation</u> (i.e., sense perception) tells you that something exists; <u>thinking</u> tells you what it is; <u>feeling</u> tells you whether it is agreeable or not; and <u>intuition</u> tells you whence it comes and where it is going.[11]

A few critical remarks seem called for. Like all typologies, this one undoubtedly oversimplifies humankind's heterogeneous diversity; exceptions will always appear that simply defy neat categorization. That point having been made, the extrovert and introvert terms do have some descriptive utility (as their adoption into popular language indicates), so long as we remind ourselves that these <u>are</u> purely descriptive labels that do not explain a personality but themselves need explanation. Unfortunately, the functional types seem less satisfactory. As described, their differences are by no means clear; the intuitive and feeling functions in particular seem to overlap and shade into one another. Still, they can be distinguished at an operational, if not at a theoretical, level; measurement techniques are available, such as the Myers-Briggs Type Indicator,[12] that will indicate the category to which a person should be assigned.

In addition, we can certainly conceive, as Jung himself admitted[13], of other possible responses besides these four. For example, a <u>remembering</u> type might be preoccupied with past events; it would be personified by our historians, and by those

239

sportswriters who neverendingly complain that today's athletes aren't a patch on the giants of yesteryear.

Creativity

The article Psychology and Literature[14] provides Jung's seminal statement about creative work, but he discussed it extensively elsewhere as well. At base, he recognized some similarities between neurosis and creativity. Both phenomena arise from so-called autonomous complexes[15], psychic processes that are independent of the person's control and, having a life of their own, go their own way. No amount of willing can hasten a creative inspiration; it will reach consciousness on its own sweet time. Like Plato, then, Jung sees the "divine frenzy of the artist" as similar to a disturbed state.

But not identical. As we saw earlier (see Chapter 3), he agrees that the two may go hand in hand, and that one may even produce the other, but if anything, creative talent will cause neurosis, rather than vice versa. An artist almost inevitably will encounter conflict, because "two forces are at war within him: on the one hand, the justified longing of the ordinary man for happiness, satisfaction and security, and on the other a ruthless passion for creation which may go so far as to override every personal desire."[16] The artist is a virtual prisoner of desires beyond control. He or she is called to a greater task than the rest of humankind, "chosen for that high office by nature herself."[17] Therefore, the artist may well "pay dearly for the divine gift of creative fire."[18] Dylan Thomas verifies this point:

> Asked if his self-criticism might lead him to give up poetry in favor of prose, he replied....'You don't give up poetry. It may give you up, but you don't abandon it. It's always chasing you relentlessly--a nine foot goblin with two noses.'[19]

The creative gift may lead to problems for another reason as well. In yet another manifestation of the ubiquitous human tendency for compensation, gifted children, in Jung's opinion, often develop their narrow, special talent at the expense of other parts of their personalities.[20] In other areas, they may remain quite immature, or even disturbed. Clearly, in his eyes, a "creative gift" is one-sided, and lacks a wide-ranging "g" factor.

But having admitted the correlational link, Jung emphatically and repeatedly rejects the Freudian dogma that masterpieces result from and express personal neuroses.[21] Art can arise from these

240

sources, but the result is neurotic art, interesting only as a symptom. In Jung's view, most "modern art" (of which he was no admirer[22]) should also be tarred with this brush. James Joyce's Ulysses, for example, was not necessarily produced by a neurotic, but in trying to capture and express the inherent franmentation of our age, its contents became neurotic. (In a diatribe against Ulysses[23] which is itself almost monomaniacal, Jung openly admitted that it had not only puzzled him completely, but bored him intensely and put him to sleep. His inability to appreciate this landmark of twentieth century literature perhaps says more about Jung than about Joyce.)

Likewise, Jung dismisses the possibility that therapy might threaten creative productivity. Here is a typical passage:

> True creativity is a spring that can't be stopped...Disease has never yet fostered creative work; on the contrary, it is the most formidable obstacle to creation. No breaking down of repressions can ever destroy true creativeness.[24]

Admittedly, artistic activity can serve a confessional, exorcistic purpose. Jung himself pioneered the use of art therapy for that very reason, to encourage his patients to express their unconscious conflicts in artistic work, which would provide another pathway to that murky region.[25] As well, when those patients produce things of value, their self-images could thereby be improved. Still, Jung never pretended that the results had any aesthetic merit. They might be of interest to the patient and therapist, but not to a paying public.

But what, then, defines genuinely great artists and distinguishes them from the ordinary, neurotic version? They do not express themselves; rather, in what Jung called the unconscious animation of the archetype[26] they tap the material of the collective unconscious and express the various archetypal forms which we all share. In so doing, the great artist functions as a collective person, as a kind of medium who allows these universal ideas to express themselves through him or her. (In this regard, Jung notes with approval the statement of Neitzsche, cited previously here that "one can hardly reject completely the idea that one is the mere incarnation, or mouthpiece, or medium of some almighty power."[27]) Thus, for example, "It is not Goethe that creates Faust, but Faust that creates Goethe."[28] Putting it differently, the artist's personality quirks do not explain the work; rather, the work accounts for those quirks.

According to Jung, then, great art communicates widely because it depicts these primordial matters, "(rising) above the personal and (speaking) from the mind and the heart of the poet to the

241

mind and heart of mankind."[29] He agrees with Freud that its symbols provide a window into the unconscious, but for him the view faces the collective rather than the individual landscape. In particular, they express those mysterious archetypes, whose presence gives masterpieces their special, almost hypnotic power.

Concerning the theory of types, Jung mainly tried to show how exaggerations of the various tendencies might lead to quite different sorts of pathologies. Nevertheless he does, in passing, suggest some applications to creative personalities. First, he openly avows that an introverted outlook, less influenced by fashion and the opinions of others, will more likely yield originality and excellence (since he himself, by his own admission, fitted this type, his opinion may be somewhat suspect). In addition, more preoccupied with inner matters, the introvert should be more sensitive to the murmurings of the collective unconscious. This belief--that ultimate value is to be found in the inner psyche rather than in the external world--places Jung squarely in the tradition of Plato and Eastern mysticism and outside the empirical/scientific lineage fathered by Aristotle.

Still, in our view, extraverts might enjoy some advantages over their more reclusive alter egos. More concerned with the opinions of others, they might well be more committed to the crucial exercises of verification. Extreme introverts might have greater access to seemly inspiration, but they might shirk the demanding labor of converting it into tangible, communicative products. They might find even a sloppy result so compelling and self-evident that they would expect others to automatically share their vision. In the extreme, they could degenerate into fantasy-ridden "idea persons" who never finish anything.

Jung himself elsewhere admits that the introverted and extroverted temperaments might both produce quality work, but of notably different styles (here he attempts to explain variations in form of expression, a puzzle that quite defeated Freud). More specifically the introvert, denying external life and preferring subjective phenomena, would tend to produce forms unlike anything in reality. Thus, abstract, oriental, and primitive artists have not immersed themselves in but have tried to "overpower" the outer world. The extrovert, on the other hand, would lean toward representing and expressing external objects.

Jung also, at least by implication, tackles the choice of medium riddle by way of the various functional types (although the reader should be forewarned that we here somewhat read between his lines). The thinking type should prefer such rational endeavors as science and philosophy. The extroverted version would enthusiastically practice Bacon's inductive method,[30] gathering many empirical facts first and then abstracting theoretical ideas from them to summarize "what happened." In the extreme, this type might accumulate such chaotic masses of isolated observations that no discernibly coherent pattern could possibly emerge. As well, he or she might insist on tying even such personal matters as morality and beauty to empirical, objective criteria (a case in point being the experimental aesthetician). Forms expressing such passionate experiences as religion and love will be haughtily dismissed with the damning epithet, "subjective". For Jung, Darwin provided the classic example of this type, and Kuhn's normal scientist[31] seems another likely candidate. A note of caution, however: Roe's studies of the scientific personality hardly bear out these assertions.[32] The archetypal scientist turned out to be, as a rule, a social introvert, aloof and even inept in interpersonal relations.

But what of the introverted thinker? If a scientist, she or he would prefer a more __deductive__ approach, beginning with internally generated ideas and then collecting facts to validate them. Since that subjective idea would have priority, he or she might reject any discordant facts as errors of observation. Kuhn's revolutionary scientists, the Einsteins and Newtons, seem to fit this description, as in philosophy does Kant, with his a priori ideas that were true before and independent of experience (and certainly both Kant and Newton were textbook introverts in their personal demeanor, as well). Obviously, the two thinking types would be on quite different wave lengths, perhaps actually becoming antagonistic. The extroverted thinker might dismiss the introspective one as a pie-in-the-sky dreamer, while the latter would regard all that compulsive data gathering as so much unimaginative banality.

Feeling types would probably migrate to artistic pursuits, yet their produce would again vary. Introverts, more in tune with their inner voices, would be more likely to express the archetypes; extroverts, external phenomena. Sensation? These types shade into the preceeding, but again we would suspect a preference for artistic representation, with the extroverted type depicting concrete objects from perceptual experience (it would provide our landscape and portrait painters, nature poets, and--the definitive example?--photographers). The intuitive type's indistinct persona quite defeats our analyses, but with its never-ending search for novelty, it should be drawn, in the extreme, to the shocking and the revolutionary. Diaghilev, especially in his later years, seems to personify this type, with his demands that works for the Ballet Russe above all surprise and astonish him.[33]

Other implications are also worth noting. First, regarding the sex difference in creativity, Jung suggests (somewhat arbitrarily to modern eyes) that, based on his clinical

243

observations, the thinking types will usually be male, the feeling
and intuition types predominantly female. However, MacKinnon's[34]
results with his architects somewhat complicate this picture.
He administered the Myers-Briggs Type Indicators Test, which
yields scores on four dimensions, viz., introversion-extroversion,
feeling-thinking, judging-perceiving, and intuition-sensation.
Whereas the bulk of the general population prefers sensation,
his most creative individuals almost invariably leaned towards
intuition. If Jung's suspicion is accurate, then, women should
be _more_ creative than men. However, MacKinnon also found that
creatives tended to be perceptual rather than judgmental. Since
the feeling type is predisposed to evaluate, and since women
supposedly incline towards this type, this might work against
their productivity.

Secondly, a predisposition to judge, surely, should
characterize prospective critics. Will their results on this
test bear out this prediction? The judging person, MacKinnon
informs us, will prefer a life that is controlled and regulated
rather than spontaneous and flexible, which certainly fits our
earlier speculations about the critic's personality.

Susanne K. Langer

Many creative works, notably Melville's Moby Dick,[35] suggest
archetypal themes susceptible to Jungian analyses. Yet a creator's
personality, from Jung's standpoint, has little influence over
and is irrelevant to understanding the work that results. In
fact, an empty shell, devoid of any assertive qualities whatever,
would seem the prime candidate for collective forces to adopt.
Thus, Melville, for example, cannot be shoehorned easily into
the Jungian mold since he possessed appreciable knowledge, insight,
and some marked personal quirks.[36] Therefore our selecting an
exemplary personality for this approach becomes rather difficult,
and indeed superfluous.

Instead, we have chosen to consider the philosopher Susanne
K. Langer, who has so profoundly influenced the fields of aesthetics
and the psychology of art. We do so because the ideas propounded
in her classic works, Philosophy in a New Key,[37] and Feeling
and Form,[38], bear an uncanny resemblance to Jung's. In fact,
with a few minor exceptions to be noted later, the differences
seem largely ones of terminology. She begins, like Jung, by
distinguishing between signs and symbols. Signs are stimuli
that refer to other specific events, e.g., in Pavlov's classical
conditioning procedure, the conditioned stimulus "stands for"
the unconditioned stimulus.* Symbols, however, representing or

---

*   For the uninitiated, the unconditioned stimulus is an event

244

expressing feelings and ideas that are only vaguely understood, possess many associations and connotations. As well, signs are always useful for adapting to the environment; when this is no longer the case, their signaling function terminates (in Pavlovian terms, it extinguishes). Symbols, on the other hand--such as religious rituals, dreams, and works of art--often lack any discernible purpose or value. They may even be harmful, e.g., human sacrifice during religious worship. Yet they persist.

Langer maintains that, while animals use signs, the human mind alone seems built to and has an almost inherent need to symbolize.* Our growing awareness of this fact provides what she calls the generative idea of our time, and any description of our psychology that neglects it (as do the more radical forms of behaviorism) will be incomplete. Why do we use symbols? To shape and form feelings, ideas and emotions that by their very nature are inexpressible in verbal discourse. A symbol, such as a work of art, translates into another language an idea that otherwise could not be represented at all. In this sense, all art is abstract. For example, a musician does not aim to stimulate feeling in the onlooker but to express feelings of his own. An artist's central purpose, the creation of symbols, is guided by a vague original conception or commanding form (cf. Flaubert's "Idea" and Arieti's endocept) that emerges from the substratum of the mind (unconscious?).

These "original conceptions" closely resemble Jung's archetypes. Langer is quite as adamant as he that an artist expresses universal rather than personal matters and that it is art's almost objective character that gives it such special power. It also gives us, intuitively, a sense of its significant form, and it is this "gut reaction" that defines and indicates

---

that regularly and automatically produces an involuntary, reflex response; in Pavlov's work, food in the mouth of a dog elicited salivation. He then selected another, neutral stimulus (i.e., one that did not initially produce this response), such as a bell, to act as the conditioned stimulus. The classical conditioning procedure simply presented the two stimuli together to the subject over and over. Eventually, Pavlov showed, the previously neutral conditioned stimulus would also elicit salivation, suggesting that it had come to signify the unconditioned stimulus.

* Recent research indicates that in this ostracism of the lower orders she is wrong. Observable activities during sleep, such as distinctive eye movements and EEG patterns, now reliably indicate when dreams are occurring.(39) Since animals also produce these,(40) it would appear that they too may dream.

greatness. A work eliciting this response may not be pleasurable or beautiful, but it will somehow seem important. The various arts all seek to express these fundamental matters and differ only in the techniques and forms that they use to this end. Hence, her definition: "art is the creation of forms symbolic of human feeling,"[41] where "human" refers to collective rather than individual affairs. The artist's personal feelings matter not a whit (one can "feel deeply" and still produce garbage, as so much adolescent poetry clearly reveals), because art is not a symptom but an expression or representation of such feeling. It is, in the words of even such an avowed romantic as Wordsworth, "emotion recollected in tranquility."[42]

Other similarities with Jung abound. She cites the same evidence in support of these ideas: cultures having no contact with one another display similar mythical themes, decorative forms, and religious rituals. She adopts a similar stance towards the neurosis/creativity issue: creative activity may well cause disturbance because artists will be continually driven to seek new expressions of these universal feelings. Obsessed physicians unable to heal themselves, they no sooner complete a product than they are off on another tangent. They once more "pay dearly for the divine gift of creative fire." Lastly, she too hypothesizes organic substrates for these mystical psychic processes. Jung assumed the archetypes to be somehow represented structurally in the physical apparatus; for Langer, they are latent in the structure and organization of our perceptual system.

There are, however, some differences between them. Langer downplays the ancient, primeval origins of these universal matters. She does not define, as does Jung,[43] a few "archetypal themes" that exhaust the possible content of great art. Nor does she encumber the psyche with such vague anatomical baggage as the collective unconscious.

A noticeable point of departure is that, for Jung, it is not only possible but also therapeutically useful to interpret the meaning of a symbol in words. But in Langer's opinion this is not only misinforming but "vicious." A symbol, such as a piece of music, stands for itself; if its meaning could be verbalized, then words would have been used in the first place. The symbol would then have no raison d'être because it is precisely when "words fail us" that we use symbols. In agreement, choreographer George Balachine frequently repudiated those who must scrounge some sort of "meaning" out of every ballet they witness. He pointed out, correctly, that we don't ask what a rose "means," we simply experience and enjoy it.[44] Why can we not respond equally directly to works of art?

On this point, we heartily agree with Langer. Symbols easily decoded and obvious result in works of, not depth, but mere bombastic heavy-handedness. Witness those which in order to promote some social or political message must be crystal clear.* For the moment they may be effective but, with the changing winds of sociological fashion, custom will soon stale their finite variety. For example, the novels of Sinclair Lewis, such as Babbitt and Main Street, once lauded as scathing indictments of the American middle class, are now seldom read.

Judy Chicago's much discussed Dinner Party, in our opinion, falls into the same trap. Its technical accomplishment and visual power are stunning, but the ponderously blatant feminist message weakens the overall impression. And just in case we miss the point, Ms. Chicago's tape-recorded guide for our journey around the famous table laboriously explains the precise meaning of every symbol. Why do the plates of modern women rise up in space? To reflect their increasing assertiveness. Why do the cloths sometimes infringe on the plates? To proclaim how repressive social forces (male, naturally) have overwhelmed the female psyche. As Langer reminds us, a symbol that needs explaining is a symbol that is not doing its job. Chicago professes to be flattered by one woman's statement that[45] "(Dinner Party) was the first work of art she had ever seen that she had completely understood." But in our view the three-dimensional, multileveled heroines of Austen, the Bröntes, Ibsen, Shaw, and Chekhov have captured the complexities of femininity far more effectively. Hedda Gabler will be performed long after Dinner Party has been mercifully forgotten.

A second departure from Jung is that for Langer, the direct, intuitive "gut reaction" of significant form, the immediate sensation of importance, is the only sure indication that something deserves to be called "art." Excessive intellectualization can destroy the authenticity of this reaction. Logical, aesthetic rules and critical canons may try to explain it by studying the properties of works that produce it, but these linear processes must follow that initial, impulsive response. Admittedly, this

---

*   Those super-realistic Soviet ballets, such as The Flames of Paris, Spartacus, et al., unceasingly depict heroic workers/slaves/plebians, after much travail, overthrowing the exploitive ruling classes. The clenched fist of dauntless revolt and the courageously lifted chin are much in evidence. It is excruciating to watch the superb dancers of the Kirov and Bolshoi companies wallowing in such propagandist pap. Thus, Nureyev, Makarova, Baryshnikov, and others defected not for political "freedom" but to try roles that did not insult their talent and intelligence.

rather romantic attitude is both quite compatible with, and indeed tacitly present in, Jung. But in Langer it is emphatic.

Lastly, she confronts an embarrassing problem that Jung, to our knowledge, ignored. If great art taps such universal matters, its appeal should be widespread. Some commentators evidently assume this to be the case, but the facts are rather different. Within even the most enlightened segments of society, only a small minority will partake of artistic offerings. As a rule of thumb, live theatre of even the most fluffy, commercial kind can hope to attract about 2 percent of a large city's population. Moreover, as any manager knows full well, the box-office revenues will be even lower for King Lear, while something like Faust, in North America at least, will be lucky to lure the friends and relatives of the cast.

How can this be? Langer's answer is that artistic work, languishing in remote galleries and museums, is less an everyday, integral part of our lives than once it was, so people are simply ignorant of its overwhelming power. Admittedly, John Q. Public must actually experience King Lear to be converted to it, but once this is said, Langer's explanation simply does not ring true. Surely art is more ubiquitous and accessible than ever, what with much greater literacy and education, mass communication, and modern advances in producing cheap, high quality products such as recordings, prints, paperbacks, and the like. Yet John Q. isn't having any. You may drag him to King Lear, he may even stay awake, and he will, it is guaranteed, afterwards avow "Gosh, that Shakespeare isn't nearly as boring as he seemed in school." But given his druthers, he will opt for Three's Company on the telly every time. We cannot lie about these things and hope to achieve a genuine understanding.

At any rate, we might note that the close agreement between Langer and Jung adds further weight to their conclusions. If something like the collective unconscious does exist in the psyche, then one of its archetypal residents might well be the idea of the archetypes and of the collective unconscious, i.e., the dormant potential to conceive such possibilities. That being so, several individuals could well, quite independently, reach similar conclusions about their role in the creative process.

Commentary

In our experience, when creative people themselves become acquainted with the Jung/Langer viewpoint, they find it perhaps the most appealing of all. Let us, then, without further ado, contemplate its strengths. Since, like the theological perspective, it attributes inspiration to sources independent of creators' psyches, the medium experience is not only

248

understandable but entirely predictable. This perspective can also encompass, even more convincingly than can Freud's, creators' unwillingness and inability to explain their own products. If these originate in the collective unconscious, then they are truly not the creators' doing. They have done their job by giving formal expression to these universal affairs; others must supply the interpretations.

By implication at least, here critics make their entrance. Their main job, presumably, is not to decide yay or nay but, like therapists decoding dreams, to help artists discover what they have done (and many critics enthusiastically accept this job description). Moreover, they should not impose a meaning by fiat a la Freud but rather should suggest several alternatives for artists to ponder. Perhaps would-be critics could benefit from extensive training in the techniques of Jungian analytic psychology.

Still on the idea of archetypal expression, it likewise becomes reasonable that artists might continually return to the same themes--van Gogh to his self-portraits, Graham Greene to his Roman Catholic angst, and so on. After finishing Death of a Salesman, Arthur Miller found in some ten-year-old notebooks an outline for virtually the same play.[46] Multiple discoveries in science, when several workers quite independently reach the same conclusions (e.g., evolution by both Darwin and Wallace, calculus by Newton and Leibnitz, and, as just mentioned, archetypal explanations of creativity by Jung and Langer), likewise become understandable. So too does creative inspiration's whimsical unpredictability. If personal expression was more intimately involved, then perhaps the process should be much more manageable than it is.

Most notably, this perspective, unlike any others that we have met, provides at least some rudimentary standards for identifying great art, along with some hypotheses, however undeveloped, about the differences between those who produce quality and those who foster swill. Expression of, and access to, the archetypal themes are the distinguishing traits. Perhaps, then, by analyzing those products that do elicit that mysterious sense of "significant form" we can begin to develop some reasonably predictive laws of aesthetics.

Moreover, the notion that inherited, genetic determinants might subsume our shared psychic paraphernalia seems less arbitrary than once it did. Consider language. As Miller, among others, has argued, it now seems unavoidable that much of our linguistic competence rests on inborn, biological tendencies.[47] First, all human societies possess some kind of language, and all of these share some common features, called language universals. In

249

addition, if language depended entirely on experience and trial-and-error practice (as Skinnerian/behaviorist dogma would have it[48]), then how could children acquire it as quickly and efficiently as they do? Without an innate component, how could we comprehend sentences that we have never heard before? According to Miller, even to listen once to all possible 20-word sentences (and never mind those containing say 19 or 21) we would need 1000 times the age of the earth (since there are 10^{20} such sentences possible, give or take a few billion!).

Now the language universals, which supposedly make it all possible, closely resemble Jungian archetypes. They too are inherited entities that we all possess. They too provide only a potential, which can be expressed in many ways, as evidenced by the marked dissimilarities among the various languages. And if human language usage is anything, it is creative. How often, for example, do we produce sentences <u>that</u> <u>we</u> <u>have</u> <u>never</u> <u>heard</u>, as when we paraphrase, or "put something into our own words." If it be acceptable that this type of creative behavior might depend on universals, why might not other types?

Let us also mention some other questions that Jung and Langer, at least by implication, can address. At least two other creative personality characteristics become comprehensible. First, the paradoxical personalities. The spiritualist's medium will change personality dramatically when he or she goes into a trance. So, too, should creators as they vacillate between their own individual psychic life (when they are "themselves") and the collective unconscious (when they function as artists). In addition, given that the unconscious compensates for conscious tendencies, they should display precisely opposite characteristics while wearing their two <u>personas</u>.

Second, Jung intimates that creative alienation is not only to be expected but is almost inevitable.[49] Just as a later dream will correct any earlier interpretations that were off-base, so too do artists, voices of the collective unconscious, correct any one-sidedness of their age by bringing out any universal elements neglected by the prevailing culture. In Ezra Pound's phrase, artists are "the antennae of the race,"[50] anticipating developments before they become generally accessible. If this is so, then they will always be at odds with, and ahead of, the prevailing currents of their times.

We might also note that Jung, incidentally at least, expresses agreement with two positions taken here (which obviously enhances his credibility). At one point, he emphasizes that creative ability is not identical to intelligence and that too much of the latter can actually be harmful,[51] producing the overly analytic intellectual who loses touch with intuitions through a "craven

250

scruple of thinking too precisely on the event." Second, he repeatedly avows that talent is an innate gift, with which the chosen few are specially and mysteriously endowed. Thus, we surmise, he would nod affirmatively to the antidemocratic sentiments we expressed in Chapter 1.

For Jung also, it would seem, environmental experiences could either encourage or inhibit an already latent talent, but they could not, by themselves, initiate such talent. Freud, on the other hand, would seem more comfortable with an environmental emphasis. Creativity, for him, depends on unconscious conflicts, which frustrate intrinsic needs and wishes. Hence, such experiences seem necessary for creativity to bloom.

1. Difficulties with Jung. But, as always, there are problems, so we must now don our more abusive garb. A particularly thorny one we have already discussed, viz., that on both the producing and consuming sides of the ledger creativity is a minority activity. If great art possesses such self-evident power, then surely it should assert that power once it is experienced. Often it does not. Yet we will rarely find our own dreams boring. To this embarrassment, the Jungian might rejoin that most individuals release their archetypal strivings in other ways, e.g., through their religious and/or nocturnal pursuits, so they have no need of art. Is there any evidence that actively creative people dream less than others?

Along similar lines, why can some persons, but not everyone, communicate with and tame those collective Muses? From whence cometh the divine gift of creative fire? Now admittedly our own elitist stance also implies some vague, inborn potential (for which genetics has, as yet, provided no empirical evidence whatsoever). But in Jung there is a curious contradiction. Everyone, it would seem, inherits the necessary ingredients to create, i.e., the constituents of the collective unconscious. Furthermore, we all demonstrate that we have access to them, in some manner at least, because we all dream. Yet, we are told, only a chosen few can express them in creative work. If everyone can paint a Guernica while they sleep, why can they not do so on canvas? Jung's typology supplies some descriptive beginnings but, as things stand, poses more questions than it answers.

The real problem, in our view, is that talent depends not only on special access to content, unconscious or otherwise, but at least equally on formal skill, technique, and the like. It is these conscious, linear abilities, which come into play during the verification stage, that nature selectively endows. Now the Jung/Langer tradition has nothing whatever to say about individual differences in these abilities. Which is

251

understandable, because mediums, whether spiritual or creative,
need expend no conscious effort to clarify an inner message
for others. However "the voices" choose to express it, that
is how it will be expressed. But genuine creators certainly
must, and their ability in their regard will, as much as anything,
determine their success. As the artist Kandinsky put it:

> The horse bears the rider with strength and
> speed. But the rider guides the horse. Talent
> carries the artist to great heights and speed.
> But the artist guides his talent. This is the
> element of the "conscious," the "calculating."[52]

Several related difficulties follow directly. How do we
bring under the Jungian umbrella the obvious idiosyncrasies,
the touches of personal style, that separate the first- from
the second-rate? From whence came that mysterious individual
stamp that tells us, after a few bars, that "Mozart wrote
that"? We do not know. Neither did Mozart:

> But why my productions take from my hand that
> particular form and style that makes them
> Mozartish, and different from the works of other
> composers, is probably owing to the same cause
> which renders my nose so large or so aquiline,
> or, in short, makes it Mozart's and different
> from those of other people.[53]

But because we lack an answer does not mean that we can ignore
these crucial matters in our theories. Even if we allow that
art might begin with the archetypes, the fact remains that
these are portrayed in highly individualistic manners, and it
is the form of the expression that most distinguishes quality.
Nothing here tells us how or why this quality comes about.

In like vein, if all great art eternally rehashes a few
ancient, enduring themes (as Jung, if not Langer, certainly
implies), then would it not be much more stereotyped than seems
to be the case? Even allowing for a certain leeway in archetypal
expression, would it not be simply so much old wine in new
bottles? Jung openly asserts this to be so,[54] and a strong
case can be made in defense. It has been stated, for example,
that all the plays ever written eternally rehash a very few
basic plots. Still, as we contemplate the various masterpieces
of the ages, it is their diversity more than their similarity
that first strikes us. They all may or may not say the same
things, but they say them in very different ways, and the
present perspective tells us nothing about how or why this
comes about.

252

We have earlier taken Freud to task for viewing creation as entirely self-expressive. We must now admit, in the interests of inconsistency, that some persuasive arguments favor his position. In addition to those just presented, creators undeniably feel extraordinary responsibility for their work, particularly when it is criticized (recall Henry Miller's comment that to fail as a writer meant to fail as a man[55]). As parents will cherish even their plainest offspring, so will creators lose perspective when it comes to the progeny of their own imaginations. What we here recognize, of course, is that these feelings provide us with still another creative paradox. A detached, aloof, "I didn't do that, did I?" somehow coexists with a strong sense of personal involvement. The collective view of art finds the first emotion entirely comprehensible but the second inexplicable.

2. Further problems. We move on now to other, but still related, difficulties. From the Jung/Langer standpoint, judgments of merit should surely be much more reliable and agreed upon than in fact they are. If quality is defined by the presence of universal entities to which we all have access, then we should all "know it when we see it." Actually, of course, arguments about merit are rife; it is not an objective matter, but a highly controversial one. In the immortal words of George S. Kaufman, "One man's Mede is another man's Persian."[56]

We have intimated that the present perspective has much in common with the theological. It also shares the same susceptibility to circular reasoning. The force subsuming creative success, whether it be archetypal "commanding forms" or the voice of the Almighty, is both evidenced by the creative product and also used to explain the existence of that product. Moreover, Jungians have unquestionably been as guilty of dissecting masterpieces to arbitrarily prove their points as the most ardent fundamentalists have been of dissecting the Bible to prove theirs. Given sufficient persistence and imagination, something vaguely resembling an archetypal theme can be discovered in even the most obtuse work. Just as compulsive perusal of the Bible will most certainly locate a passage that verifies what one already wishes to believe. Even if an archetypal theme is genuinely present, and not simply a figment of the interpreter's wishful fantasies, that does not prove that the said theme produces the work's magical powers.

That having been said, the logical circularity and the arbitrary use of a deus ex machina to magically explain creativity seem somewhat less ominous in the Jung/Langer than in the theological perspective. Supposedly, the collective unconscious and its constituents can also be observed in other manifestations, such as dreams, so they can be assessed by independent means.

253

We should also mention briefly two other, more peripheral matters for which Jung's opinion seems debatable. First, as we have seen, he seems to deny a creative "g" factor; a specific talent is endowed at the expense of other abilities.[57] Not all authorities would agree (see Chapter 3). Second, he asserts that only untalented, neurotic artists need fear the dread disease of going dry; genuine creativity is a "spring that can't be stopped."[58] Our impression here would be that eminently talented people also succumb to the illness. For example Picasso, as a rule extremely productive, experienced several lengthy inactive spells, usually because of difficulties in his personal life.[59]

We finish with a criticism that others might direct towards Langer in particular, but one with which we do not agree. She emphasizes intuitive, non intellectual responses as the primary criterion for identifying quality. The problem seems obvious. Some of the worst tripe imaginable is also the most certain to elicit an emotional response in even a relatively sophisticated consumer. We think of soap opera, Gothic novels, tear-jerkers, greeting-card poetry, velvet paintings of little boys with huge eyes, and the like. Combine a kid and a dog, the saying goes, and you've got a sure-fire hit! On the other hand, undoubted masterpieces often yield up their secrets reluctantly; at first glance, they may elicit only incomprehension. They require concentration, leisurely contemplation, and repeated exposure.

This being so, how can we trust our intuitive reactions? Admittedly, they can be wrong, but an experienced consumer at least is quite able to criticize his or her own emotions and to recognize whether they stem from admirable or from exploitive sources. We can laugh at a wisecrack in a cheap comedy while simultaneously realizing that it is no more than a clever gagster's hack work. As the saying goes, "They were laughing, but they weren't enjoying it." We can drench three handkerchiefs at, say, Love Story, knowing all the while that both the work itself and the resulting emotions are pap.

How can we tell? In such cases, human emotion is not being represented but only elicited; dimly, we would argue, audiences can sense this. In fact, perhaps the most influential playwright of the twentieth century, Bertolt Brecht, advocated an alienation effect.[60] An audience should remain detached, contemplating the stage action analytically and remotely; empathy, for Brecht, interferes with a genuine aesthetic experience.

Moreover, we would agree with Langer that not to assign first priority to these intuitive responses poses much greater hazards. Judgment will thereby become a vapidly sterile, intellectual exercise in which we like something because we think we should. It will then have no more to do with genuine "quality" than will choosing a washing machine. As with so many issues within this prickly topic, we are being chased by a bull. He is called "dilemma" and he has two finely-honed horns, neither of which is particularly inviting. But if we cannot escape a goring, then let us by all means choose the cleaner antler.

Otto Rank

Here is another Freudian disciple who eventually escaped from the tender paternal embrace to develop his own creed. Rank persistently emphasized an inevitable conflict in the human psyche between two powerful, opposing drives, which we will label identification and individuation.[61] The first arises from the trauma of birth.[62] When first separated from the mother and the womb, we experience isolation and solitude; to overcome it, we strive to surrender our individual identity, to once more immerse ourselves anonymously in a larger "collectivity." Hence, this search represents a fear of life.

The opposing tendency, for individuation, reflects the opposite fear, of death. Before elaborating, we must first introduce another central Rankian notion, that of the will.[63] It denotes an active force within the organized, integrated personality, so human activity is inherently decisive, assertive, and even creative. Thus Rank takes issue with Freud's arch-deterministic, mechanistic views, allowing much greater scope for active decision making and personal choice. The ego acts rather than being acted upon. Still, Rank does accept some degree of external, antecedent control over our destiny, so he here more closely approximates Adler and the humanists (see below) than the existentialists.

The individuation tendency, then, reflects our enduring will to self immortalization, our heartfelt fear of, and desire to overcome death, and to live forever. Now death is the definitive loss of selfhood, the ultimate anonymity, so in seeking its defeat we also seek to assert ourselves as individuals, to grow towards our unique potential, and to remain separate from, and to dominate, external phenomena. Thus resembling Adler again, every healthy self is inherently creative. It develops through free choice and "will power" a product that is unique and therefore immune to complete description by general, universal laws.

This desire for immortality has also caused the human race to evolve a belief that each of us possesses something called a soul.[64] This mystical entity will survive our mortal demise and again allow us to defeat death. We all inherit this belief from the race (by almost Jungian mechanisms, apparently), so

255

while the soul's reality cannot be proven empirically, our faith is unshakable. According to Rank, many people reject modern psychology simply because it persistently debunks this arbitrary but invincible belief. But for us, the crucial point is that these two mutually exclusive drives (plainly resembling Jung's extroverted and introverted tendencies, incidentally) struggle neverendingly for dominance.

As one result, neither drive can be completely satisfied. As well, guilt and anxiety become, recalling existentialism, inevitable (albeit for different reasons). More specifically, humans face a ceaseless quandary, damned if they either do or don't. Emphasizing individuation and the growth towards uniqueness means separation from, even rejection of the mother; guilt as well as anxiety due to isolation will follow. But renouncing this growth, and therefore abandoning one's particular possibilities, also invites guilt. In addition, when we create, either a self or external products, we risk the guilt that arises from hubris, or excessive pride. Yet paradoxically, creating can also expiate guilt, through the realization that one has exercised the will and reached toward one's destiny.

Art and Artist

As is apparent, creativity is in one sense, for Rank, inherent in human nature, an act of which everyone is capable. Still, achieving tangible creative products is in some ways another matter. In Art and Artist,[65] his major work on the topic, he begins by proposing a typology of personality that somewhat recalls Jung. Two main types, the neurotic and the productive, are distinguished from the third, the normal, by their particularly intense fear of death and of "self dissolution." The normal type, largely accepting itself for what it is, encounters less conflict, but the others both wish to become something that they are not, i.e., immortal. Hence, they both begin by reconstructing themselves and, in this sense, both are creative.

However, their respective developments thereafter diverge. Productive types try to overcome death by perpetuating themselves in products in which they can live on, such as works of art. Because of their healthy will, their impulsive life instincts are "pressed into service" to achieve this goal. In a real sense, then (to use another common saying about creators), "they put their souls into their work." Like Freud, therefore, Rank holds that art taps and redirects a basic reservoir of energy. However, he disliked, as had Jung, Freud's decidedly negative portrayal of creativity, with its emphasis on repellant forces in the unconscious. Rank insisted that the act was much more positive and affirmative, with its initiating energy arising

256

not from sexuality but from an even more pervasive and fundamental drive, nothing less than the will to live itself.

Neurotic types, in contrast, are afraid of affirmative, impulsive action, because their will is inadequate. Excessively fearing life, they withdraw from it, inhibit their flamboyant instincts, and become predictably compulsive in their actions. Hence, Rank's treatment system, will therapy, aimed to strengthen assertive tendencies.[66] In his opinion, the neurotic type is a "failed artist," driven by many of the same fears and desires as her or his productive companion but too inhibited to convert them into constructive action.

As concerns the neurosis/creativity relationship, therefore, Rank clearly occupies a point somewhere between Freud and Jung. Both his creative types resemble one another more than they do the normal, so artists are, for him as for Freud, decidedly different. But they also differ from one another, especially in their responses to their excessive death fears. Productive types can accept themselves sufficiently as to express and even glorify themselves, transfering their fear onto an external, tangible product. Neurotics, unable to do this, become excessively self-critical.

But Rank's main purpose in Art and Artist was to understand the productive type. He was, of all the psychoanalysts, probably most fitted for this purpose, since he was not originally a physician but a highly-trained scholar in philosophy, history, and art.[67] Furthermore, since he clearly considered himself to be a member of this creative category,[68] much of his thinking undoubtedly developed introspectively.

Given artists' desires to overcome death, they retreat from life, which for them reeks of mortality and decay, into the artificial world of their fantasy, where something ephemeral can attain permanence. Nonetheless, not only will they themselves fail to attain immortality, they will, ironically, only temporarily gain even the illusion or feeling of being immortal. Ultimately, their purpose must fail both physically and psychologically. In Rank's words, "(The artist) desires to transform death into life, though actually he (or she) transforms life into death."[69] Evidently, he here refers to the artist's common experience of no longer feeling connected to the work once it is finished. The euphoric sense of timelessness during creation's white heat will only briefly cover existence's fundamental wound. Once expended, the energizing force only intensifies intimations of mortality and temporality.

Rank now shows how this drive for immortality might affect artistic style. He delineates the same two types of art as

257

did Jung and Camus, holding that each of them stems from one of life's two great drives. Individuation, propelled by the fear of death, produces individual, expressive, romantic art; identification, fuelled by the birth trauma, leads to abstract, classical art. All art unites these collective and individual tendencies and in fact arises from the struggle between them, between "artist" (denoting the self-assertive drive) and "art" (representing personal anonymity). In fact, that same struggle breeds not only art but all civilized activities. Depending upon which tendency becomes dominant, one style or the other will prevail. Therefore, the psychological conflict within everyone is exacerbated in the artist (which may explain those psychological problems to which they are supposedly so predisposed).

Art and Artist has another main purpose: to understand the historical development of art. Briefly put, Rank persuasively argues that it resembles the development of the individual after birth. A fetus is completely anonymous, part of a larger entity. At birth, it becomes more individualized but is still largely a dependent. However, it gradually gains more independence as it matures. So too did art mature over time. More specifically, primitive art, according to Rank, aimed not to imitate nature at all but, in good introverted fashion, to express a collective concept, the soul. It tried to give form to this highly amorphous, metaphysical concept and so bring it "down to earth." But the soul is so abstract that, in comparison, even the most unrealistic art will be hopelessly concrete. Therefore, this approach necessarily resorted to forms unlike any in nature. Hence abstract or classical style developed for the typical Jungian/Langerian reasons and we can now understand why a primitive carving of the human figure only slightly resembles the genuine article.

Immediately, this type of art becomes linked to religion, because both endeavors are in different ways seeking the same goal, i.e., to give concrete expression to a mystical concept. Now religion is the collective, self-negating activity par excellence. It appeals to our need for dependence and group membership. In like manner, abstract art does not reflect an individual's desire to attain personal immortality but rather the need to represent a universal idea. So the artist herein functions as a "collective person," humbly serving the needs of his or her fellows. Which may explain why such art is invariably unsigned. Anon. was an abstract artist.

However, as history advanced, the opposing drive for independence gradually asserted itself. A highly personal approach to art evolved in which artists sought self-expression. For the first time they signed their work, and they became as important as that work. Classical Greece first brought this approach to the fore. Its sublime endeavors, according to Rank,

258

harmoniously balanced the two competing tendencies in dynamic equilibrium. As Gothic and Romanesque products clearly reveal, identification once more achieved pre-eminence during medieval times, (perhaps corresponding to human adolescence when, as "peer group" influence shows, we apparently undergo a renewed need for identification). But the Renaissance reinstated individuation with a vengeance. The concept of "the genius" was introduced, the specially gifted artist as superstar. Personality (including neuroses) became of major interest, and creativity became a psychological rather than a sociological matter.

Since then, individuation has become ever more dominant, as evidenced by the rise of Romanticism and even more by that ultimately subjective, idiosyncratic pursuit, "modern art." Ever more life-affirming, art has increasingly tried to express external reality. The landscape painter, the nature poet, and even the empirical scientist all seek to justify and therefore to portray life and our sensory experience of it.

The first, crucial act of such individualists is to "appoint themselves artists," accepting the label and adopting the trappings--such as dress, habitat, and behaviors--of their chosen role. Once this is done, they have initiated a self-fulfilling prophecy that will motivate all their subsequent work. They must then justify their appointment by working persistently towards ever more transcendent achievements. If they do not, presumably their self concept will be given the lie, and conflict will result. (In Festinger's terms,[70] they will experience cognitive dissonance, an aversive state produced when one's attitudes and actions do not coincide.) This seems to suggest one reason for labeling's supposed importance.

Since such artists do not try to function as spokespersons for all humanity but to express their own particular vision, their potential audience is probably limited to those who share their personal attitudes. In the extreme, their drive for individuation can focus on pleasing only one special person (a "significant other," in the clumsy parlance of current psychology). In this, the artist comes to resemble a knight who sought honor only for the glory of "his lady" and who carried her token into battle. In support, some artists do report being motivated, at least in part, by a need to prove something to some particular individual, such as a parent or admired teacher. Thereby, their exercises become a mammoth "show and tell."

Rank clearly feels that things have gone too far in this direction. Sharing Jung's distaste for modern art, he points out the dangers of such a descent into a narrow subjectivism, which lacks any shared, collective basis or meaning. We approach decadence when individual artists become more important than

259

their art and when, as in our age, they become overvalued to the point of becoming cults. In Rank's opinion, an excess of either tendency will debilitate art. For this true disciple of the classical canon Méden Agán, (reportedly, the slogan over the entrance to the Temple of Apollo at Delphi, translated loosely as "Everything in moderation, nothing excessively") a masterpiece will balance the two tendencies, with the artist functioning as both an individual and collective person. In Rank's words:

> The highest type of artist is he who can use the typical conflict of humanity within himself to produce collective values which...are yet individual, and new creations of these collective values in that they present the personal ideology of the artist who is the representative of his age.[71]

Poet Earle Birney expresses the idea even more persuasively:

> It's by this very outpouring of his humanness that a poet establishes his kinship with others, and brings that sense of confirmation of the unity of mankind which is one of the exhilarations for the reader of his poems. The listener hears at once both the peculiar voice that is the bizarre identity and separateness of the poet, and the human cry that is his certificate of humanity.[72]

We wish also to impart Rank's explanation of the sex difference in creativity, since it bears on the portrait to follow. In general, he pioneered within psychoanalysis a more positive approach to feminine psychology, turning Freud's patronizing account on its head. By inviolate biological decree, the greatest of creative acts, producing another human being, is restricted to women, and they can satisfy their desires for self-immortalization in this way. But men must turn elsewhere, so to compensate for their biological inadequacies, they have been driven to sire artificial progeny.[73] Another Freudian successor, Karen Horney, makes a similar allegation.[74]

Isadora Duncan

This celebrated, colorful personality helped initiate the modern dance movement that has subsequently given us so many luminaries. Ironically, her actual dancing style is largely a mystery. She refused to be filmed, the extant photographs are merely tantalizing, and eyewitness descriptions are too often laden with abstract nouns. Her "imitators" also mislead.

260

Saccharine, coy impressions of To a Wild Rose? Anarchic "free movement" with much waving of arms and little skill? "Doing whatever you feel?" Surely these misrepresent the woman whom Europe's most discriminating critics applauded and sundry artists (notably Rodin) sought to portray. The woman who enraptured a wartime audience by interpreting The Marseillaise. Whose every performance caused a box-office stampede. On whom German students bestowed their ultimate tribute, unhitching the horses to pull her carriage themselves.

What, then, characterized her art? Above all, we suspect, was an unsurpassed charisma as a performer. Her almost hypnotic personal magnetism must have been incredible to be able to convert audiences to such a radically new dance form, whereas even today, when we have infinitely more acquaintance with "modern dance," similar daring frequently produces only derisive laughter.

For one biographer,[75] Isadora also had an extraordinary feeling for phrasing, dynamics, and tempi. This "musicality," for not only staying on the beat but also visually expressing music so its wedding with movement seems not arbitrary but inevitable, this is one of great dancing's most mysterious, unteachable, but crucial attributes. Amazingly, then, Isadora was musically untrained (although hardly ignorant, since her mother was a competent pianist--and her remarkably loyal accompanist during the early travail). Indeed, as one of her greatest contributions, she radically altered the dance/music partnership. Previously, hacks like Minkus and Drigo wrote most of the accompaniment, tailoring their work to the choreographer's needs. Even Tchaikovsky, while composing Swan Lake, bowed to Petipa's wishes. As a result, few composers of eminence stooped to writing for dance, and dancing to the great masters was seen as unthinkable sacrilege. But since Duncan believed that music should stimulate rather than kowtow to the movement, she employed Bach, Beethoven, Chopin, et al., ignoring the outrage and gradually proving that great dancing supplemented rather than debased them. Nowadays, of course, their choreographic expression is commonplace, and many notable moderns, e.g., Stravinsky, Debussy, Bartók, Ravel, and Satie, have seen fit to compose dance music. Duncan is as responsible as anyone for this development.

Duncan's communicating an overwhelming power of "the moment," of the frenzy of inspiration, probably provided her third remarkable trait. Her performances were largely improvised, expressing her momentary feelings towards her music. She prepared, not with specific choreography, but by "putting a motor in my soul,"[76] so she could move independently of her conscious will. Thus, her approach closely resembles the renowned Stanislavsky acting method, which also preaches getting inside and virtually becoming one's character. Upon meeting, Duncan and Stanislavsky felt an immediate rapport, at one point almost becoming lovers.

Technically, her fluid, expressive arms and hands received special praise, but her movement aimed above all to be "natural." While admiring the technical prowess of ballerinas like Pavlova, she abhorred ballet's artificiality--its "every movement shocked my sense of beauty and (its) expression seemed to me mechanical and vulgar"[77]--and its separation of the body's gymnastics from the mind. For this terpsichorean interactionist, "the body becomes transparent and is a medium for the mind and spirit."[78] Likewise, by emphasizing the lower spine ballet, in her opinion, caused stilted rigidity. Her movement grew from the solar plexus, the "seat of the soul."

But perhaps Isadora's major influences more clearly suggest her art. Consider her three revered masters: Beethoven, Wagner, and Nietzsche (her "dancing philosopher", whose Thus Spake Zarathustra, well marked, lay on her night table). Consider the countless hours she spent devouring Greek sculpture and pottery, seeking ideas for movement, costumes, and setting. Still, her work seemed to her more American than Greek. Witness her vision of the future:

> Let (our children) come forth with great strides, leaps and bounds, with lifted foreheads and far-spread arms, to dance the language of our Pioneers, the Fortitude of our heroes....When the American children dance in this way it will make of them beautiful beings, worthy of the name of the Greatest Democracy. That will be America Dancing.[79]

Surely the influences of her masters and this passage indicate not cloying sentimentality but heroism. Not cluttered baroque but frugal clarity. This must have been Isadora dancing!

But how does she vindicate Rank's hypotheses, other than as a fellow Greekophile? Briefly, she clearly combines individuated with collective aspects. On the one hand almost the stereotypic "modern artist"--headstrong, impetuous, and altogether fascinating --she proclaimed and practiced a colorful, even bizarre lifestyle. Even her death (by strangulation, when her scarf caught in a moving automobile's wheel) was romantically grotesque. Thus, her views on women's roles bulwarked the struggling suffragettes. She openly practiced "free love" with, among others, the brilliant director/designer Gordon Craig, bearing three children out of wedlock and only marrying late in life:

I began to look enquiringly at the faces of
the married women friends of my mother, and I
felt that on each was the mark of the green-eyed
monster and the stigmata of the slave. I made
a vow that I would never lower myself to this
degrading state.[80]

Yet according to Seroff,[81] Duncan was actually quite
traditional in these matters of the heart and adopted her public
views because she knew that Craig would never marry her (he
fathered many illegitimate children and showed no responsibility
towards any). Other signs of conservatism: her many lovers
notwithstanding, she clung to the romantic's belief in "one
true love." She saw herself as completely faithful to each
lover; they always left her, rather than she them. Yet elsewhere,
rather poetically, she advocated alternative practice:

The miracle of Love is the varied themes and
keys in which it can be played, and the love
of one man compared to another may be as different
as hearing the music of Beethoven compared to
the music of Puccini, and the instrument that
gives the response to these melodious players
is Woman. And I suppose a woman who has known
but one man is like a person who has heard
only one composer (italics mine).[82]

Judging by her varied love life, Duncan was no exemplar of
sublimation. Thus she supported communism with fervor, often
badgering her audiences about this "wave of the future." Yet
she apparently barely understood its principles, so that even
ardent fellow travelers were less than enthralled by her advocacy.
One politician of pinkish hue muttered that if Isadora kept
preaching communism, he would do a Greek dance.[83]

Believing that the body was beautiful, she counseled public
nudity. Her pseudo-Greek apparel left little to the imagination,
and during one public harangue she reportedly bared her breast
to proclaim that this, this was beauty.[84] An early press report
warned of things to come:

Under the patronage of sixty-seven society women
from the inner ranks of the One hundred and
Fifty of New York...an impressive function was
held yesterday. Miss Isadora Duncan has recently
had the misfortune to lose her wardrobe by the
Windsor Hotel fire, which probably accounts for
and excuses the fact that her sole costume for
yesterday's dance was a species of surgical
bandage, which floated merrily or mournfully.

263

Miss Duncan's melancholy brother kindly read extracts from Theocritus and Ovid as an accompaniment to the writhings and painful leaps and hops of his sister while...the audience of tortured souls gazed at one another and blushed or giggled, according to the individual form of nervousness. When the final dance was finished, there was a sigh of relief that it was over and that Miss Duncan's bandages hadn't fallen off, as they threatened to do during the entire show....(Miss Duncan will introduce her work) to London drawing rooms in May...which is sad, considering we are at peace with England at present.[85]

Later, the opposition remained equally (if less intentionally) hilarious. Note this comment from the mayor of Indianapolis:

Isadora ain't foolin' me any. She talks about art. Huh! I've seen a lot of these twisters and I know as much about art as any man in America, but I never went to see these dancers for art's sake. No, sir, I'll bet that ninety percent of men who go to see those so-called classical dancers just say they think it's artistic to fool their wives....No sir, these nude dancers don't get by me. If she goes pulling off her clothes and throwin' them in the air, as she is said to have done in Boston, there's going to be somebody getting a ride in the wagon.[86]

As also befits Rank's individuated artist, she labeled herself early. "Whatever one is to do in one's after life is clearly expressed as a baby. I was already a dancer and revolutionist."[87] Her commitment to dance she attributed to two decidedly unorthodox factors: (a) her birth by the sea, which bestowed a sense of movement and rhythm, and (b) her mother's ingesting, during her gestation, only iced oysters and champagne--the food of Aphrodite.[88] And she certainly displayed Rank's dogged will power to persist through every obstacle. Her reaction to a typical bourgeois woman trapped in dull dependency could almost serve as her motto:

For I was never able to understand, then or later on why, if one wanted to do a thing, one should not do it.[89]

In sum, in keeping with Rank's analysis, the unquestionably productive Isadora resembles the highly individual, even neurotic,

264

rather than "normal" personality. Yet here too lie collective
elements. In her eyes, she was not so much a <u>dancer</u> as a
living embodiment of <u>the</u> dance--eternal, impersonal, and spiritual.
Once (admittedly while seeking employment) she claimed:

> I have discovered the dance. I have discovered
> the art which has been lost for two thousand
> years...I bring to your theatre the vital soul
> that it lacks, the soul of the dancer.[90]

And elsewhere, in more contemplative, less flamboyant mood:

> I spent long days and nights in the studio
> seeking that dance which might be the divine
> expression of the human spirit through the medium
> of the body's movement...the source of the
> spiritual expression to flow into the channels
> of the body filling it with vibrating light--the
> centrifugal force reflecting the spirit's
> vision.[91]

She also verified, introspectively, the Rank/Horney account
of the sex difference. Isadora represents not only the relatively
rare eminent female creator but the even rarer eminent female
creator who had children. She seemed, despite her egocentric
public persona, a devoted and concerned parent to her three,
who tragically all died prematurely, one in infancy, the other
two in a bizarre accident. A car in which they were passengers
stalled and the driver, getting out to restart it, left it in
reverse. It ran down a hill into the Seine, drowning its
occupants.

Still, Duncan seems uniquely qualified to discuss possible
conflicts between motherhood and creativity. Here she is, upon
experiencing the former:

> Oh, women, what is the good of us learning to
> become lawyers, painters or sculptors, when this
> miracle exists? Now I knew this tremendous love,
> surpassing the love of man...Oh, where was my
> Art? My Art or any Art? What did I care for
> Art! I felt I was a god, superior to any
> artist.[92]

Admittedly, this sounds like Isadora playing to the gallery,
lacking only soft violin obligato, but she later, more credibly,
verifies the sentiments:

> How strong, egotistical and ferocious a possession
> is Mother Love. I do not think it very admirable.

It would be infinitely more admirable to be able to love all children.[93]

Does this not suggest that maternity might stifle any creative need?

However, one important Rankian tenet remains, namely, that the productive type fears and tries to overcome death. At first glance practitioners of that most ephemeral of the arts, dance, would seem unlikely to verify this hypothesis; their work, it would seem, must die with them. Nevertheless, using perhaps slightly Procrustean methods, we can also find some latent evidence for this mechanism in Isadora's case. Her joyful affirmation of worldly pleasures certainly betrays a strong love of life, which is the complement, the mirror image, of a fear of death. Moreover, she devoted appreciable amounts of both energy and financial resources to founding a school in which talented youngsters could learn her styles both of dance and of life. Might this not suggest a desire to overcome dance's notorious ephemerality and bequeath something that would survive her? Sadly, she was here unsuccessful; ignoring the pale imitations, which she herself disavowed, no current approach lies directly in her lineage (although in a larger sense of course, the entire modern dance movement is her memorial).

Commentary

We agree with both MacKinnon[94] and Becker[95] that Rank has been unduly neglected in the creativity literature. His discussion of the neverending war between the self-assertive and identification needs, and the revelations about how these might affect artistic style, seem particularly useful. His account of the historical development of art, based on the strikingly apt analogy with human ontogeny, seems to us equally enlightening, although those with greater expertise in the details of art history might locate some embarrassing holes. As well, Rank corrects the omissions for which we took Freud and Jung to task, i.e., their ignoring, respectively, the collective and self-expressive experiences that artists report. From Rank's standpoint, it is quite comprehensible that artists might feel now like mediums and now like captains of their souls.

Likewise, Rank certainly implies an explanation for the creative's paradoxical personality, one which from some angles closely resembles McMullan's. Intuitively, nonlinear thought seems more personal and subjective, while linear thought's more logical, analytic attributes suggest a more detached, objective, and therefore collective attitude. When the identification (linear) tendencies are dominant, one set of characteristics will result, whereas dominance of individuation (nonlinear) will bring forth the alternative, incompatible set.

Rank has also called attention to several rarely noted aspects of creative work. First is the inevitable sense of failure. Like Sisyphus, creators attempt the impossible, to get their rock to the top of the mountain or to square the circle. Similarly, they can never succeed in attaining genuine immortality and, in their perfectionism, their unreachable standards do seem to sentence them to make "death out of life." Second is the importance of labeling themselves artists and incorporating this role into their self-image. In our view, persistence and consistent productivity could well result, as much as anything, from the desire to avoid cognitive dissonance. How can people who have painted nothing for five years still call themselves painters?

Let us turn now to the notion that a creator produces something in order to survive death. It has much to recommend it. First, an often-noted analogy makes good sense. The similarities previously noted between sex and the creative process are even more marked between the latter and the act of giving birth, both in terms of "what happens" and in the experiences reported by the participants.[96] Samuel Butler reportedly said:

> A poet writes a poem as a hen lays an egg,
> and both feel better afterwards.[97]

Einstein was fond of the same simile, often saying about bright ideas, "Cheep...suddenly there it is."[98] We recall, too, A. E. Housman's labeling of the creative product as "a secretion."[99] Let us note, then, some similarities.

An act of conception, or fertilization, initiates both processes. However, this fetal "germ of an idea" must then incubate for a lengthy period, lying fallow to mature without its parent exerting much conscious control. And since gestation will take its own sweet time, periodic discomfort may accompany it, whether creative frustration or maternal morning sickness. The moments of inspiration and birth itself are plainly comparable. In both cases, a new event bursts upon an unsuspecting world, fully developed, noisy, and above all unquestionably perfect. Its parent feels quite passive at this time, little more than a tool of awesomely impersonal events.

Postnatal developments likewise coincide. Both progeny will rapidly take on lives of their own, going their own way to become what they will. Modern psychology asserts that parents exert a great influence over the destinies of their children. While there is some truth to this rumor, all parents know that

267

it is grossly exaggerated. In reality, it is often all they can do to scramble desperately along in the wake, exerting roughly the same control that creators do over their offspring. Last, no matter how objective creators may be about other matters, they can no more critically evaluate their own work than parents can judge their own children. Any ugliness or inadequacy is quite indiscernible.

Given that the birth metaphor obviously has special validity, how does this buttress Rank's position? One inducement for having children has always been that they will carry on the family name, allowing parents to symbolically triumph over and live on after death. This being so, then it becomes understandable that creativity and reproduction should so resemble one another, reflecting as they do the same fundamental drive.

The same reasoning, of course, subsumes Rank's explanation for feminine unproductiveness, and Barron's studies[100] of art students are somewhat supportive. Although the women were, by general agreement, as talented and effective as the men, they seemed less dedicated to art. Becoming wives and mothers frequently received first priority, whereas the men saw art as the most important thing in their lives; a prospective career. Still, these observations could reflect either cultural conditioning or, as Barron prefers, biased subject selection. Domestically inclined women have long dabbled in art while awaiting marriage, but only extremely committed men will study it, given its rather shoddy social image and its healthy prospects for economic insecurity.

Rank also faces other problems. Weissman, in a psychoanalytically-oriented study of critics,[101] found most to be childless. If they generally lack creative ability (see Chapter 5), then should they not, by Rank's tenets, become compulsive progenitors of human offspring? Furthermore, emotional involvement with and fulfillment in one's children is hardly restricted to women. Admittedly, those of us who are male cannot bear children, nor be absolutely certain that those credited to our accounts are actually our doing. Yet paternal feelings can be extremely powerful. Do they detract from creative drives? We remain to be convinced.

Turning to another matter, that the need to defeat death may motivate creativity, also recalls Camus, except that in Rank there is nowhere near the same note of rebellion or of attempting to blaspheme and supplant God. Rather, it would seem, a creator attempts to become God, i.e., immortal. Putting it differently, creativity resembles a defense mechanism against our ultimate adversary; by producing something, perhaps we can overcome it. Certainly we rarely feel more alive than during the intensity of creative activity and it does seem, however temporarily, to draw a blind over our inevitable end.

We will peruse the hypothesized connection between creativity and death more closely in Chapter 16, but we might mention now that we find it, in the last analysis, intuitively unappealing. Consider poets who sit down daily to struggle with "the words." Do they actually have, in the forefront of their minds, the desire to produce something in which they can live on after death? It taxes credulity. Admittedly, introspective reports[102] now and then suggest the authenticity of this motive, but they are rare and, prior to the Romantic era, virtually nonexistent. There is nothing in J. S. Bach's leavings, for example, to indicate that he expected his compositions to survive his death or cared much if they did.[103] Naturally, such a motive could operate unconsciously, but more frequent overt expressions of it would be reassuring, given its questionable face validity.

Moreover, it simply does not fit many creative endeavors, which are as inherently ephemeral as the last rose of summer. A performing artist, for example, cannot possibly live on in his or her work because, to paraphrase Yogi Berra's immortal words, "When it's over, it's over." Likewise, a choreographer's creations are notoriously transient. Until quite recently, a notational system to record dances did not exist. The highly fallible memories of participants provided the only means of passing them on to prosterity. Thus, Swan Lake as we know it today may or may not resemble the version that Petipa originally conceived, and we have almost no idea how the dances from, say, the court of Louis XIV actually appeared. These problems have never discouraged people from composing dances; in fact some, such as Balanchine,[104] actually seem to enjoy this situation.

Several other soft spots should also be noted. That creation expresses some fundamental will to live generates at least one implausible prediction. Should the drive to create not intensify with age, as time, mortality, and death become every more imminent, tangible adversaries? Putting it differently, the manner in which many young people drive their automobiles, to say nothing of their motorcycles, suggests that they see their own demise as highly unlikely. Yet it seems that those same young people do more of the creative work.

We might also question the specifics of Rank's explanation of stylistic variation. It is an admirable, provocative attempt but, as things stand, quite arbitrary. Could not the need for individuation cause us to turn inwards to our personal imagination, away from empirical sensation, resulting in subjective, abstract rather than realistic art? By the same token, the external world being an experience we all share, could not its capture in such realistic art qualify as a collective act, satisfying identification? It remains to be seen whether empirical studies can untangle this knot.

Another objection. Rank plainly feels that modern art has become excessively "individuated" in style. This may or may not be so. But to thereby assert that these days only the artist matters, while art does not, sounds like sentimental nostalgia. Admittedly, artists who live particularly colorful lives, such as Salvador Dali or Brendan Behan (not to mention that modern sex symbol, the jet-setting music conductor), do garner headlines. We have all learned about the virtues of flamboyant promotion from P. T. Barnum and Mohammed Ali. But those who contrive worthwhile products will still obtain preeminent reputation, even if their personal lives are mundane, as Stravinsky clearly verifies. A bizarre persona will not hurt, but it will be unhelpful in the studio, on the podium, or in the ring unless genius is also present. Mohammed Ali could also fight!

But now we come to that which, for us, is the biggest problem with Rank. He can be very hard going for the reader. Part of this reflects his penchant for heavy-handed, ponderous prose. Riddled with impressive sounding but ultimately uninformative abstract nouns, it leaves even a sympathetic reader, after wading through a passage such as the following, longing for the stylistic economy of a Hemingway:

> Before we follow the development of this originally physioplastic faculty into the ideoplastic expression-art of the poet and its aesthetic remoulding in the generally intelligible collective language, we will illustrate the ideological character of language-creation from the example of the soul-concept itself.[105]

An unsympathetic translation may be partly to blame for such monstrosities, but unfortunately Rank brings other problems on himself. He tends to introduce theoretical ideas without sufficient explanation, implying rather than overtly volunteering them, so we must excavate them from between the lines. Most troublesome of all, his writing is riddled with blatant inconsistencies and contradictions. For example, his typology of personality does seem attractive. In particular, his assumption that creatives are neither normal nor neurotic but something else again, provides an alternative with which most of us can live. Unfortunately, once this is said, his description of these types and his hypotheses about their antecedents are nothing short of incomprehensible.

Consider. We find that the productive type suffers both from an excessive fear of life and also of death. We learn that "Modern art's...compelling motive is fear of life and experience,"[106] but also that,

In the neurotic the fear of life predominates and so checks all expression in life, while the artist type can overcome this fear in his creation and is driven by the fear of death to immortalize himself.[107]

We discover the distinction between the neurotic and productive types, i.e., the former turns creative activity in on the self, the latter redirects it towards external phenomena. Well and good. Unfortunately, we are later informed that artists' first task is to remake their own personality into one compatible with their calling. How does this differ from the neurotic's behavior?

Then again, do only individuating artists so appoint themselves? Such behavior would seem rather out of keeping with a collective, anonymous approach. Yet Rank sees it as typical of the productive type, which apparently means both types of artists. We even encounter such jungles as the following:

In general, a strong preponderance of the fear of life will lead rather to neurotic repression, and the fear of death to production--that is, perpetuation in the work produced. But the fear of life, from which we all suffer, conditions the problem of experience in the productive type as in other people, just as the fear of death whips up the neurotic's constructive powers.[108]

After such a conundrum, we can perhaps be forgiven for throwing up our hands in dismay and groaning, "What is Rank really saying?" Clearly he has followed the psychoanalytic custom of trying to have things both ways. As those who practice creativity sometimes contradict themselves, so too do those who write about it. In short, Rank is not exactly a master of the art of communication, leaving unheeded Camus' plea for "clear language and simple words."

271

Chapter 11

PSYCHOANALYTIC APPROACHES III: MISCELLANEOUS

Apparently the founding father bequeathed his lifelong
fascination with artistic work to his successors, for the
psychoanalytic tradition has spawned a huge literature on this
topic. Would that disciples of some other approaches had evinced
the same interest! At any rate, we cannot hope to review this
mountain of scholarship in detail here, or even to give every
contributor a moment in the sun. Regretfully, we must confine
ourselves to glancing briefly at a few influential
representatives. For $_1$ elaboration, the$_2$ reader is referred to
Rothenberg and Hausman^1 or to Slochower.^{2}

Ernst Kris

We begin by reminding the reader of several Freudian ideas
on which Kris heavily leans. Primary process, closely related to
the functioning of the id, aims to satisfy its basic instincts.
Secondary process, on the other hand, ties in with ego function
and provides a realistic awareness of the external world's
demands. Another defense mechanism, regression, will also be
relevant here. Periodically, the ego may renounce its usual
functions, abdicating its responsibilities as it were. At such
times, more primitive, childlike behavior, characteristic of an
earlier phase of development, can temporarily appear. Regression
is exemplified by an adult's indulgence in baby talk or immature
play.

So far, so Freud. The master, however, insisted that
primary and secondary process must always remain separate.^{3}
Kris, on the other hand, suggested that they can fuse, or
supplement one another, and indeed it is just such an occurrence
that underlies creative thought.^{4} Usually, the well-adjusted
adult mind suppresses primary process, but the artist is capable
of regression in the service of the ego, or returning to this
primitive material, modifying it, and bringing it under the
control of the more realistic secondary process, so that it can
be expressed in work. Its energy is converted to constructive
use, like a wild animal harnessed to the plow. Essentially,
then, Kris has simply expanded another idea that Freud advanced
rather incidentally, viz., that a creator has flexibility of
repression which allows him or her to use this normally
inaccessible material. As Kris puts it:

> In the work of art, as in the dream,
> unconscious contents are alive; here too,
> evidences of the primary process are
> conspicuous, but the ego maintains its

273

control over them, elaborates them in its
own right, and sees to it that distortions
do not go too far.[5]

From this beginning, Kris suggests that the creative process
consists of two distinct, essentially opposite phases, which he
calls inspiration and elaboration. The first of these depends
largely on primary process. In common with other examples of
regression, childlike, fantastic impulses and drives are allowed
an airing. The symbols that emerge, like those in dreams,
possess great emotional power. They also possess ambiguity,
because they refer vaguely to many things (in Kris' terms they
are overdetermined). In this stage, then, creators typically
feel occupied by external forces, perhaps by God. It seems not
to be their own voice speaking and in a sense, suggests Kris,
this is so, since a usually suppressed part of their psyche has
now come to the fore. As a result, they may feel that they have
learned something new about themselves (hence what we have called
the "that sort of bear" experience), that they are as much
onlookers as is any member of the audience, and that they are not
responsible for the resulting content. They can thus avoid
guilty or anxious feelings if that content is obnoxious.

Still, this regression is not completely anarchic. The ego
may relax its controlling reins, but it still grasps them firmly,
so that the process develops "in its service." Like a permissive
nanny who allows her immature charges to romp gleefully while she
keeps a look out for authoritarian parents, so too the ego, in
obeisance to the reality principle, remains vigilant. Even now
the artist identifies partly with his or her potential public,
viewing this primitive material through their eyes. Thus, the
regression is only partial and temporary. Still, secondary
process comes much more into play during the elaboration stage,
when the ego assumes more control. There is a shift to a more
organized, logical, detached perspective, so that the id's
chaotic contributions can be polished and shaped into a work
understandable to others.

These two phases of the process may follow one another in
rapid or slow succession, or alternate, or even occur together.
But, emphatically, they are both necessary if the process is to
bear fruit. Kris thereby aligns himself with the so-called ego
psychologists, an increasingly strident voice in recent times
within psychoanalytic circles.[6] Freud himself tended to focus on
the id's unrealistic needs, its strivings for satisfaction, and
its inevitable frustration and suppression. Kris, on the other
hand, pays environmental, cultural, and socioeconomic factors
more heed. Hereditary characteristics, for example, establish
only potentials that the environment can either encourage or
smother. Kris recognizes that artistic work is not produced in

an environmental vacuum. Experiences during infancy and childhood will influence one's creative products just as they will affect one's dreams and other cognitive processes. So will a host of historical and traditional factors, notably the contributions of predecessors in a field. Whereas for Freud, a work of art depended more on factors that boil up from the psychic underworld, regardless of external circumstances (as long as these were somehow inhibitory).

Kris devotes considerable space to the art of psychotics, partly to shed light on their mental processes but also to help us understand genuine art by comparing the two. Many psychotics, including those having little pre-illness talent or training, turn voluntarily to, and become quite preoccupied by, creative activity. Several differences to normal art are, he asserts, reliably evident. First, the activity may be quite as important and absorbing, but the healthy artist always wishes, at least in part, to depict the outer world for others and to communicate with them. Psychotics labor only for personal satisfaction, so that their work resembles such casual, introverted normal activities as doodling.

Why this difference? According to Kris, in healthy art the ego only "momentarily abandons its prerogatives,"[7] tolerating id mechanisms to let them briefly free. But the psychotic's ego, completely overwhelmed by primary process, has quite abandoned the field of battle, so that reality testing is in absentia and the elaboration stage suffers. The psychotic is quite unconcerned, since he seeks not to communicate with others but only with himself. In this solitary dialogue, "basically his speech is soliloquy"[8]; he wants only to reassert control over personal demons through artistic work. In short, for the psychotic, "art has deteriorated from communication to sorcery."[9]

A second, immediately evident difference is that a healthy person who is serious about creating will practice an occupation conscientiously and submit to training in order to improve. As a rule, therefore, she or he will do so. The psychotic, however, may be amazingly prolific but the level of proficiency will not rise. It is this lack of development, in Kris' opinion, that is the mark of psychotic art. Only when we view a large catalogue of someone's work, produced over an extended period, will we begin to notice its peculiarities. To verify this argument, Kris scrutinized a psychotic artist, one F.X. Messerschmidt, who was, by all reports, a skilled, respected sculptor before his illness. Even his later busts of human physiognomy show obvious technical skill, but he produced a huge number of them and, when seen together, they do seem incredibly repetitious, little more than monotonous harpings on a theme.

275

Children's art, says Kris, is similarly controlled by
primary process, again lacking the regulating function and the
sense of detachment provided by a mature ego. With its
preponderance of rhyming responses and nonsense utterances (Alice
in Wonderland provides a delightful imitation) it cannot easily
be shared by others. Likewise, such adult activities as wit,
humor, and caricature also reinstate childlike mental
functioning. But (when these are successful, at least) the ego,
still supreme, finds ways to express inner dangers without
upsetting the restricting social conscience present in the
superego. (Kris' account of these activities is highly similar[10]
to Freud's in Wit and its Relation to the Unconscious.)
Caricature, for example, such as a political cartoon that
radically exaggerates Reagan's wavy hair or Mulroney's jaw, is
invariably aggressive in connotation because it ridicules its
subjects. Now blind aggression presumably stems from primary
process, but in effective caricature it must be tempered by
secondary process if it is to tap some deeper truths.

In sum, creative activity is, for Kris, only one
manifestation of regression in the service of the ego; this
mechanism pervades every sphere of adult life. In his words:

> The contrast between an ego overwhelmed by
> regression and a 'regression in the service
> of the ego'...covers a vast and imposing
> range of mental experience...It is not
> confined to the sphere of wit and caricature
> but extends to the vast domain of aesthetic
> expression in general, and that it applies
> to the whole field of art and of symbol
> formation, preconscious or unconscious,
> which, beginning with cult and[11] ritual,
> permeates the whole of human life.

We might also mention several tangential matters that Kris
tackles. Audience psychology is the first. Freud, in discussing
this topic[12] had leaned heavily on the ancient idea of
catharsis. Supposedly, an audience, by identifying with the
protagonist of, say, a play can surreptitiously work off, through
the character's passion, various suppressed psychological needs
such as pity and fear. For Freud, art gives pleasure by
providing a socially approved occasion, free from guilt, for
parasitically releasing and working through rather more odious
impulses.

Kris' account is rather different. In keeping with his
usual bias for balance, he sees cathartic pleasure as coming not
only from the discharge of but also from the reassertion of ego
control over these impulses. Audience members, like creators,

must also balance primary and secondary process, and hence inspiration and elaboration. If their ego control is excessive, they will experience the work only intellectually, and "the aesthetic response (will be) replaced by pedantic connoisseurship or historicism."[13] Too little ego control, and their responses will degenerate to the blind rapture and vapid emotionalism of adolescents at rock concerts. Then there will be only "enjoyment rather than appreciation."[14]

So for Kris (as for Sartre) audiences do not passively receive an artistic product; rather, its inherent ambiguity and multiple meanings invite their active participation in re-creation. Forms such as soap opera and propaganda art, which "too easily open their chaste treasures to our unmastered importunity," will, like any pleasure too easily won, soon become dull. Likewise, an ambiguous work will more likely withstand the ravages of time, while that which is abundantly clear is probably doomed to an early demise.

Secondly, Kris adds his perspective to the debate about disturbed artists seeking psychological therapy. Will they be helped or will that therapy alleviate both problem and talent? Again, he parts company with Freudian orthodoxy. Creative work may be initially undertaken because of some psychological difficulty, but mature individuals must detach themselves from it or it will lessen ego control and so be detrimental. Therapy can help them do so and thus should help productivity. Kris' psychoanalytic successors have by and large sided with him on this point. Kubie, for example, has persistently indicated the dangers of neurotic affliction for creators[15] and, as we have learned earlier, such meagre evidence as there is does suggest therapy's benefits.[16]

Some critical comments are now in order. Kris' account can handle a large number of typical creative phenomena (such as their "medium" feelings and the kaleidoscopic alternations in their personalities) and suggests some intriguing hypotheses for others. For example, artists should not feel responsible for or anxious about the content of their work, because it arises from primary process, during inspiration. But by implication, they might experience these emotions with respect to its formal aspects, which presumably develop through more conscious, egocentric secondary process. Which, we might ask, more often causes creators to lose sleep: what they have said or how they have said it?

Kris, like Rank before him, can also plead innocent to an indictment often levelled against Freud, i.e., that his is a "theory of sickness." Freud studied, almost exclusively, disturbed, neurotic patients and from them developed his theory of personality. He then proceeded to overgeneralize outrageously, applying it indiscriminately to both the sick and the healthy. Supposedly the same mechanisms affect everyone, albeit with varying severity. Now the practice of studying the sick (or even the dead) to understand the healthy has a long and honorable history in medicine, but Freud tells us precious little about how the two populations differ. Kris, like Rank and Arieti, has tried to rectify this problem; in his eyes the schizophrenic, lacking a fully functioning ego, once more becomes a "failed artist."

We should also mention that the empirical research on primary process seems, on balance, rather encouraging for Kris.[17] Projective test studies, for example, suggest that artistic people have both more access to and more "integrative control" (read secondary process/ego control) over primary process than do others. As well, it is held in some quarters that hypnosis involves a regression to the unconscious; if this is so, then creative people, having easier access to primary process, should be particularly susceptible to hypnosis. In Suler's opinion, the evidence is again favorable, although not overwhelmingly so. He cautions, however, that some types of creativity, such as artistic endeavours, may well require larger doses of primary process than do others, e.g., science and problem solving.

We must now become more negative. Kris' avowed differences between healthy and psychotic artists are compellingly defended in his study of Messerschmidt. But other personalities do not so comfortably fit this model. Again Franz Kafka commands our attention; his approach to art epitomized that of Kris' psychotic. He evidently worked largely for himself (since he left instructions that his manuscripts be destroyed) and he reiterated the same themes neverendingly. Still, by any reasonable standards, his art is also highly successful, which must call Kris' criteria to account. Sometimes, self-absorption and monotonous repetition indicate not only psychosis but also rare achievement.

Next, a more serious problem. The theory has some descriptive value, as the wide attention it has received will attest. Unfortunately, it does not seem to predict creative ability or even explain it in any other than a post hoc manner. Creative activity is as yet, despite Kris' claims to the contrary, virtually the only means available for demonstrating that regression in the service of the ego has occurred. Unfortunately, it is precisely the activity that the latter purports to explain. In other words, the concept is viciously circular. Why are people creative? Because they can regress with the ego intact. How do we know that they can do so? Because they are creative. Certainly the disease of circularity

278

has reached almost epidemic proportions within the psychoanalytic tradition (Freud himself fell ill on more than a few occasions), and Kris seems also to have succumbed.

A host of related difficulties follow. The theory defies scientific evaluation, because a person or product's creativity supplies the self-evident proof that regression in the service has taken place. We are not told how the ego accomplishes this adaptive regression. Or what sorts of environmental events, or training conditions, might facilitate this ability. Or why it is that a few sublime archaeologists of the psyche can plummet to its submerged tombs and return laden with treasure, while the rest of us either bog down in the endless labyrinths or find that grave robbers have beaten us to the punch. To Kris' credit, he openly admits his inability to explain differences in talent. We do not yet know, nor do we have the tools to learn, why apparently similar environmental circumstances will in one case produce a neurotic and in another a genius.

Lastly, Kris has also fallen victim to another illness that has ravaged the psychoanalytic constituency, viz., a propensity for brutal, sometimes violent acts against the dignity of the English language. Admittedly, Kris' symptoms are less severe than, say, Rank's and in places he is genuinely poetic. But then we are forced to cross swords with a passage such as this:

> We all know what is generally accepted as the explanation of this phenomenon; a repressed, condemned, and usually aggressive thought has presented itself, has disturbed the pathognomic activity and has turned it into parapathognomy. The topography and dynamics of the process are easily discernable; it is a matter of pathognomic parapraxis.[18]

This is little more than pollysyllabic babble. When someone in this tradition writes that a phenomenon is "easily discernable," we reflexively wince. For we have learned over the years that a torrent of verbiage will invariably follow, full of sound and fury, signifying, all too often, not very much!

Silvano Arieti

In his book Creativity: The Magic Synthesis,[19] Arieti has provided a rarity: a wide-ranging, scholarly survey of the creativity literature.[20] As well, he has advanced, both therein and elsewhere, some theoretical notions that deserve attention. Most of these, in fact, elicit a strong sense of déjà vu, for they frequently differ more in terminology than in substance from

279

other contributions. We hasten to add that Arieti has himself pointed out many of these antecedents. Still, we must compare and contrast the particularly obvious ones as we proceed.

Reminiscent of Langer, he begins by arguing that the human psyche naturally and spontaneously produces imaginary mental events that do not resemble reality. Dreams, of course, provide the most compelling evidence for this assertion. These images may distort or even replace that reality, but they also free the mind, allowing it to do more than simply mirror external events passively. Images also represent our first hesitant steps towards creating something new, for they produce desirable, intriguing possibilities that are not available in real life. The most important of these are the endocepts, which are potentials to feel or act in a particular way.

We have touched on this notion previously, which to our mind is Arieti's most compelling contribution. To repeat, an endocept is a mysterious image hovering in the mind's eye just out of reach, like the sirens for the tortured Odysseus or the Holy Grail for King Arthur's wandering knights. Like Langer's commanding forms and Jung's archetypes (to which it is closely related), it can but vaguely be communicated to others or even grasped by the person, because it is seen only indirectly, as "through a glass darkly." By definition, any attempt to express it in words will seem unsatisfactory. Yet the creative process is fuelled by the need to give form to this vague, subjective "airy nothing." If this attempt is not made it may, like an itch left unscratched, cause frustration and irritation. As Arieti admits, the endocept may be an hypothesis that cannot be empirically verified, but on introspective grounds its validity as an important "springboard to creativity" seems indisputable.

Hence for Arieti, as for Jung and Langer, creative work attempts, through symbols, to express the inexpressible. Arieti likewise follows them, as well as most psychoanalysts, ' in preferring reductionistic explanations. Why does mind have this propensity for imaging? Probably because the nervous system's physiological structure is designed that way. Although this is not clearly stated, the endocept seems to differ from its predecessors mainly in its arising from individual rather than collective psychic material.

But how does the creative process occur? In pursuing this riddle, Arieti follows Kris' footsteps rather closely; again, primary and secondary process are held to interact. As well, he likewise sees disturbed mental functioning, notably the schizophrenic, as a pure manifestation of primary process; it therefore offers a route to studying the workings of this process. However, Arieti emphasizes rather different aspects of

280

schizophrenic thinking than did Kris. Apparently, schizophrenics often use unusual criteria to connect ideas, seeing similarities not obvious to the healthy mind and forming categories that have an intuitive rather than a logical base. Nevertheless, these categories are often understandable after the fact, for they are not haphazard but obey their own perverse brand of logic. As an example, Arieti mentions a patient who thought that she was the Virgin Mary because she shared at least one characteristic with the Holy Mother. She too was a virgin. As this example also reveals, the elements, once combined, can lose their separateness, becoming not only similar but actually interchangeable. Thus, the patient saw herself not only as resembling but as being the Virgin Mary.

Another property of schizophrenic thought is its tendency for over-inclusion. Events that ordinarily would be denied membership in a category receive full active privileges. Hence Hamlet, to substantiate his supposed insanity, pretends to perceive yonder cloud as being a camel; for befuddled Polonius, desperately anxious to cooperate, the only evidence for this label is that, well, yes, "It is backed like a camel." Furthermore, these categories are not only illogical but also unreliable, fluctuating with changing mood and environment; a moment later, Hamlet's cloud is "very like a whale." The schizophrenic will also use words differently, attending more to their physical attributes, such as sound or visual appearance, than to their connotative meaning. Thus, the primary associations to a word such as "bang" may be other words that sound the same, such as "rang" and "prang." (Such rhyming responses are called clang associations.)

In short, primary process thinking, while hardly routine, seems far from randomly chaotic. Though this be madness, yet there is method in it. The later-developing secondary process, however, obeying as it does the reality principle, draws similarity relationships and forms categories based on objective, logical rules (such as knife, fork, and spoon or breakfast, lunch, and dinner). Unlike its primary counterpart, it is capable of critical detachment, allowing it to accept or reject particular possibilities and to recognize the difference between fantasy and reality.

Arieti, like Kris, suggests that a fusion of the two processes, which he labels the tertiary process, can and does occur to produce creative thinking. More specifically, the primary process is not rejected, as it usually is, but is modified by and brought under the control of the more realistic secondary process. However, Arieti then shows (much more precisely than does Kris) how this interaction might lead to some of creativity's characteristic qualities. In his view, themes and ideas needing expression come from secondary process, while the possible forms for expressing them emanate from primary process. When the two come together and the creator suddenly discovers "how to say what he or she wants to say," when the dramatic "click" or "aha" that we call inspiration occurs, that is the tertiary process. At that moment, too, the creator gains a deeper understanding of each constituent.

As well, the primary process, with its talents for overgeneralization, can provide unusual similarity relationships that are the basis of metaphor, that most fundamental of artistic tools. For example, consider again Macbeth's soliloquy:

> Out, out brief candle!
> Life's but a walking shadow, a poor player
> That struts and frets his hour upon the stage,
> And then is heard no more; it is a tale
> Told by an idiot, full of sound and fury,
> Signifying nothing.

Logic would not, in all probability, note that the human condition resembles a "poor player," yet after the fact it is strikingly evident. Scientists, too, supposedly more reliant on linear thought, often try to increase their understanding of one phenomenon with a "model" or analogy relating it to another. For example, Einstein's visual metaphors helped clarify his ideas for himself and others.

Thus, in what Arieti calls the magic synthesis, the primary process material is scrutinized by secondary process. The latter selects the worthwhile images, then shapes and refines them in accordance with the reality principle so that their special qualities can be communicated to others. We know that an apt metaphor's connection is not entirely valid - human beings and strutting players are not, after all, identical - yet it forces us to suspend disbelief and transports us into the depths of schizophrenic experience. Fortunately, for us the trip is only temporary.

So too for the artist. The schizophrenic, claims Arieti, lacks an adequate secondary process and so will accept uncritically all the primitive material coming to his or her attention. But the poet, selective and discriminating, the master rather than the slave of the primitive beast, can convert its contributions to expressive form. As well, to the schizoid mind, combined components, like humans and strutting players, will henceforth be interchangeable, but secondary process reminds both the artist and the audience that they are still distinct. Thus, their fusion is not completely "consummated."

Or consider symbolization, where again a connection that was not at first apparent suddenly becomes valid. When primary process runs rampant, a symbol will totally obscure or "immerse" the thing it represents. To borrow from Arieti again, someone dreaming of a gorilla will only realize through the probings of depth psychology that it is actually his father, since for him the event has become the symbol. In art, however, we still vaguely sense the symbolized object, because it remains subliminally present. In summary, for Arieti as for so many others, the disturbed and creative minds have both similarities and differences. Once more, the schizophrenic becomes a failed artist.

Arieti then attempts to show how these ideas can help us to understand such seemingly diverse matters as humor and wit, science, religious experience, and painting. In the last named, for example, he demonstrates that in the works of a Chagall or Dali various primitive possibilities are given perverse yet somehow acceptable form. Like dreams, such works juxtapose elements in a manner that may be unusual but that obeys its own mysterious logic, reflecting the "hidden order of the tertiary process."[21] This we intuitively sense, but the paintings of a permanent, rather than temporary, schizophrenic will lack this subtle logic of "emotion recollected in tranquility."

Arieti devotes special attention to poetry, where the primary-secondary interaction seems particularly manifest; poetry uses metaphor perhaps more than any medium. Unfortunately, here he is less successful. Many of his examples seem strained and his critiques of various poems, as well as his musings on the nature of poetry, are rambling and unenlighten- ing. Freud, never noted for his excessive humility, nevertheless pretended to be nothing more than an interested layman when it came to art. Perhaps Arieti might have profitably followed his lead.

To his credit, Arieti has openly acknowledged the similarities between his theories and others. Having noted several of these, now let us mention others. That creative thinking combines two previously unrelated ideas resembles Koestler's notion of bisociation,[22] which we will later discuss. However, Arieti does specify a likely source for these unusual combinations, i.e., primary process cognition, whereas according to Koestler they "just happen." As well, Arieti's argument that two different types of thought are necessary reiterates the popular assertion that both linear and nonlinear components are necessary.

The greatest overlap is with Kris, but Arieti has pointed out what, in his opinion, are some differences (although he admits these may be largely semantic). He maintains, correctly,

283

that Kris but vaguely shows how primary process is made acceptable to ego function or how it is tempered to fit the reality principle. Yet it is debatable that Arieti's answers to these questions are any more satisfactory. The key difference, he asserts, is that "the use of primary process is not necessarily to be viewed as a manifestation of regression, but as an emerging accessibility or availability."[23] This seems to mean that Kris' creator somehow must journey back to primitive mentation, while Arieti's stays firmly in place, waiting for it to rise up. Does the mountain come to Mohammed or _vice_ _versa_? If we have accurately captured Arieti's distinction, then it seems a rather unimportant one, for the results would surely be much the same. As Columbus so dramatically demonstrated, the same territory can be reached by traveling in diverse directions.

Since Arieti's hypotheses are so imitative, it seems pointless to repeat criticisms already levelled at his predecessors. Let us simply note one further problem, i.e., that he focuses almost exclusively on one aspect of creative thought: the discovery of metaphor. Certainly this is important but, as we know, there is much more to it than that. About these other matters, his account remains mute. But we must mainly wonder whether he has in fact said much that is new at all, or whether he has simply poured old wine into new, colorfully labeled containers.

Phyllis Greenacre

Her recurring interest in the gifted, first piqued by Kris' stimulation and prodding, has produced some readable and stimulating contributions, fortunately now collected in one source.[24] At least one writer, burning his bridges, has found them "the most convincing portrait yet offered of the conditions of creativity."[25] According to Greenacre, potential artistic talent is inborn; while not necessarily hereditary (Galton's studies that so concluded,[26] she finds flawed), it is certainly biological. Four special abilities comprise such talent: (a) rare sensitivity to sensory stimulation, (b) heightened awareness of relationships among stimuli, (c) a strong predisposition to empathy, and (d) sensory-motor equipment especially capable of expression.[27]

In other words the prospective artist, verifying popular belief, is unusually "sensitive," to both inner emotion and external stimulation. For example, she suggests, most children will at some point encounter an over-powering experience that elicits awe mingled with dread and veneration.[28] However, the gifted - especially sensitive to attributes like light, color, and rhythm - will respond to it with rare imagination and unusual associations. Thus, an ordinary infant, while nursing, would

284

relate the breast's sensory qualities largely to itself, deciding that "breasts are like that." But to the more talented tippler, they would resemble A, B, and C, and, given a predilection for empathy, he or she might even imagine what being a breast would be like. So this child who will parent an artist reveals that artist's "love affair with the world."[29] The child relates primarily not to individual persons such as the mother but to people in general and even to empirical, worldly phenomena, or collective alternates, the "range of extended experiences which may surround or become attached to the main focus of object relationships."[30] From these will come achievements in art, science, religion, and so on.

But these biological factors only set the stage. Unlike fervent hereditarians, Greenacre also recognizes that if this potential is to be realized, experience must provide supplementary abilities and drives. In particular, the family romance problem[31] seems omnipresent in talented lives (as she shows with several case histories). Supposedly, every child longs at some point for blissful infancy when adults seemed perfect, their love reliable and uncontingent. But the unduly sensitive budding artist's desire is acute. For the same reason, the oedipal stage develops earlier, is unusually intense, and is less easily relinquished. For all these reasons, this child often undergoes identification with an adult, who becomes a lifelong hero figure. Parents will most probably receive this[32] "mantle of greatness." But so may an acquaintance or someone heard or read about, through "a chance encounter with some individual...which strikes a decisive harmonizing note with a part of the hidden image of the father."[33] (Even so, the parents' role remains important, e.g., by showing their belief in the child's talent they will encourage its development.) At any rate, while talent, for Greenacre, has wide applicability (in our language, a large "g" factor), the desire to follow in the hero's footsteps often determines the choice of field.

Freud's developmental stages (oral, anal, phallic, and so forth) will also differ. Usually, children either fixate in one, or renounce it and move on to the next, but the gifted's sensitivity "diminishes the boundaries between libidinal phases,"[34] so all retain their influence. As well, the gifted's primitive, childish impulses have greater access to consciousness. From all these factors, then, comes that more flexible, even unpredictable adult personality.

As gifted children mature, other differences appear. Their attributes may induce two virtually incompatible self-images,[35] a split personality most clearly shown, perhaps, in those who use pseudonyms, e.g., Samuel Clemens/Mark Twain and Charles Dodgson/Lewis Carroll. First, they have for everyday wear, an

ordinary self. But increasingly aware that they are "different"
(which in a real sense they are) they develop a second, creative
self. This split may also cause tension, distress, and hence
suppression of the troublesome creative self, particularly by
adolescents who so fervently wish to be like everyone else.
Because of this split, Greenacre compares artists to imposters,
those strange actors who pretend to be someone distinguished or
famous.[36] Their illegitimate roles and real persona often differ
as dramatically as do artists' two selves, and they too,
Greenacre claims, also have an insufficiently developed ego due
to inadequate oedipal resolution. Therefore, like the artist
imitating a hero, imposters assume, in each imposture, a father
figure's identity. Moreover, both dissemblers, she suggests, can
languish temporarily "between engagements" in the
pipe-and-slippers comfort of their real selves. Until the
dormant, restless alternative demands an airing. Therefore both
are trapped by their personality splits, by their "ego hunger and
need for completion."[37] Imposters can no more retire than can
genuine artists forego again taking up their formidable cross.
Both of them resemble, then, multiple personalities, such as that
documented in the book/film The Three Faces of Eve.[38] Here too
each independent persona will at times dominate until a
suppressed alternative demands its turn in the sun.

Greenacre clearly accounts nicely for many creative
personality quirks, e.g., the feelings of alienation, the erratic
personal relationships, the inconsistent (even paradoxical) and
childlike demeanors, and the sexual escapades infrequent and/or
androgynous. She also explains some experiences, overtly or by
implication. That an inspired person may feel almost religious
unity with the natural world and even with God, again reveals
that empirical sensitivity, that "love affair with the world."
Likewise, relationships to individuals may be unsatisfactory,
even stormy, while that to humanity en masse is intense. In
fact, this collective love motivates work, which is offered as a
kind of "love gift" to this unseen, infinite audience (and many
creators do report such aims). Lastly, why the notorious
"medium" experience and the frequent suspicion that someone else
did that work? Presumably the creative self supervises its
production, so it might well seem unfamiliar when the ordinary
alternative regains dominance.

Greenacre's extensive discussion of female creators[39] admits
that no sex differences in those crucial biological sensitivities
have as yet been detected. However, anatomical differences might
affect their actualizing any potential giftedness. Specifically,
the male's more developed musculature, suited to mobility,
exploration, and physical aggression, induces a need for
externalization. He must test himself against and express
himself in forms outside himself. This exterior focus

286

(reminiscent of Jung's extroverted tendency) also encouraged by his genitals' clear visibility, could tilt him towards tangible productivity. In contrast, women are inclined to <u>receptivity</u>, both by social conditioning and by the hidden internal location of their sexual organs.*

Various environmental/developmental factors, she suggests, also discourage the gifted female. If the ordinary self dominates the creative, or if they become "fused," then productivity will obviously suffer. Supposedly, this is more likely for women, since the culture emphasizes such common priorities as living for others and bearing children. Thus far many perspectives would travel, but she pursues her argument with some uniquely psychoanalytic concepts. For one thing, girls who have the artist's special sensitivity will develop "greater degree of clitoral pressure"[40]; in other words, sexual awareness will probably arrive earlier and more intensely. Thereby susceptible to fantasies about having an imaginary phallus, they may associate it with their creative selves, so the latter becomes their "masculine side" (presumably they are even more prone to bisexuality than are gifted males). In an environment promoting femininity, that creative self may hence be suppressed.

The girl's messier resolution of the Oedipus complex provides another difficulty. Imagining herself <u>already</u> castrated by her mother, she supposedly is harder put to forgive and forget and to later identify with that same-sex rival. Suspicious resentment may color their relationship into adulthood but, since they must live together, the child must learn to hide these feelings, to dissemble with tactful caution, to master "infantile diplomacy."[41] While this may help social success at cocktail parties, it will devastate creativity, where one must honestly expose one's inner being.

In short, Greenacre argues, a biologically gifted girl must choose, at puberty, between her femininity and her creative urges. By fully expressing the latter, she will compromise her sexual identification. One result, Greenacre wryly understates, is that "on the whole women artists--in whatever medium--do not seem to have been conspicuously excellent

---

*For Greenacre, women envy not the penis <u>per se</u> but the unambiguous concreteness it gives to sexuality. Their uncertainty about the location and source of their sexual sensations makes their sexuality notably more mysterious and inexplicable. This version of "penis envy" seems decidedly more acceptable than does Freud's.

mothers."[42]   Another is that they may thereafter remain ambivalent about their identities, both sexual and personal. It is noteworthy, for example, that none of Gertrude Stein's four "autobiographies" is exclusively about herself; thus, the famous Autobiography of Alice B. Toklas focuses on her lifelong, intimate friend.

We now compare Greenacre with some psychoanalytic predecessors. While accepting many Freudianisms, she rejects sublimation's role in creative work, guessing that the nongifted actually use it more.[43]   The gifted, having "mobility of libidinal energy," can openly express their sexual impulses, so need not redirect them. In some ways she treads closer to Jung, although he is cited but once in her index. For example, any coexistence of neurosis and creativity she blames on the war between the two antagonistic selves. Since this is inevitable in the gifted personality, does this not resemble the artist receiving "the divine gift of creative fire" and then paying dearly for it? As well, she too sees genius as a fountain whose "pressure" is difficult to resist, although she admits (unlike Jung) that it can be blocked; indeed, this frustration often induces neurosis. Hence the young Helen Keller's explosive, anarchic personality. Being deaf, dumb, and blind, she was unable to express her exceptional potential. Like Kris, Arieti, et. al., Greenacre sees the creative personality's primitive impulses as having easier access to consciousness, but she goes them one better by suggesting how and why this might be the case. Those inborn biological tendencies might induce atypical experiences.

Lastly, there are similarities in Schachtel,[44] who also emphasizes the artist's unusual sensitivity to and relationship with external events (although he attributes this to environmental/maturational rather than biological factors). Specifically, he distinguishes between two perceptual styles, the autocentric and allocentric. The former, dominating early childhood, is self-centered; we relate every sensed object to its effects on ourselves, judging it by the experiences of pleasure or pain it induces. The more mature allocentric perception accepts the object for what it is, and its right to exist independently, as itself, without our changing it. We wish simply to contemplate and explore its many possibilities.

For Schachtel, allocentric perception is crucial for creativity, allowing artists to approach the world with "freshness, spontaneity, interest and openness."[45]   In fact, they are motivated to work because they need this allocentrism, and achieving it is their main problem. Unfortunately, society frequently discourages it, preferring that we exploit phenomena for our benefit, which stunts our perceptual development and alienates us from our world.

The time has come, the walrus said, to talk of Lewis Carroll. Greenacre's discussion of Jonathan Swift[46] (certainly a succulent morsel for psychoanalytic rumination) was apparently conceived before her own ideas had quite solidified, for it is heavily Freudian. So too[47] is her Carroll study, but it is supplemented by later work[48] and we can also, delving between the lines, find inklings of her future thinking. Clearly, Carroll displays many of her gifted individual's special quirks. He showed early and rare imagination, being continually occupied in inventing puzzles, word games, marionette theatres, and the like. Later, suggesting acute sensitivity to his surroundings, he became a fine photographer. Similarly, both <u>Alice in Wonderland</u> and <u>Through the Looking Glass</u> mix the worlds of fantasy and reality in a dream-like surrealism, betraying his capacity for unusual associations to everyday events. Animals and even nonliving objects become human. Bodies appear and dissolve. Appendages expand or contract at the sip of a drink. Flamingoes function as croquet mallets, hedgehogs as balls, and playing cards as kings and queens.

But despite his works' cheerful innocence, Carroll himself was troubled. From childhood he felt decidedly alienated and "different"; witness his education at Rugby School, where his scholarly/literary interests conflicted with the prevailing esteem for manly ruggedness. And of sexual problems he had a closetful. Greenacre finds no evidence of a mature heterosexual relationship. Instead, he was passionately devoted to prepubescent girls (although he disliked little boys), notably Alice Liddell, the heroine of his famous fantasies, for whose entertainment they were spun.

Several other Greenacrian themes are sounded. The artist will regard work as a gift? <u>Through the Looking Glass</u> was <u>literally</u> offered to Alice Liddell. Family romance should lurk in the wings? Carroll remained, in both his writing and life, nostalgic for childhood's innocence and beauty (at least as his imagination romanticized it). A venerated hero should be in evidence? Carroll loved, wrote about, and identified with little girls, [49] supposedly because he related closely to his sister Louisa.

But perhaps the personality split is the concept most clearly exemplified. Charles Dodgson represents the ordinary self, an Oxford don of mathematics, by all reports rather unsuccessful and even dull. Apparently annoyed more than somewhat by his alter ego's fame, he on occasion denied knowing Lewis Carroll, and refused to answer mail addressed to him.[50]

But that creative self, literally labeled differently, allowed dormant imagination free reign, mastered literature and nonsense poetry, and attained immortality. In fact, Greenacre suggests, this almost schizoid personality split may explain the attractions of the nonsense form. Confusion about one's identity, when coupled (as in Carroll) with worries about sexuality, castration, and even annihilation (witness the Queen of Heart's persistent cries for beheadings), obviously provides a potential for difficulties. But expressing such fears in highly exaggerated nonsense might disarm them. In short, Carroll's talent rescues him from neurosis, allowing him to separate himself from his problems. In this, Greenacre clearly follows Rank and anticipates Becker (see Chapter 16). Furthermore, she also approaches Freud's notion of sublimation, despite her denial that the gifted employ it.

Becoming editorial, as previously intimated we find much to admire in Greenacre. Above all, unlike most theorists, she seems to have openly addressed many creative phenomena, both of personality and process. These, apparently, she first discovered through interview and observation, later advancing some tentative explanations. In several ways, then, her methods contrast favorably with prevailing psychoanalytic practices. Her ideas were evolved inductively from, rather than imposed arbitrarily on, the data, so she more deserves to be called "scientist" than do many of her colleagues who vociferously claim that title. As well, she advances those ideas not as inviolate truths but, with attractive humility, as suggestions for further investigation.

We focus now on two major postulates, the first being that talent is biologically based. It concurs with most psychoanalysts' expressed sentiments, and with our own, but she specifies much more precisely both the nature of these antecedents and their possible interactions with experience. Hence, it seems not entirely inconceivable to evaluate them empirically, e.g., to determine whether talented youngsters do possess the hypothesized sensitivities. If verified, they might provide reliable, accurate predictors of talent. To the second postulate, however, we must raise more objection. If creators do possess two antagonistic selves, their paradoxical personalities, sexual ambivalence, and perhaps their rampant insecurity are thereby explained. The lastnamed, in turn, could motivate that "quest for identity" of which Storr[51] and the existentialists speak. Yet most studies endow those creators with unusually high ego strength. Does this not suggest well integrated rather than fragmented personalities? But this point aside, we find Greenacre's to be a welcome contribution.

290

Alfred Adler

Although chronologically Adler preceeds most of those already discussed, we have left him to the last. He is, as we shall see, in many ways a rather unorthodox member of the psychoanalytic tradition, who in later years parted company rather severely with much of the party line. Indeed, a case could be made that he should not be placed within it at all[52] since many of his ideas anticipate and influenced the humanists. Still, he was initially an important member of Freud's inner circle and he never relinquished the most fundamental dogma of all, i.e., that factors in the unconscious are of great importance. Hence we will consider him here, as a convenient bridge to some quite different approaches.

1. Overcoming inferiority. For Adler, a person's feelings of inferiority are the basic fact of existence. Initially, Adler attributed these feelings to actual physical, organic defects, but subsequently he concluded that they arose inevitably during early childhood and so were universal.[53] In a preponderantly adult world, children feel smaller, weaker, and less influential. Thus, inferiority was in the eye of the beholder, stemming not from objective, physical events but from the person's attitude (already, then, we can sense Adler's propensity for explanations based on more subjective, individual processes). To compensate for and to gain victory over these feelings, the individual is driven to seek superiority. This impetus from "minus to plus" and from "below to above"[54] - the striving for power, for victory over life's difficulties, and ultimately for perfection - is universal. All human beings are pushed for a desire to overcome inferiority and pulled by the complementary desire to be superior. (Early on, Adler labeled this will to power the masculine protest.[55] However, this suggested a sex difference that quite missed his meaning; in his view, women strove for superiority just as persistently as did men.)

What is crucial, then, is how they try to satisfy these motives. The healthy choice, in Adler's opinion, is for social interest, in which we relinquish personal ambition and selfishness, and seek cooperation and solidarity with our fellow humans. He was adamant that we are, by nature, social beings. We need one another not only physically, for survival and mutual protection, but also psychologically (in this, of course, he reminds us of Camus in The Rebel). This tendency for togetherness is not learned through experience but is innate, although it can be discouraged or suppressed, and it must be developed in children, primarily through infant-mother interactions.

The neurotic choice, on the other hand, seeks superiority and power at the expense of others, indulging in competition rather than cooperation. In excess, when the need for dominance becomes an all-pervading obsession, it is called overcompensation. Unfortunately, persons opting for this alternative can never find peace of mind. They may imagine, beforehand, that they will be able to transform their "poverty...into wealth, ...subordination into domination, ...suffering into happiness and pleasure, ...ignorance into omniscience."[56] But they will always be vulnerable to insecurity, because there will be persistent threats to their status. Furthermore, this path will lead to social isolation and thus go against their natural grain. Their repellent intolerance and paranoia will leave them with only a small circle of long-suffering intimates (usually family or loyal friends). Estranged from reality, living in a world of fantasy, they will seek to satisfy their needs for domination at the expense of those intimates (see Macbeth for a textbook example).

The characteristic, generalized methods by which a person seeks these goals and approaches the day-to-day business of living, Adler called the style of life. Everyone has a personal style that is unique because each of us has a different way of reaching for superiority and different criteria for feeling it achieved. One of us may wish to be a fine athlete, another a political success, and so forth. Particularly important determinants of the style of life, therefore, are certain fictional goals or ideal wishes that people have contrived for themselves. People are motivated more by future aims than by past experiences. A neurotic's lifestyle, for example, seeks to fulfill dreams of godlike power. Anyone seeking such unrealistic goals will obviously be forced to flee from real life, with its inevitable compromises and failures, into a life of fantasy, neurosis, or crime.

At any rate, if we wish to understand someone's style of life (as would a therapist trying to modify one that is unacceptable), we must first determine the person's fictional goals, the set of assumptions under which he or she operates, and the imaginary scenarios or ideal selves that she or he has constructed. To complicate matters even more, both goals and styles are established early in life and so are extraordinarily resistant to change. As well, the person is usually unaware of them, for they are hidden in the unconscious, being by far the most important constituents of that murky region.

Let us now pause briefly to point out how sweeping are Adler's departures from orthodoxy and why, in later years, he became almost persona non grata to the psychoanalytic powerbrokers. While remaining in the tradition of depth psychology by recognizing the importance of the unconscious, his depiction of its properties is worlds away from Freud (although it in some ways resembles Jung). Most heretically, he clearly implies an active, decision-making organism, freely selecting its own, individual goals and then deciding, equally autonomously, how to reach them. It is our decision, for example, whether to cooperate or compete in seeking superiority. In short, the Adlerian self is inherently <u>creative</u>. Heredity, environment, and, yes, even organic inferiorities <u>contribute</u> to the fictions it invents but, in the last analysis, our personalities are molded not by deterministic factors beyond our own control but by our own choices. As Adler put it, we are "both the picture and the artist. (We are) the artist of (our) personality."[57]

We can also recognize how greatly Adler influenced the humanists. Anticipating Allport's <u>idiographic approach</u>,[58] he held that a particular person must be studied individually in order to be understood, since each person is unique. We similarly experience anticipatory déjà vu when we learn that an individual freely chooses a day-to-day lifestyle, and that the human mind is naturally inventive, so that creativity is as indigenous as breathing. Lastly, that human behavior should be influenced, not by external reality but by the person's interpretations of that reality, so that a would-be therapist must try to perceive the world through that person's eyes - all of this recalls Rogers' <u>client centered therapy</u>.[59] In fact, a case could be made that the humanists have added little to Adler other than jargon.

But what of creativity? In one sense, of course, it is basic to Adler's views, which assume us to be inherently creative in our approach to the business of living. Therefore, as with Maslow, there is no more reason to query our creating than our eating, reproducing, or defecating. And, also as with Maslow, there is a discomforting sense of a <u>fait accompli</u>, of an assertion that leaves little more to be said about the matter. Fortunately, Adler implies the same distinction as does his humanist successor, reserving the term <u>creativity</u> specifically for this attribute that everyone possesses. The rare gift that allows the special few to accomplish quality work he labels <u>genius</u>. The latter, obviously, is more relevant here, so we shall concentrate on his account of it.

Adler paid less attention to the phenomenon of genius than did his psychoanalytic colleagues. A few, rather incidental observations, remarks, and hypotheses are scattered throughout his writings and, as we shall shortly discover, they are decidely contradictory, making his precise position rather difficult to fathom. Consider, for example, the role of organic inferiority. Does genius arise in order to compensate for it? Early on,

Adler's reply is clearly affirmative. He mentions Demosthenes, afflicted with a speech defect, attaining eminence as an orator, as well as Beethoven, with his notorious hearing difficulties, being driven to seek eminence as a musician. (This example is unconvincing. It is well known that Beethoven's deafness struck him well on in his career, when he was a successful, established composer. Surely the organic inferiority should have come first if it was the precipitating factor.) We might also mention the club foot of which Byron was so intensely sensitive.[60] Did his wounded pride give rise to his arrogant independence?

Later, Adler's position becomes more obscure. At one point he avows that "We are not so foolish as to suppose that organic imperfection is the efficient cause of genius,"[61] in another, that "Often (geniuses) started with gravely imperfect organs. In almost all outstanding people, we find some organic imperfection."[62] Furthermore, the ambivalence does not reflect a change in his views over time, since both comments were written relatively late. Clearly, Adler also lies comfortably within the psychoanalytic tradition in his desire to have things both ways! Still, the notion of compensation does provide attractive explanation for some creative phenomena. Might it not instil, for example, that dash of insecurity which provides the crucial stubborn persistence? Consider Nietzsche, who not only renounced but spent the rest of life denouncing Christian beliefs[63] Perhaps his overly strict religious upbringing was the culprit.

But for us, Adler's most troublesome waffling concerns the method that a genius chooses in order to compensate for inferiority (whether organic or "felt"). We have seen that a person can make either a healthy choice and seek social interest, or a neurotic choice and strive for superiority at the expense of others. Which path does the genius take? Or, to put it another and more crucial way, in Adler's view is genius healthy or neurotic? At first glance, his position seems unambiguous. In his major statement on genius, he asserted that:

> A man of genius is primarily a man of supreme usefulness...(It is) socially affirmative action...We note that (artists and poets) serve a social function more than anyone else. It is they who have taught us how to see, how to think and how to feel...Genius is to be defined as no more than supreme usefulness...Mankind only calls those individuals geniuses who have contributed much to the common welfare.[64]

Well and good. Judging by this frequent reiteration of the same point, he did not wish to be misunderstood. And furthermore, in another place he would write:

> In the great and small religious movements;
> in the great achievements of philosophy,
> science, art and political wisdom; as in the
> individual men and women who strive to
> penetrate to the truth, or seek to refine
> and dignify the thought, emotion, sight and
> hearing of mankind, consciously or
> unconsciously, there is expressed the most
> exalted ideal purpose: 'Love thy
> neighbor.'[65]

In short, geniuses represent the ultimate in healthy compensation because they, more than anyone, labor for the good of mankind. Now Adler realized that the nature of such work may require a genius to lead a rather reclusive, introverted life and "exile himself" in pursuit of higher goals. But these seemingly anti-social tendencies are not neurotic because they still have a social character. They will eventually enrich society. Where, then, is the ambiguity? Unfortunately, some of Adler's other, more incidental comments suggest quite a different viewpoint. For example, we are told that neurotic seekers of power, establishing their vision of godlike superiority within their fictional schema, may flee from life into fantasy, "if fortunate in art, but more generally in pietism, neurosis or crime" (italics mine).[66] Thus, here he attributes the artistic drive to precisely those same sources that also fuel more deviant pursuits. Again, we are told that such neurotic compensation can lead to:

> the positing of a goal, an imagined goal of
> superiority, whereby his poverty is
> transformed into wealth, his subordination
> into domination, his suffering into
> happiness and pleasure, his ignorance into
> omniscience and his incapacity into artistic
> creation (italics mine).[67]

And yet again (this time, admittedly from a passage produced earlier in his career):

> Such (spoiled, pampered) children, in their
> everlasting greed for triumph, may at times
> even become the material from which, under
> favourable conditions, the great personages,
> the artists and poets develop.[68]

295

Which portrayal is more accurate? Is the genius more often a healthy, socially interested laborer for the good of humanity, or an obsessed neurotic, driven by an insatiable lust for power? Before we respond, let us, as usual, consider an individual case history that may help us. To avoid swaying the reader's biases, we shall, for the moment, keep our subject's identity hidden. Let him be called, in good cloak-and-dagger fashion, simply "R."

2. **A case study.** [69]Rarely has there been a character more egocentric or arrogant. In the opinion of many, it approached megalomania. A biographer more sympathetic than most could write, "(R) was the most self-absorbed egoist of all time, and every one of (his products) was part of a lifelong drive to externalize his ego."[70] He openly believed that he was predestined for greatness and that therefore the world owed him a living while he set about achieving it. And a luxurious one at that. No matter how immense his income, he managed to outspend it, so he continually borrowed enormous sums from his harrassed intimates, often without so much as a "thank you." In his eyes, evidently, they were lucky to be allowed to serve genius. Repayment, naturally, he saw as a trivial matter, with the result that he may actually have spent time in a debtor's prison.[71] All in all, here is precious little of what a business person might call "financial responsibility."

His headstrong self-assurance meant that few teachers, either in school or in his chosen calling, could teach him anything. That he had little training in or knowledge of that calling did not discourage him in the least. The ultimate "do-it-yourselfer" (by some opinion, little more than a dilettante), he simply borrowed an instructional book from the local library and set to work. His early efforts were hardly earth shattering. In fact, for some years he lived as both a social and political outcast, wandering penniless throughout Europe. However, his ego remained unscathed, for at this very time he conceived a project on a scale unheard of either before or since. It would do nothing less than unite all the art forms into an epic Gestalt that would require four dramatically linked performances given over four days. Total running time? A mere 13 hours. As if this were not enough to discourage even the most dedicated viewer, a continuous spirit of seriousness would reign, uninterrupted by any lightheartedness or comedy. A household name would have been hard pressed to sell such a project to prospective sponsors. For a virtual nonentity, it seemed hopeless.

Still, as always, R was unwilling to compromise his artistic standards or make it easier for the public. Either they accepted him on his own terms or they would be denied the privilege of experiencing his work. Furthermore, that experiencing had to take place under nothing less than ideal conditions. Therefore, as a final act of self-aggrandizement, he conceived a facility appropriate for, and solely dedicated to, the displaying of his own work. True, it was to be situated in a somewhat out-of-the-way niche, but undoubtedly the grateful public would make its pilgrimages from the earth's four corners to partake of his largesse. Needless to say, this memorial edifice would cost the earth, but his followers would see to raising the necessary funds.

He cut an equally wide swath through the world of sexual relations. His series of extramarital dalliances, only thinly hidden from his long-suffering wife, he defended on the grounds that, since she did not completely share his high opinion of himself, he needed the comfort of partners more understanding. One of his most faithful benefactors was repaid most curiously: by R's conducting a torrid and widely publicized affair with his wife. Likewise, R sired several children by the wife of another close friend while the latter was still married to her. Only after years of thinly veiled pretense and scandal did R condescend to marry her.

Nevertheless, despite such callous treatment of his intimates, he expected total devotion in return. As one biographer put it,

> A friendship with (R) required the total
> subordination of the friend, for (R) could
> only conceive a relationship in terms of his
> own domination of that relationship...All
> those, men and women alike, who befriended
> him, helped him, loved him, came to
> experience the suffering that accompanied a
> relationship, any relationship, with
> him...All passed out of his life the moment
> he had sucked from them, like a vampire,
> whatever intellectual, financial or
> emotional sustenance they had to offer.[72]

His social and political sensitivity was equally undernourished. At one point he had a steady job, with a guaranteed if moderate income. He thereupon proposed to the head of the rigid hierarchy that sweeping changes in personnel, facilities, and aims were needed. This inability to know his place quickly led to his ouster. His sense of national obligation was so tenuous that he could cheerfully take a job in another country largely to avoid military service. Later, when he came to realize that the world would not easily bow down in grateful veneration to his genius, he became embroiled in several revolutionary movements. Narrowly escaping arrest, he again had to flee his native land and live as an exile for some twelve years.

Most deplorable of all, he became a violent anti-Semite. Moreover, stereotypic Aryan figures, worthy candidates for the SS, people his work. For these reasons, he became a revered cult figure in the Third Reich, gaining the dubious distinction of being Hitler's particular favorite. Of him the Feuhrer could say, "Whoever wishes to understand National Socialism must first know (R)." Yet his persuasive powers were such that he could convince a Jew to oversee one of his last, most grandiose projects.

Also in keeping with Adler's textbook neurotic, he continuously retreated into the world of fantasy. From childhood he was fascinated by the dark, sinister myths and legends of his native land, and by the world of the supernatural. These caused him such persistent nightmares and fits of screaming that none of his family would sleep anywhere near him.[73] Later, these foreboding occupants of his imagination received repeated expression in his work.

In short, here is a personality with an unsurpassed need for power and dominance, a textbook example of Adler's overcompensating neurotic, lacking any sign of "social responsibility." To complete the Adlerian portrait, we must now ask, "For what was he compensating?" From whence came the inferiority complex he tried so compulsively to overcome? To answer, we must search R's background and, verifying the psychoanalytic motto "Seek and ye shall find," we quickly locate some suggestive material. First, he was quite short--under 5'5" in height--and, even more discomforting, his second wife was much taller. Adlerian principles have it that the physically inferior often overcompensate by lusting insatiably after power, as witness Napolean, Stalin, and Hitler, among others. As well, R was continually ill as a child and was afflicted throughout his life by a variety of disorders, particularly by erysipelas.[74] Combined with his rather unimpressive physical appearance, which featured an overly large head and prominent nose, perhaps this explains his lifelong need to attract and dominate members of the opposite sex.

Moreover, there was some doubt, even in his own mind, about his paternity. His supposed father died when he was six months old and indications are that the gentleman who rather quickly became his step-father may have been his natural father as well.[75] For R, the anti- Semite, the crucial point is that this step-father is alleged to have had some Jewish blood, which could have compounded R's problems of identity. And finally, he perceived his mother as rather remote and aloof. In his words,

298

I can scarcely remember that she ever
caressed me...In fact there never were any
displays of tenderness and affection in our
family.[76]

Admittedly, there are no indications that these matters troubled
R whatsoever. But to doctrinaire psychoanalysts that would
matter not a whit, since the conflict would at any rate function
unconsciously.

At last we can return to the question posed earlier, viz.,
is the genius more likely to be socially interested, or
neurotically power hungry? Since Adler apparently could not make
up his mind, we will suggest on his behalf that the latter
alternative seems more likely. We chose our case history to
buttress this stance, for our definitive overcompensating,
power-hungry R is none other than the composer Richard Wagner,
arguably the preeminent figure in the world of grand opera and
undoubtedly the most influential figure in the entire world of
music during the latter half of the nineteenth century. His
integrated "music dramas," such as Tristan und Isolde and Die
Miestersinger, and especially his four-part epic, Der Ring des
Nibelungen (The Ring of the Nibelungs), were every bit the
masterpieces he believed them to be. People actually did (and
do) come from all over the world to the Bavarian town of
Bayreuth, to the theatre and festival dedicated solely to
perpetuating his work. Obviously his delusions of grandeur were
not delusional at all.

Wagner, while alive, was a figure of unprecedented
controversy, dividing the musical world into two warring camps,
the "pro-Wagnerians" (such as Franz Liszt) and the
"anti-Wagnerians" (notably Brahms and his followers). Some, like
Nietzsche, managed to reside at different times in both camps.
Even today, almost exactly a century after his death, he provokes
disagreement. Recent performances of his work in Israel perhaps
understandably brought storms of protest. Unlike virtually any
other great composer, his music is openly disliked[77] in some
quarters, primarily for its melodramatic bombast. Predictably,
one of Oscar Wilde's characters voiced the most telling
indictment:

> "Yes, it was at dear Lohengrin. I like
> Wagner's music better than anybody's. It is
> so loud that one can talk the whole time
> without other people hearing what one says.[78]
> That is a great advantage."

3. Commentary. Despite numerous negatives, however, of
Wagner's genius there can be little doubt. In our view,

299

therefore, Adler's image of the neurotic more closely resembles the typical creative than does his socially interested personality. Consider. The neurotic sets high, even unattainable goals, craves satisfaction and success, and is egocentric and even arrogant. We have argued that these qualities all contribute to the creative's necessary perfectionism, along with a persistence in the face of adversity. As well, they make alternations between self-confidence and insecurity somewhat more comprehensible. It may be, as Adler asserts, that,

> The superiority complex and the inferiority complex agree on one point, namely that they are always on the useless side. We can never find an arrogant, impertinent child...on the useful side of life.[79]

But we are inclined to disagree.

Consider too. The neurotic always seeks a situation in which he or she can excel (while presumably the healthy, cooperative person does not). In many creatives, do not the drives to compete and to defeat others seem to be alive and well? Does not Watson's Double Helix[80] merely admit openly those motives to which many others surreptitiously succumb? Consider, for example, those unseemly battles to establish someone's priority in making a scientific discover, the Newton-Leibnitz struggle over calculus being but one of many.[81] Consider too the unmistakably aggressive, dominant tendencies displayed by the scientists whom Mitroff interviewed.[82] This extraordinary statement from one individual perhaps best captures the trait:

> If you want to get anybody to believe your hypothesis, you've got to beat them down with numbers: you've got to hit them again and again over the head with hard data until they're stupified into believing it.[83]

And surely creative people are attracted to their eventual field, as much as anything, by their awareness that they are "good at it." Their evident ability will usually yield some sort of recognition, perhaps from friends or teachers, that will encourage them to continue. We are all creatures of reinforcement, more persistent at behaviors that succeed than at those that fail. In fact, Adler's early theory, emphasizing compensation for organic inferiority, is intuitively unattractive because it implies precisely the opposite, i.e., that we should persist more at pursuits for which we are unsuited. Demosthenes may have done so, but the vast majority will not.

Consider also. The neurotic confines herself or himself to a small circle of intensely loyal, usually downtrodden friends. Thus did Wagner and thus do many other creatives. As for the notion that the work of a genius is always socially useful, it simply will not stand scrutiny. Admittedly, many creatives feel, when they produce something, that they are "giving a gift to others," which does suggest alturistic motives. In addition, some have shown a well-developed sense of social conscience and involvement. Einstein, for example, quickly realized that his findings about nuclear energy had dangerous implications and thereafter worked unceasingly for the causes of peace and brotherhood.[84] In the same vein, he helped promote the founding and development of the state of Israel.

Be that as it may, genuinely innovative creative work is, in some sense at least, much more often a threat to the entrenched social order, destructive and even revolutionary in its psychological, and sometimes in its political, effects. Therefore, to repeat, in our view creators more closely resemble Adler's neurotic than his socially interested personality. Now it might be charged that Wagner is highly atypical. Rather, we suggest, he is an exception that proves the rule, simply personifying, albeit unattractively and in the extreme, many qualities that other creators also less flagrantly possess. Whether we like it or not, most of them are intensely antisocial and alienated, working not for the common good but for selfish, egocentric purposes. Putting it differently, it seems doubtful that a genuinely altruistic personality would be much driven to create.

But, the reader may rejoin, does this not contradict our persistent assertion that creatives are not neurotic? Not at all, for our real quarrel is with Adler's description of neurosis. Many of the above-mentioned qualities, while undesirable in excess, are in moderation the very stuff of achievement. In addition, excessively cooperative, social behavior is not necessarily always healthy, either. The person who almost compulsively lives for others can be equally disturbed, not to say nauseating.[*] Our case rests.

---

[*]Melanie, in Gone With the Wind (to jibe lagging memories, played in the film by Olivia de Havilland) is a case in point. Excessively concerned with the welfare of others, she becomes so repellent that the viewer is tempted to throw stinkbombs at the screen whenever she appears to counteract the overwhelming odor of syrup and cotton candy.

Chapter 12

NATURALISTIC VIEWS I: THE PASSIVE SUBJECT

Approaches which blame creativity on material, empirical,
and possibly measurable events within our hereditary and/or
environmental history comprise this collection of miscellany.
Not surprisingly, they usually lean heavily on the attitudes and
practices of science. Such a heterogeneous group defies a label,
but naturalistic seems less misinforming than most. There is
much ground to cover, so treatments will sometimes be cursory,
unenlivened by representative personalities. In justification,
these approaches have often paid creativity scant heed either.

We begin with two conflicting views of humanity, whose
persistent, seesaw battle has in this century surfaced once more.
One combatant, exemplified by John B. Watson's behaviorism,[1] sees
us as passive, almost machine-like robots. Our actions are
dictated by stimuli beyond our control, our learning efficiency
by considerations external to ourselves (such as frequency or
speed of presentation) rather than internal mechanisms (such as
thought or attention). Advocates of this position, which
dominated psychology until the 1960's, form the present chapter.
But psychology's recent so-called cognitive revolution,
anticipated by the Gestalt approach and by E. C. Tolman, has,
temporarily at least, consigned this adversary to the garbage can
of ideas. Equally committed to empirical science, albeit less
rigorously objective, the new heresy promotes an alternative more
flattering: the active subject. One's thoughts, perceptions, and
the like, determine one's responses to experience; one's
interpretations decide how and what one will learn. So the
important variables lie within a person, not outside. The next
chapter will pay our obeisance to the major proponents.

Hereditary and Evolutionary Views

These clearly related approaches agree that creative ability
is inborn, but they differ in emphasis. For the fervent
hereditarian, such ability is fixed irrevocably at conception,
bequeathed not by gods but by ancestors, perhaps a great uncle
twice removed and now put away for good. For the evolutionist,
following Darwin, our creativity probably appeared first as a
biological mutant but its possessors, advantaged in survival's
struggle, would be selected to flourish. Apart from the vague
biological/organic explanations of the psychoanalysts, neither
version has been popular hereabouts, and we might first ponder
the reasons. Watson also encouraged another prevalent bias: to
explain someone's personality, intelligence, and the like, "When
in doubt, blame the environment." It was his fervent belief that
we acquire virtually every important behavior through experience,

303

so the laws of learning became the most avidly investigated topics of psychology. Yet Watson et al. seem simply to have voiced a widespread, almost knee-jerk tendency in our culture. How often do we unthinkingly, for example, blame family backgrounds, economic privations, or peer groups for criminal or deviant acts while ignoring possible inborn causes?

From whence cometh this bias? Consider the pioneers. They left everything, including friends and relatives in Scotland, Russia, and elsewhere for unknown lands because they believed that through their own perspiring toil they could forge a better life. Ever since, our North American heritage has been shot through with optimism, sometimes almost naively so. The American Dream. The dominion from sea to sea (courtesy of the Canadian Pacific Railway). Can do. George M. Cohan as Everyman. Now environmental explanations of behavior are supremely optimistic because they imply possible modification and control; desirable acts can be encouraged, others eliminated. Whereas inborn antecedents make nuts seem more difficult to crack, so their emphasis implies fatalistic pessimism, an acceptance of "whatever is," as in "that's human nature" or "boys will be boys." They contradict our heritage. Hence they remain unpopular.

Nevertheless, a few exemplars merit mention. Francis Galton[2] found that members of one family displayed genius/eminence far more frequently than chance would allow, e.g., among the Bachs, several other fine musicians preceeded or followed the preeminent J. S. Galton therefore concluded that "Each generation has enormous power over the natural gifts of those that follow."[3] Ergo, if race horses can be bred to run and dogs to hunt, why should we not replace indiscriminate, rabbit-like breeding with judiciously selected marriages, whose gifted bloodlines would benefit future generations?

Due to their methodological weaknesses, Galton's studies now possess mainly historical interest. First, the subjects he chose for their reputations include not only artists and scientists but also such figures of dubious originality as military commanders and politicians. Yet in another sense he was overly selective: "(I have taken) little notice. . . of modern men of eminence who are not English or at least well known to Englishmen."[4] Rule Brittania! Actually, he regrets omitting Germans and Americans, but the French worry him less, since "The Revolution and the guillotine made sad havoc among the progeny of abler races."[5] Like a good Victorian, he found it unthinkable, apparently, that genius might occasionally arise from the laboring classes.

As a second problem, we might question that his numbers demand his conclusions. How many geniuses would by chance arise from one family? And finally, environmental rather than hereditary factors may be responsible, given that talented relatives could enrich either. The Mozart family was musical. Did their genes, or music's presence in the domestic air, give rise to Wolfgang Amadeus? In other words, Galton stumbles over that enduring issue, nature versus nurture. Are behaviors learned or inherited? Often, it is difficult to resolve, because subjects who differ in creativity* invariably differ in both heredity and environment, providing a confounded, subject variable comparison (see Chapter 3). Thus, the jury remains out on Galton's conclusions, but we would wager on their accuracy. Encouraging environments, it seems to us, are necessary to bring out innate, biological "gifts," but without the latter they will be ineffective. Silk purses come not from sow's ears, as Mozart himself hints:

> Why my productions take from my hand that particular form and style that makes them Mozartish, and different from the works of other composers, is probably owing to the same cause which renders my nose so large or so aquiline.[7]

We turn now to evolutionary analyses (although deferring those, such as Skinner[8] and Campbell,[9] that see natural selection as a metaphor for the creative process). Could our creative ability have originated as a mutant, and been selected? After all, its evolutionary value seems obvious. Strangely, such notions have rarely been advanced, but Storr[10] provides an exception. Scientific/technological abilities, obviously beneficial, have enhanced our safety, comfort, and longevity, but they involve mainly problem solving. How could genuine creativity, epitomized by the arts, help survival? Isn't a great painting or poem biologically useless? In fact - if these result, as Freud suggests, from dreamy wish-fulfillment and fantasy - might they not be inefficient and maladaptive?

Storr rejects Freud's view. Artistic products may not themselves help survival but, like play, they arise from and are symptomatic of impulses that certainly do. First, art grows from realization, from our need to work out and then display our interpretations of experience. (Storr here approaches Chapter 6's existential territory.) It grows too from our need for

---

*Identical twins can surmount this difficulty. Having the same inheritance, their differences must reflect environmental influence. While intelligence has often been scrutinized in this way (6), comparable studies of creativity have not come to our attention.

abstraction (which is the beginning of wisdom), for putting those experiences into imaginary, symbolic form. Lastly, it reveals our desire to communicate our understandings to others; a great artist pinpoints otherwise overlooked realities. But from whence do these useful motives arise? Supposedly, from our lengthy, helpless dependency during infancy. Frustrated by our inability to understand or control our destiny, we want to explore and understand. So for Storr, as for Adler, childhood's insecurities fuel later achievements.

This analysis has several implications, the first being the sex difference. That noted geneticist G.B. Shaw, in his preface to Man and Superman, argues that we have gradually evolved a division of labor[11] because of its great efficiency. The ordinary man's job is to provide the economic wherewithal for nourishment, shelter, and the like; the ordinary woman's, to insure the race's procreation by marrying and having children (the so-called Life Force). Yet by convention's quirk, the male must initiate the serious business of sex (the female's bailiwick), while she passively awaits his enterprise. In Shaw's play the heroine, whose prospective mate is avoiding marriage because of some specious "higher calling," tires of waiting for him to realize first priorities and, abandoning pretence, openly pursues him:

> It is assumed that the woman must wait, motionless, until she is wooed. Nay, she often does wait motionless. That is how the spider waits for the fly. But the spider spins her web. And if the fly, like my hero, shows a strength that promises to extricate him, how swiftly does she abandon her pretence of passivity, and openly fling coil after coil[12] after him until he is secured forever.

Where is creativity implicated? According to Shaw, only the genius escapes the Life Force. He has been chosen, like Woman, for higher purpose, to raise our consciousness, so his priorities are as well defined and as ruthlessly pursued as hers. He is not, contra Freud, driven by sex but supersedes it:

> The genius will risk the stake and the cross, starve, when necessary, in a garret all his life, work his nerves into rage without payment, a sublime altruist in his disregard of himself, an atrocious egoist in his disregard of others.[13]

It follows, we surmise, that Woman has rarely created because of her other biologically ingrained, implacable aims, to which the ordinary man easily succumbs. But when she confronts Genius, irresistable force meets immovable object and the clash may be tragic. And when Woman <u>is</u> Genius, and both obsessions are combined in one individual:

> Then the game is one for the king of critics; your George Sand becomes a mother to gain experience for the novelist, and to develop her, gobbles up men of genius, e.g., Chopin, as mere hors d'oeuvres.[14]

A second implication. Our ubiquitous tendency to judge everything could also reflect an ingrained, adaptive trait. Do critics spring from mutations--perhaps genes exposed to excessive radiation? This tendency does seem more prevalent at evolution's more advanced levels; paramecia rarely become critics (although worms and parasites sometimes do). But how might such a tendency help survival? Like our seemingly ingrained tendencies to selectively attend (notice some events and ignore others) and to categorize (group similar stimuli into sets), it would simplify the potentially overwhelming bombardment of stimuli, the "blooming, buzzing confusion." As well, residents of primitive environments must judge stimuli quickly and accurately. Which can be ingested safely? Which are dangerous? Which provide safe domicile? Since some events <u>are</u> better and/or more important <u>biologically</u>, a species that chooses should prevail over one that treats every stimulus as equivalent.*

Yet judgment has its maladaptive aspects. Insensitive, premature criticism can, and has, overvalued the trivial, ignored the worthy, and destroyed germinal talents. In fact, our judgmental propensities may cause psychological disturbance. For humanists such as Maslow,[15] we have basic needs to assert ourselves creatively; their stifling because of fears of rejection or ridicule invites neurosis. We must also raise objection. If this evaluative tendency be biological, how do adherents of Hinduism, Zen Buddhism, and similar beliefs apparently learn to receive empirical experience with receptive neutrality? Perhaps, instead, we learn to judge through

---

*The choice of mates provides an intriguing puzzle. Lower orders may breed like rabbits, but the higher tend to be selective. Yet the criteria used to choose partners, notably physical beauty, often seem but tenuously related to survival. Do those strange institutions known as beauty pageants reflect evolutionary values?

socialization. Suggesting that paranoia may be Western culture's defining illness.

Environmental Views

Given that same Western culture's aforementioned optimism, environmental approaches have been decidedly more popular. The ubiquitous searchings for techniques to stimulate creativity[16] obviously assume that certain experiences can be helpful. So too does Arieti's listing of the characteristics of a <u>creativogenic culture</u>, i.e., one conducive to creativity.[17] Therein, education and training will be widely accessible, innovation valued, divergent views tolerated, and gifted persons encouraged to interact. That Jewish society promotes many such values may explain its far exceeding others in <u>per capita</u> eminent scientists, such as Nobel Prize winners. So too with epochs such as Periclean Greece and Elizabethan England, in which geniuses suddenly arose in multitude. Still, unlike doctrinaire environmentalists, Arieti recognizes paradox. Few cultures parade more creativogenic attributes than does the U.S.A., but dismal is its record for fostering eminence. Whereas German society, rigidly authoritarian, intolerant, and feudal, has sired Bachs, Goethes, and Schillers by the score. Arieti argues, therefore, that the individual-environment relation is actually two-way. Each affects the other. Put in the language of history's most enduring debate (conducted at length in <u>War and Peace</u>) great men both make great events and are made great by them. Be that as it may, we turn now to the environmental spectrum's colorful array.

Associationism
<u>   </u>

Associationism's central ideas have long been available, so we can introduce them through some early proponents (Boring[18] and Watson[19] provide elaboration). Aristotle seems to have pioneered two: 1) that elements of knowledge can be acquired through the senses, and 2) that our minds can connect or <u>associate</u> those elements, so that upon experiencing one, we will think of the other. For Aristotle, elements will become associated if they are <u>similar</u>, <u>contrary</u> (i.e., opposite), or frequently occur in <u>contiguity</u>, (i.e., together in space or time).

However, the empiricist/associationist philosophers of the 18th and 19th centuries, such as Locke, Berkeley, Hume, and the Mills (father and son) have been particularly influential.[20] Locke's landmark <u>Essay Concerning Human Understanding</u> - in which he sought the origin, certainty, and extent of human knowledge - contains most of the relevant hypotheses. Locke began with the <u>idea</u>, the unit or element of mental life. Supposedly, none are innate. At birth, mind is a <u>tabula rasa</u>, or blank sheet, on which sensation, the source of experience, enscribes knowledge as does a pen on paper or chalk on blackboard. But the Lockian mind is not completely passive. Individual ideas can be combined into complex ones, not only because of such external considerations as contiguity or similarity, but also through a second, more active mental process called reflection. Moreover, mind can perceive, analyze, and note the properties common to several simple ideas. In other words, reflection, too, can provide ideas. Yet these, in the last analysis, originate in sensation, so Locke might reasonably be accused of seeking the best of both the active and passive subject. But the latter seems more consistent with his extreme empiricism. If ideas are not innate, and mind has no more than sensation's provisions, how could it conduct activities like reflection, not provided by sensation?

But the important matter here concerns the handling of creativity. If mind merely collects experiences, how could it ever produce novelties not present in the environment? Wouldn't painters, like living cameras, merely spew forth reproductions of reality? Admittedly, this is part of artistry, as Hamlet advised the players:

> Suit the action to the word, the word to the action; with this special observance, that you o'erstep not the modesty of nature; for anything so overdone is from the purpose of playing, whose end, both at the first and now, was and is, to hold, as 'twere, the mirror up to nature; to show virtue her own feature, scorn her own image, and the very age and body of the time his form and pressure.(3.2)

But artists usually modify or interpret nature as well. The empiricist would agree that individual ideas, available to many minds, must lack novelty. But what of combinations of ideas, which bring several together as never before, as in a startingly original metaphor? Could not each old be together new? The empiricist thinks so. Thus, creativity becomes for him, as Koestler notes,[21] a reshuffling of experience; there is nothing really new under the sun.

In this context, then, mind's activity or passivity comes down to this. Can it influence the combinations that occur and select those that are preferable? If so, then it is creatively active. Thus, Bain proposed an ability for constructive association or imagination, which some empiricists like Gerard used as a deus ex machina for "explaining" our every mysterious capacity, such as wit and genius.[22] But if these questions are

309

answered negatively (as did James Mill), then worthwhile contiguities must occur accidentally. Creativity relies on random chance, and mind becomes like a machine seen at bingo games that flings variously labeled ping-pong balls about, to collide or separate at fate's whim. Swift's Gulliver's Travels mercilessly lampoons such a view:

> The first professor I saw was in a very large room, with forty pupils about him. After salutation, observing me to look earnestly upon a frame, which took up the greatest part of both the length and breadth of the room, he said perhaps I might wonder to see him employed in a project for improving speculative knowledge by practical and mechanical operations...It was twenty foot square, placed in the middle of the room. The superficies was composed of several bits of wood, about the bigness of a die, but some larger than others. They were all linked together by slender wires. These bits of wood were covered on every square with paper pasted on them, and on these papers were written all the words of their language, in their several moods, tenses, and declensions, but without any order. The professor then desired me to observe, for he was going to set his engine at work. The pupils at his command took each of them hold of an iron handle, whereof there were forty fixed round the edges of the frame, and giving them a sudden turn, the whole disposition of the words was entirely changed. He then commanded six and thirty of the lads to read the several lines softly as they appeared upon the frame; and where they found three or four words together that might make part of a sentence, they dictated to the four remaining boys who were scribes...The professor showed me several volumes in large folio already collected, of broken sentences, which he intended to piece together, and out of those rich materials to give the world a complete body of all arts and sciences...I made my humblest acknowledgement to this illustrious person for his great communicativeness, and promised if ever I had the good fortune to return to my native country, that I would do

him justice, as the sole inventor of this wonderful machine.[23]

1. <u>S-R psychology: John B. Watson</u>. Associationism's most visible modern representatives have emphasized connections between environmental stimuli (S) and responses (R). Supposedly, our every act is induced by a stimulus we experience and, apart from a few inborn reflexes such as blinks to air puffs on eyelids and knee jerks to hammers, these connections are learned. Such theorists might argue among themselves about the conditions necessary for learning, but they agreed that S-R associations, occurring in sequence, comprised every behavior, regardless of its complexity. The S-R unit was behavior's fundamental elemental unit. At least in early versions, moreover, the subjects clearly remain passive, their associations dependent on environmental events such as contiguity, frequency of repetition, and the like, and their responses on the stimuli striking their sensory receptors. Like a coffee machine, their spewings out depend entirely on the puttings in.

Pavlov's famous <u>classicial conditioning</u>[24] provides the prototype of S-R acquisition, even its <u>reductio ad absurdum</u>. Ingredients. One <u>unconditioned stimulus</u> (such as food in a dog's mouth) that automatically elicits a reflex <u>unconditioned response</u> (such as salivation). One <u>conditioned stimulus</u> (such as a tone) that does <u>not</u> initially induce that response. Present the two stimuli together in contiguity. Repeat. Eventually, the conditioned stimulus will now elicit a facsimile of the unconditioned response. A new S-R association has been acquired.

<u>Instrumental</u> (or <u>operant</u>) <u>conditioning</u> provides another procedure for chiselling in these associations. We must first describe a fundamental principle, that of <u>reinforcement</u>. Sidestepping endless controversy, we define it empirically as any event whose presence increases a response tendency and whose removal causes the disappearance, or <u>extinction</u>, of that response. Thus psychology's Everyman, the rat, will learn to press a lever or run through a maze if it consequently receives food; if food no longer forthcomes, it will desist. Similarly, capitalists will invest money to obtain profits, and laborers will work for pay checks. Such rewards, or <u>positive reinforcers</u>, which we acquire behaviors to obtain, are the most obvious but not the only variety. Rats will also learn to jump hurdles to avoid electric shock, and children will reluctantly solve the mysteries of table manners to escape scoldings. Such unpleasant or <u>negative reinforcers</u> also fit our definition, since a behavior is again acquired, this time if it eliminates the reinforcer.

But how do organisms discover the response that produces reinforcement? Supposedly through trial and error, by randomly emitting various possibilities until one "works." Initially, then, their behavior will be unpredictable, but as they learn the appropriate alternative and strengthen its association to the stimulus situation, it becomes more probable. Thus, in instrumental tasks, agents who deliver the reinforcers, such as experimenters and parents, cannot do so until the desired response is forthcoming. So they are, in a real sense, at the subject's mercy, helpless when he or she is unwilling or unable to perform.

Over creativity, S-R theorists dallied but little. For one thing, it implies that stimulus conditions might not always totally dictate responses. As well, such theorists were invariably fanatic Darwinians who believed that animals would also display any human behaviors worth notice. Consequently, they spent their lives watching rats run, jump, and even, on occasion, swim. (Amazingly, these competitors rarely had to hurl javelins or put the shot to receive their sustenance.) Now rats have not practiced the arts or sciences with notable vigor. Ergo, creativity doesn't exist.

But above all, S-Rists neglected our topic because of their obsessive commitment to science. To earn this awesome mantle, a discipline must study empirical, measurable events. For this reason, Watson's behaviorism[25] held that psychology should concern itself with the actions of organisms (which qualify) rather than the mind's inner workings (which apparently do not), a revolutionary change in nothing less than the discipline's subject matter that was nevertheless quickly accepted hereabouts. But what of mentalistic mysticisms such as thought or emotion? Watson's famous description of thinking, as mere subvocal speech, implies the answer. They were usually classed (not without some justification) as simply special behaviors, albeit particularly difficult to measure. Being similar in kind to the overt variety, they could be conveniently ignored. Eventually, science's miraculous technological leaps would surmount the problem of their measurement. Creativity suffered a similar fate. For Watson, it was nothing more than a special instance of instrumental learning:

> How the 'new' comes into being: ...How do we ever get new verbal creations such as a poem or brilliant essay? The answer is that we get them by manipulating words, shifting them about until a new pattern is hit upon...The elements are old, that is, the words that present themselves are just our standard vocabulary--it is only the arrangement that is different...Why can't those of us, who are not literary, write a

poem or an essay?...The answer is, it is not
our trade, we do not deal in words, our word
manipulation is poor...How does Patou build
a new gown? Has he a 'picture in his mind'
of what the gown is to look like when it is
finished? He has not...He calls his model
in, picks up a new piece of silk, throws it
around her; he pulls it in here, he pulls it
out there, makes it tight or loose at the
waist, high or low, he makes the skirt short
or long. He manipulates the material until
it takes on the semblance of a dress. <u>He
has to react to it as a new creation before
manipulation stops</u>...His emotional reactions
are aroused one way or another by the
finished product. He may rip it off and
start over again. On the other hand, he may
smile and say 'Voila, parfait!'...Not until
the new creation aroused admiration and
commendation, both his own (an emotional
reaction either verbalized or unverbalized)
and others', would manipulation be complete.

The painter plies his trade in the same
way, nor can the poet boast of any other
method.[26]

This passage implies other analyses to follow, i.e., the
associationist's reshuffling, and also Skinner, so we shall delay
comment until later.

2. <u>S-R psychology: Clark Hull</u>. This most ambitious of S-R
approaches[27] was the most influential of the learning theories
that bestrode yesterday's psychology like colossi of Rhodes. It
presents its principles as formal postulates, using equations,
parameters, and other paraphernalia of the devout mathematician
posing as psychologist. Consequently, Hull makes foreboding
reading for those who have seizures at the mere glimpse of an
equation. Since he pays creativity no heed whatever (words like
"originality" or "innovation" do not soil his indexes), much is
irrelevant here. Still, we shall pursue a few concepts that can
be developed in our direction (although simplifying them
somewhat, while hopefully retaining their essential spirit).

We begin with the equation $sEr = sHr \times D$. sEr, <u>reaction
potential</u>, measures the tendency to produce a particular response
R to a stimulus S. sHr, <u>habit strength</u>, represents the strength
of S and R's association to one another; sHr increases whenever R
occurs in contiguity with S, and is reinforced. D, or <u>drive</u>, the
organism's overall level of motivation, increases with
deprivation of various needs, such as hunger and thirst. (Note

313

especially that sHr and D combine <u>multiplicatively</u> to determine sEr.)

Hull's views of drive and of reinforcement need brief elaboration. He did not regard various drives, such as hunger or thirst, as separate or distinct. Instead, "drive" is a general state of arousal or activation, a pool to which these various <u>sources of drive</u> contribute. We often describe "intelligence" or "personality" as nonspecific attributes, operative in many situations. Similarly, this overall level of drive supposedly energizes every behavior. And what distinguishes those events that function as reinforcers to encourage behaviors? For Hull, they invariably reduce drive[28], restoring a state of homeostasis or physiological equilibrium. (Here, Hull's Darwinian colors show. Only behaviors that help survival by satisfying needs will be encouraged.)

Experimental evidence but weakly supports the drive reduction postulate.[29] In particular, many activities (including creativity) seem to <u>increase</u> drive by inducing frustration, euphoria, or anxiety. Yet the mountain climber, the golfer, and the poet compulsively persist. Still, Hull's views on motivation have interesting application.

We must first introduce the <u>habit-family hierarchy</u>. Presumably, several alternative responses can be associated to one stimulus. A rat in a maze can turn either left or right, run in circles or straight ahead, and crash, kamikaze-like, into a barrier. Similarly, a word like "table" may remind us of "chair," "furniture," "food," or "log." But these responses are mutually exclusive; only one can be produced at a time. Such competing responses can then form a hierarchy, ranked in order of their habit strengths. The <u>dominant</u> response, that most strongly associated to S, is most probable in its presence (most of us will respond "chair" to "table") but is by no means certain. However, it becomes more likely as the <u>absolute difference</u> in sEr increases between it and its weaker alternatives. When this difference is zero, various responses become equally probable.

The effects of an increase in D (motivation) provides the interesting implication. A simple example will help exposition. Consider a situation allowing two responses, R1 and R2. Let us assign arbitrary values of sHr to each, R1's being 4 and R2's being 2; the first, possessing more habit strength, is dominant. Now note the reaction potentials when D is low or high--say equal to 2 and 4, respectively--and we plug these values into Hull's equation:

Low D (D = 2)   High D (D = 4)
sEr = sHr X D   sEr = sHr X D
sErl = 4 X 2 = 8   sErl = 4 X 4 = 16
sEr2 = 2 X 2 = 4   sEr2 = 2 X 4 = 8

difference in sEr = 8 - 4 = 4   difference in sEr = 16 - 8 = 8

Thus, as D increases, the difference in sErs in the hierarchy, and in turn the dominance of the strongest response, <u>must</u> increase. But will more motivated individuals necessarily perform more efficiently? Hull answers, "It depends." When the dominant response is correct in the situation, higher D will

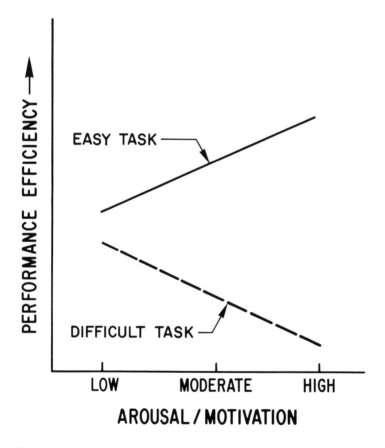

FIGURE 12.1   The Yerkes-Dodson Law.

315

help, but when it is incorrect, and a weaker alternative desirable, D will worsen performance because that incorrect tendency will persist. The Yerkes-Dodson law,[30] that the optimum level of motivation decreases with greater task difficulty, makes the same point. It follows that high motivation will help an easy task but hinder a difficult one (see Figure 12.1). Now surely a task is "easy" because the correct response is dominant and obvious. But a difficult task requires a weaker, less obvious alternative.

These predictions do contradict some dearly held Puritan suppositions about the virtues of hard work. "The harder you try, the better you do." "You've got to want it enough." To say nothing of that beloved by victorious coaches, "The guys were 'up' for this one" (an innuendo with which Freud could have had a field day.) In fact, Hull maintains, sometimes the harder we try, the worse we do. Moreover, a variety of anecdotal evidence (see Chapter 3) as well as experiments in both simple learning[31] and problem solving[32] verify his accuracy. Excessive motivation leads to inflexibility, to the ignoring of alternatives, which can be disastrous.

Hull sought a theory not of rat-in-maze learning but of learning. His postulates, he believed, should hold in any and all situations. In vindication, while he himself ignored cognition, Maltzman[33] has applied the habit-family concept to thinking and problem solving, and Mednick[34] to creativity (see below). We too shall extend its boundaries. First, recall the stage of incubation/frustration, when interfering responses cause blocking. The more we struggle, the more hidden is the forest by its trees. Let us assume (as seems reasonable) that dominant responses will be conventional, and weaker, less obvious alternatives more original. Inspirational pay dirt, then, would require access to the latter. But, according to Hull, the harder we try the less likely this becomes. Given that we have exposed ourselves to the S situation, "ahas" should strike when D, or arousal, is low, when we are dozing or running on automatic pilot, e.g., while bathing or climbing on a bus. Which is precisely what many anecdotes report.

Second, Neil Miller, a Hull adherent, has helpfully analyzed conflict,[35] which occurs when we must choose between two mutually exclusive responses. In the approach-avoidance variety, one goal has both attractive and negative features (marriage, perhaps, providing the definitive example). Approaching it obtains both; avoiding it, neither. Now supposedly both tendencies increase closer to the goal (see Figure 12.2) but (the key assertion) avoidance, having a steeper gradient, increases more rapidly. (Brown[36] verified these principles empirically by attaching rats to a harness and measuring the strength with which these galley

316

slaves pulled either towards food or away from electric shock, at varying proximities.) At a distance the dominant tendency is probably to approach and we move closer, but inevitably we reach a point of equality where conflict ensues. Beyond it, avoidance now dominates. We retreat to the conflict point, and past. And so on. Ad infinitum.

Does this not accurately describe the emotions of brides and grooms as nuptial bliss draws ever nigh? And more to the point, does not creativity, too, offer such mixed blessings of satisfaction, honor, fame, and the love of women, weighted against frustration, nights uninterrupted by sleep, and days discoloured by society's scorn and/or apathy? Thus, as positive aspects initially prevail, creators should set eagerly to work.

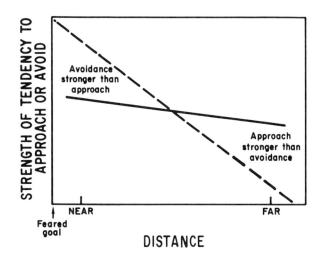

FIGURE 12.2   Approach-avoidance conflict.   Where the approach gradient is stronger, the organism advances toward the goal; where the avoidance gradient is stronger, it retreats (Adapted from N. E. Miller, "Experimental Studies in Conflict." In J. McV. Hunt (Ed.), Personality and Behavior Disorders. Copyright 1944, The Ronald Press Company. Used with permission of John Wiley & Sons.)

But as negatives loom larger, conflict begins. Those creators desist. But later, removed from the goal once more, they begin again. And again. And again. Hence the plethora of sonatas, novels, and theories of the cosmos that lie unconsummated in countless bottom drawers.

3. <u>Commentary</u>. The idea that creative thought might reshuffle existing elements into novel combinations seems widely accepted. Witness the frequency with which Poincaré's similar description is approvingly cited.[37] Furthermore, many of Part I's data are hereby encompassed. Mental flexibility, naivete, and youth should all help achieve novel combinations, as would a personality of paradox. And of course this view describes that seminal experience, inspiration, with notable validity. Often, it seems, we realize, not a new idea, but a new relationship between several familiar ones, which suddenly click together with the smooth inevitability of a space docking.

Furthermore, a solution is implied for at least one overlooked conundrum. Why are we driven to form such novel combinations at all? It is preeminently human to group events that are similar to one another into categories or sets - such as sports, flowers, violins, and lawn mowers - and then to respond identically to all members. Presumably this tendency simplifies that multitudinous sensory input, that blooming, buzzing confusion[38] of stimuli that would otherwise, as Bruner points out, quite overwhelm us. Were we to treat each stimulus as unique, as never-seen-before-or-again, we would not know how to respond to it. Thus, to seek similarities and combinations, including novel ones, has survival value, and this tendency may well be "built in."[*]

But enough of compliments, for associational accounts face a host of problems. Admittedly, some reflect mere negligence, since such accounts have typically been sketchy. Why might someone choose a certain style of expression or field or endeavor? Hull informs us how motivation might affect insight, but why are creators' levels so remarkably, persistently high? We gain apt description of frustration and inspiration, but what of creativity's other stages, notably verification? And of course the various reliable experiences, such as of mediumhood, receive short shrift, since such subjectivities are anathema to rabid behaviorists. These oversights may eventually be corrected, but other problems seem beyond help, at least when the creator is depicted as passive, a grateful slave to random, accidental combinations. We defer detailed discussion of these

---

[*]However this helpful sword is two-edged. Sometimes we overgeneralize, ignoring important differences among stimuli, as when we utter sweeping statements about all members of a minority group. Such stereotyping sows the seeds of prejudice.

318

difficulties, since they also afflict Skinner, who follows momentarily. We merely note Arnheim's succinct critique:

> The mere shuffling and reconnecting of items of experience leads...to nothing more than a clever game <u>unless it is</u> <u>steered by an</u> <u>underlying vision of what is to be attained</u> (italics mine).[39]

How and why, if necessary environmental elements are available to all, do some persons achieve and recognize fortuitous combinations more frequently? In other words, what distinguishes a Beethoven?

We will later enlarge also on objections raised by Kant and the Gestalt psychologists, but in essence they deny that creators merely internalize, then reproduce or reshuffle sensory phenomena. Creators' products are editorial statements, <u>interpretations</u>, of experience, which their unique vision modifies and supplements. According to Gestalt's motto, "The whole is greater than (or different from) the sum of its parts".

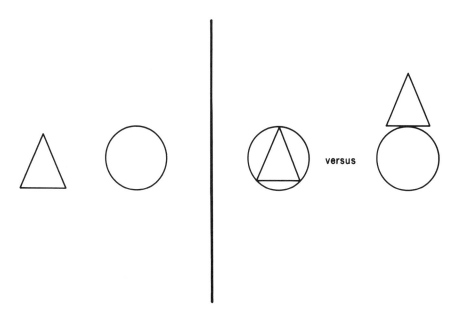

FIGURE 12.3   Two relations between the same elements.

319

Similarly, creators integrate rather than summate their components; these blend together, losing their distinctive properties in deference to the whole. A Bach fugue's component sounds may each exist in nature; the complete entity does not. Apparently there are new things under the sun.

And one criticism from this quarter does deserve present discussion. Associationism implies that all connections among elements are of one kind, i.e., that an association is an association is an association. Asch[40] retorts that elements can combine in many ways, of which association is only one, and that these various relations may possess quite variant properties. Consider the two elements in Figure 12.3's left panel. On the right are two relationships between them that obviously induce different impressions. The components seem more integrated in the one, separate in the other (as they would in association). Asch's point also applies to creative ideas. When Darwin combined the ancient concepts of evolution and natural selection,[41] each retained its distinct properties in his theoretical edifice. But in inspirations such as Einstein's, a metaphor may not be involved in, but simply provide a way of getting to a theoretical idea with which it combines. Alternatively, when an artist realizes how to say what she or he wishes to say, form and content may be entwined so inextricably that the two truly do become one.

The associationist's scenario[42] also seems simplistic in another sense. Gruber has shown that even in apparently supportive cases like Darwin, the component ideas do not suddenly collide by chance, thereafter to cling together like oppositely charged particles. Inspiration is not one but a series of "clicks." Components come and go, wax and wane continuously. So creative work is not a random thrashing around but a purposive, persistent striding towards a goal now dim, now crystal clear. Finally, Holton[43] rightly points out that associationism completely misrepresents many scientific, philosophical, and mathematical inspirations that are more analytic than synthetic. They do not combine, they take apart.

Radicial Behaviorism: B.F. Skinner

This most controversial, probably most visible figure in contemporary psychology (who else has achieved that pinnacle of renown, the cover of Time?) has, unlike other behaviorists, paid creativity repeated attention.[44] We will in due course debate whether his anglings for explanation have landed trophies or old boots. But first, some fundamentals.

1. Basic principles. On the face of it, Skinner describes not a theory (these he has deplored as pointless[45]) but a set of

320

techniques to teach behaviors efficiently. These techniques have long been familiar to those in the instructional business, such as animal trainers and parents. So Skinner's main contribution, as he readily admits, is to elucidate their underlying principles and important variables. A behavior, to be acquired, must be reinforced; otherwise, nothing is learned. In this sense, everyone is selfish, knowing on which side their food pellets are buttered. We will not perform without some reason. But as we have seen, for reinforcement to be effective, the subject must first respond appropriately. Can we help bring this about? We can. First, we can design the environment, so that therein the desired behavior, rather than other competing possibilities, becomes most probable. Consider the famous/notorious Skinner box, that supposed exemplar supreme of acquisitional situations. It is nothing more than an empty cage, barren but for a lever that must be pressed, or a disc that must be pecked for reinforcement. But note its peculiar genius. One can do precious little in such a situation except press or peck. So sooner or later, one will probably do so, allowing that response to be reinforced and its probability increased. But in more complex situations, wherein many responses are possible, that desired response, and hence success, becomes less likely.

Second, we can resort to shaping, or successive approximations. If an improbable behavior is desired, we need not wait eons for the subject to get around to emitting it. Initially, we reinforce any response that remotely resembles it. Given reinforcement's power, that first approximation will soon prevail. Next, we restrict reinforcement to an act somewhat closer to the end desired. That acquired, we now demand one still more proximate. And so on. In short, we work our subject up through a series of steps to the final goal. An example may clarify. Suppose we wish (for whatever reason) to teach a pigeon, that exterior decorator extraordinaire, to stand on its head, something it will not, of its own volition, frequently do. Now shaping cannot instill responses that exceed physical limitations (humans cannot thereby learn to fly unaided), but let us assume that ornithological anatomy does not preclude such gymnastics. We first reward any minuscule lowering of the head. Then demand that it be lowered further, and then that it contact the floor. Eventually, a pigeon ready to storm Hollywood. Similarly, pigeons have learned to play cards and peck out tunes on pianos.[46]

A third principle. Minimize delay of reinforcement (the time between a correct response and resultant reinforcement). Even short delays destroy efficiency (perhaps because the subject will be otherwise engaged when reinforcement arrives, causing that alternate behavior, rather than the one desired, to become dominant). If these principles are followed, Skinner

321

neverendingly asserts, learning should be _easy_. When it isn't, it is never the subject's fault. It is not "stupidity" or "laziness" or whatever, but inefficiences in the environment - in design, shaping, and the like - that are invariably to blame.

Reinforcement schedules present another important principle. Sometimes, both laboratory and reality provide _partial reinforcement_, in which not every correct response but only some of them are reinforced; gambling and fishing are exemplary. Various patterns or schedules of reinforced and nonreinforced instances can then be designed* that will differentially affect behavior.[47] But the highly reliable _partial reinforcement effect_ is here most relevant. Behaviors acquired under partial as opposed to continuous reinforcement are more persistent and difficult to extinguish. This effect has many explanations.[48] Perhaps subjects simply learn that "If at first you don't succeed, try, try again."

Now these basic principles supposedly apply to animals of every variety, including ourselves. Lever-pressing rats and disc-pecking pigeons analogize our every act. Skinner denies any important differences between animals and humans, or between controlled, artificial laboratories (wherein these principles have been demonstrated) and the "real world":

> It is often asserted...that there are fundamental differences between the real world and the laboratory in which behavior is analyzed...(but) the difference...is not a serious one.[49]

This allegation may not allay our doubts, but that Skinner's principles have been applied successfully to many fields does suggest their appreciable validity. Behavior modification techniques,[50] such as the token economies rampant in institutions both penal and psychiatric, can help alleviate disturbed or deviant behaviors by reinforcing more desirable alternatives. The classroom has provided a particularly inviting target for Skinner's missionary zeal.[51] Our current educational malpractices quite ignore the aforementioned principles and so to him border on the criminal. Their gross inefficiency destroys

---

*A _fixed-ratio schedule_, for example, delivers reinforcement with predictable regularity, e.g., every third correct response in a 1/3 schedule, whereas a _varied-ratio schedule_ reinforces an average proportion, such as 1/3, but whether any particular response will be reinforced cannot be predicted.

children's intrinsic desire to learn, so they soon regard school as involuntary penal servitude. Only with wholesale mechanization of instruction via teaching machines can preferable procedures be implemented on a mass scale. Now this may seem like automatized depersonalization of the ancient and honorable teaching profession, but many otherwise reluctant youngsters do respond enthusiastically.

Notwithstanding Skinner's antitheoretical pose, beneath these simple principles lurk some assumptions about human nature, which he has made explicit in Beyond Freedom and Dignity[52] and About Behaviorism.[53] First of all, let us applaud his genuine concern for our welfare and happiness. Worlds removed from the detached, amoral scientist, he is clearly saddened and frustrated that we pursue these commodities so inefficiently. For Skinner, our foreboding problems--warfare, nuclear proliferation, pollution, and the like--invariably reduce to the idiocies of human behavior, making its understanding and control nothing less than matters of survival. Unfortunately we insistently cling to an incorrect view of ourselves, called autonomous man, that hampers progress. Autonomous man possesses two basic properties: freedom (unencumbered, one can choose and is therefore responsible for one's actions) and dignity (one gains credit for one's achievements, since they seem so inexplicable).

Having long been taught that freedom and dignity are desirable, we are reluctant to relinquish this illusory view, but Skinner, that compulsive zealot, has persistently tried to convince us.[*] Control, not autonomy, is our actual situation, like it or not. Our biological and environmental histories determine our every act. Moreover, both antecedents follow the same principle of selection by environment; desirable characteristics/behaviors are encouraged and flourish, while others disappear. That being our situation, let us perforce design a culture that will reinforce survival-oriented behaviors at the expense of undesirables. (Skinner's Utopian novel, Walden II,[54] describes such a culture.)

"But," interjects the sceptic, "don't inner psychological processes, such as thought, feelings, and the like, also affect our acts?" Contrary to wide misconception, Skinner does not deny

[*]Ironically, in this enterprise he has ignored his own principles. His countless articles, books, and lectures, relentlessly belaboring the same themes, from his standpoint would seem hopelessly inefficient techniques for changing our attitudes and practices.

the existence of such mentalisms; he admits that they are often produced by reinforcement as by-products and so may well accompany learned behavior. What he denies is what we too often conclude, that they have therefore caused the behavior. In actuality, reinforcement induces both mental states and behavior. An example. I may assert that "I don't go out at night because it makes me feel anxious," erroneously attributing an act (staying home) to a feeling (anxiety). In fact, negative reinforcers delivered by my previous nocturnal ventures have elicited both. As much as anything, therefore, Skinner seeks to change our language usage, so we blame actual rather than apparent causes for our acts (since Skinnerian language is woefully lacking in style, precision, it would seem, is more to be desired than elegance).

However, the most vociferous objections to Skinner concern possible abuses of power. Any learning task requires an "experimenter," who decides the behaviors to be encouraged and delivers the reinforcers when they occur. Who will occupy this awesome position in Skinner's designed culture? On what basis will he/she/it choose the preferable behaviors? Won't this "great experimenter" be able to exploit us, to sacrifice our personal freedom to the gods of social conformity and blind obedience, as did so many of history's philosopher kings and enlightened despots? They too supposedly knew what was best for everyone and so were allowed to rule with iron hands and disastrous results. Might we gain, not Utopian bliss, but empty hedonism, even misery, as novels such as 1984, Brave New World, and A Clockwork Orange so poignantly warn?

The reinforcement situation's very nature, answers Skinner, provides our protection. A revealing cartoon has one Skinner-boxed rat observing to another, "Have I got this guy shaped. Whenever he gives me food, I press the bar." The point? That delivering reinforcement to someone else is also an emitted behavior. Therefore, like any other, it can be encouraged or extinguished via reinforcement. Which changes the learning procedure from a one-way street, wherein the experimenter gives and the subject receives, to one in which each both gives and receives reinforcement to/from the other. Or as Skinner puts it, reinforcement is reciprocal. Consider the cartoon again. From the experimenter's perspective, bar pressing is the behavior to be encouraged and feeding the subject is the resultant reinforcement. But from the rat's perspective, the analysis is reversed. The behavior it desires from the experimenter is delivering food, so it presses the bar (since that seems to reinforce the experimenter). In fact, designating one participant as "experimenter" and the other as "subject" now seems decidedly arbitrary.

324

But how does this reciprocity prevent Skinner's "great experimenter" from exploiting us? He too must receive from us, his loyal subjects, reinforcement for his acts. If he abuses his position, encouraging behaviors we dislike and shaping a repellent culture, we can withhold <u>his</u> food pellets and extinguish these tendencies. Control being symmetrical, rulers and ruled can journey together, hand in hand (or paw in paw) towards Utopia. Or is it Oceania?

2. <u>Creativity</u>. At least as a causal personality trait, Skinner denies our topic's importance; it is merely another of autonomous man's trappings:

> We gain nothing in asserting that (someone) behaves creatively because he possesses something called creativity.[55]

We should focus instead on creative <u>behavior</u>, which is controlled like any other by reinforcement contingencies. But wouldn't society more often encourage conventional activities, given its suspicion of originality? Skinner's answer is both simple and provocative. Evolutionary analyses propose that by chance, novel biological mutants periodically appear, and the environment then selects those that are desirable. Similarly an organism, during trial-and-error searchings for reinforcement, may emit unusual responses, or <u>behavioral mutations</u>; for example, a rat might press the bar with its tail, or crawl through a maze breaststroke fashion. But again, the environment will encourage such responses, if they are desirable, with reinforcement. In short, "Creative thinking is largely concerned with the production of 'mutations'.[56]

The author of such happy accidents is no more responsible for them and deserves no more credit than biological mutants for their strange characteristics. He or she needs mysterious, special talents no more than do mothers who bear children or hens that lay eggs.[57] Feelings of inspiration, responsibility, frustration, and the like may accompany the final results but play no causal role whatever. Darwin demystified creation in the natural world by substituting the book of evolution for that of Genesis. Skinner (to his own satisfaction at least) has done likewise for the human variety:

> The autonomous is the uncaused, and the uncaused is the miraculous, and the miraculous is God. For the second time in a little more than a century a theory of selection by consequences is threatening a traditional belief in a creative mind.[58]

325

Now if creativity be mere behaviors, presumably they can be[59] shaped and encouraged like others, via Skinner's technologies. We cannot teach someone to produce <u>particular</u> such mutants (for they would not then be original), but we can certainly design environments and teaching machines that reward mutations and discourage conventionalities. These machinations should also encourage sheer quantity of responses, since creative mutants would thereby become more probable. We could even shape subjects to design their own environments, such as puzzles or problems, wherein they could then seek and be reinforced for creative responses. None of this denies each person's uniqueness or individuality--in fact these are assumed. But they are attributed to one's biological and environmental history rather than to an internal "self."

3. <u>The avant-garde</u>. Before criticizing Skinner's arguments, let us examine visual artist Marcel Duchamp,[60] composer John Cage, choreographer Merce Cunningham, et al., whose practices strikingly support them. Consider Duchamp's <u>readymades</u>. Everyday objects such as snow shovels and toilet seats were designated as "art" merely by his signing and placing them in a gallery. Or Cage's <u>Imaginary Landscape Number 4</u>. Each of twelve radios had two performers, one diddling the station selector however he wished, the other the volume and tone controls[61]* acting, as Cage put it, "like fishermen, catching sounds." Consider too Cunningham's <u>How to Pass, Kick, Fall and Run</u>, which features familiar movements like walking, running, and skipping, "accompanied" by Cage reading stories from stage right while sipping champagne.

These varied, nefarious practices disguise some shared beliefs that depart severely from orthodoxy. Artists should not interpret experienced reality for the rest of us. Nor should they impose their own biases, or express emotions or universal truths. They should never suggest or even imply underlying thematic messages, which are rejected outright. Hence Cunningham: "I don't work through images or ideas, and I don't[63] want a dancer <u>ever</u> to think that a movement <u>means</u> something". No, art is much less interesting, it is believed, than real life, so artists should simply point out its fascinations. Thus when a toilet seat languishes in a gallery, we contemplate its unique wonders that ordinarily we take for granted. Similarly, during

---

*At the premiere, late at night after most stations had left the air, the fishermen's acoustic nets caught mainly a conglomeration of static. Hence it was, in[62] Cage's modest understatment, "certainly not a rabble-rouser."

Cage's 4' 33" (in which the "pianist" merely sits before his keyboard for that length of time without playing a note*), we notice everyday sounds emanating from traffic, air conditioners, and rumbling stomachs.

In other words, these heretics invite the audience (shades of Sartre) to participate actively by interpreting a work however it please, with every impression being equally valid. Ironically, that audience will frequently respond to the challenge with distaste, hostility, catcalls, and walkings out.[64] Nor are professionals more receptive. The New York Philharmonic musicians openly made fun of a Cageism while performing it, hissed him when he took his bow, and in general acted like the worst of reactionary know-nothings.[65] Why these reactions? "It isn't art! Anyone could do it!" is one common complaint. A Cage would likely reply, "So what?" But this does reveal our resilient belief that artists should be "special," able to do what most of us cannot and therefore deserving of our admiration. Enraged Ticketholder may also object that it is all a joke, a put-on. To which Carolyn Brown, Cunningham's peerless former leading dancer, provides telling rebuttal:

> Do you really believe that a man would spend
> his whole life, working this hard, even
> going into debt, merely to pull your leg?[66]

The abdication of artistic authority also decrees that methods of chance, or indeterminancy, will frequently be used to make artistic decisions. Thus, the I Ching may determine the notes of a Cage composition, and coin flips the movement sequences in a Cunningham dance. (Contrary to popular belief, however, his dancers do not "make it up as they go along." Such spontaneous improvisation would risk collisions and serious injuries, so movements are carefully rehearsed.[67]) Such methods minimize the artist's role by preventing his/her preferences from exerting an influence.

The vagaries of chance also determine those events from music and dance which will coincide. Traditional choreographers invariably select their music beforehand, then design movement to in some sense express it. But Cage and Cunningham will typically agree on a dance's length, then work independently. The dancers

---

*The dance equivalent. In 1957, Paul Taylor stood on stage in everyday apparel, making only minuscule, perfunctory movements. Fittingly, The Dance Observor's review consisted of a quarter column of blank space.

learn to produce the various movement passages in set amounts of time (itself an amazing accomplishment--try simply walking across a room in _exactly_ 12 seconds) but do not hear their "music" until opening night (and given Cage's penchant for the acoustically unexpected, their introduction may be jarring).[68] This practice also lessens music's usually excessive influence over dance, which both collaborators dislike.

And now to our point. Surely such practices personify Skinner's portrait of the artist as a producer of behavioral mutations whose products grow not from "talent" but from the whims of chance, or trial and error. The environment suggests but also restricts the possible alternatives that he might emit and then, through its applause or derision, selects those that have worked. As he would doubtless agree, a Cage is no more responsible and deserves no more credit for his achievements than does the hen who accidentally lays a golden egg.

4. _The sex difference_. Some circles[69] unquestioningly assume that this phenomenon demands environmental explanation and that it will diminish if and only if environments become more encouraging to women. Certainly, differential child rearing practices have (to use Skinnerian language) reinforced feminine politeness, passivity, conformity, and selflessness, along with wifely/motherly social roles, while ruthlessly extinguishing any hint of independence or originality. As Germaine Greer puts it:

> There is then no female Leonardo, no female Titian, no female Poussin, but the reason does not lie in the fact that women have wombs, that they can have babies, that their brains are smaller, that they lack vigour, that they are not sensual. The reason is simply that you cannot make great artists out of egos that have been damaged, with wills that are defective, with libidos that have been driven out of reach and energy diverted into neurotic channels.[70]

In view of their ubiquity, then, such explanations deserve separate scrutiny. In this enterprise, we will lean heavily on comments by several noted women. Virginia Woolf's _A Room of One's Own_[71] muses on the fate of Judith, a hypothetical sister of Shakespeare as gifted as he. Germaine Greer's epic _The Obstacle Race_[72] discusses the lives and works of female oil painters, as well as the formidable barriers they have faced. She does find a few Artemisia Gentileschis, who overcame the odds to attain genuine greatness but they are far between. Lastly, Agnes de Mille's _And Promenade Home_,[73] wittily discusses similar

328

difficulties, as well as reasons for the marked feminine successes in choreography.*

As we note those formidable obstacles, it is not women's comparative creative infertility but their considerable achievements that seem amazing. First, confined to unstimulating domestic environments, they have historically lacked access to education/training and therefore the elements for associational reshuffling. Typically, Woolf's Judith, unlike brother Will, was sent not to school but to the kitchen to mend stockings. Indicatively, those fields such as science, mathematics, and music in which women's success is especially rare, are also fields in which formal training is most crucial. Oil painting is another such field, and women have long been barred from the two main roads to technical proficiency, the academies and professional apprenticeship. Similarly, de Mille notes that women were denied the most powerful patron of all, the Church, allowed neither to officiate in, compose music for, or perform in, a service nor build or design churches. For which de Mille blames Christianity's historic suspicion of women. Look at Eve's presumed role in the Fall! Look at their intimate involvement with procreation! Which requires sex. Which is sinful. Even recently, the notorious double standard decreed that, while men could draw female nudes in life drawing classes, women would be barred from these important training devices.[75] Presumably their overly sensitive <u>psyches</u> might cause them to faint at merest glimpse of genitalia and spill all the paint!

For Greer, that seeming benefice, <u>love</u>, provided a second deterrent. Women, taught to emphasize relationships and others before self, have often lacked the ruthlessness needed to actualize their potential. Instead, they either sacrificed it to support a sometimes lesser lover or relative, or chose to labor in his shadow and imitate him. Indicatively, such women as did paint almost invariably had a male painter as close relative. Not only did they alone have access to training but also, Greer suggests, they frequently painted <u>for the wrong reasons</u>, for love

---

*De Mille's choreography for <u>Oklahoma</u>, <u>Carousel</u>, and <u>Brigadoon</u> revolutionized American musical theatre, demonstrating that dance could do more than titillate fantasies and provide rest for the singers. It could advance both plot and overall aesthetic experience. Her ballets, notably <u>Rodeo</u>, made such indigenies as tap, soft shoe, and hoedown legitimate theatrical forms. Her descriptions of her early problems, chronicled also in <u>Dance to the Piper</u>,[74] are both moving and hilarious.

of family rather than of art, to please not themselves but others. Which may explain their frequent mediocrity, since such motives do not usually herald genius. Goya's natural daughter, Maria del Rosario, provides an almost textbook example. Trained from infancy, she became a remarkable child prodigy, but her style was invariably Goyaesque, never original. Appropriately, she eventually became an art counterfeiter.

Woolf's room of one's own, or lack thereof, provided another obstacle, since both privacy and opportunity for independent thought were thereby lost. Men, de Mille agrees, wanted their wives attentive. She then wryly adds,

> Sixteen children, without benefit of pediatrician, nursery school, or corner drugstore guaranteed attentiveness.[76]

Certainly with multitudinous offspring and one adult screaming for not only attention but also supper and clean linen, the time and energy to foster the elusive Great American or Canadian Novel would be difficult to find. The underlying problem, of course, has been poverty. Women, lacking their own incomes, could not afford independence: marriage was an economic necessity. Which is why, for Woolf, productivity needs, besides space, "500 a year."

As well would be distaff creators faced denigrating reactions from society, not only its predictable apathy but also its outright ridicule:

> The world did not say to her as it said to (men of genius), Write if you choose, it makes no difference to me. The world said with a guffaw, Write? What's the good of your writing.[77]

They faced humiliation, notably from vicious rumors about their private lives:

> It is of no consequence whether a male artist leads a truly debauched sexual life; if a woman artist is convicted of any sexual irregularity the stigma clings to her forever.[78]

But above all they have faced a debilitating self-fulfilling prophecy. Because women have produced little thus far, they have come to accept their inherent inferiority, made few attempts, and so substantiated the myth:

330

> Put any gifted child at the keyboard, train
> her, exhort her six hours a day, but let it
> be borne in her that there never has been in
> recorded music a first-rate female composer,
> that no man will consider her work without
> condescension and...you may get results, but
> they won't be Beethoven.[79]

Moreover, that formidable barrier to Greer's researches, the disappearing oeuvre, has augmented the myth. A woman's painting was often consigned to a basement or warehouse, or accredited to a male of greater reputation, to increase its value. Novels have been signed by masculine nom de plumes (George Eliot) or not signed at all (antiquity's supremely productive Anon , Woolf suspects, may have been female). Critics and commentators,[80] invariably male, have judged by the biases of their sex, making oil painting important but weaving and handicrafts (wherein women have excelled) "minor."

> Football and sport are "important"; the
> worship of fashion, the buying of clothes
> "trivial." And these (masculine) values are
> inevitably transferred from life to fiction.
> This is an important book, the critic
> assumes, because it deals with war. This is
> an insignificant book because it deals with
> the feelings of women in a drawing room.[81]

According to Greer, poisonous praise has also wrought damage. Oftentimes, even childish, sentimental, and altogether amateurish output from women has earned extravagant critical and commercial reinforcement. According to Skinner excessive reinforcement of a first approximation will retard shaping toward greater attainment. Unfortunately:

> A young, pretty woman, with obliging
> manners, who also painted reasonably well,
> had no need to fear destructive criticism
> ...Even men who regarded themselves as
> responsible critics felt no shame in
> debasing all their standards in order to
> flatter a woman's work...When (men)
> patronise and flatter (women) they assert
> the unshakability of their own
> superiority.[82]

In the same vein, inappropriate motives were often reinforced. Women were frequently encouraged to dabble in the arts as suitable pastimes, or hobbies, to increase their attractiveness as matrimonial goods. But heaven forbid that they should take

331

them seriously![*] Nochlin describes the archetypal "lady painter," enshrined in etiquette books and in advice from one Mrs. Ellis:

> (I would not advocate) as essential to woman, any very extraordinary degree of intellectual attainment, especially if confined to one particular branch of study. To be able to do a great many things tolerably well, is of infinitely more value to a woman than to be able to excel in any one. By the former she may render herself generally useful; by the latter, she may dazzle for an hour...So far as cleverness, learning and knowledge are conducive to woman's moral excellence, they are therefore desirable and no further...All that would tend to draw her thoughts away from <u>others</u> and fix them on herself, ought to be avoided as an evil.⁸³

Remember first priorities, young lady. Serve your husband and breed like a rabbit! Such nonsense has, of course, damaged both women and art. Society's macho segments have therefore dismissed the latter as mere "women's (read frivolous) work," fit only for idle hands awaiting pregnancy.

But why, then, have women succeeded in a few forms? Why the novel? Woolf explains Jane Austen, the Bröntes, George Eliot, and by implication herself, partly by the easier access to the necessary preparation, simple literacy. Furthermore, writing needs no "room of one's own": to avoid accusations of reclusive selfishness, one can work in a family sitting room surrounded by conversation. Also, she suggests, women have invariably been reinforced for the talents that fiction demands, such as sensitivity to character, interpersonal relationships, and emotions. Still, even here masculine values have too often prevailed, causing must women to suppress their unique perspectives. But a great novel must possess <u>integrity</u>, an expression of the author's genuine personal vision, and it is

---

[*]Nochlin likewise explains the dearth of eminent creators amongst aristocrats. Despite every advantage of education, leisure time, etc., they too were encouraged, for reasons of image, merely to dabble. As a result, women and gentry have provided art's primary audience and patrons, but rarely its producers.

this unwillingness to compromise that distinguishes the great
female writers:

> (Only they) held fast to the thing as they
> saw it, without shrinking...It is another
> feather, perhaps the finest, in their caps.
> They wrote as women write, not as men
> write.[84]

And why that other exception, choreography? First, de Mille
suggests, men did not discourage a woman from tackling dance
because they have always been suspicious of and largely ignored
it, censoring it more severely than any activity except sex
itself. So, "The rejected art and the rejected artist (met) in
apt congress."[85] Furthermore, in this most ephemeral art,
techniques for permanently recording work have only recently
become available, so there has been no overwhelming, intimidating
male tradition of "old masters." Swan Lake and Giselle are
hardly classics in the sense that Hamlet or the Ninth Symphony
are, providing ultimate standards of quality. Lastly, dance
offered women opportunity in that most crucial arena, attracting
men to marry:

> We are told...women more than men, that to
> win love...we must be beautiful. It is a
> terrifying threat...Every girl has known
> from time immemorial that she had better
> have a dowry or looks and if she possessed
> neither, there was usually nothing for her
> but to be the family drudge or enter the
> church, where God could be counted on to
> overlook what husbands would not.[86]

A woman not naturally endowed can become beautiful through dance,
where beauty depends not on appearance but on function, not on
how you look but on what you can do. Witness that supreme image
of romance, the ballerina (perhaps quite plain at close quarters)
borne aloft by her cavalier while thousands sigh. Dancing offers
a road to love and freedom from sex.

But what of a woman drawn towards other forms, in which
success was a forlorn hope? For her, Woolf prognosticates
frustration, self-denial, and eventual psychological damage.
(This scenario contains tragic forecast, for Woolf herself fought
recurring manic-depression and eventually committed suicide.)
Those reported as possessed by devils, condemned for witchcraft,
or pursued by dogs may have been mute Jane Austens. Such, in all
probability, would have been Judith Shakespeare's fate:

Who shall measure the heat and violence of
the poet's heart when caught and tangled in
a woman's body? (At last she) killed
herself one winter's night and lies buried
at some cross-roads where the omnibuses now
stop outside the Elephant and Castle.[87]

Ibsen's <u>Hedda Gabler</u> personifies this scenario. Clearly a
woman of ability, she is trapped in 19th century convention,
expected to entertain relatives and have babies in concert with
her husband, a mediocre scholar and excruciatingly dull
personality. As she neverendingly complains, she is <u>bored</u> but,
unlike Nora of <u>A Doll's House</u>, she cannot bring herself, because
of her fear of scandal, to walk out and slam the door. On the
scene appears her former lover, bearing the manuscript of his
masterpiece. Mrs. Elvsted can, in classic female manner, give
him generous helpings of support, faith, and TLC, but Hedda
cannot. Resentful that he has fulfilled his potential while hers
languishes, she goads him into killing himself romantically,
"with vine leaves in his hair," burns the only copy of his
manuscript, and later kills herself. Those with stifled fires
can only destroy.

By now the reader can appreciate some of the problems women
have faced, and we certainly do not deny the foregoing's ring of
verity. Nonetheless, we must momentarily play devil's advocate,
for we dislike the thoroughgoing feminist's knee-jerk citing of
environmental factors while dismissing alternatives as both
unthinkable and symptomatic of chauvinism. As Chapter 4
suggested, excellence frequently arises from adverse rather than
sympathetic circumstances. As Riley points out,[88] many <u>men</u> have
faced and overcome poverty, unhappy marriages, geographic
isolation, parental discouragement, and so on. The question of
sex seems to her simply irrelevant, since art is
"hermaphroditic," both masculine and feminine. And for dogmatic
feminism she has little use:

> Women's Liberation, when applied to artists,
> seems to me to be a naive concept. It
> raises issues which in this context are
> quite absurd. At this point in time,
> artists who happen to be women need this
> particular form of hysteria like they need a
> hole in the head.[89]

5. <u>Commentary</u>. Skinner's general philosophy has been
debated in many elsewheres,[90] so we will dwell only on his
descriptions of creativity. Since these will undoubtedly strike
some discords, we begin with some positives. Creators undeniably
employ trial and error, especially during the

334

incubation/frustration and verification stages as they seek effective expression; witness the angry revisions that dot Beethoven's manuscripts like the smallpox. Furthermore, these random thrashings about frequently seek environmental reinforcers, despite our cherished beliefs that creators are above such crass motives. Roe documents[91] that recognition from colleagues is the food pellet that impels many scientists; witness Watson's[92] open admission that he and Crick sought DNA's structure because the winner of "the race" would assuredly capture a Nobel Prize. Playwright Moss Hart comments:

> If we could ever glimpse the inner workings
> of the creative impulse... I am afraid that
> to a larger degree than we choose to admit
> of so exalted a process, we would discover
> that more often the siren enticements of
> worldly pleasures and rewards spark it into
> life than the heroic and consecrated goals
> we are told inspire it. I have noticed that
> the lofty and lonely pinnacles inhabited by
> the purely creative are sometimes
> surprisingly and most comfortably furnished
> by Westinghouse, and a new convertible
> generally waits outside.[93]

As well, the polishing from rough first draft to finished product obviously resembles shaping. A writer may at first emit sentences only distantly resemblant to what she or he wishes to say, but for now they will suffice. Later, with editors and readers looming, he or she seeks performance more approximate. And certainly partial reinforcement principles can convincingly explain creators' amazing persistence/ compulsiveness.[94] They toil on varied ratio schedules of whimsical unpredictability, reaping both praise and condemnation. The well documented[95] correlation between quantity and quality of output is also supportive. The rat who emits his trial and error responses in greater number should also, by chance, more frequently strike mutational pay dirt.

And does not the relationship between creator and consumer resemble that between experimenter and subject, particularly in the reciprocity of reinforcement? Neither participant is exclusively puppeteer or marionette; each manipulates the other's behavior. The creator displays novel responses. The creator's judges, if reinforced, reciprocate with praise, invitations to dinner, and even money, thus encouraging more such responses. But their much-touted critical power, while not imaginary, is offset because that creator can either deliver or withhold his or her work of quality.

As previously noted, Skinner has little to say about such mentalisms as insecurity, inspiration, and the like, since they are supposedly mere by-products rather than causes of behavior. Creators' confidence or arrogance results from reinforcements previously received, their insecurity from a varied ratio schedule's unpredictability. Similarly, their felt responsibility or pride is misplaced; the credit, and hence the "dignity," should go not to them but to their environments. However, when they feel like mediums, manipulated by forces beyond their own control, Skinner would heartily approve. At last they appropriately assign the credit. Note his observation about his own accomplishments: "If I deserve any credit at all, it is simply for having served as a place in which certain processes could take place"[96] (an utterance worthy of mediumhood's most noted apostle, Jung, except that "certain processes" here refers to environments, not archetypes).

Unhappily, our obeisance now must end, for we find in Skinner some serious, even incapacitating flaws. We begin with a famous metaphor with many similarities (although also, as we shall see, a few differences). To demonstrate the laws of probability, statisticians sometimes claim that an infinite number of monkeys, each pecking away at a typewriter for an infinite amount of time, would eventually, purely by chance, write all the great books. Skinner appreciably apes this portrait with his creators who randomly produce mutations, among which the environment then chooses. Those creators deserve no more credit than does the monkey who accidentally emits "To be or not to be".

Several difficulties are implied. First, it is often forgotten that Skinner is an eternal optimist. While on occasion he pays lip service to individual differences within species, when pressed to the wall he fervently believes that given a well-designed environment and efficient shaping, every individual can learn anything within its species capabilities, admitting only that some might need more training to reach this potential. As well, creative behaviors are mere mutations, accidentally emitted by anyone and everyone. Combining these two notions, it follows that every monkey--and every human--has roughly equal capacity to emit works of genius. But it is inescapable. A minuscule proportion of humanity has in fact produced these, and in biological terms in an infinitesimal amount of time, so it seems not completely indefensible to hypothesize unequal portions of that mysterious disease called "talent." Furthermore, so far as we know, absolutely no emissions comparable to King Lear, Geurnica, the Ninth Symphony, or even Beyond Freedom and Dignity have come from lower animals. The rudimentay "creativity" that Skinner's pigeons under decidedly contrived circumstances have shown is worlds removed from these. It seems, then, that his position flies in the face of history's facts and so bears the burden of proof.

Now Skinner would explain humanity's "greats" as simply fortunate beneficiaries of advantageous environmental training; anyone else receiving similar shaping, selective reinforcement, environmental design, etc., could achieve as much. Here, in fact, is one important departure from the monkey metaphor. Since these auteurs are left to respond randomly, with minimal training technology to guide them, he would expect minimal accomplishment. He thus avoids one absurd implication of the metaphor, i.e., that someone's past success should not influence his/her chances in the future, any more than a previous dice roll affects the next. The monkey which produces one quality item may be no more (or less) likely to do so again than any others, but as Skinner would agree, a Mozart with years of accomplishment behind him is a more likely candidate to achieve Don Giovanni than is some heretofore nonentity. From Skinner's standpoint, however, the reason is not Mozart's "talent," but his history of reinforcement.

Unfortunately, Skinner's explanation again contradicts the facts. Given society's ambivalent attitudes towards creativity, its reinforcers are often, to put it charitably, either not terribly obvious or out and out negative--scorn, apathy, starvation, and the like. Which suggests that creators, at the very least, must possess a healthy masochistic streak. Thus, Storr points out,[97] Mozart's family provided every incentive, Handel's surgeon father nothing but discouragement, yet both composers attained eminence. Skinner would reply that this very ambivalence provides the varied ratio schedule that induces creative persistence. But, we rejoin, laboratory animals are not, as a rule, trained from the outset on such a schedule, for their progress would be minimal. At first, every response even vaguely approximate will be reinforced; only when these are well indoctrinated will they be shaped gradually towards the more unpredictable state of affairs. But in the creative arena, it is the novice who receives the fewest, most unpredictable rewards. Why nonetheless does he or she persist and progress?

We now consider two other problems with the monkey metaphor, because Skinner's answers to these are related. First, creative behavior is again seen as accidental, so the monkey who happens to type "to be or not to be" deserves no more credit than does a human emitter of same. But as Gruber[98] points out, neither chess players nor creators randomly generate every possible response before choosing appropriate alternatives. Rather, they use strategies to isolate promising possibilities and then confine their exploration within these limits. Likewise, we have seen that they seem to have a vague mental vision, an endocept, of the

337

desired product, which trial-and-error responses try to approximate; thus these are not emitted indiscriminately.

The second point grows from Skinner's assertion that reinforcement must always be, in the last analysis, controlled extrinsically, delivered by an environmental agent external to the subject. Intrinsic reinforcement, wherein subjects reinforce themselves for appropriate behavior, such as by saying to themselves "That's good" or "I like that," seems to imply, unthinkably, (1) that mentalistic events can control behavior, and (2) that organisms can autonomously choose their own actions. The monkey metaphor carries similar implications, since neither monkey, rat nor pigeon can judge its own emissions for worthwhile alternatives. Human observers would therefore be needed to monitor the random simian output for anything worthwhile. They would undoubtedly be inundated with mountains of gibberish. But now and then they might encounter morsels more tantalizing, such as

> Is this a dagger which I see before me,
> The handle toward my glplesex?

"Yet again," these watchpersons would moan, "So near and yet so far!"

The conclusion, however, seems inescapable. Human creators must evaluate their own produce for merit, reinforcing themselves for behaviors they find desirable and chastising results deemed unworthy. To hold otherwise would be to demand a patently absurd scenario, (especially since producing a complexity such as a symphony or play requires not one "response" that needs reinforcement, but thousands). Some furtive environmental agent would have to hover in the background and peer over, say, Shakespeare's shoulder, ready to deliver some symbolic food pellet the moment he accidentally pencils in "to be or not to be." But since most creators actually work alone, it must be that such reinforcers as the environment does provide arrive only after long delays. They should therefore, by Skinner's own reckoning, be ineffective.

To deny these self-controlling mechanisms would be to make the process even more inefficient and frustrating than it is. But in fact, these abilities, as much as any, probably separate the successes from the also-rans. 99 Without exception, Getzels and Csikszentmihalyi's art students reported working not for external rewards (material or otherwise) but for those from the process and the work itself. And Norman Mailer adds, while discussing another writer who had difficulties:

> And I asked him, "Why do you do it? You can
> do many other things well. Why do you

338

bother with it?" I really meant this.
Because he suffered when writing like no one
I know. He looked up in surprise and said,
"Oh, but this is the only way one can ever
find the truth. The only time I know that
something is true is at the moment I
discover it in the act of writing." I think
it's that. I think it's this moment when
one knows it's true.[100]

Now to Skinner's answers to these two points. That
strategies, visions, self-reinforcement and other such cognitive
paraphernalia should control the process might seem guaranteed to
earn his wrath, parading as they do the trappings of autonomy.
Actually, he quite admits our abilities for "self-managment;" for
example, it might help counteract those lengthy delays of
external reinforcers. He insists only that these mentalisms are
themselves behaviors previously encouraged by the environment's
feedback. Therefore it still retains <u>ultimate</u> control. They
simply internalize its standards.

Unfortunately, such an argument wildly oversimplifies the
realities of creative work, and the term's usual connotations.
As "behavioral mutation" implies, creative behavior for Skinner
clearly equals originality, novelty, etc. Admittedly such
criteria are precise and reliable, and also simplify training.
Since the target behaviors, novelties, are relatively clear-cut,
we know exactly what we want our subjects to learn, and also when
they have done it. However, since "creativity" usually implies
quality, and since not all creative work is markedly "original"
(See Chaper 1), actual reinforcement is likely to be much more
unpredictable. "The environment" will not easily make up its
mind about those mutations that deserve it.

Therefore, the creator who attempts to follow its standards,
to play it safe and "give the public what it wants" invites
neurosis. And indeed, as even the most commercially oriented
will invariably verify, to try and predict what will earn
applause, and to produce same, is hopeless. Usually, the
environment does not decide what it wants until long after the
event, so creators must lead rather than follow, relying on their
<u>own</u> standards of quality. These may partly reflect environmental
input, but must also include appreciable idiosyncracy.

A creator's typical feelings of alienation further
substantiate this point. Such feelings would seem unlikely if
he/she merely internalized cultural standards while planning,
evaluating and reinforcing his/her own work, and it <u>would</u> then
fit those standards. But as often it does not. Can we imagine a
James Joyce, for example, contriving the revolutionary mutations

339

in _Ulysses_ based on standards he had "borrowed" from the culture? Nothing remotely like it had ever occurred before. He could have few clues about its likely reception, and those he did have, such as his notorious difficulty in finding a publisher, were hardly encouraging. Yet he persisted and eventually prevailed.

We admit, therefore, that some creators probably <u>have been</u> shaped according to Skinner's scenario. They garner hefty, if transient reinforcers in such places as Burbank, Calif., and Nashville, Tenn. It is possible too that some others <u>can be</u> so shaped towards more admirable achievements, but only if some special, endowed potential exists. But this hardly means that those we most revere have been. Their lives seem as often immune to environmental influence. They march not to an external drum beat, but to their own.

Amabile has provided empirical support for these assertions in some studies deserving elucidation.[101] For not only do they castigate Skinner's position, they also augment that rare breed, the impressive empirical study of creativity. As a first attraction, her subjects, rather than answering test questions of doubtful relevance, actually had to produce something, such as a collage or short story, which seemed to require genuine "creativity." As well, she avoided an exercise in probable futility by accepting creativity as something that we cannot precisely define but that we know when we see. She therefore relied on a <u>consensus definition</u>: the creative is that which people agree to <u>call</u> "creative." Several judges independently evaluated the merit of her subjects' products and reassuringly, almost invariably agreed.

Amabile then sytematically studied the effects of some promising variables. We cannot review her every finding but her comparison of <u>intrinsic</u> with <u>extrinsic motivation</u> must give us pause. In the firstnamed, her subjects were motivated by instructions to create something for their own interest and enjoyment. Extrinsic subjects, however, were offered various tangible rewards for creating. Invariably the latter displayed less creativity. Relevant too is another finding, that when subjects expected to be judged afterwards by someone else, their creativity again suffered (possibly because such external evaluation reduced their intrinsic interest in the task). In short, the very conditions which by Skinner's reckoning are necessary to foster creative activity, invariably inhibited same.

Amabile's main conclusion is decidedly more comforting to the humanistic persuasion. Creativity seems a completely natural activity if we simply stay out of its way. It is not so much that situations such as intrinsic motivation foster it; rather, others such as the external variety are detrimental. The typical

340

creator provides powerful verification. When we ask "Why do you do it?" his/her invariable response will be "Because I enjoy it" or "because it's 'fun'." Now admittedly "fun" is a slippery concept which can easily collapse in circularity. Nevertheless, perhaps we should not ignore these responses.

The question must be asked of Skinner, therefore. If I am able to select and reinforce someone else's behaviors, and they can do likewise for mine, why is it unthinkable that we each might do the same for our own behaviors? If we can monitor and judge others, why not ourselves? Skinner's stance here seems inconsistent, yet he remains adamant. When behaviors reoccur, external reinforcers must invariably be present in some form. Although he too often remains mute about their possible identity, at least for everyday situations, admitting merely that they are frequently "inconspicuous."

Which intimates another, more pervasive problem. In practice, Skinner's concept of reinforcement is blatantly circular. Why do behaviors occur? Because they have been reinforced. How do we know that they have been reinforced? Because they occur. The logical circle is broken if those reinforcers are specified in advance, but this Skinner, at least for real-world situations, rarely does. Ironically, then, this purportedly scientific, empirically-based system becomes as vague and as untestable as Freud's. As indoctrinated psychoanalysts can find post hoc evidence for sexual repression in every neurotic, so can devout Skinnerians locate possible reinforcers for even the most selfless, altruistic behaviors.

There is even further irony, when we note Skinner's silence on a crucial point. Why does a behavior occur in the first place? Why does a rat press the bar, or the writer commit words to paper, for the first time? Accident. Such random events "just happen." Yet it is these initial responses, when innovatively mutant, that provide the irreplaceable beginnings of subsequent "creativity," because a reinforcer can control behaviors once they are emitted, but can hardly be said to "cause" them. When their explanation is left to chance's whim (which is really no explanation at all), this seemingly arch-deterministic system teeters on the brink of the existential, admitting at least tacitly that certain supremely important events defy explanation.

Therefore creators do deserve, in our view, special credit. In fact, by Skinner's own reckoning, is it not crucial that they receive it? For to eliminate their reinforcers of praise, recognition, and the like, would extinguish their endeavor. Skinner seems tacitly to accept this argument, since he signs his own books and, we gather, accepts royalties rather than donating

341

same to Harvard University, presumably the actual fostering environment. Sometimes actions do speak louder than words.

In sum, then, from our vantage point Skinner provides appealing explanation for some creative behavior (the avant-garde variety) some of the time, and for some of its aspects (trial and error, the sex difference) all of the time. But not for all of its aspects all of the time.

Physiological Views

To explain behavior, these persuasions refer to the body's physical phenomena, such as its anatomy, physiology, and biochemistry, with·particular emphasis on brain and central nervous system processes. Obviously these factors are important, but ardent proponents such as Hebb[102] deny our spiritual side entirely, reducing even such concepts as[103] "mind" and "consciousness" to material events. Lombroso provided an early such explanation of creativity. He imaginatively, even fancifully, related various psychological disorders to brain damage and noted that several talented persons had suffered from rickets, sterility, and other ailments. They therefore, he concluded, owed their abilities to these conditions. This notion has only historical interest now, but let us glance more closely at some contributions of greater allure.

For Arieti,[104] creative thought must combine primitive, primary process material with realistic secondary process (see Chapter 11). This integrative ability, he suggests, depends on two cortical areas: the prefrontal (PF) and the association cortex, which includes parts of the temporal, occipital, and parietal lobes (hence, TOP area). Malfunctioning of these areas, earlier work suggested, might cause schizophrenia, which Arieti believes closely resembles creative thought. Therefore, might not the latter rely on these same areas? Indicatively, they control our most abstract mental functioning, yet also receive input from many other areas, not only cortical but subcortical. And the latter, presumably, gives rise to primary process material. Arieti guesses, then, that creative persons' PF and TOP areas receive more input from these other areas and thus have access to mentation of greater variety:

> The mind of the creative person...
> participates consciously or unconsciously in
> a dialogue between these two areas and the
> rest of the cortex.[105]

Conceivably, then, even extensive brain damage that debilitates other functions should leave creativity intact, so long as these areas are unaffected. Several cases Arieti mentions seem to verify this prediction, but his analyses, while suggestive, nevertheless need more empirical backing.

Prentky, Hebb, and Others

That creativity and psychopathology frequently coexist has also fuelled Prentky's recent speculations.[106] He first describes two possible responses to incoming information. The abstract, A-type, scans broadly, preferring stimulus diversity, while the concrete, or C-type, attends in depth to a narrow range of events. Run-of-the-mill persons prefer neither, but the potentially creative or disturbed do, with the former's leanings being moderate and the latter's excessive. Still, Prentky may link the two, but he emphatically denies that psychopathology helps creativity or accompanies it. Rather, when creative work's inherent stresses change moderate deviation to severe deviation, productivity plummets.

At any rate, the creative's preferred form of expression, and the disturbed's type of problem, then depends on the direction of their deviation. The A-type, having a "strong" nervous system with weak inhibitory processes, is emotionally responsive, even unstable, prone in the extreme to paranoia and severe mood changes such as manic-depression. The C-type, with a "weak" nervous system and excessive inhibition, displays concrete rather than imaginative cognition and stereotyped moods, which in excess can become apathy, listlessness, and obsessive-compulsion.

Supposedly, these types display a raft of physiological differences; two deserve mention. First, the hippocampus and amygdala seem to work in opposition, balancing one another's effects. For example, damage to the first-named lessens distractibility to irrelevant stimulation, damage to the second increases it. Thus, Prentky concludes, the A-type is hippocampal dominant, the C-type amygdaloid. Another difference. The linguistic cerebral hemisphere (generally the left) and the nonlinear right hemisphere seem suppressed in the C and A types, respectively. Which suggests an addendum vis-a-vis the sex difference. Given that females usually excel in linguistic[107] skills and men in spatial, creative C-types should be predominantly masculine, creative A-types feminine. We await verification.

To complete his typology, Prentky introduces the second, by now familiar dimension of preferred thought, i.e., linear vs. nonlinear (although these now read analytic and synthetic, respectively). The former are "splitters" who prefer to contemplate elemental bits and pieces; they will dismantle a carburetor (and then, probably, forget to reassemble it). The synthetic "lumpers" prefer visualizing complex wholes. With two

alternatives on each of two dimensions, then, we have four
possible types in all, each of which displays a distinctive
personality and creative product. Moreover, when they deviate
excessively, their psychological afflictions will also differ.
Table 12.1 shows some scientists whom Prentky nominates for each
category (presumably exemplary artists could also be specified).

Table 12.1

Examples of Prentky's Four Creative Types
(after Prentky, 1980, p. 89)

Synthetic

Isaac Newton	Michael Polanyi
Albert Einstein	Jacob Bronowski
Edwin Schrödinger	Theodosius Dobzhansky

C-type   A-type

Henry Cavendish	Enrico Fermi
Wilhelm Roentgen	Robert Oppenheimer
Albert Szent-Gyorgyi	Neils Bohr
Max Born	Werner Heisenberg
	Bertrand Russell
	Alfred North Whitehead

Analytic

Let us pursue the two types of thought for, unsurprisingly,
the mushrooming interest in hemispheric specialization has
infected $_{108}$even discussions of creativity. Unfortunately,
Gardner's^{108} studies of gifted persons with brain damage finds a
picture more complicated than the literature often suggests. The
left hemisphere (LH) does, by and large, service linguistic
skills and the right hemisphere (RH) tasks more spatial. But
specific abilities often seem to be localized in several areas,
and moreover those areas can differ among individuals. (Too
often, Gardner asserts, investigators have ignored such
complexities, as well as methodological and interpretive problems
with frequently cited evidence.) Since Gardner's findings vary
by artistic sphere, we shall consider these separately.

LH damage invariably causes language deficits; witness the
poet Baudelaire's incapacitation by a stroke therein. But RH
effects, while quite different, are hardly unimportant for these
activities. Appropriate use of humor and metaphor is lost; as

344

well, its victims can remember only a story's details, not its integrated, narrative structure. Visual art paints a more complex picture. LH damage has remarkably little impact. Indeed, although it may debilitate linguistic communication, simplicity and clarity of work may actually improve, so like a child's it omits details but retains an overall structure. But RH patients produce woefully incomplete drawings that largely ignore the left side of the canvas. They include details individually relevant but not forming an integrated unity. And their sense of style seems lost since, unlike the LH patient, when shown others' paintings, they cannot group those together that are similar. Lastly, Gardner judges, their produce becomes "more directly expressive, more raw and sensuous...as if an inhibitory mechanism has been released".[109] Does the RH, perchance, house the superego?

However, music's case is the most complicated.[*] As the most reliable generalization, it can survive LH damage. The Russian composer/teacher Shebalin's abilities were undimmed by a severe stroke therein that devastated his linguistic competence. Other victims, unable to read, can still understand and interpret musical notation (which suggests independence of the two "languages"). Also, like LH visual artists, they retain their sense of style. Fortunately, musicians suffering RH damage are rare. But one, while still able to teach, lost interest in composing because he could no longer "conceive of the whole piece." Yet again, the RH's talents for integration are suggested.

As the bottom line, a few artistic abilities, such as musical pitch, may be precisely localized and so can be damaged or spared independent of others. But more commonly, such abilities are not confined even to one hemisphere, let alone area. Lashley's pioneering studies of brain damage in rats revealed that behavioral deficits generally depend much more on an injury's extent than on its location.[110] He therefore favored a law of mass action, that the brain acts as a whole, while rejecting any localization of function for higher cognition (presumably including creativity). Gardner's conclusion is similar:

> To produce something well-organized, let
> alone something fresh and original, it may
> be necessary to have an essentially intact

---

[*]Even here, exceptions appear. Some of Ravel's abilities remained after LH damage, but he ceased composing nevertheless. Perhaps, Gardner guesses, he lost his motivation.

nervous system...Only large amounts of 'uncommitted' or 'intact' cortex may allow an individual to go beyond workaday routine activity and to fashion newly conceived and highly original works of art...One needs to have all, or at least most, regions of the brain performing at top form.[111]

Bogen and Bogen[112] have also been led to physiological speculation by the seeming involvement of both linear and nonlinear thought (in their terms, propositional and appositional, respectively), and therefore of both hemispheres, in creative activity. Since the corpus callosum's nerve fibres cross the midline and connect the two hemispheres, perhaps this structure fiddles a crucial tune. It might help integrate the two types of thought, or control their dominance, insuring in particular that nonlinear aspects, often suppressed, attain freer rein. Which implies[113] another rudimentary attack on the sex difference. Goleman[113] has reviewed evidence for organizational differences between male and female brains. Among other things, localization of linear and nonlinear functioning in LH and RH respectively seems less clear-cut in women and, of particular relevance, they seem better "cognitive specialists," able to activate only areas needed for the task at hand while suppressing others. Hence, "Men... seem to be better at tasks that require two different cognitive approaches at the same time."[114] Does this not describe creative thought? Might not (following Bogen and Bogen) the corpus callosum's integratory role be played differently (for whatever reason) in each sex? Unhappily, this analysis contradicts Prentky's assertion that men are usually C-types, of narrower sensory focus. Can this be reconciled with greater cognitive inclusiveness?

But Hebb's classic conjectures[115] provide a particularly influential physiological perspective. Supposedly, for every stimulus we experience, a unique sequence of brain cells, or cell assembly, is established, which forms a closed circuit and stores the experience in memory. An insight for, say, a problem comes about when several of these assemblies interact and combine in a new way. Moreover, in a later paper[116] Hebb clearly implies a similar explanation for creative thought. Since we have here what amounts to a physiological version of the reshuffling of ideas,* familiar difficulties predictably arise. For example,

---

*Eccles[117] advances a similar explanation. He suggests, furthermore, that creative individuals possess more such traces

(Footnote Continued)

Hebb asks at one point, "how does the thinker recognize the creative combination when it occurs?"[120] How is gold separated from dross? Hebb's answer? That no answer is available.

However, Hebb earlier provided a more helpful physiological explanation[121] for creative motivation, for why we produce and consume. The brain's <u>reticular formation</u> maintains alertness and arousal in other areas. Its destruction causes permanent coma; sensory stimulation is still received but is not processed or acted upon. Now for the reticular formation to remain alert and perform its duties, it too must receive arousing stimulation, especially of <u>variety</u> and <u>novelty</u>. Repetitive experience induces lethargy, the state we call boredom. Hebb was much struck by the effects of sensory deprivation,[122] in which subjects are placed in isolated situations with their survival needs - eating, drinking, and so on - wonderfully met, so they simply need laze about. It sounds idyllic and should be if, as Hull maintains, we invariably seek homeostatic drive reduction. Yet subjects found the situation soon discomforting and eventually unbearable. Their cognitive and problem solving abilities suffered, they became irritable, some suffered hallucinations, and many could not remain for the planned duration. Although later research[123] has found these situations sometimes much less debilitating, it was the early studies that influenced Hebb.

Hebb therefore proposed that the reticular formation controls our general level of arousal (which resembles Hull's "drive"). More specifically, a U-shaped function relates arousal level and performance efficiency. We prefer not (as Hull has it) minimal but moderate amounts. Too little produces boredom; too much, panic, terror, or even immobility (see Figure 12.4). Under high arousal we seek, as Hull predicts, homeostatic experience; shipwreck survivors will desire no 1812 overtures to serenade them. But low arousal initiates a "taste for excitement," for golf, bridge, or Agatha Christie.

(Footnote Continued)
and also "a peculiar potency for unresting activity."[118] (Suggestions that their dreams, unlike what Freud would predict, seem unusually varied and rich in meaning[119] support Eccles' supposition.) At any rate, both of these eventualities would allow for more recombinations.

347

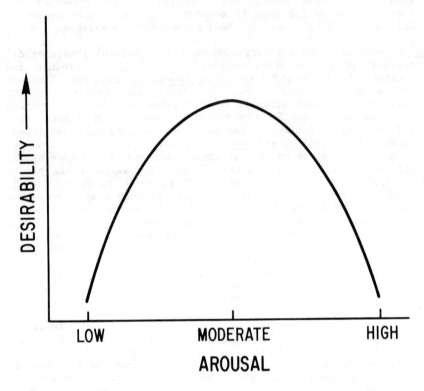

FIGURE 12.4. *Hebb's arousal function (adapted from Hebb,[121] p. 250).*

Now Hebb's arousal simply <u>energizes</u> behavior; it does not <u>guide</u>, or point us towards that which is appropriate. To this purpose, every stimulus supposedly possesses two functions: (1) <u>arousal</u> (which augments the energy pool) and (2) <u>cue</u> (which guides behavior). Be that as it may, it is presumably the aforementioned taste for excitement that leads us to produce or to contemplate creative works. Such behaviors may seem to have little biological value, but this is incorrect. They help maintain our optimal state of arousal and, in turn, response efficiency. Certainly such activities must, above all, stimulate. Their one unforgivable, even mortal, sin is to bore.

Martindale's physiological extension,[124] of Kris' regression in the service of the ego (see Chapter 11) is pertinent here. Seeing both primary and secondary process as necessary for creative thought, Kris emphasized efficient shifting between them. Supposedly, low arousal should increase access to the ordinarily suppressed primary process, with high arousal facilitating the secondary. Therefore, creative persons should accomplish such arousal shifts more readily. Martindale and associates, using EEG recordings to assess arousal levels have obtained, in Suler's judgment at least, "marginal support"[125] for these hypotheses.

We finish with a foreboding problem. To verify physiological explanations empirically, a physical structure, such as a brain area of interest, must usually be modified in some way - that is, damaged or stimulated - to observe the physiological effects. However, human subjects usually object to having electrodes implanted in or tissue carved out of their brains, regardless of the benefits to science. Two alternative tactics, each seriously flawed, must therefore suffice.

An investigator may observe, as did Gardner, the results of brain damage due to illness or injury. However, he can control neither the location nor extent of damage, nor the types of subjects who suffer it. Thus, his attempts to study creativity, for example, may founder because brain injuries to talented persons are, happily, rather rare. Putting it crudely, then, he must take what he gets, also bearing in mind that, since his subjects are not randomly assigned to groups, his comparisons with controls are inevitably confounded.

Modifying the anatomies of lower animals provides a second, more popular possibility. Although rats and monkeys are not completely comparable to ourselves, it can be helpful to study behaviors of which they are capable, which include many of the higher, cognitive sort.[126] Unfortunately, judging by the tasks used, animals can accomplish the problem solving but not creative variety (at least we have heard of no animals able to compose symphonies or choreograph dances) and these two kettles contain similar but hardly identical fish (see Chapter 5). In the face of these difficulties, then, conclusive empirical evidence about physiology's role will be hard to come by.

Experimental aesthetics: Berlyne

The donors rather than consumers of creative gifts form our main concern. Still, we have occasionally taken brief tours of this neighbouring country, so let us do so once more. Berlyne's influential and (in quantity at least) staggering output shows Hebbian tinges. Berlyne too assumes a general, nonspecific state of arousal that energizes behavior, and contemplates its possible physiological substrates.[127] He too denies that reducing arousal towards homeostasis is our invariable purpose. In fact, he was even more taken by intrinsically motivated behaviors[128] (exploration, play, humor, artistic participation, and the like) that satisfy no biological drive but seem to contain their own rewards.

Notwithstanding this heresy, however, Berlyne was also much influenced by Hull.[129] He too described us in the passive rather than active voice; for example, our aesthetic pleasure from a work of art depends almost entirely on its stimulus properties but very little on our interpretive or personal powers. Like Hull again, Berlyne propogandized the scientific investigation of observables, and therefore manipulated such properties of stimuli as their novelty, complexity, and uncertainty (the so-called collative, or attention-grabbing properties) to determine their effects on arousal and aesthetic pleasure. Perhaps his greatest contribution, then, is to reveal the advantages (and also failings) of approaching such a mentalistic concept as "aesthetic experience" in this manner. Finally, he followed Hull in his preference for elementalism, for analyzing a complex phenomenon, such as a work of art, into its various components, such as novelty, which he then studied separately. Berlyne recognized that such a work combines many such properties and paid periodic lip service to Gestalt warnings (see Chapter 13) that relations between these components might change their individual effects. But in practice he largely ignored these problems.

Berlyne's empirical predictions follow from a basic assumption: increased arousal will always be repellent (see the top panel of Figure 12.5).[130] However, unlike Hebb, he postulates a U-shaped relation between arousal and the amount of collation* in a stimulus (see Figure 12.5's center panel). Either too much or too little novelty, complexity, and so on, induces high arousal. Bored, we feel not homeostatic but irritable and tense. The U-shaped function in Figure 12.5's bottom panel, predicting that we will prefer moderate amounts of stimulus collation to either the overly simple or complex, provides the crucial prediction for his aesthetic theory, and a host of studies[131] have sought, and often found, this Holy Grail. Supposedly, successful work has both arousal inducing and reducing properties; it combines simplicity with complexity, harmony with dissonance, the familiar with the strange. Still

---

*Berlyne uses the term arousal potential but his continuous interchanges between "arousal" (denoting a state of the organism) and "arousal potential" (denoting a property of stimuli) is confusing, so we have substituted another.

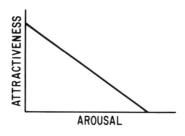

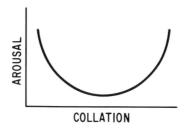

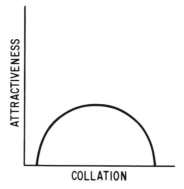

FIGURE 12.5 Berlyne's functions (adapted from D. E. Berlyne, "Motivational Problems Raised by Exploratory and Epistemic Behavior." In
S. Koch (Ed.), Psychology: A Study of Science. (Vol. 5). New York:
McGraw-Hill, 1959, pp. 318-319. Reproduced with permission of the
publisher.

(to complicate matters), the amount of collation we prefer could
change with our base arousal level.[132] The tired business
person, beset with bills, boss, and backache, may seek innocuous
"easy listening" music, while a collegiate offspring opts for the

megadecibel onslaughts of the Creatures of Ooz. Important too might be the amount of arousal change, with moderate amounts being more attractive than the sudden or unexpected.

Berlyne rarely commented about the producing side of the creative ledger, probably because of his commitment to the passive subject. Nor have his disciples, to our knowledge, done so. Therefore, let us briefly risk putting unsavory words in his mouth. Presumably intrinsic motives, particularly the curiosity that seeks arousal, would also impel creators. Thus, Berlyne implies that creativity is but one member of a more general category of activities, which also includes play, sports, and humor. Those who do not create must satisfy this mysterious basic need in other ways.

But what of Berlyne's success on his own ground, that of aesthetics? We earlier expressed our doubts (see Chapter 1). Countless subjects have been run and graphs drawn, but has our understanding of Hamlet's greatness increased many iota? Several flaws seem to us incapacitating. First, Berlyne emphasized, evidently because of his desire for objective standards, the aesthetic preferences of the majority. That which it prefers is intrinsically superior. We cannot agree. To repeat, the judgments of the enlightened and experienced must "o'erweigh a whole theatre of others." Clarification of two other problems requires the next chapter, but briefly, the aesthetic experience we receive from that work probably depends as much on our own intrinsic abilities as on its intrinsic stimulus properties. Also, the elemental, one-component-at-a-time strategy quite distorts these elements' effects within the context of a work. There they interact with and relate to one another.

Admittedly Eysenck, in an extensive defense of experimental aesthetics and the objectification of beauty,[133] provides some empirical rebuttal to the last objection at least. Suppose several artistic components such as color and texture are each manipulated separately and their effects on beauty judgments noted. If these components are then combined, the judgments obtained are precisely those we would expect were the components' effects simply to add together. We remain, however, adamantly resident in Missouri. As Eysenck admits, it remains doubtful that this additive effect would remain in phenomena as complex as symphonies or paintings. These unite a host of sometimes subtle component attributes.

Part IV

THEORIES OF DETERMINISTIC FREEDOM

According to these approaches, while we lack complete
freedom, neither are we totally passive victims of events beyond
our control. Nature and nurture do affect us, but we can modify
or interpret them to put our own stamps on any products that
emerge. In short, we have appreciable capacity for choice.
Depending on one's viewpoint, then, these approaches exemplify
either the virtues of liberal moderation or the vices of fence
sitting.

Chapter 13

NATURALISTIC VIEWS II: THE ACTIVE SUBJECT

These approaches, like those preceeding, prefer empirical science, but since they view the subject as active rather than passive, their tone differs markedly. For example, they willingly discuss such subjective determinants of behavior as thought, attention, and mental imagery, topics that in behaviorism's heyday were banished from print as effusions of the devil. But today they may be found in the Tables of Contents of many journals. Why this change? Probably because psychologists intuitively found S-R portraits increasingly unsatisfying. In contrast to most disciplines, psychology's investigators and its subjects of study are not distinct, but are in both cases human beings, making the scientist's objective detachment here difficult, perhaps impossible. Every idea those investigators will evaluate introspectively, asking, "Does it hold water in light of my own experience?" If it does not, then sooner or later they will reject it, no matter how weighty its logical, empirical, or mathematical support. Behaviorism's portraits seemed naïve and degrading, cognitive approaches more flattering,[1] so the latter have prevailed.

Philosophical Antecedents: Kant

As usual, we can identify anticipatory pundits, but this Prussian pedestrian (by whose daily walk around Königsberg one could reportedly set the clock) discussed fine art and creativity directly[2] and influenced many others in those arenas. For Kant,[3] like the associationists, all knowledge begins with experience. But Kant also endows our minds with various principles, or categories, such as causality, space, and time, which exist a priori, rather than being produced by experience. These inborn talents allow our apperception, whereby we can interpret, modify, and give meaning to our sensations, thus becoming their masters rather than slaves.

Talent, or genius, is for Kant another innate entity, requiring hefty endowment of that favorite faculty of the romantics, the imagination. Its powers allow artists to remold, rather than merely reshuffle, the elements provided by Nature and thus achieve genuinely new products:

> (The Imagination allows) freedom from the laws of association (so that) the material supplied to us by nature...can be worked up into something different which surpasses nature...The poet ventures to (make concrete) rational ideas of invisible

beings, the kingdom of the blessed, hell,
eternity, creation, etc., or even if he
deals with things of which there are
examples in experience--death, envy, and all
vices - ...he tries, by means of
Imagination$_4$..to go beyond the limits of
experience.

It is unfettered imagination, maintains Kant, that gives those
products their intangible spirit (we might now call it pizazz),
that sine qua non that sets art apart from the merely
workmanlike. Thus, great art's defining properties are tacitly
nonlinear, defying verbal description.

According to Kant, then, the genius does not imitate, nor[5]
abide by inviolate canons. Instead, he or she "gives the rule,"
freely evolving work that then provides art's rules, from which
those less talented can learn and by which they are ruled. This
trailblazer may also awaken other geniuses to exercise their
gifts and evolve their rules.[*] They thereby can also earn the
awesome label. For were they merely to follow, they would by
definition lack genius. Yet Kantian artists in some ways lack
autonomy. They also functions as mediums through whom impersonal
forces speak, so "Nature gives the rule to art."[7] They cannot
tell how they came by their ideas or show others their secrets of
success. They cannot work by systematic plans nor consciously
control their works' eventual character.

Thus, Kant avoids passivity's more objectionable, even
ridiculous pronouncements. Still, he raises other difficulties
that will persistently trouble us here. When genius is
"explained" through a hypothetical faculty such as imagination,
the quicksand of circularity is courted, since that faculty is
both revealed by and used to explain the products that result.
As well, while we enthusiastically agree that genius probably
grows from special, innate abilities, we are less ready to admit
that its origins are inherently mysterious, as Kant at least
implies, thereby to regress to that "gift of the gods," that fait
accompli that leaves us little room to maneuver. Whatever their
deficiencies, passive views at least see genius as potentially
explicable by empirical observables.

---

[*]Kant's own situation fits this scenario. Apparently,
reading Hume "awoke him from his dogmatic slumbers," to take
account of but also overcome Hume's skepticism.[6]

Gestalt Psychology

The Gestalt organization arose in Germany prior to World War I as an avowed psychology of protest. For its founding "big three" (Max Wertheimer, Wolfgang Köhler, and Kurt Koffka) the target was the prevailing system of the time: Wundt's structuralism, which attempted to study mental life, or consciousness, scientifically, using the method of introspection. Subjects, exposed to stimuli such as lights flashing or bells ringing, examined and then described their resulting experience. In these exercises, Wundt attempted to break that experience down into its component elements, thus epitomizing science's well-washed practice of analysis. Now as chemistry, for example, verifies, this strategy can pay off, but the Gestaltists objected that experiences's complex phenomena cannot be described accurately by their component sensations.

These rebels were past masters at devising elegant demonstrations to devastate their opponents and one such, Wertheimer's phi phenomenon, opened their blitzkrieg of the Wundtian heartland. When two lines are presented in alternation at an appropriate rate, we experience not separate lines but one line that seems to move between their locations. Advertising signs exploit this principle, as in a series of lights that flash in sequence, and suggest a moving arrow that repeatedly flies towards an adjacent restaurant.

This seemingly trivial parlor demonstration signified more than meets the eye. Clearly our perceptual experience does not always coincide with the stimulus sensations we receive. To further buttress this principle, a musical melody transposed to a different key, and therefore involving different notes, will seem the same melody, (except to such sensitive ears as Mozart's), and ideas paraphrased in different words will retain their essential meanings. Yet such things could not be if component sensations retained their individual character, and simply added together to produce an experience (a notion Wertheimer ridiculed as "the bundle hypothesis"). Ergo, the slogan emblazoned on Gestalt's banners: "The whole is greater than the sum of its parts."

Hitler's arrival drove Gestalt's triumvirate to America, the home of S-R behaviorism, which also practiced analysis. It believed that every activity, no matter how complex, consisted of many individual S-R associations occurring in sequence, making the S-R unit the fundamental element, the building block of all behavior. Gestalt's wrath had a new target!

Let us now confront the word Gestalt itself. It defies precise translation, but an organized unit possessing a sense of form will suffice. A Gestalt is an independent, self-contained,

357

integrated unity, defined in the last analysis by our experience, i.e., a unit seems to have unity and we so respond to it. Its qualities neither reside in nor are a sum of its parts. Still, its proponents reject not any and all analyses (after all, gestalts can reside within gestalts, as witness sentences within essays and themes within symphonies) but only those that seek artificial bits and pieces not present in experience. At base, therefore, Gestaltists, like existentialists, stressed our everyday, genuine experience, with its essential unity and structure.

Let us return to one objectionable aspect of the various bundle hypotheses, i.e., that as components summate to form conglomerates, they retain their original qualities. Does not the small square in Figure 13.1 change character depending on the figure within which it is placed?[10] Therefore, must we not

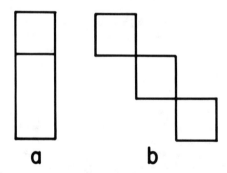

a   b

FIGURE 13.1   The effect of the whole on the qualities of the parts.   In the contexts of a and b, the top square seems different (after Hans Kreitler and Shulamith Kreitler, Psychology of the Arts, pp. 83, Figure 4.1.   Copyright C 1972 by Duke University Press.)

conclude that components become integrated, relating to one another variously and blending into the whole, so that perceptual

fields display organized groupings? Many Gestalt demonstrations
sought the laws governing such organization. For example, some
components seem almost automatically to stand out as discrete
foreground figures (areas 2, 3, and 4 in Figure 13.2) while
others, less defined, fade into the background (areas 5, 6, and

2   3   4

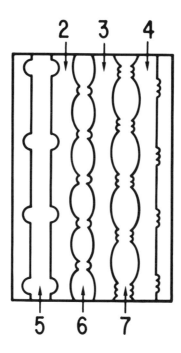

5   6   7

*FIGURE 13.2   Figure and ground (after J. E. Hochberg, "Nativism and
Empiricism in Perception."   In L. Postman (Ed.), Psychology in the
Making, 1962.   With permission of Alfred A. Knopf, Inc.)*

7).[11] Moreover, all else being equal, components in proximity or
having similarity seem to belong together (see the top and centre
panels of Figure 13.3).[12] Lastly, when components are
incomplete, we tend to invoke closure, to mentally "fill in the
blanks." Thus, we experience the brackets in Figure 13.3's
bottom panel as closed rectangles and will so recall them later.
Again, these experiences contradict our sensations, yet they are
too common to be ignored. We are inherently given to
organization. Our wholes may not exceed their parts, but they
usually differ.

We next note the Gestalt principle that underlies all these
phenomena, the Law of Prägnanz.[13] Perceptual fields will become

359

as articulated as conditions allow, with groupings of maximal simplicity, balance, and equilibrium. We seek feelings of coherence and "goodness" rather than tension, disorder, and chaos, to which ends organizational practices are simply means. Furthermore, for Gestaltists (showing Kant's influence) these practices are innate. Swimming against modernity's environmental

PROXIMITY

SIMILARITY

CLOSURE

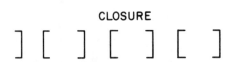

FIGURE 13.3   Gestalt principles of organization (from Edna Heibredder, SEVEN PSYCHOLOGIES, © 1933, renewed © 1961, pp. 348, 349, 350. Reprinted by permission of Prentice-Hall, Inc., Englewood Cliffs, New Jersey.)

tide, noncomformists to the end, they admitted the importance of learning, but deplored the rote repetition and trial and error methods advocated by behaviorists. Subjects who learn by such passive "chiselling in" methods cannot generalize their indoctrinated habits to other situations and often act rather stupidly.

But can these critics <u>par excellence</u> suggest better alternatives? Köhler's classic experiments[14] do. Marooned on Tenerife during World War I, with time to spare, he required, in the manner of Skinner or Thorndike, that some apes discover a response to satisfy some purpose. Thus, a banana might beckon just beyond reach of paw or stick. Does a famished primate bash wildly about, randomly emitting trials and errors in hope of accidental success? It does not. Instead, after placid, professorial pondering it notices, in its chain-linked study, two hollow tubes of differing diameters. It connects them and, using this miracle of simian technology, attains a virtuous reward. Furthermore, it thereafter solves the problem immediately, suggesting that it acquired the correct response not gradually by sheer repetition but suddenly, through <u>insight</u> (although Köhler reports no emotional "Eurekas" in apespeak). Hence, Gestalt principles of learning. The subject senses a goal and seeks behaviors that approach it. One "discovers." One "understands,"* so acquisitions are both flexible and practical. But since these matters are germane to the next topic, we defer further discussion.

Wertheimer: Productive Thinking[16]

This discussion of cognition from the Gestaltist's standpoint begins with two alternatives to it. According to formal logic, thought proceeds in systematic, step-by-step sequences, as do mathematical proofs or logical arguments. On the other hand, associationism argues that the impotent subject either discovers a problem's rules by trial and error, or memorizes same by rote repetition. Does effective cognition actually use either method? Wertheimer, after studying the solving of actual, usually mathematical problems (such as finding a parallelogram's area), answered "no." In productive thought, a sequence's various components are grouped, reorganized, and integrated, with their relationships to one another and to the final overall picture always recognized. Such thought is <u>goal directed</u>. It seeks a clear, simple structure that, once achieved, will further clarify relationships among those components; so long as these seem isolated, understanding is incomplete. Such thought, too, unlike rote learning's blind recitation of specific rules, bestows principles applicable to other situations.

---

*Bruner[15] likewise argues that skills acquired by discovery rather than rote memorization are more flexible and better retained. As further bonus, learning becomes more enjoyable, so
(Footnote Continued)

361

A jigsaw puzzles provides apt metaphor. Initially, individual pieces lie heaped before us. How, we wonder between pensive sips of coffee, do they combine to form a comprehensible picture? Obviously not any and all connections will suffice. Trial and error is used, but always guided by that final picture and by various clues such as colors and formal patterns. Later, the finished result clarifies each piece's role in the overall effect. However, productive thought, once completed, is not usually consigned to dusty top shelves or donated to the Salvation Army.

Supposedly, a sense of incompleteness or gap in a situation, a tension from "structural problems," reveals a problem and initiates the productive process. According to Henle,[17] these gaps are "active." Like dogs that scratch and howl for readmission, they demand attention. Still, we need preparatory knowledge of the problem's area to notice them; asking reasonable questions requires first knowing some answers.* Lastly, gaps beckon towards the goal; they contain, says Wertheimer, vectors whose "direction, quality and intensity"[18] mysteriously indicate the route to their elimination and also provide cognition's sense of goal-directed, linear progress. And subsuming all is our need for Prägnanz and good Gestalts, to "straighten out what is bad, to get at the good inner relatedness."[19]

To clarify this description, Mansfield and Busse[20] show how scientists avoid pursuing every conceivable solution to a problem, and remain goal oriented. Usually, various contraints - whether empirical (data already available), theoretical (prevailing biases or paradigms), or methodological (available procedural and analytic techniques) - will limit the scope of their enquiry. Only if it founders will they set aside these constraints and entertain more radical alternatives. Similarly, artificial intelligence/computer simulations of cognition have described so-called heuristics that limit the range of searchings for solutions.[21] For example, in a maze with a series of choice points, our first decision should eliminate from further

---

(Footnote Continued)
sheer discovery can motivate children and render external reinforcers, such as grades, superfluous.

*Teachers will know whereof we speak. It is cause to worry when, after a difficult presentation, questions are not forthcoming. The gloomy silence that hangs like a black cloud, the glum faces staring fixedly off into space, usually betray not understanding but bewilderment. Good questions follow when one grasps, but then on a deeper level does not.

consideration not only the rejected alternative but all remaining choices that follow from it.

To return to the gap. Its hypnotic, tantalizing promise of imminent solutions will, like Macbeth, murder sleep. Yet its closure requires so-called recentering, viewing the problem from another perspective or (in common parlance) looking at it a different way. For Wertheimer, creative blocking invariably reflects an inappropriate center, and certainly when we contemplate a painting from the front we will discover many elements and relationships we missed from one side.

So what, then, distinguishes the Galileos and Einsteins? Unlike others who fall by the wayside on the royal road to Prägnanz, they are able to get an effective center before a problem. They are also more relentless in their pursuit of same, forever changing perspectives until they find it. As well, these giants seek and often find gaps[22] where others see none (cf. Getzels et al.'s problem finding). Feelings of tension or harmony being feelings, they depend on our reactions. Most of us avoid upsetting a misleading but comforting state of affairs. We either ignore gaps or settle for band-aid solutions that overlook remaining stresses. An Einstein will grasp, and state clearly, the essence of a gap to gain precise structural insights. And nothing less than genuine closure will satisfy such a tenacious perfectionist, driven by an unquenchable thirst for "truth as against petty views--the desire not to deceive oneself".[23]

These analyses obviously describe science better than art but Wertheimer, briefly visiting the latter, admits that it begins not with a gap's tension but with a vision of a final result (cf. Arieti's endocept). Its concrete capture is the artist's[24] main problem. Witness the composer mentioned by Gardner whose latest composition was almost finished; he had only to select the notes.

But what, then, of step-by-step logic, and the rote recitation and regurgitation of the associationist? The former is a romantic fiction, perhaps evident in a finished product like a mathematical proof, but divorced from actual events. And the latter is[25] inefficient, even dangerous educational malpractice. Luchins has shown how such inflexible, robot-inducing techniques can lead even reasonably bright students into inappropriate, even stupid behavior. They solved a series of arithmetic problems by the same general rule, to instil a set, or tendency to perceive a situation in a particular way. Later, given other problems demanding different lines of attack, they could not switch horses. Wertheimer, therefore, deplores the frequent supposition that rote reproductive learning is more basic and natural than the Gestalt variety. Whereas effective

thinking is rarely bound by slavish habits, rote recitation
hinders cognitive development by ignoring organization among
elements and treating them piecemeal. It "cuts to pieces living
thinking.[26] does nothing but dissect... and thus shows a dead
picture."[26] Children so trained miss the forests behind all
those separate trees.

　　1. The thought of Albert Einstein. From countless hours
spent in discussion with Einstein, Wertheimer concluded that the
theory of relativity arose from cognition that epitomized the
productive kind. Although Einstein was preoccupied with his
project for seven years, he needed only five weeks to write the
revolutionary first paper (even with time away for his duties at
the famous Patent Office) once he had achieved the critical
recentering that provided the final insights. For this
inveterate problem finder, who often used striking visual
metaphors to pursue his solutions, the [*]Michelson-Morley
experiment seemingly provided the crucial gap. Simplifying it
outrageously, a boat moving with a river's current will obviously
travel faster than one struggling upstream. Similarly, it was
generally accepted that light would move faster when traveling in
the earth's direction than in another. Except that according to
the experiment, light's speed didn't vary with its direction.

　　Einstein's recentering led him to question a heretofore
inviolate assumption, i.e., that time is an absolute. Consider
the concept of simultaneity. Will two events in different
locations, such as two lightening flashes, seem simultaneous to
every observor? The prevailing answer was "yes," but Einstein
showed that, while they might appear so to someone stationed half
way between them, another observor moving towards one of them
would perceive it as happening first. Hence simultaneity is not
an absolute but depends on, or is relative to, the observer's
state. So, in turn, for time itself.

　　And now the puzzle's last piece. If time is not absolute,
what provides the invariant standard to which everything else
compares? Without something of the sort, the universe would
become a morass of shifting phenomena, of mutually rotating,
interacting cogwheels lacking any central core. To Einstein,
wholeheartedly committed to the universe's order and harmony,

_____

[*]Apparently, Einstein later doubted that he had known [27]of
their results before publishing his special theory in 1905.[27]
Still, many others were familiar with and puzzling over them, so
he was certainly privy to the prevailing sense that the time was
out of joint (in more ways than one, as he eventually showed).

unthinkable. His choice fell on the speed of light, previously only marginally more interesting than that of bicycles, turtles, or soap-box derbies. It was plucked from ignominy in physics' bargain basement, dressed in medalled regalia, and coronated with orb and sceptre while proud time, previously monarch _assoluta_, had to abdicate its palatial throne and mingle with the unwashed multitudes. By this master stroke the gap was obliterated, for in one fell swoop, in classic Gestalt fashion, a host of puzzling pieces, notably the Michelson-Morley results and the paradox of simultaneity, now took their place in the integrated Einsteinian structure. Their previously opaque relationships to one another and to the overall picture were now crystal clear.

And yet in print, Einstein's pronouncements march past with inexorable development. First parade axioms (e.g., that light's speed is an absolute), followed by various proofs, predictions, and implications derived from them. Does this not vindicate traditional logic's descriptions of cognition? Not a whit! Einstein's introspections, at least, suggest a different story. As he himself avowed, "No really productive man thinks in such paper fashion."[28] His axioms did not begin but grew out of the process, notably from the crucial recentering. His first thoughts, he claimed, seemed visual or even "muscular."[29] Only later were they converted to words or symbols.[*] Also (a gauntlet flung before associationists and Skinnerians) they were invariably goal directed rather than blindly groping. Even in grappling with the Michelson-Morley results, Einstein considered only possibilities having some reasonable connection to the final development. And subsuming all was his innocent naivete. Through it he saw not elegant integration but lamentable anarchy. Hence his purported remark that he proposed a new theory of the universe because he simply couldn't grasp the old one.

Festinger: Cognitive Dissonance

Why are creative persons persistently productive, when tangible reward is so rare? Because of its strong nativist bias, early Gestalt ignored this puzzle, but Festinger, once a student of Gestalt pioneer Kurt Lewin,[32] implies some possibilities harmonious with its tenets. Supposedly we experience tension, or _cognitive dissonance_,[33] whenever we observe inconsistency between our attitudes on the one hand and our actions on the other, i.e.,

---

[*] Interestingly, Einstein's letter to Hadamard[30] provides less than categorical approval for Wertheimer's descriptions; it states only that he (Einstein) cannot judge how well the psychological ideas catch the crucial point.[31]

when our acts contradict our beliefs. Thus, someone who appreciates smoking's dangers should undergo dissonance whenever lighting another cancer stick.

Festinger, true to his heritage, proposes that we will try to replace this aversive tension with Prägnant consistency by modifying either our actions or our beliefs. Our smoker may forego the weeds, or may use various rationalizations to lessen the contradiction. The research is not conclusive. Not everyone gets cancer (look at Uncle Joe, two packs a day, and still going strong at 93). Only other people get cancer. And so on. However, dissonance will not develop if external circumstance seems to have forced the inconsistency, because we thereby receive a reasonable excuse for it, e.g., "I know I shouldn't do this, but (he/she/it/they/all of the above) made me." Then acts and beliefs may still go their separate ways without reconciliation.

Let us extend these notions (as Festinger, apparently, did not[34]) to creativity, for here lies comely explanation for creatives' compulsive work habits. Recall the importance that Rank attached to labeling oneself as writer, painter, and the like (and, evidently, creative persons do perceive themselves as creative[35]). It follows, then, that lack of productivity would contradict this self concept and should induce dissonance. The alternatives? Either get to work or change one's self concept. Guilt being a powerful motivator, once more, with a heavy sigh, one will remove the dust cover from the typewriter, or book model for 10 AM sitting. Lurie[36] implicitly verifies this scenario. He notes, as have so many, the importance of persistence and stamina. But where do these originate? Elsewhere he refers to his work as "the results that justify my existence."[37] Translation: the results that confirm my self-image.

Dissonance theory also insinuates other possibilities. First, by discovering seemingly legitimate excuses for inactivity, creators can sidestep guilt/dissonance. And is it not undeniable that some are never more ingenious than in finding same? The kids need a bath. I have to visit the dentist. How can anyone concentrate with the racket from those mushrooms growing outside? Second, dissonance mechanisms could sometimes inhibit creativity. If we think ourselves untalented, any attempt we make will fly in the face of this belief and induce dissonance. All too soon we will sigh resignedly, "Whom am I trying to kid?", perhaps to nip some possibilities in the bud. Thus, novelist Saul Bellow dismissed his early writings as "timid," because "I still felt the incredible effrontery of announcing myself to the world... as a writer and an artist."[38]

Aesthetics and the Psychology of Art: Gestalt and the Kreitlers

According to the Kreitlers' scholarly, encyclopaedic survey,[39] Gestalt has mainly tackled questions about artistic form. Why do we prefer particular shapes, lines, or harmonies? Why do certain forms arouse tension? Thus, in marked contrast to Freud, content, when discussed at all, is closely linked to overt appearance. The medium is the message. As befits the Law of Prägnanz, a host of studies[40] have shown that we preponderantly prefer forms having "good Gestalt:" organized, regular, symmetrical, simple, and so on. If allowed, we will modify stimuli so as to improve their Gestalt and reduce the unsettling tension.[41] Understandably, then, although such "good" forms as straight lines, circles, and regular curves[42] are rare in nature, they were much employed by primitive artist. Perhaps they were believed to communicate with god (or devil) simply because they brought harmony out of chaos.

Still, after subjecting the various arts to lengthy Gestalt analyses, the Kreitlers recognize difficulties. Clearly we do not always prefer good forms. Unresolved dissonance and asymmetry often inhabit great work, especially nowadays; witness Martha Graham's harsh contortions, Schoenberg's atonal wanderings, and (perhaps the definitive rebuttal) those strident, fortissimo blasts in the Eroica Symphony's first movement, unresolved and off-key, that singlehandedly announce classicism's death knell and the birth of romanticism. On the other hand, are good Gestalts anywhere more ubiquitous than in unredeemed schlock? In velvet paintings of mountains and/or swans cunningly, even cynically designed for suburbia's color schemes and aesthetic appetites? In vapid MOR music, that bane of the grocery shopper and elevator occupant, with its sweetly flowing melodies and lush harmonies, to market a relentless, depressing good cheer?

Experimental evidence, too, verifies that good Gestalts,[43] like cotton candy and peaceful, homeostatic environments, are at first preferred but become, over the long haul, boring and even repellent. Thus, a Prägnant figure lengthily exposed will eventually elicit searchings for, and discoveries of, less cosy alternatives, as Sakurabayashi's study demonstrates (see Chapter 4). In fact, the Kreitlers point out, the nervous system itself is prejudiced towards the novel and unexpected; it responds intensively to stimulus change and literally tunes out monotonous repetition.

In short, Gestalt, like Hull, runs afoul of our sometime rejection of homeostatic equilibrium. In attempting to overcome this problem the Kreitlers venture far beyond the shallow wadings of Hebb and Berlyne and clearly reveal the many essentials of art that these latter overlooked. For the Kreitlers, as for Freud, Gestalt, Hull, et al., cycles of tension and relief provide part of art's attraction. A novel's plot is resolved by a "happier ever after" or a "the butler did it." A symphony's wandering theme, after many a varied elaboration, is comfortingly recapitulated. But why, then, do we seek art in the first place, if it _increases_ arousal?[44] To answer, they borrow Hebb's notion that effective stimuli possess not only arousal but also cue function, which indicates paths to resolving that arousal. Artistic consumers, they then suggest, are suffering vague, diffuse tensions, perhaps from job, evening news, or even existential _angst_, which they know not how to reduce because they lack cue function. In their tribulation, they turn to stimuli such as works of art, which generate new but specific tensions and do suggest means for resolution--in other words, they displace their tension. Presumably, then, we can enjoy increased tension so long as we foresee its imminent reduction.

With a plethora of empirical studies (the kind that only an experimental aesthetician could love), the authors then show how each art, through formal manipulation, accomplishes tension and relief. In comparison to these studies, even the telephone directory would provide more stimulating literary company. But matters improve when they admit, unlike their predecessors, that tension and relief mechanisms cannot explain art's every complexity. Otherwise, why would we (to borrow their examples) prefer a dance about boxing to the genuine article, reread a novel whose conclusion we already know, or study a score before a concert? Obviously, art provides other incentives, which next they contemplate. First, even severely formal, abstract works will provide some _emotional involvement_, some _empathy_ as we internalize and reflect on the feelings they represent. Nevertheless, since excessive empathy bespeaks soap opera's bathos, they must also provide some _aesthetic distance_, the objective scrutiny that Brecht so cherished. The best work, then, balances these two antagonists, appealing to both heart and mind.

It may also, in good Freudian fashion, fulfill wishful fantasies and provide insights into both personal and existential problems. But how, the authors ask, can it do these things both for everyone and also for each person with unique wishes and problems? How can it have both universal and individual appeal? Several devices serve these contradictory purposes, notably Freud's _sublimation_ (which allows base needs to be satisfied on higher levels) and _multileveledness_ (the best seller or pop hit wears its charms on its sleeve but great art, allowing various and equally valid interpretations, encourages continuous return). In particular, those oft-used devices, _symbols_, carry Jungian universal meaning for general impact, yet their inherent ambiguity also allows differing individual interpretations.

Fourth, the cartoonist's favourite device, abstraction, downplays stimuli's unique features while emphasizing their similarities to others; notice how a Nixon's wildly exaggerated jowls, nose, and five o'clock shadow link him to central casting's archetypal villains. But a complementary device, concretization, introduces individuality (to show us not only life but our lives) by placing collective themes within specific, unmistakable milieu. The characters in War and Peace are Everypersons but are also specific to Russian society during the Napoleonic era. Kutuzov, the military leader who dozes through strategy meetings, is a wonderfully evocative character, but he also personifies every unruffled fatalist who attributes events to preordained destiny rather than to humankind's puny interventions. To repeat, inferior work lacks this balance between opposites. For example, Ayn Rand's characters (see Chapter 16) - mere stereotyped, one-dimensional marionettes of bulldozer subtlety - are devoid of concretization; we turn without regret from them to the psychological complexities of Batman and Robin.

But the Kreitlers attach special importance to the quality of cognitive orientation. Apparently we need intellectual stimulation; we often strive, even in the face of death, to learn and comprehend. Therefore, art should clearly communicate some beliefs, or ideas, in manner both intellectually persuasive and emotionally involving:

> The peculiarly colloquial expressions of a character in a Damon Runyan story may be remembered even more accurately and vividly than an actual conversation with a hustler in New York...Charlie Chaplin's Monsieur Verdoux may teach us more about real and symbolic killing of women than the confessions of a person who has actually committed seven acts of murder.[45]

In fact, we will willingly confront, in art, unsettling or even repellent ideas which elsewhere, e.g., in a political speech, we might reject. We ask only that art say something new and stimulating. Furthermore, cognitive orientation interacts with and contributes to the usual tension-relief cycles, and so partly motivates our consumptions of art. Particularly if a work is highly original, it will often at first elicit shock or perplexity. Searching desperately, even angrily for meaning, we will cry forlornly, "What is it?", while loudly wondering why

artists must be so perversely obscure. But with further
contemplation, hopefully, enlightenment will begin to dawn.

Now, the Kreitlers conclude, a work of art must do all these
things at least to some extent (although their priorities may
vary across styles, forms, and media) if it is to earn our
praise. Thus, cheap thrillers probably provide more tension and
relief than even Macbeth (beside whose violence even Texas
Chainsaw Massacre resembles The Waltons), but lack the
multileveledness and symbolization, to say nothing of cognitive
orientation. They lend themselves to pool-side ingestion between
sips of Tom Collins. The Kreitlers' standards for aesthetic
excellence, then, seem far more comprehensive than we have met.
Moreover, they also imply a helpful distinction between art and
related pastimes. Philosophy, science, and scholarship also
provide cognitive orientation, sports and games equal tension and
relief, but only art combines all these entities in one package.
Although the Kreitlers do not extend their principles to the
producing half of the creative dyad, this would seem a step both
logical and useful. Readers needing dissertation, publication,
or merely cognitive orientation might take note.

Commentary

Early Gestalt provided appealing analyses of some topics
relevant here and, by implication, it can do likewise for others
over which it passed. Festinger's prism shed some helpful light
on creative motivation, and Kuhn's widely cited recipe for
scientific progress (see Chapter 5) also has a Gestalt aroma.
Supposedly, discomforting anomalies ruffle a discipline's
tranquil waters and unlatch the door to a revolution. But then a
new paradigm provides the necessary recentering, to relate the
various elements to one another and to the whole, in manner
heretofore unnoticed, allowing peace, harmony, and good Gestalt
once more to reign. Furthermore, Adair[46] has extended this
analysis by incorporating some cognitive dissonance principles,
i.e., that when two elements are inconsistent, the one whose
change will cause less disruption will be changed, while its
adversary is left intact. Kuhn's assertions follow directly: a
few anomalies will either be ignored or revamped to fit the
prevailing paradigm, since it carries much investment. But as
anomalies accumulate, the scientific community increasingly
senses something out of whack and experiences dissonance. Now
the paradigm itself must change to restore equanimity.

As for creatives' personality characteristics, Gestalt's
commitment to nativism would render these both inborn and
universal. But if everyone is called, why are so few chosen?
Undoubtedly Gestaltists would blame inappropriate habits, or
sets, usually reflecting abominable educational practices. Thus

has women's potential been stifled. Similarly, mental rigidity, due to excessive practice, would prevent aging dogs from not only learning but inventing new tricks. On the other hand, qualities such as naivete, flexible thinking, and dislike of regimentation would suggest a readiness to perceive unnoticed gaps and to seek productive recenterings. Moreover, successful pursuit of the same would require boundless self- confidence and persistence.

But note delightful irony. Once jargonistic differences are removed, do not Gestalt's analyses skirt the acreage of the villainous, black-hatted Hull gang? If we replace "set" with "dominant response tendency," do we not find virtually identical explanation for rigidity? When Wertheimer blames excessive "ego needs" for overly hasty, inappropriate solutions, does he not once more indicate the debilitating effects of excessive motivation? Granted, perceptual rather than behavioral tendencies are here emphasized, but, more often than not, the resulting predictions coincide.

Which leads us to become objectionable. We pass with a nod some problems previously raised, i.e., that Wertheimer's descriptions (as he admits) fit science/problem solving more comfortably than art, and that often the latter seeks dissonant tension rather than balanced simplicity. Instead, we focus on two major difficulties, both of which stem from Gestalt's nativist bias. First, as the study of Einstein's thought shows, individual differences in productivity are ignored. Many others failed in the race that he won and, most of us could not even file entries. In fact, has it not been observed that at first only a handful of scientists could even understand relativity, let alone have conceived it independently? What special abilities or rare motivations drove him to find and solve these mindboggling problems? We are not told.

Why not? Because it is clearly implied that Dame Nature has endowed us all with the equipment to perceive gaps, achieve recenterings, and even discover relativity. That most of us do not reflects our inhibiting environments, particularly of education. Herein we have repeatedly avowed an inborn, mysterious disease called talent, but in our opinion it seems not a universal but a rare affliction. Were rote recitation and piecemeal analyses banned from every classroom, the Einsteins would still be few.

The other problem we would note is that Gestalt analyses are decidedly vague and therefore difficult to implement, e.g., in the classroom. Presumably, Gestaltists lost little sleep seeking clarity because their principles, being inborn, should not need to be taught. Everyone should be able to grasp them intuitively. However this does not seem to be the case. Imagine a steamy

371

Friday afternoon in May: baseball diamonds and swimming pools beckon seductively. Harried educators exhort their charges to "notice gaps," "grasp the inner relations," and "seek balance within the whole, (to realize) equilibrium with regard to whole features."[47] Would not this list of abstracts induce, in the reluctant initiates, a demeanor even more than usually cantankerous? Would not those educators themselves eventually throw principle if not principal to the winds, and require their underlings to write down verbatim, memorize, and later regurgitate said principles? In other words, they would fall back on those very methods of rote learning to inculcate the worthlessness of rote learning.

Cognitive Associationism

Since "associationism" raises the passive subject's spectre, its pairing with cognition might seem contradictory. However, several theorists attribute originality to unusual combinations of familiar elements. They assume that subjects can control the combinations that occur and select those worth retaining. We survey such contributions now.

Henri Poincaré

No discussion of creativity, we would wager, has been so frequently referenced, or borrowed from, than this mathematician/philosopher's Mathematical Creation.[48] And this popularity is richly deserved, for a stylish, evocative presentation it is. In fact, its successors in "cognitive associationism" have advanced little beyond its terrain. Poincaré agrees with classical associationism that to discover unusual combinations and "divine hidden harmonies and relations"[49] is the key to invention in mathematics (and, by implication, in other fields as well). After laboring long and unproductively over something called Fuchsian functions, during a night untroubled by sleep, he reports:

> Ideas rose in crowds: I felt them collide until pairs interlocked, so to speak, making stable combinations.[50]

But how do these combinations arise? To psychoanalytic cheers, Poincaré invokes unconscious mechanisms, whose role in creative thought seems to him "incontestable." The seemingly fruitless stage of frustration/incubation is actually not only unavoidable but beneficial. It "sets agoing the unconscious machine,"[51] so inspirations (such as his famous specimen, received while boarding a bus) can eventually arrive. Still, most combinations will be trivial, and Poincaré unambiguously aligns himself with the active subject when he says, "invention

372

is discernment, choice...not making useless combinations".[52]
This burden is also carried by the unconscious. Like a filtering
censor, it experiments with and eliminates most combinations so
that only the worthwhile, possessing "brevity, suddenness and
immediate certainty,"[53] reach consciousness:

> (The unconscious) is not purely automatic;
> it is capable of discernment...having
> divined by a delicate intuition that these
> combinations would be useful...All goes on
> as if the inventor were an examiner for the
> second degree who would only have to
> question the candidates who had passed a
> previous examination.[54]

Moreover, even in such seemingly objective areas as mathematics,
aesthetic criteria largely determine the choices made by the
unconscious:

> (Good ideas have) beauty and
> elegance...(They) are precisely the most
> beautiful, I mean those best able to charm
> this special sensibility.[55]

But conscious processes also play a role. In Poincaré's apt
metaphor, the elements of thought resemble overcoats hung from a
wall, awaiting use. Preliminary, conscious effort selects those
that seem likely to harmonize with the other accoutrements of
one's cognitive ensemble:

> The mobilized atoms are therefore not any
> atoms whatsoever; they are those from which
> we might reasonably expect the desired
> solution...(So) the only combinations that
> have a chance of forming are those where at
> least one of the elements is one of those
> atoms freely chosen by our will (italics
> mine).[56]

Again, active decisionary processes are invoked.

Obviously, Poincaré's hypotheses rest entirely on
introspective, subjective evidence. They are not, and probably
cannot be, verified empirically. Yet, judging by their wide
dissemination, they strike responsive chords in both students of
and participants in the creative process. When ideas "feel
right" to most responsible individuals, should this reliability
not be heeded? Certainly introspection can err. But so too can
empiricism, by rejecting worthwhile ideas that cannot be

373

scrutinized by its rules. Poincaré provides telling rejoinder to those who would so limit creativity's investigation.

Sarnoff A. Mednick

Chapter 2 mentioned the RAT (Remote Associations Test),[57] which purportedly evaluates creative potential. We are now ready to discuss its underlying rationale. Mednick first cites introspective reports from such as Einstein, Coleridge, and (naturally) Poincaré to verify that, as associationism would have it, novel combinations provide creative thought's essence. Presumably, the remoteness of the component ideas, i.e., the likelihood that they have not combined previously, will determine the originality of the result.

Mednick then suggests three mechanisms for achieving such combinations. The first is serendipity. If by chance the environment joins heretofore independent elements in happy contiguity, a fortunate witness can reap the dividends. Similarity provides a second such factor which, suggests Mednick, operates particularly during the writing of rhymes. Ideas may be connected if they are already similar or if each is elicited by stimuli that are themselves associates of one another. Mediation provides Mednick's third factor. If two unrelated elements, e.g., soldier and ship, have a common element, e.g., sailor, associated to both, it can bring them into contiguity, and hence novel combination. Now these notions only ambiguously imply an active subject (in fact, serendipity suggests the reverse). Similar associations could reflect contiguities either passively experienced or actively discovered (as in a striking new metaphor). Likewise, mediation could follow pre-existing connective routes automatically, or consciously chart some previously overlooked. However, when Mednick specifies gifted persons' qualities, he firmly chooses the active portrait. To achieve creative combinations one must first have a need for associative elements. With more bingo balls placed in the machine, new combinations become more likely; prospective creators willingly undergo the necessary enlargement of their repertoires. Second, (recalling Hull), those creators have a distinctive associative hierarchy. When the various associations to a stimulus differ but little in strength, more elements will be available for combination, and particularly those from a hierarchy's lower reaches, which are probably more unusual. But with a few overwhelmingly dominant responses, thought will become inflexible, those weaker alternatives beyond recall. Mednick therefore suggests that creative persons possess (for reasons unspecified) a hierarchy more gently sloped (see Figure 13.4)--and they do, he asserts, produce more unconventional associates to verbal stimuli[*] (a finding that others have been unable to confirm.)[58]   Thirdly, creators will also produce <u>more</u> associates to stimuli, allowing more permutations among elements. Finally, creators can <u>select worthwhile combinations</u>, so for Mednick they can obviously decide not only originality but also merit.

On these foundations the RAT rests.   To evaluate the aforementioned abilities, subjects are given triplets of unrelated words and must discover an associate, or mediator,

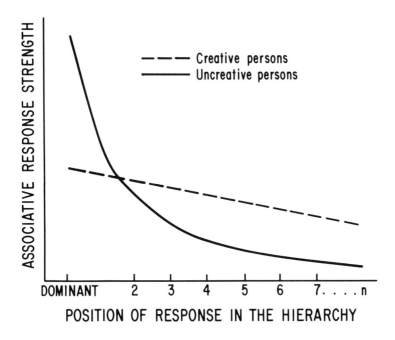

FIGURE 13.4   Mednick's hierarchy (adapted from S. A. Mednick, "The Associative Basis of the Creative Process." *Psychological Review*, 1961, *69*, 220-232.   Copyright 1962 by the American Psychological Assocation. Adapted and used by permission of the author.)

---

[*]As Mednick admits, originality could also result if a hierarchy is steeply sloped but unusual responses dominate.   In fact this may, he suggests, describe "one-shot" successes who are heard from no more.   But the longevity of a Haydn, Picasso, or Molière requires the gradual slope.

common to all three, e.g., "cheese" reasonably satisfies "rat, blue and cottage". The test purports thereby to predict creative potential, and Mednick's preliminary data suggests that it does so quite well.[59] Unfortunately, later evaluations have been less flattering. The RAT's shortcomings, we suspect, reflect its emphasis on problem solving rather than creativity. A mediator's appropriateness is immediately, generally apparent; few will dispute "cheese's" adequacy for the preceeding example. And how and why do creators separate combinatorial wheat from chaff? Mednick does not guess but merely provides some anecdotes to show that they can, anecdotes that invariably feature problem solving, not creative processes. We must insist, yet again, that these differ appreciably. Responding correctly, or appropriately does not prove that one can respond meritoriously.

Arthur Koestler

If someone were to ingest but one book about creating, Koestler's The Act of Creation[60] is likely to be the consumee. We have delayed its presentation because it contains both associationistic and Gestaltist trappings, with some psychoanalytic touches for good measure. We begin with his notion of the matrix of thought, which is "any ability, habit, or skill, any pattern of ordered behavior governed by a code of fixed rules",[61], i.e., a matrix is one way to conceive a situation, such as a problem, and resembles, then, the Gestalt concept of set. Now when we function within one matrix, we use our learned habits, making our behavior predictable and unoriginal. But, contrary to behaviorism, Koestler argues that we can also function otherwise. Animals may be exclusively creatures of habit, but we are not.

So long as a matrix succeeds, we do employ ingrained habits, but sometimes, particularly in strange situations or creative tasks, it may become blocked and lead to dead ends. Like rats unable to solve a maze, we run aimlessly about, frustrated, tension-ridden, and insomniac. But then our attention may switch to a different matrix, wherein solution suddenly appears. This process of bisociation, the combination or amalgamation of two previously unrelated matrices of thought, Koestler sees as creative thought's fundamental requisite. The humble joke provides for him (as for others) useful analogy. Supposedly its preamble builds tension by strengthening one matrix, but the punch line suddenly introduces another, bringing the two into "collision" (cf., the combat, in a pun, between a word's various meanings). Our outbursts of laughter release the tension and also signify our progress beyond bestiality and habit's bondage. For no other animal, it seems, has a sense of humor.

376

So too with creative thought. As Koestler shows by examples multitudinous, a problem's solution often lurks in a previously unrelated area. History's most famous bather, Archimedes, observed, as have many, that the water rose when he immersed himself. But he alone leaped to a different matrix. Eureka! Thus could volume be measured. Evolution was an ancient notion, but no method for achieving it could be specified. The equally ancient technique of selective breeding to improve a species gave Darwin his idea of natural selection, of survival of the fittest, which provided the puzzle's missing piece.

But how and why do fortuitous conjunctions come about? We must first introduce Koestler's concept of <u>ripeness</u>. At a particular time, certain ideas may be "in the air," preoccupying many parties, so the puzzle's pieces lie about awaiting convincing assembly. Nevertheless, Koestler asserts (firmly embracing the active subject), it requires genius to fit the pieces together; random accident has no place in his lexicon, as witness his fondness for Pasteur's dictum that fortune favors prepared minds:

> Ripeness (by itself) seems a very lame explanation, and "chance" no explanation at all...It still requires a Newton or a Leibnitz to accomplish the feat.[62]

Given this scenario, it becomes reasonable that several contemporaries might independently have the same insight, and such <u>simultaneous discoveries</u> do dot the history of science, e.g., evolution by Darwin/Wallace and calculus by Newton/Leibnitz. As another result, great discoveries will afterwards seem obvious, causing those who missed them to moan, between teeth gnashings, "Of course!"

> (Hence) the paradox that the more original a discovery the more obvious it seems afterwards. The creative act is not an act of creation in the sense of the Old Testament. It does not create something out of nothing; it uncovers, selects, reshuffles, combines, synthesizes already existing facts, ideas, faculties, skills. The more familiar the parts, the more striking the new whole.[63]

But why does a genius succeed where others fail? At times, he or she may simply occupy the right place at the right time, to notice that which everyone else has missed. As well, such an individual knows better where to look, realizing other matrices which may be helpful. But above all (and here Koestler follows

Poincaré), she or he relies on underground games in the unconscious. Here, where primary rather than rational secondary process holds sway, mental elements may combine strangely, perhaps fortuitously. Even scientists and mathematicians use such nonlinear processes. Only later, when convincing others, do they become more logical.

We must now ask whether Koestler says much that is new. In some respects, the answer must be "no." His discussion of the unconscious' role adds little to Poincaré or Kris--indeed, they develop their arguments more fully. For example, if everyone can play underground games during dreams, why does only a genius use them productively? Kris (and Arieti) at least discuss the question, however unsatisfactorily, but Koestler does not. We remain in the dark, therefore, about genius' possible requisites. Then too, Koestler's "bisociation of matrices" might seem, at first blush, to differ but little from the associationist's reshuffling of ideas. Still, we find Koestler's contribution to be a genuine departure.

First, Koestler's element for combination, the "matrix of thought," seems in theory a different animal. It seems a more general, abstract concept than does the associationist's "idea." A matrix labels the set of rules that determine the permissible ideas in a certain context. We produce different free associates to "dog" if told to think of opposites ("cat"), verbs ("bark"), or proper nouns ("Rover"). Similarly, every game has rules that specify acceptable behavior. Arbitrary they are, but if we ignore them, e.g., by moving a pawn like a queen in chess, or overcoming a tactical disadvantage by kicking over the board, we change the matrix.

Koestler mainly leaves associationism, however, with his notion of hierarchies;* their explanation requires brief digression. Supposedly, many natural phenomena form hierarchical systems, or networks, like the successively branching limbs of a tree (see Figure 13.5's left panel). Various components combine

---

*This analysis, as Koestler admits, owes much to biologist von Bertalanffy [64]. Briefly introduced in The Act of Creation's Book I, it is only developed and related clearly to creativity in Book II and in the later The Ghost in the Machine [65] (for which Book II was a prior sketch and in which it is applied so relentlessly that it becomes tedious) [66] These points need mention because Book II of the first edition [67] is omitted in some later versions so that in these, Koestler does seem unduly associationistic.

to form a unit called a holon at the next level; in turn, holons there can combine, forming a yet more complex holon at the third level, and so on. For example, human anatomy's cells form tissues, tissues become organs, which form organ systems, which form individuals, who form social systems.

Holons have two notable properties. First, they are semi-autonomous, behaving like dependent parts of larger entities in some respects, like autonomous Gestalten in others. Thus, in military hierarchies (platoon, company, regiment, and so on), a leader at each level makes some independent decisions. But when the unit must function as part of, and in relation to, other units, the leader must defer to higher authority. In short, holons tend, rather incongruously, to both self-assertion of their individuality and integration into larger entities. (These recall Rank's individuation and identification (see Chapter 10).) Secondly, holons' properties differ fundamentally from their components. Siding with Gestalt, that wholes exceed the sum of their parts, Koestler rejects behaviorism's belief that components merely combine additively. To understand a holon, we must study that holon. Yet Koestler's Gestaltism is hardly thoroughgoing either. A holon is partly an integrated entity but also, in part, a component, making analysis of higher levels into lower not entirely misinforming.

According to Koestler,[69] bisocation differs from ordinary association in several ways. First, the former, in contrast to behaviorism's (though not psychoanalysis') association, achieves its novel combinations via unconscious processes. Second, bisociation is destructive as well as constructive: these novelties arise, phoenix-like, from the ashes of their departed predecessors. (This distinction seems artificial, since associational analyses of transfer and forgetting emphasize similar destructive events.)[70] But to us the crucial distinction

---

*Koestler's[68] vitrioloic hatred of all things behavioristic on occasion verges on paranoia. He blames Watson, Skinner, et. al. for psychology's supposed failure, unlike other sciences, to progress. Yet his criticisms sometimes do ring true, to wit: behaviorism's carte blanche rejection of mind and consciousness has provided a "flat earth" view of humanity. Attributing creativity to random processes is no explanation at all and wildly oversimplifies it. Lastly, if we study animals exclusively, our knowledge of humans will remain incomplete.

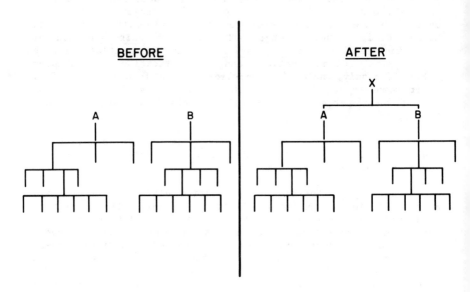

BEFORE

AFTER

FIGURE 13.5 *Koestler's hierarchies of holons.*

is that in bisociation, unlike association, a holon's component
parts meld to lose their individuality; they are not only
reshuffled but[71] integrated into something genuinely new.
(Morgan's point[71] seems similar. Familiar components can combine
to yield an entity with fundamentally different properties, as
when hydrogen and oxygen become water.) Putting it differently,
an association combines ideas within a matrix, whereas
bisociation joins previously independent matrices to form a
higher supraordinate level. Consider Figure 13.5's right panel.
Matrices A and B's top levels, when bisociated, form the more
complex holon X and lose their previous separateness.

Koestler, however, allows that only bisociations in science
follow this example:

380

> (Science) achieves the permanent integration
> into a cumulative and hierarchic order...the
> amalgamation of the two realms as wholes,
> and the integration of the laws of both
> realms into a unified code of greater
> universality.[72]

As a result, the bisociative insight releases the built-up tension in an emotional reaction of "aha." But in humor, a different matter, the bisociated matrices collide, causing the release of "ha-ha." And in art, they become juxtaposed, or placed side by side, producing the reaction, upon insight, of "ah." Which seems to suggest that for Koestler, in art combined components retain their separateness, making the results more "associationistic." In any event, since the various bisociations differ one from another, it is meet to wonder whether they reflect similar mechanisms.

To conclude, Koestler has forcefully integrated Gestalt and associationistic motifs to provide, as it were, a bisociation to explain bisociation. Yet his holon seems to retain many properties of the components, including their deficiencies. It too assumes a single "click" of combination, which may misrepresent actual inspiration (see Chapter 5). It too neglects important matters such as motivation and other stages of the process,[73] notably verification. Furthermore, according to Perkins, creativity actually relies heavily on such mundane psychological activities as recognizing, reasoning and the like. Therefore, in his opinion Koestler's emphasis of such supposedly unique processes as bisociation is misplaced.

However, two endemic problems with Koestler demand special attention. First, his many descriptions of bisociation in science are credible, but those in art leave more to be desired. Perhaps the latter does wed several components, e.g., form and content, or metaphor and theme, but Koestler has not convinced us.

Second, The Act of Creation provides a wealth, even a surfeit, of fascinating anecdotes and case histories, yet unexpectedly (Koestler being a renowned novelist/essayist and literary Nobel Prize winner) it is rather poorly written--as is The Ghost in the Machine. Meandering, irritatingly repetitive, and including huge chunks of extraneous material, they disguise the merit of his views. As a result, several readers of my acquaintance have found less there than meets the eye, and dismissed Koestler as much ado about rather little. The problem seems to be that while discussing creativity, he briefly mentions hierarchies, and when he summons hierarchies to center stage, he banishes creativity to the dressing room. As a beneficiary of associationistic principles, Koestler might have realized that if our <u>psyches</u> are to readily perceive the connection between elements, those elements must occur in contiguity.

Albert Rothenberg

This author's recent book, <u>The Emerging Goddess</u>,[74] seeks the essential components of the creative process. Like Koestler, Rothenberg invokes aspects of several traditions and so defies easy categorization. He first asked a number of experienced creators to introspect while they labored over a product such as a poem. He then compared their observations with those from others less productive and concluded that creativity depends on <u>Janusian thinking,</u>* or actively conceiving two or more opposite or antithetical ideas, images or concepts simultaneously."[75] Supposed incompatibilities now seem equally plausible and complementary.

A related mechanism called <u>homospatial thinking</u> also operates. It involves "actively conceiving two or more discrete entities occupying the same space, a conception leading to the articulation of new identities."[76] Among other things, it provides effective metaphors, those basic tools for both artist and scientist. It also, by physically uniting heretofore separate or even contradictory elements, helps to integrate them into that harmonious whole that is the effective composition.

Rothenberg then systematically examined products from many arts and sciences, as well as from other fields such as religion, and in all of these found evidence of these hypothesized processes at work. A painting apparently unites opposite elements of composition or of theme. An Einstein asserts that an observer in a free fall experiment is both in motion and at rest simultaneously. A famous religious symbol integrates the opposing forces of Yin and Yang.

Thus far associationistic and Gestaltist tenets prevail, but Rothenberg also plays some psychoanalytic themes. Most notably, he asserts (somewhat arbitrarily to the less indoctrinated) that an idea or image invariably captures a creator's interest because it relates in some way to his/her unconscious concerns. In a stimulating comparison between creative products and dreams,

---

*The reference is to the Roman god Janus, who possessed several disparate countenances, each facing in a different direction.

Rothenberg agrees with oft-expressed opinion that they have striking similarities but he also, as is less common, points out some important differences. He concludes, therefore, that a creation is a <u>mirror image</u> of the dream; the two products must serve essentially opposite purposes. (For comparable reasons he sees, like Kris and Arieti, differences as well as similarities between creative and neurotic thinking.)

More specifically, a dream seeks to disguise the unconscious content by cloaking it in vague symbols, whereas a creation attempts to reveal and clarify it. Latent content is in early drafts only dimly expressed, but during the revision process it gradually comes to the fore and moves closer to conscious realization (cf. Arieti's "endocept"), so that creators do come to "know themselves" more fully. Yet they do not actually seek complete enlightenment for, as Oedipus learned to his sorrow, this can have dangerous consequences. From his extensive studies of creators' revisions, Rothenberg has concluded that they will eliminate any aspects that are too close for comfort. Therefore, creative activity may originate in unconscious conflicts and the desire to deal with same, but it does not seem to him to represent a form of genuine therapy. These conflicts are certainly touched on and recognized to some extent, but they are not completely worked through as should be the case during treatment. As a result, a creator will probably return to them repeatedly in various works during his/her career. This itch will continue its demands to be scratched!

It seems appropriate now to raise a few notes of critical commentary. We might first ask whether Rothenberg genuinely breaks any new ground, once we surmount differences in jargon. Indeed Gedo[77] finds great similarity to Ehrenzweig, a theorist of Gestalt persuasion, but it is the spectre of Koestler that rises before the present writer's eyes. To his credit, Rothenberg has foreseen and attempted to refute this objection. One distinction, he suggests, is his own emphasis on "juxtaposition" rather than mere combination of component elements; however, from our vantage point Koestler seems of like opinion here. A second difference seems more genuine, which is the cardinal importance that Rothenberg attaches to the active opposition and contradiction of these components, rather than their mere unrelatedness.

But given the undeniable similarities, it is not surprising that Rothenberg should face at least one criticism which can also be levelled against Koestler. Both theorists place perhaps undue emphasis on one or two simple processes (be it Janusian and homospatial thinking, or bisociation) to explain each and every aspect of that supreme complexity, the creative process. To support their suppositions, these theorists then search for, and invariably find (to their own satisfaction at least) evidence for this (these) presumed process(es) in all manner of seemingly diverse products. Unfortunately, more skeptical onlookers may find these discoveries sometimes arbitrary, forced or even imaginary, and may once more come to feel like the little boy viewing the Emperor's parade, unable to perceive what they are told is there. In Rothenberg's case, "opposition" is, as he himself shows at some length, a vague and many-faceted concept; two commodities can oppose one another in a number of ways. Therefore, it is not entirely surprising that inklings of it can be found virtually anywhere.

Onlookers may wonder too, even when the theorist's conclusion does seem plausible, whether the cavalier application of a label such as Janusian thinking always adds much additional understanding of a product's existence. The lovelorn Juliet reminds us that perhaps we should attach less importance to names than we are wont to do.

Once again Rothenberg strides one step ahead of would-be critics and provides several telling rejoinders, both empirical and rational, to their objections. As a result, The Emerging Goddess is a book that undeniably grows on one as it progresses. For one thing, Rothenberg eventually admits that his favored processes hardly provide a complete explanation for creativity. They merely contribute. As well, he presents some suggestive results from word association experiments. Creative persons are more likely to respond to a word such as "hot" with its opposite, "cold," than are other subjects, suggesting that they may fathom such oppositions more readily. Indeed, Rothenberg proposes the tantalizing possibility that such tests may accurately predict one's potential for creative work.

Finally, he provides a persuasive answer to a particularly fundamental objection, i.e., that the opposition of component elements receives far too much emphasis. According to Doris Humphrey's classic treatise on choreography,[78] the uniting of opposites is but one possible device of many that creators can employ depending on the effects they wish to achieve. It is undeniably visible in some works but in others it is, to put it charitably, not immediately apparent. Rothenberg replies that we understand all our great concepts—determinism, continuity and the like—primarily as one side of a polar opposite. Indeed, without our implicitly conceiving their opposites, such concepts are virtually devoid of meaning. Therefore, such conception helps clarify a vague or difficult concept, and it is this clarification, especially of unconscious entities, that creators seek.

But why should the seeking of opposites (as opposed to other possible relations among elements) particularly facilitate the creative process? Supposedly they temporarily disrupt the ordinary smooth causality of our lives, the relentless flow of our dominant associations, which depends on continuity and sameness. Janusian thinking jars this ordinary determinism, allowing more unusual alternatives to intrude. When we contemplate opposites, we throw an eminently useful spanner in our psychological works.

Hence Rothenberg's assertion: creative thoughts are in part at least not caused at all. They are both determined and undetermined at the same time (a statement which itself seems to exemplify Janusian thinking) and certainly they cannot be predicted before they have occurred. Elsewhere, in company with Hausman, he has put the matter as follows:

> Basically, there is an unavoidable paradox: creations...are in some way recognizable and familiar to us and, therefore, they must have something in common with antecedent experiences. However, creations...are also radically new and therefore, in some respect, unfamiliar. Their specific natures cannot be predicted from a knowledge of their antecedents.In this sense, creations are undetermined.[79]

Creators' basic purpose, then, is a struggle towards freedom, and it is in the service of this struggle that they invoke Janusian thinking. They are driven towards the new, to free themselves from determinism's rigid dictates, which may partially explain why we value and admire the products that result. In such products, we glimpse that very struggle for freedom that the human spirit has always fought. (Which may explain too why products emanating from machines such as computers seem, whatever their technical merits, somehow unsatisfying. Where is the sense of human struggle?)

Other Cognitive Environmental Views

We will end this chapter with two theorists who do have some undeniable similarities to others discussed before. Nevertheless, their departures are sufficient that to force them into more specific categories would be decidedly Procrustean.

D.T. Campbell

This intriguing approach[80] sounds a few associationistic chords (e.g., it quotes Poincaré at length), but its dominant themes recall Skinner, so a comparison between the latter and Campbell seems justified. Campbell also likens creative thought to natural selection which, he notes, needs methods to (a) introduce new variations, (b) select the preferable alternatives, and (c) preserve and/or reproduce them. Thus, in biology, mutation accomplishes the firstnamed, environmental adaptation the second, and biological reproduction of selected alternatives the third. Specifying similar mechanisms for creativity will be Campbell's quest.

Like Skinner again, cognitive processes, including creativity, exemplify for Campbell trial and error, or blind responding. Subjects cannot anticipate preferred possibilities before trying them out. But hereafter, Campbell parts company. He agrees that the design of the "response occasion," i.e., environment, crucially determines the possible responses, but not that creators need it contrived for them by a godlike Significant Other. They can, by trial and error, invent it themselves, generating various situations in their imaginations and then selecting those that warrant further exploration. Thus, once more the ability to find problems becomes critical to success.

Furthermore, creators need not bash indiscriminately about, like the infinite number of monkeys or Stephen Leacock's knight who rode wildly off in all directions. Rather, they can restrict their trial responses to those of promise. Finally, they can play both subject and experimenter; they, rather than an external agent, can select the criteria that signal desirable occurrences, deliver self-reward for same, and then ingest it. Or (to switch metaphors) they design their own race tracks, enter only those horses having some hope of victory, select the winner's necessary accomplishments, and then pin the ribbon on its owner. Themselves. For Campbell then, in sharp contrast to Skinner, the occasion for responding, the responses emitted therein, and the selection criteria are all substitutes, i.e., internally generated by the subject. By this deviation, Campbell advocates the active subject and also avoids difficulties that earned Skinner rebuke.

In fact, Campbell thereby ventures towards Gestalt encampments, even more so when he agrees that thought may feature quiet contemplation, followed by sudden, remunerative insight. But his Gestalt fellow travelling is not wholehearted. Even in such instances, he asserts, blind trial and error occurs, but implicitly. Does not so-called "thought" sometimes consider various possibilities, wondering "What if I do this? Or this?"

386

Only those that match our personal criteria for selection and produce the dramatic "aha" will be emitted overtly, so they may seem insightful. Thus, Campbell recognizes the insight experience, but denies that it somehow explains success.

He then tackles one question completely ignored by behavioristic apostles of random processes. If these be creativity's tobacco, why the individual differences in lucky strikes? We have, Campbell notes, too readily credited vague entities like "talent" or "genius," which can become wonderfully circular, both verified by and used to explain creative achievement. Skinner himself could well have penned this passage:

> Let a dozen equally brilliant men each propose differing guesses about the unknown in an area of total ignorance, and let the guess of one man prove correct...In such a case, however, we would ordinarily be tempted to look for a subtle and special talent on the part of the lucky man. However, for the genuinely unanticipatable creative act, our 'awe' and 'wonder' should be directed toward the antecedents of the discovery. Just as we do not impute special 'foresight' to a successful mutant allele over an unsuccessful one, so in many cases of discovery, we should not expect marvellous consequents to have had equally marvellous antecedents.[81]

Yet the problem remains. Some mutants hit gold more often, and Campbell must ponder the reasons. First, they may have special "accuracy and detail of their representations of the external world, of possible locomotions in it or manipulation of its elements."[82] In plain words, their preparatory training has provided necessary basics, along with various exploratory responses that might work.

Second, being persistent, singleminded fanatics, the gifted practice more exploration. Those who emit few responses to puzzling situations will probably not attain immortality. Third, the gifted use constraints to restrict their responses to likely possibilities. Like untrained rats, neophytes browse indiscriminately. But the creative shopper, more systematic, imposes successively more restrictive criteria to guide the search, as if climbing one of Koestler's hierarchic trees. When seeking a library's Dickens holdings, the gifted would first locate the fiction section, then the 19th century shelves therein, then within these the English novelists, and then at

387

last the quarries. Finally, the gifted more efficiently apply their selection criteria to choose the worthwhile accidents; perhaps they possess more effective memories and so can invoke more varied criteria.

As befits North American optimism, Campbell sees these abilities as not godgivenly inherent; potentially, they can be widely instilled by imaginative instruction, so "(we) do not place the joys of creative innovation beyond the reach of the less gifted."[83] We would here agree that this may be possible for his first two abilities, but for the others we are less hopeful. Knowing where to look for quality, and how to recognize it are talents both crucial and, we suspect, difficult to impart, being innately but rarely endowed. Hopefully, further developments will give the lie to our pessimistic prognostications.

Social Learning Theory: Albert Bandura

Although his various literary endeavors include but one brief discussion of creativity,[84] along with a few casual anecdotes elsewhere, Bandura's empirical and philosophical contributions[85] have much potential. He clearly avows active subjects, whose cognitive and self-regulatory abilities can select, organize, and transform stimulation. Consider his studies of modeling[86] which investigate behaviors acquired by observing and copying others. Were we limited to trial and error, learning to, say, cross a busy street would be an inefficient, even dangerous affair. Fortunately, we can discern a situation's possible responses and their results by observing others and *imagining* ourselves therein. Which implies our active, cognitive powers.

Several factors, including attentional, retention, and motor reproduction processes,[87] supposedly influence observational learning, but only motivational processes seem relevant here. In Bandura and Walter's classic studies,[88] children who saw a model rewarded for belaboring a Bollo doll imitated his aggression more completely than did those who saw him punished. (These studies fueled fears that children might copy the rampant violence on television. The problem is large. So too is the literature on it.) Thus, the extrinsic reinforcement that a behavior produces does influence its copying (probably by insuring that we notice it). But thereafter Bandura's views depart behavioristic orthodoxy. For a Skinner, reinforcement works backwards, or "retroactively," strengthening events that have already occurred. For Bandura, it acts as a future incentive, inducing an expectancy that a certain act will achieve it; "If I do this," we surmise, "this will happen."

388

As well, reinforcers need not, for Bandura, be extrinsically administered by environmental machinery. We can set standards of expected performance efficiency for ourselves. When we reach them, we can reinforce ourselves with pride, self-satisfaction, and the like, and can also deliver punishment, such as self-criticism, when we fall short. Even the attractions, and thus effects, of such externals as praise or paycheck depend on comparisons we draw between them and those internal standards. Thus, the same reward might satisfy one individual and disappoint another. For a self-perceived journeyman hockeyist, merely warming an NHL bench might represent the thrill of a lifetime; for another, the same result will seem dismal failure. Furthermore, if the former's standards later increase, he will desire more ice time. In short, a reinforcer's effects depend not on its objective properties such as its amount, but on our subjective assessment of it.

But from whence cometh these internal, regulatory standards? First of all, when we observe others controlling their own behaviors, we realize that we need such standards. We then internalize those provided by environmental sources, particularly by models. If they set high standards, we will likewise demand more of ourselves, but lax prototypes breed lax replicae.[89] (Which suggests yet another danger of humanistic education. When anything goes, will children learn to challenge themselves?) Moreover, if we adopt standards unacceptable to those sources and reward ourselves excessively, we will face sanctions, such as, accusations that our heads are inflated and our grandeurs delusional. Lastly, our internal standards continually fluctuate due to previous actions and the results of same. As conscientious joggers run farther or faster each day, we may demand ever more of ourselves; success breeds "self-confidence," but failure may stimulate "I'm not very good at this" beliefs, expectations of failure, and premature giving in to difficulties. The self-fulfilling prophecy strikes again!

Several complications arise. Since our standards continuously fluctuate with these various influences we may now be perfectionist, now lackadaisical. We may also set different standards for activities of varying significance. Professors will (ideally at least) demand much of their lecturing while cheerfully/resignedly accepting golf scores that threaten the ozone layer. Lastly, our internal standards may be unrealistic, as witness those creators who are their own worst critics and whose excessive severity threatens their productivity.

We turn now to Bandura's[90] philosophic views, called reciprocal determinism. Typical deterministic approaches, e.g., Freud or Skinner, are unidirectional; recalling the 19th century's push-pull machineries (see Figure 13.6's left panel) they attribute our every response to antecedents beyond our control, such as environment or unconscious. Existentialism, promoting complete free will and minimal external control, represents the other extreme. Bandura derides both these options, proposing instead that we interact with rather than merely respond to our environment. As the arch-determinist forgets, it is almost entirely of our own making; so we are not only acted upon by, but act on it, making the actual relationship not one way but reciprocal.

But Bandura goes further. A third factor, intermediate cognitive processes, such as thought, attention, and those internal standards of comparison, interact with both environment and behavior. For example, the environment obviously affects these mental states, yet they also influence our impressions of that environment, that is, our attentional mechanisms determine those aspects which we notice. The relationship with overt behavior is similarly reciprocal. Our thoughts and standards influence our actions and our evaluations of same, but those same actions affect our self concepts and in turn our standards for

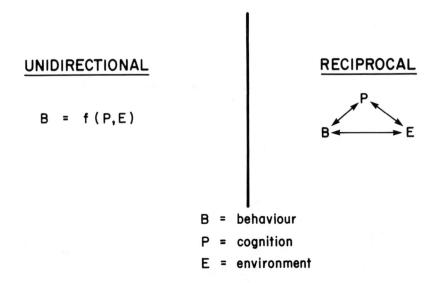

UNIDIRECTIONAL

$$B = f(P,E)$$

RECIPROCAL

B = behaviour
P = cognition
E = environment

FIGURE 13.6   Two types of determinism (adapted from A. Bandura, "The Self System in Reciprocal Determinism." American Psychologist, 1978, 33, 344-358.   Copyright 1978 by the American Psychological Association.   Adapted and used by permission of the author.)

future activities. In sum, these factors of environment, behavior, and cognition continuously interplay (see Figure 13.6's right panel), with their priorities a chicken-and-egg question. We allow Bandura the final word:

> It is within this framework...that the concept of freedom assumes meaning...Individuals are neither powerless objects controlled by environmental forces, nor entirely free agents who can do whatever they choose.[91]

Does this not seem a reasonable base for attacking creativity, especially given Rothenberg and Hausman's aforementioned, thoroughly compelling paradox?[92] While creativity in some respects conforms nicely to classic determinism, in others it is undeniably undeterministic, so that it is both at once.

We leave philosophers to debate whether Bandura avoids this quandary and move to apply him to our topic. That he has rarely done so himself is surprising, for we find almost a surfeit of explanatory riches. Most appealingly, the creative process receives realistic rather than (as with Skinner or Camus) fictional depiction. Indeed, his chastisement of Skinner recalls our own:

> Authors do not need someone sitting at their sides selectively reinforcing each written statement until a satisfactory manuscript is produced. Rather, they possess a standard of what constitutes an acceptable piece of work.[93]

Like amateur athletes, they motivate themselves in activities offering few tangible rewards. They set their own standards, comparing their behaviors to them, and reinforce themselves when appropriate. Extrinsic reinforcers may be involved, but even these creators may deliver to themselves, as when writers allow themselves a break or recreation once they meet a self-established quota of lines or pages.[94] Nothing prevents their taking these pleasures without first fulfilling the bargain. Nothing but pride, self-image, and the demands they have voluntarily placed on themselves.

In discussing modeling's role in creativity,[95] Bandura begins with a familiar problem. How could environmental stimuli, so widely available, possibly lead to novel behavior? In this context, would observers not emit mere <u>verbatim</u> copies of their models? Bandura's answer, equally familiar, employs unusual

391

combinations. Those observors reshuffle inputs from various sources (presumably using, not randomization, but enlightened cognition). As well, when models are reinforced for their creative acts (if only by evident self-satisfaction), this might encourage onlookers to try their hand. However, on the darker side, if overly competent, they may intimidate onlookers from taking the risk. Lastly, modeling helps the "diffusion of innovation."[96] New fads, trends, and styles of production are thereby passed on to the next generation, which must yet put its own stamp on them if the culture is to evolve rather than stagnate.

Beethoven's early compositions clearly owe much to the prevailing Haydn/Mazart classicism, but nevertheless hint at the more expressive, individual style to come. And it, in turn, influenced Schubert and later Brahms and Wagner, who yet found their own ways as well.

We find further application; one being modeling's therapeutic benefits. Enthusiastic colleagues can dispel apathy, that pernicious source of creative blocking. Furthermore, as Greenacre notes, modeling unquestionably influences choices of style and of field of endeavor. As child athletes so often imitate worshipped heroes, so too will others come to dance, sing, or compose. Surely it is suggestive also that so many Nobel Laureates served early apprenticeships, such as postdoctorates, under other Nobel winners;[97] Enrico Fermi alone trained six future Laureates. Thus talented students will seek out the best teachers, and vice versa. And how will those students benefit from the modeling opportunity? By all reports, not by acquiring specific bits of knowledge or techniques, for these any decent textbook can provide. Rather, as one student put it:

> It's the contact: seeing how they operate, how they think, how they go about things. Certainly not (the specific knowledge). It's learning a style of thinking...a method of work that really got things done.[98]

In particular, Amabile surmises[99] that students can thus learn to be intrinsically motivated, to work for the sheer love of the task rather than for external rewards. Such motivation, her research convincingly demonstrates, markedly benefits creative effectiveness.

Then too, as both de Mille and Woolf suggest, modeling has probably enhanced the sex difference. Girls frequently witness older women acting as wives, mothers, nurses, and teachers, but less often as creators. And does not the creator-critic dyad exemplify reciprocal determinism? Neither has priority but, bound together like prisoners in a chain gang, each stimulates, reinforces, and infuriates the other to further achievement.

In fact, modeling influences virtually[100] every aspect of creative behavior. As studies of art schools reveal, students learn to dress, speak, and even drink "like an artist" (or musician, or dancer) largely by imitating their elders. Which raises a troublesome possibility. Do the various creative personality characteristics, such as sexual androgyny, simply reflect self-fulfilling prophecies? Are they adopted by neophytes wishing to resemble their successful elders, and so perpetuated? If so, they become rather less important for understanding creativity.

Other Bandurian principles also provide explanatory aid. Creators' insecurities unquestionably stem at times from the excessive standards they set for themselves, making that which others admire seem to them a foul and pestilent congregation of vapors. For example, Hemingway constantly demeaned his own achievements, labeled himself a failure, and eventually became suicidal.[101] Even the finest orchestras have dissatisfied members, who once dreamed of soloistic renown, but now must settle for less.[102]

Obviously, then, we find in Bandura much that is worthwhile, and await with interest a fuller discussion of creativity. Yet, as always, we find problems. First, if our standards of evaluation reflect environmental input from models and other sources, why do our judgments of beauty and value differ? Why is one man's meat another's haggis? In the same vein, creators must, of necessity, possess unusual, even revolutionary standards, for they direct work. Would those creators not, therefore, as often react against as internalize those of others? Admittedly this is external influence of a sort, but the particular alternate standards that creators develop become much less predictable. For this problem, Gestalt tenets may provide medication. Perhaps environmental inputs furnish the components of the standards, but creators integrate them into a genuinely new holon, that visionary Arietian endocept that leads the verification[103] process. A recent Bandurian reply to his critics is apposite. He admits that thoughts are not limited to sensory experience, but include fantasies, imaginings, and other "novel symbolic structures" having no counterpart in reality. He does not guess at their source but, as we read him, perhaps he would find our extrapolation not completely objectionable.

Secondly, reciprocal determinism seems so intuitively reasonable that it seems a pity to quibble, but we must ask, if each factor influences every other, where does <u>explanation</u> begin?

393

Now Bandura does specify variables that affect each factor, but nevertheless, do we not end by playing intellectual ring-around-a-rosy? Whether this system even constitutes explanation as opposed to description, is another ball we hurl toward the philosophers. At least unidirectional determinism has simplicity's virtues, clearly indicating both horse and cart. Lastly, Bandura's literary style is not exactly a paragon of virtues. The polysyllabic jargon, the needlessly complicated turns of phrase, tumble forth[104] relentlessly, not only in writings addressed to professionals,[105] but in those intended for the more general populace.

Chapter 14

NATURALISTIC VIEWS III: THE ACTIVE SUBJECT PROLONGED

The philosophy underlying Chapter 13 - that of a subject endowed with decision making, cognitive powers - is here retained. However, it will now take different directions.

Developmental Approaches

Developmental psychology examines changes in behavior, cognition, and so on, with chronological age. Some of these, the inevitabilities such as puberty's onslaught and aging's graying of hair and wrinkling of skin, seem genetically prescribed, while others, such as skills of the piano-playing ilk, require specific environmental experience. However, the perspectives to be surveyed here all lie in one lineage, so let us first glance its way.

Jean Piaget

This Swiss pioneer's lifelong quest was to describe the knowledge we possess and explain its acquisition.[1] His investigations typically posed a situation, such as a problem to solve, and asked, not "Can children learn to do it?" but "What can and will they do?" In a real sense, therefore, their every response was acceptable, for it indicated how they conceived their worlds. Piaget concluded that intellectual development proceeds through a series of stages. During each of these, the child's thinking differs qualitatively. The child functions on a unique wave length, so he or she is not a miniature adult, of similar, albeit less efficient cognition. She or he is different.

Since most general psychology texts extensively describe Piaget's various stages, we will simply note one example of a stage change. Consider how the preoperational child (typically age 2-7) and the concrete operations child (age 7-11) conceive one of Piaget's famous conservation problems, that of weight. Two similar plasticene balls possess identical weight. Then, as the child watches, one ball's shape is changed by rolling it. Is the weight of ball and sausage, the child is asked, the same? An older child, realizing that weight and form are independent, votes affirmatively but a younger, unable to conserve, supports the negative. Such tests, then, reveal children's typical cognition and so their stage of development.

But let us leave empiricism for several basic Piagetian assumptions identified by Feldman.[2] According to universal achievement, every child advances through the same stages and in

395

the same order, although not at the same rate. This means, however, not that the stages are biologically programed, but that everyone, regardless of their specific cultural environment, will confront certain fundamental problems that initiate stage changes. More specifically, as we attempt to solve such problems, they interact with our current cognitive system. They may be molded to fit that system (the process of assimilation), since it affects our interpretations of and responses to our experiences. Still, those experiences, and the results of our responses to them, can also modify the cognitive system (the process of accommodation) and, in turn, the stage of development.

Supposedly, cognition seeks balance, or equilibrium, between assimilation and accommodation, which new, incomprehensible experiences upset. It can be restored (the process of equilibriation) only if the cognitive structure moves to a more mature stage, a different world view, which can encompass the unsettling experience as the old one could not. Similarly, our various cognitive systems presumably interact with and modify one another, and this process of organization can likewise impel stage changes. Thus, for Piaget, cognition is actively constructed through the child's interactions with his or her world:

> The child is neither a blank slate nor a solipsist, but rather a scientist. He is constantly building models of the world and testing those models against his experience, often in ways that facilitate changes in the models themselves. These changes...are universal, invariant.[3]

Spontaneous acquisition provides another of Piaget's assumptions. While development depends on experiences, its route is essentially inevitable, since no particular such experiences are necessary. Yet another assumption is invariant sequence. Everyone passes through the same stages in the same order. We cannot skip one, or regressively backtrack from a more advanced level. Lastly, transition rules explain how earlier stages' unique outlooks are not cast aside but reorganized to fit those that come later. And why do children thusly interact with their environments, to drive cognitive growth? Why do they not rest on their oars?[4] Apparently, Piaget finds such questions meaningless. To be human is to inquire about the world. The musical Showboat asserts that "fish gotta swim and birds gotta fly." So too must we humans progress to higher thought.

We noted that Piaget emphasized cognitive phenomena found in everyone. As a result he largely ignored, and seemed curiously unconcerned about, the rare varieties, including the creative thought he so clearly practiced himself.[5] As well, he rarely discussed nonlinear mentations, those emotions, feelings, and so forth that pervade both art and science. Significantly, his most advanced stage, formal operations, is almost exclusively rational in outlook; maturity, it seems, implies control. For these reasons, Piaget has little direct relevance here. However, a few of his (sometimes prodigal) progeny do. We might first mention, although it is somewhat tangential here, Blatt's use of some Piagetian concepts to describe the history of art.[6] He suggests that each of the main movements in culture over the ages resembles one of Piaget's stages, and that these cultural stages have arisen in the same order as that found in the child. For example, ancient Egyptian forms, while certainly admirable, indicate that Piaget's early, sensorimotor stage then prevailed, while the characteristics of "modern art" supposedly indicate that we have achieved the final stage, that of formal operations (which raises the intriguing possiblility that artistic development may have reached its terminus). Thus as Blatt shows at some length for painting at least, the preferred methods of representing forms seem to have become more complex and "mature." Still, a new development does not overthrow its predecessors but instead integrates them into a more advanced style, just as maturing children build upon rather than reject their previous outlooks.

To consider the many implications of Blatt's speculations would take us too far afield. However, we would point out the parallels with Rank's description of art history (see Chapter 10) which also used developmental concepts, albeit ones more psychoanalytic in tone. But we move on to consider several others of Piaget's heirs who relate more directly to our primary interests.

Howard Gruber

The New England area currently houses an enclave of Piagetians studying creativity. Since Gruber seems to have blazed their trails (although he has recently emigrated to a position in Geneva, Switzerland), he will raise their curtain. Creative thought, for Gruber, is a growing, developing system that may not recapitulate ontogeny but certainly resembles it. Therefore, his method of study, the evolving systems approach[7] uses a particular creator's journals, notebooks, diaries, and the like, to study the development of that person's thinking from a project's dim beginnings to its completion. Thus, as Piaget tracked down cognition's development, so Gruber tries, through retrospective, longitudinal study, to "reconstruct the growth of a creative product."[8] And whereas Piaget ignored the later years, Gruber hereby extends his boundaries by tracing creativity's progress well into adulthood (although delineating discrete stages less emphatically).

But does this method not smack of historical or biographical studies? Not exactly. Gruber stresses the unfolding of intellectual, emotional structures rather than life events, his subjects' psychological processes once beginning their creative endeavor rather than their reasons for doing so (although he sometimes does discuss environmental influence[10]). His method is avowedly phenomenological; it seeks to "get inside the subjects' heads" as it were, to view their work from their angles. Which again recalls Piaget. Yet Gruber seeks, not universal structures, but those resident in the person studied--in other words, a theory of the individual. He argues, persuasively, that since each creative product is by definition unique, its antecedent processes must in some respects be so as well; thus, to understand that product, these processes must be described (a decidedly romantic, even existential position). It would be quite arbitrary to assume that one creative act resembles and can be generalized to another.

The method possesses further attractions besides its descriptive power and recognition of creative uniqueness. By studying persons of undoubted eminence, it avoids the problem of definition; few would dispute the credentials of such Gruber targets as Darwin[11] and Piaget. Another virtue of the method is that it can provide dramatic results of compelling immediacy that studies of large groups lack. After all, what is more fascinating reading than a genuinely insightful biographical study?

Still, the method has flaws. Most notably, it invites chaos. Potentially, the number of such studies equals the number of creative persons, which, while small, is hardly infinitesimal. Will we not accumulate many individual data points but little closure on creativity in general, eventually to bog down completely?[12] Fortunately, Gruber has shown his willingness, on occasion, to practice inductive generalization. But to understand creativity, he finds it efficacious to "work backwards."[13] Begin by studying adults whose abilities are already established beyond question and find out how they do whatever it is that they do. Then try to comprehend how they came to do it, from which may come some generalizations about creativity's antecedents.

Resource availability - of notebooks, diaries, and the like - presents another difficulty, notwithstanding assurances that "there is often an embarrassment of riches."[14] Many potential candidates, Shakespeare for one,[15] are thereby eliminated. Moreover, interpreting these resources is problematic. Their

398

progenitor may, consciously or otherwise, therein play a role, as did Isadora Duncan and (as we shall soon learn) Darwin. Even private material must be ingested with saltish seasoning, given that creatives may not be overly insightful about their own processes.[16] And notebooks, like any stimulus, can provide various interpretations depending on observers' biases. Darwin's thought, to Gruber, resembled some Piagetian mechanisms, but this may simply reflect his (Gruber's) theoretical sympathies. When Gruber is, in turn, interpreted by ourselves, and we by our readers, phenomenology, we discover, can provide infinite regress. In similar vein, an investigator's biases may affect the subjects chosen to study in the first place, if they comfortably fit any theoretical axes he or she wishes to grind. Lastly, such studies, given their developmental framework, have tended to overlook some seemingly important aspects of the creative enterprise, notably personality characteristics and especially motivation. It seems to us perhaps the most seminal question of all. Why do creators do what they do?

This list by no means exhausts the difficulties with psychobiographical studies. Others have been pointed out by Perkins[17] and Runyan.[18] Their thoughtful criticisms, along with their suggestions for overcoming same, deserve consideration by those contemplating such studies. Nonetheless, the Darwin study shows the method's rich potential when practiced with commitment, (reportedly, Gruber devoted some ten years to this study). And since that study clearly affected Gruber's conclusions about creativity, we turn to it now. The notebooks from 1837-1839, (i.e., shortly following the voyage on the Beagle) suggest that Darwin's process hardly resembles a relentless "stately march" impelled by one dramatic insight. Instead, there are doubts, retreats, and leaps into the dark. Ideas wax and wane. They disappear to reappear later in different guise or changed relationship to the overall picture--for example, several versions of evolution and natural selection are contemplated. Thus, in good Piagetian fashion Gruber pursues, not Darwin's moment of inspiration, but his cognitive structure's continuous reorganization as it gradually incorporates these and other ideas.

Still, for Gruber, creative thought lacks Piaget's smooth, one-way progression through inevitable stages. On this thoroughfare, traffic flows in both directions. Sometimes, stalled vehicles block progress, so one must backtrack to take a different route[19] or perhaps lose one's way completely. Thus, Gruber doubts[19] that "unilinear" theories like Piaget's, which portray development as both continuous and inevitable, are applicable to creativity. Consider Darwin during the actual voyage. His main interest was not biology but geology. His observations verified a then-popular hypothesis, that the world had changed markedly since Day One. But that being so, how could living species have coped with their environments unless they too had changed? This was the puzzle, or gap, that forced Darwin, clearly by 1837 and perhaps even during the voyage itself, to contemplate organic evolution.

His first attempt to explain same, the so-called monad theory, propounded spontaneous generation, that new species have sprung periodically de novo from nonliving matter. Therefore, not all had been created during the magical six days, later to sailor on the ark. This version was soon relinquished, but it provides a useful beginning for studying the development of Darwin's thinking and the changing roles played by various ideas. Consider species variation. The monad theory, and several successors, tried to explain it, but the final version uses it as an explanation, assuming its occurrence and leaving its explanation to others (in this sense, Gruber suggests, The Origin of the Species has more modest scope than its predecessors, leaving unanswered this and other questions previously posed).

Or consider the idea of superfecundity, that species reproduce themselves in excessive numbers. Darwin had long realized this fact but, like Malthus, invariably viewed it negatively, as causing overpopulation and thus destruction and misery. Only when reading Malthus in 1838 was Darwin's cognitive structure ready to assimilate the notion that superfecundity might help survival. It could provide sufficient variation among species for nature to select the superior alternatives. Thus, earlier drafts virtually ignore superfecundity; it came to the fore only when Darwin's cognitive system had developed sufficiently to perceive its possibilities. Lastly, consider selection. Darwin had long known, as does every follower of horse racing, that judicious, selective interbreeding can improve bloodlines. Only later did he realize that selection could happen not only artificially, under human control, but naturally.

In short, then, an idea, to "cause the imagination to wince as at the prick of some sharp point,"[17] must be planted on sufficiently nurtured cognitive soil. And even then does one flash of inspiration convert a Darwin suddenly from perplexity to complete closure? As Gruber replies, "not really."[18] The process, he concludes, involves neither a sudden change due to one great insight, nor an uneventful monotonic progression of gradual growth. Rather, many small insights provide moments of qualitative change within a development that is on the whole continuous.[19] In Darwin's case, doubts remained even following the Malthusian awakening, and it was some weeks before the theory's final essentials were committed to paper. Yet ironically, he had previously proposed a virtually identical explanation for the development of coral reefs. But he did not

400

then see its applicability to biological systems, for in that sphere the monad theory was at that time holding sway, to block other possibilities.

Still, Darwin's cognitive system was not entirely shifting flux. A few components appear repeatedly in the notebooks, notably the branching tree of nature image, with a common trunk dividing successively into ever more divergent limbs. In fact, its very ubiquity suggests that Darwin sought a theory to fit a metaphor rather than vice versa. (And that final theory does so, holding not that humankind is descended from the apes but that both species have the same ancestry.) Indeed, many networks of thought may be similarly influenced, since one's preferred metaphors do affect one's approach to problems. But in general, Darwin's thought resembles, not a static system suddenly and dramatically reorganized, but a growing organism like a "circular argument or, better, a helical process".[25] Switchback roads on mountain sides continually double back at successively higher levels. They may seem inefficient, but they provide the surest routes to summits.

Gruber also illuminates another fascinating question. Twenty-odd years intervened between Darwin's drafting of the final theory and The Origin's publication. Biology's Hamlet, why did he delay so long? The notebooks implicate his fears of opposition and persecution. He repeatedly mentions the ancient astronomers, the Galileos and Brunos who questioned prevailing beliefs and suffered retribution. Several of his contemporaries, he knew, had known persecution as well. The notion of evolution worried him less (it was very much "in the air" in his day) than the thinly veiled advocacy of materialism, that physical entities might subsume our most intellectual, even spiritual capacities. This, to most Victorians, was unthinkable, so The Origin neatly sidesteps the entire matter. But the notebooks betray Darwin's sympathies.

His public posture, notably in his autobiography, as an arch-inductionist, driven reluctantly to his views by overwhelming empirical evidence, probably reflect these fears as well. In fact, the notebooks show, he was from early on a convinced evolutionist, interpreting his observations from that standpoint. And why did these fears so trouble Darwin, whereas a Shaw would have sailed gleefully into battle with guns ablaze? Gruber guesses that Darwin, a Victorian Willy Loman, "wanted to be well-liked" and detested conflict and controversy. Surely ironic, in view of the wrath to come.

What, then, can we say about creative thought? For Gruber, like Piaget, the cognitive system features a complex network of "incredible density,"[24] in which various ideas interact, modifying one another:

> It is essential to respect this dense network, to examine it closely, for only in such scrutiny can we discover the web of relationships that gives the individual's work its unique and creative quality.[25]

These ideas continually alternate in dominance, as witness Darwin's shifting concerns for variation, mechanisms of selection, and even the natures of man, mind and materialism (giving the lie to Koestler's description of him as a "one idea man"[26]). As Gruber puts it, Darwin, like most creators, resembles a juggler. He "orchestrates" his life to keep several interests in motion simultaneously and integrates them to form a lengthier project. Several of these, in turn, comprise a complex, overriding enterprise that may be lifelong.[27] Darwin's enterprises were two, to present a viable account of evolution, and to obtain evidence favoring it over Divine Creation.

In universal cognitive development as Piaget describes it, we progress blindly towards unforseen goals. But in another of his departures, Gruber stresses that creators consciously and purposively pursue long-term destinations. Indeed, the child who progresses most rapidly through the universal stages may not necessarily be the most likely candidate for "creativity," since a tendency to cling to the naivete of earlier stages, to the ability to wonder, may be more indicative.[28] At any rate, those creators are worlds removed from behaviorism's fabrications, who bash aimlessly about seeking accidental insights. Nor is creative thought invariably "divergent," wide ranging, and flexible, as Guilford, among others, would have it. Actually, says Gruber, it can become quite narrowly constricted in a project's final stages, when the goal looms nigh.

It is these lifelong goals that provide the incredible dedication, the continuous effort of which Gruber frequently speaks as a defining attribute of the genuinely creative, of the Einstein or Picasso. Thus, creators must be virtually self-regenerating, constantly refuelling their energies, like the burning bush within which God appeared to Moses and which, according to Exodus III:2 "was not consumed."[29] How can creators burn interminably? Their project networks cause them to look, not backwards to past accomplishments but onwards to new vistas. They seek the intellectual and emotional satisfactions of discovery, "the sensuous pleasure (of) the creative activity itself."[30] Even Piaget, that slighter of our emotional side,[31] sought all these.[32] Perhaps, then, a prospective creator more willingly devises and takes on such lifelong projects? Past experiences, such as reinforcers, may motivate others, but to the creator the future beckons, making him or her a proactive rather than retroactive individual.

Before leaving Gruber, we must pose a final question. Is his method workable for artists? Do they bequeathe materials similar to a scientist's notebooks and lab reports[30] to help cognitive reconstruction? In answer, Arnheim's study of the evolution of Picasso's masterpiece, Guernica, shows that successive drafts, sketches, trial runs, and the like, can likewise suggest the development of an artist's conceptions.[*] Thus, Arnheim actually anticipates Gruber, with his strikingly similar rationale and procedure. Similar too are his depictions of the creative process. As Picasso's sketches progress, we again see a "waxing and waning" of various elements in the composition. Some, initially dominant, later disappear (sometimes to crop up later in another work), while new recruits replace them. Often there is variation between several versions of one component (e.g., the bull figure that dominates the final composition), but a few ideas seem, at least in their essentials, remarkably resilient. Once more too the relations shift between components' dominance/submission, compositional relationships, and so on. In fact, this continuous reorganization of relations is an important aspect of a Guernica's development.

This last point clearly reveals Arnheim's Gestalt sympathies, but there are detours. Like Gruber again, he seems decidedly skeptical about the "one great insight" that makes the course thereafter crystal clear. Rather, the infinitude of Picasso's additions, subtractions, multiplications, and divisions suggest a host of small awakenings. Also, Arnheim repeatedly emphasizes that insight must combine with conscious rationality. Creativity is much more than a mere uncontrolled welling up of unconscious forces.

But Arnheim joins both Gruber and Gestalt in stressing the creative process' goal directedness--in his case, its movement towards a mental vision/endocept that is present from the start

---

[*]Some might wonder that we have omitted detailed discussion of Arnheim here, given his important contributions to the psychology of art.[34] However, he focuses mainly on the characteristics of works of art and of consumers of same (e.g., their perceptual processes), rather than on those who produce such works. And his discussions of the latter largely reiterate others herein (e.g., like Kris, he stresses the interplay between conscious and unconscious processes).

and that the artist tries to externalize. Trial and error there is, but always controlled by, and within limits set by, this consummation. Whether the latter changes as the work progresses, or whether it remains obdurate and simply becomes more intelligible, is unclear. Picasso himself hinted at both possibilities, and Arnheim seems equally tentative:

> A germinal idea, precise in its general tenor but unsettled in its aspects, acquired its final character by being tested against a variety of possible visual realizations.
>
> When, at the end, the artist was willing to rest his case on what his eyes and hands had arrived at, he had become able to see what he meant.[35]

At any rate, given these various findings, Arnheim dismisses the idea that creators simply combine elements additively, either in accidental or even "cognitive" manner. That underlying vision of "what is to be achieved" controls not only combination, but organization. In this, "the complexity level of the performance remains farly constant,"[36] i.e., depth and breadth of treatment trade off. At some times, the artist seems to work "extensively" on the overall composition, with less regard for individual components' fine details, at others, more "intensively," revising small units in isolation (and then revising them again when they relate unsatisfactorily to other components).

Thus, the work is gradually refined. But not necessarily towards greater complexity, at least in form. Admittedly the links between components, the various functions served by each in the overall composition, the depth and subtlety of meanings--all these increase. But as often a Picasso simplifies, eliminating redundant or extraneous material, making the renderings less detailed, more abstract. He himself stated that he makes a picture and then "destroys" it by taking things out, apparently seeking a level of abstraction appropriate to his vision. Or as Arnheim puts it, "The creative process has systolic and diastolic stages."[37] A product's growth is not consistent but fluctuates between adding complexities and eliminating the irrelevant. As someone said about sculpture, "It's easy; I simply cut away all the marble I don't need."

David Feldman

Another charter member of the Piagetian New Englanders, Feldman, in his Beyond Universals in Cognitive Development,[38] nevertheless proposes some appreciable departures. In his opinion, orthodoxy unduly emphasizes universals at the expense of esoteric achievements that depend more on specific experiences. Yet many domains (fields of expertise, such as chess or mathematics) also display distinctive stages, or progessions of developing prowess, and these potentially can be specified. To Feldman, Piaget's assumptions of sequentiality and hierarchical rules still apply in such circumstances, but universality and spontaneity do not.

He then proposes that various achievements form a continuum according to their prevalence (see Fig. 14.1), with those further to the right being more rare. At extreme left lie the universal domains such as conservation, which everyone everywhere accomplishes. The next, culture-based domains such as a certain language, are limited to members of a particular culture and depend more on environmental circumstances such as formalized education or folklore. At the other extreme lie the never-seen-before unique achievements, epitomized by creative acts. They may involve innovation within an existing domain--a new mathematical proof, say--or inventing an entirely new domain, such as video art.

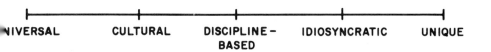

| NIVERSAL | CULTURAL | DISCIPLINE-
BASED | IDIOSYNCRATIC | UNIQUE |

DECREASING FREQUENCY OF ACCOMPLISHMENT ──►

FIGURE 14.1   Feldman's continuum: Regions of achievement (adapted from D. Feldman, Beyond Universals in Cognitive Development. Norwood, NJ: Ablex Publishing Corp., 1980, p. 9. Adaptation used with permission of the publisher.)

Feldman now introduces a key notion, the evolution of knowledge; its Darwinian debts will be evident. Supposedly a novel idea first emerges, as does a biological mutant, at the continuum's unique end, due to rare achievement. If uninteresting or unclear it will disappear like an unsuccessful mutant, but if "creative," i.e., somehow worthwhile or useful, it will survive, gradually to flourish. In other words, it begins a sort of "journey" towards the left, so the continuum's various points are, in Feldman's words, linked by time. An achievement at first unique later becomes discipline based and still later, perhaps, cultural. Consider calculus. Initially a product of individual brilliance (whether from Newton or Leibnitz), it was subsequently adopted by researchers, education systems, and textbooks of ever greater number and divergent interest.

Unique and universal achievements are linked in another sense as well. Similar mechanisms underlie their transitions, the cognitive changes accompanying advances from lower to higher levels of understanding. Supposedly, these transitions are caused by novelties, or anomalies, phenomena we either experience or conceive, that are incompatible with, and defy assimilation into, our existing cognitive structure. Disequilibrium results from the gap-like feeling that something has gone awry. Only a change in the structure to a higher outlook can eliminate it. The Gestalt tone is obvious but Feldman proposes, as one modification, that moderate disparity between novelty and structure should induce the most disequilibrium and therefore cognitive change. Slight anomalies the existing structure will simply reinterpret to fit. Gross ones it will either ignore or dismiss as "wierd." At any rate, both unique and universal transitions follow similar, recentering-like patterns. Everychild, whose transition boosts him or her to the next universal stage, and a creator, whose transitions reveal worldshaking originalities, undergo highly comparable processes.

Not surprisingly, their experiences also coincide.[39] Both insights are irreversible (reversion to earlier outlooks is unlikely) and both elicit astonishment at their simplicity (rueful amazement that they weren't realized before). They differ mainly in their receptions by others. A creative insight will garner widespread applause, but the universal variety, although profound to the child, will hardly cause anyone else to do handsprings (except, perhaps, the proud parents).

As a brief case history, Picasso claimed to have an undeviating mental vision, that guided his successive drafts and was captured by them ever more accurately.[40] Thus, he conducts "a dynamic ongoing process of comparison with an inner criterion until he is satisfied with the match of painting to 'dream'."[41] Feldman sees this description as vindicating his hypotheses. (Although he does not exactly belabor the connections, so we have had to excavate them from between his lines.) This Arietian endocept, being presumably nebulous, may induce disequilibrium and thus attempts to clarify it by capture "out there." But these external renderings will not only reflect but also alter that vision (here Feldman revises Picasso's own introspection). Thus, assimilation and accommodation dynamically interplay, with

406

internal and external events in mutual influence until equilibrium is restored. Hopefully our assimilation does not unduly distort Feldman's intent.

Which raises another of his departures from Piaget. According to the latter, we can occupy but one cognitive stage, such as concrete operations, at a given time, and this dominant outlook influences every aspect of our cognitive life. We cannot, so to speak, place different feet simultaneously in different camps. Therefore, when we progress to a higher stage, our entire cognitive structure must move as one, in lock step.

But in fact, Feldman argues, cognition often exemplifies several stages simultaneously. He therefore prefers, as he puts it, to place stages within domains rather than, as does Piaget, within heads. We may designate different achievement levels for different endeavors (one set for chess, another for math, still another for raquetball, and so on), and someone then might well be further advanced in one of these than another. Whereas for Piaget, this could not be.

Feldman defends this revision impressively, first with his studies of map drawing, in which a child makes repeated renderings, over several years, of a miniature village's essential features. Even on one such occasion, different features are drawn with varying degrees of sophistication and, even more indicatively, novelties will periodically appear, when one feature is portrayed at an atypically mature level. These lone wolf vanguards are apparently tentative tests of deeper waters, for at next opportunity they are usually withdrawn to more conservative, stripling representation (almost as if the leap ahead had intimidated its producer).

But Feldman's fascinating studies of extraordinary child prodigies most convincingly rebuff the lock-step model. Their general IQ's, although well above average (usually 120-160), are hardly extraordinary and in general they seem to be typically innocent, effervescent children. Nevertheless, in one narrow domain such as chess or music, they totally outstrip both other children and their own overall cognitive development; similarly, their passionate, persistent commitment is here remarkably adult. Even in their gifted domains they do move through the usual stages of progress, but with incredible speed. Thus they verify Piaget's invariant sequence, but not lock step.

Some child prodigies like Mendelsohn, Mozart, and J.S. Mill fulfill early promise, to disprove "early ripe, early rot." Others do not. (Those astonishingly accomplished Suzuki-trained violinists, for example, rarely persist into adulthood.) Where lies the distinction? Gardner[42] offers some guesses (as Feldman does not). Even a precocious child will not threaten superior adult standards; Mozart's early produce, so charming and amazing for one so young, lacks the depth and originality of the later. To attain this maturity, Gardner suggests, the individual will at some point, probably during adolescence, undergo a sort of mid-life crisis, questioning the meaning of heretofore obsessive labors. And this crisis, Gardner feels, is eminently desirable. Although some may desert their callings, others will reaffirm their work's importance, now with the depth and scope that is essential. For innocent naivete may be charming in a child of eight, but is somewhat less winsome in someone of forty-five.

The prodigies also provide another challenge to Piaget. Their development, unlike the universal kind, seems to depend crucially on the occurrence of specific environmental conditions. They display, not only special talent, but a remarkable coincidence of many factors, such as an enriched environment (including parents willing and able to assist) and a domain in which quality instruction is both available and possible. This lastnamed factor may explain why prodigies are generally found in a few fields, notably chess, music and math, but are rare in, say painting. (Gedo,[44] however, points out that fields such as literature simply require a fair amount of life experience for success.) Since his prodigies invariably displayed all these requisites, Feldman asserts that without every one, potential will languish. A Bobby Orr resident in Brazil rather than Parry Sound, Ontario, would never have donned the hallowed blades (although hockey's loss might have been soccer's gain). Thus, universal developmental phenomena, of Piagetian ilk, are "robust," and will occur under many circumstances.[45] But talent is "delicate." To be actualized, it requires a perfect coordination of many factors.

From this same angle, Feldman trains his guns on trait approaches such as Guilford's (see below). These imply, first, that personal qualities are fixed immutably (whereas Piagetians find continuous developmental flux--which explains their largely ignoring the various personal qualities of creatives) and second,

---

*Recently Bamberger, while accepting the ubiquity and importance of this adolescent mid-life crisis, has provided a slightly different explanation.[43] Briefly, she suggests that mature achievement requires two kinds of cognition, the child prodigy's only one, so unless the individual can make the "leap" to the more complex adult cognition, his or her work will stultify.

that traits are bequeathed by biology rather than by complex environment-individual interaction.

But Feldman's most provocative proposals, which obviously owe much to his experiences with the prodigies, concern education. He views children as craftsmen, as wanting naturally to be good at something. Primarily, therefore, their education should explore various possibilities until their niches are found. Supposedly once this occurs, they will need no threats of whipping to induce persistent labor; dilletantes no longer, they will, like the prodigies, gleefully pursue excellence. At this stage, educators should encourage this commitment by setting high standards of performance and by providing the wherewithal to progress. For example, each domain has its invariant stages of achievement, and these children should be taken through at their own pace (as Feldman's child prodigies clearly had been). Every child will thereby attain, not necessarily geniushood, but feelings of competence and self worth. It seems, then, that stereotypic suburban practices are initially recommended, i.e., swimming lessons on Monday, piano on Tuesday, jousting on Wednesday, and so on, while parental chauffeurs perfect their freeway skills. But once the niche is found, these attitudes should be sent to cold storage, for suburbia does not usually approve of highly specialized, intense commitment. "Keep it in Perspective" preach the stationwagon bumperstickers.

Comments are in order, first regarding the parallel drawn between insights of the universal, and of the unique, creative kind. The similarities are certainly striking but Gruber[46] has rightly admonished Feldman for overlooking some essential differences. For one thing, a Darwin's creativity involves a series of insights, whereas a Piagetian stage transition requires but one disequilibrium and recentering. Furthermore, a universal insight is rarely foreseen by its eventual recipient, whereas creativity is consciously goal directed. And lastly, universal achievements generally decrease social distance between children and elders; the two warring factions will now think more alike. But a unique discovery encourages the victim's separation, even alienation, from others.

---

[*]Here Feldman may be somewhat unfair. In his opinion, trait approaches cannot recognize the influence of the environment; otherwise, as it changed, so too must the supposedly irreversible traits. But could not a learned trait, once firmly implanted, resist further change? Do we not ever after recall how to swim, or to ride a bicycle?

These objections seem well placed. The two types of insight must somehow differ, since everyone can accomplish the one but not the other--otherwise, Einsteins would languish on every streetcorner. Indeed, Feldman here recalls Rogers' unintentional witticism equating discoveries of meat sauce and of relativity.[47] Feldman would not, we trust, wish to board this rickety bus, and indeed he later states that he wished to portray the two insights as similar, not identical.

The remainder of our editorial examines Feldman's provocative but problematic educational proposals. Some underlying assumptions seem a mite cavalier. First, since his important studies of prodigies have obviously influenced his thinking, we wonder whether it is reasonable to generalize from this small, highly atypical group to the larger population? Can instructional techniques workable on this small scale be implemented on one much larger? Also, allowing for the moment that each child has a potential niche, will the child, upon discovering it, necessarily take to it like the proverbial duck to water? At least for some domains, children both talented and enthusiastic will nevertheless often put in the requisite practice only at gun point, even if they fervently desire excellence. At 5 a.m. on an Arctic January, no reasonably sane ten-year old will voluntarily plunge into a pool, draw figurative patterns on arena ice, or even saw away at a cello. Sometimes those children must be prodded, because these are the prices that must be paid.

Moreover, do ability and enthusiasm invariably coincide? How many have pursued callings with avid ineptitude, while others have combined great ability with underwhelming apathy? Given such discrepancy, should the child be channeled towards talent or fervor? We would vote for the former. If one is good at something, enthusiasm should eventually develop, but its initial absence may necessitate some instructional force-feeding.

And leave us not forget that supply and demand still rules. Will society provide tax dollars and jobs to support any and every chosen pursuit--even such aberrations as, say, bird watching? On the other hand, will anyone joyfully embrace such unromantic, aromatic necessities as garbage collection? Feldman replies that society's long-term interests are best served when each person is competent at what he or she does and enjoys it, for productivity will thereby skyrocket. Ideally, perhaps, but will advocates of Reagonomics or Mulroney-gyrations cooperate? And what of those children whose interests change, as happens even with many child prodigies (Yehudi Menuhin notwithstanding)? One's passions at 18 and at 45 often differ dramatically (the nucleus of the much-discussed mid-life crisis). Will Feldman's approach not train narrow specialists who are stuck ever after

410

with their choices? And since the modern world's main constant is rapid change, perhaps educators would be better advised to stress wide-ranging nonspecifics, so the end-product is a flexible, capable learner able to **adapt** to change. Which is precisely a primary aim of the classic liberal arts and science tradition.

Lastly, are Feldman's proposals not wildly unmarketable in these days of government cutbacks and fervent cries for "back to basics"? If every child pursues her or his interests, huge resources of equipment, space, and instructional expertise will be needed, and the "three R's" will be in large part ignored (although Feldman suggests they may be acquired incidentally as the specialty is perfected). However, Feldman elsewhere recognizes realities:

> The foregoing discussion...should not be taken as an argument that **all** educational effort should be expended (towards the special interest). It is not enough for a young woman to be a skillful swimmer if she is unable to read and write. It is unacceptable to society that a child devote his total energy to mastery of the balletic form; he should also learn to participate fully in the political, economic and social life as a member of society.[48]

But despite our frownings, Feldman has provided a stimulating discussion about the education of the talented. In this age of scholarly tranquilizers, that is no small achievement.

Howard Gardner

Having extensively studied children's art in several media, Gardner in his <u>Art, Mind and Brain</u>,[49] discusses artistic development. Piagetian stage concepts are evident but so too is some departure. Apparently, between ages 2-7 creativity is rampant; art, singing, dancing, and the like are spontaneously enacted and enjoyed. As Gardner points out, children at this time are learning about and mastering their culture's symbols, notably language, so the arts provide "practice." As well, they are attempting to understand the world around them and are developing feelings about it, including profound fears of baffling phenomena. These, the fledgling existentialists, like adults, seek to understand and master through artistic expression.

The produce from this <u>golden age of art</u> is often delightfully lively and sometimes stunningly organized. It may

411

even suggest synesthesia, in which the various sensory systems intermingle; the child may sing as he draws or tell stories while prancing around the living room. Therefore he might seem an adult artist in miniature, working for similar reasons, albeit with less technical skill. Gardner, a true Piagetian, disagrees; this early artistry is but a "first draft" for maturity and different in kind, although possibly portending greater things. For one thing, an adult consciously, even cynically manipulates a medium to attain desired effects, but a child hardly understands the rules, conventions, or implications of his or her work (which enhances its uncontrived innocence). Thus, children's refreshing metaphors often express striking sensitivity to worldly similarities - one tot described a bald man as having a "barefoot head" - but these metaphors lack something of the adult's. For one thing, the similarities they express are decidedly literal and/or formal rather than abstract or emotional--an adult might find a pencil "angry," a child would not. In other words, a great artist (cf. Kris) must retain some vestiges of the child, but these must be tempered with linear, secondary process to attain depth and to avoid precociousness. As André Malraux (cited by Gardner) put it, the child's gift controls him, while the adult controls his gift.

But after the golden years' flying start, tepid stagnation sets in. Admittedly, children between 7 and 11 can now better appreciate quality and, with their heightened reasoning powers, can interpret such devices as metaphors, cliches, and figures of speech more accurately, but in this literal stage, they undertake art less enthusiastically, with decidedly more realistic, less imaginative results. Similarly, in others' work, they prefer realistic accuracy to surrealistic fantasy. (Winner[50] reviews the development of perceptual skills in several arts.) Now some authorities of Rousseauian inclination have blamed enculturation and formal education for this decline, for ravaging the natural proclivities of infant noble savages. Leave children to go their own way. Then the golden years will wax, not wane, and masterpieces will descend in torrents. Gardner hoists Piaget's colors to disagree. The stage of concrete operations, with its more realistic, down-to-earth world view, fills these years. Temporarily, rules and techniques - the "right way to do things" - and acceptance by others (notably peers) seem more important than experimentation or novelty. Thus, the decline probably reflects inevitable developmental tendencies. In support, both these initial stages appear in cultures of extremely variant socialization practices.

Furthermore, during adolescence the decline reverses. The initial level of involvement rarely returns (children now usually prefer to watch rather than do) but appreciation of stylistic and technical differences improves notably, as does tolerance for new approaches. In sum, then, artistic development follows a U-shaped curve, with the preschool and adolescent years providing the arms, and the trough lamenting the literal period. These stages invariably appear, even in dazzlingly productive lives such as Picasso's, albeit with more rapid dispatch.

Piaget's stage analyses have greatly influenced education, and Gardner also attacks this sphere. He contemplates two alternatives. We might, following humanist advice, allow children free reign to go their own way and unfold natural proclivities. Or we might intervene with more controlled regimentation to impose necessary technical skills. For Gardner, predictably, the developmental stage determines the choice. During the golden years' inherent enthusiasm, the first option seems preferable, while the literal stage, with its desires to "learn the right way," calls for the second. This later skill practice may also rectify one of Gardner's major concerns. Why does creative involvement rarely revive during adolescence? The culprit, he suspects, is excessive self-criticism. Adolescents judge everything, including their own work. If it fails to pass muster, they will quit in disgust and turn to opposite sex watching. But if some firm technical grounding can be implanted during that time of readiness, the literal stage, greater proficiency should result. Perhaps the self-flagellation to come can thereby be weathered.

Still, Gardner also reveals some important departures from Piaget. First, he agrees with Feldman that individual differences within stages deserve more attention than Piaget paid them. Consider musical development. Some children learn new songs easily while others (including some of otherwise superior intelligence) are almost literally "tone deaf," insensitive to key or interval. Or consider the literary realm. Some children fly spontaneously on wings of whimsical, imaginative fantasy; others remain firmly grounded in the here and now. But above all, consider Nadia. Severely autistic, neither understanding nor communicating with others, she nevertheless from early on showed astonishing sophistication in drawing. Even talented children draw first in scribbles, then in geometric forms such as circles and triangles. For none of these stages did Nadia pause. Did her language deficiencies allow her nonlinear talents to develop unimpeded? Certainly her drawings did decline in both quantity and quality when she eventually learned to talk (leading one breast-beating Cassandra to bemoan that therapy destroyed her sole talent). Gardner dismisses this attitude. Other autistic children show nothing like Nadia's skills, and "normals" show the same decline around age seven. Their interest later returns and so, by all appearances, has Nadia's. So she seems merely to relive the usual developmental story. Rise, fall, and resurrection.

413

Gardner also leaves Piaget's company by identifying quite different stages for artistic as opposed to cognitive development. Thus he implicitly denies that one outlook, such as concrete operations, influences every aspect of cognition. In artistic development, a rudimentary "adult" outlook appears much earlier, and fewer stages intervene. Undoubtedly, full maturity demands further growth in technical craft and awareness, but these are changes of quantity rather than quality. In fact, as we have seen, the later cognitive stages, with their exaggerated critical propensities, may impede artistry.

The foregoing implies a genuinely fundamental departure from Piaget, which Gardner has recently taken.[51] Like Guilford (see below), he denies that all types of cognition are related. There is no nonspecific "intelligence," no overriding "g" factor applicable in any and all situations, but several relatively independent domains of knowledge. Each has its own genetic origins, system of symbols, localization in the brain (as evidenced by the highly specific, selective effects of brain damage discussed in Chapter 12), and stages of progress. At last report,[52] Gardner had identified seven such "intelligences": linguistic, musical, mathematical/logical, visual-spatial, bodily-kinesthetic, social- interpersonal (i.e., ability to interact effectively with others), and intrapersonal (knowledge of oneself). However he makes no claim that this list is exhaustive. Since these faculties are "natural," every normal person has some potential for each. But since they are largely independent, their amounts will typically differ, so that someone will be better at some things than others.

In fact, Gardner proposes that certain individuals possess great potential, or are "at promise" for high achievement in a particular domain. This potential is inborn (a biological/genetic emphasis that places Gardner somewhat outside mainstream developmental thinking), but still needs appropriate environmental experiences to be actualized. He agrees with Feldman, then, that the educational sphere should stress the child's finding a niche by judicious exploration, testing, and so on. He agrees too that each domain probably features a prescribed, and distinctive, developmental path (since artistic and cognitive developmental stages differ).

The implications for our topic are several. Gardner clearly rejects the concept of a unitary faculty called "creativity." Instead, each domain may lead to a particular sort of, say, artistic expression, but the forms will differ (thus a high degree of bodily-kinesthetic ability might lead to dance expertise, spatial intelligence to geometry or sculpture, and so on). A person might well have talent in one sphere but little in another. Moreover, the classic psychological faculties, such as memory and perception, are not unitary but are separately represented in each domain. Therefore, one does not have a good memory; instead, one might remember linguistic material well but not music. Hence the Mozarts who can recall an entire composition after one hearing, but forget such trivialities as paying the rent. Similarly, one's artistic "sensitivity" might differ across domains, being torn by tortured, stormy passions in the musical sphere while evincing remarkable insensitivity in interpersonal relations (cf. Wagner).

As will become clear momentarily, Gardner's position here is reminiscent of Guilford's, although the specific domains Gardner proposes are different and (thankfully) far fewer in number. However, Gardner's main departure, it would appear, is to stress, given his developmental biases, the dynamic growth of these various faculties over the life span. Whereas for Guilford they are fixed, static traits. At any rate, given the similarities, we shall defer discussion of such analyses and pass on to commentary on other Gardnerian proposals.

Many of these we find reasonable and presented, thankfully, in style both scholarly and literate. His proposals that laissez-faire education during the golden years be followed by rigorous skill training later, and that the crucial second named be introduced at a developmentally advantageous time, seem particularly compelling. But our informal observation makes us wonder whether the literal stage provides that time. The archetypal pianist of nine will practice scales or exercises only under threat of bombardment by an entire artillery regiment. Likewise, athletes of this age (whom we have periodically instructed, to stimulate our ulcers and decrease our hair density) will endure, say, hockey drills in skating, passing, and shooting for all of three minutes. Then the cries commence. "Aw jeez. Can't we scrimmage?" In fact, did not the artistic education of earlier eras emphasize just such technical training at this very age? And did it not cause more subsequent disinterest than even adolescent self-criticism? Granted, some basic skills are best instilled early, notably those of ballet, which need the greater physical flexibility of that age. But might not adolescents more fully understand the need for, and more willingly endure, this dry but necessary groundwork?

Which raises another quibble. We agree that adolescents do abandon the artistic trough too frequently, just as they become passive spectators of rather than active participants in athletics. But is self-criticism the main culprit? Does not interest sometimes decline for precisely the opposite reason? If one possesses appreciable natural ability, it can all seem too easy. Laboring to prove that ability may seem pointless. A dab of insecurity, of a need to "show them," can provide powerful motivation. And also, of course, priorities do change when the cataclysm called puberty arrives. It is difficult to conjure up masterpieces while mooning over the latest crush or anxiously awaiting the semi-hourly phone call from Present Person Perfect. Admittedly, the output of self-pitying poetry may rise dramatically. But all else will suffer.

Psychometric Approaches: J.P. Guilford

The term psychometric implies psychological measurement and these avenues do, in the main, devise tests of such presumed commodities as intelligence, personality, and creativity. Test scores certainly provide unambiguous criteria for evaluation and prediction. Their accuracy is another matter. At any rate, psychology's resolute scientists have frequently favoured such approaches, but we restrict ourselves to one influential example.

J.P. Guilford's long, productive career advanced such topics as statistics, psychophysics and scaling, and personality theory,[53] but only his ruminations about intellect warrant our attention. Few have surpassed Guilford's commitment to empirical methods[54] as the corkscrew for liberating nature's genies. For creativity to be understood scientifically, it must be quantified so individual differences can be expressed numerically. His discussion of incubation reveals his discomfort with mystical possibilities:

> (A belief in unconscious processes) merely chases the problem out of sight and thereby the chaser feels excused from the necessity of continuing the chase further.[55]

The suggestion that psychoanalytic sympathizers are merely lazy should both amuse and infuriate them.

But while Guilford clearly inhabits naturalistic lodgings, his address re our activity/passivity is unlisted. On the one hand, he repeatedly stresses creativity's hereditary and environmental antecedents[56] (although sidestepping debate about their relative importance), as well as factors physiological. Yet his catalogue also includes some decidedly "cognitive" abilities, which suggest our interpretive powers. As well, his 1950 presidential address to the American Psychological Association[57] deplored mainstream psychology's lengthy neglect of creativity. Such missionary zeal hardly suggests his contentment with behaviorism's passive robot. In that same speech, Guilford also introduced the now accepted distinction between creativity and intelligence, and the denial that IQ tests adequately measure the first named. They overlook some of its basic requisites,

416

e.g., so-called <u>divergent thinking</u>. But to understand his objections, we must elaborate his position.

1. <u>The structure of intellect</u>. Guilford's studies emphasize <u>traits</u>, or "distinguishable, relatively enduring ways in which one individual differs from another".[58] Several assumptions about these traits deserve mention. (For Guilford, heredity and environment interact to determine our traits, so neither has primacy.) First, they are <u>variable</u>. Everyone has some amount of each, but it can differ. Second, as this statement implies, traits are <u>continuous</u>. Each varies along a dimension, or continuum, so their presence is not a yes-no, either-or matter. One cannot be slightly pregnant but (to paraphrase Polonius) one's intelligence can be slight, moderate, superior, slight-moderate, moderate-superior, or slightly-moderately-superior. Now this assumption embraces every presumed intellectual ability, including creativity, so Guilford denies that it demands special talents. The successful few differ in quantity, not quality:

> The important consideration here is the concept of continuity. Whatever the nature of creative talent may be, those persons who are recognized as creative merely have more of what all of us have.[59]

Let us immediately correct one common misconception. This approach may deny the uniqueness of traits, but it does <u>not</u> deny the uniqueness of <u>persons</u>. Each individual occupies a certain point on each trait dimension, and the <u>collection</u> of such points describes his or her personality. There being many dimensions and an infinitude of points along each, one person's aggregation of qualities, like the proverbial snowflake's, may well differ from any other.

Finally, Guilford assumes, predictably, that the various traits are <u>scalable</u>, or measurable, his preferred[60] technique for this endeavor being <u>factor analysis</u>. Its mathematical machinations are both foreboding and for us irrelevant, so we simply note a few essentials. Various suspected intellectual abilities are first hypothesized and a large number of tests constructed that seem, intuitively, to measure them. These tests are administered to large numbers of subjects, chosen indiscriminately (if everyone possesses every trait one need not delineate a set of, say, creative persons to test). Factor analysis of scores reveals groups of tests that seem to measure the same thing, so they are inspected for skills they all seem to require. Hypotheses are then advanced concerning an intellectual factor that might underly these skills, and new tests are invented to assess it more precisely.

417

Early on, Guilford[61] proposed some plausible candidates for factorhood, particularly in creativity, but some of these have subsequently been replaced by others. Therefore these early papers mainly reveal his theoretical metamorphosis over the years. Still, the philosophy of traits in essence has remained steadfast, so we will focus on the so-called structure of intellect model's final version, pictured in Figure 14.2. Supposedly, intellect varies along three independent dimensions, each containing several categories. The first dimension, content, concerns the various types of information with which someone might prefer to deal. The first of these is figural stimulation, "generated rather immediately from input from sense organs as what we call perception."[62] This category contains two sub-classes, visual and auditory, since figures can take either form. Other persons might prefer semantic stimulation (in the form of language), others symbolic stimuli (such as the mathematical or logical), and still others behavioral (those emanating from organism's actions).

The second major dimension, products, denotes various preferred means of expressing oneself. These include units (or Gestalts), classes, implications, and relations. Each involves a way of grouping units and each is but vaguely described,[63] but presumably they can be distinguished operationally. However, the last product category, transformations, is both more intelligible and here more relevant; it describes our tendencies to change the information we receive.

The final dimension, operations, includes various types of thought we might prefer. Memory, cognition and evaluation (judging) seem self-explanatory, e.g., the first might pinpoint those prone to nostalgia or living in the past. Convergent thinking, resembling the present writer's notion of problem solving, searches with narrow focus for a certain idea. Divergent thinking, akin to our "creativity," surveys a broad range of ideas, none of which is unquestionably "correct."

A particular combination of any three categories, or one cell in Figure 14.2's matrix, designates a psychological factor. By current computation there are 120 in all (6 products X 5 operations X 4 contents). Guilford aims first to identify and name each factor (e.g., divergent production of semantic units is called ideational fluency, and divergent production of symbolic units is word fluency) and then to invent a test that measures it. Thus, the Plot Titles Test assesses ideational fluency. How many titles, clever or otherwise, can one devise for a presented short story? Or (to test word fluency) how many words can one spew forth that contain a specified letter such as "r"?

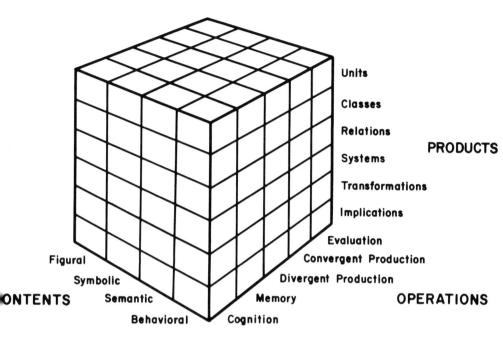

Units

Classes

Relations

PRODUCTS

Systems

Transformations

Implications

Evaluation

Convergent Production

Divergent Production

Figural

Symbolic

Semantic

Memory

OPERATIONS

Behavioral   Cognition

ONTENTS

FIGURE 14.2   Guilford's structure of intellect model (after J. P. Guilford, 1975, [62] p. 41.   Used with permission of the author.)

We turn now to Guilford's depiction of creativity. Although the factor of transformation is implicated,[64] since it allows changes to familiar information, divergent thinking provides the main constituent. And since this category embraces 24 cells, Guilfordian creativity obviously comes in many guises. For example, different cells within divergency represent not only self-evident factors like flexibility and originality, but also less obvious candidates like fluency. For Guilford, creative persons should produce <u>more</u> ideas in a situation, because the chance of quality emerging is thereby greater. At any rate, the tests for these various factors reportedly correlate somewhat with indicants of creativity, such as teachers' ratings.[65] However, Guilford stresses not only these intellectual factors but various motivational, social, and temperamental ones.[66] He has even used the flow diagrams beloved of computer simulators and cyberneticians[67] to describe the creative process's stages. But the results defy simplification and add little to understanding, so we pass on to some implications of the intellectual model.

Guilford rejects overriding, nonspecific "g" factors for creativity or any other aspect of intellect: "Creative potential is not a single variable any more than intelligence is."[68] Instead, each of many specific abilities supposedly affect some but not every endeavor. The oft-ignored question of specialization provides the first corollary of this provocative stance. Why might someone choose a particular field of work? Why does talent's range seem limited? (Unlike Camus, Jung or Rank, however, Guilford does not tackle differences in style. These, matters of taste rather than intellect, are peripheral to his model.) According to the model, prospective novelists should prefer semantic and perhaps behavioral content (revealing an interest in people), whereas musicians should occupy the auditory-figural, symbolic category. Similarly, those loaded with visual-figural information might lean towards visual artistry, architecture or inventing, while behavioral longings might symptomatize salespeople, politicians, judges, or even psychologists.

A second implication follows directly. Guilford favors many tests, each for a specific ability, over one grandiose test of general "creativity." Thirdly, the rejection of "g" dictates that in education, children should first sample widely, until[69] they find activities where their talents lie. From aptitude, presumably, will evolve enthusiasm (since success usually brings rewards), so specialization is now called for. Thus Guilford, from very different premises, reaches conclusions remarkably similar to Feldman and Gardner.

Guilford also confronts other creative phenomena. Concerning the sex difference, factorial evidence indicates male and female superiority in figural and verbal abilities, respectively. Which means, not that either sex has more "creativity" (such statements imply the odious "g") but that they typically will prefer different fields. Guilford would probably blame nonintellectual factors, such as discouraging environments, for women's infrequent success. And why is creativity wasted on the young? Because many divergent thinking factors, notably fluency and flexibility, decline with age. Lastly, his model might seem to encompass the critic through the category of "evaluation." But actually its tests, having correct answers, seem to measure problem solving and so may not predict ability to judge matters more arbitrary. Guilford concurs:

> There appears to be no overlap between evaluative functions...in the (structure of intellect) model and value[70] behavior of the personal preference type.

2. Commentary. Having raised the critic's specter, we too must evaluate. As Guilford himself maintained,[71] his model's main virtue is its provision of a unified, general theory of intelligence, but it can also handle, as we have seen, many creative phenomena. Still, when all is said, perhaps his main success - and a notable one it is - has been to legitimize creativity within orthodox psychology and to show how it might be attacked empirically. In 1950, when he nailed his theses to psychology's door, by his own reckoning only .2 percent of its studies during the preceeding 25 years had concerned creativity. The proportion has since grown geometrically, due in part to his own prodigious productivity. Furthermore, his model has stimulated much research (for some, an automatic proof of its value) and his equally influential tests have, through their frequent use as criterion measures, decided whether various stimulating procedures have helped creativity and whether certain individuals possess it.[72]

But now, we become less laudatory. First, we dislike Guilford's unremitting analytic propensities. Like so many of the empirically inclined, he is an unrepentant "splitter" of gross phenomena (in this case, intellect) into their components. But does not his mammoth Rubik's cube describe more than explain mind? Do we not learn something about the "what" but little about the "why"? Once we have specified the points that a Beethoven occupies on each dimension, do we understand him any better? In the same vein, as we contemplate this mind-boggling array of categories, we harbor Gestaltist doubts that Humpty Dumpty can be reassembled. Can intellect be so complicated and still function? Underwood has chastised students of memory for "overloading" it with too much structural and functional paraphernalia.[73] Guilford invites similar criticism, particularly when we include his nonintellectual components, to say nothing of other plausible categories that we might add to his list.

The Piagetians, Gruber and Feldman, have voiced another telling objection. Creativity, for Guilford, involves, not the developing, dynamic system that they see but an unchanging, static set of fixed traits. Now one might view these as changeable commodities, but Guilford would hardly do so. His tests would thereby be rendered useless, since characteristics identified at one point in time would not necessarily predict those to come.

Which raises a practical, even (given Guilford's priorities) vital difficulty. His tests have enjoyed but mixed success in prediction. Guilford, perhaps whistling past the graveyard, publically proclaims their validity, but Stein, among others, is less convinced.[70] He admits that they possess some face

421

validity, in that they demand abilities that seem intuitively related to creativity. However, their correlations both with one another and with later success are hardly of a magnitude about which to write home. And those with intelligence are rather higher than seems desirable, given Guilford's fervent avowals of creativity's independence. Why the tests' inadequacies? Guilford retorts,[71] often with justification, that they have been misused to predict general creativity. Which assumes the very thing his model denies, a creative "g" factor, so naturally they have come up short. Since each test was designed to predict a more specific ability, it would seem more appropriate to compare, say, scores on visual-figural divergent thinking with later success in art/painting.

However, the tests may still fail to pass muster. While Guilford asserts[72] that he has, on occasion, faced the problem of quality, in practice his dogmatic scientism will usually not allow it. The tests' validities, both face and other kinds, must therefore suffer. For example, naming objects both white and edible - quite apart from the tenuous connection to, say, writing poetry - hardly demonstrates one's ability to produce worthwhile responses. An answer's acceptability is objectively defined (sugar qualifies, tar doesn't), raising the specter of problem solving rather than creativity. Moreover, sheer quantity of responses is stressed; the more the merrier, regardless of their imaginative content. Now Guilford pleads that such fluency should help creativity, and we have learned of its undeniable[77] correlation to quality of output, but some such as Gruber nevertheless disagree. Creativity, especially in its later stages, demands focused goal direction, a restricting to essentials (one of Einstein's oft-noted talents). Gruber also questions the tests for being validated on large, randomly selected subject populations; he denies Guilford's assumption that everyone possesses something of creativity's requisities. Actually, he points out, most of us have not shown that part and parcel of the genuine article, the readiness for lifetimes of concerted effort, and in this sense we hardly resemble a Darwin or Einstein.

We finish with a reprimand too often earned by writers herein discussed. Reading Guilford's many emanations has not been a labor of love. His prose, although precise and unambiguous (if somewhat wordy) nonetheless evokes Kuhn's problem-solving normal science[78]--the type Maslow cashiered as allowing uncreative people to become creative.[79] Little lurks between Guilford's lines to spark further associations or set our minds awhirl. What we see is what we get. But still and all, let us not lose sight of his appreciable accomplishments, nor underestimate his honorable, highly productive career.

Chapter 15

THE THIRD FORCE I: NEO-ROMANTICISM

Third stream psychology, or the third force,[1] arose as revolt against yesteryear's two prevailing psychologies, behaviorism and psychoanalysis, which it saw as not necessarily incorrect but decidedly limited, even insulting.[2] Early apostles, notably Allport[3] and Murray,[4] formed a small minority in the rat-running wilderness, but more recently, psychologists dissatisfied with orthodoxy have flocked to its banners in large, even alarming numbers. The new religion is also called humanistic psychology because, generally deploring behaviorism's knee-jerk Darwinism and its preoccupation with lower animals, it persistently wonders what it means to be human. While not denying Darwin, the heretics insist that we are in some ways unique. Witness Allport's sentiments:

> A colleague, a good friend of mine, recently challenged me to name a single psychological problem not referable to rats for its solution. Considerably startled, I murmured something, I think, about the psychology of reading disability. But to my mind came flooding the historical problems of the aesthetic, humorous, religious, and cultural behavior of men. I thought how men build clavichords and cathedrals, how they write books, and how they laugh uproariously at Mickey Mouse; how they plan their lives five, ten, or twenty years ahead; how, by an elaborate metaphysic of their own contrivance, they deny the utility of their own experience, including the utility of the metaphysic that led them to this denial. I thought of poetry and puns, of propaganda and revolution, of stock markets and suicide, and of man's despairing hope for peace.[5]

Humanists have also questioned psychoanalysts' customary subjects, the neurotically disturbed. Should one focus only on our shortcomings and not our health? Is not the latter more than absence of illness?

> (Research psychology and psychiatry have) so far revealed to us much about man's shortcomings, his illnesses, his sins and his weaknesses, but rather little about his virtues, his potentialities, or his highest

423

aspirations. To identify realism with darkness, misery, pathology and breakdown as so many novelists have done in our time, is idiotic. Happiness is just as real as unhappiness, gratification is just as real as frustration, love is just as real as hostility....We must know what men are like at their best; not only what they are, but also what they can become.[6]

In the same vein, humanists accept the unconscious, but as a source of our greatest potential, not as a garbage dump for primitive unmentionables. In brief, whereas <u>Beyond Freedom and Dignity</u> could well entitle Freudian as well as Skinnerian attitudes, humanists prefer optimism, even flattery.

In addition, while agreeing that past and present stimulation affect our behaviors, they also avow Kantian internal structures that affect our interpretation of stimuli.[7] We are active determiners as well as passive determinees. Similarly, they admit that we often try to satisfy needs and restore homeostasis, but also stress other motives. Many activities, notably creativity, increase tension. Our persistent, essentially insatiable life goals (reminiscent of Adler) render our personalities consistent and predictable, even in situations widely diverse. Furthermore, these future plans are usually consciously held, so for humanism, unlike establishment faiths, we are able to understand our own actions.

Still, it alleges our personal stability only up to a point. We also possess appreciable free choice and hence responsibility for our lives. As Maslow's question, "Existential psychology--what's in it for us?[8]" suggests, virtually every humanist has been influenced by Kierkegaard, Sartre, et al., and has felt obliged, on occasion, to display a knowledge of them (while sometimes watering them down beyond all recognition). Why this paternity? Because third-forcers, usually clinicians rather than academics, must deal,

with human beings who are immediately suffering, struggling, and experiencing conflicts in a myriad of protean forms. This immediate experience is our mileau....We have to deal with patients whose anxiety and suffering will not be healed by theories no matter how brilliant, or by abstract laws no matter how comprehensive.[9]

Such clinicians would therefore listen sympathetically to the classic existential preachings about freedom, responsibility, and unpredictable individuality. (It is unclear whether existentialism clarified humanists' previously vague opinions, or whether the latter reached these views independently and subsequently had them confirmed. Maslow's statement that "We Americans have been talking prose all the time and didn't know it"[10] suggests the second possibility.)

However, humanists have not purchased existentialism whole hog either. To opt for complete freedom and deny our partial debts to biology and evolution, to heredity and environment seems, in Maslow's pungent phrase, "just plain silly."[11] As well, the rampant, pessimistic paranoia has held little attraction, seeming mere "high IQ whimpering on a cosmic scale."[12] We face, then, a decidedly North American existentialism, tempered by strains of utilitarianism, pragmatism (William James' influence is often admitted[13]), and scientific determinism, to say nothing of that pioneering optimism that challenged the frontiers and propounded the American Dream. Yet humanists here differ among themselves. Some, recognizing our capacities for anxiety, anguish, and evil, purvey a more pungent "existential" aroma; they will be discussed in the chapter to follow. Their more rosy-spectacled brethern provide our present focus.

In short, eclectic psychology seems yet another apt label for the humanists. These selective shoppers extraordinaire have borrowed unashamedly from many traditions, so that much to follow may seem familiar. Allport, for one, defends this practice:

> Eclecticism is often a word of ill-repute (suggesting that one lacks) a mind and style of his own. Yet...there is surely some portion of truth in every thoughtful theory or observation. How shall the broadminded theorist take this fact into account unless he holds an eclectic perspective?[14]

Yet one of their most obvious forefathers has largely been overlooked. Therefore, after examining its main sentiments, we shall point out the humanists' many similarities (and also some differences) so its representatives will serve as humanism's exemplary creatives (although in beliefs more than practices).

Romanticism[*]

This reaction against the Enlightenment's[15] intellectual, analytic excesses represents, according to Furst, that rarity, a genuinely new artistic movement. Unlike the Renaissance, it did not simply revitalize old ideas but, by emphasizing the artist's personal feelings, imagination, and taste, it replaced fixed canons of quality with a veneration for experimental nonconformity. Thus, our current assumption that creativity must include novelty expresses a romantic bias, as do the plethora of modernisms, such as Joyce's _Finnegans Wake_, which portray the world of dreams, fantasy, and inner reality. In fact, many movements of recent note, including surrealism, expressionism, and existentialism/absurdism, have romantic inclinations.

Nonetheless, as with existentialism, we can, once we know for what to look, find some influential predecessors, notably Kant, Rousseau, and the German _Sturm und Drang_ movement; indeed, Abercrombie[16] finds inklings in Spenser, Aeschylus, and even Plato. Actually, he argues, great poetry must always include some romantic tinges, for these artistic elements are basic; in the genuine article, they merely predominate. Unfortunately, like existentialism again, specifying romanticism's elements is difficult[17] since few literary terms have accumulated so many meanings. To complicate matters further, European romanticism was hardly a unified school with agreed on principles. The English, for example, revered their predecessors (especially Shakespeare), whereas the Germans and especially the French, driven by the era's revolutionary fervor, sought new beginnings. Likewise, the English, with their traditions of personal freedom, took individualism largely for granted while the French, of enduring political repression, trumpeted it to the heavens. For all these reasons, authorities disagree (recalling existentialism yet again) about those who deserve membership; for example, Furst would exclude Wordsworth, usually an automatic choice. But again we shall leave the wise man racked by dilemma and rush inwards. Hopefully by concentrating on one fairly well defined category, the English romantic poets--Wordsworth, Blake, Keats, Shelley, Byron, Coleridge, en suite--we can avoid excessive foolishness.

We begin with Abercrombie's observation that not only style or technique but also attitudes reveal romanticism. Its opposite

---

[*]We speak here of the movement in literature, especially poetry. Musical romanticism, announced by Beethoven's Eroica Symphony and epitomized by Chopin, Schumann, Liszt, et al., flowered somewhat later.

is not classicism but realism; the first named actually incorporates both extremes in virtuous moderation. And what are these romantic attitudes? Three deserve mention, the first being the aforementioned emphasis on the individual as primary, the source of ultimate truth. Humanity in the singular rather than the plural, personal experience rather than objective observation, "what it seems to me" rather than "what is," have priority. Admittedly, the English (Byron excepted) rarely struck this chord fortissimo, but it was certainly sounded. Now such beliefs obviously require abundant self-confidence, so genuine romantics relate to the surrounding world through their inviolate egos, with suspicious, high-handed arrogance.

The second theme involves the _imagination_, that presumed mental faculty mentioned earlier. Supposedly it mediates between raw sensation and the experience we obtain, modifying and enriching that sensation with images and symbols. Mind can thereby actively interpret rather than passively receive external stimulation, or can even withdraw entirely from it into an inner reality of things conceived that "never were, nor are, nor e'er shall be," things such as demons and fairies that are, well, imaginary. Here lies one distinction between romanticism and its great descendant, existentialism. Kierkegaard's revolt vociferously rejected this escape from existence into fantasy, this "inauthenticity,"[18] as Kaufmann reveals:

> What we perceive (in existentialism) is an
> unheard-of-song of songs on individuality;
> not classical, not Biblical, and not at all
> romantic. No, individuality is not
> retouched, idealized, or holy; it is
> wretched and revolting, and yet, for all its
> misery, the highest good...Nothing could be
> further from that softening of the contours
> which distinguished all romantics from the
> first attack on classicism to Novalis, Keats
> and Wordsworth. Romanticism is flight from
> the present, whether into the past, the
> future, or another world, dreams, or most
> often, a vague fog. It is self-deception.
> Romanticism yearns for deliverance from the
> cross of the Here and Now; it is willing to
> face anything but the facts.[19]

At any rate, to the romantics, the artist's rare imagination made possible creativity, by determining perceptual experience. (Although here lurks further national difference. The English avowed the imagination more fervently than did more externally inclined continentals.) Thus, this faculty, before the Enlightenment virtually unmentioned[20] but whose importance for

427

art we nowadays take for granted, came to prominence, allowing Furst to claim:

> This revolutionary evaluation of imagination represents the greatest single advance made by the Romantic movement as a whole, its most valuable contribution to the development of criticism; indeed no modern aesthetic is conceivable without some such notion of a creative imagination as one of its cornerstones.[21]

Romanticism's third attribute, the spontaneous, uninhibited expression of personal _feeling_ or emotion, is often seen as its very hallmark, but actually follows from the preceeding. After all, emotions _are_ more individual, more subjective, and therefore, supposedly, more valid than are logical arguments or empirical inductions. Although emotion in art was hardly unknown before the romantic era, it was now promoted as never before. Enlightenment priorities were jettisoned; now the heart, not the mind, became truth's seat, so that

> Instead of intellectual ardor we have cordial passion. Roughly, in fact we may say...that philosophy gave way to poetry.[22]

Now Wordsworth could describe poetry as "the spontaneous overflow of powerful feelings."[23]

But we must correct misconception. These days, we often equate romanticism with sloppy, superficial sentiment, with wide-eyed boys and cuddly dogs, with the melted butter of The Waltons and greeting card verse. Actually, the true romantic spirit is worlds removed from such supermarket art, for the latter's emotion is not spontaneous, but calculated, contrived, even cynical. Still, predictably, romantics promoted spontaneity with varying fervor. The English usually tempered it with detachment--recall that for Wordsworth, poetry is emotion recollected in tranquillity--so a first draft's passionate outpourings could presumably be revised. But a Shelley would likely leave them untouched, since the moment of frenzied inspiration for him provided truthful revelation supreme.

Some corollaries flow from these nuclei, the first of which is the artist's, especially the poet's, special status. This summit of individualism supposedly possessed rare imagination and particularly acute perceptual powers. He or she thus attained greater awareness of feelings and, in turn, of the universe and its workings. Where art was formerly a mere skilled craft, therefore, it now became mysterious, dependent on whimsical inspirations available only to the few. Nevertheless, the poet's powers of expression made her or him a prophet, a revealer of Divine Truth who awakened similar feelings in an audience and led them towards enlightenment. Unfortunately, since prophets are frequently misunderstood, alienated, and even martyred, the stereotypic romantic artist had to suffer.

The poet's imagination, whether gift or curse, supposedly also allowed communication with the Godhead resident within us, providing insight into such matters as the meaning of life and the order beneath experience's flux. Blake particularly propounded this theme, seeing the poet as a mediating Moses whose virtually sacred activities revealed God to humankind. Alternatively, for Shelley and Coleridge, that poet served largely as a "vessel" or medium through whom God communicated. More used by than using imagination, the poet might well misconceive the messages conveyed. The similarities to Jung are apparent. Indeed, the romantic imagination, when portrayed as an impersonal force at whose mercy the poet labors, does resemble the collective unconscious.

At any rate, by these various tenets the romantic poet became a virtual law unto himself, his every whim accepted and even revered. Whatever he felt, went. Thus, romanticism could degenerate into the egoistic posturing of a Byron or Wagner. Those crass inhibitors of spontaneous emotionality called form and technique could sometimes go by the boards, resulting in uncommunicative, subjective bathos. Such excess led Rank, among others, to condemn "modernism's" stressing of artists more than art.

To return to the imagination, one of its most lauded talents was to reveal the harmony beneath experience's chaos, by combining the many into the one. Perhaps reacting against the Cartesian split of mind from body, the romantics longed to regain our sense of unity in diversity. In fact, they trusted feelings partly because these capture that very sense which empirical sensations, with their fluctuations and illusions, quite lack. When we know the world, we know many things. When we know ourselves, we know but one. The search for unity had several implications. It provided a popular criterion for beauty, as in Coleridge: "The beautiful..is that in which the many, still seen as many, becomes one."[24] It affected romantic produce. Supposedly, the poet/sorcerer's magical imagination, through what Coleridge called its modifying power, could unify sensation's various components into those integrated Gestalts, artistic images. Making these, therefore, became creativity's main task and in a Blake or Shelley, they march past neverendingly, like a veritable Red Army. An ideal image unites in one entity the poet's various visions. In the extreme, he might feel himself

429

blending with the external in a sort of mystical Nirvana, or "encounter" (a reliable experience during both creative inspiration and religious frenzy).

Lastly, the quest for unity subsumed the famous preoccupation with <u>love</u> as the ultimate, perfect bliss. The romantics, ever optimistic, fervently believed that interpersonal feeling could unite all things to achieve truth, and this message it was the poet's duty to preach. Now realists, too, may promote love but for them, like Leonardo, it will require <u>intimacy</u>, extensive knowledge of the object of one's sighs. But the true romantic prefers distance, to <u>idealize</u> he/she/it. Familiarity breeds contempt. Dante's lifelong infatuation for the immortal Beatrice, the inspiration for his greatest work, is exemplary.[25] Apparently he met her briefly, on a total of three occasions.

The cult of individualism and the artist's special status also engendered the romantic superheroes, the Werthers and Childe Harolds who have so influenced our stereotypes of creative personalities. Invariably their frenzied egos and their unduly sensitive self-awareness conflicted with their unsympathetic environments. Unable to do their own things unencumbered, they perforce sank into neurosis--emotional instability, melancholy self pity, and dreamy fantasy. Yet they rather enjoyed their self-indulgent gloom, for it proved that they were "different." Unfortunately, invariably directing their feelings toward themselves, they evaluated others selfishly, which precluded genuine love.

But one famous romantic concern seems at first blush paradoxical. To Wordsworth, Keats, and Shelley at least, the poet enjoyed a rare intimacy with the surrounding world, especially nature. He or she could therefore enlighten ordinary mortals about that world, which was not the empiricist's static, lawful machine but a dynamic, living organism. But when internal feelings have priority, should not such sensory experience be downplayed? Actually, a Byron or Shelley contemplates, not nature <u>per se</u>, with its mountains, abbeys, cows, and crabgrass, but the feelings that these evoke:

> In their approach to nature they were not so much looking at extraneous objects with a life of their own as seeking a symbolic counterpoint to something within themselves.[26]

Thus, nature merely extended internal life, becoming a means to an end. In fact, a Wordsworth who could contemplate nature with detachment might find his romantic credentials thereby questioned.[27]

The Neo-Romantic Humanists

These recent resuscitators of romanticism, whom we will now discuss, have many similarities with their predecessors. They too rebelled against excessive scientism, in this case represented by behaviorism, but in rather less sweeping manner. Maslow, for instance, comes not to bury science but to broaden it:

> It is quite clear to me that scientific methods (broadly conceived) are our only ultimate ways of being sure that we have truth....I certainly wish to be understood as trying to enlarge science, not destroy it.[28]

Narrow science has erred by ignoring topics such as cognition and creativity that fit neither its methodologies nor its preferred subject populations. Unfortunately, it has thereby distorted human beings, because:

> It is tempting, if the only tool you have is a hammer, to treat everything as if it were a nail.[29]

Similarly, it has too often legitimized trivial rather than crucial questions:

> What isn't worth doing, isn't worth doing well, (and) what needs doing is worth doing, even though not very well.[30]

But psychology needs a different brand of science because it deals (or should) with human beings, who pose problems that other objects of study do not. A rock or rat will not hide its properties if it mistrusts the observer or does not wish to be studied. Moreover, that observer will rarely identify with it. But the observer cannot remain objectively detached from a subject who is human, so he or she may feel empathy, love, or anger. Yet these seeming disadvantages in fact permit a more intimate understanding and a more accepting, Taoistic science,[31] one that passively observes, rather than classifying or manipulating. After all, might not humans resent and resist attempts to "control" or "predict" their behaviors? And given the ethical problems, do we really wish to do these things, Skinner's arguments notwithstanding? In short, religion can promote either boldness and genuine understanding, or caution, defending against insecurity by denying unsettling phenomena.[32] Science provides the same alternatives and the second, too common in psychology, will attract careful, compulsive dehumanisers. In this way (to repeat Maslow's attractive aphorism) the uncreative may seem to practice creativity.

Maslow's recommendations for broadening science reveal his romantic lineage. He agrees that theory needs a data base but as a particularly avid inductionist, he would broaden it. Otherwise theories will not express everyday reality and, like his existential bretheren, he deplores those that are pie-in-the-sky. Science must also face up to our feelings, subjective experiences, and indeed all the vague, mysterious aspects of our reality, for these are paramount. A Freudian will willingly, nay eagerly discuss them, but only if they are neurotic, while the behaviorist completely ignores them. The humanist, however, welcomes introspective self reports to study feeling. The dangers of these inclusions, revealed by romanticism's excesses, that humanist _sometimes_ realizes. Vapid anti-intellectualism.[33] Touch-feely freakishness. "Navel watching and solipsism." And a clumsy one-upmanship in which each sympathiser attempts to prove that "I can outfeel any person in this movement." Whoever sobs longest and loudest to a Mozart quintet, it sometimes seems, gains the presidency of the Humanistic Society.

Like the romantic too, the humanist trumpets individuality. The behaviorists, like most scientists, sought similarities between and general statements valid for many phenomena (in this case, persons), using statistical paraphernalia such as averages and probabilities. The humanist, while accepting our many affinities, also avows our differences. Thus, Allport ardently advocated _idiographic methods_[34] to study each person's unique properties. Pigeon-holing,[35] categorical statements that "rubricize" us misinform because:

> (I suspect) that all of the infrahuman
> vertebrates in the world differ less from
> one another...than one human being does from
> another.[36]

A valid science will pursue both general and unique knowledge. It will begin with the individual, derive tentative generalizations, and apply these to other persons, modifying them where necessary. It will then return to the individual to verify their lingering suitability.[*] Too often this final step is omitted.

---

[*]Relevant to creativity, Howe[37] advocates the study of biographies of gifted persons to reveal possible antecedents for

(Footnote Continued)

Finally, like the romantics again, the humanists prefer holism to atomism. Whereas behaviorists enthusiastically analyzed complex phenomena into simple S-R associations, the humanists, heeding Gestalt's message, have viewed personality as an organized, integrated structure. Likewise profound experiences. When I am excited, it is not my stomach, nor my spleen, nor my pineal gland that feels. It is me. Indeed, Maslow sees indiscriminate analysis as another attribute of narrow, cautious science. By taking something apart, we can avoid confronting its discomforting uniqueness. But if we boldly seek genuine knowlege of a person, such analysis is "just a nuisance."[39]

Abraham Maslow: Basic Postulates

Maslow, by providing in our view the most fully developed, provocative humanistic analyses, at least of creativity (Allport, for example, rarely mentions it), earns our main attentions, although we will glance in other directions when appropriate. We will also mention some further debts to romanticism, but one difference deserves immediate notice. In contrast to the latter's heterogeneous diversity, the humanists' messages have been virtually indistinguishable, at least about matters relevant here. Which also vindicates our Maslowian focus. When everyone's speech is interchangeable we can, without grievous loss, concentrate on the superior expositor.

According to Maslow, we each possess a unique inner nature, the real self, which is partly hereditary and partly acquired. (Here he departs from those romantics like Blake who saw inner reality as not personal but collective, representing the Godhead.) It is also inherently healthy, representing our maximum potential. So once more the romantic themes of individualism, optimism, and subjectivism appear; the highest good exists within ourselves. For Maslow, then, it is invariably healthy to accept and express this real self and reach towards our potential. The crotchety but canny Polonius summarizes this creed:

> This above all--to thine own self be true,
> And it must follow, as the night the day,
> Thou canst not then be false to any man.
> (Hamlet, 1.3)

(Footnote Continued)
their abilities. Such studies have problems, which Howe discusses, but Allport[38] suggests some remedies.

In this process of self actualization[40] or becoming it is crucial, Allport adds,[41] to acquire a conscience, so that long range rather than transitory goals gain priority. This conscience is not a Freudian superego that internalizes social values and stifles impulses. It is ruled not by the dread of "I must" but by the challenge of "I ought," encouraging obligation to ourselves, so that both our self-images and growth are consistent. Thus, recalling Adler, we strive towards these unique ideals or intentions and when these change, perhaps because of religious conversion, illness, or bereavement, so will our actions. And since these intentions provide our individuality, idiographic methods become de rigeur for understanding them and, in turn, ourselves.

We turn now to perhaps Maslow's most compelling proposals, which concern motivation.[42] Most theories, he claims, lose relevance by stressing the somatic drives such as hunger, which are atypical. They are localized physically (in stomach, throat, and so on), are clearly separable (whereas most drives interact), and, above all, can momentarily be satisfied. Actually, he suggests, human needs form a hierarchy of priority (see Figure

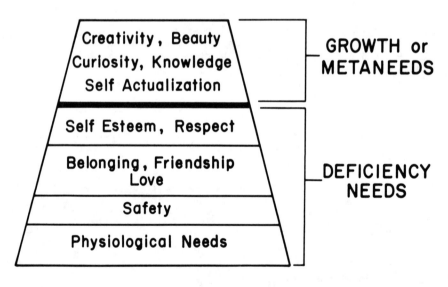

FIGURE 15.1   Maslow's hierarchy of needs.

15.1) in which these physiological needs,[*] no longer the entire story, merely occupy first place. Admittedly, we must satisfy them to live and until we do, little else will matter. A hungry person dreams about food, not love or brotherhood. Similarly,

> We should never have the desire to compose music or create mathematical systems, or to adorn houses, or to be well dressed if our stomachs were empty most of the time, or if we were continually dying of thirst.[43]

But once these survival needs are quenched, others emerge, the first being those for safety, for protection from danger. Children, for example, require parental assurance to risk exploration; otherwise ambiguity, even freedom, may threaten them. Next, the needs for belonging, friendship, and love rise to prominence, followed by those for self-esteem and respect (which drive us towards achievement, prestige, and the like). Many individuals spend their lives satisfying these deficiency needs. But if and when they succeed, the so-called growth or metaneeds can come to the fore, and it is these that distinguish living from existing.[**] They include the needs for self actualization (to become what potentially we can be); for curiosity, knowledge, and understanding; and for beauty in both surroundings and activities. Though often suppressed, these needs are supposedly as natural and "instinctoid" as eating (we do not have to learn them) and as universal. They reside within us all.

Deficiency and growth needs differ in several respects. The former, requiring external events such as other people to satisfy them, lessen personal autonomy, but the latter, being internal, enhance it. Growth needs are also individual. At this level,[45] each person is different, whereas everyone, even animals, shares the same deficiencies. The latter can also be temporarily, sometimes permanently gratified, so they come and go. Children who receive enough love and safety, for example, will always feel lovable and secure. Thus, Maslow asserts, we needn't worry about spoiling children. The more need gratification the better, for they can thereby advance further

---

[*]Maslow classified motives, not by the drives which impel them such as hunger or thirst, but by the goals, or needs, which satisfy them, because these remain stable. Love needs, for example, demand only love and anything else is mere bandaid.

[**]Goldstein[44] first described, and named, this need.

towards metahood. In contrast, growth needs, though pursued to exhaustion, seem unattainable[46] and must remain forever unsatisfied. We can have enough to eat. But enough knowledge? Or beauty? Lastly, by satisfying deficiencies, we prevent illness or neurosis, but meta satisfaction is more positive, promoting growth <u>towards</u> healthy fulfillment.

Supposedly a motive's relation to survival determines its place in the pecking order, so all needs might seem equally admirable. Nonetheless, Maslow obviously prefers the growth needs because they encourage health, individuality, and achievement of potential. Above all, they make us <u>feel</u> more delightful and joyful, and for this romantic, feelings tell the important story. No one, having once lived at this higher level,[47] will return voluntarily to the lower.

Some implications. First, for human beings to satisfy their every need completely becomes a futile, Sisyphian prospect. It is both our glory and tragedy that one need having been met, another will emerge to be frustrated and elicit moans. No one permanently surmounts Figure 15.1's mountain (although some do ascend higher on its face). Admittedly, priorities may differ; some may stress, say, esteem over love and others the reverse, but generally a need once satisfied will seem unimportant, even trivial. We gaze upwards at obstacles before us, almost never down from whence we have come (a clever tactic for avoiding unseemly tumbles). And what clues reveal someone's level of attainment? A sense of humor, for one thing. Sarcastic or cruel jokes amuse the deficient, not the actualized. Complaints, for another.[48] Like soldiers, everyone will find something to grumble about. But the deficient bemoan their cold, hunger, loneliness, or lack of love; the self-actualized their personal inadequacy, virtue unrewarded, or some such:

> A wife who complained about her husband
> forgetting to bring her flowers once...is
> certainly at a different level from the wife
> who complains that her husband broke her
> nose or knocked her teeth out.[49]

Good point!

A second implication. Our growth needs, pleading weakly for satisfaction, presumably give rise to our instinctive impulses. Therefore (recalling romanticism yet again) spontaneously expressing those impulses, even when they are not completely understood, is usually healthy. Still, Wordsworthian realism tempers Maslow's optimism. We must sometimes stifle impulses in the interests of long-term achievement and because some of them are undesirable, even evil, as our checkered history so clearly

436

demonstrates. Not even Maslow blames every human outrage on environmental factors! Thus he does not advocate <u>complete</u> permissiveness for children. They should sometimes experience frustration and the challenging struggle to overcome obstacles. But pressed to the wall, Maslow invariably chooses freedom over constraint. Excessive need gratification damages children less than does impulse suppression. Late Victorianism's <u>enfant terrible</u>, Oscar Wilde, may have spoken partly in jest, but humanists will seriously agree that:

> We are punished for our refusals. Every impulse that we strive to strangle broods in the mind and poisons us....The only way to get rid of a temptation is to yield to it.[58]

In passing, we might point out that here lurks an unusual view of "instincts." Whereas Freud, like all Puritans, saw them as inherently evil, for Maslow they lead to health and welfare. Moreover, he rejects the common belief that highly evolved species, like ourselves, are less ruled by them. Our instincts are <u>different</u>, but quite as powerful. In addition, an instinct is often thought to be something possessed by every member of a species. Again, not so. Retardates, for example, lack the need to understand, and satisfiers of a particular need can certainly differ amongst us. Lastly, it is often assumed[51] that instincts cannot be suppressed. But for Maslow, metaneeds not only can be, but are, until lower needs receive attention.

But if growth is both natural and healthy, why do so many remain stunted? Why is it that, as Martha Graham perceptively observed, "Everyone is born a genius, but in most people, it only lasts a few minutes."[52] Perhaps basic needs remain unsatisfied. Perhaps the environment inhibits spontaneity by stressing "adjustment" and instilling repetitive, derivative habits. Perhaps, since we all possess lazy streaks, we avoid the necessary hard work. Finally, perhaps we <u>fear</u> our own destiny, the attaining of our potential[53] (Maslow's <u>Jonah complex</u>). Society, in its ambivalence, suspects that creators may exceed their station; so too may we see our own actualization as arrogant, even gods-threatening. Then too, growth risks failure, alienation, and the loss of friends and lovers. And discovering our abilities implies responsibility to use them; as Allport recognized, "guilt, doubt and anxiety are the penalty men pay for having a conscience."[54] For all these reasons, we are torn between desires to fulfill our potential and to wallow in comfortable mediocrity.

One obvious departure from the romantics emerges here. Whereas they preferred to withdraw from reality into subjective fantasy, humanists have enthusiastically tackled such practicalities as education, mental health, and therapy. Over these peripheral matters we need not dally long, but they do deserve brief elucidation. If we naturally seek growth then everyone, even children, will of their own accord choose healthier, "better" alternatives. Needs and frustrations are not absent in the healthy; they are merely different. But need gratification always helps growth. Mental illness, then, with its boredom, underachievement, and unrealistic perception, indicates failure to grow.[*] Most neurotics, lacking belonging, love, and security, are obsessed with them. Denied knowing and understanding, they find uncertainty intolerable and weakness or ignorance[**] inadmissable; they must needs seem decisive and in control. Illness is often defined by a culture's prevalent norms, with majority behavior being "normal" and the unusual, disturbed. Not so for Maslow. He vehemently denies that the well-adjusted, conforming person necessarily exemplifies health, for cultural standards may themselves be sick. In a Third Reich, is it the deviant/criminal or the well adjusted pillar of the community that represents health? Another good point! For Maslow, the criteria of health are universal, not culture relative, because health involves the pursuit of growth and metaneeds and these are similar everywhere. Measles is measles, whether in New York, Tokyo, or Pago Pago. So is stunting.

Thus humanist[55] therapy systems, such as Rogers' client centered therapy, seek not "coping" or "adjustment" but personal growth. The therapist avoids power or dictatorial control, and tries, not to manipulate patients but to remove obstacles to, and establish an atmosphere for, such self actualization.[***] Since patients, supposedly, realize intuitively what is best for themselves, they assume

---

[*] Tennessee Williams' A Streetcar Named Desire demonstrates the dangers of frustrating aesthetic needs. Blanche sensitively hungers after beauty, but is trapped in a squalor personified by the brutish Stanley Kowalski. She is driven insane.

[**] Thus, as with Freud, every pathology has the same underlying cause, in this case, stunting. And similar difficulties arise in explaining the "choice of the neurosis." Has an obsessive-compulsive, say, denied different needs than a depressed person?

[***] To this end, humanists have sometimes plumped for such questionable techniques as marathon groups and psychedelic drugs. To put it charitably, the jury remains out on their efficacy, and on the lastnamed, a negative verdict is already returned.

responsibility for decisions about therapy's directions and thus for its success. In Rogers' helpful metaphor, the therapist acts like a gardener, providing conditions in which a plant can fulfill its potential. The therapist's training, credentials, or what she or he <u>does</u>, Maslow adds,[56] matter less than his or her abilities in human relationships, or what that therapist <u>is</u>.

Likewise, in the educational sphere, schools should encourage not culturally valued skills and attitudes but need gratification and impulsive spontaneity, the climate for growth. A pox on those popular priorities, restrictive control and impulse suppression. The scenario extends even to society itself. Its institutions should provide the wherewithall for need gratification, freeing members to seek not social but personal fulfillments:*

> (The good society will) get out of the way
> and stand aside to let the organism itself
> utter its wishes and make its choices.[57]

1. <u>Self actualization, values, and peak experiences</u>. The first of these Maslowian concepts represents another existential wolf in humanistic clothing. That target of growth, the real self, is partly a fundamental project created by our actions. Might not Sartre, rather than Maslow, have stated that "Every person is, in part, 'his own project' and makes himself"?[58] Yet Maslow's optimism decrees this quest to be not futile but exhilarating and remunerative. In fact, he has sought out <u>self-actualized people</u> who seem to have accomplished it. These ultimately admirable individuals are exemplary models of how to live and so in some ways descend from the romantic superheroes. But they are hardly escapist, world-weary misfits. In fact, with their spontaneous, "natural" behavior, they will replace animals and neurotics as the prototype for a new psychology, one of health and of values.[59] Maslow clearly accepts the hoary doctrine that "the good" (and the healthy) is that which good (and healthy) people do, and self actualizers will model universal standards that transcend cultural differences. In his willing provision of statements about values and moral behavior,

---

*Maslow thus implies, as we read him, an unusual blend of socialism and laissez-faire individualism. Presumably, only a centrally controlled socialist economy insures satisfaction of each person's basic needs. But the aim would be to free everyone for personal fulfillment. In such a utopia, then, the state would serve the person rather than <u>vice versa</u>. The result? That ultimate socialist no-no, the cult of the individual.

then, he typifies third forcers. Perhaps because they have often been children of or themselves clergymen,[60] they have deplored the scientist's typically amoral, value-free attitude as crass dereliction of duty. It has harmed both science and ethics/religion.

But how are self actualizers identified? Maslow, ever the romantic truster of feeling, admits to vague "holistic impressions" rather than precise, objective criteria, but his several lengthy catalogues list their innumerable qualities. Self-confident and self-accepting, they feel guilt only when lazy or unproductive, because these threaten their self-images. Therefore they find novelty or ambiguity not threatening but fascinating. Possessing childlike spontaneity, openness, and perceptual accuracy, and so especially sensitive to dishonesty or pretence, they invariably display B-cognition in their interpersonal relations. They see the best in others, valuing them for what they are (cf. Schachtel's allocentric perception) with sympathy, affection, even love. Predictably, therefore, they attract many admiring disciples, yet their friendships, while deep, are relatively few.

Love, then, for Maslow as for the romantics, becomes a desirable high road to interpersonal understanding. Yet to him it features not idealizing worship from afar but intimate knowledge, accepting the beloved as he or she is. As well, the romantic hero's self centeredness prevented his giving himself to another, but for Maslow, those who love themselves can better love others, a seeming inconsistency that self actualizers nevertheless verify. Yet they do retain aloof detachment. Certainly not "well adjusted," they resist enculturation and any threats to their autonomy; they do accept norms, but only those not cramping their styles. In short, in daily life, they are invariably creative.

However they also are in some ways far from admirable. Ruthless in pursuit of their self-centered priorities. Boring. Stubborn. Vain. Absent minded and antisocial. Their B-cognitions can become indiscriminate, rose-colored acceptance of everything, in which evil is overlooked, value judgment avoided even when desirable, and standards lowered. Yet these definitively paradoxical personalities - intimate/ aloof, rational/impulsive, kind/ruthless - can resolve their antagonisms into integrated Gestalts to become "synergistic."

Their predominant motives, meta rather than deficit, deserve special mention. Often their activities are not means to ends but practiced for their own sake (a phenomenon that Allport labelled functional autonomy[61]); note the gourmet whose sole hesitation about dining was that it reduced one's appetite.[62]

440

Thus, self actualizers, although dedicated and hardworking, cannot easily distinguish work from play. As well, they seek and are especially susceptible to mystical peak experiences of ecstacy and awe, which often arrive when activities totally engross us. The romantic briefly glimpsed spiritual reality in moments of imaginative insight. So too do peaks, to the humanist, reveal the meaning of life and our real selves, because at such times we drop all pretense. The experiences associated with peaks[63] need no mention, since they resemble those of creative inspiration (see Chapter 5). But their universality (self actualizers merely have them more frequently and intensely) indicate, as do dreams, that we are all artists on occasion. Furthermore, peaks occur not only during creation but also in religious, athletic, and intimate endeavor, and this ubiquity means that a genuine science of persons must pay them heed, despite their messy subjectivity.

And what of the individual who denies having peaks? It must be that such a person suppresses them. In fact every religion, nay every human activity, may, encompass two personality types:

> The two religions of mankind tend to be peakers and non-peakers, that is to say, those who have private, personal transcendent, core-religious experiences easily and often and who accept them and make use of them, and, on the other hand, those who have never had them or who repress or suppress them and who, therefore, cannot make use of them for their personal therapy, personal growth, or personal fulfillment.[64]

Is formal religion, perchance, simply a means for communicating peaks to non-peakers?*

2. Creativity. As Maddi and Costa cogently point out,[65] the humanists, by stressing individuality, must do likewise for creativity. Since each self is unique, a healthy life actualizing that self must feature creativity; it is a natural, instinctive need that everyone can and should pursue:

---

*The Grand Inquisitor episode in Dostoevsky's Brothers Karamazov is instructive. A "peaker," Christ himself, confronts a nonpeaking scion of formal religion, the Inquisitor. Their fundamental differences in outlook and priorities lead the latter to see Christ as a threat. If He returned to earth, the Church
(Footnote Continued)

> Creativity is a fundamental characteristic
> of common human nature--a potentiality given
> to all human beings at birth...akin to the
> naive and universal creativeness of
> unspoiled children.[66]

Rogers' sentiments are similar:

> The mainspring of creativity appears to
> be...man's tendency to actualize
> himself, to become his potentialities.[69]

Similarly, since aesthetic needs are instinctive, we should all
enthusiastically consume attractive, original produce.

In humanistic jargon, then, "creativity" labels, not a
tangible <u>product</u> (for there may be none) but a <u>process of
living</u>--spontaneous, perceptually fresh, and uninhibited.[*] It is
not limited to art or science but surfaces everywhere. An
immaculate tackle in football can be as "creative" as a sonnet, a
fine soup more stirring than a mediocre painting. So
"creativity" becomes a general, holistic character trait, a "g"
factor radiating from the entire person and affecting his or her
every act.[69] (For this reason Maslow dismisses most research of
it as overly atomistic/analytic.) Henry Miller's views seem
exemplary:

> Writing, like life itself, is a voyage of
> discovery...I am a man telling the story of
> his own life, a process which appears more
> and more inexhaustible as I go on. Like the
> world-evolution, it is endless...Somewhere
> along the way, one discovers that what one
> has to tell is not nearly so important as
> the telling itself...Immediately I heard my

(Footnote Continued)
would have to muzzle Him to protect the religion founded in His
name.

[*]Although here Rogers differs. Creativity <u>is</u> evidenced by
products, but <u>good</u> creativity requires appropriate processes,
which differ from those of <u>bad</u> creativity: "When the individual
is 'open' to all his experiences...then his behavior will be
creative and his creativity may be trusted to be essentially
constructive."[68] In other words, creativity is judged by worth
of process, not of product; in fact, Rogers refuses to evaluate
the merit of the latter.

own voice, I was enchanted: the fact that
it was a separate, distinct, unique voice
sustained me...My life itself became a work
of art.[70]

In short, both the creative and aesthetic motives are
functionally autonomous, sought for the pleasures and peaks they
provide. Witness the multitudes who have labored with passionate
commitment, though tangible rewards were few.[72] The passion
itself sufficed.

But is not this a major departure from romanticism with its
blatant elitism and its artists specially endowed? Perhaps,
except that Maslow repeatedly distinguished two meanings of
"creativity," the aforementioned and another, so-called secondary
creativity that does yield masterpieces and that more resembles
the romantics' rare, lonely, often tortured genius. Certainly
the two overlap; witness the correlation between self
actualizers' and creatives' personality traits, which Craig[72]
found to be almost perfect, e.g., both display paradoxical
personalities. Still, the two creativities do differ appreciably
and to treat them interchangeably is, Maslow repeatedly warns, a
gross oversimplification. Many self actualizers produce nothing
concrete, while many secondary creatives (notably Wagner, Kafka,
and van Gogh) hardly personify admirable living.[73] The latter
variety, he admits, is a mystery but is certainly not universal;[74]
it probably depends on special, inborn talents. As well, in
its service, impulsive spontaneity must be tempered by
disciplined techniques and self-denial. Yet here the humanists,
like the romantics, differ among themselves. Maslow,
Wordsworth's heir, stresses these linear aspects, approving Kris'
regression in the service because it does so as well.[75] But
Rogers, modernity's Byron or Shelley, generally advocates the
frenzy of letting all hang out.

Also, the stereotypic secondary creator lacks many
self-actualized qualities, such as equanimity, kindness, and
generosity; he or she is neither a good citizen, nor a good
parent, nor liberal in politics or religion. Even the
self-actualizer's detached aloofness sounds less extreme than the
secondary's outright alienation. Finally, the latter often seeks
to satisfy not growth but deficit needs such as esteem,
belonging, or even nutrition.[76] The secondary is probably
"multimotivated" and the visage of his or her drives can vary.
In contrast, growth-type creativity is invariably healthy and its
suppression neurotic, so effective therapy (contra Freud) should
help it.[77] For its facilitation, Rogers advocates,[78] within the
person, openness to experience (extensionality), an internal
locus of evaluation (judging by our own criteria rather than
others), and a readiness to toy flexibly with elements and

443

concepts. To the same end the environment, delightfully permissive, should increase safety, freedom, and (of course) spontaneity, while minimizing threatening evaluation.

3. <u>Commentary</u>. If for nothing else, we must applaud the humanists for breathing some needed fresh air into psychology and for resurrecting such neglected topics as creativity. Unquestionably the mighty labors of experimentation and logical analysis too often brought forth empirical mice. The humanists used such methods so long as they served the purpose, but discarded them cheerfully when they did not. For example, Maslow's definition of self actualization is blatantly circular, both revealed by and used to explain a certain style of living and behaving. And he openly admits the problem, but argues that we must sometimes put up with such sophistries to "get on with it". (Furthermore, to break the circularity, self actualizers are, in the last analysis, identified by gut feelings of admiration. A dogmatic scientist/logician might deride such criteria, but to us they seem both legitimate and reliable.)

In like vein, humanistic optimism provided welcome contrast to the gloomy veneers of behaviorism and psychoanalysis. Psychology <u>was</u> too preoccupied with the disturbed and the animal; its catalogue of human traits was woefully barren. The healthy deserved attention, not least because they fling down the gauntlet of challenge to the rest of us to demand more of ourselves. Lastly, the humanists remind us that "selfishness" can be a complimentary rather than pejorative quality (an attitude the next section will defend even more fervently), its absence rather than presence a sign of neurosis.

Furthermore, some Maslowian ideas, particularly the need hierarchy, are ingratiating, and creativity thereby receives some useful explanation. We might wonder <u>why</u> growth as opposed to deficit needs cannot be satisfied, but we can certainly thereby understand the remarkable persistence of not only creators but also athletes and gardeners. Similarly, that creative work might seek the excitement of peaks seems eminently reasonable. Boredom has received insufficient emphasis as an aversive motivator; once we have felt adrenalin flow, we will settle for no less.

But having discharged our chivalrous duties, we must now express overall dissatisfaction, especially with Maslow's vague, imprecise theoretical statements. While he may have rejected some aspects of psychoanalysis, he unfortunately retained its fervor for having things every way. As a result, an eel is more easily pinned down than is his theory. The distinction between the two creativities is partly responsible for this failing. About the secondary variety (our main concern here) he says rather little, so when his statements about "creativity" contradict our data, we must always wonder whether we refer to the same phenomenon. As well, Maslow continually pays lip service to valid objections, to "the other fellow's point of view." Torn between his romantic and empirical streaks, between head and heart, he forever compromises what he has said. In the face of such vacillation, what can we deplore except vacillation?

Consider. At first it seems clear: gratifying lower needs should liberate[80] higher ones and promote health. But (as Amsel's theory implies[80]) might not a child continually loved and fussed over, who rarely encounters frustration and so learns no responses to overcome it, be woefully unfitted for the real world? There, sadly, our every whim is not always satisfied. (In similar vein, basic need gratification was almost epidemic in Huxley's Brave New World. Precious little individualistic behavior resulted.) Perhaps "withdrawal of love is no great threat to one who has been loved throughout his life,"[81] but we remain doubtful. And so does Maslow. He too admits[82] elsewhere that overcoming frustrating obstacles can be healthy.[82] We are left to wonder. When is frustration desirable, and when permissiveness? For whom? How often? Undoubtedly Maslow would answer, "It depends." Harried parents, wishing to heed contemporaneity's all-seeing, all-knowing guru, the psychologist, will doubtless sigh, "Thanks a lot. For nothing."

Similarly, if creativity only emerges once lower needs are gratified, what of those who create to satisfy the latter? We repeat Moss Hart's assertion:

> I am inclined to believe that (vanity, fury and the savage necessity to be liked) often seductively quicken the wheels of creation...to a larger degree than we choose to admit of so exalted a process...More often the siren enticements of worldly pleasures and rewards spark it into life than the heroic and consecrated goals we are told inspire it.[83]

And what of those who sacrificed love, belonging and even basic sustenance for their art? Shaw's observation also bears repeating:

> The genius will risk the stake and the cross, starve, when necessary, in a garret all his life, work his nerves into rags without payment, a sublime altruist in his disregard of himself, an atrocious egoist in his disregard of others.[84]

445

Maslow will reply that secondary creativity waives these rules, being "multimotivated," oftentimes by deficiencies. To repeat, such complications may be necessary, but they do compromise clarity and predictive power. They will trouble us continually as we proceed.

Having objected earlier to the democratic "everyone can do it" bias, we need only reiterate. In one sense, of course, creative activities are and should be for everyone. Dance, for example, can improve physical and psychological health, as the current jazzercise craze verifies. But when a paying audience is involved, such activities must be restricted to the few; then, not everyone should perform Swan Lake. Moreover Maslow, by distinguishing between the two creativities, clearly agrees. It is not he, but followers, who have promoted the lie that, like Socrates' slave, we all carry unfathomed potential. As Rothenberg and Hausman[85] warn, we must be clear whether we study the common or rare variety, for the subjects we select and thus the conclusions we draw will vary. We extend findings indiscriminately from one variety to the other at our peril.

One result has been particularly pernicious. A "creativity" for everyone can become a mere buzzword, cheapened beyond measure. So too can be its genuine achievements, for now the discovery of relativity[86] can be bedded down comfortably with that of a meat sauce. Humanists insist, rightly, that psychology ignores human values at its peril, yet they have themselves been far too reluctant to evaluate creative products-- their publications, for example, parade syrupy, touchy-feely poetry that would hardly pass muster on greeting cards. Their direct progeny, the so called "me generation" of the 1970's, provides perhaps their crowning chastisement. In the reductio ad absurdum, self expression, "getting in touch with yourself" (suggesting nothing so much as psychic masturbation) and "creativity" became mere staples of cocktail-party chit-chat.

The promotion of spontaneity and impulse expression, while a needed corrective to excessive regimentation (e.g., in the classroom) has also sired evils. Again Maslow's pleas for moderation have reached deaf ears and the pendulum has continued to swing. First, we doubt that children invariably realize their own best interests. Without some constructive guidance, even discipline, they will probably become, not cheerful scions of preferred values, but spoiled brats. As usual, Maslow disarms the critic by immediately agreeing:

> Only to the self-disciplined and responsible
> person can we say 'Do as you will and it
> will probably be all right'.[87]

However, another victim of this "doctrine of spontaneity", creativity, is our main concern. All humanists should be forced to read (at gun point if necessary, and never mind the compromising of their individual spontaneity) an article by Maddi.[88] He denies, vehemently, that creativity is "easy" and automatic if we "let it all hang out" and that inhibition or authoritarian control are dangerously stifling. So do we. Such sentiments will encourage not achievement but licentious sloth. Consider Maslow's advice about dancing:

> Let yourself go to the music--when we try to be directed, controlled, studied, we lose the essence of good dancing...Most good dancers became good without training.[89]

Now there is some truth here, both for social dancing (of which we presume he speaks) and the stage variety. Many so-called "classroom dancers" parade formidable techniques - casually tossing off, say, the notorious thirty-two fouettes from the Black Swan pas de deux - but on stage fade into the scenery. It is a Fonteyn, often quite defeated by those same fouettes, whom customers will cue overnight in a drizzle to see. Her distinctive qualities far surpass technique. Yet that having been said, many exhuberantly spontaneous dancers are merely klutzy, their flying knees and elbows a danger to every passerby. They send their partners, red-faced with embarrassment, to hide in the washroom. And Maslow's final observation is pure bunkum. Unless some technical training channels--not inhibits but channels--that spontaneity, the dancer will be not free but hamstrung. As Martha Graham, who should know if anyone does, reminds us, in dance and elsewhere, discipline is needed to achieve freedom.[90]

We turn now to the various data of creativity. If everyone has the potential, why are certain qualities usually found in those who actually "do it"? In explanation, humanists will invariably cite those supreme threats to individuality, inhibiting environmental factors. It is these that stifle the female and the elderly. Abundant self-confidence is needed to surmount their pernicious influence, along with a readiness to risk, and a hatred of their spokespersons such as pedagogues. And so on. Presumably, matters such as the choice of field or style of expression would be similarly explained. Unfortunately, humanists have rarely advanced beyond such shadowy beginnings and when they have, their fondness for abstract nouns too often renders the discussions incomprehensible. Even so, they would seem hard put to account for creativity's collective aspects such as the medium experience, since for them, as for Freud, it expresses a uniquely individual self (albeit one admirable rather

447

than reprehensible). Therefore, Chapter 9's objections once more apply.

However the critic's labors do receive attention, albeit derogatory. If process rather than product is creativity's hallmark, if feelings matter more than results, then criticism becomes not only superfluous but undesirable, a danger to expressive spontaneity.[91] Now admittedly it can have such effects, but if everything is permitted, anarchy will follow and quality be buried beneath piles of refuse. And when Maslow equates the critic with the religious nonpeaker,[92] he is merely contentious. As Chapter 5 argued, the best critics are not linear-dominated mediocrities, casting their gray, envious shadows over the true artist's sublime frenzy. They too are creative. Few have trumpeted frenzy's virtues more enthusiastically than Coleridge or Schumann, yet few have surpassed their commentary.

We finish with some literary reflections. Maslow evokes impressions decidedly mixed. Thankfully, he avoids academic pretense, his style leaning to the informal, even folksy. Tentative, even humble in advancing ideas, he is not afraid to admit ignorance or the flying of kites. Furthermore, we admire the existentialist's commitment, the honest integrity of one who feels deeply about a topic and speaks from the heart. These are all, all honorable virtues. Unfortunately, Maslow also displays the romantic's weaknesses, particularly in the verification stage. He is too often disorganized, unclear, and lax in pursuing implications of his ideas. He can therefore convey an unfortunate sense of superficiality, especially when his romanticism gallops out of control (as happened increasingly in his later writing), causing him to plead uncritically for, say, wholesale permissiveness. Particularly irritating is his ad nauseum repetition, in book after book, of virtually the same ideas. Much as Maslow disliked critics and therefore, we presume, editors, he badly needed a good one.

For all these reasons Maslow - or indeed any humanist within our gaze - rarely bowls us over by opening new vistas, or shortens our breath by the sheer depth of insight or bravura turn of phrase. But then Maslow, to his credit, admitted his stylistic limitations. Let these not demolish his not inconsiderable achievements.

Ayn Rand

The philosophy of objectivism[93] has attained a high profile through Rand's popular novels, The Fountainhead[94] and Atlas Shrugged.[95] A self-styled neo-romantic, nostalgic for that age whose last gasps she witnessed as a child, she can call it "the greatest achievement in art history (whereas) our day has no art and no future."[96] Its art expresses her vision of ideal, moral humanity, so in her eyes she has become its lone modern prophet, plugging its messages to a world too ignorant to listen:

> In regard to romanticism, I have often thought that I am a bridge[97] from the unidentified past to the future.

These romantic streaks justify her inclusion here, although we shall find some appreciable departures.

John Galt, of **Atlas Shrugged**, is clearly a Randian mouthpiece, and his interminable speech cements her cornerstones. As a rugged individualist, she advocates **selfishness** as the preeminent value. Emphasizing oneself and one's own existence is not evil but essential for moral living. Pride goeth before, not a fall, but attainment of one's perfection and, in turn, of **happiness**. And what is human perfection? We are by nature thinking organisms endowed with **consciousness**. Through it we can know and discover, but it is only a potential that we must choose to actualize. Otherwise, we will languish in lazy, brutish docility. In objectivist ethics, then, anything that promotes consciousness is "good," notably **thinking** and **productive work**. The latter, for example, frees us from animalhood by increasing our control over our lives. The competence, even magnificence of its results matter not, so long as it taxes our mental capacities completely and purposefully. Our greatest vice, then, is to deny our humanity by suspending our consciousness. By acting like animals, we cannot survive.

Thus, moral behavior invariably exploits our **reason**, that faculty which "identifies and integrates the material provided by man's senses."[98] It flows directly from consciousness, but again we must **choose** to use it. To be human is to integrate and conceptualize the information we receive from our senses; therefore, infants invariably form a **sense of life**:

> a pre-conceptual equivalent of metaphysics, an emotional subconsciously integrated appraisal of man and of existence.[99]

This sense of life, largely emotional, guides our early values; something is good because it **feels** good. But with maturity, reason gradually emerges so we can now understand those values consciously rather than feel them intuitively, and therefore can express them verbally. In short, reason now determines ethical standards that in turn influence, rather than result from, emotion. Being human, we cannot avoid value-based decisions.

449

But will we rely on reason or on emotion to make them? Need we say that the former, for Rand, is preferable?

> In any hour and issue of your life, you are free to think or to evade that effort. But you are not free to escape from your nature, from the fact that <u>reason</u> is your means of survival--so that for <u>you</u>, who are a human being, the question 'to be or not to be' is the question 'to think or not to think'.[100]

Thus, reason is invariably truth's fountainhead, providing ethical standards that are objective and universal rather than arbitrary or culturally relative. Following its dictates, we will act with independent <u>integrity</u>, never sacrificing our convictions to those of others. With <u>honesty</u>, never disguising reality. With <u>justice</u>, allowing neither ourselves nor others something unearned, but demanding an honest day's work for pay. And the ultimate evil? <u>Altruism</u>. Sacrificing our wishes and needs to those of others has caused virtually every injustice and immorality in history. According to altruistic philosophy, anything done to benefit oneself is inherently bad, so,

> An industrialist who produces a fortune and a gangster who robs a bank are regarded as equally immoral since they both sought wealth for their own 'selfish' benefit.[101]

But the evil, Rand retorts, lies not in the self-interest but in what is <u>seen</u> as the self-interest, in what is <u>valued</u>. That is the robber's (but not the industrialist's) error.

Contrary to wide suspicion, objectivism does not countenance obeying our every whim. The same act may be evil or virtuously selfish depending on the values behind it. Altruism sacrifices one's values, not welfare:

> Do not call your best actions a 'sacrifice': that term brands you as immoral. If a mother buys food for her hungry child rather than a hat for herself, it is <u>not</u> a sacrifice: she values the child higher than the hat, but it is a sacrifice to the kind of mother whose higher value is the hat.[102]

Nor do these ethics promote the exploitation, injury, or enslavement of others. Such acts are immoral because they are not human but animal. They display not reasoned thought but emotion at work.

Rand particularly extolls selfishness in the economic arena, in the person of _laissez-faire_ capitalism. She's for it. Not the pale imitations of even such supposed bastions of private enterprise as Wall Street, but the real thing (which, she asserts, has never been tried). Since everyone should be free to do their own things unencumbered, they should face no restricting interference from others. Including and especially governments. But as the coin's flip side, we should expect no charitable welfare or largess, for these too allow someone else to impose his or her values on us. Let the law of the marketplace rule. Supply and demand. If our personal initiative can yield the proverbial better mousetrap for which others will pay, we will have earned just profits. But if our produce is unwanted, we deserve to fail and probably to starve.

1. _Creativity and art_. Let us note at the outset that the preceeding economic analysis does not draw exception for these matters. Art too must obey the marketplace's implacable laws. It is a commodity like any other, no more deserving of government support or charitable handouts. Symptomatically, Rand has one of those liberal socialists whom she so despises utter these words:

> Culture should be taken out of the hands of the dollar-chasers. We need a national subsidy for literature. It is disgraceful that artists are treated like peddlars and that art works have to be sold like soap.[103]

She deplores, we may assume, this sentiment's every syllable.

And yet art is, for Rand, not a frill but an admirable example of productive work, promoting our consciousness and hence fulfillment:

> Art _is_ inextricably tied to man's survival--not to his physical survival, but to that on which his physical survival depends: to the preservation and survival of his consciousness.[104]

And again:

> All work is creative work if done by a thinking mind, and no work is creative if done by a blank who repeats in uncritical stupor a routine he has learned from others.[105]

More specifically, one's art expresses one's sense of life. Artists' values guide their choices as they develop their work,

so it becomes a concrete statement of and a means for them to
understand* their own value system:

> Art is a selective recreation of reality
> according to an artist's metaphysical value
> judgements. It is the integrator and
> concretizer of man's metaphysical
> abstractions.[106] It is the voice of his sense
> of life.

In their enterprise, artists do not fake or escape from reality
but, by selecting its significant properties, they do stylize it.

The consumer's sense of life also comes into play,
determining responses to and interpretations of artistic work.
By these reactions, that consumer will learn something of his or
her own values. And these the work should never try to dictate;
attempts to educate or preach immorally infringe on precious
individuality (cf. Sartre's What is Literature?). Art should
merely show. Thus, artistic creation resembles scientific
deduction (abstract values determining specifics) and artistic
consumption, induction (from specific events, abstractions are
comprehended). It is because it either affirms or denies our
conscious views of reality that a novel, although fictional, may
seem more personally relevant than does a news story. That is
why art seems so important. But why, then, is it frequently
neglected? As usual, the bogeyman of altruism is to blame.
Artistic production and consumption both seek personal pleasure
and enhancement. Art may be universal, but it is not social; it
benefits not collective society but each individual member. Such
inherently selfish acts, we are taught, are dangerous. So art
suffers.

Still, not only what people are, but what they ought to be
provides its legitimate domain, and here it may actually better a
philosophical treatise. Its concrete portrayals of such
phenomena as heroes and villains makes it "the indispensable
medium for the communication of a moral ideal."[107] Supposedly,
the artist's particular values matter not, so long as he or she
depicts values of some kind and our willingness to suffer and die
for same. Only value-free art is contemptible:

----

*This resembles existentialism's "that sort of bear"
motives, and also the doctrines of Langer and Jung.

> The fact that one agrees or disagrees with
> an artist's philosophy is irrelevant to an
> aesthetic appraisal of his work qua art.[108]

Rand then blithely ignores her own tenet and judges others almost exclusively by their opinions. Great work, for her, evinces her version of romanticism, so her favorite novelists (after herself) are Victor Hugo and Dostoevsky, her playwrights Schiller and Edmund Rostand. From our decadent era, those solitary romantic outposts, detective and spy thrillers (especially Mickey Spillane's Mike Hammer and Ian Fleming's James Bond) alone earn her cheers. (So too, we would have thought, would that pinnacle of lone-wolfery, the western.) Their heroes fight singlehandedly for what they believe, overcoming formidable odds. Their enduring popularity, she argues, demonstrates our hunger for figures to admire, our desire still to be shown that "it can be done."

Believing, like the romantic and the humanist, that art should depict admirable, not average or stunted, humanity, she too unveils her superheroes, the Howard Roarks and John Galts, to shame the rest of us. These Clint Eastwoodian individuals par excellence are throwbacks to the romance of the old west, when men had to do what men had to do. If they rode horses, the final reel would see these, not the heroine, receiving their bashful kisses. In line with Frank Sinatra's greeting-card philosophy, they do it their way. In like vein, her heroic artists, such as the composer Richard Halley of Atlas Shrugged, provide a central-casting stereotype of the romantic artist struggling against an unsympathetic environment:

> The story of his life had been like a
> summary written to damn greatness... It had
> been a procession of years spent in garrets
> and basements... It had been the gray of a
> struggle against long flights of unlighted
> tenement stairs, against frozen plumbing,
> against the price of a sandwich in an
> ill-smelling delicatessen store.[109]

Halley lacks only consumption!

Her pet bugaboos also earn their lofty status through their portrayed values. Tolstoy's Anna Karenina is "the most evil book in serious literature"[110] because it preaches resignation to and self-sacrifice for social entities. But like Jung and Rank, her favored bete noire is that symptom of our sick age, "modern art." Partly, its grunts, random noises, and splashes of paint demonstrate our decline from human consciousness to bestiality, but also it often (see Chapter 12) avoids self expression, which for Rand is the main purpose of art. Thus, she dismisses modern dance as "neither modern nor dance,"[111] asserting that its abominations have all but destroyed interest in this art (a strange observation, since by both box-office and participation criteria, dance is the most rapidly growing of the arts). Indicatively, she prefers tap dancing, which expresses "gaiety, and every shade of emotion pertaining to the joy of living."[112]

2. Commentary. Is Rand's self image accurate? Does she qualify as a genuine romantic, perhaps the last? Certainly there are similarities, notably in the advocacy of individualism. Moreover, she recalls the neo-romantic Maslow when she seeks an objective base for values and when she promotes self actualization as the highest value, which potentially we can all reach if we choose. But we wish to focus instead on her departures. Most notable is the elevation of coldly intellectual reason over spontaneous emotion as the source of truth. Actually, this much-touted "reason," this supposed route to objective, infallible decision-making, seems on closer scrutiny as arbitrarily subjective as the romantic's "feeling." At one point Galt/Rand admits,

> The most depraved sentence you can now utter is to ask: whose reason? The answer is: yours... It is only with your own knowledge that you can deal.[113]

Actually, Rand believes this not a whit. She follows the medieval Church's example. Certain conclusions--hers--are unquestionably correct because they stem, not from Holy Writ or some such, but from that same "reason." One has "reasoned" correctly if one reaches them; otherwise one deserves burning, eternal damnation, or even a month's vacation in the Soviet Union. So the concept is hopelessly circular to boot.

Be that as it may, her views on friendship and love are decidedly unromantic. For these are bestowed, not in blind, frenzied obsession, but rationally, as payment for the other's acting well. Love is not a high road to interpersonal understanding, but simply a commodity like any other, paid in good Skinnerian fashion for services rendered:

> (Love is) the expression of one's values, the greatest reward you can earn for the moral qualities you have achieved in your character and person, the emotional price paid by one man for the joy he receives from the virtues of another.[114]

454

We fall in love thoughtfully, with the other's values. Any emotional attachment (hopefully at least) will follow after, so love expresses philosophy; it involves the mind, not the heart.[115] Presumably, then, we worship not idealistically from afar, but realistically, after subjecting the prospective mindthrob to several attitude surveys and perhaps an MMPI. All of which sounds absolutely compelling if love amongst computers be the matter of interest, the dry rapture of a Mr. Spock or Space Odyssey's Hal.

Rand also avoids the romantic's typical admiration for nature. The workings of man rather than God earn her approbation. Productive work provides tangible commodities for buying and selling, so her heroes are architects, railway builders, and investors who walk not amongst daffodils but in the corridors of business. Their musings about the lake country would contemplate its potential for supermarket or scrap metal storage. And what reveals their integrity? The size of their profit margins. One of them can say, without a twinge of conscience, "I want to be prepared to claim the greatest virtue of all--that I was a man who made money."[116]

Rand likewise rejects the romantic's other escape, into inner fantasy. We must never disguise reality, but face up. Which by Abercrombie's distinction[117] would seem to classify her as the romantic's opposite, the realist. Rarely does she promote the imagination's desirability, because external, worldly phenomena are of prime interest. Even creative work for her seems to depend more on conscious intellect that on "imagination." Moreover, whatever that work requires, clearly everyone potentially has it. Poets/artists may provide exemplary models, but we can all aspire to their status if only we get our acts together.

Now romanticism's attributes are admittedly debatable. Nevertheless, Rand's version is, to put it charitably, somewhat unusual. Yet in her view, romanticism stood not for feeling but for volition, or the freedom to choose, with our values being our most crucial decisions:

> (Romanticism was) a category of art based on
> the recognition of the principle that man
> possesses the faculty of volition.[118]

The more familiar variety - with its emotions and nonrational, even supernatural sources of knowledge - she cryptically dismisses as mysticism. It defers to others' opinions by allowing whim rather than reason to influence decisions. Which renders it altruistic and therefore sinful.

Yet despite these departures Rand, in her extremism, does provide a _reductio ad absurdum_ of romantic individualism to highlight its less desirable aspects. Of all the perspectives surveyed herein, we find hers the least attractive. Hence we are grateful that she avoids the humanist's waffling because we may now, in good romantic fashion, trust our feelings and try to explain them. Ironically, this supposed steely-eyed realist's world is as much a pipe-dream fantasy as the most romantic escapist's. Given such modern realities as urbanization, rapid communication, and travel, when events not only in Baltimore but in Buenos Aires and Bangkok affect us, nowadays no one is or can be an island. Opposing value systems must collide, and if everyone insists on individual integrity, competitive struggle will follow. We will almost certainly, thereby, blow ourselves to smithereens. Peaceful, relatively harmonious coexistence, in marriage and elsewhere, requires _compromise_, not giving _in_ but _giving_.

And what fantasy diverted Rand's attentions while we have harvested rampant individualism's more bitter crops? Free enterprisers, in the name of their inviolate rights to make a profit, have polluted our environment, converted our cities into uninhabitable concrete jungles, and run roughshod over even minimal standards of human decency. Government restrictions are needed _because_ what's good for General Bullmoose is not always good for the USA. (This archetypal free enterpriser was, in Al Capp's comic strip _L'il Abner_, a figure of satire. But Rand would, we suspect, applaud him heartily.) Now admittedly, such abominations may represent animalistic rather than human behavior, but they are the realities of individualism _in practice_. In other words, as Rand's novels prove, she was a woefully unperceptive observer of actual human behavior.

To compound our animosity, her repellent world lacks romanticism's attractive aspects. An icicle-like rationality replaces emotionality's tempering warmth. Competition supersedes love, friendship, and other accruements of interpersonal empathy; dog heartlessly devours dog, and no quarter is either given or requested. Her relentlessly pathological superheroes, lacking any of human kindness's milk or indeed most of the attractive emotions, personify these repugnancies, thus verifying Maslow's contention that not only self actualization, but also belonging, love, and compassion are ingredients of health. Admittedly, her heroes never impose their standards on others, but in lurching compulsively along their individualistic paths they are (recalling romantic elitism) high-handedly merciless towards those who fall short. Viewing false modesty as sinful, they both accept and parade their own virtues. Bluntly honest, they call a spade a spade. "Arrogance" could be their middle names.

Now few would deny that, in moderation, these are virtues. Neurotic and boring are those who live exclusively for others; similarly, thoroughgoing economic socialism promotes a dull average in which "a common greyness silvers everything".[119] But surely "civilization" - towards which we have trekked so torturously over the ages - represents, if anything, <u>victory</u> over the jungle's law of survival of the fittest. It includes compassionate responsibility for the weak and the unfortunate, even when our selfish interests might dictate otherwise. In a civilized society, we are all partly our brothers' keepers.

But in present context her views on artistic charity deserve special condemnation. Organizations such as symphonies, theatrical companies, and the like cannot survive on profit; a major ballet company, for example, does well to recoup 50 percent of its costs at the box-office. By inviolate decree, such organizations engender red ink; in fact, their artistic success usually breeds heftier, not diminished, losses. If placed at the mercy of supply and demand, they will be forced to cater to the lowest common denominator a la Broadway or (the direst warning) commercial television. Forced to increase ticket prices beyond reach of all but the wealthiest. Above all, forced to compromise the most precious of all their freedoms--the freedom to fail. Supply and demand encourages playing it safe. An adventurous artistic policy, with innovative works by authors of less than household reputation, <u>guarantees</u> mishaps. And even ultimately successful products are often not at first well received, so their profits will not be quick.

Now Randians will retort that private largesse, voluntarily given, should rectify the debts. It is the <u>forced</u> support, via increased taxation, to which they object. This attitude, while understandable, is fatal. The principle of <u>noblesse oblige</u> unfortunately no longer holds much sway when oil barons, not titled princes, form the wealthy aristocracy. And private donors have always resisted innovation. Too much of even Brahms, let alone Bartók or Stravinsky, may be risky, and Varèse or Cage we will not even discuss. Let's program more Tchaikovsky or, better still, "Great Themes from the Movies" and "Beethoven meets Duran Duran." Or best of all, "The Stars and Stripes Forever" guest conducted by the local furniture magnate, with his prepubescent daughter winningly tweeting the piccolo solo.

In Europe, where these realities are recognized, public support for the arts is long established practice. Organizations such as Britain's Royal Shakespeare and National Theatres, the Berlin Philharmonic, the Royal Danish Ballet, the Louvre and the Moscow Art Theatre (to name a few) are the happy result. Canada's federal government in the 1950's came to the same realization and created the Canada Council as its cultural funding arm. Its monies are invariably insufficient, and political machinations can influence the distribution of its largesse. But at least its arms length principle protects the* fundees from ruinous penalty whenever they contravene taxpayers' or politicians' preferences. Unquestionably the myriad theatres, musical and dance companies, art galleries, and so on that have sprung up since the Council's inception and would quickly perish without it, have made Canada a more stimulating, desirable place to live. Even that bastion of private enterprise, the USA, finally recognized reality and founded The National Endowment for the Arts (although this beachhead the unsympathetic Reagan administration has somewhat set back). Thus, we may well debate the pros and cons. But as the proverbial bottom line, many of the arts we cherish would simply not survive without public support. Would the most ardent Randian risk such loss?

As for Rand's views on artistic creation, her own novels verify their dangers. When intellectual (as opposed to emotional) values dictate artistic decisions, bombastic propaganda may result. Contrary to her own edict that art should never preach, hers rank among the most didactic novels in existence. Her remark that "I approach literature as a child[120] does: I write--and read--for the sake of the story" must rank among the least self-perceptive ever made. In actuality, she writes like a college sophomore, with her philosophical values controlling both her creakily predictable plots and her one-dimensional, cartoon characters. As a result (once more, irony) those supposed monuments to rugged individuality, her superheroes, all run to a type, as interchangeable as peas in a pod. Her writing does come alive when momentarily she forgets philosophy, but usually it remains front and center.

Her repellent style compounds the negativity. She practices what might be called the Chinese water torture school of writing, like Maslow repeating the same points ad nauseum but without his

---

*The government funds the Council with a set amount each year. Council members then decide funding for applicants, based largely on jury evaluations by professionals in the various fields, e.g., musical experts will evaluate a symphony orchestra. Thus, politicians can only influence the Council's overall funding, not that of individual applicants. This policy was recently (in 1984, symbolically) endangered by a government bill seeking greater accountability from all its crown corporations. But the arts community set up such a hue and cry that an exception was made for artistic organizations. When they bother, artists can gain appreciable political power!

folksy humility. Entire episodes could be transposed from one book to another without missing a beat. Her dauntless ego adds to the problem. Symptomatically, in describing superior writing's attributes, she frequently cites examples <u>from her own work</u>. If false modesty be sinful, what of delusions of grandeur? We forgive a Shaw his arrogance, tempered as it is by humor and equalled by deeds. But in this paragon of heavy-handed banality, who yet fancies herself as not only philosopher but <u>litterateur</u> supreme, it is merely irritating. For the Rand novel, incredibly wordy and relentlessly humorless, provides the same doubtful pleasures as being hit on the head with a mallet for several hours. In comparison, even Visconti's films seem lyrically pastoral and we long for the subtle, warm humanity, the wry humor of a Jane Austen. If <u>Pride and Prejudice</u> be the proverbial book we cannot put down, <u>Atlas Shrugged</u> is its antithesis, the book we cannot pick up. Unless we fancy weight lifting.

Chapter 16

THE THIRD FORCE II: THE EXISTENTIAL HUMANISTS

After gazing at ourselves through Maslow's rosy glasses, we now don others stained by metaphysical anxiety to darker hue.

Rollo May

This widely read therapist/author avows many of the aforementioned humanistic tenets. Therefore we concentrate on his idiosyncracies, particularly manifest in Love and Will[1] and The Courage to Create,[2] relevant to his views on our topic.

1. Eros, the daimonic and death. Essentially, May provides two accounts, which differ more in emphasis than in substance, and which he forged while facing a puzzle. By Freudian orthodoxy, neurosis stems from denial of basic instincts, particularly the sexual. Ergo, given our much-trumpeted modern liberality, neurosis should be dwindling. Yet while physicians' waiting rooms display different problems than did those of yore, the legions of the troubled are actually larger--and not simply because neurosis is now more fashionable. Feelings of insecurity, apathy, and loneliness are rife. Permissiveness, it appears, has solved some problems but engendered others.

According to May, where once we denied our sexuality, we are now obsessed with it. Where once guilt descended if we did (particularly, given Victorian double standards, if we were female), now it comes if we don't. Why this preoccupation? Because sex implies that we are liberated and "with it." Because it adds temporary excitement to otherwise drab and lonely lives. Because it symbolizes our power and assertiveness--a heady attraction to the many who feel powerless. And because when sexually active, we feel young and attractive. But these inducements, besides being selfish, betray what May calls the New Puritanism,[3] our suppression of some basic facts of existence. We may discuss sex neverendingly but seem remarkably uptight about other matters that Victorians openly acknowledged. Ironically sex, once repressed, now represses other unmentionables. In other words, we are rather less liberated than our self-congratulatory propaganda would have it.

We will examine two victims of the New Puritanism, the first being some basic needs summarized as eros. To overcome our lonely isolation, we desire encounter, to reach for physical and emotional union with external phenomena, especially other persons. This apparently unique need to escape self's boundaries, our acts of love must satisfy. Otherwise, although we carve ever more notches on our bedposts, we will feel

461

unfulfilled. Jane Austen, that unrivalled observer of behavioral nuance, archly reveals how love transcends mere logical interaction:

> A very few hours spent in the shared labor of incessant talking will dispatch more subjects than can really be in common between any two rational creatures, yet with lovers it is different. Between them no subject is finished, no communication is ever made, till it has been made at least twenty times over.[4]

Unfortunately, the modern propoganda from Playboy et al. preaches that we choreograph the two-backed monster strictly for sexual satisfaction, via orgasm. For men especially, passionate commitment must never intrude, for this signifies weakness. No, "keep your cool" and selfishly exploit your partners:

> The Victorian person sought to have love without falling into sex; the modern person seeks to have sex without falling into love.[5]

Thus, eros is suppressed. The results? Love making becomes mechanistically impersonal, and partners virtually interchangeable means to ends. Such tomes as Comfort's The Joy of Sex (John Bunyan and Sigmund Freud, please call the operator), sell astronomically, because in unerotic love making, technique becomes a goal rather than a tool. YAP (Yet Another Position) becomes the Holy Grail, and its contortions must challenge Olympic gymnasts, its employed materiel, The Prop Master to The Inquisition. Our sex symbols supreme, Playboy centerfolds, become remarkably unsexy, dehumanized Sartrian objects of perception resembling nothing so much as dressmakers' dummies in store windows. No one like Miss October, airbrushed, pancaked, and midriff-stapled, has ever lived.

But surely, were these love making's sole purposes, prostitutes would make ideal partners and masturbation, uncomplicated and efficient, a satisfactory outlet. Sexual health would be indicated by success at the local singles bar (otherwise known as Meat Market). But in fact such woeful wrongheadedness forgets that sex seeks not only orgasm but that erotic need satisfaction perhaps best captured by the word intimacy. As May insightfully points out, only human beings make love face to face (usually). Why? To share the partner's

462

reactions and experiences, so the act becomes more personal.[*]
Satisfactory lovemaking features give and take of both passion
and tenderness; to May, not orgasm but initial penetration, when
eros is fulfilled, seems especially significant. Following mere
sex we slumber. But after eros we remain awake, savoring that
special person with whom we have shared so much of ourselves.

In sum, having sex is worlds removed from making love, a
truth we seem to have forgotten. The price we pay? Those modern
neuroses. Now we realize why Meat Markets are so profoundly
depressing. The air hangs heavy with frustrating emptiness, with
desires unexpressed and unfulfilled by inhabitants who seek
erotic satisfaction but gain only the transitory pleasures of the
one night stand. When we deny those other needs, we invite
neurosis. Feeling impotent and isolated, we either pursue power
via violence and aggressiveness (not only power, apparently, but
powerlessness corrupts) or retreat into innocence, a childish,
fantasy-ridden naivete typified by movements like "flower power"
and the "greening of America."[6]

Which brings us to May's concept of the daimonic:

> (The daimonic is) any natural function
> which has the power to take over the whole
> person. Sex and eros, anger and rage and
> the craving for power are examples. The
> daimonic can be either creative or
> destructive and is normally both. When
> this power goes awry and one element usurps
> control over the total personality, we have
> "daimonic possession."[7]

The daimonic, then, represents the urge to assert ourselves.
Capable of either good or evil, it may seek to integrate the self
with, or alienate it from, other things, to dominate, even
destroy them. Emotional and arational, it can be somewhat
directed by reason, but it demands release of some kind. So when
its normal channels are denied, it will erupt in psychopathology.

If readers find this notion unclear, we must agree. It
seems unduly reminiscent of Freud's id/primary process (although
its purely sexual power receives less emphasis) and its

---

[*]The film Quest for Fire, depicting our evolution during
caveman times, attached great significance to the first couplings
in this human rather than animal style. They revealed a desire
(Footnote Continued)

possibilities for either healthy social interaction or neurotic
domination of others surely recalls Adler. Reeves, too,
chastises the daimonic concept as but vaguely described and
insufficiently distinguished from _eros_ (which also seeks
self-assertive union and which also initiates both creativity and
destructiveness). May's commentary/rejoinder tried to clarify
the daimonic. The optimistic humanists have either denied our
nature's darker side or blamed it on environmental inadequacies,
frustrations, and the like. But May, like Freud, recognizes our
proclivities for evil, and the daimonic represents his attempt to
face them. He admits its appreciable overlap with _eros_, but
nevertheless asserts its distinctiveness. Unfortunately, he has
not allayed our doubts.

At any rate, we move on to the New Puritanism's second
victim. Death. Nowadays, to be sexually out front, even gross,
may be permissible, but to be morbid is definitely non-U.
Refusing to admit our mortality, we surpass any age in our
obsessive, Dorian Gray-like searchings for the fountains of youth
and sexiness. We no longer care for aging or terminally ill
relatives at home, but ship them to institutions where, apart
from occasional visits, we can forget them. We thereby avoid
admitting that one day we too will occupy the same boat. How
many of us have never seen anyone dead or dying! When death does
arrive, those ceremonies in make- believe called funerals
cunningly disguise reality, camouflaging corpses so we can
murmur, "He looks just like he's sleeping," and outfitting
luxurious caskets with piped-in Muzac, no less, presumably for
the gastronomic pleasure of the worms. (Evelyn Waugh's novel _The
Loved One_[11] scathingly satirizes the funeral industry's
excesses.) Perhaps because of his long battle with tuberculosis
May believes, like his existential forefathers, that we must
confront death and the anxiety it engenders. Only then will we
renew our responsibilities to grow towards fulfillment.

(Footnote Continued)
to make love, not indiscriminately, but only with a certain
someone.

*Wuest's poignant short story, _A Sense of Tribe_,[10] portrays
our loss. An elderly man, lying on a special bed in the family
home, listens to his descendents playing outside. He remembers
doing likewise as his grandmother lay on the same bed, from which
"you never came out alive," and realizes, without undue anxiety,
that his family has gathered to witness his demise. It seems to
him quite fitting that, like the seasons, life should have this
sense of inevitable progress, making death not a feared adversary
but the logical, inevitable ending to life.

But the less courageous deny death and thereby once more invite neurosis because, strangely enough, they suppress eros as well. To May, love and death seem intimates. Each has both creative and imaginative aspects--death may end life but it also helps evolutionary progress, and the act of love may elicit ecstatic vitality (and it can, of course, literally conceive new life) but such feelings, like life, cannot last. But above all, truly erotic love constantly reminds us of death (whereas mere sex disguises it). Loving parents continually worry about their children's health. Similarly, when we give ourselves completely to others, their mortality becomes as important as our own. While recovering from a heart attack, Maslow wrote:

> Death, and its ever present possibility makes love, passionate love, more possible. I wonder if we could love passionately, if ecstacy would be possible at all, if we knew we'd never die.[12]

Obviously, true love of another risks devastating loss.

Which raises another of May's favorite themes. Authentic living, with eros front and center, requires the courage to gamble. As an old song reminds us: "Here I go again, taking a chance on love." We risk rejection and loss, yet this mixture of anxiety and joy from "walking on the razor's edge" adds to love's excitement. Without it, life is barren.

May has also, perhaps more than any third forcer, stressed unconscious mechanisms, although he here departs but little from orthodox psychoanalysis. Like Freud, he admits the unconscious' instinctive, primitive, and anarchic tendencies, notably in the daimonic. But otherwise it is Jung that he recalls. Consider: the unconscious has a collective as well as individual aspect, expressing archetypal themes. It compensates for conscious deficiences. Illogical and unrealistic it may be, but it does prevent consciousness from "drying up in banal, empty, arid rationality."[13] It can foretell the future and impel us towards realizing our potential. In fact, it is "intentional." It desires that we understand its meaning. Still, May on occasion leaves psychoanalysis' yellow brick road for the black asphalt of existentialism. We can still choose among the various unconscious influences, to find and affirm our genuine selves.

However, his writings about the psychic nether regions[14] attend especially to symbols. These seem to provide, as dreams reveal, the unconscious' special language, which is more artistic than logical. Why do we use them? Indicatively, "symbol" combines the Greek sym and bolein, meaning literally "to throw together" or "to unite." Reflecting our need for encounter, therefore, symbols unify (as rational communication cannot) our inner and outer worlds and also various aspects of our mental life. In short, we produce symbols to contact both our surroundings and ourselves--an innovative, if somewhat vague explanation.

But in the matter of interpreting symbols, May provides little fresh fodder. He agrees with Freud that they do carry hidden messages, but since both the patient and his or her unconscious desire understanding, these should eventually become clear when the patient is ready to recognize them. Indeed, as patients progress in therapy, their dreams do seem to gain in clarity[15] (perhaps because treatment increases self-understanding). Otherwise, May again treads Jung's path. He rejects Freud's pejorative attitudes towards symbols. Dreams and myths communicate not only news unfit to print but also our most profound hopes and experiences, often of a primordial kind. And May too distinguishes symbols from signs. The former allow many interpretations, among which their producer can best choose. As well, symbols are never arbitrary, since the unconscious chooses forms that best suit its vague themes. Thus, symbols are:

> an organic expression of the meaning of the total living experience of the person at that time in...history.[16]

May's major innovation in this area is to suggest that external as well as unconscious environments may determine a symbol's form, so it may differ across cultures; a mandala may have similar meaning everywhere, but a handbag probably does not. As another departure from psychoanalysis May, like Langer, deplores overly intellectual symbol interpretation as misinforming, even dangerous. Patients and therapists may both use fashionable jargon as a defense against direct, open encounter with a dream's emotional meanings. But these, mere words cannot capture, and symbols will resist such dodges, reappearing in various guise until the actual message is faced.

2. Creativity. May's helpful discussions[17] of inspiration's typical experiences and of the creator's ambivalent relationship with society, we have previously divulged. We turn here to other matters. Why do we create? May has strewn several answers, uncompared and unintegrated, haphazardly through his writings. First, our minds possess a passion for form. While seeking understanding of experiences, we often convert them into symbols, so creativity illustrates this more general purpose, which is more emotional and intuitive than intellectual. But May's views on love underly his most satisfying suggestions.

Creativity expresses our erotic needs for union with the
external, temporarily providing the experience of encounter:

> Creativity is the encounter of the
> intensively conscious human being with his
> or her world...Creativity occurs in an act
> of encounter and is to be understood with
> the encounter as its centre.[18]

And again:

> Our feelings, like the artist's paints and
> brush are ways of communicating and sharing
> something meaningful from us to the world.[19]

In support, Barron's interviews[20] found creators to have
strong feelings of isolation and loneliness that - unlike the
rest of us, Barron feels - they openly face and try to overcome.
Their works seek bridges not only to their audience but also to
their forefathers and successors (since culture provides a sense
of community). In other words, their feelings of alienation may
motivate their creativity, rather than vice versa. Hutchinson[21]
extends the notion of encounter to audiences. For a product to
affect us and elicit "understanding," it must induce an almost
mystical sense of union or empathy, causing a flood of
associations from earlier life that will obliterate our awareness
of present surroundings.

For May, creative encounter invariably evokes feelings of
intensity (from complete involvement in activity) and of joy
(from actualization of potential). The presence of encounter
distinguishes genuine creativity from the dilletante variety and
also from purely intellectual pursuits in which subject-object
separation remains. However creative thought is not uncontrolled
frenzy. Recalling Kris/Arieti's tertiary process, the logic of
form must temper encounter's passion (although about these
Appollonian aspects, May says little).

His final theme concerns death's motivating power.
Admitting debts to Camus, he sees creators as rebelling against
it, refusing to go gently into that good night. Their most
pervasive emotion, then, is rage, seemingly directed against
wordly evils such as cruelty and injustice but ultimately against
this greatest of all injustices.

But to us, May's musings about courage[22] comprise his
greatest contribution. As a good existentialist, anxiety seems
to him not neurotic but the necessary price of authenticity. And
creators need the courage to accept and even welcome this mixed
emotion, since their activities invite it. Thus, courage becomes

467

ontological, essential to our being if we would realize our potential. Timidity betrays both ourselves and our fellows who need our talents (whether they know it or not). If neurosis accompanies creativity, then, it is because the latter guarantees anxiety. So again May follows Jung, not Freud; creators may well "pay dearly for the divine gift."[23]

But why does creativity invite anxiety, making courage so necessary? Chapter 2's answers we briefly recapitulate. Note creativity's demands. Taxing labor to "will ourselves to the encounter with intensity of dedication and commitment."[24] One must tolerate, even enjoy, solitude, loneliness, uncertainty, and thus insecurity, along with feelings of personal inadequacy and failure--especially when that ideal vision in the mind's eye eludes capture. Thus, Goodman's[25] self actualized/creative subjects moved blithely ahead without assurance of success, whereas the "unfulfilled," of equal potential, held back from fear of failure. The genuinely creative, May adds, realize the dangers and that they could be wrong, but leap in with both feet nevertheless. Which provides the paradox of courage. Creative work is healthiest when it occurs not without but in spite of doubt.

Creators also need courage because, like explorers, they journey into the unknown--indeed, in their encounters they abandon their normal individual selfhood, their sense of separation, to immerse themselves in the world. Because their supposedly assertive acts paradoxically require some self renunciation, notably during inspiration (an experience that can be terrifying, as psychedelic trips, via LSD-25 or mescalin reveal). And of course because creativity involves rebellion--rejecting the status quo, knocking props from under accepted ways to invite slings, arrows, and poverty, and above all through its aspects of metaphysical rebellion, risking (as so many legends preach) omnipotent wrath and eternal damnation. Lastly, because creators must dare to confront the unconscious' seedy matters consciously, assuming that inspiration needs hefty doses of same (and May agrees with Poincaré that it does). Dauntless Lears, they must welcome strange and unnatural horrors, crying open-armed in invitation to the firmament:

> Blow, winds, and crack your cheeks! rage!
> blow!
> You cataracts and hurricanoes, spout
> Till you have drench'd our steeples, drown'd
> the cocks!
> You sulphurous and thought-executing fires,
> Vaunt couriers to oak-cleaving thunderbolts,
> Singe my white head!
>   (3,2)

Thus for May, as many others, both artists and neurotics communicate more easily with the unconscious. However, the artists' psychic hot line helps them, because they can share its revelations with others, while neurotics (for unexplained reasons) cannot. But again here we see May's fondness for Jung. The daimonic, a particularly rich source of artistic material, is primarily collective in nature, so "the great artist serves as an artesian well through which eternal patterns spring into expression,"[26] (a statement which his great predecessor might well have uttered). Similarly again, May assigns both art and neurosis a predictive, future-foretelling function, citing Ezra Pound's dictum that artists are "the antennae of the race."[27] Moreover, they also help <u>form</u> the future, by first conceiving new possibilities in their unconscious imaginations and then, like psychic test pilots, trying them out. And modern art's futuristic messages contain warnings of a "schizoid" world in which apathy, isolation, and loneliness abound and <u>eros</u> is suppressed. These messages gave May his first clues about the reasons for those modern neuroses.

This observation notwithstanding, May has often interpreted dreams but seldom artistic symbols. However, his principles for the former suggest an intriguing possibility. Supposedly themes at first expressed subtly become more obvious in later dreams. Should not works of art, then, display similar development? If so, someone's mature produce could help understanding, retroactively, of that which came before.

We finish by revisiting courage and yet another of its various contributions. May, perhaps more than anyone we have met, stresses creativity's intimate connection to death. Not only can our foreboding adversary drive us to create, but also "the creative act itself is an act of dying, (and) this is the reason <u>par excellence</u> why it takes courage."[28] When we relinquish ourselves to those inspirational visions, when we leap into encounter, the resultant loss of self does resemble a psychological death. So here again lurks paradox in this most paradoxical of acts. Like the mythical firebird, we must symbolically sacrifice ourselves if a new entity is to arise, phoenix-like, from our ashes, an entity that yet may provide our symbolic victory <u>over</u> death:

> I believe that eternity comes only when we are willing to give up our claim to immortality, only when we are willing to die, only when we can give up the claim that God made the universe with us at its centre.[29]

We shall return to this topic forthwith.

3. __Commentary__. His clarification of courage's various roles provides May's most telling bequest. Think, for example, of Copernicus, standing the world on its ear, overthrowing humankind's prevailing image of itself and of its relationship to the universe. Copernicus' upbringing, education, revered predecessors, and the prevailing dogma of the time would all weigh against him. He must be wrong! Some subtle, crucial flaw must stain his reasoning! And yet he had the resolution to leap past these restraints. From where does it come? As we saw in Chapter 2, persons of Copernicus' breed must possess, first, boundless self-confidence, even arrogance. These may not be particularly likable or socially advantageous traits, but we probably wrong talented youngsters by teaching _excessive_ politeness, consideration for others, and deference to elders. Courage's other necessity, presumably, is naive innocence. The child, like the fool, blissfully ignorant of the dangers, will rush in while wise men deliberate and so, on occasion, surpass them.

May's deliberations on _eros_ are also meet. The notion of the encounter recalls Sartre's fundamental project, although the former seeks to unite, not two aspects of being, but subjective being with external phenomena. Moreover, as befits humanistic optimism, May nowhere implies this quest to be hopeless. But first and foremost, a linkage of creativity with our needs for interpersonal interaction immediately calls up Freud. May's energy may be more widely erotic than narrowly sexual, but its implications are nevertheless similar. Most obviously, creators' everyday lives should less evidence the need their work satisfies. And is it not conceivable that innovation's altar sacrifices not _sex_ but _love_, those broader intimacies that require appreciable time, energy, and self? Creators' sexual lives, _contra_ Freud, have frequently been rich. But rarely have their erotic lives. In like vein, since their work should quench their needs for encounter, creators could tolerate the necessary solitary confinement, even alienation. Even the choice of field may hereby receive explanation. Some activities (poetry, painting) require more isolation than do others (choreography). Perhaps they elicit more intense or different encounters and thus attract different persons to them.

But negativity becomes necessary. Writing about May has been difficult because, while he has added some new armaments to our arsenal, when compared to some of the admittedly fast company discussed herein, he comes up rather short. The Courage to Create, his major statement on the subject, seems decidedly barren in its abilities to increase our sense of understanding, to elicit far-reaching associations, or warm gut reactions of aesthetic excitement. Love and Will is vastly superior and genuinely provocative, but it is only incidentally about creativity.

Why our middling impression? First of all, May's presentation style shares many of Maslow's failings. Meandering, even chaotic, it too often resembles a first draft that tries to "get everything down," while postponing refinement. Furthermore, he not only displays Maslow's vacillation but he also too frequently contradicts himself outright. Consider his definition of creativity. He several times insists that it must involve encounter, which certainly indicts an experience as its distinguishing sine qua non. Yet elsewhere he is as adamant as ourselves that a tangible product must result. Perhaps by systematically exploring his topic's various aspects, he might have avoided these problems. But instead he jumps haphazardly about, to return later, or in another book, to virtually the same subject, sometimes to reverse his position, sometimes to repeat himself virtually verbatim. On occasion May, like Maslow again, could sue himself for copyright infringement.

But other weaknesses are more idiosyncratic. The Courage to Create seems needlessly padded with superfluities, and such meat as there is deserves more succinctness. Also, next to May's penchant for vagueness, even Freud seems a model of precision. The encounter, for example, is admittedly an inherently fuzzy concept, but a Sartre will usually find a tactic such as a metaphor to clarify ambiguities. Unfortunately, May relies mainly on unedifying personal experiences or on clinical anecdotes of doubtful relevance.

In like vein, he too often ignores his ideas' implications. For example, between his lines lurks a possible explanation for individual differences in creativity. Since he nowhere implies a talent differentially doled out, we must suspect that his answer reduces to differences in courage, i.e., successful creators are those able to "damn the torpedoes, full speed ahead!" in pursuit of their fleeing muses. But is this May's conclusion? The issue is avoided, as are some worm cans thereby opened. Why, for example, does self-confident courage often yield garbage, as it does in the deluded psychotic? Why is courage differentially endowed? How does creative courage differ from that needed to, say, gamble on the stock market, snorkel in the Bermuda Triangle, or even coach in the NHL? Similarly, we are told (as if it were self-evident) that death, eros and cosmic rage are major motivators. But what of those who dismiss encounter as a romantic fiction and deny any such experience (see Chapter 5)? Or of those who, apropos of the supposed importance of "rage," retort that "mere indignation does not make an artist of any kind."[30] Or of those who have all the appropriate experiences but produce only dogs' breakfasts? And what of encounter's

471

inherent paradox? If we create to overcome isolation, why does this activity so often increase it?

Now no theorist can handle every eventuality, but most will anticipate and face some objections, however unsatisfactorily. But May's irritatingly superficial discussions merely scratch the surface, leaving us suspecting that he has not thought deeply enough about what he has said. For all these reasons, his perspective defies extensive application to Part 1's phenomena. Admittedly, few theorists have tackled these, but at May's answers we are often hard put even to _guess_.

But perhaps most offensive of all is his loyalty to predecessors far beyond duty's call. Always excepting the musings on courage, his main ideas, apart from details, have too often been advanced previously and more effectively, his most obvious creditors being Freud, Sartre, Camus, Rank, and especially the Jung/Langer consortium. As a result, May smothers us with overwhelming déjà vu, intensifying our suspicions that we have learned little. Perhaps we have missed some genuine originalities, but surely a writer should try to anticipate such problems by discussing other approaches and the differences in his own (as both Jung and Rank, for example, do with Freud). But too frequently May neglects such mundane scholarly labor, as well as the scholar's almost compulsive tendency to acknowledge sources. Ideas cast, either overtly or implicitly, in the first person pronoun should sometimes be in the third; for "I Suggest", read "X has suggested." Perhaps May's main contribution, in retrospect, is to simplify and make more widely palatable, important ideas from others. At any rate, a hasty, informal poll conducted by Calgary Straw Votes, Inc., found that among writings on creativity, only Koestler's The Act of Creation[31] and Ghiselin's The Creative Process[32] rival The Courage to Create in size of readership on our topic. Without this wide consumption, May would hardly deserve the extensive attention we have paid him.

Creativity and Death

May is hardly alone in suspecting a connection between these two activities. We have previously heard Sarte, Camus and Rank propose it, and we shall now learn of others. Matson's Short Lives[33] describes a number of eminent persons - such as comedian Lenny Bruce, novelist Malcolm Lowry, and poet Dylan Thomas - who not only died prematurely but seemed almost to foresee this eventuality, judging by their excessive preoccupations with death (Thomas' works, for example, is laden with it). Unfortunately, Matson's portraits, potentially so rich, are mere thumbnail sketches of each person's "lifeandwork." How and why might death have affected that work? What (besides their early demise) do

they have in common? Precious few such theoretical kites are
flown, so we receive, in the immortal words of Dragnet's Jack
Webb, "just the facts, ma'am." For greater sustenance, we must
turn elsewhere.

    1. Lisl M. Goodman. Her Death and the Creative Life[34]
proposes that our knowledge of mortality impels virtually our
every advance, because

> If we didn't know that our future was
> limited, our only goal would be the
> satisfaction of immediate parochial needs,
> as witness it on the animal level.[35]

Goodman surmises, like Camus, that only with death's tangible
proximity do we live fully and, like May, that great art
invariably struggles and comes to terms with death. But mainly
she wonders whether we resent death because it prevents our
accomplishing everything we wish. Do we fear, not dying per se
but dying prematurely? If so, might those who have achieved much
perhaps fear death less? To find out, she interviewed more than
700 subjects, some of them self actualized, i.e., highly
productive in art or science.

    Verifying our suspicion that artists and scientists may be
different animals, the latter think more about death and are also
more concerned with past and future, with what has and will
happen, whereas artists focus on the here and now. Perhaps,
Goodman guesses, their locus of death differs. Artists may see
it as an everpresent potential within ourselves that they
fatalistically accept and even take for granted. Scientists,
however, with their external focus, their desires to control
events, might locate it outside themselves and believe that if
one tries one can, if not eliminate, at least delay it.

    But her actual results only marginally vindicated her major
hypothesis. Fear of death does decline with age for the self
actualized, while increasing overall. But to complicate matters,
the former remain dissatisfied; they always have "more to do."
Which after the fact seems predictable, since resting on one's
laurels does seem tantamount to dying. Self actualization, in
contrast, implies a Browningesque pursuit of the impossible:

> Ah, but a man's reach should exceed his
> grasp,
> Or what's a heaven for.[36]

Thus, such persons might find death both less and also more
intimidating (having accomplished more, but also having more
still to accomplish). Furthermore, these ever paradoxical

personalities voice both possibilities when interviewed. Fortunately, we espy resolution. One of these (perennial dissatisfaction) has existential immediacy; they apply it to themselves. But they avow that for people in general, a rich, full life should disarm death's grip.

Hindsight's benefits also suggest that the study's conceptualization worked against it. First, Goodman defined self actualization mainly by the objective criterion of tangible accomplishments. Yet is not a satisfactory life in the eye of the beholder? Might not those who seem successful to others seem less so to themselves and believe (as did Goodman's subjects) that they still have much to do? Putting it differently, by setting minimal goals we virtually guarantee success. Which suggests that underachievers might fear death less, that (with apologies to both Caesar and Shakespeare):

> Self actualizers die many times before their
> deaths
> The wishy-washy never taste of death but
> once.

Thus, had Goodman emphasized one's beliefs about one's level of achievement, her hypothesis might have received fairer hearing. Second, her interviews, judging by the excerpts provided, may not have tapped attitudes toward death precisely. For example, to the question "Do you ever think about death?" a response of "hardly ever" could indicate either a healthy fatalism more concerned with living, or excessive fear and denial.

Be that as it may, since even self actualizers showed appreciable fear of death, Goodman saw her initial hypothesis as only marginally supported. Therefore she argues, in a provocative conclusion, that to lessen angst we should try to regard death not as a terrible adversary but simply as life's logical last act (as did the rational Houyhnhnms in Gulliver's Travels). Sound advice. But perhaps easier said philosophically than done psychologically, since attitudes are emotional as well as intellectual, more easily changed on the second level than the first. Can we learn to accept death emotionally? Measure for Measure's Claudio, sentenced to death for fornication, expresses our fears:

> Ay, but to die, and go we know not where;
> To lie in cold obstruction and to rot;
> This sensible warm motion to become
> A kneaded clod; and the delighted spirit
> To bathe in fiery floods, or to reside
> In thrilling region of thick-ribbed ice;
> To be imprison'd in the viewless winds,

474

And blown with restless violence round about
The pendent world; or to be worse than worst
Of those that lawless and incertain thought
Imagine howling:--'tis too horrible!
The weariest and most loathed worldly life
That age, ache, penury, and imprisonment
Can lay on nature is a paradise
To what we fear of death.

                                        (3,1)

2. Ernest Becker. The assumption underlying Becker's The
Denial of Death[37] seems more realistic. Death so intimidates us
that we must lock it away in the unconscious to remain sane.
Becker imaginatively combines Freudian and existential
(particularly Kierkegaardian) themes, but his greatest debt,
gratefully acknowledged, is to Rank.* He begins with what he
sees as the most glaring paradox in that collection of same, the
human condition. We combine animal materialism with spiritual
longings and capabilities. We can appreciate, even create beauty
and soar on fancy's boundless flights. Yet we house these
sublimities within a physical body that is earth bound and time's
fool, that emits foul odors, performs distasteful functions, and
withers and decays. That is our dilemma. Reaching for the
stars, we are ultimately food for worms. Witness Hamlet's
musings as he contemplates the skull of a deceased companion:

> Alas, poor Yorick! I knew him, Horatio. A
> fellow of infinite jest, of most excellent
> fancy. He hath borne me on his back a
> thousand times. And now how abhorred in my
> imagination it is! My gorge rises at it.
> Here hung those lips that I have kiss'd I
> know not how oft. Where be your gibes now?
> your gambols? your songs? your flashes of
> merriment that were wont to set the table on
> a roar? Not one now, to mock your own
> grinning? Quite chapfall'n? Now get you to
> my lady's chamber, and tell her, let her

---

*Becker feels, as do we, that Rank has been too much
ignored. This state of affairs he attributes partly to Rank's
split with Freud (which made him persona non grata among
psychoanalysts, who should have been most sympathetic) and partly
to his inadequacies as a writer (which we have implicated as
well). According to Becker, Rank realized his literary
deficiences and asked Anaïs Nin, a devoted disciple, to rewrite
his work. Unfortunately, she never did so.

> paint an inch thick, to this favour she must
> come. Make her laugh at that...Dost thou
> think Alexander look'd o' this fashion i'th'
> earth?...And <u>smelt</u> so? Pah!...Why may not
> imagination trace the noble dust of
> Alexander till a' find it stopping a
> bunghole?
>
> (5,1)

Thus Becker, following the existentialists, finds human anxiety to be not neurotic but eminently reasonable, given our awareness of our own mortality:

> What does it mean to be a <u>self-conscious</u>
> <u>animal</u>? The idea is ludicrous, if not
> monstrous. It means to know that one is
> food for worms. This is the terror; to have
> emerged from nothing, to have a name,
> consciousness of self, deep inner feelings,
> an excruciating inner yearning for life and
> self-expression and with all this yet to
> die.[38]

To make matters worse, this fear cannot be alleviated, for death <u>is</u>, after all, inevitable. Our only recourse, for comfort and sanity, is to banish this overwhelming fact from consciousness. Becker's Freudian debts here show clearly, except that for him (like Rank) our fundamental trauma is not sex but death.

This immediately raises a problem for therapy, one that troubled Freud. If hidden fears are restored to consciousness, might anxiety not diminish but flourish? Should these sleeping dogs not be left aslumbering? After all, they were repressed for good reason. Ibsen's <u>The Wild Duck</u> dramatizes the dangers of recognizing reality. A family, by consigning some threatening skeletons to its psychic closet, has remained comparatively content. Unfortunately, a fervent "missionary" convinces some members to eliminate what Ibsen calls <u>life lies</u> and live truth. He thereby destroys them. Moral:

> Take the life-lie away from the average man
> and straightaway you take away his
> happiness...Life wouldn't be too bad if only
> these blessed people who come canvassing
> their ideals around everybody's door would
> leave us poor souls in peace.
>
> (<u>The Wild Duck</u>, 5)

Becker voices similar suspicions. Perhaps psychoanalysis did little harm because, by focusing on matters sexual, it left the _illusion_ of our immortality firmly in place, masking the one trauma we _cannot_ confront. But how, then, can we _retain_ this illusion? For Becker, as for Rank and Fromm, some of us identify with larger groups; unity, it seems, provides not only strength but comfort. Others resort to so-called _causa-sui projects_. When our accomplishments, to us at least, deserve admiration, we thereby deny our physical bestiality.

Thus, _heroism_ seems to Becker a basic problem. How can we become, to ourselves at least, important objects in the universe? Now creators commonly display such inflated egos, as we know, yet we shall now learn that their causa sui projects face obstacles. Again recalling Rank, Becker first compares them to neurotics. Both feel keenly individuated and therefore alone. Both have unduly vivid imaginations and overly developed spiritual, symbolic sides. As a result, while they can replace actual experience with their private worlds of fantasy, they also, paradoxically, perceive reality most accurately. In fact, they take in more than is healthy, living "on the brink of danger."

But only neurotics fall in. What saves artists? In a word, _talent_. Using their expressive powers, artists can sidestep self-knowledge's dangers by re-working them in products that, by bringing satisfaction, acclaim, and symbolic immortality, can substantiate their heroic illusions. Neurotics, however, equally realistic* but lacking talent's protection, must work through their traumas either by excessive self criticism or by retreats into fantasy where they can glorify themselves. Their clumsy defences against truth, their attempts to ward off anxiety, merely interfere with their daily living, e.g., the obsessive-compulsive who neverendingly washes hands, cleans floors, or checks zipper of fly. In short, Becker's neurotic, like Rank's, is a failed artist:

> Both the artist and the neurotic bite off more than they can chew, but the artist spews it back out again and chews it over in an objectified way, as an external, active, work project. The neurotic can't marshall this creative response embodied in a specific work[40] and so he chokes on his introversions.

---

*Apparently depressed neurotics do perceive their actual status particularly accurately, while the less afflicted labor under exaggerated (and seemingly healthy) delusions of their own importance, competence, and the like.[39]

And who touches reality most accurately of all? Paradoxically, it is the woefully deluded schizophrenics. Supposedly most in touch with their spiritual side, most sensitive, and therefore creative (or at least imaginative), their defences against recognizing their mortality fail completely. Anxiety, and thus insanity, must be their fate.*

Becker also implies artist-scientist divergence. Both provide answers, but of differing kind, to the problem of death. Artists confront this trauma openly but transfer it to their work, while the scientists' defence is to deny it entirely and pretend a comprehensible, orderly world that does not exist. In this regard, Becker especially chastises various modern psychologies. Reincarnations of Voltaire's Dr. Pangloss, they don't take life seriously enough, legislating out its terrors by completely ignoring our mortality. Both pop psychology's pendant-clad guru and the rat-running behaviorist imply that existence can be both understandable and "happy" if only we heed their messages (and buy their books).

We might also note another of Becker's departures from Freud. For the latter, artists, like everyone else, bury their traumas in the unconscious, so these must be subtly sublimated in their products. But for Becker, artists are less repressive; their traumas hover nearer consciousness. Yet may we suggest that perhaps this is not true of their death fears? Perhaps these alone are fully repressed, to provide the latent content of their work? At any rate, Becker does suggest that artists, sometimes dismissed as superfluous luxuries, perform valuable service. By risking greater realization themselves, they provide comforting illusions for the rest of us. When we admire their work, we intuitively conclude that humans, at their best, are more than mere worm fodder. In addition, that work often suggests purpose and meaning for life and shows death in defeat. Hence the frequent criticism that modern art is unduly pessimistic may, in this context, have validity. The emanations of existentialism, for example, of lean and hungry look, may be dangerous, resolutely undermining our every life lie and serving not to comfort but remind.

---

*Schizophrenics do sometimes surpass "normals" in perceptual accuracy. In one instance, some reasonably healthy individuals pretended symptoms of psychopathology to gain admittance to a psychiatric institution.[41] They completely fooled the staff but indicatively, not the other patients, who quickly realized that the interlopers did not belong.

Becker deserves comment. First of all, he is a pleasure to read. A genuine scholar, of wide-ranging interest and expertise, he nevertheless avoids the dégagé quality far too common in academic writing. He enthusiastically discusses and gleefully credits the work of others, dotting his references to them with superlatives such as "magnificent" and "outstanding." As well, he implies some intriguing possibilities. As the saying goes, fear is a great motivator, so if the most traumatic of all actually drives creators, their persistent dedication becomes eminently understandable. By implication also, those neverending dreams, eternal life and/or the fountain of youth, would be mixed blessings if attained. Our death fears might thereby become mere historical curiosities, but so too might some treasured activities that make life worthwhile.

Nonetheless, as previously intimated, we find the notion of death's motivating powers unappealing. First, predictably, it suits not every creative figure. While some have been unusually preoccupied by death--the composer Gustav Mahler springs immediately to mind[43]--many others, notably Picasso[44] and Goethe[45] denied and feared death with almost phobic intensity. Second, as the legend of the Resurrection clearly reveals, religions have always served, as perhaps their prime purpose, to provide comfort in the face of, and even a kind of victory over, death. Illusions, leaps, even opiums of the people they may be, but surely existential anxiety should less trouble people of faith. Therefore, according to Becker, their creative fires should wither. In fact, this is hardly the case, as the Bachs, Leonardos, and countless Anonymi of earlier days verify. And what of poet Earle Birney's incontestable observation, that these days "who believes in any kind of permanence of human beings?"[46] To create in order to defeat death would seem pointless when any day we may all be blown to smithereens. Yet creativity seems to be as rampant as ever.

As well, few of us, admittedly, think of death frequently and fewer still can imagine themselves actually dead. But perhaps these oversights reflect not repression (which implies active suppression below consciousness and special techniques for

---

*Solomon & Wynne's avoidance learning studies[42] validate this truism. Dogs learned to jump hurdles when a light came on, to avoid shock. Presumably the light became a feared warning of incipient danger. The response, once acquired, proved much more difficult to eliminate than any that obtain positive reinforcement, although the dogs never again experienced the shock.

resurrection) but simply that <u>no one living has ever experienced death</u> (unless reincarnation be conceded). As the parent and the aged will verify, often we must undergo an experience ourselves before we can identify with it. Perhaps, then, artists' preoccupation with death (if indeed it exists) simply reflects their special abilities to imagine the extraordinary. Which renders that preoccupation a mere by-product rather than cause of their abilities.

In addition, both Becker and Camus maintain that facing death as an immediate possibility should drive us to accomplish more, to live fully. Such empirical evidence as we have seems decidedly mixed. On the one hand, the terminally ill do often respond with bursts of activity in hobbies, travel, and the like, to "make up for lost time" and their priorities do frequently change dramatically, e.g., in personal relationships. (I am grateful to Dr. Jerry Devins for supplying this information.) However, Kübler-Ross' classic study of such persons, <u>On Death and Dying</u>,[47] concluded that they typically pass through five stages: denial, anger, bargaining, depression, and finally acceptance. Perhaps excepting bargaining, these suggest not Camusian intensity but the opposite, especially so the final stage, with its detachment from life's typical activities, its movement toward not <u>more</u> but <u>less</u> living. In like vein, we repeat that those psychologically most segregated from death, the young, are also the most creatively active. It would be helpful to learn, then, whether creative persons who become terminally ill evince bursts of productivity.

In sum, as we have said before, we find it intuitively implausible that the desire to defeat death should serve, unconsciously or otherwise, as a <u>fundamental</u> motive for creativity. Its occasional role we willingly admit; its ubiquity we question. Admittedly, one's intuitions hardly justify rejecting hypotheses, especially in the shadowy realm of human motives and more especially still when these are thought to be unconscious. Nevertheless, when our gut reactions do not indicate face validity, we will not be converted without appreciable evidence. Such evidence is simply not as yet available. Why our introspective doubts? Above all, these explanations seem to us unduly pessimistic. Behaviorists teach that either positive carrots or negative sticks can motivate. Why must creativity necessarily seek to avoid something discomforting, be it sex, death, or overly large feet? Why could we not retreat into imaginative fantasy, not to suppress reality's unpleasantries but to <u>obtain</u> the pleasures therein? A recent film about Molière[48] captures this point. We see him fascinated from childhood by ritual, by human pretense, and by dissemblance, so that eventually he rejected more practical pursuits to pursue and express their hypnotic magnetism.

Erich Fromm

Placing Fromm among humanists may raise some eyebrows. He is, after all, by his own admission[49] ensconced firmly in Freud's tradition, outdoing many fellow neo-Freudians in ratifying the party line, e.g., in interpreting symbols[50] and in rescuing the founder's major discoveries from revisionist tinkerings. As well, Fromm has explicitly forsworn the existentialist label, since he cannot agree that we possess complete freedom or lack universal values. Actually, his other preeminent forefather, besides Freud, is Karl Marx. Symptomatically, he has labeled his framework for developing Freud as _dialectic humanism_, no less, and he has stressed personality's social, political, and cultural as well as psychological antecedents. Therefore, as a trip to one's library will verify, Fromm's output relates to sociology, political science, history, and even medicine. As a result, it is scattered throughout the cataloguer's firmament; tracking it down provides excellent exercise for would-be marathoners. Nevertheless, Fromm does accept the main planks of humanism's platform, and his thoughts on creativity clearly march in step with May's, so his concurrent treatment is vindicated.

However, Fromm's ruminations are intimately entwined with other speculations. At base, he distinguishes between creativity as a _product_ and as an _attitude towards living_.[51] The second is necessary for the first to result, but can also exist on its own. This creative attitude requires, among other things[52] a readiness to be puzzled (cf. Getzels et al.'s problem finding[52]), to accept and even seek out conflict and stress, and above all to break out of self boundaries and feel united with the external (cf. May's encounter). Now because this creative attitude surfaces repeatedly throughout Fromm's writing we shall, in the interests of brevity, discuss relevant topics and raise creativity's specter within these contexts rather than separately.

1. _Existential needs_. Recalling Maslow's hierarchy, Fromm's _The Sane Society_[53] posits some uniquely human motives that do not reflect physiological tension but are nevertheless influential. We can choose either to meet them and grow, or to suppress them and regress to animal status. The first such need is for _identity_. Separation from the mother causes individuation and a search for a sense of ego, or "I." Secondly, we need a _frame of orientation and devotion_. Having both reason and imagination, we try continually to understand our situation's every aspect, and lacking explanations, we will devise our own, however inappropriate. Both these motives, obviously, are conducive to creativity, but others seem even more so. That same reason and imagination makes us dissatisfied playing the passive animal to whom things happen. We desire _transcendence_ beyond this bestial status, and creating - whether through love, art,

481

religion or manufacturing - can provide it. If no such outlets are available (perhaps because of stifling environments) we will become destructive, because both love and hate, both creation and destruction, answer this same need. Which course we choose is fundamental. Thus, Fromm, like May, recognizes a diabolic as well as sublime side to our nature:

> It would be difficult indeed for anyone who has had a long clinical experience as a psychoanalyst to belittle the destructive forces within man.[54]

Indeed, anyone familiar with history would face the same difficulty!

The last, but for us certainly not least, need is for relatedness. Fromm planted the seeds for these thoughts earlier in Man for Himself,[55] but brought them to blossom in The Art of Loving,[56] so we follow him there. Isolation induces anxiety, so we seek unification with others. This quest, both neverending and resolute, keeps the human race, and its various subunits such as clans and families, together. It has impelled such varying activities as animal worship, human sacrifice, military conquest, artistic creation, and the love of God. But these are bandaids. Only complete physical and psychological fusion with another person in the act called love is entirely satisfactory.

What is this thing called "love?" First, it is giving not only sex's physical donations but our most precious qualities, like joy, humor, and sadness. Therefore, love is not simply a warmth in heart or stomach that "just happens" and is caught, like measles. It is an act. It demands knowledge, persistence, and practice, making it an art. And these strictures apply to both participants, so love must be reciprocated, these gifts received in equal measure from the other. If we are not loved persons, Sartrian beloveds as well as lovers, then our love is unfulfilled. Secondly, genuine love treats the partner, not as an object for selfish exploitation, but with care (an active concern for his or her life and growth, epitomized by a mother's love for her child). With responsibility (a voluntary agreement to satisfy the other's various needs). With respect (cherishing the other for what he or she is instead of for our selfish preferences--which prevents possessive domination). And with knowledge (trying to understand the other, not superficially but to his or her very essence--which prevents blind, romantic idealization). Lastly, genuine love is paradoxical. Fromm repeatedly stresses our various polar opposites, notably life/death and masculine/feminine. Similarly, love unites individuals completely, yet each retains personal integrity (otherwise, that competing need for identity could be threatened). A twosome in love can perhaps live as cheaply as one, and may even become one. Yet they remain two. In W. S. Gilbert's immortal words, "a most ingenious paradox."

Let us pause to compare other views of love with these. They immediately recall May, although Fromm emphasizes separateness as well as encounter. Sartre is clearly rebuffed. Fromm admits that perversions such as sadism and masochism do occur, but sees these symbiotic unions as not prototypic but deviant because each partner seeks total unity with the other. Whereas genuine love's egalitarian partnership preserves personal integrity. Each member is both lover and beloved. As well, Fromm carefully separates himself from Freud. Love is not simply a physical, even chemical matter of sex, to be satisfied by orgasm; it requires both physical and psychological union between the polar opposites of male and female. In Biblical legend, Eden's twain, first one, became separate. Ever since, we have striven to again Fly United.

But what of creativity? For Fromm, like May, it seeks to satisfy relatedness, but it seems to him an unsatisfactory solution. Admittedly, creators do unite themselves with their materials and so with the external. Also, they plan, produce, and witness their results, in contrast to menial mass production that isolates producer from product. (By deploring industrialization's alienation of workers from means of production, Fromm shows his Marxist lineage.) Still, such unions are only transitory and, more important, are not interpersonal; creators relate to things, not to people.

Yet elsewhere[57] Fromm portrays one species of creativity more positively. Denial or incomplete satisfaction of those unique human needs invites psychosis or neurosis, respectively, so

> Mental health is characterized by the ability to love and to create, by the emergence from incestuous ties to clan and soil, by a sense of identity based on one's experience of self as the subject and agent of one's powers, by the grasp of reality inside and outside of ourselves, that is, by the development of objectivity and reason.[58]

Something called collective art, "(a responding) to the world with our senses in a meaningful, skilled, productive, active, shared way"[59] best achieves these various goals. Examples are such group artistic activities as communal singing and dancing. Now that these activities might satisfy needs for transcendence and relatedness is obvious. But how could they do likewise for

483

orientation? Fromm answers that we need to understand, not only logically via philosophy, theology and science, but also sensually and intuitively through art and ritual, which therefore resemble one another. Not, perhaps in superficial form but certainly in the needs they satisfy.

Such collective pursuits, therefore, become not mere leisure-filling frills, of less import than making money or waging war. They are absolutely basic for secure lives devoid of anxiety. Any purportedly "sane society" provides for them--in fact, singing and dancing, in Fromm's opinion, rival scholarly literacy in importance and deserve at least the emphasis sports and games currently receive.* Unfortunately, he asserts, both production and consumption of art is nowadays a largely individual endeavor. Only woefully pale imitations like fraternities and spectator sports fill the communal void:

> There is no active productive participation, no common unifying experience, no meaningful acting out of significant answers to life...What help is it to have almost no illiteracy, and the most widespread higher education which has existed at any time--if we have no collective expression of our total personalities, no common art and ritual? Undoubtedly a relatively primitive village in which there is still real feasts, common artistic shared expression and no literacy at all--is more advanced culturally and more healthy mentally than our educated, newspaper reading, radio-listening culture.[60]

2. <u>Character orientation</u>. Another Frommian description arises from his discussions of ethics and values, most fully realized in <u>Man for Himself</u>.[61] The essential argument recalls Maslow, so we merely repeat its gist. Ethical questions must not be avoided while discussing personality and culture; we should ask both what humans do and what they <u>ought</u> to do. Prevailing

---

*This may be laudable in theory. But will such bastions of combative higher education as Alabama or Nebraska sacrifice their famous football teams so students can gambol gleefully on the green in, say, Morris dancing? Let us not hold our collective breaths for Howard Cosell to bring us The Wide World of Collective Art, this week spotlighting Sing-Along Madrigals, with Michael Jackson countertenoring the Fa-la-las.

belief to the contrary, it is possible to determine universal values if we discover our healthy, natural best interests. However, Fromm's pessimistic streak (courtesy of Freud) leads him to deny, unlike the humanists, our inherent goodness. Rather, we possess potentials for good and evil in equal measure.[62] Various factors, e.g., environmental, can sway us toward one or the other, but we can also choose whether to give our lives meaning and develop our potential. Yet to take control of our existence implies both freedom and responsibility, attributes that many find threatening. To avoid them, they will resort either to authoritarianism (domination of or submission to others), conformity (immersion in a larger group), or destructiveness (aggression and violence).

Fromm's basic character orientations represent different solutions to these problems. Each displays a distinctive, reliable style of responding to and relationship with the surrounding culture and so lends consistency to personality. At base we can choose (cf. Maslow again) between nonproductive orientations, which are neurotic and even evil (leading to depersonalization, apathy, personal dissatisfaction, and occasionally violence) and the productive orientation--self actualized, fully mature, integrated, and (in some sense at least) creative.

Let us dally briefly over the four nonproductive types. The receptive and exploitive both believe that all things worthwhile exist external to themselves. However, the first named assumes an inability to control their attainment, so he receives them passively; in love, therefore, he prefers dependency and masochism. In contrast, the exploitive, assuming that he must use force and cunning to get what he wants, grabs and steals; his love is sadistic, aimed at targets currently attached to others. The hoarding orientation, a suspicious wolverine, distrusts the outside world. Since he values only things under his lock and key, he saves compulsively. He usually surrounds himself with a protective emotional wall, but once bitten by love he becomes extraordinarily possessive. The marketing orientation, a relative newcomer, arose with capitalism. He evaluates everything by its dollar value, including other people and their accomplishments. Since he views even himself as a mere commodity, his self esteem is minimal.

Turning to the productive orientation, we need note, since it closely resembles Maslow's self actualization, only a few distinctive highlights. Again, a desire to realize the potential within oneself defines it, but Fromm frequently[63] corrects a possible misinterpretation. Unlike, say, Rand he does not advocate selfishness over altruism or personal licentiousness over social responsibility, but distinguishes forcefully between selfishness and self-love. Only the latter accompanies the true productive personality. Selfish persons cannot love others. Only taking gives them pleasure, so the worth of another depends on usefulness. Those who would truly love must first love themselves, since they must love all mankind. Therefore healthy living requires not selfishness but self-interest, whose meaning, Fromm feels, has become severely compromised. It is actually the first named's antonym rather than synonym:

> The failure of modern culture lies not in its principle of individualism, of self-interest, but in the deterioration of the meaning of self-interest; not in the fact that people are too much concerned with their self-interest, but that they are not concerned enough with the interest of the real self; not in the fact that they are too selfish, but that they do not love themselves.[64]

Thus for Fromm - as for Maslow, Rand, and indeed old Polonius - seeking one's own interests, striving to preserve one's being, is virtuous; not to do so is neurotic, even criminal. But Fromm rejects the romantic ideal of loving only one person at others' expense. Such narrow infatuation is mere symbiotic attachment, not love. It follows, strangely, that selfish persons have less in common with the self interested than with the neurotically unselfish, those who care excessively and live only for others. They too are unproductive, incapable of genuine love.

The productive orientation also displays, simultaneously, two distinct relations to the outside world; the lack of either begets sickness. The reproductive relation perceives and evaluates that world as it is (thus preventing deluded fantasy), while the generative relation conceives new possibilities to improve that world (to enhance spontaneity and imagination, and to preclude excessive preoccupation with realistic detail). The productive orientation also features a distinctive cognition. We become involved with and concerned about our objects of thought, rather than indifferent to them, thus blurring our separation from them. Still, we will retain enough objectivity that we can respect them for their genuine, unique qualities.

As Maslow too proclaims, such a person's tangible "creativity" may be moot. On the one hand, it seems to Fromm eminently natural for us to transform available materials with our imaginations, so works of art may well result--in fact the real artist provides the productive orientation's definitive representative. Yet living is also an art, its products being nothing less than actualized human beings. Some creators are woefully unproductive in this sense, while the healthy often produce nothing concrete. In the last analysis, the person's attitudes, not output, identify productivity--"we are concerned with man's character, not his success"[65]--and this creativity everyone (except the mental or emotional cripple) can achieve. Still, even those who succeed will occasionally display various nonproductive symptoms, for these simply exaggerate universal tendencies. After all, survival demands periodic receptivity, exploitation, and so on. But the productive hold these tendencies firmly in moderation, not excess.

But what determines one's dominant orientation? The Heart of Man speculates. Three tendencies, love of death, narcissism (excessive self-love) and symbiotic-incestuous fixation (immature, selfish relations with others) lead to destruction and evil rather than actualization. Only the first merits discussion here. Certain necrophilious persons, fascinated by death, worship force, power, and everything mechanical and nonliving. They wish to change even people into things, "the organic into the inorganic."[66] They fear life's messy, disordered uncertainty, its lack of control; the past, which is immutable, they prefer to the future, which is unknown. Supposedly the necrophiliac's morbid attitudes influence even his appearance. Central-casting's Ebeneezer Scrooge, he is cold, his skin looks dead, and "often he has an expression on his face as though he were smelling a bad odor."[67] His counterpole, the biophilious orientation, however, prefers life to death, construction to destruction, novelty over certainty, and love over power. It follows that "the pure necrophiliac is insane; the true biophiliac is saintly."[68] Now biophilia, unsurprisingly, is invariably present in productive persons, so the choice of life over death seems the fundamental one for inducing health.*

As regards the conditions that encourage this choice, Fromm admits doubt, but security (due to basic need satisfaction), justice (due to protection from exploitation), and freedom (to become responsible members of society) seem to him likely candidates. Especially, children must experience others who love life ("love of life is just as contagious as love of death"[69]) and who provide warm affection. As well, they must receive

---

*As Fromm recognizes, he here recapitulates Freud's notion of competing life and death instincts. However, he differs when he sees the former as primary, as more "natural." A death preference resides within us all but dominates only in perverted circumstances.

teaching by example rather than by preaching, so they are free to explore and to wonder without threat. Again Maslow's hierarchy rises to memory. Again "the good" is what healthy, productive persons do, and a moral society is one that facilitates the doing of it.

3. <u>The sex difference</u>. Masculinity/femininity to Fromm seems a particularly important dichotomy.[70] His most extensive discussion of our need to unify these, while not tackling creativity directly, certainly suggests possibilities. As usual, he straddles several traditions. Like Freud, he attributes sex differences partly to biology, but he assigns the primary role to cultural conditioning and he deplores Freud's equating of <u>differences</u> with <u>deficiencies</u>, which brands one sex (usually the female) as second class. Indeed, the differences between the sexes seem to him insignificant compared to their similarities (since both represent the same species) and to variations within the <u>same</u> sex.

The sexes' variant roles during intercourse suggest to him such differences as there are. To demonstrate potency, the male must achieve erection, but the female need only display willingness. Thus his inadequacies will be more evident. She can pretend but he cannot (his readiness being under involuntary, not voluntary control). Therefore intercourse becomes for the male a test that he may fail. This, his main sexual anxiety, makes him sensitive to ridicule, especially from women. They too experience anxiety in this sphere, but more about their ability to <u>attract</u> males, whom they require for satisfaction.

The male's desire to "prove himself" fuels his persistent need for prestige and recognition. Given his fear of failure, he becomes more competitive, driven to prove his superiority. Moreover, our culture accentuates these tendencies by rewarding them. Therefore,

> There is probably no achievement of men,
> from making love to the most courageous acts
> in fighting or thinking, which is not
> colored to some degree by this typical male
> vanity.[71]

As for the distaff side, Fromm agrees with Freud that women desire possession of the male organ, but not because they feel inadequacy or envy. Rather, they thereby demonstrate their adequacy and also avoid frustration. And, as is usual with Fromm, we can choose to satisfy these various desires either morally or neurotically. From the male's seeking after prestige and his fear of failure comes initiative, activity, and courage, but also vanity and boastfulness. Likewise, women frequently display reliability, intense love, and patience, but also excessive dependency and passivity.

It seems straightforward to extend these ideas to the sex difference in creativity. Producing admirable products can satisfy those typically masculine needs, self worth and vanity. On the other hand women, perhaps, might prefer to receive, admire, and even buy such products (and audiences do seem weighted, casual observation suggests, toward the distaff side). Also, Fromm at least implies (as do Rank and Horney) that men's inability to bear children might drive them to sire artificial progeny, although their aim, for him, is not to overcome death but to prove themselves capable of this exclusively feminine talent. In contradistinction to Freud, might we call this "uterus envy"?

4. Commentary. At first blush, Fromm's analyses seem typically humanistic. Creativity is inherent to the human psyche, a life attitude rather than a road to masterpieces. So when it remains dormant, stifling environmental/social factors are invariably to blame and creators are not neurotic but paragons of health. In fact, to Fromm, living itself seems an art form, quite as worthwhile as any other. The superior works of the genre, healthy actualized persons, possess not novelty and value but happiness and joy, indicating that they have satisfied those uniquely human needs. Thus "happiness is the criterion of excellence in the art of living."[72]

In the humanistic pantheon, Fromm clearly stands closest to May, and like his compatriot he gives us nothing like a full blown account of creativity. Yet despite this reticence he provides decidedly more stimulating company. He does not pretend to discuss our topic to any depth, so we are less disappointed when he does not do so. In addition, while he too fails to develop some of his ideas, quite bewildering their applications to Part I's data, others, notably those about personality types and human motives, possess obvious fecundity. He too borrows copiously from his predecessors. Yet he usually explains his diversions from, and his additions to, their largesse.

Likewise, the distinction between productive and nonproductive orientations certainly recalls Maslow, so similar commentary is called for, e.g., the ethical system that results is blatantly circular; "the good" is what healthy/productive persons do, and those same good deeds verify their productive status. Furthermore, the various orientations, like all such stereotypes, wildly oversimplify the hilarious heterodoxy of the genuine article and, unlike Jung's, they have not as yet been defined by objective criteria, such as psychometric tests, to insure that they actually differ empirically. Nevertheless, the

489

nonproductive types do breathe an air of legitimacy. They also suggest possible answers to some questions, such as the choice of creative field and of preferred style of expression. Perhaps a neo-Frommian in the readership will undertake these embellishments.

Fromm again resembles Maslow, and here even surpasses him, in stressing our essentially paradoxical nature. We contain a plethora of polar opposites, but can resolve them in that greater unity, the integrated personality, to overcome the potential anxiety. He does not pretend to explain how this comes about, but we can now understand, at least descriptively, the paradoxes endemic to the creative personality. This most developed, integrated exemplar of humanity simply dramatizes phenomena latent in us all.

But on further examination, Fromm's humanism seems in some ways atypical, notably when The Art of Loving depicts creativity as a sign of inadequacy, a compensation for an inability to love completely. But this departure does help explain several phenomena. As Frommian lovers must both give and take, so too should creators view their produce as gifts to others, and often they do. As well, love must, for Fromm, be reciprocated to be fulfilled. A rejected lover is a contradiction in terms. But his or her torment will not exceed a creator's whose gift of self to audience and critics is spurned. The streets joining both audience with creator, and lover with beloved, must be two-way; even Sartre, that advocate of struggle in matters of the heart, admitted as much for the first named.

This position also implicates critics. Because their relationship with creators inevitably includes judgments of worth, it smacks of a Sartrian dominance struggle. In Fromm's terms, it becomes an incomplete, neurotic form of love, one-sided and lacking in give and take. True lovers do not evaluate one another! Love may be blind, but the critic's senses must remain alert. Yet that critic wonders. Why do they resent my negative judgments and not accept them in a spirit of constructive camaraderie? I'm only trying to help. In this dreamy naivete, the critic resembles the beloved who, having spurned a would-be lover's advances, avows, "But we can still be friends". No they can't, as spurned lovers and creators will both agree. Critic Stanley Kauffmann recognizes reality:

> A work of art of any kind is a tremendous
> investment of ego, of self, of nakedness
> (Note: as is a declaration of love). Even
> if it's the worst play or film ever made,
> you still exposed yourself in it. If
> someone tells you you're deformed after

you've exposed yourself, the more truthful
he is, the more you hate him...If a man or a
woman hates me for negative things I've
written about him, I never resent it in the
slightest. Why shouldn't he? Why shouldn't
she? How could I in reason expect him or
her to like me or to say, "Well, that's
reasonable."[73]

However, Fromm renews his humanist membership when he holds
that we must choose between productivity and barrenness, between
growth and deficiency, health and neurosis. We might now mention
Dabrowski's theory of positive disintegration[74] which sounds a
rather different chord. Supposedly, neurosis becomes a
necessary, ultimately beneficial stage through which we must pass
to reach personal fulfillment, or secondary integration--a sort
of Khumbu ice-field barring our challenge to Everest's heights.
Conflicts, depressions, and anxieties provide "psychic
loosenings" that force us to "muster (our) own forces and engage
in self-education."[75] They induce us to escape ordinary
mechanical routine, to become more internally oriented, more
fully individual, and yet also less self centered and more
altruistic. We also will become more creative, both in the
humanist's life attitudes and in tangible productivity (which may
explain such neuroses as eminent creators have sometimes had).

Thus, Dabrowski agrees with Fromm (and Maslow) that fully
actualized persons resolve seemingly paradoxical needs, but for
him they climb a different route towards their lofty state. He
also, like Becker and Rank, sees neurotics as climbing higher in
some respects than do the "normal". Their greater sensitivity,
e.g., to existential anxieties, is precisely the reason for their
problems. Therefore to classify them as "mentally ill" may be
cavalier; sometimes they occupy a half-way house on the road to
creativity. But only sometimes. Dabrowski distinguishes between
various levels of disturbance. One type immobilizes the person
and prevents growth, e.g., "self centered" depression, due to
feelings of personal loss, inferiority, and the like. The second
type spurs him to greater heights, e.g., "creative" depression,
due to dissatisfaction with oneself. The psychopath, supposedly,
has the least growth potential of all. While oftentimes
perceptive and intelligent, he or she lacks emotionality or
concern for others.

The remainder of this discussion we devote to what is for us
Fromm's most intriguing concept, that of collective art. The
term obviously has a Jungian aura (ironically, since Fromm seems
to have admired Jung neither as theorist nor, we suggest, as man;
at one point,[76] he describes Jung as a textbook example of a
necrophilious person.) Closer inspection, however, suggests

491

mirror imagery. More specifically, Jung's artist, by withdrawing from social intercourse to work alone, thereby expresses the unconscious' collective aspects. Whereas Fromm's artist favors communal activities in order to satisfy personal psychic needs. Actually, Fromm seems more Rankian when he hypothesizes competing drives of individuation and identification (here called identity and relatedness, respectively) and when he deplores modern art's excessively individualistic streak. But he repudiates such art for psychological, not aesthetic reasons. Unless creators and consumers both partake of art socially, it will not satisfy the needs that it should. As well, for Rank the two opposing needs struggle eternally for dominance, to provide the tension essential to both life and art. But for Fromm, apparently, both can be fully met, and in actualized persons, they are.

Be that as it may, we must take issue with Fromm's assertion that we nowadays lack adequate social interaction. Admittedly, we less frequently practice group art; most of us passively consume rather than actively produce it, and rarely will we see dancers frolicking around maypoles in Times Square or Piccadilly Circus. But do we not satisfy these various needs in other ways, notably by sports, and games which, as Michener's wide-ranging Sports in America[77] persuasively shows, play such an important role in our culture? Nor are we mere tube-bound passivities, slumping corpulently, beered and popcorned, to peer at Hockey Night in Canada or Howard and Dandy Don. Myriads of young and old, rich and poor, male and female sweatily pursue those very Frommian motives on playing fields (at Eton and elsewhere), racquet courts, and jogging trails. Perhaps hockey provides the quintessential example of this dedication. Even Canada's arctic climate provides insufficient ice to meet the demand, so otherwise sane persons, foregoing the arms of nod, can be seen dragging their protesting corpulences to deserted, hypothermic arenas at 2 a.m. merely to play shinny.

Now because sports are inherently competitive, Fromm explicitly rejects them as adequate answers to those cooperative needs. But these rabid pucksters harbor few dreams of NHL. They seek mainly exercise, personal fulfillment, and the communal feeling that arrives both during combat and afterwards, whilst sharing cool bubblies in a steaming dressing room. They compete only with themselves, to maximize their own abilities, a drive they share with teammates and opposition alike.

Having raised this point, we may as well exorcise some demons. We certainly agree that creative work can provide one path to psychological Nirvana. But when Fromm dismisses, as do too many of the scholarly inclined, athletics as somewhat base or supercilious, as less uplifting than, say, madrigal singing, we jib. Actually, sports at their best become art forms second to

none. Witness. Hockey (for us, the jock art supreme): Team
Canada vs. the Soviet Union (September 1972), Montreal Canadiens
vs. Red Army (New Year's Eve, 1975), or U.S.A. vs. Soviet Union
(Lake Placid Olympics, 1980), or Team Canada vs. the Soviet Union
(September 1984). Baseball: Boston Red Sox vs. Cincinatti Reds
(World Series, 1975). Soccer: France vs West Germany (World
Cup, 1982), or England vs. West Germany (World Cup, 1966). Golf:
Watson vs. Nicklaus (final round, British Open, 1977). Tennis:
Borg vs. McEnroe vs. the officials at Wimbledon--the list is
endless. In fact even football, usually an unrivalled soporific,
occasionally approaches these aesthetic heights. Competitions
these were, but to us, and probably to the participants, there
were no losers. Do the trumpets defeat the flutes in Beethoven's
Ninth merely because they play louder? Does not each contribute,
in its own way, to the peerless Gestalt that emerges?[*]

Similarly, as Michener has also observed, great athletes
blur the distinction between physical and aesthetic activity, and
thus resemble dancers. Bobby Orr, Sandy Koufax, Billie Jean
King, Pelé, Lynn Swann, Nadia Comenici, Julius Erving, et al.
tread the exalted turf of Baryshnikov, Graham, Fonteyn, and
Astaire. Without question, great athletes and great artists
both, even in memory, take our breath away and bring tears to our
eyes at the sheer colossal beauty of their endeavors. They
restore our faith in our species' sublime possibilities.

---

[*]Former Montreal Canadiens goalie Ken Dryden, in his
wonderful book, The Game[78] points out that great athletes, to
achieve their potential, need great opponents. Thus Ali should
be grateful to Frazier for bringing out his best and helping
realize that greater unity, which is the unforgettable event.
The Boston Bruins, Dryden reports, served a comparable role for
Les Canadiens.

Chapter 17

EPILOGUE

Bottom: Will it please you to see the epilogue, or to hear a Bergomask dance between two of our company?

Theseus: No epilogue, I pray you; for your play needs no excuse.
(A Midsummer Night's Dream, Act 5,1)

Our revels now are ended, but we must nevertheless, risking lèse majesté, contravene Duke Theseus' desires. The literary realm being unsuited to choreographic expression, Bergomask or any other, an epilogue it shall be. And one of visible perceptibility, to fit Bottom's unwitting witticism. At the outset, we suspected that our perspectives might, almost by definition, fail to tame the prodigious peak called creativity and, in verification, they have all displayed serious weaknesses and/or oversights. Yet on balance we remain optimistic; most of them also contain ideas of value that can convincingly handle some creative phenomena and also (of equal importance, perhaps) "feel right." Of even greater moment, the strengths of one often correspond to the gaps in another, suggesting that all might benefit from some judicious combination. If we borrowed, reshuffled, and integrated the best features of each, might we not obtain an account both comprehensive and compelling? We have here displayed some component building blocks so such a Gestaltist enterprise might follow - which, in retrospect, may have been our primary purpose from the start.

Several of our students have commented that seeking such combination seems a reasonable road to travel. So has more than one authority in the field. Guilford, whose devotion to our topic few have surpassed, observes that, "Just as all roads once led to Rome, many approaches lead to a better understanding of creativity."[1] Likewise Allport, that pioneering humanist, in defending its frequent eclecticism, pleaded for more "mututal respect (among differing theorists) and a larger breadth of outlook."[2] He went on to quote another noted eclectic, perhaps the most widely admired (and least imitated) American psychologist, William James:

> Let your approaches be diverse, but let them
> in aggregate do full justice to the heroic
> qualities in man. If you find yourselves
> tangled in paradoxes, what of that? Who can
> say that the universe shall not contain
> paradoxes simply because he himself finds
> them unpalatable?...I'm sure there's a

495

harmony somewhere, and that our strivings
will combine.[3]

We share James' faith. Eventually, with imaginative enterprise,
our strivings will combine. So, lazy or cowardly as it might
seem, let us mimic the magpie and borrow the constructions of
others.

But what of the fact that the various perspectives often
reflect diverse, even contradictory philosophical underpinnings?
Can we reconcile, for example, the arch-determinism of a Freud
with the anarchic freedom of a Sartre? Here Maslow has shown us
the way. First, it seems eminently reasonable to us that, as his
hierarchy of needs suggests, human beings might, in various
circumstances, behave in a manner befitting all of these models.
Each is correct some of the time. Why should this not also be
the case when those humans create. We agree with Maslow also
that although philosophers may shudder (to say nothing of the
theorists themselves, dragged into unalluring armistice with
unsavory opposition) we must sometimes overlook, not fundamental
distinctions certainly, but niceties of same to get on with the
job. Furthermore, some succulent appetizers have already been
placed before us. Becker's imaginative integration of
Kierkegaard and Rank, with a dash of Freudian curry to season the
dish. Koestler's blending of Gestalt and associationism. Even
Sartre's tacit admission, with his so-called "existential
psychoanalysis," that some Freudian and Adlerian tenets were not
totally inedible.[4] We ourselves have pondered a possible
Camus-Jung nuptial to describe creative motivation.[5]

We see every possibility for more such enterprise since,
fortunately, a theorist's most fruitful ideas vis-a-vis
creativity in practice do not always demand his or her
philosophy. During our arduous journey, how often have we seen
supposed antagonists reaching surprisingly similar conclusions,
and apparent colleagues differing completely? Not only politics,
it seems, makes strange bedfellows! Camus, Rank, May, and Becker
all vouched for death's motivating power. Freud, Rank, Koestler,
and Sartre stressed the similarities between creativity and play.
Both Freud and the existentialist emphasized the role of
neurosis/anxiety in creating, while Jung and the humanists saw it
as health's epitome and Rank and Kris fell somewhere in between.
The humanists, Skinner and Guilford, held creative potential to
be universal, whereas Freud, Greenacre, Gruber, and this writer
posited special talents. And does creativity express a need for
power and dominance, or for cooperative sharing with others?
Sartre and Rand favored the first alternative, Greenacre and
Fromm the second, while Adler, Rank, and Camus tried valiantly to
remain mounted on both these spirited steeds simultaneously.

496

Lastly, does the creator's work require conscious involvement, to evoke a sense of personal expression and responsibility? Jung, Skinner, and Poincaré all reply in the negative, whether they use medium, mother, or egg-laying hen as metaphor. Whereas for Freud, the humanists, and the existentialists, the creator, masterfully Godlike, personified individual self-expression. Now the noteworthy point, to repeat, is how often these shared attitudes cut completely across philosophical lines. As a first step, therefore, it might be fruitful to examine a particular creative person from the standpoint of many perspectives. What, for example, would Freud, Sartre, Adler, Skinner, Gruber, and so on each have to say about such a complex, many-faceted individual as Isadora Duncan? Again, we might well find that each answer supplements the others, to provide one more piece towards completing the puzzle. Therefore, we cry out with Lear. Let integration, like copulation, thrive!

We would also encourage couplings of another kind. We suspect, as have others, that creativity is but one manifestation of a much more pervasive tendency, one that also subsumes other activities that are uniquely human. Hence the striking parallels that some theorists have drawn between creativity and religion, humor, play, love, and the like. And we would add sports and games to this list; it seem obvious that a Wayne Gretzky and a Beethoven have many personal qualities and talents in common. But what might be the identity of this basic, nonspecific energy? Freud, of course, provided some trail-blazing guesswork but his candidate, sexuality, seems rather too narrow in scope. Similarly the Rank/Becker/May nominee, death, failed to capture our own fancy. But let us have more musings on this matter. Eventually, creativity, and for that matter squash and chess playing, may turn out to be "multimotivated," as an uncharacteristically pessimistic Maslow would have it. But for now we prefer the strategy of seeking one reason rather than several, of stressing unity, not diversity.

We would warn, however, that virtually all approaches shared a few weaknesses, so not even borrowing their best aspects will correct these. First, Greenacre and Guilford aside, they have not grown from or attempted to encompass "the facts" presented in Part I. That being so, it is not their explanatory failings, but their appreciable successes that seem surprising. Therefore, let those evolving those mammoth entries of the future address the data.

We would also request attendance to a fundamental antecedent which we call <u>fascination</u>. Creative acts begin with events perceived in the external world and/or imagined in the internal. Since these experiences are available to all, the genuinely productive person is distinguished, surely, by a <u>need to capture them in form</u>, to give them external materialization so they can be contemplated at leisure. To a productive person, they seem almost hypnotic; like the proverbial itch, they demand scratching, and herein lies the <u>sine qua non</u>, the germ, of success (although it will demand other abilities as well, e.g., for improving those forms' effectiveness during verification). Thus we repeat. Most theories have unduly stressed the escape from unpleasantries aspect of creativity, from sex, death, and so on. We suspect, instead, that its incentives may as often be carrots as sticks.

In short, we here follow Langer; creation seeks not so much communication as expression. We clearly overlap too with Arieti's endocept and Getzel's problem finding--although we stress the need to <u>externalize</u> more than <u>obtain</u> these experiences. None of our perspectives explain why only some of us are so driven (although Greenacre's hypothesized biological gifts represent a start). When we solve this problem, that Sphinxly riddle, the creative person may become somewhat more comprehensible.

REFERENCES

Introduction

01. Taylor, I. A. "A Retrospective View of Creativity Investigation." In I. A. Taylor & J. W. Getzels (Eds.), Perspectives in Creativity. Chicago: Aldine Publishing Company, 1975, 1-36.
02. Busse, T. V., & Mansfield, R. S. "Theories of the Creative Process: A Review and a Perspective." Journal of Creative Behavior, 1980, 14, 91-103.
03. Vernon, P. E. (Ed.) Creativity. New York: Penguin Books, 1970.
04. Rothenberg, A., & Hausman, C. R. (Eds.) The Creativity Question. Durham, N. C.: Duke University Press, 1976.
05. Bloomberg, M. (Ed.) Creativity: Theory and Research. New Haven, Conn.: College & University Press, 1973.
06. Kreitler, H., & Kreitler, S. Psychology of the Arts. Durham, N. C.: Duke University Press, 1972.
07. Winner, E. Invented Worlds: The Psychology of the Arts. Cambridge, Mass.: Harvard University Press, 1982.
08. Wadeson, H. Art Psychotherapy. New York: Wiley, 1980.
09. McNiff, S. The Arts and Psychotherapy. Springfield, Ill.: Charles C. Thomas, 1981.
10. Freud, S. Leonardo da Vinci: A Study in Psychosexuality. New York: Vintage Books, 1947.
11. Kuhn, T. The Structure of Scientific Revolutions. Chicago: University of Chicago Press, 1962.

Chapter 1

01. Mooney, R. L. "A Conceptual Model for Integrating Four Approaches to the Identification of Creative Talent." In C. W. Taylor and F. Barron (Eds.), Scientific Creativity: Its Recognition and Development. New York: John Wiley & Sons, Inc., 1963, 331-340.
02. Taylor, I. A. "A Retrospective View of Creativity Investigation." In I. A. Taylor and J. W. Getzels (Eds.), Perspectives in Creativity. Chicago, Ill.: Aldine Publishing Company, 1975, 1-36.
03. Stein, M. I. Stimulating Creativity, Vol. 1: Individual Procedures. New York: Academic Press, 1974.
04. Nijinsky, R. Nijinsky. New York: Penguin Books, 1954.
05. Holton, G. The Scientific Imagination: Case Studies. London: Cambridge University Press, 1978.
06. Pirsig, R. M. Zen and the Art of Motorcycle Maintenance. New York: Bantam Books, 1974.
07. Maltzman, I. "On the Training of Originality." Psychological Review, 1960, 67, 229-242.

08. Arieti, S. _Creativity: The Magic Synthesis_. New York: Basic Books, 1976.
09. Arnheim, R. _Toward a Psychology of Art_. Berkeley, Calif.: University of California Press, 1966, p. 20.
10. Stobart, J. C. _The Glory that was Greece_. London: Four Square Books, 1962.
11. Lang, P. H. "Introduction." In P. H. Lang (Ed.), _The Creative World of Mozart_. New York: W. W. Norton & Co., 1963, p. 12.
12. Hertzmann, E. "Mozart's Creative Process." In P. H. Lang (Ed.), _The Creative World of Mozart_. p. 29.
13. Guilford, J. P. _The Nature of Human Intelligence_. New York: McGraw-Hill, 1967.
14. Gruber, H. "The Evolving Systems Approach to Creativity." In S. Modgil & C. Modgil (Eds.), _Toward a Theory of Psychological Development_. Atlantic Highlands, N.J.: Humanities Pres, 1980, 269-299.
15. Arieti, S. _Creativity: The Magic Synthesis_. p. 11.
16. Kleitman, N. "Patterns of Dreaming." _Scientific American_, 1960, Reprint #460.
17. Miller, G. A. "Some Psychological Studies of Grammar." _American Psychologist_, 1962, 17, 748-762.
18. Perkins, D. N. _The Mind's Best Work_. Cambridge, Mass.: Harvard University Press, 1981.
19. Rothenberg, A. _The Emerging Goddess_. Chicago: The University of Chicago Press, 1979.
20. ibid. p. 32.
21. Rogers, C. R. "Towards a Theory of Creativity." In P. E. Vernon (Ed.), _Creativity_. New York: Penguin Books, 1970, 137-151.
22. ibid. p. 140.
23. Maslow, A. H. _Toward a Psychology of Being_. Toronto: D. van Nostrand Company (Canada) Limited, 1962.
24. Magee, B. _Popper_. Glasgow: Fontana/Collins, 1973.
25. ibid.
26. Ghiselin, B. _The Creative Process_. New York: New American Library, 1952.
27. Hutchinson, E. D. _How to Think Creatively_. New York: Abingdon Press, 1949.
28. Nisbett, R. E., & Wilson, T. B. "Telling More Than We Can Know: Verbal Reports on Mental Processes." _Psychological Review_, 1977, 84, 231-259.
29. Dickens, C. _Hard Times_. New York: Penguin Books, 1949.
30. Polanyi, M. _The Study of Man_. Chicago: University of Chicago Press, 1959.
31. Kuhn, T. _The Structure of Scientific Revolutions_. Chicago: University of Chicago Press, 1962.
32. Hutchinson, E. D. _How to Think Creatively_.
33. Kreitler, H., & Kreitler, S. _The Psychology of the Arts_. Durham, N. C.: Duke University Press, 1972.

34. Clark, R. W. Einstein: The Life and Times. New York: Avon Books, 1972, p. 243.
35. Wallas, G. "The Art of Thought." In P. E. Vernon (Ed.), Creativity. New York: Penguin Books, 1970, 91-97.
36. Stein, M. I. Stimulating Creativity, Vol. I: Individual Procedures. New York: Academic Press, 1974.
37. Hutchinson, E. D. How to Think Creatively.
38. Stein, M. I. Stimulating Creativity, Vol. I.
39. Wallas, G. "The Art of Thought."
40. Poincaré, H. "Mathematical Creation." In B. Ghiselin (Ed.), The Creative Process. New York: New American Library, 1952, p. 38.
41. ibid. p. 36.
42. Hutchinson, E. D. How to Think Creatively.
43. Stein, M. I. Stimulating Creativity, Vol. I.
44. May, R. The Courage to Create. New York: W. W. Norton & Co., Inc., 1975.
45. Cited in Holton, G. The Scientific Imagination: Case Studies. London: Cambridge University Press, 1978.
46. Seroff, V. The Real Isadora. Avon Books, 1972.
47. Getzels, J. W., & Csikszentmihalyi, M. The Creative Vision. Toronto: John Wiley & Sons, Ltd., 1976.
48. Stein, M. I. Stimulating Creativity, Vol. I.
49. Cobos, J., Ribio, M., & Pruneda, J. A. "A Trip to Don Quixoteland: Conversations with Orson Welles." In R. Gottesman (Ed.), Focus on Citizen Kane. Englewood Cliffs, N. J.: Prentice-Hall, 1971, 7-24.
50. Wolfe, T. "The Story of a Novel." In B. Ghiselin (Ed.), The Creative Process. p. 194.
51. Nietzsche, F. "Composition of Thus Spake Zarathustra." In B. Ghiselin (Ed.), The Creative Process. p. 203.
52. Roukes, N. Personal communication.
53. Stein, M. I. Stimulating Creativity, Vol. I.

Chapter 2

01. Lombroso, C. "Genius and Insanity." Abstracted in A. R. Rothenberg & C. R. Hausman (Eds.), The Creativity Question. Durham, N. C.: Duke University Press, 1976, 79-86.
02. Cattell, R. B. "The Personality and Motivation of the Researcher from Measurements of Contemporaries and from Biography." In C. W. Taylor & F. Barron (Eds.), Scientific Creativity: Its Recognition and Development. New York: John Wiley & Sons, Inc., 1963.
03. Cattell, R. B., & Butcher, H. J. "Creativity and Personality." In P. E. Vernon (Ed.), Creativity. New York: Penguin Books, 1970, 312-326.

04. Barron, F. "The Psychology of Creativity." In New Directions in Psychology, II. New York: Holt, Rinehart & Winston, Inc., 1965.
05. MacKinnon, D. W. In Search of Human Effectiveness. Buffalo, New York: Creative Education Foundation, in association with Creative Synergetic Associates, Ltd., 1978.
06. Goldstein, K., & Scheerer, M. "Abstract and Concrete Behavior: An Experimental Study with Special Tests." Psychological Monographs, 1941, 53, Whole No. 239.
07. Guilford, J. P. "Creativity: A Quarter Century of Progress." In I. A. Taylor & J. W. Getzels (Eds.), Perspectives in Creativity. Chicago: Aldine Publishing Company, 1975, 37-59.
08. Mednick, S. A. "The Associative Basis of the Creative Process." Psychological Review, 1962, 69, 220-227.
09. Koestler, A. The Act of Creation. London: Pan Books Ltd., 1970.
10. Quoted in Hyslop, T. P. The Great Abnormals. London: Philip Allan & Co., 1925, p. 239.
11. Clark, R. W. Einstein: The Life and Times. New York: Avon Books, 1972.
12. Pearson, H. George Bernard Shaw: His Life and Personality. New York: Atheneum, 1963.
13. May, R. The Courage to Create. New York: W. W. Norton & Co., Inc., 1975.
14. Spender, S. "The Making of a Poem." In B. Ghiselin (Ed.), The Creative Process. New York: New American Library, 1952, p. 118.
15. Powys, L. "Letter to Werner Taylor." In B. Ghiselin (Ed.), The Creative Process. p. 178.
16. Kauffmann, S. "Literary criticism." In S. Rosner & L. E. Abt (Eds.), The Creative Expression. Croton-on-Hudson, New York: North River Press, Inc., 1976, p. 218.
17. Spender, S. "The Making of a Poem." In B. Ghiselin (Ed.), The Creative Process.
18. McDonagh, D. Martha Graham. New York: Popular Library, 1973.
19. ibid.
20. Koestler, A. The Act of Creation.
21. McDonagh, D. Martha Graham.
22. Miller, H. "Reflections on Writing." In B. Ghiselin (Ed.), The Creative Process. p. 179.
23. Pearson, H. George Bernard Shaw: His Life and Personality. p. 279.
24. Quoted in McDonagh, D. Martha Graham. p. 48.
25. Duncan, I. My Life. New York: Liveright, 1955.
26. de Mille, A. Dance to the Piper. Boston: Little, Brown & Co., 1952.
27. Hutchinson, E. D. How to Think Creatively. New York: Abingdon Press, 1949, p. 155.

28. Foss. L. Speech at Dance in Canada Conference, Waterloo, Ontario. June, 1979.
29. Cropley, A. J. "S-R Psychology and Cognitive Psychology." In P. E. Vernon (Ed.), Creativity. New York: Penguin Books, 1970, 116-125.
30. Barron, F. "The Needs for Order and for Disorder as Motives in Creative Activity." In C. W. Taylor & F. Barron (Eds.), Scientific Creativity: Its Recognition and Development. New York: John Wiley & Sons, 1963, 153-160.
31. Goertzel, M. G., Goertzel, V., & Goertzel, T. G. Three Hundred Eminent Personalities. San Francisco: Jossey-Bass, 1978.
32. Fromm, E. The Fear of Freedom. London: Routledge & Kegan Paul, Ltd., 1960.
33. Rotter, J. B. Social Learning and Clinical Psychology. Englewood Cliffs, New Jersey: Prentice-Hall, 1954.
34. Rand, A. The Fountainhead. New York: Signet Books, 1959; Rand, A. The Virtue of Selfishness. New York: New American Library, 1961.
35. Brod, M. "Postscript to the First Edition." In F. Kafka, The Trial. New York: Modern Library, 1956, 326-335.
36. Tolstoy, L. The Death of Ivan Ilych and Other Stories. New York: New American Library, 1960, p. 296.
37. Quoted in Storr, A. The Dynamics of Creation. Markham, Ont.: Penguin Books, 1976, p. 239.
38. Simon, N. "Interview." In S. Rosner & L. E. Abt (Eds.), The Creative Experience. New York: Dell Publishing Co., Inc., 1970, p. 374.
39. Koestler, A. The Act of Creation.
40. Holton, G. The Scientific Imagination: Case Studies. Cambridge: Cambridge University Press, 1978.
41. Rainey, F. G. "Interview." In S. Rosner & L. E. Abt (Eds.), The Creative Experience. p. 19.
42. Quoted in Koestler, A. The Act of Creation. p. 113.
43. Clark, R. W. Einstein: The Life and Times.
44. Maslow, A. H. Toward a Psychology of Being. Toronto: D. van Nostrand Co., (Canada) Ltd., 1962.
45. McMullan, W. E. "Creative Individuals: Paradoxical Personages." Journal of Creative Behavior, 1976, 10, 265-275.
46. May, R. The Courage to Create.
47. ibid. p. 21.
48. Holton, G. The Scientific Imagination: Case Studies. p. 280.
49. McMullan, W. E. "Creative Individuals: Paradoxical Personnages."
50. Ornstein, R. The Psychology of Consciousness. San Francisco: W. H. Freeman and Co., 1972.
51. Polanyi, M. The Study of Man. Chicago: University of Chicago Press, 1959.

52. Tart, C. T. <u>Altered States of</u> Consciousness. New York: John Wiley & Sons, Inc., 1969.
53. Poincaré, H. "Mathematical Creation." In B. Ghiselin (Ed.), <u>The Creative Process</u>. 33-42.
54. Clark, R. W. <u>Einstein: The Life and Times</u>.
55. Nietzsche, F. <u>The Birth of Tragedy</u>. New York: Vintage Books, 1967.
56. Rothenberg, A. "The Process of Janusian Thinking in Creativity." In A. R. Rothenberg & C. R. Hausman (Eds.), <u>The Creativity Question</u>. p. 311-327.
57. Dellas, M., & Gaier, E. L. "Identification of Creativity: The Individual." <u>Psychological Bulletin</u>, 1970, <u>73</u>, 55-73.
58. Roe, A. "Psychological Approaches to Creativity in Science." Abstracted in A. R. Rothenberg & C. R. Hausman (Eds.), <u>The Creativity Question</u>. 165-175.
59. Helson, R. "Women and Creativity." Abstracted in A. R. Rothenberg & C. R. Hausman (Eds.), <u>The Creativity Question</u>. 242-250.
60. Dellas, M., & Gaier, E. L. "Identification of Creativity: The Individual." <u>Psychological Bulletin</u>.
61. Gedo, J. E. <u>Portraits of the Artist</u>. New York: The Guilford Press, 1983.
62. Lehman, H. C. <u>Age and Achievement</u>. Princeton: Princeton University Press, 1953.
63. Greer, G. <u>The Obstacle Race</u>. London: Secker & Warburg, Ltd., 1979.
64. Boswell, J. <u>The Life of Johnson</u>. Markham, Ont.: Penguin Books, 1979, p. 116.
65. Wooley, H. T. "A Review of the Recent Literature on the Psychology of Sex." <u>Psychological Bulletin</u>, 1910, <u>7</u>, 340-341.
66. Quoted in Getzels, J. W., & Csikszentmihalyi, M. <u>The Creative Vision</u>. New York: John Wiley & Sons, 1976, p. 44.
67. ibid.
68. Zervos, C. "Conversation with Picasso." In B. Ghiselin (Ed.), <u>The Creative Process</u>. p. 56.
69. Cattell, R. B. "The Personality and Motivation of the Researcher from Measurements of Contemporaries and from Biography." In C. W. Taylor & F. Barron (Eds.), <u>Scientific Creativity: Its Recognition and Development</u>. New York: John Wiley & Sons, Inc., 1966, p. 121.
70. Simon, N. "Interview." In S. Rosner & L. E. Abt (Eds.), <u>The Creative Experience</u>. New York: Dell Publishing Co., Inc., 1970, 358-359.
71. Hart, M. <u>Act One</u>. New York: Vintage Books, 1976.
72. Arieti, S. <u>Creativity: The Magic Synthesis</u>. New York: Basic Books, 1974.
73. Nin, A. <u>The Diary of Anaïs Nin</u>. Chicago: Swallow, 1966.
74. Woolf, V. <u>A Room of One's Own</u>. Toronto, Ontario: Granada Publishing, 1977, p. 51.

75. Fast, H. "The First Men." In H. A. Katz, P. Warrick & M. H. Greenberg (Eds.), Introductory Psychology through Science Fiction. Chicago: Rand McNally, 1974, 314-343.
76. Rosner, S., & Abt, L. E. (Eds.) The Creative Experience. New York: Dell Publishing Co., 1970; Rosner, S., & Abt, L. E. (Eds.), The Creative Expression. Croton-on-Hudson, New York: North River Press, Inc., 1976.
77. Lurie, R. "Interview." In S. Rosner & L. E. Abt (Eds.), The Creative Expression. p. 102.
78. Rossman, J. The Psychology of the Inventor. Washington: Inventors Publishing, 1931.
79. Graham, M. A Dancer's World. N.A.C.C.:, 1957 (Film).
80. Storr, A. The Dynamics of Creation. New York: Penguin Books, 1976.
81. Spender, S. "The Making of a Poem." In B. Ghiselin (Ed.), The Creative Process.
82. Graham, M. A Dancer's World.
83. Kerr, W. God on the Gymnasium Floor. New York: Delta Books, 1973, p. 259.
84. Rosner, S., & Abt, L. E. (Eds.) The Creative Experience.
85. James, H. "Preface to the Spoils of Ponton." In B. Ghiselin (Ed.), The Creative Process. p. 147.
86. Simonton, D. K. Genius, Creativity and Leadership. Cambridge, Mass.: Harvard University Press, 1984.
87. ibid. p. 83.
88. Gruber, H. "The Evolving Systems Approach to Creativity." In S. Modgil & C. Modgil (Eds.), Toward a Theory of Psychological Development. Atlantic Highlands, N.J.: Humanities Press, 1980, 269-299.
89. Cary, J. The Horse's Mouth. New York: Penguin Books, 1948.
90. Maslow, A. H. Toward a Psychology of Being.
91. Greene, G. The End of the Affair. New York: Penguin Books, 1962.
92. Wilde, O. The Picture of Dorian Gray. New York: Penguin Books, 1949, p. 85.
93. Duncan, I. My Life.
94. Clark, R. W. Einstein: The Life and Times.
95. Davies, S. G. James Joyce: A Portrait of the Artist. London: Granada Publishing, 1982.
96. Torrance, E. P. Guiding Creative Talent. Englewood Cliffs, N.J.: Prentice-Hall, 1962.
97. Quoted in Koestler, A. The Act of Creation. p. 124.
98. Kuhn, T. The Structure of Scientific Revolutions. Chicago: University of Chicago Press, 1962.
99. MacKinnon, D. W. In Search of Human Effectiveness. Buffalo, N.Y.: The Creative Education Foundation, Inc., and Creative Synergetic Associates, Ltd., 1978.
100. Simonton, D. K. Genius, Creativity and Leadership.

101. Lehman, H. C. Age and Achievement. Princeton: Princeton University Press, 1953.
102. Hardy, G. H. "A Mathematician's Apology." In R. S. Albert (Ed.), Genius and Eminence. New York: Pergamon Press, 1983, p. 389.
103. Gedo, J. E. Portraits of the Artist.
104. Butler, R. N. "The Destiny of Creativity in Later Life: Studies of Creative People and the Creative Process." In S. Levin & R. J. Kahana (Eds.), Psychodynamic Studies on Aging. New York: International Universities, 1967.
105. Dennis, W. "The Age Decrement in Outstanding Scientific Contributions: Fact or Artifact?." American Psychologist, 1958, 13, 457-460.
106. Dennis, W. "Creative Productivity Between the Ages of 20 and 80 Years." Journal of Gerontology, 1966, 21, 1-8.
107. Simonton, D. K. Genius, Creativity and Leadership.
108. Krebs, H. A. "Comments on the Productivity of Scientists." In A. Kornberg, B. L. Horecher, L. Cornudella, & J. Oro (Eds.), Reflections on Biochemistry. New York: Pergamon Press, 1976.
109. Camus, A. Caligula and 3 Other Plays. New York: Vintage Books, 1958, p. v.
110. Horney, K. Neurosis and Human Growth. New York: Norton, 1950.
111. Wilson, S. "Interview." In J. Gruen (Ed.), The Private World of Ballet. New York: Penguin Books, 1976, 244-253.
112. Tudor, A. "Interview." In J. Gruen (Ed.), The Private World of Ballet. 258-267.
113. Spender, S. "The Making of a Poem." In B. Ghiselin (Ed.), The Creative Process. pp. 120-121.
114. Craik, F. I. M. "Age Differences in Human Memory." In J. E. Birren & K. W. Schaie (Eds.), The Handbook of the Psychology of Aging. New York: Van Nostrand Reinhold, 1977, 384-420.
115. Peter, L., & Hull, R. The Peter Principle. New York: Bantam Books, 1970.
116. Krebs, H. A. "Comments on the Productivity of Scientists." In Reflections on Biochemistry.
117. Taylor, C. W., Smith, W. R., & Ghiselin, B. "The Creative and Other Contributions of One Sample of Research Scientists." In C. W. Taylor & F. Barron (Eds.), Scientific Creativity: Its Recognition and Development.
118. Simonton, D. K. "Dramatic Greatness and Content: A Quantitative Study of eighty-one Athenian and Shakespearian Plays." Empirical Studies of the Arts. 1983, 1, 109-123.
119. Edel, L. "The Artist in Old Age." The Hastings Center Report. April, 1985, 38-44.

Chapter 3

01. Dryden, J. "Absalom and Achitophel." Quoted in G. Pickering, The Creative Malady. New York: Delta Books, 1974, p. 286.
02. Plato. "Inspiration." In A. Rothenberg & C. R. Hausman (Eds.), The Creativity Question. Durham, North Carolina: Duke University Press, 1976, p. 32.
03. Kretschmer, E. "Psychology of Men of Genius." Quoted in E. D. Hutchinson, How to Think Creatively. New York: Abingdon Press, 1949, p. 75.
04. Lombroso, C. "Genius and Insanity." In A. Rothenberg & C. R. Hausman (Eds.), The Creativity Question. p. 79-86.
05. Russell, B. Satan in the Suburbs and Other Stories. New York: Simon and Schuster, 1953.
06. Hutchinson, E. D. How to Think Creatively.
07. Pickering, G. The Creative Malady. New York: Delta Books, 1974.
08. Storr, A. The Dynamics of Creation. New York: Penguin Books, 1976.
09. Sandblom, P. Creativity and Disease. Philadelphia: George F. Stickley Co., 1982.
10. Storr, A. The Dynamics of Creation. p. 258.
11. Stein, M.I. Stimulating Creativity: Vol. I: Individual Procedures. New York: Academic Press, 1974.
12. Fried, E. Artistic Productivity and Mental Health. Springfield, Ill.: Charles C. Thomas, 1964.
13. Jung, C. G. "Psychology and Literature." In The Collected Works of C. G. Jung (Vol. 15). Princeton, New Jersey: Princeton University Press, 1966, 84-105.
14. ibid. p. 102.
15. Wilde, O. The Picture of Dorian Gray. New York: Penguin Books, 1949, p. 65.
16. Slater, E., & Meyer, A. "Contributions to a Pathography of the Musicians: 1. Robert Schumann." Confinia Psychiatrica. 1959, 2, 65-94.
17. Woolf, V. A Room of One's Own. Toronto, Ontario: Granada Publishing, 1977.
18. Ellis, H. A Study in British Genius. London: Hurst & Blackett, 1904.
19. Juda, A. Hochstbegabung: Ihre Erbverhaltnisse sowie ihre Beziehungen zu psychischen Anomalien. Munich: Urban and Schwarzenberg, 1953.
20. Terman, L. M. (Ed.) Genetic Studies of Genius: Vol. 5. Palo Alto: Stanford University Press, 1959.
21. Barron, F. "Creativity." In New Directions in Psychology II. New York: Holt, Rinehart & Winston, 1965, 1-134.
22. Grant, V. W. The Great Abnormals. New York: Hawthorn Books, 1968.
23. Esslin, M. The Peopled Wound. London: Methuen & Co., Ltd., 1970.

507

24. Brod, M. "Postscript to the First Edition." In F. Kafka, The Trial. New York: Modern Library, 1956, 326-335.
25. Camus, A. "Hope and the Absurd in the Work of Franz Kafka." In The Myth of Sisyphus and Other Essays. New York: Vintage Books, 1955, p. 92.
26. Grant, V. W. The Great Abnormals. New York: Hawthorn Books, 1968, 70-71.
27. Kreitler, H., & Kreitler, S. Psychology of the Arts. Durham, North Carolina: Duke University Press, 1972.
28. Cox, C. "The Early Mental Traits of 300 Geniuses." Genetic Studies of Genius, Vol. II. Palo Alto: Stanford University Press, 1926.
29. Guilford, J. P. "Creativity." American Psychologist, 1950, 5, 444-454.
30. Dellas, M., & Gaier, E. L. "Identification of Creativity: The Individual." Psychological Bulletin, 1970, 73, 55-73.
31. ibid; Golann, S. E. "Psychological Study of Creativity." Psychological Bulletin, 1963, 60, 548-565.
32. Simonton, D. K. Genius, Creativity and Leadership. Cambridge, Mass.: Harvard University Press, 1984.
33. Gardner, H. Frames of Mind: The Theory of Multiple Intelligences. New York: Basic Books, 1983.
34. Guilford, J. P. The Nature of Human Intelligence. New York: McGraw-Hill, 1967.
35. Stein, M. I. Stimulating Creativity: Vol. I; Dellas, M., & Gaier, E. L. "Identification of Creativity: The Individual." Psychological Bulletin.
36. Tate, A. "Narcissus as Narcissus." In B. Ghiselin (Ed.), The Creative Process. New York: New American Library, 1952, p. 137.
37. Getzels, J. W., & Jackson, P. W. "The Highly Intelligent and the Highly Creative Adolescent." In P. E. Vernon (Ed.), Creativity. New York: Penguin Books, 1970, 189-202; Wallach, M. A., & Kogan, N. "A New Look at the Creativity-Intelligence Distinction." In P. E. Vernon (Ed.), Creativity, 235-256.
38. Getzels, J. W., & Jackson, P. W. "The Highly Intelligent and the Highly Creative Adolescent." In P. E. Vernon (Ed.), Creativity. p. 198-199.
39. Tynan, K. Tynan Right and Left. London: Longmans, 1967, p. 171.
40. Spearman, C. The Abilities of Man. New York: MacMillan, 1927.
41. Guilford, J. P. "Traits of Creativity." In P. E. Vernon (Ed.), Creativity. 167-188.
42. Quoted in Koestler, A. The Act of Creation. London: Pan Books, Ltd., 1970, p. 461.
43. ibid. 461-462.
44. Hutchinson, E. D. How to Think Creatively. p. 150.

45. Cited in Terman, E. L. "Psychological Approaches to the Biography of Genius." In P. E. Vernon (Ed.), Creativity. 25-42.
46. MacKinnon, D. W. In Search of Human Effectiveness. Buffalo, New York: The Creative Education Foundation and Creative Synergetic Associates, Ltd., 1978.
47. Barron, F. "Creativity." In New Directions in Psychology, II.
48. Roe, A. "Psychological Approaches to Creativity in Science." In A. Rothenberg and C. R. Hausman (Eds.), The Creativity Question. 165-175.
49. Barron, F. "The Disposition towards Originality." In P. E. Vernon (Ed.), Creativity. p. 273-288.
50. Cattell, R. B., & Butcher, H. J. "Creativity and Personality." In P. E. Vernon (Ed.), Creativity. 312-326.
51. ibid. 322-323.
52. Engell, J. The Creative Imagination. Cambridge, Mass.: Harvard University Press, 1981.
53. ibid. p. 275.
54. Lehman, H. C. Age and Achievement. Princeton: Princeton University Press, 1953.
55. Cropp, M. Personal communication.
56. Stobart, J. C. The Glory that was Greece. London: Four Square Books, 1962.
57. Hess, T. B. "Great Women Artists." In T. B. Hess & E. C. Baker (Eds.), Art and Sexual Politics. New York: MacMillan, 1973, 44-54.
58. Simonton, D. K. Genius, Creativity and Leadership.
59. Seroff, V. The Real Isadora. Avon Books, 1972.
60. Ferris, P. Dylan Thomas. New York: Penguin Books, 1978.

Chapter 4

01. Stravinsky, I. An Autobiography. New York: W. W. Norton & Company, 1962, p. 20.
02. Torrance, E. P. Guiding Creative Talent. Englewood Cliffs, New Jersey: Prentice-Hall, 1962; Roe, A. "A Psychological Study of Eminent Psychologists and Anthropologists and a Comparison with Biological and Physical Scientists." Psychological Monographs, 1953, 67, No. 2 (Whole No. 352); Stein, M. I. Stimulating Creativity, Vol. 1: Individual Procedures. New York: Academic Press, Inc., 1974.
03. Mansfield, R. S., & Busse, T. V. The Psychology of Creativity and Discovery. Chicago: Nelson-Hall, 1981.
04. Simonton, D. K. Genius, Creativity and Leadership. Cambridge, Mass.: Harvard University Press, 1984.
05. MacKinnon, D. W. In Search of Human Effectiveness: Identifying and Developing Creativity. Buffalo, New York: The Creative Education Foundation, Inc., & Creative Synergetic Associates, Ltd., 1978.

509

06. Albert, R. S. "Exceptional Creativity and Achievement." In R. S. Albert (Ed.) Genius and Eminence. New York: Pergamon Press, 1983, 19-35.

07. Eisenstadt, J. M. "Parental Loss and Genius." American Psychologist. 1978, 33, 211-223.

08. Getzels, J. W., & Csikszentmihalyi, M. The Creative Vision. Toronto: John Wiley & Sons, Ltd., 1976.

09. Torrance, E. P. Guiding Creative Talent.

10. DeHaan, R. F., & Havighurst, R. J. Educating Gifted Children. Chicago: University of Chicago Press, 1957, p. 208.

11. Getzels, J. W., & Csikszentmihalyi, M. The Creative Vision; Barron, F., Artists in the Making, New York: Seminar Press, 1972.

12. Getzels, J. W., & Csikszentmihalyi, M. The Creative Vision.

13. Kahn, A. E. Days with Ulanova. New York: Simon & Schuster, Inc., 1962.

14. Lawrence, D. H. "Making Pictures." In B. Ghiselin (Ed.), The Creative Process. New York: New American Library, 1952, 68-73.

15. Maddi, S. R. "The Strenuousness of the Creative Life." In I. A. Taylor and J. W. Getzels (Eds.), Perspectives in Creativity. Chicago, Ill.: Aldine Publishing Company, 1975, 173-190.

16. Potok, C. My Name is Asher Lev. New York: Fawcett Crest, 1972.

17. Nietzsche, F. "Composition of Thus Spake Zarathustra." In B. Ghiselin (Ed.), The Creative Process. p. 201-203.

18. ibid. p. 202.

19. Eisenstadt, J. M. "Parental Loss and Genius." American Psychologist.

20. Barron, F. "The Needs for Order and for Disorder as Motives in Creative Activity." In C. W. Taylor & F. Barron (Eds.), Scientific Creativity: Its Recognition and Development. New York: John Wiley & Sons, 153-160.

21. ibid. p. 157.

22. Mead, M. "Creativity in Cross Cultural Perspective." In H. H. Anderson (Ed.), Creativity and Its Cultivation. New York: Harper, Row, 1959, 222-235.

23. ibid. 224, 228.

24. Jones, J. "Interview." In G. Plimpton (Ed.), Writers at Work: The Paris Review Interviews. New York: The Viking Press, 1968, 231-250.

25. Arieti, S. Creativity: The Magic Synthesis. New York: Basic Books, 1976.

26. Henle, M. "The Cognitive Approach: The Snail Beneath the Shell." In S. Rosner & L. E. Abt (Eds.), Essays in Creativity. Croton-on-Hudson, New York: North River Press, Inc., 1974, 23-44.

27. Spender, S. "The Making of a Poem." In B. Ghiselin (Ed.), The Creative Process. p. 118.

28. Moore, H. "Notes on Sculpture." In B. Ghiselin (Ed.), The Creative Process. p. 74.
29. James, H. "Preface to The Spoils of Poynton." In B. Ghiselin (Ed.), The Creative Process. p. 147.
30. Cited in Housman, A. E. "The Name and Nature of Poetry." In B. Ghiselin (Ed.), The Creative Process. p. 91.
31. Cited in Hutchinson, E. D. How to Think Creatively. New York: Abingdon Press, 1949, p. 19.
32. ibid. p. 117.
33. Getzels, J. W., & Csikszentmihalyi, M. "From Problem-Solving to Problem Finding." In I. A. Taylor & J. W. Getzels (Eds.), Perspectives in Creativity. p. 90-116; Getzels, J. W., & Csikszentmihalyi, M. The Creative Vision.
34. Einstein, A., & Infeld, L. The Evolution of Physics. New York: Simon & Schuster, 1938, p. 92.
35. Getzels, J. W., & Csikszentmihalyi, M. The Creative Vision.
36. Yeats, W. B. "Adam's curse." In R. K. Alspach (Ed.), The Varorium Edition of the Poems of W. B. Yeats. New York: MacMillan Co., 1956, 204-205.
37. Stein, M. I. Stimulating Creativity, Vol. I.
38. Underwood, B. J. Experimental Psychology. New York: Appleton-Century-Crofts, 1966.
39. Koestler, A. The Act of Creation. London: Pan Books Ltd, 1970.
40. Osborn, A. F. Applied Imagination. New York: Scribner's, 1963.
41. Maltzman, I., Belloni, M., & Fishbein, M. "Experimental Studies of Associative Variables in Originality." Psychological Monographs, 1964, 78(3, Whole No. 580); Maltzman, I., Simon, S., Raskin, D., & Licht, L. "Experimental Studies in the Training of Originality." Psychological Monographs, 1960, 74(6, Whole No. 493).
42. Gall, M., & Mendelsohn, G. A. "Effects of Facilitating Techniques and Subject-Experimenter Interaction on Creative Problem Solving." In M. Bloomberg (Ed.), Creativity: Theory and Research. New Haven, Conn.: College & University Press, 1973, 178-189.
43. Hutchinson, E. D. How to Think Creatively.
44. Sakurabayashi, H. "Studies in Creation IV: The Meaning of Prolonged Inspection from the Standpoint of Creation." Japanese Journal of Psychology, 1953, 23, 207-216, 286-288.
45. Gall, M., & Mendelsohn, G. A. In M. Bloomberg (Ed.), Creativity: Theory and Research.
46. Hutchinson, E. D. How to Think Creatively.
47. Arieti, S. Creativity: The Magic Synthesis.
48. Rosner, S., & Abt, L. E. (Eds.) The Creative Experience. New York: Delta Books, 1970; Rosner, S., & Abt, L. E. (Eds.) The Creative Expression. Croton-on-Hudson, New York: North River Press, Inc., 1976.
49. Stein, M. I. Stimulating Creativity, Vol. I.

50. Lumet, S. "Interview." In S. Rosner & L. E. Abt (Eds.), The Creative Experience. 187-206.
51. Tynan, K. Tynan Right and Left. London: Longmans, Green & Co., Ltd., 1967.
52. Mazo, J. H. Dance is a Contact Sport. New York: Da Capo Press, Inc., 1974.
53. Tudor, A. "Interview." In J. Gruen (Ed.), The Private World of Ballet. Markham, Ont.: Penguin Books, 1976, 258-267.
54. Mailer, N. "Interview." In G. Plimpton (Ed.), Writers at Work: The Paris Review Interviews. 251-278.
55. Zervos, C. "Conversation with Picasso." In B. Ghiselin (Ed.), The Creative Process. p. 56.
56. Russell, B. The Autobiography of Bertrand Russell: The Middle Years: 1914-1944. New York: Bantam Books, 1969, pp. 71 & 62.
57. Zuckerman, H. A. "The Sociology of the Nobel Prize." Scientific American, 217, 25-33.
58. Kimble, G. A. Hilgard and Marquis' Conditioning and Learning. (second ed.). New York: Appleton-Century-Crofts, Inc., 1961.
59. Greer, G. The Obstacle Race. London: Secler & Warburg, 1979.
60. Stein, M. I. Stimulating Creativity, Vol. I.
61. Blume, H. Personal communication.
62. Olivier, L. Confessions of an Actor. London: Wiedenfeld & Nicolson, 1982.
63. Gedo, J. E. Portraits of the Artist. New York: The Guilford Press, 1983.
64. Spence, K. W. Behavior Theory and Conditioning. New Haven: Yale University Press, 1956; Glucksberg, S. "The Influence of Strength of Drive on Functional Fixedness and Perceptual Recognition." Journal of Experimental Psychology, 1962, 63, 36-51.
65. Yerkes, R. M., & Dodson, J. D. "The Relation of Strength of Stimulus to Rapidity of Habit Formation." Journal of Comparative Neurology, 1908, 18, 459-482.
66. Costello, C. G. Anxiety and Depression: The Adaptive Emotions. Montreal: McGill-Queens University Press, 1976.
67. Foley, C. "The Legend of Rachmaninoff." Music Guide. 1963.

Chapter 5

01. Moore, H. "Notes on Sculpture." In B. Ghiselin (Ed.), The Creative Process. New York: New American Library, 1952, p. 73.
02. Albee, E. "Interview." In G. Plimpton (Ed.), Writers at Work: The Paris Review Interviews. New York: Viking Press, 1967, p. 341.

03. Cited in E. D. Hutchinson. How to Think Creatively. New York: Abingdon Press, 1949, p. 141.
04. ibid. p. 134-135.
05. May, R. The Courage to Create. New York: W. W. Norton and Co., Inc., 1975.
06. Hyslop, T. P. The Great Abnormals. London: Philip Allan & Co., 1925.
07. Cited in E. D. Hutchinson. How to Think Creatively. p. 161.
08. Tart, C. T. (Ed.) Altered States of Consciousness. New York: John Wiley & Sons, Inc., 1969.
09. Poe, E. A. "Creation as craft." In A. Rothenberg & C. R. Hausman (Eds.), The Creativity Question. Durham, N.C.: Duke University Press, 1976, 57-61.
10. Stravinsky, I. An Autobiography. New York: W. W. Norton & Co., 1962.
11. Balanchine, G. "Interview." In J. Gruen (Ed.), The Private World of Ballet. Markham, Ont.: Penguin Books, 1976, p. 281.
12. Gruber, H. E. Darwin on Man: A Psychological Study of Creativity. New York: E. P. Dutton, 1974.
13. Hutchinson, E. D. How to Think Creatively.
14. Cited in E. D. Hutchinson. How to Think Creatively. p. 181.
15. Ghiselin, B. "Introduction." In B. Ghiselin (Ed.), The Creative Process. p. 28.
16. Wolfe, T. "The Story of a Novel." In B. Ghiselin (Ed.), The Creative Process. 186-199.
17. Storr, A. The Dynamics of Creation. Markham, Ont.: Penguin Books, 1976.
18. Arieti, S. Creativity: The Magic Synthesis. New York: Basic Books, 1976.
19. Langer, S. Philosophy in a New Key. New York: New American Library, 1951.
20. Wilde, O. The Picture of Dorian Gray. Markham, Ont.: Penguin Books, 1949, p. 128.
21. Duncan, I. My Life. New York: Liveright, 1955, p. 213.
22. Tweney, R. D., Doherty, M. E., & Mynatt, C. R. (Eds.) On Scientific Thinking. New York: Columbia University Press, 1981.
23. Polanyi, M. "The Creative Imagination." In D. Dutton & M. Krausz (Eds.), The Concept of Creativity in Science and Art. The Hague: Martinus Nijhoff, 1981, 91-108.
24. ibid.. p. 101.
25. Magee, B. Popper. Glasgow: Fontana, 1973.
26. Bogarde, D. A Postillion Struck by Lightning. Triad Granada, 1978, p. 285.
27. Miller, H. "Reflections on Writing." In B. Ghiselin (Ed.), The Creative Process. p. 181.
28. Housman, A. E. "The Name and Nature of Poetry." In B. Ghiselin (Ed.), The Creative Process. p. 91.

29. Nietzsche, F. "Composition of Thus Spake Zarathustra." In B. Ghiselin (Ed.), The Creative Process. p. 202.
30. Milne, A. A. The House at Pooh Corner. McLelland & Stewart, Ltd., 1925, p. 31.
31. Wood, J. "Playing a Ghostly Tune." The Calgary Sunday Sun. Oct. 5, 1980, p. S 15.
32. Esslin, M. The Peopled Wound: The Plays of Harold Pinter. London: Methuen & Co., 1970.
33. Evans, R. I. Psychology and Arthur Miller. New York: E. P. Dutton, 1969, 40-41.
34. Preston, J. H. "A Conversation with Gertrude Stein." In B. Ghiselin (Ed.), The Creative Process. p. 160.
35. Hutchinson, E. D. How to Think Creatively, p. 169
36. Bourne, L. E., Ekstrand, B. R., & Dominowski, R. L. The Psychology of Thinking. Englewood Cliffs, N.J.: Prentice-Hall, Inc., 1971.
37. Mednick, S. A. "The Associative Basis of the Creative Process." Psychological Review, 1962, 69, 220-232.
38. Finney, T. M. A History of Music. New York: Harcourt, Brace & Co., 1947.
39. Kohut, H. The Analysis of the Self. New York: International Universities Press, 1971.
40. Magee, B. Popper.
41. Popper, K. The Logic of Scientific Discovery. London: Hutchinson, 1972.
42. Langer, S. K. Feeling and Form. New York: Charles Scribner's Sons, 1953, p. 40.
43. Kant, I. "Genius Gives the Rules." In A. Rothenberg & C. R. Hausman (Eds.), The Creativity Question. 37-42.
44. Bruner, J. "Art as a Mode of Knowing." In J. Bruner, On Knowing: Essays for the Left Hand. Cambridge, Mass.: Harvard University Press, 1979, 59-74.
45. Maslow, A. H. "The Creative Attitude." In R. L. Mooney & T. A. Razik (Eds.), Explorations in Creativity. New York: Harper & Row, 1967, p. 46.
46. Hadamard, J. The Psychology of Invention in the Mathematical Field. Princeton, N.J.: Princeton University Press, 1945.
47. Poincaré, H. "Mathematical Creation." In B. Ghiselin (Ed.), The Creative Process. 33-42.
48. Cited in Koestler, A. The Act of Creation. London: Pan Books Ltd., 1970, p. 117.
49. ibid. p. 117.
50. ibid. p. 124.
51. Dickens, C. Hard Times. Markham, Ont.: Penguin Books, 1949.
52. Kuhn, T. The Structure of Scientific Revolutions. Chicago: University of Chicago Press, 1962.
53. Schonberg, H. The Lives of the Great Composers. New York: W. W. Norton, 1970.

54. Watson, J. D. The Double Helix. New York: New American Library, 1968.

55. Judson, H. F. The Eighth Day of Creation: Makers of the Revolution in Biology. New York: Simon & Schuster, 1979.

56. Gabor, D. "Holography." In S. Rosner & L. E. Abt (Eds.), The Creative Expression. Croton-on-Hudson, N.Y.: North River Press, Inc., 1976, 36-53.

57. Watson, J. D. "Competition in Science." Dialogue. 1977, 10, 18-24.

58. Torrance, E. P., et al. "Role of Evaluation in Creative Thinking, Revised Summary Report." U.S. Office of Education, Department of Health, Education and Welfare, Cooperative Research Project No. 725. Minneapolis: Bureau of Educational Research, University of Minnesota, 1964.

59. Popper, K. The Logic of Scientific Discovery.

60. Hull, C. L. "The Conflicting Psychologies of Learning--A Way Out." Psychological Review, 1935, 42, 491-516.

61. Hull, C. L. A Behavior System. New Haven, Conn.: Yale University Press, 1952.

62. Clark, R. W. Einstein: The Life and Times. New York: Avon Books, 1972.

63. Kreitler, H., & Kreitler, S. Psychology of the Arts. Durham, N.C.: Duke University Press, 1972.

64. Kuhn, T. The Structure of Scientific Revolutions.

65. Freud, S. "Introductory Lectures on Psychoanalysis (Part III)." In The Complete Psychological Works of Sigmund Freud. (Vol. 16). London: Hogarth Press, 1963, p. 376.

66. Kuhn, T. The Structure of Scientific Revolutions.

67. Cannon, W. B. "The Role of Hunches in Scientific Thought." In A. Rothenberg and C. R. Hausman (Eds.), The Creativity Question. 63-69.

68. Kaplan, N. "The Relation of Creativity to Sociological Variables in Research Organizations." In C. W. Taylor and F. Barron (Eds.), Scientific Creativity: Its Recognition and Development. New York: John Wiley & Sons, Inc., 1963, 195-204.

69. Kuhn, T. The Structure of Scientific Revolutions. p. 110.

70. Knapp, R. H. "Demographic Cultural and Personality Attributes of Scientists." In C. W. Taylor and F. Barron (Eds.), Scientific Creativity: Its Recognition and Development. 205-216.

71. Roe, A. "A Psychologist Examines Sixty-four Eminent Scientists." In P. E. Vernon (Ed.), Creativity. Markham, Ont.: Penguin Books, 1970, 43-51.

72. Roe, A. "Painters and Painting." In I. A. Taylor & J. W. Getzels (Eds.), Perspectives in Creativity. Chicago: Aldine Publishing Co., 1975, 157-172.

73. Knapp, R. H. In Scientific Creativity: Its Recognition and Development.

74. Hudson, L. *Frames of Mind*. Harmondsworth, Great Britain: Penguin Books, 1970; Hudson, L. *Human Beings*. London: Jonathan Cape, 1975.

75. McClelland, D. C. "On the Psychodynamics of Creative Physical Scientists." In L. Hudson (Ed.), *The Ecology of Human Intelligence*. Harmondsworth, Great Britain: Penguin Books, 1970.

76. Schonberg, H. *The Lives of the Great Composers*.

77. *ibid*.

78. Stein, M. I. *Stimulating Creativity: Vol 1, Individual Procedures*. New York: Academic Press, Inc., 1974.

79. Buckle, R. *Diaghilev*. London: Weidenfeld & Nicolson, 1979.

80. Stravinsky, I. *An Autobiography*.

81. *ibid*.

82. Lieven, P. A. *The Birth of the Ballet Russe*. New York: Dover Publications, 1973.

83. McDonagh, D. *The Rise and Fall and Rise of Modern Dance*. New York: New American Library, 1971.

84. Tynan, K. *Curtains*. London: Longmans, 1961; Rosner, S., & Abt, L. E. "Interview with John Simon." In *The Creative Expression*. 168-183.

85. Magee, B. *Popper*.

86. Boswell, J. *The Life of Johnson*. Markham, Ont.: Penguin Books, 1979, p. 263.

87. Rosner, S., & Abt, L. E. "Interview with Stanley Kauffmann." In *The Creative Expression*. p. 218.

88. Pirsig, R. *Zen and the Art of Motorcycle Maintenance*. New York: Bantam Books, 1974.

89. Russell, B. *The Autobiography of Bertrand Russell. The Middle Years: 1914-1944*. New York: Bantam Books, 1969, p. 326.

90. Goldman, W. *The Season: A Candid Look at Broadway*. New York: Harcourt, Brace & World, Inc., 1969.

91. Rosner, S., & Abt, L. E. "Interview with Martin Bookspan." In *The Creative Expression*. 221-234.

92. Rigg, D. *No Turn Unstoned: The Worst Ever Theatrical Reviews*. London: Arrow Books, 1983, p. 17.

93. Duncan, I. *My Life*. New York: Liveright, 1955.

94. Rosner, S., & Abt, L. E. "Interview with Stanley Kauffman." In *The Creative Expression*.

95. Rosner, S., & Abt, L. E. "Interview with John Simon." In *The Creative Expression*.

96. Rosner, S., & Abt, L. E. "Interview with Stanley Kauffman." In *The Creative Expression*.

97. Ferris, P. *Dylan Thomas*. Markham, Ont.: Penguin Books, 1978.

98. Rosner, S., & Abt, L. E. "Interview with Anna Kisselgoff." In *The Creative Expression*. 153-167.

99. *ibid*. p. 156.

100. Rosner, S., Abt, L. E. "Interview with Martin Bookspan." In The Creative Expression.
101. Rosner, S., & Abt, L. E. The Creative Expression.
102. Kerr, W. Thirty Plays hath November. New York: Simon & Schuster, 1970.
103. Kerr, W. Journey to the Centre of the Theatre. New York: Alfred A. Knopf, 1979, p. 288.
104. Boswell, J. The Life of Johnson. p. 100.
105. Rosner, S., & Abt, L. E. "Interview with Anna Kisselgoff." In The Creative Expression.
106. Rosner, S., & Abt, L. E. "Interview with Judith Crist." In The Creative Expression. p. 188.
107. Russell, B. The Autobiography of Bertrand Russell. The Middle Years: 1914-1944. p. 326.
108. Tynan, K. Curtains; Tynan, K. Tynan Right and Left. London: Longmans, 1967.
109. Rosner, S., Abt, L. E. "Interview with John Simon." In The Creative Expression.
110. Nathan, G. J. Passing Judgements. New York: Greenwood Press, 1969, p. 19.
111. Rosner, S., Abt, L. E. "Interview with Martin Bookspan." In The Creative Expression.
112. Goldman, W. The Season: A Candid Look at Broadway.
113. Rosner, S., Abt, L. E. "Interview with John Simon." In The Creative Expression.
114. Teichmann, H. George S. Kaufman, an Intimate Portrait. New York: Dell Publishing Co., 1972.
115. Quoted in Nathan, G. J. Passing Judgements. p. 11.
116. Rosner, S., Abt, L. E. "Interview with John Simon." In The Creative Expression.
117. Rigg, D. No Turn Unstoned: The Worst Ever Theatrical Reviews.
118. Stein, M. I. Stimulating Creativity. Vol. 1: Individual Procedures.
119. Rosner, S., Abt, L. E. The Creative Expression.
120. Tynan, K. Tynan Right and Left. p. 171.
121. Getzels, J. W., & Jackson, P. W. "The Highly Intelligent and the Highly Creative Adolescent." In P. E. Vernon (Ed.), Creativity. Markham, Ont.: Penguin Books, 1970, 189-202; Wallach, M. A., & Kogan, N. "A New Look at the Creativity-Intelligence Distinction." In P. E. Vernon (Ed.), Creativity. 235-256.
122. Brill, A. A. (Ed.). The Basic Writings of Sigmund Freud. New York: Random House, 1938, p. 193.
123. Bruner, J. "The Act of Discovery." In On Knowing: Essays for the Left Hand. 81-96.
124. Hall, C. S., & Lindzey, G. Theories of Personality. (2nd ed.). New York: John Wiley & Sons, Inc., 1970.
125. Maddi, S. R. Personality Theories: A Comparative Analysis. (rev. edition). Homewood, Ill.: The Dorsey Press, 1972.

126. Sahakian, W. S. (Ed.). Psychology of Personality: Readings in Theory. Chicago: Rand McNally & Co., 1965.

Chapter 6

01. Kaufmann, W. Existentialism from Dostoevsky to Sartre. New York: The World Publishing Co., 1956.
02. Stern, A. Sartre: His Philosophy and Existential Psychoanalysis. New York: Dell Publishing Co., 1967.
03. Kerr, W. "The Playwright as Existentialist." In God on the Gymnasium Floor and other Theatrical Adventures. New York: Dell Publishing Co., 1973, pp. 151-152.
04. Barrett, W. What is Existentialism?. New York: Grove Press, Inc., 1964.
05. ibid.
06. Kaufmann, W. Existentialism from Dostoevsky to Sartre.
07. Stein, A. Sartre: His Philosophy and Existential Psychoanalysis.
08. Fromm, E. The Fear of Freedom. London: Routledge and Kegan Paul, Ltd., 1960.
09. Camus, A. The Rebel. New York: Vintage Books, 1956.
10. Sartre, J. P. The Age of Reason. New York: Alfred A. Knopf, 1947, p. 249.
11. Milne, A. A. Winnie the Pooh. Toronto: McLelland & Stewart, Ltd., 1925.
12. Kreitler, H., & Kreitler, S. Psychology of the Arts. Durham, N.C.: Duke University Press, 1972.
13. Getzels, J. W., & Csikszentmihalyi, M. The Creative Vision. Toronto: John Wiley & Sons, Ltd., 1976.
14. Camus, A. The Myth of Sisyphus and Other Essays. New York: Alfred A. Knopf, 1969, p. 70.
15. Esslin, M. The Theatre of the Absurd. Garden City, N.Y.: Doubleday, 1961.
16. Kerr, W. "The Playwright as Existentialist." p. 128.
17. ibid. p. 131.
18. ibid. p. 132.
19. Pinter, H. The Homecoming. London: Methuen & Co., Ltd., 1965, p. 51-52.
20. Pugh, M. The Daily Mail. London, March 7, 1964. Cited in Esslin, M., The Peopled Wound. London: Methuen & Co., Ltd., 1970, p. 38.
21. Cited in Esslin, M. The Peopled Wound. p. 37-38.
22. Esslin, M. The Peopled Wound.
23. Pinter, H. The Caretaker. London: Methuen & Co., Ltd., 1960.
24. Gruber, H. E. "The Evolving Systems Approach to Creativity." In Modgil, S., & Modgil, C. (Eds.), Toward a Theory of Psychological Development. Atlantic Highlands, N.J.: Humanities Press, 1980, 269-299.

518

25. Getzels, J. W., & Csikszentmihalyi, M. The Creative Vision; Tate, A. "Narcissus as Narcissus." In B. Ghiselin (Ed.), The Creative Process. New York: New American Library, 1952, 134-145; Beckmann, M. "On My Painting." In R. L. Herbert (Ed.), Artists on Art. Englewood Cliffs, N.J.: Prentice-Hall, 1964, 131-137.

26. Storr, A. The Dynamics of Creation. New York: Penguin Books, 1976.

27. Rosner, S., & Abt, L. E. "Interview with John Simon." In The Creative Expression. Croton-on-Hudson: N.Y.: North River Press, 1976, p. 176.

28. Arieti, S. Creativity: The Magic Synthesis. New York: Basic Books, 1976.

29. Poincaré, H. "Mathematical Creation." In B. Ghiselin (Ed.), The Creative Process. 33-42.

30. Maslow, A. H. Toward a Psychology of Being. Toronto: D. van Nostrand Co., (Canada) Ltd., 1962, p. 12.

31. Dryden, J. "Dedication of the Rival-Ladies." In B. Ghiselin (Ed.), The Creative Process. p. 81.

32. Humphrey, D. The Art of Making Dances. New York: Grove Press, 1959.

33. Camus, A. In The Myth of Sisyphus and Other Essays. p. 88.

34. ibid. p. 21, 28.

35. ibid. p. 3, 9.

36. ibid. p. 38.

37. ibid. p. 119, 123.

38. ibid. p. 61.

39. ibid. p. 73.

40. Koestler, A. The Act of Creation. London: Pan Books Ltd, 1970.

41. Engman, R. "Interview." In S. Rosner & L. E. Abt (Eds.), The Creative Experience. New York: Dell Publishing Co., 1970, p. 351.

42. Camus, A. "Hope and the Absurd in the Work of Franz Kafka." In The Myth of Sisyphus and Other Essays. 92-102.

43. Kafka, F. "The Metamorphosis." In The Penal Colony and Other Stories. New York: Schocken Books, 1961, p. 67.

44. Grant, V. W. The Great Abnormals. New York: Hawthorn Books, 1968.

45. Kafka, F. The Trial. New York: Modern Library, 1937, p. 286.

46. Camus, A. "Hope and the Absurd in the Work of Franz Kafka." In The Myth of Sisyphus and Other Essays. p. 100.

47. Maddi, S. R. "The Strenuousness of the Creative Life." In I. A. Taylor & J. W. Getzels (Eds.), Perspectives in Creativity. Chicago, Ill.: Aldine Publishing Co., 1975, 173-190.

48. Leigh, M., & Darion, J. "The Quest." From Man of La Mancha. Kapp Records, KRL-4505.

49. Sorell, W. <u>The Dancer's Image: Points and Counterpoints</u>. New York: Columbia University Press, 1971, p. 4.
50. Langer, S. K. <u>Philosophy in a New Key</u>. New York: Mentor Books, 1951.
51. Camus, A. <u>The Rebel</u>.
52. Tynan, K. <u>Curtains</u>. London: Longmans, 1961, p. 343.
53. Camus, A. <u>The Rebel</u>. p. 5.
54. <u>ibid</u>. p. 10.
55. Thomas, D. <u>Collected Poems</u>. London: Dent, 1954.
56. Camus, A. <u>The Rebel</u>. p. 283.
57. <u>ibid</u>. p. 16.
58. <u>ibid</u>. p. 22.
59. Camus, A. <u>Caligula and Three Other Plays</u>. New York: Vintage Books, 1958.
60. Camus, A. <u>The Rebel</u>. p. 283.
61. Camus, A. <u>The Rebel</u>. p. 253.
62. <u>ibid</u>. p. 256.
63. <u>ibid</u>. p. 253.
64. <u>ibid</u>. p. 270.
65. <u>ibid</u>. p. 255.
66. May, R. <u>The Courage to Create</u>. New York: W. W. Norton and Co., Inc., 1975.
67. Camus, A. <u>The Rebel</u>. p. 256.
68. <u>ibid</u>. p. 256.
69. Camus, A. "The Artist and His Time." In <u>The Myth of Sisyphus and Other Essays</u>. p. 147-151.
70. <u>ibid</u>. p. 151.

Chapter 7

01. Stern, A. <u>Sartre: His Philosophy and Existential Psychoanalysis</u>. New York: Dell Publishing Co., 1967.
02. Sartre, J. P. <u>Being and Nothingness</u>. New York: The Citadel Press, 1969.
03. <u>ibid</u>. p. 55.
04. Grimsley, R. <u>Existentialist Thought</u>. Cardiff: University of Wales Press, 1960.
05. Stern, A. <u>Sartre: His Philosophy and Existential Psychoanalysis</u>. p. 168.
06. Sartre, J. P. <u>Being and Nothingness</u>. p. 519.
07. Grene, M. <u>Introduction to Existentialism</u>. Chicago: University of Chicago Press, 1948.
08. Sartre, J. P. <u>Being and Nothingness</u>.
09. Maslow, A. H. <u>The Psychology of Science</u>. Chicago: Henry Regnery Co., 1969.
10. Sartre, J. P. <u>Being and Nothingness</u>. p. 231.
11. de Beauvoir, S. <u>The Second Sex</u>. New York: Alfred A. Knopf, Inc., 1962.
12. Laing, R. D. <u>The Divided Self</u>. Harmondsworth, Middlesex: Penguin Books, 1965.

13. Sartre, J. P. Being and Nothingness.
14. Sartre, J. P. "The Quest for the Absolute." In Essays in Aesthetics. New York: The Citadel Press, 1966, p. 92.
15. Sartre, J. P. The Words. New York: Vintage Books, 1981.
16. ibid. p. 83, 163-164.
17. ibid. p. 193-194.
18. Skinner, B. F. Beyond Freedom and Dignity. New York: Alfred A. Knopf, 1971.
19. Sartre, J. P. What is Literature?. New York: Harper Row, 1965.
20. ibid. p. 40.
21. ibid. p. 37.
22. ibid. p. 45.
23. ibid. p. 39.
24. ibid. p. 55-57.
25. Croce, B. Aesthetics as Science of Expression. New York: Noonday Press, 1953.
26. Sartre, J. P. Saint Genet: Actor and Martyr. New York: New American Library, 1971.
27. ibid. p. 9.
28. ibid. p. 49.
29. ibid. p. 31.
30. ibid. p. 50.
31. ibid. p. 55.
32. ibid. p. 68.
33. ibid. p. 91.
34. ibid. p. 446.
35. ibid. p. 452.
36. ibid. p. 448.
37. ibid. p. 459.
38. ibid. p. 495.
39. ibid. p. 498.
40. Festinger, L. "Cognitive Dissonance." Scientific American. offprint #472, reprinted from October, 1962. San Francisco: W. H. Freeman & Co.
41. Sartre, J. P. Saint Genet: Actor and Martyr. p. 499, 501.
42. ibid. p. 552.
43. ibid. p. 574.
44. Siegel, M. The Shapes of Change: Images of American Dance. Boston: Houghton Mifflin Co., 1979.
45. de Mille, A. Dance to the Piper. Boston: Little, Brown & Co., 1952.
46. de Mille, A. Speak to Me, Dance with Me. New York: Popular Library, 1973.
47. Mazo, J. Dance is a Contact Sport. New York: Da Capo Press, Inc., 1974.
48. Gruen, J. In The Private World of Ballet. Harmondsworth, Middlesex: Penguin Books, 1976.
49. Mazo, J. Dance is a Contact Sport. p. 100.

50. Sorrell, W. The Dancer's Image: Points and Counterpoints.
    New York: Columbia University Press, 1971, p. 11.
51. Gruen, J. "Interview with Michael Somes." In The Private
    World of Ballet. 162-168.
52. Siegel, M. The Shapes of Change: Images of American Dance.
    p. xiii.
53. Klosty, J. Merce Cunningham. New York: E. P. Dutton &
    Co., Inc., 1975.
54. Gruen, J. "Interview with Antoinette Sibley and Anthony
    Dowell." In The Private World of Ballet. p. 124.
55. Gruen, J. "Interview with Michael Coleman and Jennifer
    Penny." In The Private World of Ballet. p. 150.
56. Gruen, J. "Interview with Michael Somes." In The Private
    World of Ballet. p. 166.
57. Gruen, J. "Interview with Ivan Nagy." In The Private
    World of Ballet. p. 231.
58. Gruen, J. "Interview with Merle Park." In The Private
    World of Ballet. p. 128.
59. Sartre, J. P. Being and Nothingness.
60. McDonagh, D. The Rise and Fall and Rise of Modern Dance.
    New York: E. P. Dutton & Co., 1970.
61. Maslow, A. H. Toward a Psychology of Being. Toronto: D. van
    Nostrand Co., (Canada) Ltd., 1962.
62. Gruen, J. "Interview with Jorge Donn." In The Private
    World of Ballet. p. 189.
63. Sartre, J. P. Existentialism. New York: Philosophical
    Library, 1947.
64. de Beauvoir, S. The Second Sex.
65. Hoffer, E. The True Believer. New York: Harper Row,
    1951.
66. Toland, J. Adolph Hitler. New York: Ballantine Books,
    1977.
67. Goldman, W. The Season: A Candid Look at Broadway. New
    York: Harcourt, Brace & World, Inc., 1969.
68. ibid. p. 227.
69. Fromm, E. The Art of Loving. New York: Harper Row,
    1956.
70. May, R. Love and Will. New York: Dell Publishing Co.,
    1969.

Chapter 8

01. Plato. "Inspiration." In A. Rothenberg & C. R. Hausman
    (Eds.), The Creativity Question. Durham, N.C.: Duke
    University Press, 1976, 31-33.
02. Von Franz, M. L. Creation Myths. Zurich: Spring
    Publications, 1972.
03. Tolstoy, L. "Art is the Communication of Feeling." In
    G. Dickie & R. J. Sclafani (Eds.), Aesthetics, a Critical
    Anthology. New York: St. Martin's Press, 1977, 53-82.

522

04. ibid. p. 80-81.
05. Engell, J. The Creative Imagination: Enlightenment to Romanticism. Cambridge, Mass.: Harvard University Press, 1981.
06. Flanders, M., & Swann, D. At the Drop of a Hat. London: Angel Records, 65042.
07. May, R. The Courage to Create. New York: W. W. Norton & Co., Inc., 1975.
08. Cited in May, R. The Courage to Create. p. 27.
09. Arieti, S. Creativity: The Magic Synthesis. New York: Basic Books, 1976, p. 5.
10. Clark, R. W. Einstein: The Life and Times. New York: Avon Books, 1972, p. 37.
11. ibid. p. 502.
12. Getzels, J. W., & Csikszentmihalyi, M. The Creative Vision. New York: John Wiley & Sons, 1976.
13. Coulson, J. Religion and Imagination. Oxford: Clarendon Press, 1981.
14. ibid. p. 14.
15. Davies, S. G. James Joyce: A Portrait of the Artist. London: Granada, 1982, p. 55.
16. Foss, L. Dance in Canada Conference. (Speech), University of Waterloo, Waterloo, Ontario, June, 1979.
17. Lawrence, D. H. "Making Pictures." In B. Ghiselin (Ed.), The Creative Process. New York: New American Library, 1952, 68-73.
18. Spender, S. "The Making of a Poem." In B. Ghiselin (Ed.), The Creative Process. 112-125.
19. Quoted in Hyslop, T. P. The Great Abnormals. London: Philip Allan & Co., 1925, p. 228.
20. Hutchinson, E. D. How to Think Creatively. New York: Abingdon Press, 1949.
21. Tart, C. T. (Ed.). Altered States of Consciousness. New York: John Wiley & Sons, Inc., 1969.
22. Hutchinson, E. D. How to Think Creatively.
23. Clark, R. W. Einstein: The Life and Times. p. 422.

Chapter 9

01. Jones, E. The Life and Work of Sigmund Freud. (abridged and edited by L. Trilling & S. Marcus). Markham, Ont.: Penguin Books, 1964.
02. Salter, A. The Case Against Psychoanalysis. New York: The Citadel Press, 1964.
03. Hall, C. S. A Primer of Freudian Psychology. New York: New American Library, 1954.
04. Hall, C. S., & Lindzey, G. Theories of Personality. (2nd ed.). New York: John Wiley, 1970.
05. Freud, S. The Interpretation of Dreams. London: Hogarth Press, 1953.

06. Freud, S. The Problem of Anxiety. New York: W. W. Norton & Co., 1936.
07. Freud, S. An Outline of Psychoanalysis. New York: W. W. Norton & Co., 1949.
08. Freud, S. "Introductory Lectures on Psychoanalysis (Part III)." In The Complete Psychological Works of Sigmund Freud. (Vol. 16). London: Hogarth Press, 1963.
09. Freud, S. "The Ego and the Id." In The Complete Psychological Works of Sigmund Freud (Vol. 19). 1961, 12-66.
10. Watson, R. I. The Great Psychologists. Philadelphia: J. B. Lippincott, 1963, p. 442.
11. Suler, J. R. "Primary Process Thinking and Creativity." Psychological Bulletin, 1980, 88, 144-165.
12. Salter, A. The Case Against Psychoanalysis.
13. Magee, B. Popper. Glascow: Fontana/Collins, 1973.
14. Jones, E. The Life and Work of Sigmund Freud.
15. Watson, R. I. The Great Psychologists.
16. May, R. Love and Will. New York: Dell Publishing Co., 1969.
17. Freud, S. "One of the Difficulties of Psychoanalysis." In On Creativity and the Unconscious. New York: Harper & Row, 1958, 1-10.
18. Graves, R. Goodbye to All That. Markham, Ont.: Penguin Books, 1960.
19. Remarque, E. M. All Quiet on the Western Front. Boston: Little, Brown & Co., 1975.
20. Freud, S. "Thoughts for the Times on War and Death." In On Creativity and the Unconscious. 206-235.
21. ibid. p. 218.
22. Freud, S. "Three Essays on the Theory of Sexuality." In The Complete Psychological Works of Sigmund Freud (Vol. 7). 1953, 123-243.
23. Freud, S. "The Moses of Michelangelo." In On Creativity and the Unconscious. 11-41.
24. Carr, E. Growing Pains: The Autobiography of Emily Carr. Toronto: Oxford University Press, 1946.
25. Freud, S. "The Relation of the Poet to Daydreaming." In On Creativity and the Unconscious. 44-54.
26. Freud, S. "Introductory Lectures on Psychoanalysis (Part III)." In The Complete Psychological Works of Sigmund Freud (Vol. 16). 1963, p. 376.
27. Freud, S. "The Relation of the Poet to Daydreaming." In On Creativity and the Unconscious. 44-54.
28. ibid. p. 45.
29. Cited in Bronowski, J. The Ascent of Man. London: Macdonald Futura, 1981, p. 47.
30. Freud, S. "The Relation of the Poet to Daydreaming." In On Creativity and the Unconscious. p. 47.

31. Freud, S. "Introductory Lectures on Psychoanalysis (Part III)." In The Complete Psychological Works of Sigmund Freud.

32. Freud, S. "Civilized Sexual Morality and Modern Nervous Illness." In The Complete Psychological Works of Sigmund Freud (Vol. 9). 1959, p. 188.

33. Freud, S. "Introductory Lectures on Psychoanalysis (Part III)" and "The Claims of Psychoanalysis to Scientific Interest." In The Complete Psychological Works of Sigmund Freud (Vol. 13). 1955, 165-190.

34. Freud, S. "The Relation of the Poet to Daydreaming." In On Creativity and the Unconscious. 44-54.

35. Freud, S. "Introductory Lectures on Psychoanalysis (Part III)." In The Complete Psychological Works of Sigmund Freud (Vol. 16). 1963, p. 376-377.

36. Freud, S. "On Transience." In The Complete Psychological Works of Sigmund Freud (Vol. 14). 1957, p. 306.

37. Spector, J. J. The Aesthetics of Freud. New York: McGraw-Hill Co., 1974.

38. Jones, E. The Life and Work of Sigmund Freud.

39. Freud, S. Leonardo da Vinci. New York: Vintage Books, 1947.

40. ibid. p. 18-19.

41. ibid. p. 73.

42. ibid. p. 74.

43. ibid. p. 88.

44. ibid. p. 91.

45. Bieber, I. Homosexuality: A Psychoanalytic study. New York: Basic Books, 1962.

46. Freud, S. Leonardo da Vinci. p. 119.

47. Hutchinson, E. D. How to Think Creatively. New York: Abingdon Press, 1949.

48. Storr, A. The Dynamics of Creation. Markham, Ont.: Penguin Books, 1976.

49. Freud, S. "Degradation in Erotic Life." In On Creativity and the Unconscious. p. 183.

50. Lombroso, C. "Genius and Insanity." In A. Rothenberg and C. R. Hausman (Eds.), The Creativity Question. Durham, N.C.: Duke University Press, 1976, 79-86.

51. Freud, S. "Delusions and Dreams in Jensen's 'Gradiva'." In The Complete Psychological Works of Sigmund Freud (Vol. 9). 1959, 1-93.

52. Ferris, P. Dylan Thomas. Markham, Ont.: Penguin Books, 1978, p. 81.

53. Pearson, H. George Bernard Shaw: His Life and Personality. New York: Atheneum, 1963.

54. Weismann, P. Creativity in the Theatre. New York: Basic Books, 1965. Quoted in H. Teichmann, George S. Kaufman, an Intimate Portrait. New York: Dell Publishing Co., 1972, p. 276.

55. Plimpton, G. "Interview with James Jones." In G. Plimpton (Ed.), Writers at Work: The Paris Interviews. New York: Viking Press, 1968, p. 250.
56. Spender, S. "The Making of a Poem." In B. Ghiselin (Ed.), The Creative Process. New York: New American Library, 1952, p. 123.
57. Freud, S. "Totem and Taboo." In The Complete Psychological Works of Sigmund Freud (Vol. 13). 1955, 1-161.
58. Bruner, J. "Myth and Identity." In On Knowing: Essays for the Left Hand. Cambridge, Mass.: Harvard University Press, 1979, 31-42.
59. Freud, S. "A Metapsychological Supplement to the Theory of Dreams." In The Complete Psychological Works of Sigmund Freud (Vol. 14). 1957, p. 223.
60. Spender, S. "The Making of a Poem." 112-125.
61. Hudson, L. Human Beings. London: Jonathan Cape, 1975.
62. Freud, S. "Femininity." In J. Starkey (Ed.), New Introductory Lectures on Psychoanalysis. New York: W. W. Norton & Co., 1964, 112-135.
63. ibid. p. 134.
64. Freud, S. "Some Psychical Consequences of the Anatomical Distinction between the Sexes." In The Complete Psychological Works of Sigmund Freud (Vol. 19). 1961, 248-258.
65. Rosner, S., & Abt, L. E. (Eds.) The Creative Expression. Croton-on-Hudson, N.Y.: North River Press, Inc., 1976.
66. Freud, S. "Some Psychical Consequences of the Anatomical Distinction between the Sexes." In The Complete Psychological Works of Sigmund Freud.
67. Watson, J. D. The Double Helix. New York: New American Library, 1968.
68. Freud, S. "Femininity." In J. Starkey (Ed.), New Introductory Lectures on Psychoanalysis.
69. ibid.
70. Spector, J. J. The Aesthetics of Freud.
71. Crews, F. C. The Pooh Perplex. New York: E. P. Dutton, 1965.
72. Jung, C. G. "Dream Analysis in its Practical Applications." In Modern Man in Search of a Soul. New York: Harcourt, Brace & World, 1933, 1-27.
73. Stolorow, R. D., & Atwood, G. E. Faces in a Cloud: Subjectivity in Personality Theory. New York: Jason Aronson, 1979.
74. Freud, S. "Dostoevsky and Parricide." In The Complete Psychological Works of Sigmund Freud (Vol. 21). 1961, 175-198.
75. Ferris, P. Dylan Thomas. p. 170.
76. Jung, C. G. "Analytic Psychology and Education." In The Collected Works of C. G. Jung, Vol. 17. Princeton, N.J.: Princeton University Press, 1954, 63-132.

77. Jung, C.G. "Psychology and Literature." In The Collected
    Works of C. G. Jung (Vol. 15). 1966, p. 101.
78. Evans, R. Psychology and Arthur Miller. New York: E.P.
    Dutton, 1969.
79. Freud, S. "The Relation of the Poet to Daydreaming." In On
    Creativity and the Unconscious. 44-54.
80. Evans, R. Psychology and Arthur Miller. p. 20.
81. Freud, S. "The Claims of Psychoanalysis to Scientific
    Interest." In The Complete Psychological Works of
    Sigmund Freud (Vol. 13). 1955, p. 187.
82. Freud, S. "The Moses of Michelangelo." In On Creativity and
    the Unconscious. 11-41.
83. Spector, J. J. The Aesthetics of Freud.
84. Freud, S. "The Relation of the Poet to Daydreaming." In On
    Creativity and the Unconscious. 44-54.
85. Quoted in Slochower, H. "The Psychoanalytic Approach;
    Psychoanalysis and Creativity." In S. Rosner & L. E.
    Abt (Eds.), Essays in Creativity. Croton-on-Hudson,
    N.Y.: North River Press, 1974, p. 176.
86. Pope, A. "An Essay on Criticism." In J. H. Smith and E. W.
    Parks (Eds.), The Great Critics. (3rd edition). New
    York: W. W. Norton & Co., 1951, p. 393.
87. Freud, S. "Dostoevsky and Parricide." In The Complete
    Psychological Works of Sigmund Freud (Vol. 21). 1961,
    175-198.
88. Freud, S. Leonardo da Vinci. p. 119.

Chapter 10

01. Jones, E. The Life and Work of Sigmund Freud (abridged and
    edited by L. Trilling & S. Marcus). Markham, Ont.:
    Penguin Books. 1964.
02. Jung, C. G. "Approaching the Unconscious." In Man and His
    Symbols. Garden City, N.Y.: Doubleday & Co., 1964,
    18-103.
03. Jung, C. G. "The Archetypes and the Collective Unconscious."
    In The Collected Works of C. G. Jung (Vol. 9).
    Princeton, N.J.: Princeton Univeristy Press, 1959.
04. Jung, C. G. "On the Relation of Analytic Psychology to
    Poetic Art." British Journal of Medical Psychology,
    1923, 3, 219-231.
05. Jaffe, A. "Symbolism in the Visual Arts." In C. G. Jung
    (Ed.), Man and His Symbols, 230-271.
06. von Franz, M. L. Creation Myths. Zurich: Spring
    Publications, 1972.
07. Jung, C. G. "Symbols of Transformation." In The Collected
    Works of C. G. Jung (Vol. 5), 1956.
08. Kleitman, N. "Patterns of Dreaming." San Francisco: W. H.
    Freeman & Co., Scientific American reprint #460.
09. Jung, C. G. Psychology of Types. London: Routledge & Kegan
    Paul, 1923.

10. Grahame, K. The Wind in the Willows. New York: Scribner's, 1954.
11. Jung, C. G. "Approaching the Unconscious," p. 61.
12. Myers, I. B. Myers-Briggs Type Indicator Manual. Princeton, N.J.: Educational Testing Service, 1962.
13. Jung, C. G. "Approaching the Unconscious."
14. Jung, C. G. "Psychology and Literature." In The Collected Works of C. G. Jung (Vol. 15), 1966, 84-105.
15. Jung, C. G. "On the Relation of Analytic Psychology to Poetic Art."
16. Jung, C. G. "Psychology and Literature," p. 102.
17. Jung, C. G. "The Gifted Child." In The Collected Works of C. G. Jung (Vol. 17) 1954, 135-145.
18. Jung, C. G. "Psychology and Literature," p. 102.
19. Ferris, P. Dylan Thomas. Markham, Ont.: Penguin Books, 1978, p. 299.
20. Jung, C. G. "The Gifted Child."
21. ibid; Jung, C. G. "Analytic Psychology and Education," in The Collected Works of C. G. Jung (Vol. 17), 1954, 63-132.
22. Jung, C. G. "Is There a Freudian Type of Poetry?" in The Collected Works of C. G. Jung (Vol. 18), 1950, 765-766; "Ulysses: A Monologue." ibid., (Vol. 15) 1966, 109-132.
23. Jung, C. G. "Ulysses: A Monologue."
24. Jung, C. G. "Analytic Psychology and Education." In The Collected Works of C. G. Jung (Vol. 17), 1954, p. 115.
25. Jung, C. G. "The Aims of Psychotherapy." In Modern Man in Search of a Soul. New York: Harcourt, Brace and World, 1933, 55-73.
26. Jung, C. G. "On the Relation of Analytic Psychology to Poetic Art."
27. Nietzsche, F. "Composition of Thus Spake Zarathustra." In B. Ghiselin (Ed.), The Creative Process. New York: New American Library, 1952, p. 202.
28. Jung, C. G. "Psychology and Literature," p. 103.
29. ibid., p. 101.
30. Watson, R. I. The Great Psychologists. Philadelphia: J. B. Lippincott Co., 1963.
31. Kuhn, T. S. The Structure of Scientific Revolutions. Chicago: University of Chicago Press, 1962.
32. Roe, A. The Making of a Scientist. New York: Dodd, Mead, 1952.
33. Buckle, R. Diaghilev. London: Weidenfeld and Nicolson, 1979.
34. MacKinnon, D. W. In Search of Human Effectiveness: Identifying and Developing Creativity. Buffalo, N.Y.: Creative Education Foundation, Inc., in association with Creative Synergetic Associates, Ltd., 1978.

35. Edinger, E. F. Melville's Moby Dick: A Jungian Commentary. New York: New Directions Books, 1975; Pops, M.L. The Melville Archetype. Kent, Ohio: Kent State University Press, 1970.
36. Howard, L. Herman Melville: A Biography. Berkeley, Calif.: University of California Press, 1951.
37. Langer, S. Philosophy in a New Key. New York: Mentor Books, 1951.
38. Langer, S. Feeling and Form. New York: Charles Scribner's Sons, 1953.
39. Kleitman, N. "Patterns of Dreaming."
40. Jouvet, M. "The Role of Monoamines and Acetylcholine-Containing Neurons in the Regulation of the Sleep-Waking Cycle." Ergebnisse der Physiologie, 1972, 64, 166-307.
41. Langer, S. Feeling and Form, p. 40.
42. ibid, p. 176.
43. Jung, C. G. "Symbols of Transformation."
44. Taper, B. Balanchine: A Biography. New York: MacMillan, 1974.
45. Chicago, J. Through the Flower. New York: Anchor Books, 1982, p. 21.
46. Evans, R. Psychology and Arthur Miller. New York: E.P. Dutton, 1969.
47. Miller, G. A. "Some Preliminaries to Psycholinguistics." American Psychologist, 1965, 20, 15-20.
48. Skinner, B. F. Verbal Behavior. New York: Appleton-Century-Crofts, 1957.
49. Jung, C. G. "On the Relation of Analytic Psychology to Poetic Art."
50. Cited in May, R. Love and Will. New York: Dell Publishing Co., 1974, p. 21.
51. Jung, C. G. "Forward to Gilbert: The Curse of the Intellect." In The Collected Works of C.G. Jung (Vol. 18), 1950, p. 767.
52. Kandinsky, W. "Reminiscences." In R.L. Hebert (Ed.), Artists on Art. Englewood Cliffs, N. J.: Prentice-Hall, 1964, p. 33.
53. Mozart, W. A. "A Letter." In B. Ghiselin (Ed.), The Creative Process, p. 45.
54. Jung, C. G. "Cryptomnesia." In The Collected Works of C.G. Jung (Vol. 1), 1957, 95-106.
55. Miller, H. "Reflections on Writing." In B. Ghiselin (Ed.), The Creative Process, p. 179.
56. Teichmann, H. George S. Kaufman: An Intimate Portrait. New York: Dell Publishing Co., 1973.
57. Jung, C. G. "The Gifted Child."
58. Jung, C. G. "Analytic Psychology and Education."
59. Gedo, M. M. Picasso: Art as Autobiography. Chicago: The University of Chicago Press, 1980.

60. Brecht, B. <u>Brecht</u> <u>on</u> <u>Theatre</u>: <u>The</u> <u>Development</u> <u>of</u> <u>an</u>
     <u>Aesthetic</u>. London: Methuen, 1964.
61. Rank, O. <u>Beyond</u> <u>Psychology</u>. Camden, N. J.: Hadden
     Craftsmen, 1941.
62. Rank, O. <u>The</u> <u>Trauma</u> <u>of</u> <u>Birth</u>. Harcourt, Brace & Co., 1929.
63. Rank, O. <u>Psychology</u> <u>and</u> <u>the</u> <u>Soul</u>. New York: A. S. Barnes &
     Co., 1961.
64. Rank, O. <u>Art</u> <u>and</u> <u>Artist</u>. New York: Alfred A. Knopf, 1932.
65. Rank, O. <u>Will</u> <u>Therapy</u>, <u>an</u> <u>Analysis</u> <u>of</u> <u>the</u> <u>Therapeutic</u>
     <u>Process</u> <u>in</u> <u>Terms</u> <u>of</u> <u>Relationship</u>. New York: Alfred A.
     Knopf, 1936.
66. <u>ibid</u>.
67. Karpf, F. B. <u>The</u> <u>Psychology</u> <u>and</u> <u>Psychotherapy</u> <u>of</u> <u>Otto</u> <u>Rank</u>.
     New York: Philosophical Library, 1953.
68. Taft, J. <u>Otto</u> <u>Rank</u>: <u>A</u> <u>Biographical</u> <u>Study</u> <u>Based</u> <u>on</u>
     <u>Notebooks</u>, <u>Letters</u>, <u>Collected</u> <u>Writings</u>, <u>Therapeutic</u>
     <u>Achievements</u> <u>and</u> <u>Personal</u> <u>Associations</u>. New York:
     Julian Press, 1958.
69. Rank, O. <u>Art</u> <u>and</u> <u>Artist</u>, p. 39.
70. Festinger, L. "Cognitive Dissonance." <u>Scientific</u> <u>American</u>,
     1962, <u>207</u>, 93-100.
71. Rank, O. <u>Art</u> <u>and</u> <u>Artist</u>, p. 361-362.
72. Birney, E. <u>The</u> <u>Creative</u> <u>Writer</u>. Toronto: Canadian
     Broadcasting Corp., 1966, p. 13.
73. Rank, O. <u>Beyond</u> <u>Psychology</u>.
74. Horney, K. "The Flight from Womanhood." In H. Kelman (Ed.)
     <u>Feminine</u> <u>Psychology</u>. New York: W.W. Norton, 1967.
75. Seroff, V. <u>The</u> <u>Real</u> <u>Isadora</u>. New York: Avon Books, 1972.
76. Duncan, I. <u>My</u> <u>Life</u>. New York: Liveright, 1927, p. 168.
77. <u>ibid</u>, p. 142.
78. <u>ibid</u>, p. 165.
79. <u>ibid</u>, p. 343.
80. <u>ibid</u>, p. 17.
81. Seroff, V. <u>The</u> <u>Real</u> <u>Isadora</u>.
82. Duncan, I. <u>My</u> <u>Life</u>, p. 348.
83. Seroff, V. <u>The</u> <u>Real</u> <u>Isadora</u>.
84. <u>ibid</u>.
85. New York newspaper, April 19, 1899.
86. Seroff, V. <u>The</u> <u>Real</u> <u>Isadora</u>, p. 359.
87. Duncan, I. <u>My</u> <u>Life</u>, p. 11.
88. <u>ibid</u>.
89. <u>ibid</u>, p. 57.
90. <u>ibid</u>, p. 30-31.
91. <u>ibid</u>, p. 75.
92. <u>ibid</u>, p. 196.
93. <u>ibid</u>, p. 228.
94. MacKinnon, D. W. "Personality and the Realization of
     Creative Potential." In <u>In</u> <u>Search</u> <u>of</u> <u>Human</u>
     <u>Effectiveness</u>: <u>Identifying</u> <u>and</u> <u>Developing</u> <u>Creativity</u>.

Buffalo, N.Y.: The Creative Education Foundation, Inc., 1978.

95. Becker, E. The Denial of Death. New York: The Free Press, 1975.

96. Ghiselin, B. "Introduction." In B. Ghiselin (Ed.), The Creative Process, 11-31.

97. cited in Skinner, B. F. "A Behavioral Model of Creation." In A. Rothenberg & C. R. Hausman (Eds.), The Creativity Question. Durham, N. C.: Duke University Press, 1976, p. 267.

98. Clark, R. W. Einstein: The Life and Times. New York: Avon Books, 1972, p. 220.

99. Housman, A. E. "The Name and Nature of Poetry." In B. Ghiselin (Ed.), The Creative Process, p. 91.

100. Barron, F. Artists in the Making. New York: Seminar Press, 1972.

101. Weissman, P. Creativity in the Theatre--a Psychoanalytic Study. New York: Dell Publishing Co., 1965.

102. Copland, A. "Interview." In S. Rosner & L. E. Abt (Eds.), The Creative Experience. New York: Delta Books, 1970, 269-278.

103. David, H., & Mendel, A. (Eds.). The Bach Reader. New York: W. W. Norton & Co., 1945.

104. Taper, B. Balanchine: A Biography.

105. Rank, O. Art and Artist, p. 265.

106. ibid, p. 76.

107. ibid, p. 387.

108. ibid, p. 48.

Chapter 11

01. Rothenberg, A., & Hausman, C. R. (Eds.), The Creativity Question. Durham, N. C.: Duke University Press, 1976.

02. Slochower, H. "The Psychoanalytic Approach: Psychoanalysis and Creativity." In S. Rosner and L. E. Abt (Eds.), Essays in Creativity. Croton-on-Hudson, New York: North River Press, Inc., 1974, 151-190.

03. Arieti, S. Creativity: The Magic Synthesis. New York: Basic Books, Inc., 1976.

04. Kris, E. Psychoanalytic Explorations in Art. New York: International Universities Press, Inc., 1952.

05. ibid, p. 116.

06. Hall, C. S., & Lindzey, G. Theories of Personality (2nd ed.). New York: John Wiley, 1970.

07. Kris, E. Psychoanalytic Explorations in Art, p. 103.

08. ibid, p. 167.

09. ibid, p. 61.

10. Freud, S. Wit and Its Relation to the Unconscious. London: Kegan Paul, 1922.

11. Kris, E. Psychoanalytic Explorations in Art, p. 177.

531

12. Freud, S. "Psychopathic Characters on the Stage." In The Complete Psychological Works of Sigmund Freud (Vol. 7). London: Hogarth Press, 1960, p. 303 ff.
13. Kris, E. Psychoanalytic Explorations in Art, p. 256.
14. ibid.
15. Kubie, L. S. "Creation and Neurosis." In A. Rothenberg and C. R. Hausman (Eds.), The Creativity Question. Durham, N. C.: Duke University Press, 1976, 143-148; Kubie, L. S. "Unsolved Problems of Scientific Education." In M. Bloomberg (Ed.), Creativity: Theory and Research. New Haven, Conn.: College and University Press, 1973, 92-114.
16. Stein, M. I. Stimulating Creativity: Vol. I, Individual Procedures. New York: Academic Press, Inc., 1974.
17. Suler, J. R. "Primary Process Thinking and Creativity." Psychological Bulletin, 1980, 88, 144-165.
18. Kris, E. Psychoanalytic Explorations in Art, p. 231.
19. Arieti, S. Creativity: The Magic Synthesis.
20. Arieti, S. "From Primary Process to Creativity." Journal of Creative Behavior, 1978, 12, 225-246; Arieti, S. The Intrapsychic Self: Feeling, Cognition and Creativity in Health and Mental Illness. New York: Basic Books, 1967.
21. Arieti, S. Creativity: The Magic Synthesis, p. 226.
22. Koestler, A. The Act of Creation. London: Pan Books Ltd., 1970.
23. Arieti, S. Creativity: The Magic Synthesis, p. 24.
24. Greenacre, P. Emotional Growth: Psychoanalytic Studies of the Gifted and a Great Variety of other Individuals, Volume 2. New York: International Universities Press, Inc., 1971.
25. Glynn, E. "Desperate Necessity: Art and Creativity in Recent Psychoanalytic Theory." In The Print Collector's Newsletter, 1977, 8, 29-35, (quote on p. 31).
26. Galton, F. Hereditary Genius: An Inquiry into its Laws and Consequences. London: MacMillan and Co., 1869.
27. Greenacre, P. "The Childhood of the Artist: Libidinal Phase Development and Giftedness." In Emotional Growth, Vol. 2. New York: International Universities Press, Inc., 1971, 479-504.
28. Greenacre, P. "Experiences of Awe in Childhood." In Emotional Growth, Vol. 1, 1971, 67-92.
29. Greenacre, P. "The Childhood of the Artist: Libidinal Phase Development and Giftedness," p. 490.
30. ibid.
31. Greenacre, P. "The Family Romance of the Artist." In Emotional Growth, Vol. 2, 1971, 505-532.
32. ibid, p. 507.
33. ibid, p. 494.

34. *ibid*, p. 528.
35. Greenacre, P. "The Childhood of the Artist: Libidinal Phase Development and Giftedness."
36. Greenacre, P. "The Relation of the Imposter to the Artist." In *Emotional Growth*, Vol. 2, 1971, 533-554.
37. *ibid*, p. 554.
38. Thigpen, C. H., & Cleckley, H. *The Three Faces of Eve*. Kingsport, Tenn.: Kingsport Press, 1954.
39. Greenacre, P. "Woman as Artist." In *Emotional Growth*, Vol. 2, 1971, 575-591.
40. *ibid*, p. 587.
41. *ibid*, p. 591.
42. *ibid*, p. 589.
43. Greenacre, P. "The Childhood of the Artist: Libidinal Phase Development and Giftedness."
44. Schachtel, E. G. "Perceptual Modes and Creation." In A. Rothenberg & C. R. Hausman (Eds.), *The Creativity Question*, p. 153-161.
45. *ibid*, p. 155.
46. Greenacre, P. "The Mutual Adventures of Jonathon Swift and Lemuel Gulliver: A Study in Pathography." In *Emotional Growth*, Vol. 2, 1971, 399-437.
47. Greenacre, P. "'It's my own invention:' A Special Screen Memory of Mr. Lewis Carroll, its Form and History." In *Emotional Growth*, Vol. 2, 1971, 438-478.
48. Greenacre, P. "On Nonsense." In *Emotional Growth*, Vol. 2, 1971, 592-615.
49. *ibid*.
50. *ibid*.
51. Storr, A. *The Dynamics of Creation*. New York: Penguin Books, 1976.
52. Maddi, S. R. (Ed.), *Perspectives in Personality: A Comparative Approach*. Boston: Little, Brown & Co. 1971; Hall, C. S., and Lindsey, G. *Theories of Personality*.
53. Ansbacher, H. L., & Ansbacher, R. R. (Eds.), *The Individual Psychology of Alfred Adler*. New York: Basic Books, Inc., 1956.
54. Adler, A. "Individual Psychology." In S. R. Maddi (Ed.), *Perspectives in Personality: A Comparative Approach*, p. 253.
55. Ansbacher, H. L., & Ansbacher, R. R. (Eds.), *The Individual Psychology of Alfred Adler*.
56. Adler, A. "Individual Psychology as a Personality Theory." In W. S. Sahakian (Ed.), *Psychology of Personality: Readings in Theory*. Chicago: Rand McNally & Co., 1965, p. 111.
57. Ansbacher, H. L., & Ansbacher, R. R. (Eds.), *The Individual Psychology of Alfred Adler*, p. 177.

58. Allport, G. H. _Pattern_ and _Growth_ in _Personality_. New York: Holt, Rinehart & Winston, 1961.

59. Rogers, C. R. _Client_ _Centered_ _Therapy_: _Its_ _Current_ _Practice_, _Implications_ and _Theory_. Boston: Houghton Mifflin, 1951.

60. Landblom, P. _Creativity_ and _Disease_. Philadelphia: George F. Stickley Co., 1982.

61. Ansbacher, H. L., & Ansbacher, R. R. (Eds.), The _Individual_ _Psychology_ of _Alfred_ _Adler_, p. 153.

62. _ibid_, p. 213.

63. Gedo, J. E. _Portraits_ of _the_ _Artist_. New York: The Guilford Press, 1983.

64. Ansbacher, H. L. & Ansbacher, R. R. (Eds.), The _Individual_ _Psychology_ of _Alfred_ _Adler_, pp. 152-153.

65. _ibid_, p. 449.

66. Adler, A. "Individual Psychology as a Personality Theory," p. 114.

67. _ibid_, p. 115.

68. Ansbacher, H. L, & Ansbacher, R. R. (Eds.), The _Individual_ _Psychology_ of _Alfred_ _Adler_, p. 55.

69. Schonberg, H. The _Lives_ of _the_ _Great_ _Composers_. New York: W. W. Norton, 1970.

70. Brockway, W., & Weinstock, H. _Men_ of _Music_. New York: Simon & Schuster, 1939, p. 359.

71. Taylor, R. _Richard_ _Wagner_: _His_ _Life_, _Art_ and _Thought_. London: Paul Elek, 1979.

72. _ibid_, p. 31.

73. Taylor, R. _Richard_ _Wagner_: _His_ _Life_, _Art_ and _Thought_.

74. _ibid_.

75. Brockway, W., & Weinstock, H. _Men_ of _Music_.

76. Taylor, R. _Richard_ _Wagner_: _His_ _Life_, _Art_ and _Thought_, p. 20.

77. Thomson, V. "Dissent from Wagner." In R. Taylor, _Richard_ _Wagner_, _His_ _Life_, _Art_ and _Thought_, 260-261.

78. Wilde, O. The _Picture_ of _Dorian_ _Gray_. Markham, Ont.: Penguin Books, 1949, p. 54.

79. Adler, A. "Individual Psychology as a Personality Theory," p. 92.

80. Watson, J. D. The _Double_ _Helix_. New York: New American Library, 1968.

81. Merton, R. K. "Behavior Patterns of Scientists." In R. S. Albert (Ed.), _Genius_ and _Eminence_. New York: Pergamon Press, 1933, 253-261.

82. Cited in Gilhooly, K.J. _Thinking_: _Directed_, _Undirected_ and _Creative_. New York: Academic Press, 1982.

83. _ibid_, p. 126.

84. Clark, R.W. _Einstein_: _The_ _Life_ and _Times_. New York: Avon Books, 1972.

Chapter 12

01. Watson, J. B. Behaviorism. New York: W. W. Norton, 1970.
02. Galton, F. "Genius as Inherited." In A. Rothenberg and C. R. Hausman (Eds.), The Creativity Question. Durham, N. C.: Duke University Press, 1976, 42-48.
03. ibid, p. 43.
04. ibid, p. 44.
05. ibid, p. 44.
06. Erlenmeyer-Kimling, L., & Jarvik, L. S. "Genetics and Intelligence: A Review." Science, 1963, 142, 1477-1478.
07. Mozart, W. A. "A Letter." In B. Ghiselin (Ed.), The Creative Process. New York: New American Library, 1952, p. 45.
08. Skinner, B. F. "A Behavioral Model of Creation." In A. Rothenberg and C. R. Hausman (Eds.), The Creativity Question. 267-273.
09. Campbell, D. T. "Blind Variation and Selective Retention in Creative Thought as in other Knowledge Processes." Psychological Review, 1960, 67, 380-400.
10. Storr, A. The Dynamics of Creation. Markham, Ont.: Pelican Books, 1976.
11. Shaw, G. B. Preface to Man and Superman. In The Complete Prefaces of Bernard Shaw. London: Paul Hamlyn Ltd., 1965, 149-195.
12. ibid, p. 156.
13. ibid, p. 157.
14. ibid.
15. Maslow, A. H. Toward a Psychology of Being (2nd edition). Toronto: D. van Nostrand, Inc., 1968.
16. Stein, M. I. Stimulating Creativity, Vol. 1: Individual Procedures. New York: Academic Press, 1974.
17. Arieti, S. Creativity: The Magic Synthesis. New York: Basic Books, 1976.
18. Boring, E. G. A History of Experimental Psychology (2nd edition). New York: Appleton-Century-Crofts, Inc., 1957.
19. Watson, R. I. The Great Psychologists: From Aristotle to Freud. Philadelphia: J. B. Lippincott Co., 1963.
20. Locke, J. Essay Concerning Human Understanding. (1690). Reprinted by Everyman's Library. London: Dent, 1961.
21. Koestler, A. The Act of Creation. London: Pan Books, Ltd., 1970.
22. Engell, J. The Creative Imagination. Cambridge, Mass.: Harvard University Press, 1981.
23. Swift, J. Gulliver's Travels. (1726). New York: New American Library, 1960, Pp. 201-202.
24. Pavlov, I. P. Conditioned Reflexes. (Translated by G. V. Anrep). London: Oxford University Press, 1927.

25. Watson, J. B. Behaviorism.
26. ibid, p. 247-248.
27. Hull, C. L. Principles of Behavior. New York: Appleton-Century-Crofts, 1943; Hull, C. L. A Behavior System. New Haven: Yale University Press, 1952.
28. Hull, C. L. Principles of Behavior.
29. Kimble, G. A. Hilgard and Marquis' Conditioning and Learning (2nd edition). New York: Appleton-Century-Crofts, Inc., 1961.
30. Yerkes, R. M., & Dodson, J. D. "The Relation of Strength of Stimulus to Rapidity of Habit Formation." Journal of Comparative Neurology, 1908, 18, 459-482.
31. Spence, K. W. Behavior Theory and Conditioning. New Haven: Yale University Press, 1956.
32. Glucksberg, S. "The Influence of Strength of Drive on Functional Fixedness and Perceptual Recognition." Journal of Experimental Psychology, 1962, 63, 36-51.
33. Maltzman, I. "Thinking: From a Behavioristic Point of View." Psychological Review, 1955, 66, 367-386.
34. Mednick, S. A. "The Associative Basis of the Creative Process." Psychological Review, 1962, 69, 220-232.
35. Miller, N. E. "Liberalization of Basic S-R Concepts: Extensions to Conflict Behavior, Motivation and Social Learning." In S. Koch (Ed.), Psychology, a Study of a Science (Vol. 2). New York: McGraw-Hill, 1959, 196-293.
36. Brown, J. S. "Gradients of Approach and Avoidance Responses and their Relation to Level of Motivation." Journal of Comparative and Physiological Psychology, 1948, 41, 450-465.
37. Poincaré, H. "Mathematical Creation." In B. Ghiselin (Ed.), The Creative Process. 33-42.
38. Bruner, J. "Art as a Mode of Knowing." In On Knowing: Essays for the Left Hand. London: Harvard University Press, 1979, 60-74.
39. Arnheim, R. "The Aesthetic Approach." In S. Rosner and L. E. Abt (Eds.), Essays in Creativity. Croton-on-Hudson, N. Y.: North River Press, Inc., 1974, 5-21.
40. Asch, S. "The Doctrinal Tyranny of Associationism: Or What is Wrong with Rote Learning." In T. R. Dixon and D. L. Horton (Eds.), Verbal Behavior and General Behavior Theory. Englewood Cliffs, N. J.: Prentice-Hall, Inc., 1968, 214-228.
41. Koestler, A. The Act of Creation.
42. Gruber, H. E. Darwin on Man: A Psychological Study of Creativity. New York: E. P. Dutton, 1974.
43. Holton, G. The Scientific Imagination: Case Studies. Cambridge: Cambridge University Press, 1978.
44. Skinner, B. F. "A Behavioral Model of Creation."; About Behaviorism. New York: Alfred A. Knopf, 1974;

      <u>Cognition</u>, <u>Creativity</u> <u>and</u> <u>Behavior</u>. (Film). Colwell
      Systems, 1980.
45. Skinner, B. F. "Are Theories of Learning Necessary?"
      <u>Psychological</u> <u>Review</u>, 1950, <u>57</u>, 193-216.
46. Skinner, B. F. "How to Teach Animals." San Francisco: W.
      H. Freeman and Co., <u>Scientific</u> <u>American</u> reprint #423,
      Dec. 1951.
47. Kimble, G. A. <u>Hilgard</u> <u>and</u> <u>Marquis'</u> <u>Conditioning</u> <u>and</u>
      <u>Learning</u>.
48. Tarpy, R. M., & Mayer, R. E. <u>Foundations</u> <u>of</u> <u>Learning</u> <u>and</u>
      <u>Memory</u>. Glenview, Ill.: Scott, Foresman & Co., 1978.
49. Skinner, B. F. <u>Beyond</u> <u>Freedom</u> <u>and</u> <u>Dignity</u>. New York:
      Alfred A. Knopf, 1971, p. 158.
50. Wolpe, J., & Lazarus, A. A. <u>The</u> <u>Practice</u> <u>of</u> <u>Behavior</u>
      <u>Therapy</u>. New York: Pergamon, 1969.
51. Skinner, B. F. <u>The</u> <u>Technology</u> <u>of</u> <u>Teaching</u>. New York:
      Appleton-Century-Croft, 1968.
52. Skinner, B. F. <u>Beyond</u> <u>Freedom</u> <u>and</u> <u>Dignity</u>.
53. Skinner, B. F. <u>About</u> <u>Behaviorism</u>.
54. Skinner, B. F. <u>Walden</u> <u>Two</u>. New York: McMillan, 1948.
55. Skinner, B. F. <u>The</u> <u>Technology</u> <u>of</u> <u>Teaching</u>. p. 170.
56. Skinner, B. F. <u>About</u> <u>Behaviorism</u>, p. 114.
57. Skinner, B. F. "A Behavioral Model of Creation."
58. <u>ibid</u>, p. 271.
59. Skinner, B. F. <u>Walden</u> <u>Two</u>.
60. Tomkins, C. <u>The</u> <u>Bride</u> <u>and</u> <u>the</u> <u>Bachelors</u>: <u>Five</u> <u>Masters</u> <u>of</u>
      <u>the</u> <u>Avant-Garde</u>. New York: Viking Press, 1968.
61. <u>ibid</u>, p. 113.
62. <u>ibid</u>, p. 114.
63. <u>ibid</u>, p. 246.
64. McDonagh, D. <u>The</u> <u>Rise</u> <u>and</u> <u>Fall</u> <u>and</u> <u>Rise</u> <u>of</u> <u>Modern</u> <u>Dance</u>.
      New York: New American Library, 1970.
65. Tomkins, C. <u>The</u> <u>Bride</u> <u>and</u> <u>the</u> <u>Bachelors</u>: <u>Five</u> <u>Masters</u> <u>of</u>
      <u>the</u> <u>Avant-Garde</u>.
66. Brown, C. Untitled article. In J. Klosty (Ed.), <u>Merce</u>
      <u>Cunningham</u>. New York: E. P. Dutton & Co., Inc., 1975,
      p. 30.
67. Klosty, J. "Introduction." In J. Klosty (Ed.), <u>Merce</u>
      <u>Cunningham</u>.
68. Brown, C. Untitled article. In J. Klosty (Ed.), <u>Merce</u>
      <u>Cunningham</u>. 18-31.
69. Chicago, J. <u>Through</u> <u>the</u> <u>Flower</u>. Garden City, N. Y.:
      Anchor Press, 1982; Nochlin, L. "Why Have There Been
      No Great Women Artists?" In T. B. Hess and E. C. Baker
      (Eds.), <u>Art</u> <u>and</u> <u>Sexual</u> <u>Politics</u>. Macmillan Publishing
      Co., 1973, 1-43.
70. Greer, G. <u>The</u> <u>Obstacle</u> <u>Race</u> London: Secker & Warburg,
      1979, p. 327.

71. Woolf, V. _A Room of One's Own_. New York: Granada Publishing, 1977.
72. Greer, G. _The Obstacle Race_.
73. de Mille, A. _And Promenade Home_. Boston: Little, Brown, 1958.
74. de Mille, A. _Dance to the Piper_. Boston: Little, Brown, 1952.
75. Nochlin, L. "Why Have There Been No Great Women Artists?"
76. de Mille, A. _And Promenade Home_, p. 216.
77. Woolf, V. _A Room of One's Own_, p. 51.
78. Greer, G. _The Obstacle Race_, p. 90.
79. de Mille, A. _And Promenade Home_, p. 218.
80. Hess, T. B. "Great Women Artists." In T. B. Hess & E. C. Baker (Eds.), _Art and Sexual Politics_. New York: Macmillan Publishing Co., 1973, 44-54.
81. Woolf, V. _A Room of One's Own_, p. 70.
82. Greer, G. _The Obstacle Race_, p. 68.
83. Cited in Nochlin, L. "Why Have There Been No Great Women Artists?" In T. B. Hess and E. C. Baker (Eds.), _Art and Sexual Politics_, p. 28.
84. Woolf, V. _A Room of One's Own_, p. 71.
85. de Mille, A. _And Promenade Home_, p. 219.
86. ibid, p. 222.
87. Woolf, V. _A Room of One's Own_, p. 47.
88. Riley, B. "The Hermaphrodite." In T. B. Hess and E. C. Baker (Eds.), _Art and Sexual Politics_, Pp. 82-83.
89. ibid, p. 83.
90. Carpenter, F. _The Skinner Primer: Behind Freedom and Dignity_. New York: The Free Press, 1974.
91. Roe, A. "Changes in Scientific Activities with Age." _Science_, 1965, _150_, 313-318.
92. Watson, J. D. _The Double Helix_. New York: New American Library, 1968.
93. Hart, M. _Act One_. New York: Vintage Books, 1976, p. 256.
94. Skinner, B. F. _About Behaviorism_.
95. Simonton, D. K. _Genius, Creativity and Leadership_. Cambridge, Mass.: Harvard University Press, 1984.
96. Skinner, B. F. "_A Behavioral Model of Creation_," p. 273.
97. Storr, A. _The Dynamics of Creation_.
98. Gruber, H. E. "The Evolving Systems Approach to Creativity." In S. Modgil and C. Modgil (Eds.), _Toward a Theory of Psychological Development_. Atlantic Highlands, N.J.: Humanities Press, 1980, 269-299.
99. Getzels, J. W., Csikszentmihalyi, M. _The Creative Vision_. Toronto: John Wiley & Sons, Ltd., 1976.
100. Mailer, N. "Interview." In G. Plimpton (Ed.), _Writers at Work: The Paris Review Interviews_. New York: Viking Press, 1968, 251-278.
101. Amabile, T. M. _The Social Psychology of Creativity_. New York: Springer-Verlag, 1983.

102. Hebb, D. O. "What Psychology is About." American Psychologist, 1974, 29, 71-79.
103. Lombroso, C. "Genius and Insanity." In A. Rothenberg an C. R. Hausman (Eds.), The Creativity Question, 79-86.
104. Arieti, S. Creativity: The Magic Synthesis.
105. ibid, p. 397.
106. Prentky, R. A. Creativity and Psychopathology. New York: Praeger Publishers, 1980.
107. Buffery, A. W. H., & Gray, J. A. "Sex Differences in the Development of Spatial and Linguistic Skills." In C. Ounsted and D. C. Taylor (Eds.), Gender Differences: Their Ontogeny and Significance. Edinburgh: Churchill Livingstone, 1972, Chap. 6.
108. Gardner, H. Art, Mind & Brain: A Cognitive Approach to Creativity. New York: Basic Books, 1982.
109. ibid, p. 323.
110. Lashley, K. S. Brain Mechanisms and Intelligence. Chicago: University of Chicago Press, 1929.
111. Gardner, H. Art, Mind & Brain: A Cognitive Approach to Creativity. Pp. 334-335.
112. Bogen, J. E., & Bogen, G. M. "Creativity and the Bisected Brain." In A. Rothenberg and C. R. Hausman (Eds.), The Creativity Question, 256-261.
113. Goleman, D. "Special Abilities of the Sexes: Do They Begin in the Brain?" In Annual Editions in Psychology. Sluice Dock, Guilford, Conn.: The Dushkin Publishing Co., 1980, 43-49.
114. ibid, p. 46.
115. Hebb, D. O. The Organization of Behavior. New York: John Wiley & Sons, Inc., 1949.
116. Hebb, D. O. "What Psychology is About."
117. Eccles, J. C. "The Physiology of Imagination." San Francisco: W. H. Freeman & Co., Scientific American offprint #65.
118. ibid, p. 12.
119. Gedo, J. F. Portraits of the Artist. New York: The Guilford Press, 1983.
120. Hebb, D. O. "What Psychology is About," p. 78.
121. Hebb, D. O. "Drives and the C.N.S. (Conceptual Nervous System)." Psychological Review, 1955, 62, 243-254.
122. Heron, W. "The Pathology of Boredom." San Francisco: W. H. Freeman & Co., Scientific American offprint #430.
123. Suedfeld, P. "Environmental Restriction and "Stimulus Hunger": Theories and Applications." In H. I. Day (Ed.), Advances in Intrinsic Motivation and Aesthetics. New York: Plenum Press, 1981, 71-86.
124. Martindale, C. "Degeneration, Disinhibition and Genius." Journal of the History of the Behavioral Sciences, 1971, 7, 177-182; Martindale, C. "Femininity,

Alienation and Arousal in the Creative Personality."
Psychology, 1972, <u>9</u>, 3-15.
125. Suler, J. R. "Primary Process Thinking and Creativity."
Psychological Bulletin, 1980, <u>88</u>, p. 158.
126. Köhler, W. *The Mentality of Apes*. New York: Harcourt
Brace, 1925; Harlow, H. F. "The Formation of Learning
Sets." *Psychological Review*, 1949, <u>56</u>, 51-65.
127. Berlyne, D. E. "Arousal and Reinforcement." In D. Levine
(Ed.), *Nebraska Symposium on Motivation*. Lincoln Neb.:
University of Nebraska Press, 1967, 1-110.
128. ibid; Berlyne, D. E. *Conflict, Arousal and Curiosity*. New
York: McGraw-Hill, 1960; Berlyne, D. E. "The New
Experimental Aesthetics." In D. E. Berlyne (Ed.),
*Studies in the New Experimental Aesthetics: Steps
Toward an Objective Psychology of Aesthetic
Appreciation*. New York: John Wiley & Sons, 1974,
1-25.
129. Furedy, J. J., & Furedy, C. P. "'My First Interest is
Interest': Berlyne as an Exemplar of the Curiosity
Drive." In H. I. Day (Ed.), *Advances in Intrinsic
Motivation and Aesthetics*. New York: Plenum Press,
1981, 1-17.
130. Berlyne, D. E. "Motivational Problems Raised by Exploratory
and Epistemic Behavior." In S. Koch (Ed.), *Psychology:
A Study of a Science*. (Vol. 5). New York:
McGraw-Hill, 1959, 284-364.
131. ibid.
132. Berlyne, D. E. "The New Experimental Aesthetics."
133. Eysenck, H. J. *Sense and Nonsense in Psychology*.
Hamondsworth, England: Penquin Books, 1958.

Chapter 13.

01. Postman, L. "A Pragmatic View of Organization Theory." In
E. Tulving and W. Donaldson (Eds.), *Organization of
Memory*. New York: Academic Press, 1972, 3-48.
02. Kant, I. "Genius Gives the Rules." In A. Rothenberg and C.
R. Hausman (Eds.), *The Creativity Question*. Durham, N.
C.: Duke University Press, 1976, 37-42.
03. Kant, I. *The Critique of Pure Reason*. Meiklejohn, J. M. D.
(Trans.). London: Bohn, 1855 (1781).
04. Kant, I. "Genius Gives the Rules," p. 40-41.
05. ibid, p. 38.
06. Watson, R. I. *The Great Psychologists: From Aristotle to
Freud*. Philadelphia: J. B. Lippincott, 1963.
07. Kant, I. "Genius gives the rules," p. 38.
08. Heidbredder, E. *Seven Psychologies*. New York:
Appleton-Century Co., 1935.
09. Watson, R. I. *The Great Psycholgists: From Aristotle to
Freud*.

10. After Kreitler, H., and Kreitler, S. Psychology of the Arts. Durham, N. C.: Duke University Press, 1972, p. 83.
11. After Hochberg, J. E. "Nativism and Empiricism in Perception." In L. Postman (Ed.), Psychology in the Making. New York: Alfred A. Knopf, Inc., 1962, p. 298.
12. After Heidbredder, E. Seven Psychologies. New York: Appleton-Century Co., 1935, Pp. 348-350.
13. Sahakian, W. S. History and Systems of Psychology. New York: Schenkman Publishing Co., 1975.
14. Köhler, W. The Mentality of Apes. New York: Harcourt Brace, 1925.
15. Bruner, J. "The Art of Discovery." In On Knowing: Essays for the Left Hand. Cambridge, Mass.: Harvard University Press, 1979.
16. Wertheimer, M. Productive Thinking. Wertheimer, M. (Ed.). New York: Harper and Brothers, 1959.
17. Henle, M. "The Cognitive Approach: The Snail Beneath the Shell." In S. Rosner and L. E. Abt (Eds.), Essays in Creativity. Croton-on-Hudson, N. Y.: North River Press, Inc., 1974, 23-44.
18. Wertheimer, M. Productive Thinking, p. 238.
19. ibid, p. 49.
20. Mansfied, R. S., & Busse, T. V. The Psychology of Creativity and Discovery. Chicago: Nelson-Hall, 1981.
21. Newell, A., & Simon, H. A. Human Problem Solving. Englewood Cliffs, N. J.: Prentice-Hall, 1972.
22. Getzels, J. W., & Csikszentmihalyi, M. The Creative Vision. New York: John Wiley & Sons, 1976.
23. Wertheimer, M. Productive Thinking, p. 244.
24. Gardner, H. Art, Mind and Brain. New York: Basic Books, 1982.
25. Luchins, A. S. "Mechanization in Problem Solving." Psychological Monographs, 1942, 54, No. 248.
26. Wertheimer, M. Productive Thinking, p. 237.
27. Clark, R. W. Einstein: The Life and Times. New York: Avon Books, 1972.
28. Wertheimer, M. Productive Thinking, p. 228.
29. Einstein, A. "Letter to Jacques Hadamard." In B. Ghiselin (Ed.), The Creative Process. New York: New American Library, 1952, 43-45.
30. ibid.
31. ibid, p. 44.
32. Sahakian, W. S. History and Systems of Psychology.
33. Festinger, L. A Theory of Cognitive Dissonance. Palo Alto, Calif.: Stanford University Press, 1957; Festinger, L. "Cognitive Dissonance." San Francisco: W. H. Freeman & Co., Scientific American reprint #472.

34. Adair, J. G. "Scientific Method and Creativity: A View from the Psychology of Science." Paper presented at the International Symposium on Creativity and the Teaching of Science, San Jose, Costa Rica, March 24, 1982.
35. Stein, M. I. Stimulating Creativity, Vol. 1: Individual Procedures. New York: Academic Press, 1974; Taylor, C. W. "A Search for a Creative Climate." Paper presented at the Seventeenth National Conference on the Administration of Research, Estes Park, Colorado, September 11-13, 1963.
36. Lurie, R. "Political Cartooning." In S. Rosner & L. E. Abt (Eds.), The Creative Expression. Croton-on-Hudson, N. Y.: North River Press, Inc., 1976, 98-113.
37. ibid, p. 107.
38. Bellow, S. "Interview." In G. Plimpton (Ed.), Writers at Work: The Paris Review Interviews. New York: Viking Press, 1967, p. 182.
39. Kreitler, H., & Kreitler, S. Psychology of the Arts. Durham, N. C.: Duke University Press, 1972.
40. ibid.
41. Lund, F. H., & Anastasi, A. "An Interpretation of Aesthetic Experience." American Journal of Psychology, 1928, 40, 434-448.
42. Boas, F. Primitive Art. New York: Dover, 1955.
43. Heron. W. "The Pathology of Boredom." San Francisco: W. H. Freeman & Co., Scientific American, offprint #430.
44. Hebb, D. O. "Drives and the C.N.S. (Conceptual Nervous System)." Psychological Review, 1955, 62, 243-254.
45. Kreitler, H., & Kreitler, S. Psychology of the Arts.
46. Adair, J. G. "Scientific Method and Creativity: A View form the Psychology of Science."
47. Wertheimer, M. Productive Thinking, p. 137.
48. Poincaré, H. "Mathematical Creation." In B. Ghiselin (Ed.), The Creative Process, 33-42.
49. ibid, p. 35.
50. ibid, p. 36.
51. ibid, p. 38.
52. ibid, p. 35.
53. ibid, p. 37.
54. ibid, p. 39, 36.
55. ibid, p. 40.
56. ibid, Pp. 41-42.
57. Mednick, S. A. "The Associative Basis of the Creative Process. Psychological Review, 1962, 69, 220-232.
58. Maltzman, I., Belloni, M., & Fishbein, M. "Experimental Studies of Associative Variables in Originality." Psychological Monographs, 1964, 78, 3, Whole No. 580.
59. Dellas, M., & Gaier, E. L. "Identification of Creativity: The Individual." Psychological Bulletin, 1970, 73,

55-73; Taylor, I. A. "A Retrospective View of Creativity Investigation." In I. A. Taylor and J. W. Getzels (Eds.), Perspectives in Creativity. Chicago: Aldine Publishing Co., 1975, 1-36.

60. Koestler, A. The Act of Creation. London: Pan Books, Ltd., 1970.

61. ibid, p. 38.

62. ibid, pp. 110-111.

63. ibid, p. 119.

64. von Bertalanffy, L. Problems of Life: An Evaluation of Modern Biological Thought. London: Watts & Co., 1952.

65. Koestler, A. The Ghost in the Machine. London: Pan Books Ltd., 1975.

66. Koestler, A. The Act of Creation. London: Hutchinson & Co., 1964.

67. Koestler, A. The Act of Creation, 1970.

68. Koestler, A. The Ghost in the Machine.

69. Koestler, A. The Act of Creation, 1964.

70. Underwood, B. J. Experimental Psychology. New York: Appleton-Century-Crofts, 1966.

71. Morgan, C. L. "Emergent Novelty." In A. Rothenberg and C. R. Hausman (Eds.), The Creativity Question, 288-291.

72. Koestler, A. The Act of Creation, 1964, p. 658.

73. Perkins, D. N. The Mind's Best Work. Cambridge, Mass.: Harvard University Press, 1981.

74. Rothenberg, A. The Emerging Goddess. Chicago: The University of Chicago Press, 1979.

75. ibid, p. 55.

76. ibid, p. 69.

77. Gedo, J. E. Portraits of the Artist. New York: The Guilford Press, 1983.

78. Humphrey, D. The Art of Making Dances. New York: Grove Press, 1959.

79. Rothenberg, A., & Hausman, C. R. "Introduction: The Creativity Question." In A. Rothenberg & C. R. Hausman (Eds.), The Creativity Question, p. 23.

80. Campbell, D. T. "Blind Variation and Selective Retention in Creative Thought as in other Knowledge Processes." Psychological Review, 1960, 67, 380-400.

81. ibid, p. 390.

82. ibid, p. 391.

83. ibid, p. 392.

84. Bandura, A. Social Learning Theory. Englewood Cliffs, N. J.: Prentice-Hall, 1977.

85. Bandura, A. "The Self System in Reciprocal Determinism." American Psychologist, 1978, 33, 344-358.

86. Bandura, A., & Walters, R. Social Learning and Personality Development. New York: Holt, Rinehart & Winston, 1963.

87. Bandura, A. Social Learning Theory.

543

88. Bandura, A., & Walters, R. <u>Social Learning and Personality Development</u>.
89. Bandura, A. <u>Social Learning Theory</u>.
90. Bandura, A. "The Self System in Reciprocal Determinism."
91. Bandura, A. "The Self System in Reciprocal Determinism." pp. 356-357.
92. Rothenberg, A., and Hausman, C. R. "Introduction: The Creativity Question." In A. Rothenberg and C. R. Hausman (Eds.), <u>The Creativity Question</u>, 3-26.
93. Bandura, A. <u>Social Learning Theory</u>, p. 129.
94. Wallace, I. "Self-Control Techniques of Famous Novelists." <u>Journal of Applied Behavior Analysis</u>, 1977, <u>10</u>, 515-525.
95. Bandura, A. <u>Social Learning Theory</u>.
96. <u>ibid</u>, p. 50.
97. Zuckerman, H. "The Scientific Elite: Nobel Laureates' Mutual Influences." In R. S. Albert (Ed.), <u>Genius and Eminence</u>. New York: Pergamon Press, 1983, 241-252.
98. <u>ibid</u>, p. 246.
99. Amabile, T. M. <u>The Social Psychology of Creativity</u>. New York: Springer-Verlag, 1983.
100. Getzels, J. W., & Csikszentmihalyi, M. <u>The Creative Vision</u>; Barron F. <u>Artists in the Making</u>. New York: Seminar Press, 1972.
101. Yalom, I. D., & Yalom, M. "Earnest Hemingway--a Psychiatric View." <u>Archives of General Psychiatry</u>, 1971, <u>24</u>, 485-494.
102. Boyd, L. M. "The Most Disappointed Men in the World." <u>San Francisco Chronicle</u>, March 15, 1969.
103. Bandura, A. "Self Referent Mechanisms in Social Learning Theory." <u>American Psychologist</u>, 1979, <u>34</u>, 439-441.
104. Bandura, A. "The Self System in Reciprocal Determinism."
105. Bandura, A. <u>Social Learning Theory</u>.

Chapter 14.

01. Phillips, J. L., Jr. <u>The Origins of Intellect: Piaget's Theory</u>. San Francisco: W. H. Freeman & Co., 1969; Ginsburg, H., & Opper, S. <u>Piaget's Theory of Intellectual Development: An Introduction</u>. Englewood Cliffs, N. J.: Prentice-Hall, Inc., 1969.
02. Feldman, D. H. <u>Beyond Universals in Cognitive Development</u>. Norwood, N. J.: Ablex Publishing Corp., 1980.
03. <u>ibid</u>, p. 44.
04. <u>ibid</u>.
05. Gardner, H. <u>Art, Mind, & Brain: A Cognitive Approach to Creativity</u>. New York: Basic Books, Inc., 1982.
06. Blatt, S. J. <u>Continuity and Change in Art: The Development of Modes of Representation</u>. Hillsdale, N.J.: Lawrence Erlbaum Associates, 1984.

07. Gruber, H. "The Evolving Systems Approach to Creativity." In S. Modgil and C. Modgil (Eds.), Toward a Theory of Psychological Development. Atlantic Highlands, N.J.: Humanities Press, 1980, 269-299.
08. ibid, p. 271.
09. Gardner, H. Art, Mind & Brain: A Cognitive Approach to Creativity.
10. Gruber, H. Darwin on Man: A Psychological Study of Scientific Creativity. New York: E. P. Dutton & Co., 1974.
11. ibid.
12. ibid; Gruber, H. Afterword. In D. H. Feldman. Beyond Universals in Cognitive Development, 175-180.
13. Gruber, H. "On the Hypothesized Relation Between Giftedness and Creativity." In D. H. Feldman (Ed.), Developmental Approaches to Giftedness and Creativity. San Francisco: Jossey-Bass Inc., 1982, 7-29.
14. Gruber, H. "The Evolving Systems Approach to Creativity," p. 277.
15. Black, J. Personal communication.
16. Nisbett, R. E., & Wilson, T. B. "Telling more than We can know: Verbal Reports on Mental Processes." Psychological Review, 1977, 84, 231-259.
17. Perkins, D. N. The Mind's Best Work. Cambridge, Mass.: Harvard University Press, 1981.
18. Runyan, W. M. Life Histories and Psychobiography: Explorations in Theory and Method. New York: Oxford University Press, 1982.
19. Gruber, H. "On the Hypothesized Relation between Giftedness and Creativity."
20. James, H. "Preface to the Spoils of Poynton." In B. Ghiselin (Ed.), The Creative Process. New York: New American Library, 1952, p. 147.
21. Gruber, H. Darwin on Man: A Psychological Study of Scientific Creativity, p. 174.
22. Gruber, H. "On the Hypothesized Relation between Giftedness and Creativity."
23. Gruber, H. Darwin on Man: A Psychological Study of Scientific Creativity, p. 70.
24. Gruber, H. "The Evolving Systems Approach to Creativity," p. 289.
25. ibid, p. 290.
26. Koestler, A. The Act of Creation. London: Pan Books, Ltd., 1970, p. 447.
27. Gruber, H. "The Evolving Systems Approach to Creativity."
28. Gruber, H. "On the Hypothesized Relation between Giftedness and Creativity."
29. Gruber, H. "The Evolving Systems Approach to Creativity."
30. Gruber, H. "The Evolving Systems Approach to Creativity," p. 294.

31. Gardner, H. Art, Mind, & Brain: A Cognitive Approach to Creativity.
32. Gruber, H. "The Evolving Systems Approach to Creativity."
33. Arnheim, R. The Genesis of a Painting: Picasso's Guernica. Berkeley, Calif.: U. of California Press, 1962.
34. Arnheim, R. Toward a Psychology of Art: Collected Essays. Berkeley, Calif.: U. of California Press, 1966.
35. Arnheim, R. The Genesis of a Painting: Picasso's Guernica, p. 135.
36. ibid, p. 131.
37. ibid, p. 56.
38. Feldman, D. H. Beyond Universals in Cognitive Development.
39. Feldman, D. H. "The Developmental Approach: Universal to Unique." In S. Rosner and L. E. Abt (Eds.), Essays in Creativity. Croton-on-Hudson, N. Y.: North River Press, Inc., 1974, 45-85.
40. Zervos, C. "Conversation with Picasso." In B. Ghiselin (Ed.), The Creative Process, 55-60.
41. Feldman, D. H. Beyond Universals in Cognitive Development, p. 113.
42. Gardner, H. Art, Mind, & Brain: A Cognitive Approach to Creativity.
43. Bamberger, J. "Growing up Prodigies: The Midlife Crisis." In D. H. Feldman (Ed.), Developmental Approaches to Giftedness and Creativity, 61-77.
44. Gedo, J. E. Portraits of the Artist. New York: The Guilford Press, 1983.
45. Feldman, D. H. "A Developmental Framework for Research with Gifted Children." In D. H. Feldman (Ed.), Developmental Approaches to Giftedness and Creativity, 31-45.
46. Gruber, H. Afterword. In D. H. Feldman, Beyond Universals In Cognitive Development.
47. Rogers, C. R. "Towards a Theory of Creativity." In P. E. Vernon (Ed.), Creativity. New York: Penguin Books, 1970, 137-151.
48. Feldman, D. H. "The Developmental Approach: Universal to Unique." Pp. 78-79.
49. Gardner, H. Art, Mind, & Brain: A Cognitive Approach to Creativity.
50. Winner, E. Invented Worlds: The Psychology of the Arts. Cambridge, Mass.: Harvard University Press, 1982.
51. Gardner, H. "Giftedness: Speculations from a Biological Perspective." In D. H. Feldman (Ed.), Developmental Approaches to Giftedness and Creativity, 47-60.
52. Gardner, H. Invited address to Division 10, American Psychological Assoc., Toronto, Ont., Aug. 1984; Gardner, H. Frames of Mind: The Theory of Multiple Intelligences. New York: Basic Books, 1983.

53. Michael, W. B., Comrey, A. L., & Fruchter, B. "J. P. Guilford: Psychologist and Teacher." _Psychological Bulletin_, 1963, 60, 1-34.
54. Guilford, J. P. "A Psychometric Approach to Creativity." In M. Bloomberg (Ed.), _Creativity: Theory and Research_. New Haven, Conn.: College and University Press, 1973, 229-246.
55. Guilford, J. P. "Creativity." _American Psychologist_, 1950, 5, p. 451.
56. Guilford, J. P. "Creativity," 444-454; Guilford, J. P. "Traits of Creativity." In P. E. Vernon (Ed.), _Creativity_. New York: Penguin Books, 1970, 167-188.
57. Guilford, J. P. "Creativity."
58. Guilford, J. P. "Traits of creativity," p. 169.
59. Guilford, J. P. "Creativity," p. 446.
60. Guilford, J. P. "Traits of Creativity."
61. Guilford, J. P. "Creative Abilities in the Arts." _Psychological Review_, 1957, 64, 110-118; Guilford, J.P. "Creativity."
62. Guilford, J. P. "Creativity: A Quarter Century of Progress." In I. A. Taylor & J. W. Getzels (Eds.), _Perspectives in Creativity_. Chicago: Aldine Publishing Co., 1975, p. 39.
63. Guilford, J. P. "Creativity: A Quarter Century of Progress," 37-59.
64. Gardner, H. Invited Address to Division 10, American Psychological Assoc.
65. Drevdahl, J. E. "Factors of Importance for Creativity." _Journal of Clinical Psychology_, 1956, 12, 21-26.
66. Guilford, J. P. "Traits of Creativity."; Guilford, J. P. _The Nature of Human Intelligence_. New York: McGraw-Hill, 1967.
67. Guilford, J. P. _The Nature of Human Intelligence_.
68. ibid, p. 166.
69. Guilford, J. P. "Creativity: A Quarter Century of Progress."
70. Guilford, J. P. _The Nature of Human Intelligence_, p. 219.
71. Guilford, J. P. "A Psychometric Approach to Creativity."
72. Stein, M.I. _Stimulating Creativity, Vol. 1: Individual Procedures_. New York: Academic Press, 1974.
73. Underwood, B. J. "Are we Overloading Memory?" In A. W. Melton & E. Martin (Eds.), _Coding Processes in Human Memory_. New York: John Wiley & Sons, 1972, 1-23.
74. Stein, M.I. _Stimulating Creativity, Vol. I: Individual Procedures_.
75. Guilford, J. P. "Creativity: A Quarter Century of Progress."
76. Guilford, J. P. _The Nature of Human Intelligence_.
77. Gruber, H. "The Evolving Systems Approach to Creativity."

Chapter 15.

01. Goble, F. *The Third Force*. New York: Simon & Schuster Pocket Books, 1974.
02. May, R. "The Emergence of Existential Psychology." In R. May (Ed.), *Existential Psychology*. New York: Random House, Inc., 1969, 1-48.
03. Allport, G. W. *Pattern and Growth in Personality*. New York: Holt, Rinehart & Winston, 1961.
04. Murray, H. A. "Preparations for the Scaffold of a Comprehensive System." In S. Koch (Ed.), *Psychology: A Study of a Science*, (Vol. 3). New York: McGraw-Hill, 1959, 7-54.
05. Allport, G. W. "The Psychologist's Frame of Reference." *Psychological Bulletin*, 1940, *37*, p. 14-15.
06. Allport, G. W. *Becoming: Basic Considerations for a Psychology of Personality*. New Haven: Yale University Press, 1955, p. 18.
07. Maddi, S. R., & Costa, P. T. *Humanism in Personology: Allport, Maslow and Murray*. Chicago: Aldine Atherton, Inc., 1972.
08. Maslow, A. H. "Existential Psychology - What's in it for Us?" In R. May (Ed.), *Existential Psychology*, 49-57.
09. May, R. "The Emergence of Existential Psychology." In R. May (Ed.), *Existential Psychology*, p. 11.
10. Maslow, A. H. "Existential Psychology - What's in it for Us?" p. 50.
11. Maslow, A. H. *Toward a Psychology of Being*. Toronto, Ont.: D. Van Nostrand (Canada) Co., 1962, p. 12.
12. *ibid*, p. 16.
13. May, R. "The Emergence of Existential Psychology."
14. Allport, G. W. *The Person in Psychology: Selected Essays*. Boston: Beacon Press, 1969, p. 3.
15. Furst, L. R. *Romanticism in Perspective*. Toronto: MacMillan, 1969.
16. Abercrombie, L. *Romanticism*. New York: Barnes and Noble, 1926.
17. Furst, L.R. *Romanticism in Perspective*.
18. Grimsley, R. *Existentialist Thought*. Cardiff: University of Wales Press, 1960.
19. Kaufmann, W. *Existentialism from Dostoevsky to Sartre*. New York: The World Publishing Co., 1956, Pp. 12-13.
20. Engell, J. *The Creative Imagination*. Cambridge, Mass.: Harvard University Press, 1981.
21. Furst, L. R. *Romanticism in Perspective*, p. 128.
22. Abercrombie, L. *Romanticism*, p. 70.
23. Wordsworth, W. "Preface to Second Edition of Lyrical Ballads." In B. Ghiselin (Ed.), *The Creative Process*. New York: New American Library, 1952, p. 83.
24. Quoted in Furst, L. R. *Romanticism in Perspective*, p. 143.

25. Arieti, S. Creativity: The Magic Synthesis. New York: Basic Books, 1976.
26. Furst, L. R. Romanticism in Perspective, p. 88.
27. Furst, L. R. Romanticism in Perspective.
28. Maslow, A. H. Toward a Psychology of Being, p. viii, and The Psychology of Science: A Reconnaissance. Chicago: Henry Regnery Co., 1966, p. xvi.
29. Maslow, A. H. The Psychology of Science: A Reconnaissance, Pp. 15-16.
30. ibid, p. 14.
31. Maslow, A. H. The Psychology of Science: A Reconnaissance.
32. Maslow, A. H. Religions, Values and Peak-Experiences. New York: Viking Press, 1970.
33. Maslow, A. H. The Psychology of Science: A Reconnaissance. p. xvi.
34. Allport, G. W. "General and Unique in Psychological Science." In The Person in Psychology: Selected Essays. Boston: Beacon Press, 1969, 81-102; Allport, G. W. Pattern and Growth in Personality.
35. Maslow, A. H. The Psychology of Science: A Reconnaissance.
36. Allport, G. W. "General and Unique in Psychological Science," p. 83.
37. Howe, M. J. A. "Biographical Evidence and the Development of Outstanding Individuals." American Psychologist, 1982, 37, 1071-1081.
38. Allport, G. W. Pattern and Growth in Personality.
39. Maslow, A. H. The Psychology of Science: A Reconnaissance, p. 11.
40. Maslow, A. H. Toward a Psychology of Being.
41. Allport, G. W. Becoming: Basic Considerations for a Psychology of Personality.
42. Maslow, A. H. Motivation and Personality. New York: Harper and Brothers, 1954.
43. ibid, p. 69.
44. Goldstein, K. The Organism. New York: American Book, 1939.
45. Maslow, A. H. Toward a Psychology of Being.
46. Allport, G. S. Pattern and Growth in Personality.
47. Maslow, A. H. Toward a Psychology of Being.
48. Maslow, A. H. "On Low Grumbles, High Grumbles and Metagrumbles." In The Farther Reaches of Human Nature. Markham, Ont.: Penguin Books, 1976, 229-238.
49. ibid, p. 236.
50. Wilde, O. The Picture of Dorian Gray. Markham, Ont.: Penguin Books, 1949, p. 25.
51. Lorenz, K. On Aggression. New York: Harcourt, Brace & World, Inc., 1966.
52. Graham, M. A Dancer's World. N.A.C.C.:, 1957 (Film).
53. Maslow, A. H. "Neurosis as a Failure of Personal Growth." In The Farther Reaches of Human Nature, 24-39.

54. Allport, G. W. <u>Becoming</u>: <u>Basic Considerations for a Psychology of Personality</u>, p. 79.
55. Rogers, C. R. <u>Carl Rogers on Personal Power</u>. New York: Delacorte Press, 1977.
56. Maslow, A. H. <u>Motivation and Personality</u>.
57. Maslow, A. H. <u>Motivation and Personality</u>, p. 349.
58. Maslow, A. H. <u>Toward a Psychology of Being</u>, p. 193.
59. Rogers, C. R. "Toward a Modern Approach to Values: The Valuing Process in the Mature Person." In M. Bloomberg (Ed.), <u>Creativity</u>: <u>Theory and Research</u>. New Haven, Conn.: College & University Press, 1973, 115-128.
60. Maddi, S. R., & Costa, P. T. <u>Humanism in Personology</u>: <u>Allport, Maslow, and Murray</u>.
61. Allport, G. W. <u>Pattern and Growth in Personality</u>.
62. Maslow, A. H. <u>Toward a Psychology of Being</u>.
63. Maslow, A. H. <u>Religions, Values and Peak-Experiences</u>.
64. <u>ibid</u>, p.29.
65. Maddi, S.R., & Costa, P.T. <u>Humanism in Personology</u>: <u>Allport, Maslow, and Murray</u>.
66. Maslow, A. H. <u>Motivation and Personality</u>, p. 223.
67. Rogers, C. R. "Towards a Theory of Creativity." In P. E. Vernon (Ed.), <u>Creativity</u>. New York: Penguin Books, 1970, p. 140.
68. <u>ibid</u>, p. 141.
69. Maslow, A. H. "A Holistic Approach to Creativity." In <u>The Farther Reaches of Human Nature</u>, 69-77.
70. Miller, H. "Reflections on Writing." In B. Ghiselin (Ed.), <u>The Creative Process</u>. New York: New American Library, 1952, Pp. 178-179.
71. Allport, G. W. <u>Pattern and Growth in Personality</u>.
72. Craig, R. "Trait Lists and Creativity." <u>Psychologia</u>, 1966, <u>9</u>, 107-110.
73. Maslow, A. H. <u>Toward a Psychology of Being</u>.
74. Maslow, A. H. <u>Motivation and Personality</u>.
75. Maslow, A. H. "Emotional Blocks to Creativity." In <u>The Farther Reaches of Human Nature</u>, 78-91.
76. Maslow, A. H. <u>Toward a Psychology of Being</u>.
77. Maslow, A. H. "Emotional Blocks to Creativity."
78. Rogers, C. R. "Towards a Theory of Creativity, 137-151.
79. Maslow, A. H. <u>Motivation and Personality</u>.
80. Amsel, A. "The Role of Frustrative Nonreward in Noncontinuous Reward Situations." <u>Psychological Bulletin</u>, 1958, <u>55</u>, 102-119.
81. Maslow, A. H. <u>Motivation and Personality</u>, p. 166.
82. Maslow, A. H. <u>Toward a Psychology of Being</u>.
83. Hart, M. <u>Act One</u>: <u>An Autobiography</u>. New York: Vintage Books, 1976, p. 256.
84. Shaw, G. B. Preface to <u>Man and Superman</u>. In <u>The Complete Prefaces of Bernard Shaw</u>. London: Paul Hamlyn Ltd., 1965, p. 157.

85. Rothenberg, A., & Hausman, C. R. "Introduction." In A. Rothenberg & C. R. Hausman (Eds.), The Creativity Question. Durham, N. C.: Duke University Press, 1976, 3-26.
86. Rogers, C. R. "Towards a Theory of Creativity."
87. Maslow, A. H. Toward a Psychology of Being, p. 164.
88. Maddi, S. R. "The Strenuousness of the Creative Life." In I. A. Taylor & J. W. Getzels (Eds.), Perspectives in Creativity. Chicago, Ill.: Aldine Publishing Co., 1975, 173-190.
89. Maslow, A. H. Motivation and Personality, p. 182.
90. Graham, M. A Dancer's World.
91. Maslow, A. H. The Psychology of Science: A Reconnaissance.
92. Maslow, A. H. Religion, Values and Peak Experiences.
93. Rand, A. The Romantic Manifesto. New York: New American Library, 1975; Rand, A. The Virtue of Selfishness. New York: New American Library, 1964.
94. Rand, A. The Fountainhead. New York: New American Library, 1959.
95. Rand, A. Atlas Shrugged. New York: New American Library, 1957.
96. Rand, A. The Romantic Manifesto, p. viii.
97. ibid, p. vi.
98. Rand, A. The Virtue of Selfishness, p. 20.
99. Rand, A. The Romantic Manifesto, p. 25.
100. Rand, A. Atlas Shrugged, Pp. 939, 941.
101. Rand, A. The Virtue of Selfishness, p. viii.
102. Rand, A. Atlas Shrugged, p. 954.
103. ibid, p. 137.
104. Rand, A. The Romantic Manifesto, p. 17.
105. Rand, A. Atlas Shrugged, p. 946.
106. Rand, A. The Romantic Manifesto, p. 33.
107. ibid, p. 21.
108. ibid, p. 42.
109. Rand, A. Atlas Shrugged, p. 116, 70.
110. Rand. A. The Romantic Manifesto, p. 116.
111. ibid, p. 70.
112. ibid, p. 69.
113. Rand, A. Atlas Shrugged, p. 943.
114. ibid, p. 959.
115. Rand, A. The Romantic Manifesto.
116. Rand, A. Atlas Shrugged, p. 96.
117. Abercrombie, L. Romanticism.
118. Rand, A. The Romantic Manifesto, p. 99.
119. Browning, R. Andrea del Sarto. In The Complete Poetical Works of Robert Browning. New York: The MacMillan Co., 1912, p. 451.
120. Rand, A. The Romantic Manifesto, p. 163.

Chapter 16

01. May, R. _Love and Will_. New York: Dell Publishing Co.,
    1969.
02. May, R. _The Courage to Create_. New York: W. W. Norton &
    Co., 1975.
03. May, R. _Love and Will_.
04. Austen, J. _Sense and Sensibility_. Markham, Ont.: Penguin
    Books, 1975, p. 353.
05. May, R. _Love and will_, p. 45.
06. May, R. _Power and Innocence_. New York: W. W. Norton &
    Co., 1972.
07. May, R. _Love and Will_, p. 121.
08. Reeves, C. _The Psychology of Rollo May_. San Francisco:
    Jossey-Bass, 1977.
09. May, R. "Reflections and Commentary." In C. Reeves, _The
    Psychology of Rollo May_, 295-309.
10. Wuest, S. M. "A Sense of Tribe." In N. Miller (Ed.), _New
    Campus Writing, No. 2_. New York: Bantam Books, 1957.
11. Waugh, E. _The Loved One: An Anglo-American Tragedy_.
    London: Chapman & Hall, 1948.
12. May, R. _Love and Will_, p. 98.
13. May, R. _The Courage to Create_, p. 59.
14. May, R. (Ed.). _Symbolism in Religion and Literature_. New
    York: George Braziller, 1960; Caligor, L., & May, R.
    Dreams and Symbols: Man's Unconscious Language. New
    York: Basic Books, Inc., 1968.
15. Caligor, L., & May, R. _Dreams and Symbols: Man's
    Unconscious Language_.
16. _ibid_, p. 16.
17. May, R. _The Courage to Create_
18. _ibid_, p. 54, 77.
19. May, R. _Love and Will_, p. 90.
20. Barron, F. "The Solitariness of Self and its Mitigation
    through Creative Imagination." In I. A. Taylor & J. W.
    Getzels (Eds.), _Perspectives in Creativity_. Chicago:
    Aldine Publishing Co., 1975, 146-156.
21. Hutchinson. E. D. _How to Think Creatively_. New York:
    Abingdon Press, 1949.
22. May, R. "The Courage to Create." In _Creativity and the
    University_. Toronto: York University Publications
    Office, 1975; May, R. _The Courage to Create_.
23. Jung, C. G. "Psychology and Literature." In _The Collected
    Works of C. G. Jung_ (Vol. 15). Princeton, N.J.:
    Princeton University Press, 1966, p. 102.
24. May, R. _The Courage to Create_, p. 46.
25. Goodman, L. M. _Death and the Creative Life_. New York:
    Springer Publishing Co., 1981.

26. May, R. The Art of Counselling: How to Give and Gain
    Mental Health. Nashville, Tenn.: Abingdon Cokesbury,
    1939, p. 60.
27. Pound, E. Cited in May, R. Love and Will, p. 21.
28. May, R. "The Courage to Create," p. 58.
29. ibid, p. 61.
30. Birney, E. The Creative Writer. Toronto: The Canadian
    Broadcasting Corporation, 1966, p. 6.
31. Koestler, A. The Act of Creation. London: Pan Books,
    Ltd., 1970.
32. Ghiselin, B. (Ed.). The Creative Process. New York: New
    American Library, 1952.
33. Matson, K. Short Lives. New York: William Morrow and Co.,
    Inc., 1980.
34. Goodman, L. M. Death and the Creative Life.
35. ibid, p. 6.
36. Browning, R. "Andrea del Sarto." In The Complete Poetical
    Works of Robert Browning. New York: The MacMillan
    Co., 1912, p. 451.
37. Becker, E. The Denial of Death. New York: The Free Press,
    1973.
38. ibid, p. 87.
39. Lewinsohn, P. M., Mischel, W., Chaplin, W., & Barton, R.
    "Social Competence and Depression: The Role of
    Illusory Self-Perceptions." Journal of Abnormal
    Psychology, 1980, 89, 203-212.
40. Becker, E. The Denial of Death, p. 184.
41. Rosenhan, D. L. "On Being Sane in Insane Places." Science,
    1973, 179, 250-258.
42. Solomon, R. L., & Wynne, L. C. "Traumatic Avoidance
    Learning: Acquisition in Normal Dogs." Psychological
    Monographs, 1953, 67, No. 354.
43. Schonberg, H. The Lives of the Great Composers. New York:
    W. W. Norton, 1970.
44. Gedo, M. M. Picasso: Art as Autobiography. Chicago: The
    University of Chicago Press, 1980.
45. Goodman, L. M. Death and the Creative Life.
46. Birney, E. The Creative Writer, p. 27.
47. Kübler-Ross, E. On Death and Dying. New York: The
    Macmillan Co., 1970.
48. Mnouchkine, A. Molière. (film).
49. Fromm, E. The Heart of Man: Its Genius for Good and Evil.
    New York: Harper & Row, 1964.
50. Fromm, E. The Forgotten Language: An Introduction to the
    Understanding of Dreams, Fairy Tales and Myths. New
    York: Grove Press, Inc., 1951.
51. Fromm, E. "The Creative Attitude." In H. H. Anderson
    (Ed.), Creativity and its Cultivation. New York:
    Harper & Row, Inc., 1959, 44-54.

52. Getzels, J. W., & Csikszentmihalyi, M. The Creative Vision. Toronto: John Wiley & Sons, Ltd., 1976.
53. Fromm, E. The Sane Society. New York: Rinehart & Co., 1955.
54. Fromm, E. The Heart of Man: Its Genius for Good and Evil, p. 21.
55. Fromm, E. Man for Himself: An Inquiry into the Psychology of Ethics. New York: Holt, Rinehart and Winston, 1947.
56. Fromm, E. The Art of Loving: An Enquiry into the Nature of Love. New York: Harper & Row, 1962.
57. Fromm, E. The Sane Society.
58. ibid, p. 69.
59. ibid, p. 347, italics mine.
60. ibid, p. 348.
61. Fromm, E. Man for Himself: An Inquiry into the Psychology of Ethics.
62. Fromm, E. The Heart of Man: Its Genius for Good and Evil.
63. Fromm, E. Man for Himself: An Inquiry into the Psychology of Ethics; Fromm, E. "Selfishness, Self-love and Self-interest." In C. Moustakas (Ed.), The Self: Explorations in Personal Growth. New York: Harper & Row, 1956, 58-69.
64. ibid, p. 67.
65. Fromm, E. Man for Himself: An Inquiry into the Psychology of Ethics, p. 87.
66. Fromm, E. The Heart of Man: Its Genius for Good and Evil, p. 41.
67. ibid, p. 42.
68. ibid, p. 48.
69. ibid, p. 51.
70. Fromm, E. "Sex and Character." In The Dogma of Christ and other Essays on Religion, Psychology and Culture. New York: Holt, Rinehart & Winston, 1955, 107-127.
71. ibid, p. 117.
72. Fromm, E. Man for Himself: An Inquiry into the Psychology of Ethics, p. 189.
73. Kauffmann, S. "Interview." In S. Rosner & L. E. Abt (Eds.), The Creative Expression. Croton-on-Hudson, N. Y.: North River Press, Inc., 1976, p. 218.
74. Dabrowski, K. "The Theory of Positive Disintegration." Paper presented at Second International Conference on Positive Disintegration, Loyola College, Montreal, PQ, Dec. 27-31, 1972.
75. ibid, p. 2.
76. Fromm, E. The Heart of Man: Its Genius for Good and Evil.
77. Michener, J. A. Sports in America. Greenwich, Conn.: Fawcett Publications, Inc., 1976.
78. Dryden, K. The Game. Toronto: Macmillan of Canada, 1983.

Chapter 17.

01. Guilford, J. P. "A Psychometric Approach to Creativity."
     In M. Bloomberg (Ed.), Creativity: Theory and
     Research. New Haven, Conn.: College and University
     Press, 1973, p. 229.
02. Allport, G. W. "The Productive Paradoxes of William James."
     In The Person in Psychology: Selected Essays. Boston:
     Beacon Press, 1969, p. 324.
03. ibid, Pp. 323-324.
04. Stern, A. Sartre: His Philosophy and Existential
     Psychoanalysis. New York: Dell Publishing Co., 1967.
05. Abra, J. C. "Camus and Jung in Conjunction: Absurdity and
     Archetypes as Engines of Creation." Unpublished
     manuscript.

Lombroso, C., 23, 24, 49,
225, 342
Louis XIV, 269
Lowry, Malcolm, 472
Luchins, A. S., 94, 363
Lumet, Sidney, 81
Lurie, R., 366
Luther, Martin, 206

Macbeth, 282, 292
MacKinnon, D., 24, 70, 244,
266
MacMillan, Kenneth, 182
Maddi, S. R., 73, 121, 145,
441, 447
Mahler, G., 479
Maier, N. R. F., 94
Mailer, Norman, 81, 338
Makarova, Natalia, 247
Malraux, A., 412
Malthus, T., 88, 400
Maltzman, I., 6, 78, 80, 316
Mansfield, R. S., 69, 362
Marat, Jean, 188
Markova, Alicia, 110
Martin, John, 111
Martindale, C. 348, 349
Marx, Groucho, 182, 183
Marx, Karl, 211, 481, 483
Maslow, A. H., 9, 10, 33, 43,
98, 138, 184, 293, 307,
422, 425, 431-448, 454,
457, 458, 461, 465, 471,
481, 484-486, 488, 489,
491, 496, 497
Massine, L., 110
Matisse, Henri, 37
Matson, K., 472
May, Rollo, 18, 26, 33, 87,
151, 190, 206, 215, 461-
473, 481-483, 489, 495, 496
Mays, Willy, 11
Mazo, Joseph, 176-178
McClelland, D. C., 107
McEnroe, John, 493
McMullan, E., v, 33-35, 266
McNiff, S., xv

Mead, Margaret, 74
Mednick, S. A., 25, 80, 315,
316, 374-376
Medusa, the, 161
Melanie, 301
Melville, H., 244
Mencken, H. L., 118
Mendel, G., 5
Mendelsohn G. A., 80
Mendelssohn, Felix, 92, 139,
407
Menuhin, Yehudi, 410
Meredith, Don, 492
Merrick, David, 113
Mersault, 141, 150
Messerschmidt, F. X., 275,
278
Michelangelo, 35, 51, 73,
203, 217, 232
Michelson, A., 364, 365
Michener, James, 491, 492
Mill, James, 308, 310
Mill, John Stuart, 55, 308,
407
Miller, Arthur, 93, 230, 231,
249
Miller, C., v
Miller, George, 249, 250
Miller, Henry, 28, 92, 253,
442
Miller, N., 316, 317
Millikan, R.A., 32
Minkus, L, 261
Mitroff, I. I., 300
Mitty, Walter, 119
Mnemosyne, 47
Mohammed, 284
Molière, 375, 480
Moore, Henry, 76, 85
Morgan, L., 380
Morley, E., 364, 365
Moses, 402, 429
Moustakas, C., 9
Mozart, W.A., 5, 7, 8, 10,
31, 41, 43, 55, 64, 82, 93,
99, 100, 107, 108, 139,

Varèse, E., 457
Verdoux, Monsieur, 369
Verdy, Violette, 179
Villella, Edward, 179
Virgin Mary, 281
Visconti, L., 459
Vivaldi, A., 51
Volkova, Vera, 89
Voltaire, 478
von Bertalanffy, L., 378
von Franz, M. L., 236
von Goethe, J. W., 31, 37,
  55, 76, 241, 308, 479

Wadeson, H., xv
Wagner, Richard, 100, 108,
  147, 195, 224, 262, 296-
  299, 392, 415 , 443
Walker, L., v
Wallace, A. L., 101, 249, 377
Wallas, G., 16, 17, 77
Walters, R., 388
Warhol, Andy, xiii
Watson, James, 101, 228, 300,
  335
Watson, John B., 303, 304,
  311-313, 379
Watson, R.I., 308
Watson, Tom, 493
Watton, J., v
Waugh, Evelyn, 464
Webb, Jack, 473
Webern, Anton, 108
Weissmann, P., 225, 268
Welles, Orson, 20
Werter, 430
Wertheimer, Max, 357, 361-365
Wesley, John, 206
White, R. K., 59
Whitehead, A.N., 344
Wiigs, A., vi
Wilde, Oscar, 43, 52, 90,
  114, 163, 299, 437
Williams, Tennessee, 35, 438
Wilson, Sallie, 47, 113
Wilson, T. B., 13
Winner, E., xv, 412

Winnie-the-Pooh, 93, 131, 229
Wolfe, Thomas, 89
Wood, S., v
Wooley, H. T., 37
Woolf, Virginia, 36, 39, 52,
  328-333, 392
Wordsworth, William, 61, 62,
  246, 426-427, 430, 436, 443
Wuest, S. M., 464
Wundt, W., 12, 14, 357
Wynne, L. C., 479

Yeats, W. B., 48, 77
Yorick, 475

Zeffirelli, F., 81
Zeus, 47
Zola, E., 81
Zorina, Vera, 182

Poetry, 26, 40, 42, 45, 47-
48, 51, 52, 57, 58, 77, 92,
93, 97, 107, 138, 166, 171-
175, 193, 198, 199, 201,
240, 243, 246, 254, 259,
260, 269, 270, 282, 283,
290, 313, 374, 382, 416,
426-430, 442, 470, 472
Poisonous praise, 82, 331
Politics, 295, 301, 304, 369,
420, 443, 451, 457, 481,
496; and creativity, 197,
297, 298
Pornography, 232
Positive disintegration, 491
Possessed, The (Dostoevsky),
142
Post-criterion drop, 82
Power - see Competition
Pragmatism, 425
Pre-paradigmatic disciplines,
108
Prejudice, 318
Preparation stage, 16-17, 20,
41, 69-75, 223, 328-329,
332, 362, 373-374, 387,
392, 413, 415, 446, 447
Pride and Prejudice (Austen),
459
Primary process, 214, 273-
278, 280-283, 342, 348,
378, 463
Private World of Ballet, The
(Gruen), 176
Problem finding, 362-364,
386, 481, 498; and
creativity, 76-77, 94-97
Problem finding score, 77
Problem solving, 76, 78, 95,
104-107, 120, 278, 316,
326, 346, 347, 349, 361-
365, 371, 375, 377, 395,
418, 420, 422
Productive type, 256, 257,
266, 271
Projection, 170, 226, 230

Projective techniques, 24,
278
Prolonged inspection, 79-80,
369
Propaganda, 457
Propositional thought - see
Thought - linear
Prostitutes, 126, 134
Psychoanalysis, xiv, 9, 13,
27, 80, 143, 211, 298;
effects on creativity, 50,
52; distinctive beliefs,
211; criticisms of 211,
214, 215, 271, 278, 279,
294, 341, 444; system of
therapy, 212-213, 277, 476,
477; as science, 215, 290;
pessimism of, 216, 444,
482, 485; and World War I,
216-217; motivation, 211-
215; view of
psychopathology, 438;
emphasis on children, 216;
explanations of creativity,
217-220, 223-233, 236-254,
255-271, 273-276, 292-301;
and homosexuality, 222;
view of art history, 397;
Guilford's attitude
towards, 416; and
humanists, 423; in May,
465; study of critics, 268,
and development, 285; in
Poincaré, 372; in Koestler,
376, 380; in Rothenberg,
382; rejection of Rank,
475; chauvinism of, 488;
and existentialism, 496
Psychoanalysts, 170
Psychologists, 147, 161, 420;
ego, 274
Psychology and Literature
(Jung), 240
Psychology of Consciousness,
The (Ornstein), 34
Psychology - neglect of
creativity, xvii, 410, 420,

anxiety, 129, 130, 485; in love, 482
Resurrection, the, 479
Retardation, 56, 437
Reticular formation, the, 347
Retrospective criteria, 397
Retrospective IQ, 55
Return of the Jedi, 113
Revision - see Verification stage
Rickets, 342
Rigidity, 25, 33, 46, 371
Ripeness, 377
Risk, 437, 465; and creativity, 26, 28-30, 84, 110, 112, 188, 392, 457, 468, 490
Rodeo (deMille), 329
Role playing, 78
Roman Catholic Church, 26, 30, 106, 329, 441, 454
Romanesque art - see Art - Romanesque
Romanticism, 7, 34, 49, 52, 60, 61, 87-88, 96, 107, 108, 145, 151, 161, 195, 205, 230, 259, 269, 367, 398, 426-430, 431-447, 448-459
Rome, 382, 495
Room of One's Own, A (Woolf), 328
Rorschach ink-blot test, 14, 24, 106, 139
Routine science - see Science - normal
Royal Ballet, 176
Royal Danish Ballet, The, 457
Royal Shakespeare Theatre, 457
Rubik's cube, 95, 421
Rubricize, 160
Rugby School, 289
Russia, 304, 369

Sacre du Printemps, Le (Stravinsky/Nijinsky), 5, 110
Sadism, 164-165, 171, 483, 485; in the gaze, 161-162
Saint Genet: Actor and Martyr (Sartre), 169, 188
Saint Joan (Shaw), 26
Salvation Army, the, 362
Samoa, 74
Sane Society, The (Fromm), 481
Satan of the Suburbs (Russell), 50
Schizophrenia, 162, 278, 281-283, 342 (see also Psychopathology)
Schizothymia, 24
Schlock, 367
Scholars, 57, 58, 310, 334, 389, 472, 479, 484, 492
Schwanengesang (Schubert), 41
Science, 58, 138, 242, 295, 442, 483; limits of, xvii, 373; methods of evaluating ideas, 11-12, 14; advantages of, 12; value judgments in, 5, 6, 17, 112, 422; originality in, 7; theories in, 11-12, 97-98, 102-103, 317; compared to other methods, 15; nonlinear thought in, 34, 91, 97, 105, 320, 365, 378; and education, 44-45; history of, 44-45, 60-63, 99-100, 102-107, 108, 370; age effects in, 45-48; Greek, 100; competition in, 100, 101, 300, 377; as human, 101; normal, 104-107, 243, 422; revolutionary, 104-107, 243; and existentialism, 128; theological view, 208-209; and psychoanalysis, 215; intelligence in, 56;